RESONANCES

Engaging Music in Its Cultural Context

Esther M. Morgan-Ellis
Editor-in-Chief

UNG
UNIVERSITY *of*
NORTH GEORGIA™
UNIVERSITY PRESS

Blue Ridge | Cumming | Dahlonega | Gainesville | Oconee

ISBN: 978-1-940771-31-1

Produced by:
University System of Georgia

Published by:
University of North Georgia Press
Dahlonega, Georgia

Cover Design and Layout Design:
Corey Parson

Cover Image:
"Music" by Flickr User "JULIE"
CC BY 2.0

For more information, please visit http://ung.edu/university-press
Or email ungpress@ung.edu

If you need this document in another format, please email the University of North Georgia Press at ungpress@ung.edu or call 706-864-1556.

Table of Contents

Contributions and Acknowledgments

The textbook and accompanying materials were produced by a team of faculty collaborators at the University of North Georgia, each of whom contributed as follows:

Esther M. Morgan-Ellis developed the concept, managed the project, wrote the text (unless otherwise attributed), produced the listening guides (unless otherwise attributed), edited contributions from collaborators, selected/captioned the images, and created the accompanying PowerPoint slides.

Rebecca R. Johnston wrote the Chapter 1 sections entitled "The Power of Music" and "Music and Human Development, Learning, and Wellness" and produced the test bank questions in collaboration with **Marie Graham**.

Louis Hajosy wrote the Chapter 8 section entitled "The Beatles, *Sgt. Pepper's Lonely Hearts Club Band*" and the passage concerning Hendrix's performance of "The Star-Spangled Banner" that appears in the Chapter 7 section entitled "1969: An Aquarian Exposition." He also contributed to the Chapter 9 discussion of "The Star-Spangled Banner," produced the "Lucy in the Sky with Diamonds" listening guide, and created Appendix B, in addition to providing valuable feedback on the text.

David R. Peoples contributed to the Chapter 13 sections entitled "1965: The Duke Ellington controversy" and "1997: Wynton Marsalis, Blood on the Fields." He also typeset all of the listening guides and examples and produced all of the graphics, in addition to providing valuable feedback on the text.

Arielle P. Crumley wrote the Chapter 5 sections entitled "Beyoncé, *Lemonade*" and "Ancient Greece: *The Iliad*" and provided feedback on the remainder of the text.

Alexandra Dunbar wrote the Chapter 4 section entitled "Lin-Manuel Miranda, *Hamilton*" and produced the accompanying listening guides. She also provided feedback on the remainder of the text.

Philip Snyder created the notation-based videos in Chapter 2, contributed some images, and provided valuable feedback on the entire text.

Lisa Prodan created the teaching videos in Chapter 2.

Bart Walters contributed to Appendix A, provided valuable feedback on the text, and corrected the initial proof. He also created the YouTube channel that accompanies this book, uploaded videos as necessary, and built playlists in collaboration with **Serena Scibelli.**

In addition, **Jura Pintar** formatted listening examples for the typesetting process and **Noël Hahn** selected some of the images used in Chapter 1. These contributors were not compensated and we appreciate their support.

This text was piloted with the 2019 Honors Music Appreciation class at the University of North Georgia, the members of which provided edits and feedback. Participants included Bailey Bullard, Abigail Cartwright, Zoe Conoly, Camille Cowherd, Morgan Dow, Olivia Forrest, Sarah Graddy, Isabelle Pobanz, Julia Pownall, and Jessica Wood.

The development and publication of this textbook was funded by a Large-Scale Textbook Transformation Grant from Affordable Learning Georgia (**Jeff Gallant**, Program Director). Our work was also supported by a Presidential Innovation Incentive Award and a Presidential Semester Incentive Award from the University of North Georgia (**Bonita Jacobs**, President) and by the UNG Music Department (**Benjamin Schoening**, Department Head). We are very grateful to these institutions and individuals for making this project possible.

How to Use This Book

OUR VISION

Welcome to *Resonances: Engaging Music in Its Cultural Context*! Although this book is intended primarily for use in the college music appreciation classroom, it was designed with consideration for independent learners, advanced high school students, and experienced musicians. That is to say, it includes enough detail that expert guidance is not required and is written using broadly-accessible language. At the same time, it addresses advanced topics and positions music as a serious object of study.

Unlike most music appreciation textbooks, this volume is organized thematically according to the many ways that music is and has been used in human societies. It brings together examples from classical, folk, and popular traditions from around the world. The text offers a thorough grounding in the cultural and historical context of each work and a close examination of its characteristics. While the book can certainly be read from beginning to end, one can also move freely between chapters and examples without missing crucial information.

This textbook is in no sense comprehensive. There are lots of important and influential works that are not discussed in its pages, many vital musical concepts that are not addressed, and countless ideas that are left unexplored. However, this is a feature, not a bug. The authors of this book reject the idea that a comprehensive overview of "important" music is either desirable or possible. Instead, our approach values diversity and depth. Each chapter includes wildly dissimilar examples from various times and places, each of which is uncovered as both a sonic object and a cultural artifact. The result, we hope, will be renewed interest in the music one hears every day, broadened taste for music that was once unfamiliar, and expanded awareness of the music that is still waiting to be discovered.

In short, this book does not offer a definitive curriculum. What it offers is a new approach to thinking about and engaging music—an approach that we have already piloted with a variety of student audiences and know to be successful. Whether you are reading this book on your own or using it as part of a course, we hope you will find that it is full of new ideas and sounds that change the way you listen to and think about music.

NOTES TO THE INSTRUCTOR

This text is meant to be highly adaptable to your desired curricular and learning objectives, and you are welcome to use it in any way you see fit. It is accompanied by a complete set of teaching materials, including PowerPoint slides, test banks, and videos. These can be accessed through the UNG Press website and the UNG Music Department YouTube channel.

What follows are some guidelines and suggestions for using this text:

1. By our estimation, this textbook contains enough material for four semester-length music appreciation courses. This allows the instructor to select the desired chapters and/or examples and also to change the curriculum from semester to semester. We strongly advise that you **do not attempt to teach this entire text in a single semester**. You will find that the outcome is much more satisfactory if you lead students to engage deeply with a limited number of examples.

2. This textbook is designed to be modular. Any subset of chapters can be assigned in any order, and individual examples can be skipped. Although we advise that you teach one chapter at a time, choosing which examples to use and which to omit, it is also possible to reorganize this volume at the level of the musical example. For instance, one might choose to teach only works from the Western classical tradition, and to do so in chronological order. While this is not ideal, the fact that each example is self-contained means that it can be done. (You might also find that individual entries are of use in other music courses.)

3. In addition to being a textbook, this volume proposes a new approach to organizing the music appreciation curriculum. The examples reflect the expertise of the authors, but they are by no means exhaustive. It goes without saying that many important and interesting musical works are not included. As such, you are invited not only to chart your own path through the examples but to add your own. Please feel free to integrate additional material under the appropriate chapter headings!

4. Although the musical examples linked in this book are primarily audio-only, we recommend videos of live performances for pedagogical use, and have included our recommendations in the chapter playlists on the UNG Music Department YouTube channel. Live performances are also linked in the PowerPoint slides. We chose to link to audio recordings supplied to YouTube by record labels with the hope that they will remain accessible for the life of this text, which in turn means that the listening guides will remain relevant and useful. We have found, however, that students respond much more positively when they are able to watch a performance.

5. You will find that some of the musical examples are accompanied by listening guides, but that many are not. There are several reasons for this. To begin with, the authors felt that only certain examples would benefit greatly from listening guides. Although guides can be helpful, we don't want them to limit students' engagement with the examples. Finally, we thought that the creation of listening guides for the remaining examples would make a good assignment for your students to complete.

6. This textbook is only a tool in support of a great music appreciation course, the most important elements of which are listening, discussion, and reflection. The focal point of any course, whether in person or online, should be direct engagement with the musical objects under consideration. This means focused and repeated listening/watching, accompanied by guided observation. It is up to you to change the way your students perceive and understand musical objects. Happy teaching!

HELP MAKE THIS BOOK BETTER!

The authors intend to issue at least one revised edition of this book, which was developed on an abbreviated timeline and does not contain everything we could have wished. We want our revisions to reflect the needs and interests of those who use the text. Is it missing examples that you would like to teach? Is there an additional unit or chapter that could be integrated? Can information be added to a discussion? Could the text package incorporate additional teaching tools? Did you find an error? If you are interested in helping us to improve this book, please contact Esther Morgan-Ellis with your feedback and ideas.

Unit 1

MUSIC AS A FIELD OF PRACTICE AND STUDY

1

Music in Human Life

Rebecca R. Johnston and Esther M. Morgan-Ellis

WHAT IS MUSIC?

It is surprisingly difficult to define the term "music." More specifically, it can be challenging to determine what is *not* music, and to explain why.

For example, is bird song music? It is beautiful and enjoyable to listen to, and bird song often features clear, catchy melodies. Some birds learn songs from one another, thereby developing diverse repertoires. Is it a problem that birds sing primarily to communicate and attract mates? Humans certainly make music for those purposes. Does the reason for singing determine whether a song counts as music or not? Can music even be made by non-humans, or is it a uniquely human phenomenon?

Let's consider another example. Are the noises of the city music? How about when they are carefully recorded and curated for release by a record company? In 1964, Michael Siegel issued an album entitled *Sounds of the Junk Yard*[1] on

Image 1.1: Is bird song music?
Source: PxHere
Attribution: Unknown
License: CC0

Folkways Records. Does this enshrinement turn the sounds into music? Does your opinion change when you consider that the rock band Sonic Youth was directly inspired by *Sounds of the Junk Yard* and sought to replicate its sounds in their playing? How about when noises are painstakingly arranged into a collage by a composer? The 1952 work *Williams Mix*[2] by John Cage is made up entirely of pre-recorded sounds. How about when they are imitated by a musical instrument? Henry Cowell set out to capture the sounds of the New York subway with his 1916 piano composition *Dynamic Motion*[3]. Or when they are integrated into a concert work, such as the real car horns used in Gershwin's 1928 orchestral composition *An American in Paris*?

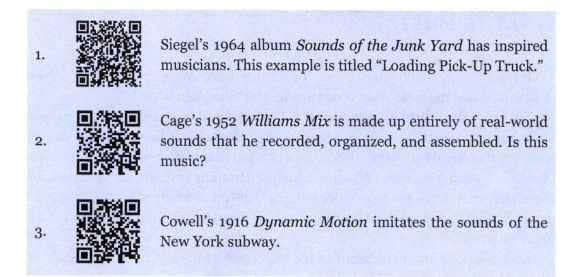

1. Siegel's 1964 album *Sounds of the Junk Yard* has inspired musicians. This example is titled "Loading Pick-Up Truck."

2. Cage's 1952 *Williams Mix* is made up entirely of real-world sounds that he recorded, organized, and assembled. Is this music?

3. Cowell's 1916 *Dynamic Motion* imitates the sounds of the New York subway.

The broadest definition of music to date was provocatively set forth on August 29, 1952, by the American composer John Cage. He made his statement not in words but with a performance of a composition that is known as *4'33"*. The premiere of *4'33"* was given by pianist David Tudor, who came out onto the stage and proceeded to sit in silence at the keyboard for the time indicated in the title, interrupting his performance only to open and close the keyboard at predetermined time markers. The musical contents of the performance, therefore, were not sounds that emanated from the piano but rather the incidental sounds that audience members happened to perceive during the allotted time: rustling programs, whispers, laughter, a passing train. The composer certainly did not know what these sounds would be and exercised no control over them—and indeed, the sounds heard during performances today would in some cases have been unimaginable to the composer, who died in 1992. The object of this composition was to make the case that any sounds could be music as long as they were listened to as music. In other words, music is in the ear of the beholder. It is defined not by its source or by the intent of its creator. It is defined by the act of listening.

There is continued debate over how to define "music." The Google Dictionary definition—that is to say, the definition that one is most likely to come across—reads "vocal or instrumental sounds (or both) combined in such a way as to produce beauty of form, harmony, and expression of emotion." This describes most music, to be sure. But does music have to be beautiful? If so, who is the arbiter of what is beautiful? Does music have to express emotion? And what about music that is created not by voices or instruments but by computers (e.g. electronic dance music)? The above definition excludes a lot.

For a more clinical take, we can turn to Merriam-Webster, which describes music as "the science or art of ordering tones or sounds in succession, in combination, and in temporal relationships to produce a composition having unity and continuity." This definition is more difficult to criticise, but it still seems lacking. What about the power of music to make us cry, or dance, or become overwhelmed with nostalgia? What about the significance of music to personal and cultural identity? A dictionary definition certainly doesn't have to address these dimensions, but they are integral to a deeper understanding of what music really *is*.

THE POWER OF MUSIC

Although we might argue over what is and what is not music, there is no question that music is important. Its significance ranges from the historical to the cultural to the biological. Music has played a role in every documented human society of the past and present. The oldest instrument found to date is an ivory flute created about 43,000 years ago—clear evidence that music is not a recent development. But why did humans start making music? The answers to that question might be discovered by examining the extraordinary effects that making and listening to music has on our brains.

Image 1.2: This bone flute from the Geissenklösterle cave Germany is the oldest known musical instrument.
Source: Wikimedia Commons
Attribution: José-Manuel Benito
License: CC BY-SA 2.5

Music, Human Experience, and the Brain

All of our activities are governed by the amazing organ situated inside of our skulls and between our ears: the human brain. And it is clear to religionists and evolutionists alike that there is something distinctly different between humans and other animals. But what is that difference? What makes us capable of complex reason and emotion? What gives us the ability to have an awareness of our own thought processes? It can't simply be the *size* of our brains, as the brains of blue whales are much larger than those of humans, yet we don't credit them with equivalent intelligence. Conversely, gorilla brains are only a little smaller than human brains, and they are not capable of the extreme creative and processing power of humanity. So what is it that makes our brains different?

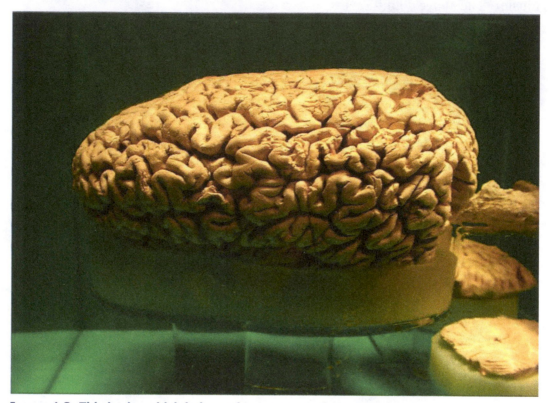

Image 1.3: This brain, which belonged to a sperm whale, is many times the size of a human brain.
Source: Wikimedia Commons
Attribution: Yohei Yamashita
License: CC BY-SA 2.0

What makes us human?

Consider just a few of the qualities that are claimed to be unique to humans. We recognize ourselves in the working order of things, and are capable of standing back as a spectator and seeing our part in the greater picture. In other words, we have *self-consciousness*, and are capable of making choices based upon that information. Scientists use the mirror test (whether or not an animal species recognizes reflections of themselves as self, rather than another animal) to measure self-consciousness. But there are many species of primates that recognize their reflections as self, so that characteristic isn't unique to humans. We have an appreciation of beauty and of aesthetic things, and are compelled as a species to create art. But there are some elephants who paint surprisingly beautiful imitations of the world around them, and some birds who decorate their nests—does this mean that they possess our same capacity for appreciation of aesthetics?

What about humor? All people possess a sense of humor (though some have less than others) and can appreciate and express humor. Not only does humor require intelligence and understanding of situational variables, but it also requires the ability to see the odd, absurd and ironic. But there are chimpanzees that "laugh" when they are tickled, and if you watch young chimps playing long enough, you will eventually see one pull a prank on another and run away "laughing."

Image 1.4: This elephant is painting a picture. Does that mean it can appreciate art?
Source: Wikimedia Commons
Attribution: User "Raki_Man"
License: CC BY 3.0

Image 1.4: This satin bowerbird has decorated its courtship stage with a wide variety of blue objects. Bowerbirds appear to have a keen artistic sense and decorate with exquisite care.
Source: Wikimedia Commons
Attribution: Joseph C Boone
License: CC BY-SA 4.0

What about awareness of death? While many creatures exhibit behaviors we could characterize as mourning when they lose a beloved human or fellow animal, humans have elaborate funeral rituals upon death. The ancient Egyptians actually buried people with physical objects so that they would have things with them in the next life. But elephants[4] have been observed burying their dead (and the dead of other species) in addition to placing food, fruit, and flowers with their bodies. That sounds a lot like a funeral.

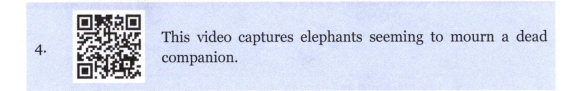

4. This video captures elephants seeming to mourn a dead companion.

What about awareness of time? Humans experience sequence of events, form memories, and then predict future outcomes, and we have ways of measuring the passing of time in equal intervals (think second hand on a watch). Dogs and other animals certainly don't have clocks or devices, but they reliably know when it is dinner time. Is this because of biological processes, or do they, too, have some sense of time?

What about love? It is arguably one of the most important motivational forces in a human's life, but are we alone in this? Animals display behaviors that clearly indicate affection, but do they love each other the way we do? Cats will rub their companions and purr, whales can deliberately save seals from attack, and dogs display extraordinary altruism towards their owners and other creatures. In humans, these behaviors signal the thing we call love. Do animals experience it the way we do?

What about language? Humanity is the only species that uses language, although we are clearly not the only species that communicates. So what is different about us? Animals communicate in many ways with one another, and some gorillas have been taught sign-language. Koko the gorilla reportedly understood over 2,000 spoken words and was able to use more than 1,000 signs to convey thoughts and emotions. She was even able to communicate compound ideas by using signs in ways they had not been taught to her. This certainly was a form of communication and language use, although Koko could never learn to speak. In addition, while some animals can understand words, sounds, and tone of voice, they do not comprehend syntax or communicate in complex sentences. Throughout history, human beings have devised hundreds of languages and endless dialects, despite the fact that we are born with no way to verbally communicate, at all. So what is it about our brains that makes them capable of complex language, when the composition of our brains is so similar to chimpanzees and gorillas?

Image 1.6: Bonobos Kanzi and Panbanisha are pictured here communicating with a pictorial "keyboard."
Source: Wikimedia Commons
Attribution: User "Wcalvin"
License: CC BY-SA 4.0

Language and the Human Brain

It comes down to the structure of our brains and to what those structures do. Generally, the human brain can be divided into three regions: the **forebrain**, **midbrain**, and **hindbrain**. This characteristic is absent in most animals. Although the *size* of the brain itself does not determine complex intelligence, the size of the brain in relationship to the size of the body matters. Humans win the rodeo with the largest brain of all animals in comparison to the size of their bodies. In addition, the human brain has more neurons in its outermost layer (the **cerebral cortex**) than do other animals, and the insulation around nerve fibers in the human brain is thicker than that of other animals, enabling more rapid signal transfer between neurons. We literally *think better and faster*. But it is the structures responsible for language production and comprehension (Broca's and Wernicke's areas) that are unique to human beings. And, interestingly, both of these areas are heavily involved in the processing of music, which brings us to the crux of the matter: human beings are the only animals who employ "music" and "language". That is what separates us from every other species on the planet. And it seems as though we do these things because we have been endowed with neuroanatomical structures that are unique to us. So what do these two critical brain regions do? And how is music cognition different from language cognition?

Early investigators learned about particular regions of the brain that control speech by observing patients' limitations and then conducting postmortem exams. A French neurologist named Paul Broca observed a patient who understood language but who was unable to produce more than a few isolated words. When that patient died, Broca conducted a postmortem exam

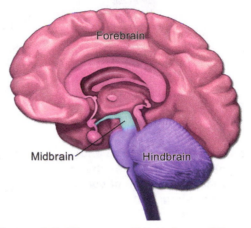

Image 1.7: These are the regions of the brain.
Source: Wikimedia Commons
Attribution: User "BruceBlaus"
License: CC BY-SA 4.0

Image 1.8: This engraving from ca. 1881 depicts Paul Broca, a French neurologist responsible for making foundational discoveries about language and the brain.
Source: Wikimedia Commons
Attribution: Unknown
License: Public Domain

and found a lesion in the man's forebrain in the **frontal lobe**. He deduced that this area was associated with the production of speech, and it was termed **Broca's area**. Persons with damage to Broca's area understand heard language and know what they wish to say but are unable to speak. They can't speak because Broca's area controls the *physical production of speech*. Essentially, our brains take in auditory stimuli, then Broca's area (in conjunction with Wernieke's area, which we will discuss in a moment) converts the stimuli to neuronal representations that are then translated into the physical motions involved in producing speech sounds. To put this more simply, that area of the brain helps us understand what we hear, formulate articulate thoughts and then convert them into speech.

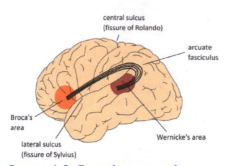

Image 1.9: Broca's area and Wernieke's area handle the input of sound, conversion of sound to understanding, and utterance of spoken language.
Source: Wikimedia Commons
Attribution: Peter Hagoort
License: CC BY 3.0

Image 1.10: The German physician Carl Wernicke, photographed here in the early 20th century, expanded on Broca's observations.
Source: Wikimedia Commons
Attribution: J.F. Lehmann, Muenchen
License: Public Domain

About ten years later, a neurologist named Carl Wernicke identified a similar, but different, problem in patients who were unable to comprehend language or to construct meaningful sentences, even though they did not experience difficulty in producing articulate words. In postmortem examination, he found lesions at the junction of the parietal, temporal, and occipital lobes. He deduced that this area, now termed **Wernicke's area**, had something to do with the understanding of language. Conjunctly, Broca's and Wernicke's areas handle the input of sound, conversion of sound to understanding, and utterance of spoken language. And these two areas are distinct to humans. The genuinely fascinating thing is that for many years, these areas were thought to be exclusively involved in the processing of language. But recent researchers have discovered through fMRI (functional magnetic resonance imaging) technology that the two language processing centers are activated during listening to and processing music, even when it contains no text. In other words, your two language centers fire when you are listening to instrumental music and are not processing language. How bizarre is that? Why might that be? How are music and language similar in such a way as to explain this phenomenon?

Connections Between Speech and Music

What two things do you think of most easily when someone asks, "What is music?" Probably variation in pitch (frequency) and rhythm (time), even though those are not the only elements of music. Is there a pitch and a rhythm to speech? Read that question aloud to yourself, and note the fact that not all words are the same pitch. This is because we emphasize more important words and increase pitch when asking a question. Read it again and note the fact that not all of the words are the same speed or length, due to the fact that we vary the rhythm of speech sounds. And not only that: there is a **syntax** (the orderly arrangement of sounds in a system) to both language and music. They behave similarly in that the arrangement of sounds is predictable and conforms to patterns. And there we have it. Our brains are uniquely constructed for the successful intake, conversion, and execution of *language and music*. And the reason other animals can't and don't make music or speech (some animals make musical sounds, but the construction of these sounds doesn't conform to syntactical rules, so these sounds aren't actually music in the way we understand it) is because their brains lack the two areas involved in the processing of orderly sound systems. How crazy is that?

But what does this really mean about the nature of music and speech? It suggests that those are the two primary things that make us human and that distinguish us from all other creatures on the planet. That's a significant point. But music isn't only processed in Broca's and Wernicke's areas, although speech primarily is.

Before we examine that, however, we need to discuss how the brain is generally structured. The brain is divided into three main parts: the **cerebrum**, the cerebellum, and the brain stem. The cerebrum is the part that gives the brain its wrinkled appearance. It is divided into a left and right hemisphere separated by the **corpus callosum**, a bundle of fibers that transmit messages from one side of the brain to the other. The cerebrum performs higher functions like receiving and analyzing sensory input such as touch, sight, and sound, and also processes reasoning, emotion, memory, and fine motor control. Both Broca's and Wernicke's areas are situated in the cerebrum. The cerebellum is located under the cerebrum. It primarily coordinates muscle movements, and processes the body's position in space for purposes of balance. The brainstem is the most evolutionarily primal area of the brain—one that we share with other primates. The brainstem performs primarily autonomous functions—those that don't involve voluntary thought, like heart rate, breathing, body temperature, digestion, swallowing, coughing, and vomiting. You

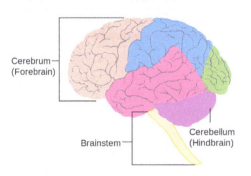

Image 1.11: The brain is divided into the cerebrum, the cerebellum, and the brain stem.
Source: Wikipedia
Attribution: Cancer Research UK
License: CC BY-SA 4.0

can see that as you move upward from the brainstem, the functions of the brain become more complex.

Now that we've handled some of the less-interesting technical information about the way the brain is structured, let's go back to the cerebrum, where most complex brain function occurs. If we can arrive at an understanding of the way the cerebrum is divided and what kinds of information are processed in each area, it will help us to understand the differences in the way the brain processes language and music—perhaps the two most significant markers of what it is to be human. As previously mentioned, the cerebrum is divided into a left and right hemisphere that communicate with one another across the corpus callosum. Not all functions of the two hemispheres are shared. In general, the left hemisphere controls the physical motion on the right side of the body and the right hemisphere controls the physical motion on the left side of the body. Also, in general terms, the left hemisphere processes speech, comprehension, arithmetic, and writing. The right hemisphere controls creativity, spatial ability, and artistic and musical skills. This explanation is a bit misleading, however.

If you look down at a brain from the top, you can see it is divided into two distinct hemispheres. But if you look at the brain from the side, you can see that each hemisphere has distinct fissures that divide the brain into chunks, called lobes. Each hemisphere has four lobes. Moving from front to back, they are the frontal, parietal, temporal, and occipital lobes. Each can be divided even further into areas that serve specific functions (like Broca's and Werneike's areas). But it is important to understand that no lobe or area of the brain functions in isolation. There are complex networks between the lobes of the brain and between the hemispheres that interact to process information. In that sense, our brains are the most complex computers on the planet! We'll quickly take a look at what is generally processed in each lobe before circling back to talk about the differences between language and music processing in the brain.

Frontal lobe processing determines personality, behavior, emotions, judgment, planning, problem solving, speech (Broca's area), fine body movement, intelligence,

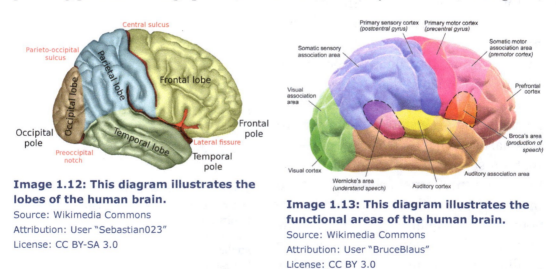

Image 1.12: This diagram illustrates the lobes of the human brain.
Source: Wikimedia Commons
Attribution: User "Sebastian023"
License: CC BY-SA 3.0

Image 1.13: This diagram illustrates the functional areas of the human brain.
Source: Wikimedia Commons
Attribution: User "BruceBlaus"
License: CC BY 3.0

concentration, and one of the other defining characteristics of human beings: self-awareness. You can see that the frontal lobe (put your hand up to your forehead—that's where the frontal lobe is) handles most of the things that make you, well... *you*. This is why traumatic injury to the frontal lobe from head-impact is often absolutely devastating to the individual. You can lose what it is to be you if that area is damaged. The parietal lobe processes senses of touch, pain, and temperature, and interprets signals from vision, hearing, motor input, memory, and spatial perception. It also plays a role in the interpretation of language and words. Moving further back, the temporal lobe handles the understanding of language (Wernicke's area), memory, hearing, sequencing, and organization. And finally, the occipital lobe interprets visual stimuli, including color, light, and movement. Whew! That was a lot of information about our highly complex human brain.

So let's go back to examine language processing a little more deeply. First, our ears take in sound waves and translate them into electrical impulses that travel through nerves to different parts of the brain. The first place they go is the auditory cortex in the temporal lobe, where the sound is translated into neuronal representations (basically, your brain's "image" of the sounds). The neuronal representations are then transmitted to the areas of the brain involved in interpreting them and deciding what to do with them. In the case of speech that is only heard, the auditory cortex and Werneike's area are primarily involved. In the case of language that is read and interpreted, the visual cortex and Werneike's area are primarily involved. In the case of speech that is produced, Werneike's area transmits neuronal representations to Broca's area, which converts them into spoken language with involvement in the motor cortex. But if language and music are so similar, what is different in the way that the brain processes language and music?

Well, to begin with, language processing is fairly isolated. As we've discussed, depending on the type of language activity a person is engaging with, there are a few areas primarily involved in processing the information. In the case of music cognition, however, the brain lights up like a Christmas tree. There is activity all over the place: in both hemispheres, in all four lobes, in the cerebellum, and even in the brain stem. With the advent of fMRI, we can see which areas of the brain light up as a person is engaging with music. As in the case of language, it depends upon the way in which you are engaging with music. But the one thing that is consistent is that no matter how you are engaging—whether you are listening passively, or listening actively (listening *and* thinking about what you are listening to), whether you are hearing music with or without words, whether you are playing music, reading music, writing and composing music, or improvising music—a unique neural network lights up all across the brain. Normally unrelated areas of the brain work in synchronicity to process music, even when they do not coordinate to process any other type of information. That is pretty crazy! Even the brain stem—the part of the brain that handles automatic and subconscious processes—assists in music cognition.

So here we come to the crux of it. The human brain is an incredibly complicated computer. It handles incomprehensible amounts of information every second, and is more complex than the brains of other animals. There are two primary things that separate us from all other animals on the planet: language and music. Our brains are structured differently than are those of other animals, and it is these specialized structures that allow us to engage in language and music. But while language processing is complex, music cognition is even more complex, involving more brain regions and involving activity in both hemispheres, all lobes, the cerebrum, and the brainstem.

Beyond this, music also activates the limbic system within which emotions and feelings are processed. It is capable of eliciting sympathetic emotional response from listeners even in the absence of words, and our memory systems are intrinsically woven into the brain's processing of music. This is why music can be used to "bring back" patients with Alzheimer's[5], and why you can remember a song even if you haven't heard it for 40 years. Suddenly, you'll find yourself singing along and wondering how in the world you still have that information in there—but it's in there because the retrieval pathways were laid down in more than one way. You won't remember a poem or a story, or any other information, the way you remember music. For this reason, it is a profound educational tool: information can be entrained quickly and permanently when connected to music. Think about how many things were taught to you as a child through song, beginning with learning your letters! The A-B-C song is the most commonly taught song in the U.S. (and many other places have their own version) because it is such an effective way of teaching children to remember otherwise unfamiliar and disconnected information (the sound of each letter and the order in which they occur in the alphabet). If it is such a profound educational tool because of the effects on memory and retention, how else can music be used?

5.  This video details the experience of Henry, a man with Alzheimer's Disease, who remembers who he is through the use of music.

MUSIC AND HUMAN DEVELOPMENT, LEARNING, AND WELLNESS

Due to the information that we have gained from the field of neuroscience, the use of music therapy has exploded in the past decades. **Music therapy** is the clinical and evidence-based use of music interventions to accomplish individualized goals within a therapeutic relationship by a licensed music therapist. And because music is processed all over the brain, music therapy can be utilized to rehabilitate patients suffering from a broad host of disorders, ranging from traumatic brain injury to cerebral palsy, from learning disabilities to Parkinson's Disease. It can be used to regain voluntary movement or return speech skills when they have been lost because of a blood clot or stroke. And the remarkable thing is how genuinely effective these interventions are.

The Field of Music Therapy

It is important to talk about what music therapy *is*, and what it is *not*. Although all people can participate in music, and music teachers spend time creating music and working with students, board certified music therapists are the only individuals who participate in an allied health profession that is research-based, and that, in the words of the American Music Therapy Association, "actively applies supportive science to the creative, emotional, and energizing experiences of music for health treatment and educational goals." Music therapy is applied in either an educational or clinical context, and music therapists must hold a music degree(s) and a degree in music therapy. The degree involves clinical internship and certification by the board of the American Music Therapy Association (AMTA). Licensing involves many hours of training in order to understand which musical activities to apply in a given context, and it may be used to improve individuals' functioning, health, or wellbeing.

So why does music therapy work? Because it is a stimulus that activates every major region of the brain simultaneously. Because music processing occurs globally in the brain, it develops more comprehensive and stronger neurologic processes. According to Sharon Graham, founder and director of the Tampa Bay Institute for

Image 1.14: Here, a music therapist works with a patient who is recovering from traumatic brain injury.
Source: Military Health System
Attribution: Caitlin Russell
License: Public Domain

Music Therapy, "Music is used as a stimulus when one encounters trauma, disease or disorder, and is the most powerful non-pharmacological tool we have to address any deficits that arise."

What is music therapy used for? The possibilities are almost limitless! It may be used for physical rehabilitation and facilitating movement, because when we hear rhythmic information, the motor cortex in our brains is activated: It is for this reason that you are compelled to move on the beat when you hear a peppy song. Have you ever noticed how people unconsciously coordinate themselves in time when music is played? Pay attention when music is playing outdoors—nearly everyone will begin to walk at the same tempo as the music. The funny thing is that they don't even realize they are doing it! The activation of the motor cortex can be utilized by music therapists to increase motor function and voluntary movement in people with Parkinson's and Multiple Sclerosis and in physically injured veterans.

Music therapy may be used to facilitate improvement of mood and reduction of depression. This works for multiple reasons, not the least of which is that music is enjoyable. However, it also works because we have an immediate physiological response to the music we enjoy. Engaging with liked music causes the release of serotonin and dopamine- neurotransmitters in the brain, which leads to feelings of happiness and well-being. It also releases norepinephrine, which can result in a sense of alertness and euphoria. The act of singing, in particular, releases endorphins—the "feel good" chemicals in the brain. Choral singing (singing in a group with others) has been shown to cause the release of oxytocin, which enhances feelings of trust and bonding and results in reduction of depression and loneliness. One study recently indicated that choral singers have lower levels of cortisol, indicating lower stress, while multiple studies have indicated that singing relieves anxiety and contributes to quality of life. And the best part is, you don't have to be a good singer to reap the rewards: A 2005 study indicated that group singing "can produce satisfying and therapeutic sensations even when the sound produced by the vocal instrument is of mediocre quality."

Image 1.15: This music therapist is visiting Renown Children's Hospital in Reno, Nevada.

Studies have indicated that music can be used to reduce insomnia and to reduce the perception of pain, and it can be used as part of a rehabilitation protocol after injury or surgery. One study from the General Hospital of Salzburg found patients recovering from back surgery had higher rates of healing and less pain when exposed to music. Music therapy can be used with older adults to lessen the effects of dementia and Alzheimer's Disease and it can be used to restore speech when aphasia (loss of ability to speak) occurs as a result of injury or stroke. Congresswoman Gabrielle Giffords used music therapy to regain speech after surviving a gunshot wound to her brain. Interestingly, music can also be used to reduce the symptoms of asthma, can be used in premature infants to improve sleep patterns and to increase weight gain, and can be used to help people with Down's Syndrome or Autism when speech is limited. In fact, it seems that there is little that music therapy cannot be utilized to improve. So what should we take away from all of this? That music is awesome, of course, and that everyone should engage with music actively throughout the course of their lives.

Why do (and should) humans make music?

If music can help rewire a brain that has been damaged or is limited in some way, it can also be used to create new brain growth and increase processing efficiency in all students. This is why there is a strong correlation (relationship) between studying music and higher grades in other subject areas. In 2015, the

Image 1.16: Studying music can lead to higher achievement in other areas.
Source: Wikimedia Commons
Attribution: F. Rodricks
License: CC BY-SA 4.0

Every Student Succeeds Act replaced No Child Left Behind, and for the first time codified music as part of a core, well-rounded academic experience with which all children should be provided. The current academic environment focuses on and prizes primarily STEM subjects, but we have learned that it is actually the A in STEAM (Arts) that provides training ground for the things employers say they prize more than subject-matter knowledge: creativity, initiative, and the ability to generate new solutions to problems not previously encountered. No child should go through school without access to these subjects.

Humans have engaged in music for as long as we have written history. Even before humans had the ability to write down the music they were creating and performing, they produced written descriptions documenting the fact that they valued music. The Biblical authors wrote about people engaging in music by playing instruments, dancing, and singing. Clearly, music was a part of those ancient cultures. We don't know what that music sounded like, because they didn't have a system to write it down, but we know they were doing it.

We also know that humans have been "musicking" since *long before* written history, as evidenced by prehistoric bone flutes found in various parts of the world. The existence of these instruments suggests that music may actually have preceded formalized spoken language as we understand it, and certainly preceded writing. To put this in perspective, humans were creating and playing instruments when wooly mammoths and saber tooth tigers roamed the earth. And to make that fact even more intriguing, when researchers blew through those flutes, they heard the pentatonic scale still in use in elementary school music today. Why would those early humans have created music, when the primary objectives were to eat, not die from the elements, and not be eaten? We can't answer this question definitively, but one theory is that they were imitating the sounds they heard in nature. Another is that humans utilized music to coordinate themselves in time together (think: *one, two, three - pull!*). Yet another is that music simply feels good and touches something spiritual in humans. We will likely never know. All we can say for certain is that music is one of the things that separates us from every other animal on the planet, including our closest relatives, and that it was part of human experience before modern humans existed.

One final consideration is that it appears as though music and language acquisition skills are innately learned by humans. No one sits down with children and attempts to formally teach them to produce language or music. They simply learn those things by listening to and imitating the sounds being used in their environment. All humans in all cultures the world over uniformly amass both language and music skills simply by being immersed in an environment in which those systems are being used. And this tells us that our brains are *hardwired* for success with those two systems. Even if we didn't have fMRI scans to show us that, we can deduce it from the informal experiences of babies. Studies have even shown that newborn infants who have had no experience in the world whatsoever recognize and respond to essential musical elements. These elements, which will be described and discussed in the next section, include tonic and dominant (I and V in the scale—the two most important chords) and meter (the way beats are grouped and divided). How is it that babies' brains are able to do this with no training? *It's hardwired!*

Music and Innate Aptitude

We have all seen that some people seem naturally to have more musical ability than others. Some children seem born singing beautifully, while others struggle to develop musical skills. We tend to look at children who sing early and well, and think, "Oh, she's so *talented*." But that perception can be a little misleading, and here's why.

Researchers have indicated that there are two primary things that contribute to musical ability. One of them is **aptitude**, which is defined as the ease and speed with which your brain processes certain kinds of information. Aptitude is innate. You're born with it. It is woven into the development of the grey matter in your brain as you are developing in your mother's womb. Strangely, research indicates that aptitude is developmental until somewhere around age eight or nine. In other words, the ease and speed with which your brain is able to process certain types of information is formative until you reach age nine, at which time it stabilizes. From that point forward, you will be reliant on whatever aptitude you developed during your earliest years. This doesn't mean you can't learn to do new things or develop new skills. We can all learn to do things within whatever aptitude we possess. It just means that the ease and speed with which we work doesn't fundamentally change beyond that point.

Image 1.17: Everyone has an aptitude for music, even though some people have a greater aptitude than others.
Source: Wikimedia Commons
Attribution: User "Sungmin Yun"
License: CC BY-SA 2.0

Interestingly, the same is true of aptitude for language, which makes sense, because the two systems are so intrinsically similar. Research has indicated that the same developmental window (birth to age nine) exists for language aptitude. For both of these, early exposure, and early development, are critical for the rest of the life of a human being. How do we know language aptitude stabilizes at that age? Obviously, it would be horribly unethical to lock children up for the first nine years of their lives and expose them to little or no language to see what would happen. We can't do that. We do, however, have multiple stories of severe neglect that shine some light on what happens when children don't develop language aptitude while they are young.

In one particularly famous case, a young girl was born to an abusive father who kept her chained to a potty chair or in a crib, and rarely let anyone speak to her or interact with her. Because there was no interactivity with the sound system, this child did not learn to speak. When she was rescued, around age 12, she was immediately taken into custody, and teams of researchers attempted to teach her to speak. She learned the use of some nouns and verbs and was able to communicate simple things, but she never learned the complex grammar that all children innately learn simply by hearing language spoken around them and having people interact with them using language. In fact, researchers estimate that all she could achieve was the basic communicative ability of Koko the gorilla (who had limited ability to form compound or complex thoughts, and did so with sign language). Why was this? Because a child's aptitude for certain kinds of processing is developmental, and is developed, during the first years of life. Once that developmental window closes, the child is working with established aptitude.

In another famous case, a child was kept contained in a room with a television on all day. The child was hearing language spoken regularly, but by abstract people on the television. In other words, no one was interacting with the child while using language. Interactivity is critical—just *hearing* language isn't enough. That child did not learn to speak just by listening. In the same way, music aptitude is not developed simply by listening. Children must hear others around them singing and see them moving rhythmically, and others must interact with them as they do these things.

In addition to aptitude, the thing that most determines a person's skill is **achievement**. This is what an individual *does* with the aptitude they have. Do they learn to sing and play an instrument? Do they learn to read and write? Do they regularly engage in creating music? If the answer is yes, then chances are, their achievement (or skill) will be relatively high. Does high innate aptitude automatically mean a person will have high achievement? No. There exists only a correlation between the two variables—not a causative relationship. A child may be born with lower aptitude but work her entire life and emerge as a person with relatively high skill after years of training. By the same token, a child may be born with relatively high aptitude but never engage with it or use it. That child is likely to have much lower achievement than the one who worked at it. Interestingly, the same seems to be true of language.

And in both cases, there is no such thing as a person with *no* aptitude. I've frequently heard people say: "Oh, I can't sing." My usual response is: "Yes, you can. Everyone can." Usually when people make statements like that, what they actually mean is: "I don't sing *well*." But our society has robbed so many people of their birthright by fooling us into thinking that music is something only the most talented and skilled should do while everyone else watches, and, as a result, these people believe their aptitude is so low that they just shouldn't do it. Knowing what we do about music and the brain, and about the benefits of engaging in music over the course of a lifetime, this is a pretty tragic thing! If I told you that simply singing, reading music, playing an instrument, or writing music over the course of a lifetime could decrease the likelihood of developing Alzheimer's when you are older, would you change your mind about whether or not you should pursue it? (I hope so!) All humans have aptitude for music and for language. This aptitude is generally distributed along a bell curve. There are people with higher aptitude and people with lower aptitude. But none of us have no aptitude, because it is a matter of our brain structure.

In fact, they had to search the world over to find only ten or so people to participate in a study in *amusia* (a condition in which the brain simply doesn't organize musical sounds into meaningful patterns). In people with amusia, the brain takes in sound, but it is disorganized and the individual can't perceive the structure. In other words, they don't hear music, they hear *noise*. While a normal individual might hear a beautiful symphony, an individual with amusia might perceive the sounds of New York City on a busy day. Obviously, both people *hear* the same thing, but one person's brain organizes the sound meaningfully into melody, harmony, phrases, meter, and other elements, while the other's brain doesn't organize it at all. What a terrible thing! Can you imagine not being able to listen to and enjoy music? Not being able to play a song back in your mind? Not being able to tap on a beat because your brain doesn't perceive the organization of meter and rhythm? Imagine how colorless life would be! Fundamentally, what I am telling you is this: *Of course you can sing and learn to play an instrument, and learn to read or write music.* Do you know how I know? Because you can listen to and enjoy music. Your brain is organizing the sound, which means you have the fundamental capacity to engage with it.

Music and Human Flourishing

So what does all of this together tell us? Music is important to the human species and always has been. Though you may remember a poem or a story, the way you remember words differs from the way you remember music. This difference is why music, like literature, belongs in the curriculum. Because information can be entrained quickly and permanently when connected to it, music is a profound educational tool. It is something that engages all areas of the brain at once, and no other activity does that.

Image 1.18: It's never too late to get involved in music!
Source: Flickr
Attribution: Garry Knight
License: CC BY 2.0

Music can be used to train and grow the brain and build connections between areas, or to rehabilitate and heal individuals. It assists in the formation of long-term memories and in the retrieval of stored information, increases processing efficiency in other modes of cognition, and assists the brain in coordinating normally unrelated brain regions. It is for these reasons that music is one of life's most miraculous phenomena. It has probably been with us for the totality of our existence as a species. And despite the fact that there are a limited number of pitches and rhythmic patterns, people throughout history, in every corner of the globe and every culture ever recorded, have engaged in the creation and performance of music that is unique to them. It truly is part of our human birthright and deserves to again take its place as a *critical curricular offering* in all of our schools.

And you know what else? Even if you didn't learn to read music, sing, or play an instrument while you were in school, it's not too late! Researchers tell us that you can begin at literally any point in life and still see benefits. It truly isn't about how well you do it—it is that you regularly do it over time. So go join an ensemble or find some private lessons!

RESOURCES FOR FURTHER LEARNING

Print

Knight, Andrew J., A. Blythe LaGasse, and Alicia Ann Clair. *Music Therapy: An Introduction to the Profession*. American Music Therapy Association, 2018.

Murph, Megan Elizabeth. "Max Neuhaus, R. Murray Schafer, and the Challenges of Noise." Ph.D. dissertation, University of Kentucky, 2018.

Patel, Aniruddh D. *Music, Language, and the Brain.* Oxford University Press, 2010.

Sacks, Oliver. *Musicophilia: Tales of Music and the Brain.* Revised and expanded edition. Vintage, 2008.

Online

American Music Therapy Association: https://www.musictherapy.org/

Alive Inside documentary: http://www.aliveinside.us/

The Elements of Music

Esther M. Morgan-Ellis

THE DIMENSIONS OF SOUND

All sound—not just music—has certain characteristics. The distinction between music and non-musical sounds, in most cases, is one of organization: sounds that we describe as noise tend to be irregular and unpredictable, while sounds that we describe as music are more likely to exhibit patterns. This is not always the case. A jackhammer, for instance, makes a regular and patterned noise, while certain composers create patternless music.

Whether we are listening to noise or music, we will perceive the same elements: **rhythm**, **pitch**, **volume**, **articulation**, and **timbre**. These elements will combine in time to produce a sonic object of a given **texture** that either exhibits or lacks **form**. In the following sections, we will define each of these dimensions and explore the roles that each plays in the creation and perception of music.

Rhythm

Rhythm is the temporal aspect of sound. It is the pattern of "on" and "off" states exhibited by any sound as time passes. Rhythm is by no means unique to music. When you speak, the consonants of your words produce rhythm. When a car drives by, the oscillating sounds of the tires and engines create rhythm.

Music often (although not always) features rhythmic patterns. The most basic of these is the **pulse**[1], which—like the pulse produced by your own heart—is a sequence of regularly-spaced sounds. The frequency of the pulses determines **tempo**[2], which can range from very slow to very fast. It makes sense that music should tend to be organized around a pulse, since our very existence is organized around pulses. Our hearts beat to a pulse, we often breathe to a pulse, we walk to a pulse, and we organize time into pulses (seconds). It is usually not difficult to detect the pulse in a musical work: simply tap your foot or clap your hands, and there it is.

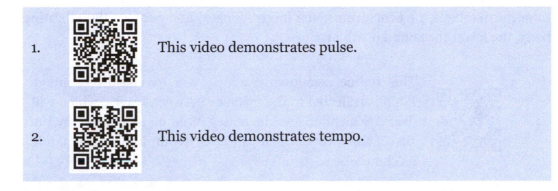

1.   This video demonstrates pulse.

2.   This video demonstrates tempo.

Pulses, however, are usually not all of equal weight. Some have a greater musical significance than others. When pulses are organized into groups containing strong and weak beats, **meter** is established. Each metrical group is called a **measure** or **bar**. In notated music, these groups are physically separated by **bar lines**, which help performers to easily perceive how the pulses are grouped and to identify which is the strongest. While measures can contain any number of pulses, the most common grouping are two, three, and four. These groupings are termed **duple**, **triple**, and **quadruple meter**. Each measure in all three of these meters will begin with a strong pulse, termed the **downbeat**. In duple meter, the pattern of pulses is [strong-weak]. In triple, it is [strong-weak-weak]. And in quadruple, it is [strong-weak-medium-weak].

Pitch

Pitch[3] refers to the "highness" or "lowness" of sound. Sound, of course, is not physically located in high or low spaces, but most listeners can easily perceive the difference between a high-pitched sound and a low-pitched sound. Our use of the terms high and low to describe pitch reflects the characteristics of sound waves.

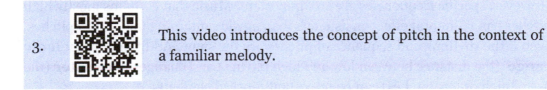

3.   This video introduces the concept of pitch in the context of a familiar melody.

All sounds are produced by vibrating bodies, which in turn produce sound waves that can be perceived by mechanisms in your ear and decoded by your brain. Pitch[4] is determined by the frequency of those sound waves. A high pitch is produced by a high-frequency sound wave, and a low pitch is produced by a low-frequency sound wave. The frequency of sound waves is in turn determined by the characteristics of the vibrating body that sparks them into action. All other parameters being equal, a long string, once plucked and set into motion, will produce a lower pitch than a short string[5]. Likewise, a thick string will produce a lower pitch than a thin string of the same length. The same principles apply when you blow across the ends of tubes, strike bells, or beat drums: the larger, longer, and heavier the vibrating body, the lower the sound it will produce.

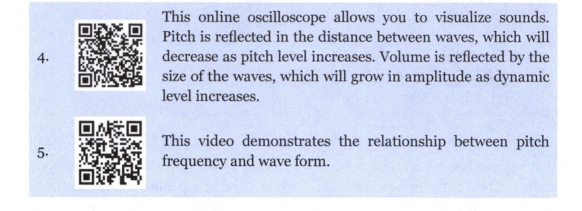

4. This online oscilloscope allows you to visualize sounds. Pitch is reflected in the distance between waves, which will decrease as pitch level increases. Volume is reflected by the size of the waves, which will grow in amplitude as dynamic level increases.

5. This video demonstrates the relationship between pitch frequency and wave form.

Music is usually characterized by the careful organization of pitches. To begin with, most musical systems recognize what is termed **octave equivalence**[6]. This is the consensus that you can halve or double the frequency of the pitch without changing its essential identity. To see this principle in action, attend any birthday party at which both women and men are present. When the guests sing "Happy Birthday," they will not sing exactly the same pitches. Instead, the women will tend to sing in a high octave, and the men will tend to sing in a low octave. In technical terms, this means that the women will probably sing pitches that have frequencies equal to twice that of those sung by the men. However, all participants will agree that they are all singing the same pitches, or in **unison**. An octave is an example of an **interval**, which is the distance between two pitches.

In the Western system, we acknowledge this phenomenon by using the same letter names to designate pitches in different octaves. For example, pitches at the frequencies of 110 hz, 220 hz, 440 hz, 880 hz, and 1,760 hz are all called "A." However, specific frequencies are still important. Music that contains mostly high pitches has a different effect on listeners than music containing mostly low pitches, even if the rhythms and sequence of pitches are the same. Additionally, **melodic range**[7] (the distance between low and high pitches) and changes in **register** (the use of high or low pitches) can be important musical elements.

6. This video demonstrates octave equivalence in the context of "Happy Birthday."

7. This video introduces the concept of melodic range.

The Western system—that is to say, the system of musical organization that was first developed in medieval Europe and continues to dominate global listening today—goes quite a bit further in its efforts to organize pitch. Let us return to the octave. Between the A at 220 Hz and the A at 440 Hz, there are a near-infinite assortment of possible frequencies at which an intermediary pitch might sound. However, we do not use all of those pitches when we create music. Instead, we identify a limited number of specific pitches to be used. The Western system is best represented by the piano keyboard, which is both familiar and useful.

Image 2.1: Each white key on a piano is assigned a letter name. Those letter names repeat at each octave, reflecting our agreement that every A (for example), whether high or low, is in some sense the "same" note. The black keys are named after the adjoining white keys: simply add "flat" to the name of the white key to the right or "sharp" to the name of the white key to the left.
Source: Public Domain Pictures
Attribution: Karen Arnold
License: CC0

As you can see, the space between the A at 220 Hz and the A at 440 Hz is divided across twelve piano keys. This is called the **chromatic**[8] pitch set, and it includes all of the pitches used in Western music. However, composers only rarely use the entire chromatic pitch set. When you do hear music that uses every available note, you will probably find that it makes you uncomfortable. This is because we are used to hearing music built using a set of only seven pitches that is called a **scale**. Most music is based on one of two scales: the **major** scale[9] and the **minor** scale[10]. If the pitches in a piece of music are drawn from a major scale, it is described as being in the **major mode**. Likewise, if the pitches are drawn from a minor scale, it is in the **minor mode**. A scale can start on any pitch, which then determines the **key** of music that is based on that scale. For example, music created using pitches drawn from the A major scale is in the key of A major.

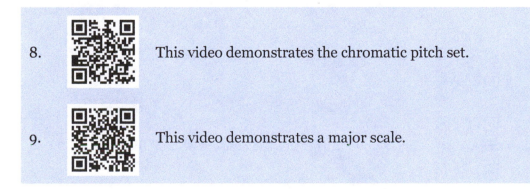

8. This video demonstrates the chromatic pitch set.

9. This video demonstrates a major scale.

10.   This video demonstrates a minor scale.

In most pieces of music, pitches are assigned to two different roles: **melody**[11] and **harmony**[12 & 13]. Melodies are constructed out of a sequence of pitches. This is the part of a musical work that you might sing along with or that might get stuck in your head. Melodies have various characteristics, including **shape**[14] and **motion**[15], which can be **conjunct** (in which the melody primarily moves up and down the scale) and **disjunct** (in which the melody contains larger intervals and leaps). Harmonies are constructed out of groups of pitches that are usually sounded simultaneously and constitute **chords**[16], while a sequence of harmonies is termed a **chord progression**. In a musical work, the harmony is usually unobtrusive and might be repetitive. A melody and a harmony sound good together when they are based on the same scale and contain some of the same pitches. However, every melody can be harmonized in many different ways, using various chords. Likewise, a single harmony can be used to accompany many different melodies.

11.   This video demonstrates the melody to Beethoven's "Ode to Joy."

12.   This video demonstrates melody and a possible harmony to Beethoven's "Ode to Joy."

13.   Here, you can hear Beethoven's melody and harmony in the context of his original composition.

14.   This video introduces the concept of melodic shape.

15.   This video introduces the concept of melodic motion.

| 16. |  | This video demonstrates chords, which are used to harmonize melodies. |

Although this text will not offer a technical explanation of harmony (which can become very complicated indeed), it is often central to the listening experience. A certain chord progression can surprise you, or excite you, or break your heart. It is not necessary to understand harmonies from a theoretical perspective to feel their impact. You also don't need a theoretical background to understand the role harmony plays in establishing and then satisfying or frustrating expectations. As long as a piece of music is in a key, one chord—the chord built on the note that the key is named after—will serve as a home base, while other chords in the key will facilitate journeys away from or back towards that home base. We get used to hearing certain chord progressions and come to expect them, so we often have a sense of where the music is going to go. If we hear an unexpected chord or—most shocking of all—a chord that is not in the key of the piece of music, we tend to respond emotionally.

Volume

Like pitch, volume—the loudness or softness of a sound—is a parameter of every soundwave. **Volume** is determined by the amplitude of the wave, such that waves with a large amplitude produce high-volume sound and waves with a small amplitude produce low-volume sounds. While volume is simple to understand and assess (we can all tell whether music is "loud" or "soft"), its significance in the creation of musical meaning cannot be overlooked. On the one hand, certain genres of music depend on volume for their identity. You cannot appreciate the impact of heavy metal by listening to it with the dial turned down, just as you cannot sing a baby to sleep at the top of your voice. Changes in volume can also communicate meaning in music. A gradual increase in volume can indicate growing excitement, while a sudden change in volume can indicate a dramatic mood shift.

A few terms will help us to talk about volume, which is also referred to as **dynamic level**. An increase in volume is referred to as a **crescendo**, while a decrease is termed a **decrescendo** or **diminuendo**. Musicians in orchestras, bands, and choirs describe volume using Italian terms including **fortissimo** (very loud), **forte** (loud), **mezzo forte** (medium loud), **mezzo piano** (medium soft), **piano** (soft), and **pianissimo** (very soft). While this book will not employ these terms, you might encounter them elsewhere.

Articulation

Articulation has to do with how pitches are begun, sustained, and released, and it is driven primarily by changes in dynamic level. In music production language, this dimension of sound is referred to as the envelope[17]. The envelope is independent of pitch, but it determines the character of that pitch. For example, a pitch might begin with a gentle increase in volume, or a sudden decrease, or no dynamic change. Once it has begun to sound, a pitch might be sustained for a long time, or it might be abruptly cut off. And when it is ended, it might be released with a decrease in volume, and increase in volume, or no dynamic change.

17.  This video explains the four elements of the envelope: attack, decay, sustain, and release.

Although the preceding description was highly technical, the effects of articulation are easy to perceive. At one end of the spectrum, a series of pitches might be heavily punctuated, with forceful onsets and no sustain. The traditional Italian term for this articulation is **staccato**—a term that means short and accented, and which is difficult to replace with an English equivalent. At the other end, a series of pitches might be smoothly connected, with gentle onsets and a great deal of sustain. The term for this articulation is **legato**. Between these extremes are an enormous variety of approaches to beginning, sustaining, and releasing notes, many of which are unique to the instruments that produce them.

Timbre

The final characteristic that is universal to all sounds is **timbre** (TAM-ber), which describes the quality of a sound. Whether one has no musical training or is an accomplished performer, we are all skilled at identifying minor variations in timbre. This ability lets you know that your mother is calling you from the other room, not your sister. It helps you to tell the difference between a guitar and a piano. Not only does every voice and every instrument exhibit a unique timbre, but performers can alter the timbre they produce by changing their technique. Timbre is also integral to genre and style: A symphony orchestra produces one range of timbres, while a rock band produces another.

Variations in timbre are made possible by the existence of the **overtone series**, which is a sequence of higher-pitched frequencies that are activated every time a pitch is produced. When you strike a key on the piano, for example, you are not only sounding the pitch associated with that key, you are also activating dozens of pitches at set intervals above that pitch, each of which might sound at a relatively high or low volume. The combination of these **overtones** produces timbre. Two instruments playing the same pitch sound different, therefore, because they are activating different pitches in the overtone series at different volumes. The complexity of this process allows for near-infinite variety in timbres.

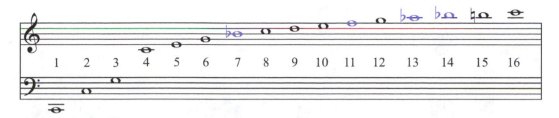

Image 2.2: These are the pitches of the overtone series as they might be notated on a staff. Even if you cannot read notation, you can see that the pitches get closer together as they get higher. When one plays a low C on any instrument, most of these pitches are sounded to some degree. The pitches in blue will be out of tune.
Source: Wikimedia Commons
Attribution: User "Hyacinth"
License: CC BY-SA 3.0

If you engage with every example in this volume, you will experience an extraordinary range of contrasting timbres. Audiences for various genres develop unique preferences and expectations for timbre, and timbre is often one of the most distinctive characteristics of a musical tradition. Variations in timbre are often not hard to identify: A piano trio, for example, had a different sound quality than a thrash metal band. These differences, however, can be very difficult to put in to words. While timbre is easy to perceive and measure, it is hard to describe.

For the most part, we will consider timbre in the context of individual examples. We will investigate different ways of producing sound with the human voice (which is capable of extraordinary diversity), the various instruments that are responsible for the characteristic sounds of non-Western classical traditions, and the electric instruments and sound processing techniques that have contributed to popular music of the last seventy years. There is one sound source in particular, however, that pervades this volume: the symphony orchestra. For an overview of the instruments that make up the orchestra, please see Appendix A.

Texture

We are now really to move from sound to music, which usually exhibits some additional characteristics. One of these is **texture**[18], which concerns the contents of and interactions between various layers or voices in a musical work. We use four basic terms to describe texture, although these terms can tell us little about what a piece of music actually sounds like. **Monophonic**[19] music has a single melody line, performed by a soloist or in unison, with no accompaniment. If you add an accompaniment that has different pitches (probably chords) but that is secondary to the melody, you have **homophonic** music. In **polyphonic** music, every voice is independent but equally important, and there is no distinction between melody and harmony. And in **heterophonic** music, multiple instruments or voices each perform a unique version of the same melody, such that unison is not achieved. We will encounter these terms in the context of specific examples throughout this volume.

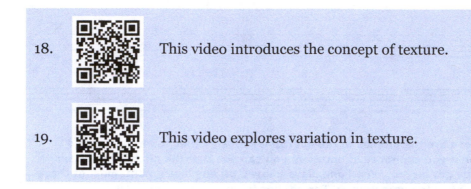

18. This video introduces the concept of texture.

19. This video explores variation in texture.

In addition, texture can be described using qualitative terms. It can be thick or dense, meaning perhaps that there are many independent and highly-active parts, or it can be thin or sparse, meaning perhaps that there are few instruments, each of which can be clearly identified and tracked. Consider, for example, two songs from *Sgt. Pepper's Lonely Hearts Club Band*, discussed in Chapter 8. The concluding thirty seconds of "Being for the Benefit of Mr. Kite" are irrefutably dense: There is so much going on that it is difficult to identify individual sources of sound, and the listener's focus is constantly attracted by new and varied voices. The first verse of "A Day in the Life," on the other hand, has a thin texture, made up only of guitar, bass, and shaker. It is possible to focus on individual instrumental parts and to hear the unique articulation of each.

Form

Finally, we need a way to talk about how music unfolds over time. This element is known as **form**. Most musical compositions exhibit formal characteristics, although some pieces are very amorphous or difficult to describe in terms of form. At the very least, creators of music usually plan the formal dimensions of their work. John Cage's *4'33"* doesn't have form, per se, since its sonic contents are always different, but at least the composer decided how long the piece was going to last.

In most cases, the creators of music rely on three organizational principles that produce form. These are **repetition**, **variation**, and **contrast**. Repetition occurs when we hear the same thing twice, whether it is a long and complicated melody, a short melodic fragment, a rhythm, or a harmonic pattern. Variation occurs when musical material returns, but with alterations. Contrast, naturally, refers to musical material that has not been heard before.

Repetition is key to our ability to understand and enjoy music. When we hear something new, internal repetition allows the music to quickly become familiar and helps us to predict what is going to happen next. For this reason, all popular music features repetition of various kinds. When an unfamiliar song comes on the radio, you can expect to hear the chorus (the catchy part with words and melody that both repeat) several times. Most popular songs also have repetitive chord progressions and some sort of repeating accompaniment, known formally as an

ostinato[20]. Ostinatos are important in many types of music and will play a role throughout this book.

20. The bass line at the beginning of White Stripe's "Seven Nation Army" provides a good example of an ostinato. This seven-note melodic figure is heard throughout the song.

Variation and contrast are what make music interesting. We enjoy and rely upon repetition, but we can only take so much. However, music that contains constant variation or lacks repetition altogether requires more of the listener. Most people cannot relax and enjoy music that is constantly changing and that offers something new and different with each passing moment. At the same time, such music can communicate a great deal and be particularly rewarding for an engaged listener.

The degree to which music relies on repetition or contrast is often linked to its purpose. Dance music, for example, tends to be repetitive. When people are dancing, they don't want much contrast. They want the music to maintain a constant tempo, rhythmic character, and mood. Minor variations might make dancing more interesting, but major changes can make dancing impossible. In addition, when you're dancing you don't pay careful attention to the nuances of the music. Music belonging to a sung theater tradition, however, is much more likely to exhibit contrast. In the first place, it is probably being used to express emotions or to portray a nuanced character. Variation and contrast allow for more complex and meaningful communication. In the second, audience members are paying full attention to the music, and, therefore, have a higher tolerance for contrast and change.

MUSIC IN THE WORLD

With the exception of its opening passages, which considered the problem of defining what music even is, this unit has so far emphasized the empirical qualities of music. We have acknowledged the documented effects of music on the human brain, and we have acquired a variety of terms and concepts that can be used to understand and describe music as a physical phenomenon. Now it is time to address some of the messier aspects of talking and writing about music.

Categories

What kinds of music do you like to listen to? Country? Hip-hop? Classical? EDM? Top 40? Whether we are talking to a friend, using a streaming service, or browsing records in a store, we like to think about music in terms of categories. These categories can be very useful. They can help us pick a radio station we might enjoy, or decide whether or not to buy tickets to hear an unfamiliar band. At the same time, these categories are both artificial and extremely limiting.

Let us begin by considering the classic tripartite division of music into the categories of "classical," "popular," and "folk." This approach has been around for a long time, and it has persevered because, in many ways, it works. If I tell you that I like "classical" music, you immediately understand that I probably mean orchestral music, or opera, and that I probably listen to music that is fairly old. But there are problems with this categorization. To begin with, much of what is "classical" today was "popular" in the past. When Mozart wrote his symphonies, for example, his object was to satisfy popular demand and sell concert tickets, and his audiences behaved the same way that fans at a rock concert do today. And what if I actually prefer experimental orchestral music composed last year? It is common practice to refer to such repertoire as "classical," but it's about as far from Mozart as you can get.

Image 2.3: "Classical" music is usually associated with certain performance conventions, including formal dress, music reading, and standard ensembles such as the orchestra and choir pictured here, but none of these are essential.
Source: Pexels
Attribution: Pixabay
License: Pexels License

How about "popular" music? This category is generally understood to contain commercial music that appeals to large numbers of people. But what about individual artists or songs that fail to achieve any popularity whatsoever? What about experimental rock bands that take the same attitude towards their work as serious "classical" composers? Mozart, a "classical" composer, might have more in common with a "popular" artist like Jimi Hendrix than Hendrix has in common with Pink Floyd. Mozart and Hendrix were both gifted instrumentalists who dazzled their audiences with virtuosic performances and wrote music to showcase their skills, while the band Pink Floyd is known more for their nuanced production, complex song structures, and unusual instrumentation. Again, however, this category is not without its value. While there is an enormous diversity of "popular" musics, they tend to be characterized by certain forms, instrumentations, styles, and performance venues. There might be much to separate Jimi Hendrix and Pink Floyd, but their music shares important elements of instrumentation and style, and it might be heard in the same types of settings.

"Folk" is also a slippery category. "Folk" music is typically described as music of unknown authorship that is passed down from generation to generation in a particular region. It tends to be fairly simple and in a distinctive style, and it is performed on instruments that are integral to the local musical culture. However, problems quickly arise as we try to label individual pieces or practices. In the United States, for example, the works of Stephen Foster have long been considered folk music. Songs like "My Old Kentucky Home" and "Camptown Races" have certainly entered folk culture, and many who sing or play them know nothing of their composer or origin. But can a commercial song, created and published by a professional composer, truly be considered "folk" music? Different problems arise as we address the musical practices of non-Western societies, many of which do not employ musical notation and reject notions of individual authorship. But do the absence of a named composer, official sheet music, and copyright notice mean that a work in the North Indian classical tradition is "folk" music? The complexity, sophistication, and technical demands of music in this category would suggest not.

Image 2.4: Woody Guthrie, pictured here in 1943, is an icon of American folk music. However, he mostly performed songs that he himself wrote and had a successful commercial career—characteristics that put him more in line with "popular" musicians.

Source: Wikimedia Commons
Attribution: Al Aumuller
License: Public Domain

A further challenge arises when we try to identify *the* "folk" music of a region or nation. Let us take the United States. If I tell you that I listen to American folk music, you will probably imagine someone like Joan Baez playing guitar and singing songs from the Anglo folk tradition. Indeed, music such as hers has come to be known as Folk music (with a capital F). If I ask Spotify to play Folk music for me, I'll hear Joan Baez and others like her. However, her music represents only one cultural strain within the United States.

What about the polka music of midwestern communities? What about the corrido ballads of Spanish-speaking communities near the southern border? What about the dance music heard at Native American pow-pow gatherings? Are any of these traditions less "folk" or less "American" than the others?

For all the reasons explored above, this narrative is going to steer clear of "classical," "popular," and "folk" as categories and terms. They have been addressed here only because their use is so widespread. Instead, we will focus on what music across these categories shares in common: the purposes for which individual works were originally created and continue to be consumed. This book is organized around categories, but these categories have little to do with the style of the works contained therein. Instead, they have to do with the roles music plays in society. These categories lead us to first understand what music is *for*. Only then will we seek to address how the music works, who created it, and how it is rooted in its historical and cultural context.

These categories also have their shortcomings. Many musical examples included in a given category could just as easily be included in another. We will admit that at the outset. All the same, these categories seem more useful than "classical," "popular," and "folk," and they tell us much more about what really matters: music as an integral aspect of the human experience.

Genres and Subgenres

This book will engage with another mode of categorization: **genre**. Genre is a way of making connections between closely-related works and musical artists that share stylistic, formal, and cultural elements. You are sure to recognize a large number of genres—rock, pop, R&B, country, hip-hop—from your own musical consumption. Each of these genre names tells us something about what the music is like and who listens to it. Each also hosts a variety of **subgenres** that communicate more specialized information about the music contained therein. For example, the genre EDM (electronic dance music) contains all computer-produced music intended primarily for dancing, whereas the subgenre dubstep contains only bass-heavy EDM that uses specific timbres, is in duple meter, and falls within a narrow tempo range. The label "dubstep" also gives us a clearer picture of who consumes the music and what a concert might be like. Finally, subgenres tend to come and go, each leading to the next, while genres remain relevant for longer periods of time.

Image 2.5: Genre is primarily a marketing tool. Customers in this store can easily find the music they are likely to be interested in because the recordings are organized by genre.
Source: NeedPix
Attribution: User "StockSnap"
License: CC0

It is important to acknowledge that genre in the 21st century is primarily a marketing tool. The main purpose of genre is to help record companies efficiently label their merchandise, identify consumers, and advertise music to the people who are most likely to buy it. Genre also helps the music industry to track sales; consider the Billboard music charts, which have been in use since 1958. Of course, genre is meaningful to consumers as well, and subgenres are often named not by faceless corporations but by the fans themselves. Genre can also help listeners to find music that they will enjoy, and it can serve to create communities of listeners and concertgoers.

At the same time, genre can be divisive. Historically, genre has been used to separate black and white performing artists whose music was stylistically identical. This happened in the 1920s, when the marketing categories of "race records" and "hillbilly records" were invented to segregate the music of black and white Southern musicians, and again in the 1950s, when the distinction between performers of R&B and rock 'n' roll was often one of race. It is important, therefore, to be critical of genre, and to repeatedly assess exactly what genre is telling us.

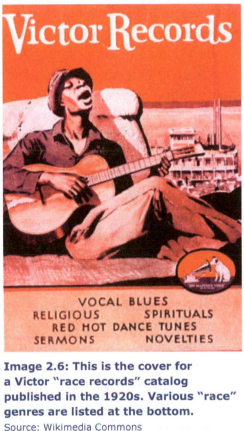

Image 2.6: This is the cover for a Victor "race records" catalog published in the 1920s. Various "race" genres are listed at the bottom.
Source: Wikimedia Commons
Attribution: Unknown
License: Public Domain

Indeed, genre can convey a wide variety of types of information, but not all genres convey the same types of information. Let's look at two examples: "string quartet" and "French reggae." The former provides us with precise information about instrumentation (two violins, viola, and cello) and suggests a multi-part concert work intended for the stimulation of players and listeners. We might also make assumptions about the consumer of such a genre, who is probably (although not always) well-educated and reasonably well-off, and we might expect to hear performances in a formal concert hall, surrounded by well-dressed and attentive listeners. However, genre in this case tells us nothing at all about style, geographical origin, historical context, or social significance. A work in this genre might have been composed in 1780, or 1880, or 1980, or yesterday. Although the string quartet originated in German-speaking Europe, this genre has been accessible to composers, performers, and listeners across the globe for at least the past one hundred years. A string quartet might be pleasant and lyrical, or dissonant and jarring. It might be fairly simple or mind-bogglingly complex. It might last eight minutes, or eighty minutes. And genre provides us no idea about what sort of meaning—political, social, or otherwise— might be contained in such a work.

The case is quite different with "French reggae." On the one hand, this genre tells us less about instrumentation. We can expect to hear certain instruments— electric guitar, electric bass, drums, and perhaps electric organ, trumpet, and saxophone—but taking away or adding instruments does not fundamentally destabilize the genre. On the other, it tells us much more about everything else. First and foremost, the "reggae" designation tells us all we need to know about style, which is a core identifying feature of the genre. It also limits the scope of time and place. Reggae has only been around since the late 1960s, and it was developed in Jamaica by Rastafarians—a nation and culture that are central to the genre's identity no matter where individual songs might come from. The subgenre identification of "French reggae" tells us even more about geographic location and language. Finally, reggae carries certain political, social, and racial connotations. It is usually performed by musicians of African descent, and it often espouses ideals of pan-African unity and social justice. These values in turn help us to understand how and why people consume the music, and how French reggae might become an integral part of someone's identity.

Fixed Composition vs. Improvisation

The two genres just discussed exhibit an additional pair of features that require deeper discussion: string quartets tend to be **fixed compositions**, such that the pitches and rhythms in every performance are identical, while reggae invites **improvisation** and variation from performance to performance, such that two renditions of the same song might sound quite different. In a tradition that relies on fixed composition, it is assumed that the creator of a work will make all decisions concerning pitch, rhythm, form, instrumentation, and length, and that performers will follow these instructions precisely. Fixed compositions are usually enshrined in notated music, although they do not have to be. This does not mean, however, that every performance of a fixed composition will be identical. Performers are usually invited to make minute adjustments to some of these elements, such as articulation, tempo, and dynamics, with the result that each rendition is unique to the discriminating listener.

Improvisation is much more difficult to sum up. This is due to the fact that there are nearly as many approaches to improvisation as there are musical traditions. Improvisation implies the production of new musical elements in the course of a live performance, but it always occurs within a set of boundaries. No improviser is free to play or sing whatever they want. Instead, an improviser will tend to apply formulas to the transformation of musical material while respecting certain fundamental characteristics of the style and composition.

In jazz, for example, improvisation is guided by the form and harmonic structure of a fixed composition that serves as the basis for a performance. While

Image 2.7: In the United States, improvisation is most closely associated with jazz. Here we see Coleman Hawkins improvising a solo in 1947.
Source: Wikimedia Commons
Attribution: William P. Gottlieb
License: Public Domain

improvising, a player is free to choose pitches and rhythms—but they must fit with the predetermined harmonies, so choices are limited. Improvisation means something different to a balafon player in West Africa, who will constantly vary a repeated melodic figure used to accompany singing (see Chapter 5). It means something different again to a member of a Javanese gamelan, who might not know how a performance will unfold ahead of time but understands exactly how to vary their melody in response to instructions from the drummer (see Chapter 4). And it means yet something else to a Baroque violinist, who performs a fixed composition but is free to add ornaments and flourishes according to stylistic guidelines.

When we talk about fixed composition versus improvisation, we are talking about different roles in the creation of music: the role of the composer versus the role of the performer. Not all traditions distinguish between these roles, which makes it particularly difficult to define our terms. Throughout this volume, we will identify and examine the contributions of different individuals—composers, orchestrators, arrangers, adapters, and performers—to the creation of unique musical objects.

Image 2.8: North Indian classical musicians, such as Shruti Sadolikar Katkar and Mulye Mangesh, also engage in improvisation. Their performances, however, are guided by entirely different principles than those of jazz musicians.
Source: Wikimedia Commons
Attribution: Joe Mabel
License: CC BY-SA 3.0

Emotional Expression and Cultural Context

Emotional expression is, for many listeners, the main reason to interact with music. It is also the most difficult to pin down or explain. While we can make some generalizations and predictions, emotional response to music happens at the individual level, and it is impossible to know exactly what impact music will have on a given listener. A piece of music might make one person cry, another feel uncomfortable, and another feel bored. The extraordinary diversity of genres is itself a testimony to the wide-ranging responses that people have to music. There is something out there for everybody to love, and something for everybody to hate.

All the same, members of a given culture tend to agree, at least to some extent, about the emotional content of music. As an example, consider two excerpts from a musical work created by the German composer George Frideric Handel in 1740 entitled *The Cheerful Person, the Thoughtful Person, and the Moderate Person* (original Italian: *L'Allegro, il Penseroso ed il Moderato*). For most of this work, two archetypal characters—the cheerful person and the thoughtful person—argue about whether it is better to be happy or pensive. Each calls forth the emotional state for which they advocate, the cheerful person with an aria (song) entitled "Come, thou Goddess fair and free,"[21] and the thoughtful person with an aria entitled "Come, rather, Goddess sage and holy."[22] Although this music was written over 250 years ago, the emotions expressed are still easy to perceive by many today. But what is it, exactly, that makes the first aria sound happy, and what makes the second sound reserved?

Image 2.9: This 1845 painting by Thomas Cole captures the allegorical figure of L'Allegro, or "The Cheerful Person."
Source: Wikimedia Commons
Attribution: Thomas Cole
License: Public Domain

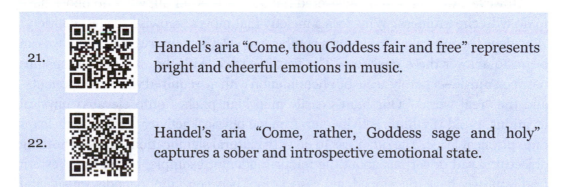

21. Handel's aria "Come, thou Goddess fair and free" represents bright and cheerful emotions in music.

22. Handel's aria "Come, rather, Goddess sage and holy" captures a sober and introspective emotional state.

The answer can be arrived at by comparing and contrasting the dimensions of sound that were enumerated above. The first aria is quick in tempo, while the second is slow. The first contains fast-moving rhythms, while the second does not.

Image 2.10: Here we see Cole's representation of Il Penseroso, or "The Thoughtful Person."
Source: Wikimedia Commons
Attribution: Thomas Cole
License: Public Domain

The first is in the major mode, which we often hear as communicating positive emotions, while the second is in the minor mode, which can sound sad or serious. The vocal line in the first aria jumps around, skipping notes in the scale, while that in the second generally does not. The articulations in the first are bouncy and accented, while those in the second are smooth and connected. The first aria features bright-timbred wind instruments—oboe and bassoon—while the second relies on the mellower strings.

However, we still haven't answered the question. After all, what do oboes have to do with cheerfulness? Why does a melody that moves stepwise suggest sobriety? Why does the minor mode signify a somber mood? There are two ways that we can begin to answer these questions. The first has to do with the web of relationships between music—a purely acoustic phenomenon with no required visual component—and the "real world." Our brains easily map high pitches onto elevated physical locations, rapid rhythmic activity onto frenetic physical activity, and melodic leaps onto physical leaps. The other has to do with cultural signification. There is nothing objectively sad or serious about the minor mode, for example, but in the Western tradition we have developed an association between minor-mode music and profound emotional expression. (This is largely due to the complex inner workings of Western harmony, which are beyond the scope of this book.) Other cultures have not made this association, and listeners in those traditions might respond to minor-mode music differently than those acculturated to Western music.

This has been only a brief introduction to questions that will occupy us throughout this book. Our object will not be to answer these questions, but rather to carefully consider how music can create an emotional experience, how we respond to it, and how it has been used by humans over the span of centuries and continents.

RESOURCES FOR FURTHER LEARNING

Print

Duckworth, William. *A Creative Approach to Music Fundamentals* (11th edition). Cengage Learning, 2012.

Online

Music theory lessons and exercises:
- https://utheory.com/
- https://www.musictheory.net/lessons

Unit 2

MUSIC FOR STORYTELLING

Music and Characterization

Esther M. Morgan-Ellis

INTRODUCTION

Music may have originally developed for the purpose of communication, and it has become a powerful tool in the telling of stories. Over the next four chapters, we will explore ways in which music has been used to convey, enhance, or transform stories in a variety of cultural contexts.

Most storytellers use music with great care. They do so because it is powerful. Music can help to set the mood in a video game, or allow a character on stage to express emotion by singing, or add interest and gravity to the recitation of an epic poem. It can encourage an audience member to get more involved in a performance, either emotionally or by joining in with the music-making. It can help a listener to remember the words to a story. And it can "say" things that go beyond words and images.

Music is used to tell stories in many different ways. Sometimes it accompanies images, such as in a film. Sometimes it is combined with stage action, as in ballets and musicals. Sometimes it is paired with a text, which might be sung or provided to the listener to read. Of course, we can choose to hear a story in any piece of music, and we will encounter examples later in this book that seem as if they must be communicating *something*, even if we can't say exactly what it is. In the next four chapters, however, we will examine pieces of music that are used to tell clearly defined stories, and we will focus on understanding how music enriches and impacts those stories.

JOHN WILLIAMS, *STAR WARS*

We will start with an example that is familiar to most listeners: the music created for the *Star Wars* films. We will examine this music on its own terms, but through it we will also encounter five other works and styles that strongly impacted the creation of this score. No art exists in a vacuum. New works are built upon old, and creators rely upon cultural memory to communicate meaning. Even the *Star Wars* films were not conjured out of a vacuum—director George Lucas based his creation on Akira Kurosawa's 1958 samurai film *The Hidden Fortress*.

You probably already have a wealth of associations with the *Star Wars* soundtrack—both personal and general—as a result of having watched these films. On the personal level, you might find that this music evokes nostalgic memories of watching *Star Wars* with your family as a child, or it might make you uncomfortable if you found the films particularly scary or sad. Such responses are valid and worth exploring. Here, however, we will focus on objective characteristics of the music that help us to explain how it enhances the story.

Williams's Career

The soundtrack to the *Star Wars* films was composed by one of the most prolific and influential of all cinema composers, John Williams (b. 1932). Williams's career took off in 1974, when director Steven Spielberg recruited him to score his first feature production, *The Sugarland Express*. The two went on to produce a string of hit films with memorable soundtracks, including *Jaws*, *Close Encounters of the Third Kind*, *E.T.*, *Schindler's List*, *Saving Private Ryan*, the *Indiana Jones* films, and the first two *Jurassic Park* films. This kind of collaboration has long played a role in the production of great music, and we will see similar partnerships at work in opera and ballet. It was Spielberg who recommended Williams to George Lucas, the director of the *Star Wars* films. His scores for the original *Star Wars* trilogy—*A New Hope* (1977), *The Empire Strikes Back* (1980), and *Return of the Jedi* (1983)—are among the best-known musical works created for the big screen.

Williams—who had studied music at UCLA and the Juilliard School—certainly knew his music history and concert repertoire. He also had decades of experience as a **session musician** in Los Angeles, recording soundtracks for television and film. He came to the task of

Image 3.1: John Williams frequently conducts live performances of his film scores, as in this 2011 appearance with the Boston Pops orchestra.
Source: Wikimedia Commons
Attribution: Chris Devers
License: CC BY-SA 2.0

Image 3.2: Director George Lucas is best known for his work on the Star Wars films.
Source: Wikimedia Commons
Attribution: Joi Ito
License: CC BY 2.0

writing film scores, therefore, with a deep understanding of how music can shape the viewer's experience of a drama.

The *Star Wars* Soundtrack

At the heart of Williams's soundtrack is a series of themes—about eleven per film—that represent individual characters, settings, or ideas. The viewer doesn't need a guide to these themes. Instead, one quickly connects music with onscreen action as themes return throughout the films. Here, we will examine themes associated with Darth Vader, Luke Skywalker, Princess Leia, Yoda, and the Force. Williams carefully crafted each of these themes to represent the character or idea, and they are used both to amplify the onscreen action and to enrich the storytelling.

		"Main Theme" from Star Wars Composer: John Williams Performance: the Skywalker Symphony, conducted by John Williams (1990)
Time	**Form**	**What to listen for**
0'00"	intro	The opening fanfare features the brass section
0'06"	A	This triumphant trumpet melody contains multiple upward leaps
0'17"		The A theme is repeated with changes in the accompaniment
0'26"	B	This melody features the strings
0'48"	A'	When the A material returns, the melody is played by violins and horns, giving it a different character
1'10"		*End of listening guide*

We will begin with Luke Skywalker's theme (officially titled "Main Theme"), which is first heard over the opening title. This is clearly the music of a hero. The opening fanfare suggests royalty, while the **duple meter** and moderate **tempo** tells us that this is a march. This, in combination with brass-heavy instrumentation, suggests a military character—a good representation of the Rebel Alliance. The melody soars into the upper **range**, confirming Skywalker's confidence and authority with a series of leaps up to the high **tonic scale degree**. (This is the first and most important note of the scale on which the melody is built.) Trumpets, with their bright **timbre**, are more prominent than the other brass instruments. And, of course, Skywalker's music is in the **major mode**. In addition, this theme has more emotional depth than Darth Vader's. It is in a three-part form, which might be described as a b a'. While the a section has the characteristics described above, the b section features the string section, thereby introducing a warmer timbre and indicating that our hero has a human side. Finally, the fact that we hear Skywalker's theme over the opening title tells us from the start who is going to emerge from this conflict victorious.

"The Imperial March (Darth Vader's Theme)" from *Star Wars* Composer: John Williams Performance: London Symphony Orchestra, conducted by John Williams (1980)		
Time	**Form**	**What to listen for**
0'00"	intro	The strings and percussion lay down a pattern of dotted rhythms suggesting a slow, militaristic march
0'09"	A	The trombones and trumpets play a low, ominous melody
0'18"	B	This section of the melody begins with a leap to the high range followed by a twisted chromatic descent
0'28"	B'	The repetition of B' concludes differently
0'38"		*End of listening guide*

The theme that represents the villain, Darth Vader, has many of the same characteristics. It, too, is a march (the theme is entitled "Imperial March"), and it features similar instrumentation. However, this theme is in the **minor mode**, which lets us know that this is the bad guy. The fact that the melody is played in a low range makes the music ominous, while the **chromatic** pitches and unusual **harmonies** make it mysterious. Darth Vader's theme is forceful and threatening, perhaps even unstoppable, but it is not heroic.

The other themes are similarly suited to their subjects. Leia's theme[1] opens with a winding chromatic melody in the flute and oboe before unfolding into an expressive melody for french horn with muted strings in the background. The music suggests seduction and romance, while largely ignoring her role as an action hero (although there is a historical connection between the horn and heroes of the opera stage). Yoda's theme[2] is heard in the cellos and oboes with a peaceful accompaniment of strings, bassoons, and harp. The instrumentation resonates with his life in the woods, while the simplicity of the melody communicates his character. Both themes are heard at the same moderate tempo—an indication of romance in one case and peace in the other. Perhaps the slowest theme is that used to represent the Force,[3] but now the tempo signifies inevitability and power. The theme itself is in the minor mode, not because it is tragic but because it is serious. It starts with a lone french horn, supported by **tremolo** in the strings, but grows dramatically in volume to embrace the whole orchestra.

1.		"Princess Leia's Theme" from *Star Wars* Composer: John Williams Performance: The Utah Symphony Orchestra, conducted by Varujan Kojian (1983)
2.		"Yoda's Theme" from *Star Wars* Composer: John Williams Performance: London Symphony Orchestra, conducted by John Williams (1980)
3.		"The Force Theme" from *Star Wars* Composer: John Williams Performance: London Symphony Orchestra, conducted by John Williams (1980)

This has been a fairly technical description of each theme's attributes, but the character of the music is easy to perceive without specialized knowledge. It is worth a reminder, however, that our understanding of what music expresses is determined by our own cultural contexts. This music builds on centuries of stylistic development and depends on each listener's lifetime of experience. We understand what it is trying to communicate because we dwell in the same musical world as the composer. Sound, however, seldom has objective meaning. We recognize the sounds of a military march because we have heard one somewhere else. We know that swelling strings signify romance because we have seen a hundred other movies, which in turn build on older theatrical traditions. A listener from a culture that had no military bands and in which, say, organ music was understood to signal romance would not make these connections.

RICHARD WAGNER, *THE VALKYRIE*

We are now going to explore that cultural context. John Williams was well educated in the Western concert and theatrical traditions. He served in the U.S. Air Force Band from 1952 to 1955, during which time he played piano and brass, arranged music, and conducted. His piano degree from the Juilliard School in New York City came with a thorough grounding in music history. And his decades recording film and television scores as a session musician in Los Angeles allowed him to become deeply familiar with the conventions of the screen.

Our examples, however, will come not from television or movies but from older traditions of theatrical music. We will begin with an example from the opera repertoire. In the European tradition, **opera** is a staged work of music theater, complete with costumes, sets, and dramatic plot twists. Most operas employ an orchestra to accompany the stage performers, who often sing throughout. While Richard Wagner's style and melodies certainly influenced Williams's work (the "Imperial March," for example, is clearly derived from a theme Wagner's wrote to represent a magical helmet known as Tarnhelm[4]), we will focus here on Williams's use of a technique that Wagner perfected: the technique of assigning a unique theme to each character, object, place, and idea in a drama. Wagner called such a theme a **leitmotif**.

4.  This theme by Richard Wagner bears a clear resemblance to Williams's "Imperial March."

Wagner's Career

Before examining Wagner's music, some biographical context is called for. It is possible that Richard Wagner (1813-1883) has had a greater impact on the development of Western art music than any other composer. For such a towering figure, however, he got off to a very slow start. He did not exhibit any particular talent as a child and never became an accomplished performer. In his twenties, he dedicated himself to the composition of operas, although it was many years before he made a success of the endeavor. In 1839 he actually had to crawl through the gutters of Riga to escape his creditors after having his passport confiscated by the municipal authorities. Then in 1849 he became involved in an attempt to overthrow the Dresden government. He not only helped to plan what is now known as the May Uprising, but actually participated, throwing grenades in the street. After the uprising failed, Wagner fled to Switzerland, where he remained in exile for most of a decade.

In Switzerland, Wagner shifted his attention from practice to theory. He quit writing music for several years and instead

Image 3.3: This portrait of Richard Wagner was painted by Franz von Lenbach.
Source: Wikimedia Commons
Attribution: Franz von Lenbach
License: Public Domain

wrote *about* music. In one 1849 essay, "The Artwork of the Future," Wagner theorized a **Gesamtkunstwerk**, or "total artwork," that would bring together all art forms—music, dance, gesture, poetry, image—into a single, ideal medium of artistic expression. Naturally, he imagined himself as the artist who was most capable of achieving this fusion. To prove the power of his ideas, he set to work on a monumental cycle of music dramas that would take him decades to complete. In a highly unusual move, Wagner not only wrote the music for these operas but also developed the narrative, wrote the libretto (the sung text), and even designed the theater in which the operas were eventually premiered. The project took him decades to complete, and the entire cycle was not premiered until 1876. By this time, Wagner had returned to Germany under the patronage of the King of Bavaria, who admired his work and offered him permanent financial support. The King also financed the construction of a grand opera house (the *Festspielhaus* in Bayreuth) to Wagner's specifications. It was there that the complete cycle was finally staged.

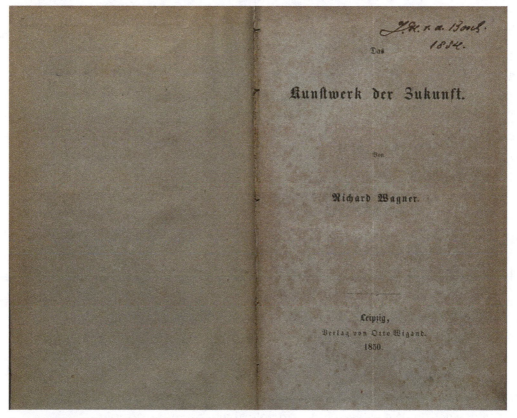

Image 3.4: This early edition of Wagner's manifesto was published in 1850.
Source: Wikimedia Commons
Attribution: H. P. Haack
License: CC BY 3.0

The Ring Cycle

Wagner's *The Ring of the Nibelungs* (German: *Der Ring des Nibelungen*)—or, as it is now known, the Ring Cycle—consists of four massive operas and takes about fifteen hours to perform. The story derives from Norse mythology, which Wagner understood to describe the ascent of his own German race. The operas enact a prolonged struggle between the gods and the humans. The gods are ruled by Wotan (the German version of the more familiar name Odin), who seeks to consolidate their power, but he is finally defeated by the human Seigfried. The story begins with the forging of a powerful ring out of gold extracted from the Rhine river and ends with the return of the ring to the river, the burning of Valhalla, and the flooding of the Rhine. These catastrophes mark a new age of human rule—the Norse myth of Ragnarök.

Like John Williams and George Lucas, Wagner relied on centuries of cultural history in crafting his masterpiece. The story outlined above is not original. His approach to setting that story to music was also not original, although he took pre-existing techniques to new heights. To begin with, Wagner expanded the size of his orchestra, introducing new instruments into the brass section. These instruments—which included the bass trumpet, contrabass trombone, and a euphonium-type device now known as the "Wagner tuba"—allowed him to produce a more subtle variety of timbres for the creation of diverse sound worlds. His musical style, like that of other composers of the time, was highly varied and expressive, although many of Wagner's contemporaries felt that his music set the bar for intensity of emotional content. Finally, Wagner adapted and transformed a practice that had long been common in opera: the use of recurring melodic themes (leitmotifs) to help tell the story.

If a listener sits through Wagner's entire fifteen-hour drama, they will hear hundreds of leitmotifs, most of which are frequently repeated. Some span all four operas, while some are restricted to an act, or even a single scene. Each is connected to an important element of the drama, and each is introduced along with that element. The first time Wotan picks up his spear, for example, we hear a forceful, march-like descending melody in the brass. This music then returns every time we see the spear or hear a reference to it. Wagner's leitmotifs are often melodically connected to each other, such that themes representing related ideas or characters sound similar to one another. The leitmotifs[5] can also be transformed as the power of an idea or object shifts over the course of the story. Most importantly, however, the leitmotifs can be used to communicate information to an audience that is not included in the libretto or onstage action. We will see this principle at work in our example.

5.  This video, produced by the brass section of the Metropolitan Opera orchestra, presents several important leitmotifs and demonstrates how they can be transformed to communicate meaning.

The Valkyrie

		"Wotan's Farewell" from The Valkyrie
		Composer: Richard Wagner
		Performance: Bryn Terfel with the Berliner
		    Philharmoniker, conducted by Claudio
		    Abbado (2002)

Time	**Leitmotif**	**What to listen for**
7'53"	Powerful destiny	Heard in the trombones as Wotan prepares to put Brünnhilde into an enchanted sleep
7'59"	Renunciation	Heard first in the horn and continued in the oboe
8'06"		Wotan announces that he is about to strip Brünnhilde of her immortality
8'40"	Magic sleep	Heard first in the woodwinds, then the strings
9'26"	Innocent sleep	Heard in the strings
9'36"	Wotan's grief	Heard in the strings in combination with "Innocent sleep"
11'10"	Powerful destiny	Heard in the tromobones in combination with "Innocent sleep"
11'35"	Wotan's spear	Heard in the low brass
11'43"	Loge as fire	The collection of leitmotifs related to Loge as fire enter the texture
11'45"		Wotan calls forth Loge, the demigod of fire
12'05"	Wotan's spear	Heard in the low brass
12'11"	Ambivalent Loge	We hear hints of this leitmotif interwoven with "Loge as fire"
12'44"	Ambivalent Loge	Heard in the woodwinds
13'19"	Magic sleep	This version of "magic sleep" moves at a much quicker tempo than that heard at 8'40"

13'33"	Innocent sleep	Heard in the woodwinds
13'43"	Siegfried's heroism	To the melody of "Siegfried's heroism," Wotan declares that any man who fears his spear will be incapable of crossing the flames
14'11"	Siegfried's heroism	Repeated in the brass
14'36"	Wotan's grief	Heard in the cellos
15'25"	Powerful destiny	Heard twice in the low brass

We are going to take a look at the final scene (Act III, Scene 3) of the second opera, *The Valkyrie* (German: *Die Walküre*). This scene contains two characters, Wotan and his favorite daughter, Brünnhilde. At this point in the drama, Brünnhilde, daughter of the god Wotan, has disobeyed her father's orders by interceding on behalf of the humans Siegmund and Sieglinde. Despite her efforts, Siegmund is killed, and Brünnhilde is left to face Wotan's fury. The punishment for disobeying the ruler of the gods is death, but Wotan takes pity on Brünnhilde,

Image 3.5: These two engravings both appeared in the 1917 *Victrola Book of Opera*. **The first depicts Wotan taking pity on his erring daughter Brünnhilde, who in the second has fallen into a magic sleep.**
Source: Wikimedia Commons
Attribution: Internet Archive Book Images
License: Public Domain

whom he loves dearly, and instead declares his intention to strip her of her immortality and powers and put her into a magical sleep on top of the mountain. He conjurs Loge, the demigod of fire, to erect a ring of flames around Brünnhilde, and declares that only a hero who does not fear his spear will be able to pass through the fire and wake his daughter.

This scene, which lasts less than twenty minutes, contains twenty-one separate leitmotifs. Indeed, the listener hears virtually no music that cannot be classified as a leitmotif. Most of the themes in this scene were introduced in the first opera and have been heard many times, although some do not return after this scene. Four themes, however, are introduced in this scene and proceed to play an important role in the remaining operas. Although various music scholars have counted and named Wagner's leitmotifs in different ways, we will use the descriptions supplied by Roger Donington in 1963.

According to Donington, the scene in question contains the following leitmotifs: love as fulfillment, Wotan frustrated, powerful destiny, unavoidable destiny, Valkyries as animus, Valhalla, Wotan's spear, relinquishment, Volsung as destiny, the love of Siegmund and Sieglinde, downfall of the gods, the curse, Siegfried's heroism, sword as manhood, magic sleep, innocent sleep, ambivalent Loge, Wotan's grief, renunciation, and Loge as fire (two different versions). As you can see, these themes connect with a wide variety of dramatic elements. Some are straightforward representations of objects or places, while others embody abstract concepts. All enrich the drama and aid in telling the story.

Like Williams, Wagner did not randomly pair themes with objects and ideas. Each leitmotif expresses meaning in sound. We will examine a few of the themes used in this scene before seeing them in action. The music associated with "Loge as fire,"[6] for example, is meant to capture the characteristics of flame. This passage features high-pitched instruments with bright timbres, such as the flute, and the sharply-articulated melody leaps about. The music almost sparkles. Swells and ebbs in the music—created using rising and falling dynamic levels and pitches—represent the unpredictable spread of fire across the ground. (This kind of music has long been associated with wind and storms.) In contrast, both of the "sleep" leitmotifs are slow and peaceful, and they feature the soothing sounds of strings and harp. "Magic sleep"[7] consists of a gradual chromatic descent that comes as close as music can to representing the act of falling asleep. "Innocent sleep,"[8] on the other hand, is easily recognized as a lullaby, with its rocking rhythms, lilting melody, and stable harmonies.

6.  The "Loge as fire" and "Ambivalent Loge" leitmotifs, both heard in this passage, capture the characteristics of a leaping flame.

7.   The "Magic sleep" leitmotif suggests the act of falling asleep.

8.   The "Innocent sleep" leitmotif sounds like a lullaby.

Wagner used his large brass section to represent strength and power. "Wotan's spear,"[9] which features the trombones and tubas, marches confidently down a scale into the very low range. "Siegfried's heroism"[10] begins with a confident leap up to the tonic and often grows in volume. (Many listeners observe that this leitmotif closely resembles John Williams's theme for "the Force.") "Powerful destiny,"[11] which is heard throughout the scene, consists of a simple but surprising shift from one harmony to another. Wagner weaves all of these leitmotifs together into a tapestry of orchestral and vocal sound.

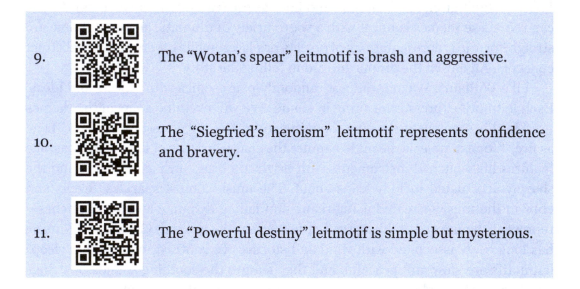

9.   The "Wotan's spear" leitmotif is brash and aggressive.

10.   The "Siegfried's heroism" leitmotif represents confidence and bravery.

11.   The "Powerful destiny" leitmotif is simple but mysterious.

Finally, this scene—which is often referred to as "Wotan's farewell"—exhibits one of the most significant powers of the leitmotif: its ability to foreshadow events yet to come. In the final moments of the scene, Wotan declares that only a hero who does not fear his spear will be able to pass through the flames and wake Brünnhilde. He sings this declaration to the melody of "Siegfried's heroism," which is then echoed by the full orchestra in a resounding climax. At this point in the story, however, Siegfried has not even been born. Sieglinde has only just learned that she is pregnant with him, and he will not appear until the next opera. At the same time, the theme is not new. It has been in use since earlier in this opera to foreshadow the appearance of a human hero, and it will be heard nine times in the next opera. When we hear this music, therefore, we know exactly who is going to wake Brünnhilde, even though Wotan—who sings the melody—does not.

Image 3.6: This engraving from the 1917 _Victrola Book of Opera_ portrays the scene in the next opera in which Siegfried awakens the sleeping Brünnhilde.
Source: Wikimedia Commons
Attribution: Internet Archive Book Images
License: Public Domain

Concerns

There is no question that Wagner's _Ring_ operas have been both influential and successful. They are staged in countless opera houses around the world every year, often at great expense. The most lavish cycle to date was produced at New York City's Metropolitan Opera House in 2012 at a cost of $19.6 million. Every year, fans travel to the Bayreuth Festival in Germany to see the _Ring_ and other Wagner operas staged in the theater that the composer himself designed. At the same time, some critics argue that we should no longer produce these operas or listen to Wagner's music. Their argument is not that the music is bad, but rather that the composer's ideology is so repugnant as to merit the erasure of his art.

Wagner's anti-Semitic views were widely known during his lifetime. In an article entitled "Jewishness in Music" (1850), he argued that Jewish composers were incapable of producing profound musical expression, and that their attempts to do so were damaging to the progress of art. Furthermore, he claimed that Jewish artists lacked the capacity to recognize or represent authentic German culture. Although Wagner first published the article under a pseudonym (presumably to

Image 3.7: This 1910 postcard captures the interior of the Bayreuth Festpielhaus, designed by Wagner himself for the presentation of his operas.
Source: Wikimedia Commons
Attribution: Ramme & Ulrich, Hoffotograf, Bayreuth
License: Public Domain

make his attacks against other composers seem less personal), in 1869 he republished it under his own name, and with a long addendum reflecting the artistic and political developments of the intervening decades. Wagner's views provoked considerable resistance among his contemporaries, but they were later embraced by the Nazi Party. Indeed, Adolf Hitler would become Wagner's most infamous admirer.

There are also concerns about the content of Wagner's music dramas. While the *Ring* is not overtly anti-Semitic, it expresses an ideology of nationhood that tacitly excludes all but the ethnically pure "German" of Wagner's imagination. Stripped of their mythology, the *Ring* operas tell the story of a human race that rises to a position of world dominance. For Wagner, this was the German race, and the German race did not include Jews.

For these reasons, Wagner's music is unofficially banned in the nation of Israel, while music lovers around the world hold his work in disdain and choose not to program or consume it. The debate over whether we can separate an artistic work from its creator, however, is far from settled. Should the sins of the artist be visited upon the art? Can we enjoy music, films, or paintings that we know to have been created by reprehensible individuals? Does it matter that Wagner died many years ago, and can neither profit nor suffer as a result of our consumption decisions? Does support of Wagner's art suggest support of his ideas? We are forced to grapple with these questions not only in the case of Wagner but every time that the creator of beloved cultural products is discovered to have committed hateful actions.

GUSTAV HOLST, *THE PLANETS*

While John Williams's approach to creating the *Star Wars* soundtrack can be traced through Wagner, his music is more heavily influenced by other composers and works. The most frequently noted of these is the orchestral suite *The Planets* (1914-1916) by British composer Gustav Holst (1874-1934). The reasons for which Williams chose to borrow from Holst are simple enough to understand. Holst was one of the first composers to write music about outer space, and he did so with a dramatic flair that has kept this work in the repertoire ever since its 1920 premiere.

Holst and *The Planets*

Holst studied composition at the Royal College of Music in London, where he met with moderate success. He was not attracted to the life of a professional musician (Holst played the trombone), but he struggled to make a living as a composer. In 1903, therefore, Holst began teaching music in schools. Although he would write some of his most successful music for the orchestras he directed, he had little time in which to pursue his craft. Nevertheless, Holst continued to produce serious concert pieces and his reputation steadily grew.

Holst finally earned national attention in 1920, first with a work for choir and orchestra entitled *The Hymn of Jesus* and then with *The Planets*. *The Hymn of Jesus* paved the way for *The Planets'* success by establishing for Holst a reputation as a mystic and spiritual composer. As we will see, these qualities are prominent in the orchestral suite. Although the entire suite was not premiered until 1920, Holst had been at work on it since 1913. He first wrote the music for two pianos, and produced the orchestral score only after the composition was complete.

Image 3.8: This photograph of Gustav Holst was taken around the time that *The Planets* premiered.
Source: Wikimedia Commons
Attribution: Herbert Lambert
License: Public Domain

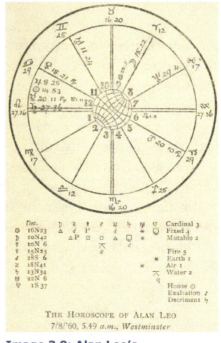

Image 3.9: Alan Leo's astrological work inspired Holst's compositions. Here, we see Leo's own horoscope, published in 1919.
Source: Wikimedia Commons
Attribution: Alan Leo
License: Public Domain

Much of Holst's work as a composer can be traced to his personal interests. This is certainly true of *The Planets*. In 1913, Holst travelled to Majorca with a group of fellow artists, who introduced him to the study of astrology. Holst became fascinated and immersed himself in the work of British astrologist Alan Leo, reading his book *What Is a Horoscope and How Is It Cast?*. The idea of composing an orchestral suite came to him almost immediately, and he began sketching the first movement, "Mars," that same year.

Holst's intent was to capture the astrological significance of each of the planets, as described by Leo. He was interested in the specific characteristics bestowed on those who were born under the influence of each individual planet. At the same time, Holst was a composer first and an astrologer second. His primary concern was musical cohesion and expression. As a result, he frequently deviated from Leo's prescription, and in the end used Leo's writings merely as an inspiration for his own creative work.

It seems that Holst was worried that audiences would not take his music seriously. An orchestral work inspired by celestial bodies, after all, might easily be dismissed as a mere novelty, especially when compared to the traditional symphonies that formed the core of the concert hall repertoire (see Chapter 7). For this reason, Holst first titled his suite *Seven Pieces for Orchestra*, only later changing it to *The Planets*. He added the individual movement names, indicating which planet the music is about, only just before the work was published. The descriptive titles qualify *The Planets* as **program music**, a term used to identify an instrumental composition that tells a story or paints a picture. Holst chose not to order the movements in order of their distance from the sun, instead swapping Mars and Mercury. The reason for this decision is clear enough: The music that Holst composed to depict Mars makes a great opener for the work.

The Planets was a massive success. It was immediately programmed by orchestras all over England and has since become one of the most familiar and most frequently performed pieces in the orchestral repertoire. All the same, Holst came to regret his biggest hit. He continued to develop and grow as a composer, and within just a few years he considered *The Planets* to be outdated. Critics, on the other hand, were disappointed when Holst's new compositions did not sound like his original blockbuster. Although Holst went on to write many beloved works, he never matched the success of *The Planets*.

We will examine the first and last movements of Holst's suite: "Mars, the Bringer of War" and "Neptune, the Mystic." "Mars" served as a model for John Williams's "Imperial March" in the *Star Wars* soundtrack, while "Neptune" seems to have had a general influence on Williams's musical portrayals of space.

Mars[12]

In astrological terms, the planet Mars is associated with confidence, self assertion, aggression, energy, strength, ambition, and impulsiveness. Leo described those born under the influence of Mars as "fond of liberty, freedom, and independence," noting that they "may be relied upon for courage" and are "fond of adventure and progress" but are also "headstrong and at times too forceful." In mythological terms, Mars is the ancient Roman god of war.

12.		"Mars" from *The Planets* Composer: Gustav Holst Performance: Chicago Symphony Orchestra, conducted by James Levine (1990)

Holst seems to have combined these influences in his music, which is overtly militaristic. The staccato rhythms heard at the beginning are the rhythms of a military march. At first they are played by the entire string section using a special technique, known as **col legno**, for which players turn their bows upside down and bounce the wooden stick on the string. Later, the snare drum—an actual military instrument—plays the same rhythm, which is heard almost throughout the movement. There is something very strange about Holst's march, however: It is in quintuple meter, with five beats per measure. It would be very difficult to actually march to this music.

Holst uses other strategies as well to communicate the character of Mars. The first melody we hear is low and ominous, consisting only of a rising gesture followed by a small descent. As the texture thickens, the volume increases and the melodic gestures seems more threatening. The introduction of trumpets and other brass instruments reinforces the militaristic flavor of the movement. In the middle section, the trumpets seem to be

Image 3.10: This ancient Roman statue depicts Mars as the god of war.
Source: Wikimedia Commons
Attribution: Andrea Puggioni
License: CC BY 2.0

sounding battle calls. Finally, the whole movement comes to a crashing close with the strings and brass playing as loudly and violently as possible.

Neptune[13]

Holst's representation of Neptune, the final planet in his suite, is entirely different. This is natural enough, given Holst's astrological mindset, for the influence of Neptune is associated with idealism, dreams, dissolution, artistry, empathy, illusion, and vagueness. Holst creates music, therefore, that captures these same qualities.

| 13. | | "Neptune" from *The Planets*
Composer: Gustav Holst
Performance: Chicago Symphony Orchestra, conducted by James Levine (1990) |

We might begin with a discussion of timbre. "Neptune" includes a sound that is completely absent from the other movements: women's voices. Holst includes two choirs of **sopranos** and **altos**, making for six separate vocal parts. The women don't sing words, however, but are instead instructed to sustain long, open "ah" vowels. The singers therefore function in the same way as instruments, bringing an ethereal, transparent quality to the upper register of the orchestra.

Apart from the voices, "Neptune" calls for the same instruments as "Mars." However, Holst deploys these instruments quite differently. He hardly uses the brass section at all, relegating them to low, sustained pitches in the background of the texture. Holst assigns the melody to wind instruments, with a preference for the airy sound of the flutes and the reedy timbre of the oboe and English horn. He also foregrounds the two harps and a percussion instrument called the celeste, which has a keyboard similar to that of a piano but produces the sound of bells.

The articulation in "Neptune" is completely unlike that heard in "Mars." While "Mars" is characterized by abrupt, accented rhythms, the pitches in "Neptune" are sustained and connected. Interestingly, this is the only movement that Holst originally composed for organ instead of piano. He felt that the organ, which can sustain pitches indefinitely, was better able to capture his musical vision. While both "Mars" and "Neptune" are in quintuple meter, the differences in articulation and tempo ("Neptune" is much slower) means that the two movements have completely different effects on the listener.

Finally, we might say something about the melody and harmony. There are no catchy tunes in "Neptune." Instead, the wind instruments and voices repeat floaty, circular melodies that don't seem to go anywhere. "Neptune" is also not in any particular key. Instead, the music rocks back and forth between seemingly unrelated harmonies. All of this creates the sensation of being unmoored. It is hard to predict where the music is going, but easy to enjoy the beautiful sounds.

IGOR STRAVINSKY, *THE RITE OF SPRING*

While the influence of Holst's "Mars" is particularly evident (after all, we hear the "Imperial March" repeatedly in almost all of the films), Williams also tapped the musical language of another prominent composer working at the same time. This borrowing did not become one of the repeated themes in Williams's score, but it is no less unmistakable. In addition, he borrowed for the same reason: Another composer of musical drama had already succeeded in setting the mood that Williams wanted to create: a mood reflecting uncertainty, suspense, and possible danger. Why reinvent the wheel?

The scene in question comes early in the first film, *A New Hope* (1977). The droids, R2D2 and C3PO, have landed on the desert planet Tatooine, where they argue and strike off in different directions. The setting is desolate and eerie, and the music serves to amplify our feeling of uncertainty about what is to come. We follow the path taken by C3PO, who doesn't know where he is, where he is going, or what might happen to him. The music that accompanies his journey is similarly uncertain. Oscillating melodies in the winds and muted trumpets are paired with high sustained notes in the strings and chromatic interjections from the bassoon and clarinet. Low, ominous sounds from the brass and reeds suggest a lurking danger. The music is in neither the major nor minor mode, there is no sense of a "home" note (the **tonic**), and we are not provided with any conclusive musical gestures (**cadences**). Instead, the pitches seem to float about. There is no sense of direction or purpose. At the end of this brief scene, the music simply fades away.

In the context of *Star Wars*, we are talking about just over 50 seconds of music. Were it not for Williams's borrowing, this scene would hold little interest. However, the work from which Williams extracted this brief passage of music was among the most influential of the twentieth century, and it is therefore worth exploring in order to understand why Williams chose this source, why the original work was composed in the first place, and how the dramatic intent of the two composers can help us to understand how music communicates meaning.

The passage adapted by Williams appears at the beginning of the second half of Igor Stravinsky's 1913 **ballet** *The Rite of Spring* (French: *Le sacre du printemps*). Like Williams, Stravinsky needed music that would create an atmosphere of mystery and suspense. Both dramas are set in an undefined, distant past: Williams's "a long time ago in a galaxy far, far away," Stravinsky's amongst the pagan tribes of prehistoric Russia. The differences arise when we examine the scenes for which each composer is preparing the viewer. C3PO is about to be captured by traders, while Stravinsky's characters are about to choose their victim for a virgin sacrifice.

Stravinsky and *The Rite of Spring*

Stravinsky wrote *The Rite of Spring* for a Paris audience (for whom Russia was indeed "far, far away"). Although Stravinsky was himself Russian, he had been living in Paris and writing ballets for three years. He was recruited for the job by Sergei Diaghilev, a wealthy Russian who had embarked on the quest of exporting Russian ballet to Paris. To do so, Diaghilev established a ballet troupe known as the *Ballet Russes* (that's "Russian Ballet" in French). His troupe specialized in flamboyant stage presentations that were meant to dazzle Parisian theatergoers with exotic stories, costumes, and music. When Stravinsky first agreed to join Diaghilev, he did so only because he had few other opportunities. He was unknown in Russia and had just begun his career in music. In accordance with Diaghilev's scheme, he participated in the production of a series of ballets with Russian themes. The first was *The Firebird* (1910), which combined various Russian folk tales with a typically Russian musical language. The second, *Petrushka* (1911), was set at a fair in the Russian countryside. *Rite of Spring* carried on this trend to a degree, but it was also startlingly new in several ways.

Like all ballets, *The Rite of Spring* was developed by an artistic team. The idea for the ballet was conceived jointly by Stravinsky and the painter Nikolai Roerich. Roerich, who was an expert on pre-Christian Slavic history, also designed the ballet's **scenario** (how the story unfolds), costumes, and sets. The choreographer—that is, the person who planned and taught the actual dance steps—was Vaslav Nijinsky, a famous dancer who had been part of the *Ballet Russes* since its founding and first performances in 1909. Working together, these three men put together a show that they knew would turn heads. At the same time, their ideas weren't entirely new. Artists working in Paris and beyond had for

Image 3.11: Although Nikolai Roerich's original costumes have been lost, replicas such as this have been created based on sketches and photographs.
Source: Wikimedia Commons
Attribution: Jean-Pierre Dalbéra
License: CC BY 2.0

Image 3.12: Nikolai Roerich created this sketch for scenery in 1912.
Source: Wikipedia
Attribution: Nikolai Roerich
License: Public Domain

Image 3.13: Here we see Vaslav Nijinsky in an earlier role with the Ballet Russes.
Source: Wikimedia Commons
Attribution: Bert. A
License: Public Domain

decades been preoccupied with so-called "primitive" cultures, which were believed to reveal fundamental truths about the human condition. At the same time, paintings of half-naked island dwellers, such as those produced by Paul Gauguin (1848-1903), were enticing and exotic. They allowed momentary escape from the constraints of Western society as they invited viewers to gaze upon supposedly innocent and uninhibited subjects.

Unlike most ballets, *The Rite of Spring* doesn't tell a particularly coherent story. It is in two parts. Over the course of Part I, which is entitled "Adoration of the Earth," members of Roerich and Stravinsky's imagined pagan tribe engage in a variety of rituals and games. In Part II, "The Sacrifice," a young girl is selected as the sacrificial victim. She dances herself to death in the final minutes of the ballet.

The Rite of Spring caused something of a stir at its premier. In what has since been described as a "riot" (although historical evidence indicates that this characterization is overblown), audience members reacted with consternation to what they saw and heard. To fully understand this response, we need to examine context, precedent, and the musical and visual elements of the ballet.

To begin with, *The Rite of Spring* was not the evening's sole entertainment. It was the second ballet on a double bill. The first ballet, entitled *The Sylphs* (French: *Les Sylphides*), was a classic from the Russian ballet repertoire. Diaghilev had included it in the first Paris season of the Ballet Russe, so the audience knew what to expect—and *The Sylphs*, which featured music by the 19th-century composer

Image 3.14: This 1898 painting by Gaugin captures Tahitian scenes.
Source: Wikimedia Commons
Attribution: Paul Gauguin
License: Public Domain

Frederic Chopin, was just the kind of thing Parisians wanted to see. The action consisted of elegantly-clad dancers cavorting gracefully about the stage. Viewers admired the beauty and poise of the artists.

The most disturbing element of *The Rite of Spring*, therefore, was not the plot or music but the dancing. Nijinsky had abandoned the graceful gestures and acrobatic leaps of traditional ballet. Instead, he had the dancers stomping around the stage on flat feet,[14] with hunched backs and awkwardly protruding limbs. He did so in an attempt to capture the primitive and raw aesthetic of the subject matter, as he perceived it. Of course, all of this came out of Nijinsky's imagination. For him, the idea of ancient pagan tribes served as an inspiration to try something new and daring. He had no way of knowing how his subjects might have actually danced.

14.  This 1987 performance by the Joffrey Ballet attempted to recreate the original appearance of Rite of Spring, including the costumes and choreography.

Nijinsky's choreography was complimented by Roerich's costumes. Instead of delicate tutus revealing stocking-clad legs and pointe shoes, Roerich's dancers appeared in cumbersome, floor-length dresses and cloaks. The women wore flat shoes and had long braids instead of neat buns. Audiences were thereby denied the opportunity of admiring the female form—a luxury that was central to the enjoyment of ballet.

Image 3.15: This photograph captures the original costumes for *The Rite of Spring*.
Source: Wikimedia Commons
Attribution: Unknown
License: Public Domain

Nijinsky was also responding to Stravinsky's music, which was unlike anything that had been heard in the theater before. The music did not contain lyrical melodies or compelling harmonic progressions. It did not express feelings of yearning, or heartbreak, or passion—the typical "human" emotions of the stage. Instead, it was alternately mechanistic, mysterious, threatening, and frenzied. Stravinsky's ostinatos and pounding rhythms inspired Nijinsky's similarly repetitive and rhythmic choreography. To understand how the music worked, we will look at two examples: the "Introduction" to Part II (later borrowed by Williams) and the "Sacrificial Dance" that concludes the ballet.

Part II: Introduction[15]

15.		Part II: "Introduction" from *The Rite of Spring* Composer: Igor Stravinsky Performance: San Francisco Symphony, conducted by Michael Tilson Thomas (2004)

The "Introduction" opens with a dissonant cluster of notes. The oboes and horns hold their notes, while the flutes and clarinets oscillate between pitches. What we hear does not suggest any particular key, major or minor. Stravinsky achieves this by having the instruments play in a number of different keys at the same time, a technique known as **polytonality**. The result is that the listener has no sense of direction or grounding. This disorienting effect serves to introduce a dramatic world with mysterious and unfamiliar characteristics.

There is no discernable melody for a long time—just the ebb and flow of Stravinsky's unusual sound colors. When a recognizable tune finally appears in the violins, it is played using **harmonics**, a string technique that causes pitches to sound much higher than usual and gives them an eerie quality. The melody uses only four pitches (it is **quadratonic**), and was probably inspired by Russian folk music.

Near the middle of the movement, the music changes. Two trumpets introduce a new melodic idea, changing pitches in alternation with one another. Starting at this point, Stravinsky employs a compositional technique that is typical of *The Rite of Spring*: He begins to build up layers by bringing in the sections of the orchestra one by one, each with its own characteristic melodic motif. First the strings begin to play quick rhythmic figures with repeated notes. Then the clarinets and violins enter with upward melodic swoops. The musical texture slowly gets denser and busier, the swoops coming with gradually increasing frequency. This ends with the return of the quadratonic melody in the horns as Stravinsky transitions into the next movement.

The "Introduction" has a pulse throughout, but the pulse is unevenly grouped into measures and phrases. For this reason, it is impossible to predict when a melodic or harmonic change is going to come. The effect is to leave the listener on edge, never certain what is going to happen next. Stravinsky uses this technique in every movement of *The Rite of Spring*, but to various ends. While uneven phrasing makes the "Introduction" seem vague and mysterious, it makes the "Sacrificial Dance," which concludes the ballet, sound violent and threatening.

Part II: Sacrificial Dance

	"Sacrificial Dance" from *The Rite of Spring* Composer: Igor Stravinsky Performance: The Chicago Symphony, conducted by Seiji Ozawa (1968)

Time	Form	What to listen for
0'00"	A	All parts of the orchestra engage in an unpredictable back-and-forth characterized by constant meter changes
0'25"	B	The texture is reduced to an uneven rhythm
0'37"		Brass interjections begin
0'52"		Strings enter to supplement the uneven rhythms and intensity builds
1'21"		Following a climactic point, the texture is reduced to a minimum and the process repeats
1'27"		Brass interjections begin again
1'35"		A whirling figure in the strings intensifies the music
1'43"	A'	Nearly identical to A
2'08"	C	The texture is dominated by brass and percussion
2'40"	A"	Brief return to A material
2'46"	C'	Return to C material
3'07"	A'''	Rhythmically, this passage can be recognized as a version of A, although the range, harmonies, and instrumentation are different
3'54"	Coda	The dance ends with an ascending flute run and a final cacophonous chord

The "Sacrificial Dance" is in **rondo form**, in which a primary melody returns throughout. It might be summarized as A B A' C A" C A''' with a brief coda, although in reality it is somewhat more complicated. However, using these letters will allow us to briefly discuss each section.

The A section is the most rhythmically jarring. The strings and winds play accented, dissonant chords in alternation with one another, culminating each time in one of two melodic figures: a short series of descending pitches or a series of repeated pitches with one higher outlier. Both figures are loud, accented, and aggressive, and, due to the rhythmic irregularity, it is impossible to predict when they will be heard.

The B section is significantly more subdued, although no more predictable. The strings provide an underpinning of irregular chords, while brass instruments periodically interject with accented, descending melodic fragments. The music builds in intensity before reverting to its original character. It then builds once more before the return of the A material (labelled A' to indicate the fact that the music is slightly different).

The C section features a wide variety of percussion instruments, including timpani and cymbals. Over these, various brass instruments enter with heavily accented melodies. Again, the music gets louder and more intense as it builds into yet another return of the A material. A", however, is very brief, for it is almost immediately interrupted by the continuation of C—now with even greater intensity.

The final return of the opening material as A''' sounds significantly different, for it employs different sets of pitches. However, the rhythmic character is the same. Once again Stravinsky builds the intensity of the music by alternating between his melodic ideas with increasing frequency, never establishing a pattern that will allow the listener to get comfortable. Finally, an ascending glissando in the flute, followed by a loud final chord, indicates that the dancing girl has collapsed.

RAGTIME AND DIXIELAND JAZZ

We will consider one more of Williams's borrowings. This time, however, we will be giving primary consideration to style, for Williams was influenced by a pair of musical traditions—specifically, those of ragtime and Dixieland jazz—rather than by a specific composition. Before we can examine the borrowing, however, we need to take a step back and consider the different ways in which music works in film.

Underscoring vs. Source Music

Think back on the scene we used to introduce the borrowing from *The Rite of Spring*. Was C3Po able to hear that music? Did the eerie, discordant sounds tell him anything about what lay in store? Most viewers would agree that he heard nothing other than the wind across the desert sands. That music was only for us, the movie-watchers, not for the character in the scene. Indeed, most of the music in *Star Wars* seems to be only for the viewer. Darth Vader does not keep an orchestra on hand to play his entrances, and Yoda certainly doesn't have one out in the swamp. When we hear music while watching the movie, we understand that its purpose is to amplify emotion and help tell the story. It is not actually a part of the story.

In the film industry, this technique is known as **underscoring**. It has been in use since the silent era, when theater organists and orchestras used to provide live music to accompany moving pictures that did not have dedicated soundtracks. Of course, this kind of music played a role in theatrical presentations long before movies came on the scene. Operas and ballets also include music that the characters on stage cannot hear, but that is nonetheless essential to the storytelling. In general terms, this is termed **non-diegetic music**.

If there is non-diegetic music, there must be **diegetic music**—music that the characters in the drama can in fact hear. In film, this is called **source music**, because the source of the sound is usually visible on screen. Almost every film and television show combines these two types of music. When a character is listening to the radio, or playing the guitar, or attending a concert, or dancing in a club, you are hearing source/diegetic music. When you can't see where the music is coming from and have good reason to doubt that it is audible to the onscreen characters (for example, when you hear an orchestra while watching someone walk down the street alone), you are hearing underscoring/non-diegetic music.

Often, it is not obvious whether the music we are hearing is diegetic or non-diegetic. In the case of the "Imperial March," for example, it is reasonable to believe that the Imperial Army might in fact have a band present that might in fact play a march. Many militaries have such musical ensembles, and even though we never see a band, we cannot prove that one is not present. At the same time, we can doubt that such a band would contain the full range of winds and strings that we hear in the soundtrack. Perhaps the Imperial forces are indeed hearing music— just not the same music that we are hearing. (The opposite can also occur. In one famous scene from Alfred Hitchcock's 1956 film *The Man Who Knew Too Much*, a live concert performance also serves to underscore the unfolding drama, such that we cannot confidently label the music as either diegetic or non-diegetic.) These problems become much more frequent and difficult to solve in musical theater genres, as we will see later.

Both diegetic and non-diegetic music can be equally important to the telling of a story, although each type tends to serve a different purpose. The most striking use of diegetic music in *Star Wars* occurs forty-five minutes into the first film, when the protagonists arrive at a bar to meet with Han Solo. In this scene, known popularly as the "cantina scene," we both hear and see a band playing a catchy tune. Because we see the performers, we can be quite certain that the onscreen characters are able to hear the music as well. At the same time, the music makes sense in this context. It is natural for a bar scene to contain a band playing lively music in a popular style.

The style itself speaks to us. Although Williams is not borrowing from a specific composition in this case, he is borrowing from a rich tradition of African

American dance music. Specifically, he is reinterpreting the rhythms and textures of two related dance music styles from the early twentieth century: ragtime and Dixieland jazz.

Ragtime

Ragtime was developed in the 1890s by African American piano players working in Midwestern entertainment venues. These highly-skilled musicians began to take a new approach to performing well-known tunes. A ragtime pianist would keep a steady beat with his left hand, alternating between high and low pitches, while performing complex **syncopated** rhythms with the right hand. (A syncopated rhythm includes accented notes that do not line up with the underlying pulse, but instead seem to fight against it.) While any melody can be "ragged" (that is, performed in this manner), African American pianists soon began composing and publishing original pieces with "ragtime" in the title or description.

The style quickly caught on across the nation. Its syncopated rhythms were fresh and exciting, and they made the listener want to dance. By 1910, ragtime rhythms and references were common in all types of popular music. At the same time, white Americans exhibited a great deal of concern about the influence of ragtime, which was associated with establishments where alcohol was served and the opposite sexes mingled freely. It was believed that the music's enticing rhythms were so powerful that they might lead young people to commit immoral acts. Most importantly, ragtime was the first in a long line of African American styles to have a major impact on mainstream popular music, and it was therefore perceived as a threat by white cultural powerbrokers.

George Botsford/Winifred Atwell, *Black and White Rag*

We will take a closer look at *Black and White Rag* (1908), a composition by the Iowa pianist George Botsford (1874-1949). Like all rags, this piece is in a form derived from that of 19th-century marches. This approach to organizing music is based on the repetition of several distinct melodies, each of which is heard twice upon being introduced and then may or may not return later in the piece. The form of *Black and White Rag* can be summarized as follows: intro A A B B A C C B'. As you can see, the A melody returns after the introduction of B. The B melody then returns (in modified form) after we hear C. The result is a musical work that balances repetition with contrast. The listener is able to identify familiar melodies as they return, but is kept from becoming bored by the regular introduction of new melodies.

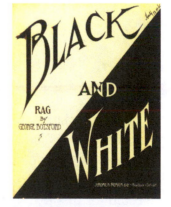

Image 3.16: *Black and White Rag* **was published as sheet music in 1908.**
Source: Wikimedia Commons
Attribution: User "Ragtimedorianhenry2010"
License: Public Domain

Time	Form	Source for the passage
	Black and White Rag Composer: George Botsford Performance: Winifred Atwell (1951)	
0'00"	Intro	Botsford
0'04"	A	Botsford
0'20"	B	Botsford
0'36"	A	Botsford
0'52"	Transition	Atwell
1'01"	D	Atwell
1'16"	E	Atwell
1'32"	F	Atwell
1'48"	Intro'	Botsford/Atwell
1'52"	B	Botsford
2'07"	A	Botsford
2'24"	Outro	Atwell

Ragtime piano compositions were never intended to be performed exactly as written. A published composition in this genre should be understood as a set of guidelines for performance. The composer supplies the basic material, but the performer is invited to reorganize and elaborate upon that material. The recording[16] selected for this text was made in 1951 by the Trinidadian pianist Winifred Atwell (1914-1983). It proved a hit, selling millions of copies in the UK and launching a craze for Atwell's style of ragtime piano playing. Atwell prefered the sound of an authentic "honky-tonk" piano, as heard in this recording. This is not a specific type of instrument, but rather a general aesthetic that is associated with the sound of early-20th century barroom pianos. Such instruments were generally cheap, damaged, and out of tune. The piano in this recording has a tinny quality, while the multiple strings that are struck each time the player depresses a key are not in tune with one another.

Atwell takes a typically improvisatory approach to her performance of Botsford's composition. She plays his introduction and A section essentially as written, although she does not repeat the A after the first time through. Then she plays the B section, followed by a repeat of the A section. Atwell omits Botsford's C section, however, and instead interpolates her own material. The new music, which includes several contrasting phrases and transitional passages, fits well within the performance but bears no relation to what Botsford wrote. To conclude, she plays the B and A sections once more, adding a final tag of her own creation. Atwell's performance, therefore, can be diagrammed as follows, with her original contributions in brackets: intro A B A [trans D E F intro'] B A [outro]. In sum, therefore, this is a performance of a piece composed half by Botsford and half by Atwell.

Image 3.17: Pianist Winifred Atwell became a sensation in the 1950s.
Source: Flickr
Attribution: User "Aussie~mobs"
License: Public Domain

The syncopated, danceable rhythms of ragtime are easy to hear in Williams's barroom music for *Star Wars*. The texture of ragtime—regular pulses in the low range, lively melody in the high range—is also evident. The instrumentation, however, echoes that of another African American dance music tradition, one that burst onto the scene just as ragtime was becoming passé: Dixieland jazz.

Dixieland Jazz

The style that would come to be known as Dixieland jazz developed in New Orleans in the early years of the twentieth century. Like ragtime, Dixieland jazz was heavily influenced by marching band music. Street bands provided an important form of entertainment in the city, and formal ensembles regularly processed between the various neighborhoods. Less disciplined musicians, known as "second line" players, would tag along behind the bands, improvising syncopated melodies on top of those being played by the ensemble.

Image 3.18: In this photograph, Dixieland musicians march in a 2016 parade in Dresden.
Source: Wikimedia Commons
Attribution: User "SchiDD"
License: CC BY-SA 4.0

This practice resulted in a new performance style, and small groups of musicians began gathering together to play syncopated music on traditional band instruments—usually clarinet, trumpet, trombone, and tuba, with banjo to provide the rhythmic underpinning. Dixieland jazz is also sometimes referred to as polyphonic jazz, due to the fact that all of the musicians play independent melodies at the same time. The term **polyphonic** means "many sounds," and is used to describe music in which all parts carry melodies of equal importance.

Image 3.19: Dixieland jazz is still popular today. Here, we see a US Army band performing in Leipzig.
Source: US Army Europe Band & Chorus
Attribution: Valerie Avila
License: Public Domain

One of the first great Dixieland band leaders was the cornet player Joseph Nathan "King" Oliver (1881-1938). Despite having established a formidable reputation in New Orleans, King Oliver moved to Chicago in 1918, hoping to secure a better life for himself and his family. He was not alone: millions of other African Americans living in the post-bellum South made the same trip in what is now termed the Great Migration. In Chicago, King Oliver was able to recruit the finest players for his band. These included a young Louis Armstrong, who had also learned his craft growing up in New Orleans. Oliver played first cornet, while

Image 3.20: Louis Armstrong was one of the most influential jazz musicians of the 20th century.
Source: Wikimedia Commons
Attribution: World-Telegram staff photographer
License: Public Domain

Armstrong played second cornet and slide trumpet. The other musicians in Oliver's band were clarinetist Johnny Dodds, Honoré Dutrey on trombone, Lil Hardin (later Armstrong) on piano, Bill Johnson on banjo and string bass (in place of tuba), and Baby Dodds on drums. King Oliver and his Creole Jazz Band quickly gained popularity, and the recordings that they began to release in 1923 sparked a national craze for jazz.

King Oliver, *Dippermouth Blues*

		Dippermouth Blues Composer: Joseph Nathan "King" Oliver Performance: King Oliver and his Creole Jazz Band (1923)
Time	**Form**	**What to listen for**
0'00"	Intro	All the melody instruments play a descending arpeggio
0'07"	Head	All of the melody instruments contribute different parts to the main theme
0'43"	Solo 1	The clarinet improvises a solo while the other instruments provide a **stop-time** accompaniment
1'19"	Solo 2	All of the instruments improvise at the same time
1'37"	Solo 3	The cornet player improvises with a plunger mute; other instruments are heard improvising in the background
2'29"	Solo 4	All of the instruments improvise at the same time

One of King Oliver's most influential compositions was *Dippermouth Blues*, which his group recorded twice in 1923 for two different record labels. We're going to examine the first recording, made in April for Gennett Records. The way this recording was made had a significant impact on how it sounds. Before the electric microphone was invented in 1925, music was recorded using acoustic technology. The musicians would gather around a horn that looked much like those you see on old gramophones. Those who played quiet instruments would stand close to the horn, while those who played loud instruments would stand further away, sometimes behind a barrier. The sound waves that entered the horn would cause a stylus to vibrate, which would in turn carve a groove into a rotating wax cylinder. The limitations of this technology meant that certain sounds could not be recorded.

Image 3.21: This photograph captures a recording session in the acoustic era.
Source: Library of Congress
Attribution: Library of Congress
License: Public Domain

In particular, instruments and voices that were very high, very low, or very loud caused the stylus to skip and ruined the recording. This explains why we don't hear string bass or very much percussion in this recording of "Dippermouth Blues." A live performance would have been slightly different.

After a brief introduction, we hear an excellent example of the Dixieland style as both cornets, the clarinet, and the trombone all play unique melodies at the same time. It is impossible to say who has "the" melody, for the music being played by each instrument seems to be of equal importance. The various instruments also take turns emerging from the texture. At one moment the clarinet seems to stand out, while at another your attention is drawn to the trombone. After a while, the clarinet really does take the melody, while the other instruments play a repeated rhythm in the background. Later, the cornet similarly takes a lead role. Near the end of the recording, we once again hear the polyphonic texture that marks this style. This music is busy and complex, but in a way it is also simple. Its object, after all, is to make you want to dance. If you feel compelled to tap your foot or otherwise respond to its syncopated rhythms, then the players have accomplished their goal.

The title of this selection also provides us with valuable information. "Dippermouth" was simply a nickname for Louis Armstrong (a fact that has led some to believe that Armstrong wrote this tune, not Oliver). The term "Blues," however, describes several important characteristics of the music we are about to hear. The **blues** was an influential style of African American popular music that emerged on the vaudeville stage and later flourished among musicians of the Mississippi delta region. There is much to say about the blues style, but here we will focus on two elements that found their way into Oliver's composition. The first has to do with harmonies. Upon listening to "Dippermouth Blues," you might notice that you hear the same chords pattern again and again. This pattern repeats every forty-eight beats (listen to the percussion), or—if we group those beats into measures— every twelve measures. What you are hearing is called the twelve-bar blues, and it provides the structure for most blues compositions.

The other element from the blues that we hear in this example is the **blue note**. All of the harmonies used in the twelve-bar blues chord progression are in the major mode, and the melodies therefore ought to be in the major mode as well. In the blues tradition, however, performers sometimes lower certain melodic notes (an act known as "blueing" the note). These are usually the third, fifth, and

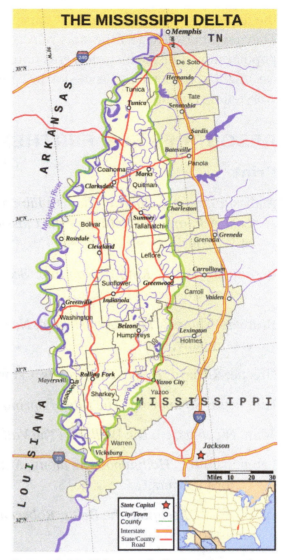

Image 3.22: This map indicates the region of Mississippi that is often referred to the as the Mississippi delta.
Source: Wikimedia Commons
Attribution: User "Philg88"
License: CC BY-SA 3.0

seventh degrees of the scale, although other notes can also be blued. Because of this, the melody occasionally clashes with the harmony as the music pulls alternately towards the major and minor modes. This gives the music a particularly expressive dimension and encourages the listener to get physically involved. Whether or not you can identify the blue notes in this recording, you certainly feel their impact.

When we examine John Williams's use of ragtime and Dixieland styles in *Star Wars*, we see how music intended for a purely practical purpose—in this case, dancing—can be used to tell a story. Ragtime and Dixieland jazz are not storytelling genres, but their sounds communicate many layers of information to the modern listener. They suggest dancing, nightclubs, drinking, and excitement. They might also suggest the story of African American contributions to American popular music, or the historical eras from which these styles emerged. In this way, we might consider all music—not just film scores or theatrical works—to have storytelling potential.

RESOURCES FOR FURTHER LEARNING

Print

Audissino, Emilio. *John Williams's Film Music: Jaws, Star Wars, Raiders of the Lost Ark, and the Return of the Classical Hollywood Music Style.* University of Wisconsin Press, 2014.

Berlin, Edward A. *King of Ragtime: Scott Joplin and His Era.* Second edition. Oxford University Press, 2016.

Brothers, Thomas. *Louis Armstrong's New Orleans.* Reprint edition. W.W. Norton & Company, 2007.

Greene, Richard. *Holst: The Planets.* Cambridge University Press, 1995.

Hill, Peter. *Stravinsky: The Rite of Spring.* Cambridge University Press, 2000.

John, Nicholas, ed. *Die Walküre (The Valkyrie).* Overture Publishing, 2011.

Lehman, Frank. *Hollywood Harmony: Musical Wonder and the Sound of Cinema.* Oxford University Press, 2018.

Wald, Elijah. *Escaping the Delta: Robert Johnson and the Invention of the Blues.* Amistad, 2004.

Online

Frank Lehman, *Complete Catalog of the Musical Themes of Star Wars*: https://franklehman.com/starwars/

The Leitmotifs of Wager's Ring: https://pjb.com.au/mus/wagner/

Not Another Music History Cliché!, "Did Stravinsky's The Rite of Spring incite a riot at its premiere?": https://notanothermusichistorycliche.blogspot.com/2018/06/did-stravinskys-rite-of-spring-incite.html

Sung and Danced Drama

Esther M. Morgan-Ellis and Alexandra Dunbar

INTRODUCTION

The notion that characters in a staged drama might periodically break out into song or dance is fundamentally strange. All the same, sung and danced dramas permeate our lives, and they have for a long time. Even if you do not regularly visit the opera or ballet, you have likely seen *Frozen* or *The Little Mermaid*. Films such as these fit squarely into a tradition of musical theater that extends back for hundreds of years.

Musical drama, as the examples in this chapter will demonstrate, is highly diverse. It can be tragic or comic. It can be realistic or self-consciously artificial. It can be emotionally compelling or merely entertaining. It also encompasses endless variety in musical style, and it can be difficult to draw lines between genres. The examples in this chapter might variously be described as "musical theater," "opera," or "ballet" (a term that both European and Javanese performers use to describe their dance drama traditions). However, there are many overlaps between these categories. European ballet first developed as a part of opera, for example, and many operatic traditions include dancing. Dance dramas often include singing—something that is true of both examples in this chapter.

The most difficult categories to differentiate are "musical theater" and "opera." For example, one does not hear *Frozen*—even in its live, staged version—referred to as an opera. But why not? Because it is in English? Lots of operas are in English. Because it has spoken dialogue? So does Mozart's *The Magic Flute*, discussed below. Because the music is written in a popular style? The Italian opera composer Giuseppe Verdi was responsible for the greatest hit tunes of his day. The most substantial difference between "musical theater" and "opera," as those categories are understood today, has to do with the training of the performers on the one hand and the venues in which they perform on the other. However, these categories are already shaky, and they will continue to change as new styles of sung and danced drama are developed and popularized.

We encourage the reader of this chapter to approach each example on its own terms, without undue preconceptions about genre. Whether we are talking about New York City in 2015 or Mantua in 1608, it is always helpful to consider the cultural context in which the work was created. Who was the audience, and how were they prepared to understand and appreciate what they saw onstage? Although our examples are diverse, each effectively uses music to enrich the storytelling.

SUNG DRAMA

LIN-MANUEL MIRANDA, *HAMILTON*

Hamilton is considered by many to be the greatest American musical theater production of the current era. The musical tells the story of Alexander Hamilton, an immigrant who travelled from the West Indies to the American colonies before the time of the American Revolution, and who came to be one of the founding fathers of the United States and the first Secretary of the Treasury under George Washington. The musical is based upon the biography by Ron Chernow (b. 1949), *Alexander Hamilton,* published in 2004.

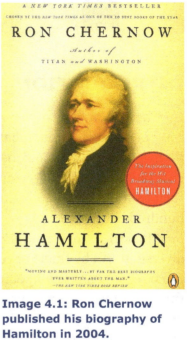

Image 4.1: Ron Chernow published his biography of Hamilton in 2004.
Source: Flickr
Attribution: Nathan Hughes Hamilton
License: CC BY 2.0

Miranda and *Hamilton*

Hamilton is the singular creation of the actor, writer, and musician Lin-Manuel Miranda (b. 1980), who, in addition to premiering the title role, wrote the music and lyrics. Miranda is one of the biggest musical theater celebrities of his generation, having won multiple Emmys, Grammys, and Tony Awards for his music, lyrics, and performances. Much of Miranda's work is influenced by his origins. As the child of parents of Puerto Rican descent, he grew up in a largely Latino neighborhood in Inwood, New York City, regularly visiting family in Puerto Rico. His musical preferences—Miranda grew up listening to salsa and American musicals (such as *West Side Story*)—reflected both an early interest in his musical heritage and a fascination with the stage. Miranda was gifted musically and academically, attending the highly competitive primary and secondary schools at Hunter College before enrolling at Wesleyan University.

Image 4.2: Lin-Manuel Miranda in the title role of *Hamilton*.
Source: Wikimedia Commons
Attribution: Steve Jurvetson
License: CC BY 2.0

In his theatrical work, Miranda foregrounds his multi-cultural upbringing and Latino identity. As a director, he has always made a conscious decision to cast actors from various cultural and racial

Image 4.3: This photograph, taken in 2015 by White House photographer Pete Souza, captures the diversity of the *Hamilton* cast.
Source: Wikimedia Commons
Attribution: Pete Souza
License: Public Domain

backgrounds. This feature of *Hamilton* has created some controversy, given the historical fact that the men and women represented in the musical were primarily white. Miranda, however, has defended this approach by drawing parallels between his casting and musical decisions. Just as he did not attempt to write music in the style of the 1770s, he did not attempt to create a visual image representative of the 1770s. Miranda's *Hamilton* was created to represent America in the current age. He makes the point that the United States was founded by immigrants. The founding fathers themselves—despite their skin color—were either immigrants or the children or grandchildren of immigrants. Hamilton himself was born in the West Indies, coming to America at a young age to make a name for himself. What is more American than that?

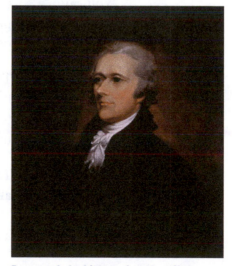

Image 4.4: Alexander Hamilton was the first US Secretary of the Treasury, serving from 1789 to 1795.
Source: Wikimedia Commons
Attribution: John Trumbull
License: Public Domain

The musical numbers in *Hamilton* incorporate hip-hop beats and rap. The use of popular styles in a musical is not unique to

Hamilton: *Hair* (1967) and *Jesus Christ Superstar* (1970) were the first modern-era musicals to incorporate rock styles, and Lin-Manuel Miranda had already used rap and hip-hop in his first musical, *In the Heights* (on Broadway from 2008 to 2011). In writing *Hamilton*, Miranda found that rap was not only musically exciting but also very useful, for he was able to fit more words into a shorter span of time. Hamilton the man was known for being poetically loquacious. In addition, rap allowed Miranda to incorporate a large amount of information from Chernow's biography, in addition to Hamilton's own words. The entire musical is 150 minutes long, but includes over 20,000 words.

Miranda also uses music to communicate with the *Hamilton* audience in ways that both complement and transcend the script and stage action. One of his favorite techniques for doing so is **allegory**, or the use of musical sounds to signify hidden meaning. We will address several ways in which Miranda employs instruments or musical styles in an allegorical manner.

Allegory

"You'll be Back" from *Hamilton*
Composer: Lin-Manuel Miranda
Performance: Original Cast Recording (2015)

Time	Form	What to listen for
0'00"	Introduction "You say…"	King George III of England addresses America to a homophonic accompaniment of sustained piano chords in a four-chord descending pattern
0'33"	Verse 1 "You'll be back…"	The accompaniment switches to short harpsichord accents; the overall tone of the text becomes more sinister, which offers an unusual juxtaposition with happy music
1'15"	Hook "Da-da-da-da-da…"	This catchy passage is sung to nonsense words and is reminiscent of the outro of The Beatles' "Hey Jude," which is similar in terms of key and melodic arc
1'29"	Bridge "You say our love is draining…"	Stop-time accompaniment; double entendre on the word subject at 1'46"

2'12"	Verse 2 "You'll be back, like before..."	Same musical material as Verse 1; harpsichord returns to the front of the mix, one octave higher than before; tempo slows, emphasizing text, until the word "Love" at 2'36"
2'46"	Hook/Outro "Da-da-da-da-da...."	The performer is joined in this catchy tune by the rest of the cast members on stage

There are several additional musical allegories in *Hamilton*. Let us consider, for example, the number "You'll Be Back," which is sung from the perspective of King George III. The music for this number is in the style of 1960s British Invasion pop. (Incidentally, The Beatles—the most famous and influential of the British Invasion bands—prominently featured harpsichord in their 1967 album *Sgt. Pepper's Lonely Hearts Club Band*.) Again, Miranda makes a connection between a British musical style (an invasive one at that) and an imperialistic British character. But that's not all: Miranda further uses the pop genre to heighten the impact of his character's words. King George sings this number to a personified America. The music is relentlessly upbeat, as if expressing the emotional state of a delirious ex-boyfriend who cannot grasp that the relationship is over. The text, which is quite disturbing at times, is hilariously juxtaposed with the some of the happiest and tuneful music of the show.

Let us also consider Miranda's use of the harpsichord. Miranda writes for two keyboard instruments in his musical: the harpsichord and the piano. The two instruments really did not coexist in history. During the course of the 1700s, the harpsichord was gradually replaced by the fortepiano, which was itself an early predecessor to the piano. In *Hamilton*, however, we do not hear a fortepiano but rather a modern, 20th-century piano—an instrument historically separated from the harpsichord by over one hundred years. The harpsichord, therefore, represents an old way of life—and, more particularly, an old way of conducting politics. Specifically, Miranda uses the harpsichord to represent British rule before the revolution.

The sound of the harpsichord was, historically speaking, the sound of the

Image 4.5: This French harpsichord was built in 1780.
Source: Wikimedia Commons
Attribution: Gérard Janot
License: CC BY-SA 3.0

Image 4.6: This 1795 fortepiano looks like a harpsichord, but, like a modern piano, it creates sound by striking the strings with hammers. In a harpsichord, the strings are plucked.
Source: Wikimedia Commons
Attribution: User "JaGa"
License: CC BY-SA 4.0

Image 4.7: A modern piano is considerably larger than the fortepiano and has a metal frame, which allows the string tension to be greater. As a result, the instrument is much louder.
Source: Wikimedia Commons
Attribution: Carl Bechstein
License: CC0

18th-century British monarchy. In order to draw a historical comparison, we might consider the music of George Frederic Handel. Handel served as music director (German: *Kapellmeister*) to the German Prince George of Hanover, who later became King George I of England. While living in London, Handel composed many great works for the King, most notably his *Water Music* and *Music for the Royal Fireworks*[1]. Handel was also one of the best-known and highly celebrated harpsichordists of his time. It is therefore fitting that the harpsichord should represent King George III, England, political oppression, and a deranged narcissistic ex-suitor.

We encounter this allegory in several musical examples. In "Farmer Refuted,"[2] Bishop Samuel Seabury, accompanied by harpsichord, defends his decision to remain loyal to England and begs Hamilton to do the same. "You'll Be Back" begins with King George III singing to a subdued piano accompaniment. When his lyrics turn sinister, however, we hear the harpsichord enter. In both of these cases, therefore, the sound of the harpsichord is a symbol for the old-fashioned values of the British monarchy.

1.	 G.F. Handel's *Music for the Royal Fireworks* incorporates the harpsichord in a way that is typical of 18th-century European music.
2.	In "Farmer Refuted," Miranda uses the harpsichord to symbolize loyalty to England.

Cyclicism

"I Know Him" from *Hamilton*
Composer: Lin-Manuel Miranda
Performance: Original Cast Recording (2015)

Time	Form	What to listen for
0'00"	Introduction "They say…"	Same introductory chords as the original introduction, despite plot changes
0'24"	"I'm perplexed…"	Unusual harmonies
0'42"		"John Adams…" is spoken in surprise.
0'45"	Verse 1 "I know him…"	Begins with the same tune and feel of Verse 1 from "You'll Be Back," but there is no harpsichord; instead, the texture consists of plucked strings, which recall the sound of the harpsichord but offer a warmer timbre; harpsichord returns to the mix in the background at 0'54" on the words, "Years ago"
1'18"	Hook	Only one iteration of this, unlike before, and there is no "everybody" joining in

King George later returns to perform "I Know Him." This song is a musical **reprise** of the first number he sang ("You'll Be Back"). At this point in the musical, the Revolution is long over and John Adams has been elected president. The harpsichord can still be heard, but it is less prominent than it was in "You'll Be Back." Instead, it is lurks behind a texture that consists primarily of strings played pizzicato. This is significant: England (harpsichord) has lost the war and King George (harpsichord) no longer rules over the Americans.

"I Know Him" is not the only example of a musical reprise. Indeed, in crafting the score to *Hamilton*, Miranda sought to unify the various parts of the work using **cyclical techniques**. *Hamilton* contains many musical ideas that harken back to earlier points in the work. This approach to creating a narrative can be compared to Wagner's use of leitmotifs. For example, the opening of the musical begins with a narrative rapped by Aaron Burr: "How does a bastard [...] grow up to be a hero and scholar?" Miranda treats this passage from Aaron Burr's opening number, which is entitled "Alexander Hamilton,"[3] as a **leitmotif**, which later returns in "A Winter's Ball," "Guns and Ships," "What'd I Miss," "The Adams Administration," and "Your Obedient Servant." Despite the recurrence of musical material, however, each of these numbers has a distinct character. In "What'd I Miss," the borrowing takes on a swinging feel as the once-straight sixteenths of the opening become dotted. In "Your Obedient Servant," on the other hand, the tone is darkened by tremolo strings and the omission of the snaps that were previously heard on offbeats: Burr, now downright angry, is resentful of Alexander Hamilton.

3.  The opening phrases of "Alexander Hamilton" become a leitmotif and return throughout the work.

Success

Upon its Broadway premiere in 2015, *Hamilton* immediately sold out. As of 2019, it continues to be nearly impossible to secure a ticket, the aftermarket prices of which have soared to record-breaking levels. The musical is currently on tour to cities across the globe, including Puerto Rico and London, England. It has won numerous awards, including ten Lortel Awards, three Outer Critic Circle Awards, eight Drama Desk Awards, the New York Drama Critics Circle Award for Best New Musical, and an Obie for Best New American Play.

CLAUDIO MONTEVERDI, *ORPHEUS*

In Chapter 2, we examined a classic opera: Richard Wagner's *The Valkyrie*. Wagner was contributing to a tradition of staged musical drama that had existed for about 250 years. Here, we will encounter one of the very first European operas ever created, Claudio Monteverdi's *Orpheus*. First, however, we will consider the social structures and values that gave rise to opera in the first place, and we will address the new ways of writing music that made sung drama possible.

The Origins of European Opera

European opera was born in the city of Florence in the late 16th century. Beginning in the 1570s, a group of intellectuals began meeting in the home of Count Giovanni de' Bardi to discuss artistic matters. They called themselves the Camerata (a name derived from the Italian term for "chamber"), and today are referred to as the **Florentine Camerata**. The members of the Camerata were courtiers, composers, poets, and scholars, and they were concerned

Image 4.8: This map shows the walled city of Florence about 100 years before opera was born there.
Source: Wikimedia Commons
Attribution: Hartmann Schedel
License: Public Domain

with the modern development of artistic forms. In particular, they believed that the arts had become corrupted, and that artistic expression could only be revived by returning to the principles of ancient Greece. Where music was concerned, however, ancient Greece could offer only limited guidance. While many theoretical and philosophical treatises on music survive, very few compositions were preserved, and we don't really know what those would have sounded like. Resurrecting the musical practices of ancient Greece, therefore, is a tricky endeavor.

Image 4.9: Music was very important in ancient Greece, both in the context of theater and as everyday entertainment.
Source: Wikimedia Commons
Attribution: Colmar Painter
License: Public Domain

The members of the Camerata drew much of their inspiration from the work of Girolamo Mei (1519-1594), a Roman scholar and the leading authority on ancient Greece. In his 1573 treatise *On the Musical Modes of the Ancients*, Mei argued that all ancient Greek poetry and drama had been sung, not spoken. He also wrote about the extraordinary power that music had over the listener. His descriptions fascinated the Florentine intellectuals, who felt compelled to develop a modern approach to sung drama. Their aim was to recapture the emotional impact that, according to Mei, sung plays had once had on audiences.

The leading music theorist of the Camerata was none other than Vincenzo Galilei (1520-1591), father of the famous astronomer Galileo Galilei. In order to facilitate sung drama, Galilei sought to develop a new approach to writing vocal music that imitated dramatic speech. It would be modelled on the way in which actors used variations in pacing and pitch to expressively declaim text from the stage. Such music would be free of repetition, of course, since every note would be uniquely tied to the word it illuminated. The rhythms would be derived from the text, while the melodies and harmonies would portray the emotional content.

Today, this style is termed **recitative**, for it more closely resembles dramatic recitation than typical singing.

Of course, a solo singer needs accompaniment. Although Galilei and his colleagues did not invent **basso continuo**, they did adopt it as the ideal vehicle for supporting sung text. The term "basso continuo" (which translates to "continuous bass") refers to a style of accompaniment that came to be used in almost all music of the **Baroque** period (ca. 1600-1750). When a composer writes an accompaniment in the form of basso continuo, they indicate only the bass line and harmonies, which are usually to be played by at least two instruments. They do not usually specify instruments or exact pitches of each chord, which are chosen on the spot by the performers. An instrument that can play chords— harpsichord, organ, and lute were most common—is required, while an instrument that can play a bass line—cello or bassoon, perhaps— is usually included.

Image 4.10: Here we see the cover of Galilei's 1581 treatise, *On Music Ancient and Modern*.
Source: Wikimedia Commons
Attribution: Vincenzo Galilei
License: Public Domain

Members of the Camerata began experimenting with short sung dramas in 1589, while the first full-length opera—now lost—was composed by Jacopo Peri (1561-1633) in 1597. In 1600, Peri created *Euridice*, an operatic portrayal of the Orpheus myth. This work, which survives, consists almost entirely of recitative, as does a second version of *Euridice* produced by another member of the Camerata, Giulio Caccini (1551-1618), in 1602. (The two men were colleagues and collaborators, but also saw themselves as being in competition with one another.)

Image 4.11: This photograph of the interior of the Medici Palace in Florence captures the splendor in which the family lived.
Source: Wikimedia Commons
Attribution: User "Sailko"
License: CC BY-SA 3.0

All of these developments took place in Florence, and were supported by the Medici court. Peri's Euridice, for example, was created and staged to celebrate the marriage between King Henry IV of France and Maria de Medici. From its inception, opera was understood to be aristocratic entertainment. It upheld noble values and catered to refined musical tastes. It also offered the opportunity for luxurious spectacle in the form of fantastical costumes and scenery. Musically, however, these early operas were a bit boring, and the art form might have lived and died in Florence had not one of the great composers of the century developed an approach to sung drama that was truly compelling.

Orpheus

Claudio Monteverdi (1567-1643) was born in Cremona—an Italian city most famous for its legendary violin makers. He secured a position at the Mantuan court in 1590, where he served the Gonzaga family. Although Monteverdi flourished under the employment of Duke Vincenzo I, he was abruptly dismissed by the Duke's son and successor in 1612. The next year he won the prestigious post of music director at St. Mark's basilica in Venice, where he remained for the rest of his long life—despite a 1620 invitation to return to his post in Mantua, which he gleefully rejected. Although we will examine an opera that Monteverdi produced early in his life for the Gonzagas, he returned to the genre in his old age, creating three operas for the Venetian public in the 1640s.

Image 4.12: This portrait of Claudio Monteverdi was painted around 1640 by Bernardo Strozzi.
Source: Wikimedia Commons
Attribution: Bernardo Strozzi
License: Public Domain

Image 4.13: This portrait of Duke Vincenzo I was produced around 1600.
Source: Wikimedia Commons
Attribution: Studio of Frans Pourbus the Younger
License: Public Domain

The oldest opera still to be regularly performed and enjoyed is Monteverdi's *Orpheus* (Italian: *L'Orfeo*). We will begin with the occasion for which Monteverdi created this masterpiece. Then we will summarize the story before examining several musical excerpts.

Like the operas developed by the Florentine Camerata, *Orpheus* was intended for the private enjoyment of courtiers and their guests. This opera was among the festive entertainments on offer for the 1607 **Carnival** season. Carnival is celebrated in Catholic countries around the world during the days or weeks preceding Ash Wednesday, which marks the beginning of the liturgical season of **Lent**. During the forty days of Lent, Catholics are expected to give up earthly pleasures and demonstrate penitence for their sins. Lent culminates in Holy Week, when the story of Christ's crucifixion is told, and ends with Easter, which celebrates the resurrection. Carnival, therefore, marks the last opportunity for the faithful to enjoy food, drink, and entertainment. Although *Orpheus* was one of the first operas written for Carnival, the genre would be associated with the Carnival season for centuries to come. Opera would also come to be prohibited during Lent.

Orpheus, like other early operas, served a dual purpose. On the one hand, it provided dazzling entertainment to accompany a courtly celebration. On the other, it put the wealth and splendor of the court on display for the purpose of impressing those in attendance. Because he was tasked with exhibiting the affluence of the Gonzagas, Monteverdi did not need to worry about keeping his production within budget. For this reason he was able to write for an enormous orchestra and cast, and the original staging would have been extravagant.

It is not difficult to guess why Monteverdi chose the Orpheus myth as the subject for his opera. To begin with, by doing so he set himself up for favorable comparison with the Florentine composers who had already produced operas on this topic. Monteverdi's boss, Duke Vincenzo, had in fact seen the production of Jacopo Peri's opera *Euridice*, which had inspired him to commission a similar sung drama from his own court composer. The story itself is also particularly well-

Image 4.14: Orpheus and his lyre have been the subject of countless paintings. In the work from the 1630s, we see him captivating woodland creatures with his musical ability.
Source: Wikimedia Commons
Attribution: Theodoor van Thulden and Frans Snyders
License: Public Domain

suited to an operatic telling. The Orpheus myth is, in essence, a story about the power of music to sway emotions. This, of course, was exactly what the architects of opera wanted to accomplish with their new art form.

Monteverdi set a **libretto** (the text for a sung drama) written by another member of the Mantuan court, Alessandro Striggio, who crafted a narrative in five acts. In the first part of the opera, Orpheus—a legendary musician fathered by the god Apollo—weds Euridice, a wood nymph. A raucous celebration follows, but the revelers are interrupted by Euridice's friend Sylvia, who reports that she has died as the result of a bite from a venomous snake. Orpheus is at first devastated, but soon resolves to pursue her into the underworld and bring her back to life. Using the power of song, he convinces the boatman Caronte to carry him across the river Styx. He then persuades the rulers of the underworld to release his beloved. She is permitted to follow him back to the Earth's surface, but Orpheus is warned that he must trust that she walks behind him, for he will lose her forever if he looks back. Unable to control himself, he looks—and she is once more taken away from him. Orpheus returns home distraught, but is comforted by his father, who carries him away to the heavens. (This is a relatively happy ending: In a more authentic telling, Orpheus is torn to pieces by the Furies.)

Image 4.15: In this 1862 painting by Edward Poynter, we see Orpheus leading Euridice out of the underworld.
Source: Wikimedia Commons
Attribution: Edward Poynter
License: Public Domain

Perhaps because they were working in a different city, Monteverdi and Striggio departed from the dogmatic prescriptions of the Florentine Camerata. Instead of setting the entire story in recitative, they interspersed recitative with different types of structured vocal music, including folk-like **strophic songs** (in which many verses are sung to the same melody), choral **refrains** (interjections by the choir), and a massive, ornate **aria** (a highly formalized song) for Orpheus. The resulting opera is full of variety, although it still relies on recitative to convey emotion at all of the key dramatic moments.

Toccata

The first thing the audience heard at the premiere of *Orpheus* was not singing but instrumental music. This would become typical of opera and other types of sung theater, which always begin with an orchestral **overture**. Monteverdi described his overture as a "toccata"[4], an Italian term that translates to "a thing that is touched" and was used at the time to indicate music for instruments. The toccata is very simple, for it served a simple purpose: It alerted the audience, with appropriate grandiosity, that the show was about to start. For his toccata, Monteverdi composed a repetitive melody in the style of a bugle call. It contains only the first six notes of a major scale, and consists primarily of ascending and descending stepwise motion. The melody is played three times using different sets of instruments. In our recording, it is heard first in the brass, second in the strings, and finally in the brass again.

4.   "Toccata" from *Orpheus*
Composer: Claudio Monteverdi
Performance: Le Concert des Nations and La Capella Reial de Catalunya, directed by Jordi Savall (2002)

This recording—and *Orpheus* in general—provides us with an excellent opportunity to encounter instruments of the Baroque era. As one can see and hear, they are similar to modern instruments, but not entirely familiar. The instrumentation in *Orpheus* is particularly interesting because, counter to common practice, Monteverdi specified it himself. Up until the Baroque era, it was typical for composers to write generic "instrumental" music that could be performed on any instrument. Monteverdi, however, took special concern with the sound qualities of his opera. In particular, he specified that the scenes on earth were to be accompanied by strings and flutes, while the scenes in the underworld were to be dramatized by the sounds of brass and the reed organ. The resulting timbres reinforce the darkness of Hades.

Most modern productions, including both referred to in this text, use what are termed **period instruments**. These are usually copies of instruments that were built in the Baroque era. In the first pass through the toccata, we see a drum, a trumpet that is a bit different in shape than the modern instrument, and two sackbuts—small predecessors of the modern trombone. During the repeat by the full orchestra, we see a variety of additional instruments: Baroque violins, which can differ slightly in shape and are played with arched bows; cornetti, which sound somewhat like trumpets but look like oboes or clarinets; recorders (the predecessor to the modern flute); a Baroque harp; theorbos, which are lutes with long necks and additional bass strings; and bass viols, which look a bit like cellos but are different in shape and have frets. The ensemble sounds familiar, but has a timbre that is notably different than that of a modern orchestra.

We will continue to address instrumentation throughout the opera, for it plays an important role. The richest area for discussion, however, is not the orchestra but the basso continuo section. Monteverdi provides a diverse selection of continuo instruments, including harpsichord, theorbo, harp, pipe organ, reed organ, bass viol, and cello. These can be combined in a variety of ways to produce a nuanced palette of sound colors. As a result, even long passages of recitative are full of variety, as accompanying instruments enter and leave the texture.

Act II

Act II from *Orpheus* Composer: Claudio Monteverdi Performance: Das Monteverdi-Ensemble des Opernhauses Zürich, directed by Nikolaus Harnoncourt (1978)		
Time	**Form**	**What to listen for**
22'27"	Ritornello & Aria A	Ritornello: strings and flutes Aria: Orpheus, one verse
23'10"	Ritornello & Aria B	Ritornello: violins Aria: a shepherd, two verses
23'50"	Ritornello & Aria C	Ritornello: violins Aria: a pair of shepherds, two verses
24'49"	Ritornello & Aria D with Chorus	Ritornello: flutes Aria: a pair of shepherds, one verse Chorus: one verse
25'44"	Orpheus's aria	Orpheus sings a four-verse aria; the ritornello is a lively dance tune played by the strings
28'20"	Recitative: Shepherd	Basso continuo: harp and cello

29'01"	Refrain: Messenger	The Messenger enters with a melodic refrain that will return throughout Act II Basso continuo: theorbo, organ, and cello
29'27"	Recitative: Shepherd	Basso continuo: harpsichord and cello
29'24"	Recitative: Messenger	Basso continuo: theorbo, organ, and cello
[...]	Recitative: various	Basso continuo: various
34'17	Refrain: Shepherd	One of the shepherds repeats the Messenger's refrain
35'29"	Recitative: Orpheus	Basso continuo: theorbo and cello
37'41"	Refrain: Chorus	The chorus repeats the Messenger's refrain, which is extended into a choral lament
38'47"	*End of listening guide*	

We will skip the wedding and start at the beginning of Act II with the party. In this scene, Orpheus is celebrating with the nymphs and shepherds who reside in an unnamed rural paradise. As might be expected on such an occasion, they sing and dance together. Monteverdi took the opportunity to abandon the solemn recitative of the previous act and compose a string of folk-like songs to be performed by Orpheus and his friends. Almost all of the songs are **strophic**, meaning that two or more verses of text are sung to the same melody. In between the songs, different assortments of orchestral instruments provide **ritornellos**, which are repeating instrumental themes. The performing forces slowly grow: first we hear a solo, then a duet, then the entire chorus. Finally, Orpheus himself sings the longest strophic song of all—containing four verses—on the topic of his extreme happiness.

All of this music can be heard in a **diegetic** framework. That is to say, we can understand the characters on stage to really be singing. This interpretation makes sense in the dramatic context. Orpheus in particular is a famed musician who would be likely to sing for his friends, while the setting—a wedding celebration—suggests the presence of music. The folk-like attributes of the songs also make them particularly appropriate for the characters to sing. However, we must also assume that the characters are not hearing *exactly* the same music that we are. Although shepherds might sing and dance, they would not have a large orchestra at their disposal. Monteverdi treads the line between the realistic portrayal of a party and the fantastical world of opera, in which everything happens to musical accompaniment.

At the conclusion of Orpheus's song, the music suddenly changes. The orchestra drops out, leaving only basso continuo in support of a solo singer (one of the shepherds). This is recitative. Suddenly, the scene is interrupted by Sylvia, who comes bearing the news of Euridice's death. In our production, her entrance is marked visually with the descent of a black cloth over the backdrop, but also musically with a change in basso continuo instrumentation. While the shepherd had sung with an accompaniment of harp and cello, Sylvia sings with theorbo and organ. The new timbres contrast with the pastoral scene, making her message all the more disruptive.

Following interjections from several of the other characters, each marked with a change in basso continuo, Sylvia tells her story. It might seem strange that one of the most dramatic scenes in the opera is not portrayed onstage, but rather described in a lengthy monologue. Compared with the party that opened the act, the next few minutes are a bit drab. Sylvia's recitative lacks variety in texture and instrumentation, and it contains no melodic repetition—indeed, it contains no memorable melodies whatsoever. However, it does allow Monteverdi to exhibit his skill at expressing emotion by means of harmonized text declamation.

We might see Monteverdi's technique at work by examining the emotional high point of the recitative, which arrives when Sylvia recounts Euridice's final words: "Orpheus, Orpheus!" These are the highest pitches that she sings, and her delivery of the text closely mimics Euridice's unsung cry, which the listener can easily imagine. The harmonies are stark and surprising. Throughout this passage, the listener is kept ill at ease as Monteverdi leads the singer through countless harmonic twists and turns. The devastating development of the story is paralleled by unpredictable, dark, and even ugly chords.

After a response from the shepherds, the first of whom repeats Sylvia's text and melody from her entrance ("Ah, bitter blow!), Orpheus finally speaks. His opening words are low, set to a murky, chromatic melody and accompanied by gut-wrenching harmonies. As he moves from disbelief to anguish, his melody becomes higher, louder, and faster. Soon, however, his mood changes again as he resolves to bring her back from the underworld. Orpheus engages in a bit of **text painting** as he sings the words "I will surely descend to the deepest abyss" to a melody that itself descends into his lowest range. His final passage, in which he bids farewell to the sun and sky, in turn ascends into his highest range.

Act III

		Act III from *Orpheus* Composer: Claudio Monteverdi Performance: Das Monteverdi-Ensemble des Opernhauses Zürich, directed by Nikolaus Harnoncourt (1978)
Time	**Form**	**What to listen for**
51'30"	Recitative: Caronte	Basso continuo: reed organ
53'13"	March	Played by cornetti, sackbuts, and harp
54'31"	Orpheus's aria - Verse 1	Basso continuo: theorbo and organ Accompanied by a pair of violins
56'31"	Orpheus's aria - Verse 2	Accompanied by a pair of cornetti
57'50"	Orpheus's aria - Verse 3	Accompanied by harp
1:00'38"	Orpheus's aria - Verse 4	Accompanied by orchestral strings
1:03'25"		*End of listening guide*

We will briefly visit Act III to hear the sounds of the underworld. Caronte, the boatman who is responsible for transporting deceased souls across the river Styx, sings to the somewhat horrible accompaniment of reed organ. This instrument's aggressive timbre underscores Caronte's gloomy job and belligerent character, expressed in his refusal to transport to Orpheus. Next we hear the music of Caronte's world: a funereal march performed principally on sackbuts.

After the march, Orpheus sets about the task of convincing Caronte to carry him across the river. He does so, of course, using the power of music. Orpheus sings a magnificent aria, "Mighty spirit and formidable god," that lasts for nearly ten minutes. Unlike his joyful song from the wedding party, this aria is slow, grandiose, and expressive. As in recitative, his singing is mostly unmetered. There is a fixed melody, and although it varies between the first three verses, the bass line remains the same. The listener, however, would be forgiven for failing to observe the repetition, for the bass line is so long and complex that it is difficult to recognize even upon repeated hearings. Recognition is made more difficult by the fact that the singer heavily ornaments the melody, and does so differently on each repetition. **Ornamentation** refers to the practice of adding notes according to accepted rules.

Orpheus's aria also provides us with one more opportunity to encounter some of Monteverdi's more interesting instruments. Each verse of the aria is decorated with instrumental interjections and completed by an instrumental refrain. First, we hear two violins: one playing from the stage or pit, and the other echoing from a distance. (Monteverdi was particularly fond of this echo effect, and used it in several dramatic contexts.) Next, we hear similar music from a pair of cornetti. This instrument—now almost extinct—employs a trumpet-like mouthpiece connected to a narrow tube, traditionally made from an animal horn and wrapped in leather. Finally, we hear from the double harp, a Baroque instrument with two rows of strings (modern harps have one row). The fourth verse of Orpheus's aria, which is accompanied by strings, is different—an indication that he is gaining control of the situation. He wins his argument with a concluding passage of comparatively simple and straightforward singing.

As with the dance songs that open Act II, we can understand this aria to be diegetic: Orpheus the character really *is* singing. Whether or not he has in fact conjured up cornetto and harps to accompany his singing, however, is up for debate. It is more reasonable to interpret these instruments as belonging only to the theater orchestra, not to the scene in the underworld. The double harp in particular can be heard as a symbolic stand-in for Orpheus's own instrument, the lyre, which is a type of small harp used in ancient Greece. This scene is expressly about the music, however, for it is Orpheus's hypnotic singing and playing, in combination with his eloquence, that wins over the reluctant Caronte.

WOLFGANG AMADEUS MOZART, *THE MAGIC FLUTE*

During his lifetime, Monteverdi saw opera become mainstream popular entertainment in Venice. Over the next few centuries, opera became the most prominent form of public entertainment across all of Europe. Although the practice was first developed in Italian-speaking cities, it soon spread to France, England, and Germany, where new forms of opera were developed that catered to local tastes and languages. Italian opera remained so dominant, however, that it was performed—most often in its original language—in every European country. Opera was not truly dethroned as the West's favorite form of entertainment until talking pictures became mainstream in the 1930s.

Although the variety and riches of the European opera tradition can reward a lifetime of study, we will examine only one more example here. This example was chosen for its historical significance, its intrinsic interest, and the many ways in which it contrasts with *Orpheus*. While *Orpheus* is a serious opera written for court performance in the early Baroque style, *The Magic Flute* (1791), composed nearly two hundred years later, is a comic opera created for commercial, public performance, and it exemplifies the pinnacle of the **Classical** style. It is also the work of the most important opera composer of the era: Wolfgang Amadeus Mozart (1756-1791).

Mozart's Career

Mozart was born into a musical family in the city of Salzburg. His father Leopold was a composer and violinist at the court of the Archbishop of Salzburg. Leopold was successful in his career, but he soon realized that his children possessed greater talent than he did. He subsequently abandoned composing to focus on their education. Mozart had an older sister, Marianne, who was his equal as a child prodigy. Both children mastered the

Image 4.16: This portrait, titled *The Boy Mozart*, was painted in 1763 by Pietro Antonio Lorenzoni.
Source: Wikimedia Commons
Attribution: Pietro Antonio Lorenzoni
License: Public Domain

harpsichord and fortepiano (a predecessor to the modern piano), while Mozart also became an expert violinist. Beginning in 1762, Leopold took his children on extensive tours to perform for heads of state across Europe. Marianne, however, was forced to abandon public performance when she became old enough to marry. Although there is some evidence that she composed music later in life, she was never given the opportunity to pursue a career.

Mozart, on the other hand, was expected to follow in the footsteps of his father, and upon the conclusion of his final tour in 1773 he took a job at the Salzburg court. Mozart, however, was dissatisfied with the provincial life he led. His exposure as a child to the great cities and courts of Europe had whetted his appetite for cosmopolitan excitement. He also wanted greater personal freedom, and resented being subservient to an employer. In 1781, he quarrelled with the Archbishop of Salzburg and was released from his position. Although his father was disappointed and concerned, Mozart was elated. He immediately moved to Vienna, an important

Image 4.17: The Austrian city of Salzburg as it appears today.
Source: Wikimedia Commons
Attribution: Henry Vagrant
License: CC BY-SA 3.0

Image 4.18: This 1764 painting captures Leopold Mozart performing with his two prodigious children.
Source: Wikimedia Commons
Attribution: Jean-Baptiste Delafosse
License: Public Domain

Image 4.19: Although this 1819 painting by Barbara Krafft was produced some time after Mozart had died, his sister approved of it.
Source: Wikimedia Commons
Attribution: Barbara Krafft
License: Public Domain

center of politics and culture in the German-speaking world, and set out to build an independent career for himself.

In the late 18th century, there were few opportunities for a freelance musician to make a living. Most composers were employed by a court or church. Mozart, however, was able to capitalize on his fame as a child prodigy, and he had many marketable skills. He taught private piano lessons—although only to the elite young ladies of the city, and for a high fee. He wrote music for publication and accepted commissions. And he put on regular concerts of his music, each of which featured an appearance by the composer himself at the piano in the performance of a new concerto.

Finally, Mozart wrote operas in every genre of his day. He was fluent in various operatic styles and experienced in the conventions of the musical stage: Mozart, after all, had composed and premiered his first opera at the age of 13. In Vienna of the late 18th century, there were audiences for both Italian and German opera. Italian opera was divided into the old-fashioned opera seria ("serious opera"), which told heroic stories of gods and kings, and the newer opera buffa ("comic opera"), which portrayed characters from various social classes in humorous situations. *The Magic Flute*, however, is an example of a **Singspiel** ("sing-play"): a German-language comic opera with spoken dialogue and catchy songs. Of the three genres, Singspiel was the least respectable and sophisticated.

Mozart poured most of his energy into opera buffa. In collaboration with the court librettist Lorenzo da Ponte, he created three works—*The Marriage of Figaro* (1786), *Don Giovanni* (1787), and *All Women Do It* (Italian: *Cosí fan tutte*; 1790)—that have maintained a central place in the operatic repertoire ever since. Although all three of these operas contain comical characters and situations, each conveys a moral and is essentially serious in its purpose. The same is true of Mozart's last opera, *The Magic Flute* (1791).

In the final years of his career, Mozart struggled to make a living. Despite early success, he found that his audiences had largely evaporated by 1787. This was due both to the vagaries of fashion and economic difficulties. Whatever the cause, he was no longer able to sell concert tickets, and was forced to abandon his rather lavish lifestyle. He and his wife moved to less expensive lodgings, gave up their carriage, and sold many of their belongings. At the time Mozart received the commission to write *The Magic Flute*, therefore, he was eager to increase his income. Although 1790 saw a general improvement in Mozart's fortunes, he became ill while in Prague for the premiere of his final opera seria, *The Clemency of Titus* (1791), and died on December 5, just a few weeks after the premiere of *The Magic Flute*.

The Magic Flute

The Magic Flute was largely conceived by the man who commissioned Mozart's participation in the project, Emanual Schikaneder. Schikaneder was the head of a theatrical troupe that performed at the Theater auf der Wieden, which was located in the Wieden district of Vienna. He and Mozart had known each other for many years, and Mozart had contributed music to several of his collaborative productions. Acting in his role as **impresario**, Schikanader had a hand in every step of the opera's development: he came up with the idea of staging a series of fairy tale operas, wrote the libretto for *The Magic Flute*, assumed financial responsibility, acted as director, and played one of the leads. He is even reported to have made suggestions to Mozart that were incorporated into the score.

Although *The Magic Flute* can certainly be described as a fairy tale, it is a fairy tale with a political message. In particular, *The Magic Flute* embodies Enlightenment values, celebrating the triumph of reason over superstition and the moral equality of individuals from different social classes. It also contains multiple references to **Freemasonry**, which, in late-18th century Vienna, was committed to the furtherance of Enlightenment ideals. Both Mozart and Schikaneder were Freemasons. The Masonic elements include various symbols that featured in the original set design, references to the four

Image 4.20: This 1784 engraving captures Schikaneder in one of his theatrical roles.
Source: Wikimedia Commons
Attribution: Hieronymus Löschenkohl
License: Public Domain

elements (earth, air, water, and fire), fixation on the number three, and the tale's setting in Egypt. Mozart also incorporated the rhythmic knock of the Masonic initiation ritual into his overture.

The plot, in a much simplified form, is as follows: The curtain rises on Prince Tamino fleeing from a serpent. Although he is rescued by three female attendants to the Queen of the Night, he awakens to find Papageno, a bird catcher, who takes credit for defeating the monster. When the women return, they chastise Papageno and show Tamino a portrait of Princess Pamina, the Queen's daughter. He immediately falls in love with her, but is told that she has been kidnapped by the evil sorcerer Sarastro. The Queen herself appears to tell Tamino that he can marry her daughter if he rescues her. The Queen's attendants give each of the men a magic instrument to help in their quest: a flute for Tamino and a set of bells for Papageno.

Image 4.21: This 1815 painting captures a stage set for an appearance by the Queen of the Night.
Source: Wikimedia Commons
Attribution: Karl Friedrich Schinkel
License: Public Domain

At the end of Act I, Tamino finds his way to Sarastro's temple, but there he learns that the sorcerer is in fact benevolent, and that it is the Queen of the Night who has evil intentions. Sarastro had taken Pamina in order to protect her from her mother's influence. Tamino and Pamina finally meet, and Pamina reciprocates his affection. Sarastro, however, refuses to permit the union before Tamino has completed a series of trials (based on Masonic ritual) to prove his spiritual worthiness.

Act II sees conflict between Pamina and her mother and suffering as Pamina awaits Tamino's successful passage through the trials. The magic flute and bells each serve their respective holders as they seek personal fulfillment. In the end, the two lovers reject the evil influence of the Queen of the Night and join Sarastro's enlightened brotherhood. And Papageno, who mourns his lonely existence, is rewarded for his faithfulness with a wife: Papagena.

The Magic Flute is rich with comedy, provided by Papageno (and, in a few scenes, the equally ridiculous Papagena), and the opera as a whole is highly entertaining. Most of the characters, however, are serious in purpose, and the story itself certainly carries a message.

The Queen of the Night represents forces that seek to suppress knowledge and clarity in favor of fear, insularity, and irrationality. Some scholars have identified her with the Roman Catholic Empress Maria Theresa, and have interpreted the opera as an attack on Catholicism. This is contentious, however: On the one hand, the Catholic Church was opposed to Freemasonry, but on the other, Mozart himself was a devout Catholic. Whatever the specifics, the Queen of the Night certainly embodies anti-Enlightenment values. Sarastro, on the other hand, is the wise, generous, and benevolent head of state. He exemplifies the political principle of rule by an Enlightened monarch, which many at the time believed to be the ideal form of government. He grants agency and freedom to his subjects, but demands that they hold themselves to high intellectual and moral standards. In the end, the protagonists—Tamino and Pamina—choose modern, Enlightened thinking over the beguiling superstitions of the past.

The opera conveys other messages as well—not all of which are so palatable. Women are certainly not portrayed in a positive light. The realm governed by the evil Queen is entirely female, while the light-filled court of Sarastro is predominantly male. Although Pamina eventually joins Tamino in his trials, her role is to support him: The couple's salvation relies primarily on his strength of character, and several musical numbers reinforce the idea that a wife must be subservient to her husband. The other female lead, Papagena, is literally a gift to a male character.

Likewise, the opera takes an ambivalent stance toward class distinctions. On the one hand, it portrays low-class characters in an essentially positive light. Papageno might be a buffoon, but he is on the side of good and capable of exhibiting strong moral character. This is an advance on previous operas, in which servants existed only to serve. At the same time, the low-class and high-class characters are kept at a distance from one another. Although Pamina and Papageno are friends and at one point sing a duet about the value of marriage, there is no question of them ending up together. A princess must marry a prince, while a bird catcher must marry within his own social class. Papageno is treated with the loving condescension that all members of his class supposedly deserve.

The Magic Flute, like many operas, also has a race problem. The synopsis above omitted the character of Monostatos, a black man who repeatedly threatens Pamina with sexual assault. Although he initially serves Sarastro as head of his slaves, he defects to the Queen's side in hopes of winning Pamina for himself. And of course, the fact that Sarastro keeps slaves should also raise eyebrows.

The Magic Flute was a product of its time and place, but all of these issues must be addressed in modern stagings. One of the strengths of live theater is that scripts can be reinterpreted by directors and actors. The challenges of doing so, however, have not been trivial. Many operatic narratives promote social values that are no longer widely accepted. Many also portray non-Western characters or societies in demeaning ways. The inclusion of non-white characters also provides interpretive challenges. While the practice of blackface performance, in which a white actor uses make-up to portray a character of African descent, has been condemned as racist in almost all spheres for the past half century, it is still sometimes used on the opera stage.

Opera companies continue to perform *The Magic Flute*, however, because the music is delightful. (A clever director can address most of its messaging problems—for example, Monostatos does not have to be black.) The arias that Mozart produced for this opera are unusually diverse and entertaining. This was the case for several reasons. To begin with, he was writing for a commercial theater that attracted a middle-class audience. Most of his listeners were looking for a fun night out, not a transcendent artistic experience. In addition, not all of the actors in Schikanader's troupe had equivalent musical capabilities. Some were highly-trained opera singers, but others—including Schikander himself, who played Papageno—could barely carry a tune. Mozart, therefore, carefully tailored his writing to each individual singer.

"I am a bird catcher"

With this in mind, we will examine four selections from *The Magic Flute*. We will begin with Papageno's first number, "I am a bird catcher."[5] This is the aria that Papageno sings to introduce himself to Tamino. In it, he sings about his simple life, wandering the countryside in search of birds, and expresses his wish to be equally adept at capturing the hearts of young women. The music created by Mozart effectively communicates Papageno's character, for he writes what is effectively a strophic folk song. It is in a cheerful major mode and contains only the simplest of harmonies, while the jaunty tempo establishes Papageno's carefree attitude. We hear Papageno's flute, which he uses to attract birds, in the second half of each of the two verses.

5. "I am a bird catcher" from *The Magic Flute*
    Composer: Wolfgang Amadeus Mozart
    Performance: Hermann Prey with the Staatskapelle
    Dresden, conducted by Otmar Suitner (1967)

In addition to being dramatically appropriate, this music is also easy to sing. The orchestra begins by playing the entire melody, and the singer, upon entering, is doubled by the violins. Both of these features would have greatly helped Schikaneder give a successful performance. In addition, the vocal range is very small, spanning only a single octave, and positioned comfortably for an average male (not too high or low). Finally, the melody moves mostly by step, with few difficult leaps. Although the role of Papageno is always sung by a highly-trained professional in modern productions, his arias could easily be learned by almost anyone.

Other members of Schikaneder's troupe were more skilled. In fact, the unusual capabilities of the actors who played the Queen of the Night and Sarastro inspired Mozart to write arias that continue to challenge modern singers. At the same time, the music sung by these two characters accurately reflects their respective roles in the drama.

"O Isis and Osiris"

The role of Sarastro was created for the bass singer Franz Xaver Gerl. Gerl had trained in Salzburg, and might have studied with Mozart's father. He had an unusually low voice, which Mozart took into consideration. Sarastro's introductory aria, "O Isis and Osiris,"[6] comes at the beginning of Act II, and its music and text both serve to establish his noble character. Sarastro calls upon the ancient Egyptian gods, Isis and Osiris (both prominent figures in Masonic lore), to guide and protect Tamino and Pamina in their pursuit of wisdom. The text exhibits his profound spiritual commitment to Enlightenment principles and his generous concern for others. The music is slow and deliberate, emphasizing Sarastro's stability and power. Although this is a strophic aria in two verses, like the one sung by Papageno, it is certainly not a folk song—the melody and harmonies are both too sophisticated. Finally, the extremely low range makes this aria inaccessible for any but a trained singer with unique capabilities.

6. "O Isis and Osiris" from *The Magic Flute*
Composer: Wolfgang Amadeus Mozart
Performance: Kovács Kolos with the Orchestra of the Hungarian State Opera House, conducted by Pál Varga (1970)

"Hell's vengeance boils in my heart"

The music that Mozart created for the Queen of the Night is different in every respect. Once again, we must start by considering the original singer, soprano Josepha Hofer (and Mozart's sister-in-law). Hofer was a singer of extraordinary skill, and she possessed an unusually high vocal range, of which Mozart took full advantage. We will examine the Queen of the Night's Act II aria, "Hell's vengeance boils in my heart,"[7] in which she threatens Pamina for refusing to kill Sarastro.

While Sarastro exhibits self-control with his singing, the Queen enacts her all-consuming rage. The most remarkable passages of her aria have no words at all, but rather require the singer to leap from pitch to pitch in the highest range using only repeated vowel sounds. Here we encounter a paradox: Although the Queen of the Night is the opera's villain, her dazzling displays are the highlight of the show. Sarastro's music is drab and forgettable in comparison.

7.		"Hell's vengeance boils in my heart" from *The Magic Flute* Composer: Wolfgang Amadeus Mozart Performance: Sumi Jo with the Berlin Radio Symphony Orchestra, conducted by Roberto Paternostro (2009)

"Ah, I feel it, it is vanished"

Finally, we will hear from Pamina. This role was created for Anna Gottlieb, who was only 17 when *The Magic Flute* premiered. (Later in life, Gottlieb specialized in parody roles that required her to ridicule operatic sopranos.) Pamina's major aria, "Ah, I feel it, it is vanished,"[8] comes in the middle of Act II. She has just been in the presence of Tamino. When she tried to speak with him, however, he refused to respond. She believes this to mean that he no longer loves her. In fact, Tamino is undergoing one of his trials, which requires a vow of silence. Pamina does not know this, and sings a mournful aria about her heartbreak and desolation.

8.		"Ah, I feel it, it is vanished" from *The Magic Flute* Composer: Wolfgang Amadeus Mozart Performance: Dorothea Röschmann with the Mahler Chamber Orchestra, conducted by Claudio Abbado (2005)

A sparse orchestral accompaniment combines with the minor mode to convey her emotions. The soprano solo soars unaided into the heights, for Gottlieb certainly did not need to be doubled by an instrument. Unlike the Queen of the Night, however, Pamina keeps her emotions under control: She is despairing, but noble.

Speaking more broadly, we can hear the ideals of self-control and rationality in all of Mozart's music. These are hallmarks of the **Classical** style. Composers working in this period preferred balanced phrases, sparse textures, predictable chord progressions, and elegant melodies. Just as the Enlightened individual placed a high value on rational discourse, the music of this period valued orderliness over emotional expression. Mozart certainly sought to convey a wide range of emotional states, but he never abandoned the rational parameters of his art.

TIAN HAN, *THE TALE OF THE WHITE SNAKE*

Europe and the United States are, of course, not alone in developing sung drama traditions. Examples of musical drama can be found around the world. Here we will examine two, each of which has a unique set of characteristics and each of which—like European opera—requires years of dedicated training for those who desire careers as performers. Each of these traditions—also like European opera—is highly heterogeneous. Different styles and forms have dominated in different eras, and one can encounter a variety of contemporary practices.

Beijing Opera

The form of musical theater known as **Beijing opera** is the most popular of the many forms of Chinese opera. Although the roots of Chinese opera extend back thousands of years, Beijing opera dates only to 1790—about when Mozart set to work on *The Magic Flute*. This particular form is said to have emerged when four regional opera troupes visited the Beijing court simultaneously to celebrate the 80th birthday of the Emperor. Although Beijing opera (like Italian opera) was available only as courtly entertainment for several decades, it soon found favor with the broader public, and by 1845 its conventions were both firmly established and widely enjoyed.

Image 4.22: Beijing is located in the Northeast of China.
Source: MapsWire
Attribution: MapsWire
License: CC BY 4.0

Image 4.23: Aristocratic female characters have ornate headdresses, fancy apparel, and complicated sleeves.
Source: Flickr
Attribution: Gustavo Thomas
License: CC BY-NC-ND 2.0

Image 4.24: The Jing, or "painted face," character is always powerful. This is the historical figure Xiang Yu, who was King of Western Chu in the second century BC. His final battle is the subject of the piece *Attack from All Sides* discussed in Chapter 6.
Source: Wikimedia Commons
Attribution: User "G41rn8"
License: CC BY-SA 4.0

Beijing opera combines a variety of different art forms, and its practitioners must be well-versed not only in singing but also in gesture, dance, makeup application, and acrobatics. Traditionally, children were apprenticed to travelling troupes. They were offered little formal education, and were instead expected to learn through imitation. Today, this system has been replaced by formal schooling. Other changes have also shaped the tradition. Until the 1890s, all Beijing opera performers were men, many of whom specialized in female roles. When women first began to perform, they were confined to all-female troupes—some members of which, naturally enough, had to take on male roles. Troupes were integrated following the founding of the Republic of China in 1911, but men continue frequently to perform female roles, especially that of the beautiful young woman.

The roles in Beijing opera are highly standardized. There are four character types: Sheng (the lead male), Dan (any female), Jing (a forceful male), and Chou (the clown). Each character type has a variety of subtypes based on age and social status. An actor must specialize in playing a specific character type, for each has a distinct manner of speaking, singing, and moving. The Jing types also wear special face paint, the designs of which reveal facets of their character and mark them as being on the side of good or evil.

Many genres of Chinese music, including Beijing opera, are categorized into "civil" and "martial" works. Civil operas concern the court intrigues and love interests of the aristocracy, while martial operas contain scenes of military conflict. Plots of both types are drawn from history, traditional stories, and novels, all of which are already familiar to the audience. A single opera will usually present only a few episodes from a much longer story, and it is typical to combine serious and comical elements.

Image 4.25: In a Beijing opera orchestra, only one person plays each type of instrument. The additional *jinghu* fiddles sitting at the feet of the performer are probably tuned to different modes.
Source: Wikimedia Commons
Attribution: Xavier Serra
License: CC BY-SA 2.0

Like the operas themselves, the orchestra that provides music for Beijing opera is divided into civil and martial instrument groups. The civil group contains string instruments. The most significant of these is the *jinghu*, a high-pitched bowed fiddle after which the genre itself is named. The other principal instrument is the *yueqin*, a moon-shaped lute with four strings. The martial group—which might also be described as the percussion section—contains gongs of different sizes, cymbals, and a pair of instruments known as *guban* that consists of a high-pitched drum and a wooden clapper. These last are the most important, as they are played by the ensemble director. This person has a challenging task, for the percussion section

Image 4.26: The *jinghu* is held upright on the left knee.
Source: Wikimedia Commons
Attribution: Metropolitan Museum of Art
License: CC0

Image 4.27: The *yueqin* lute dates to the second century BC. Its name derives from its shape: "Yue" means "moon" in Chinese.
Source: Wikimedia Commons
Attribution: Queensland Museum
License: CC BY-SA 3.0

must accompany action, punctuate speech, and provide sound effects—all of which requires precise timing. The orchestra might also contain additional lutes and wind instruments.

The division of the Beijing opera orchestra into string, wind, and percussion sections mirrors the European orchestra. However, there are significant differences both in the makeup of the ensemble and in its function. A Beijing opera orchestra usually contains only one player per instrument, and the music performed by the orchestra is **heterophonic** in texture, meaning that all of the instruments play the same melody, but not in perfect unison. Instead, each player interprets the melody in a way that is appropriate to the instrument, contributing ornaments or adding/removing pitches as considered suitable.

Beijing opera performances contain various types of orchestral and vocal music. None of this music, however, is composed for a specific opera. Instead, the melodies all belong to the tradition in general, and they are used by individual performers to characterize specific roles. Certain instrumental pieces, for example, are always played to accompany certain scenes, such as a banquet or the arrival of an important character. Onstage characters sing short arias in one of two modes: *xipi* for happy or energetic lyrics, and *erhuang* for serious or heroic lyrics. Each mode arranges the pitches of the pentatonic scale (degrees 1 2 3 5 and 6 of the major scale) in a different way, and the melodies in each tend to have different shapes.

For this reason, individual operas in this tradition do not have composers. The plots and dialogues are crafted by playwrights, but the music is drawn from a communal store. The same arias and instrumental numbers will be heard in a variety of different works. The singers themselves also have a great deal of control over the music, which will reflect their training, style, and vocal range. It is generally considered desirable to sing the arias as high as possible, so it is the onstage performers who determine what key the music will be in. While this level of flexibility will seem unusual to someone who is used to Western opera or musical theater, Beijing opera is in fact remarkably rigid when compared to other Chinese opera forms. The Shenqu opera of Shanghai, for example, can be completely improvised, with plots based on the news stories of the day.

The vocal timbre used in Beijing opera is one of its most remarkable features. Singers strive to produce a piercing, nasal sound with a slow, controlled vibrato. They will sometimes slide between pitches, each of which is carefully placed. The speech in Beijing opera is also highly stylized, and is often delivered in high range. To accomplish this, male actors frequently employ **falsetto** when singing and speaking. Actors employ an ancient dialect that is not always intelligible to modern listeners, but they communicate as much with their gestures and steps as with their voices. The Chou (clown) is the only character permitted by tradition to speak in modern Beijing dialect or to improvise onstage.

Finally, a word about the trappings of the stage. Costumes are often elaborate, and they always reflect the social status of the character. Sleeves are especially important, and are carefully managed by the actors for expressive purposes. Stage sets, however, tend to be minimal or non-existent. Audiences are expected to imagine the scene, which is brought to life through the use of symbolic props. A table, for example, might serve as a wall, a mountain, or a bed, while a single oar is enough to suggest the presence of a boat.

Image 4.28: Although the costumes used for Beijing opera are elaborate, the stage sets are minimal.
Source: Wikimedia Commons
Attribution: Chen Wen
License: CC BY 2.5

The Tale of the White Snake

We will see all of these elements at play in our example, Tian Han's dramatization of *The Tale of the White Snake*. The source of this opera is a legend concerning a white snake spirit that transforms into a young woman named Bai Suzhen after consuming a substance that grants immortality and wisdom. The legend contains many episodes, but Tian chose to focus on events that lead up to and follow Bai's marriage to Xu Xian, who through a twist of fate was originally responsible for her powers. Tian himself was a leading playwright in the first half of the 20th century, but he was condemned by Mao's government in 1966 for writing a play that was considered to undermine Communist values. He died in prison two years later.

We will examine two scenes from *The Tale of the White Snake*, which, as a typical martial opera, contains both civil and martial scenes. The first, a civil scene, comes from near the beginning of the opera. Bai Suzhen and her friend Xiao Qing (also previously a snake) have been caught in a downpour when they meet Xu Xian.

The three of them share a boat, and Bai and Xu proceed to fall in love. This excerpt will allow us to hear a variety of speech and song types, to hear the orchestra in its various roles, and to witness the conventions by which actors communicate their emotions and conjure up absent settings and props.

The second scene, which is martial in character, concludes the initial episode of the couple's romance. A few months after their marriage, Xu dies of fright after seeing his wife in her snake spirit form. Bai has journeyed to Mount Emei, home of the immortals, where she hopes to obtain a magical fungus that will bring Xu back to life. This scene contains almost no singing, but instead features acrobatics and martial arts as Bai battles the guardians of the sacred shrine.

Our first scene[9] begins with the entrance of Xu Xian, who sings an aria to explain his recent activities, describe the weather, and clarify that he has no interest in love. He sings in a high, falsetto range, as is typical of Sheng-type characters. The orchestra both accompanies and doubles him, following the contour of his melody and arriving at the same final pitches. The orchestra, however, does not play only what he sings, but also tacks on repeated motifs that add rhythmic and melodic interest. Although the aria has a regular pulse for the most part, it slows at the end as the singer adds ornaments to draw out the final notes.

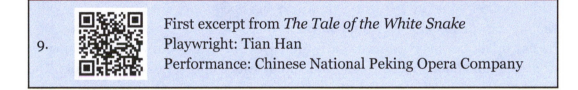

9.   First excerpt from *The Tale of the White Snake*
      Playwright: Tian Han
      Performance: Chinese National Peking Opera Company

Xu's aria is followed by spoken dialogue between the characters, which is punctuated by percussive bursts. Soon, however, they are interrupted by singing from offstage. This aria, performed by a boatman, is quite different in character from Xu's lively aria. It is slower and the notes more connected to one another—a style that would be described in the West as *legato*. Also, the boatman's aria is accompanied by the *dizi*, a bamboo flute, in addition to the standard instruments. Finally, the heterophonic texture is more clear, since the orchestral instruments double the voice without adding any additional pitches.

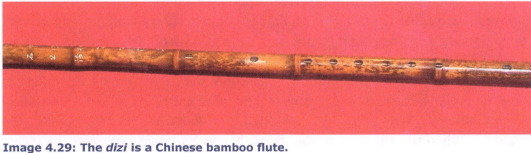

Image 4.29: The *dizi* is a Chinese bamboo flute.
Source: Wikimedia Commons
Attribution: Metropolitan Museum of Art
License: CC0

Xu engages the boatman to take him and the two ladies to their destinations, and the boatman invites them to board. There is, of course, no boat. Instead, the actors help us to imagine it using carefully choreographed actions. After Bai and Xiao step into the boat, for example, they sway back and forth in perfect unison, as if being rocked by gentle waves. The journey of the boat is accompanied by appropriate music from the orchestra, to the melody of which the boatman sings a suitable Chinese proverb.

During the journey, all three characters engage in an extended accompanied musical number that combines singing and speaking. Again, the conclusion of the aria, sung by Bai, slows gradually to a stop as she makes the vital observation that Xu is a very nice young man. Pantomime and speech follow as the boat arrives at its first destination. The scene concludes with another musical sequence, in which Bai thanks Xu for his aid. Her final warning that

Image 4.30: The *sheng*, or mouth organ, is a Chinese wind instrument.
Source: Wikimedia Commons
Attribution: User "PraktykantSiM"
License: CC BY-SA 4.0

he not break her heart is particularly effective: She draws the words out, singing unaccompanied for some time and concluding with a long series of ornaments. The phrase "gaze through autumn waters" is an idiom that indicates that one is waiting expectantly for another with tears in one's eyes.

The scene ends with orchestral music to accompany Bai and Xiao's departure from the stage. We now hear another instrument clearly: the *sheng*, or mouth organ. The *sheng* consists of a series of vertical reed pipes attached to a mouthpiece. The instrument is held with both hands, and the player positions their fingers over openings to sound the various pipes. The *sheng* will be heard during interludes such as this throughout the opera, although it seldom accompanies singing.

The scene we have just examined includes a typical mix of song, speech, and instrumental music, accompanied by symbolic movement and punctuated with percussive sound effects. As in European opera, speech (often cast as recitative in the Western tradition) moves the plot along, while song provides an opportunity for characters to express their emotions or reflect on what has happened.

Our next scene[10] is quite different. Because this scene is martial in character, the focus is not on speech or song but on action. Bai sings to mark her entrance onto the stage, but she then executes an extended martial display to percussion accompaniment. Next she sings an excited aria about her mission to save her husband. When the guardian of the shrine blocks Bai's way, she begs his mercy using speech. He refuses to assist her, and they enter into a long physical battle accompanied only by the percussion section. The battle features remarkable acrobatics from both of the guardians, who represent a Chou character type known as Wu Chou, or "military clown."

10.	[QR code]	Second excerpt from *The Tale of the White Snake* Playwright: Tian Han Performance: Chinese National Peking Opera Company

Bai is ultimately defeated by the guardians, but the scene ends with an elder immortal gifting the magical fungus to Bai and sending her away to revive her husband. The two characters do not sing, but their dramatic and highly melodic speech is executed over orchestral accompaniment featuring both the *dizi* and *sheng*. After the long stretch of percussive music, the entrance of the full orchestra effectively underscores the emotion of the scene, communicating both the mercy of the immortal and the grateful joy of Bai.

DANCED DRAMA

PYOTR ILYICH TCHAIKOVSKY, *THE NUTCRACKER*

We've already encountered one **ballet** by a Russian composer: Igor Stravinsky's *The Rite of Spring*. Now we will examine another. Stravinsky and Pyotr Ilyich Tchaikvosky (1840-1893) are, after all, two of the best-known ballet composers. The most famous choreographers and dancers have been mostly Russian as well. Ballet, however, originated not in Russia but in France. We will begin, therefore, with the story of how this art form ended up thriving nearly two thousand miles away from its birthplace.

Image 4.31: This photograph of Tchaikovsky was taken near the end of his life.
Source: Wikipedia
Attribution: Unknown
License: Public Domain

Ballet

Ballet's origins can be traced to European courts of the 15th and 16th centuries, where dance became increasingly formalized and dramatic. Early ballets, however, were quite different from the art form we might be familiar with: Dancers wore regular shoes and clothing, the steps were taken from participatory court dances, and spectators usually joined in for the finale. Court ballet reached its pinnacle under Louis XIV, who ruled France from 1643 to 1715. He was an avid dancer, and frequently took leading roles in the productions. Louis XIV also sponsored the first professional ballet company, which was attached to the Paris Opera. The two genres—opera and ballet—were closely related in this period: French operas always contained extended dance numbers, while court ballets included singing.

Image 4.32: These students at Escuela Superior de Música y Danza are performing the Dance of the Snowflakes from *The Nutcracker* in 2010.
Source: Wikimedia Commons
Attribution: Gabriel Saldana
License: CC BY-SA 2.0

Ballet as we know it today emerged in the second half of the 18th century, when a series of reforms were enacted by ballet master Jean-Georges Noverre. Noverre sought to make ballet more expressive and realistic by replacing the heavy costumes with light, form-fitting apparel, doing away with masks, and introducing the use of pantomime and facial expressions to communicate dramatic elements. The early 19th century saw the invention of the pointe shoe, which allows female dancers to balance on their toes, and the tutu, which accentuates their graceful movements and reveals the legs.

Soon, however, ballet in France was faltering. In seeking to compete with opera, ballet promoters were not successful. Ballet's association with the aristocracy made it distasteful to French audiences of the late 19th century, and it was generally considered to be less expressive than opera—and therefore inferior. Ballet might have vanished completely were it not for Russian interest in the art form. Beginning in the late 18th century, Russian courts sought to establish their cultural credentials by importing European art forms. First, they brought in Italian opera. In the mid-19th century, they turned to French ballet.

Tchaikovsky's Career

At first, the Russian ballet establishment was managed by French choreographers, scenarists, dancers, and composers. Gradually, however, Russians took over, and ballet became a distinctively Russian art form. Pyotr Ilyich Tchaikovsky was among the first Russian ballet composers, and his three masterpieces—*Swan Lake* (1877), *Sleeping Beauty* (1890), and *The Nutcracker* (1892)—are still frequently performed today.

Tchaikovsky, however, did not particularly care for his ballet scores, and he disdained their popularity. He would much prefer to have been remembered for his six symphonies, which he considered to be his greatest works. Tchaikovsky also wrote programmatic orchestral pieces, operas, and chamber music—in fact, he composed in all of the prominent European genres of the 19th century. Unlike Russian composers such as Modest Mussorgsky (discussed in Chapter 6), who rejected European influence, Tchaikovsky sought to follow in the European tradition.

Tchaikovsky was firmly entrenched in Russia's European-style musical establishment. As a young man, he was at first frustrated in his desire to pursue a career in music by the fact that there were no opportunities to study music in Russia. He instead embarked upon a career in the civil service, but in 1862 was able to enroll in the first class at the newly-opened St. Petersburg Conservatory. He impressed his teachers, and upon graduating was offered a teaching position at the Moscow Conservatory, which opened in 1866. Tchaikovsky went on to establish an international reputation as a composer, although he faced criticism at home for not being "Russian enough" in his musical expression.

It is no surprise that Tchaikovsky did not care for ballet work, for in the creation of a ballet, the composer found himself at the bottom of the hierarchy. Most of the creative work was completed by the **scenarist** (who outlined the dramatic contents of the ballet) and the **choreographer** (who designed the dance). *The Nutcracker* was conceived of by the renowned scenarist Marius Petipa, who chose and adapted the story, decided how it would be told through the ballet medium, and established a character for each of the dances. He went so far as to provide Tchaikovsky with the exact tempo and duration for each number, leaving the composer with little opportunity for creative expression. All the same, Tchaikovsky—who, while working on *The Nutcracker*, wrote to a friend that "I am daily becoming more and more attuned to my task"—was able to produce distinctive music that has charmed listeners for over a century.

The Nutcracker

The short story on which *The Nutcracker* was based required a great deal of alteration to become appropriate for the ballet stage. Indeed, the plot of *The Nutcracker* bears little resemblance to E.T.A. Hoffmann's "The Nutcracker and the Mouse King" (1816), which can be categorized as a horror story. In Hoffmann's account, a young girl, Marie (Clara in the ballet version), is subjected to terrifying nighttime encounters with the seven-headed Mouse King, who repeatedly threatens her. The tortuous plot hinges on a curse that transforms characters into hideous creatures with giant heads, gaping smiles, and long white beards. At the end of the story, Marie breaks the curse by pledging her love to the toy nutcracker that was given to her at Christmas by her godfather, the mysterious inventor Drosselmeyer.

Image 4.33: This scene, taken from a 2014 production by the New Mexico Dance Theater, includes Drosselmeyer, Clara, and the Nutcracker Prince in his human form.
Source: Wikimedia Commons
Attribution: Larry Lamsa
License: CC BY 2.0

Petipa (following an earlier adaptation by Alexandre Dumas) stripped this narrative of its horror elements, thereby transforming it into a family-friendly story about Christmas magic. The first act takes place at the home of Clara Stahlbaum, where guests have assembled for a Christmas Eve celebration. Drosselmeyer provides wonderful gifts for all of the children, including a nutcracker, to which Clara immediately becomes attached. After the party, Clara returns to the parlor to visit her nutcracker, where she witnesses a ferocious battle between the nutcracker—grown to life size and revealed to be a prince—and the Mouse King. She intercedes on the nutcracker's behalf and he emerges victorious.

In the second act, the Nutcracker Prince takes Clara to his kingdom, the Land of the Sweets, where she is welcomed and celebrated. The courtiers put on a show for her to demonstrate their gratitude, presenting a series of dances while she and the Prince sit upon thrones. At the end of the ballet, Clara returns to her home—awakening, perhaps, from a fantastic dream.

The Nutcracker was premiered as part of a double-bill at the Imperial Mariinsky Theater in St. Petersburg. The other item on the program was Tchaikovsky's newest opera, *Iolanta*, making for a complete evening of entertainment lasting about three hours. The premiere was not a success. Critics lambasted the dancing, the choreography, the adaption of the story, the sharp contrast between the acts, the prominence of children onstage, and the neglect of the principal ballerina, who, as the Sugar Plum Fairy, does not dance until nearly the end.

The music, on the other hand, was well-received, and Tchaikovsky was quick to salvage his work by transforming it into an orchestral **suite** that could be performed on concert programs. It was in this form that *The Nutcracker* first became popular. *The Nutcracker* was not staged again as a ballet until 1919, and did not enter the regular repertoire until 1934. A 1944 production by the San Francisco Ballet introduced it to American audiences. The New York City Ballet began offering annual performances in 1954, and the tradition of staging *The Nutcracker* during the Christmas season soon began to take hold across the United States. Today, *The Nutcracker* attracts millions of patrons every year, and is responsible for a large portion of the ticket sales by American ballet companies.

We will be taking a look at Act II of *The Nutcracker*. We will begin with the opening scene, in which Clara and the Prince arrive in the Land of the Sweets. Then we will examine part of the "Grand Divertissement" (that's "grand entertainment" in English) that is staged for their amusement.

Act II: Introduction

	Excerpt from Act II of *The Nutcracker* Composer: Pyotr Ilyich Tchaikovsky Performance: Semperoper Ballett

Time	Form	What to listen for
45'30"	Introduction to Act II	Clara and the Prince are welcomed to the Land of the Sweets
51'25"		The Prince tells the story of his victory over the Mouse King; we hear music from Act I
52'51"		The dancers for the "Grand Divertissement" are introduced to Clara and the Prince
53'38"	Chocolate (Spanish dance)	The melody is introduced by the trumpet, while castanets are heard throughout
55'04"	Coffee (Arabian dance)	A chromatic melody, heard first in the violins and later in the double reeds, floats above a droning rhythmic ostinato punctuated by tambourine strikes
59'00"	Tea (Chinese dance)	This dance pairs a flute/piccolo melody with pizzicato strings and a simple ostinato in the bassoon

| 1:00'16" | Russian Trepak | The fast-paced Trepak, which uses the entire orchestra, grows in intensity before culminating in a raucous final chord |
| 1:01'31" | | End of listening guide |

Tchaikovsky opens Act II with harp arpeggios and a sweeping, romantic melody in the violins. Sustained pitches in the brass create a sense of calm and repose. When Clara and the Prince arrive onstage, they use pantomime and facial expressions to indicate their wonder at beholding the magical kingdom, while the music intensifies in excitement with the addition of ascending flourishes in the flutes and piccolo. Magical sounds are created by violin **harmonics** (a technique by which the player lightly touches the string to produce a high, wispy sound) and celesta, a keyboard instrument that produces bell-like sounds when hammers strike resonant metal bars. Tchaikovsky associated this instrument, invented in Paris in 1886, with the Sugar Plum Fairy, and he was the first to use it in a major work.

The entrance of the Sugar Plum Fairy, who has been ruling the Land of the Sweets in the Prince's absence, is marked by another special effect (flutter tongue) in the flutes. She proceeds to greet Clara and the Prince, as do the subjects of the court. Next, the Prince tells the story of his battle with the Mouse King. He cannot use words, of course, so he reenacts the conflict in pantomime. He is aided by the orchestra, which repeats music from the battle scene—music that the audience heard only twenty or thirty minutes before and will easily recognize.

There has been dancing throughout the procedures thus far, of course, but nothing that could be described as a formal dance number. One of the challenges faced by any scenarist in designing a ballet is coming up with excuses for carefully-choreographed dance numbers. Ballet audiences enjoy the drama, but they want to see some good solo and ensemble dancing, not just pantomime. Petipa solved this problem by crafting a "Grand Divertissement" in which a series of dances are performed for Clara and the Prince. This "show within a show" is ostensibly put on for the benefit of the couple, but is in fact directed at the audience in the theater.

The "Grand Divertissement" consists of a diverse collection of themed dances. The first three dances are named after foods appropriate to the Land of the Sweets: chocolate, coffee, and tea. For each of these, Tchaikovsky drew inspiration from the lands from which these foods came: Spain, Arabia, and China. These are followed by a Russian dance, the "Dance of the Reed Flutes," and a dance known as "Mother Ginger and the Little Clowns." We will focus our attention on the first four dances for the purpose of considering how Tchaikovsky approached the task of representing national identity in music.

Act II: Chocolate

The Spanish dance is vibrant and exciting. The melody is first heard on the trumpet—an instrument that is not necessarily associated with Spanish music, but which introduces a bright timbre and sets the number apart from what has come before. The harmonies are simple and repetitive, suggesting a sort of generic "folk" style. What really marks the music as "Spanish" is the use of **castanets**, which are heard nowhere else in the ballet. Castanets are a simple percussion instrument

Image 4.34: The Spanish dance often features flamenco-inspired costumes.
Source: Flickr
Attribution: Gabriel Saldana
License: CC BY-SA 2.0

that consists of two concave pieces of wood. These are held in one hand and clapped together. Castanets are particularly associated with the Spanish tradition of **flamenco**, which encompasses unique forms of guitar playing, singing, and dancing. By prominently featuring castanets, Tchaikovsky clearly signalled to his audience that the music and dancing were meant to be Spanish.

But how successful was he in replicating the sounds of flamenco music? We might compare Tchaikovsky's music to a performance by flamenco musicians of the folk song "El Vito,"[11] which dates to the 16th century. This rendition is typical of Spanish music in several ways. It is in a minor mode, with the melody supported by characteristics harmonies. The guitar player executes dissonant strums. And the castanet player provides complex accompanying rhythms. The performance of flamenco most often incorporates dance[12] as well, and there is a rich vocabulary of movements and rhythmic steps that accompany and express the music. Next to these examples, Tchaikovsky's Spanish dance sounds comically cheerful and simplistic.

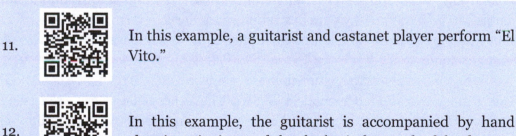

11. In this example, a guitarist and castanet player perform "El Vito."

12. In this example, the guitarist is accompanied by hand clapping, singing, and the rhythmic footwork of the dancer.

Act II: Coffee

Next is the Arabian dance. This time, Tchaikovsky employs a variety of compositional techniques to signal to his listener that this is "Middle Eastern" music. The low strings play a repeating rhythmic **ostinato** that produces a hypnotic

Image 4.35: The Arabian dance often emphasizes sensuality and mystery. These dimly-lit performers are wearing typical costumes.
Source: Pexels
Attribution: Ermelinda Maglione
License: Pexels License

effect. The ostinato features the interval of an open fifth, which leaves the question of mode open: we could be in major or minor. The ostinato also eliminates the possibility of complex harmonies, for we are to dwell on the same partial chord for the entire piece. Over the top of this, we hear a modal violin melody that incorporates both the raised and lowered seventh scale degrees and is characterized by unusual rhythms and phrasing. The melody prominently features the interval of an augmented second, which is seldom heard in European music, and it is scattered with trills. The melody is bookended by a repeated motif from the clarinets and double reeds and punctuated by the jingle of a tambourine. Later, the melody is echoed in the oboe and the bassoon. A modal shift concludes the dance on a major harmony.

For an example of authentic Middle Eastern music, one can refer to the discussion of Turkish makam music in Chapter 8. Many of Tchaikovsky's strategies for representing the Middle East in sound are indeed rooted in genuine practice. The tambourine, for example, features prominently in Persian and Turkish music. Likewise, Middle Eastern compositions use modes other than major and minor, and their melodies often feature augmented seconds. The trill is not an uncommon ornament in some instruments, such as the flute, and an ostinato sometimes provides a musical backdrop for improvisation. Finally, double reed instruments such as the *sorna* are native to the Middle East.

In short, Tchaikovsky captures the sound of Middle Eastern music with considerable success. The main differences between the genuine article and Tchaikovsky's imitation are the different timbres of the instruments, the inauthentic complexity of Tchaikovsky's orchestration, and the Western intonation of the orchestral players, who do not tune their pitches in the same way as members of a *takht* ensemble.

All the same, Tchaikovsky contributes to a musical stereotype that casts Middle Eastern music as static and hypnotic. While it can have these characteristics, it usually does not. Unfortunately, these have become the hallmarks of Western imitations, with the result that a rich music tradition is reduced to a handful of cliches.

Act II: Tea

Next up is the Chinese dance, representative of tea. Tchaikovsky again makes use of an ostinato—this time, a rapid oscillation between the first and fifth scale degrees by the bassoon player. Above this we hear a high melody in the flutes and piccolos, punctuated by pizzicato from the strings. As the music grows in intensity, clarinets provide an arpeggiated accompaniment while bells sparkle alongside the flutes.

For an example of authentic Chinese music, we need only look to the previous example in this chapter. Any listener will immediately note that the Tchaikovsky's dance has little to do with actual Chinese music. His choice of flutes for the melody might bring to mind the bright timbres often favored in Chinese music, but the similarity ends there. The steady rhythm, choice of scale, texture, and repetitive form all suggest that he had never actually heard Chinese music at all—or at least had no interest in creating a faithful reproduction.

Creating a faithful reproduction, of course, was never Tchaikovsky's goal in any of these cases. Whether or not he accurately reflected the music of the cultures he parodied was purely incidental. Tchaikovsky's only task was to entertain the Moscow audience members that purchased tickets to see the ballet. His audience was Russian, and he knew that they enjoyed exotic escapism as part of their theatrical entertainment. They were not alone.

Exoticism—the use of stereotypes to portray other cultures as exciting or mysterious—has a long history in European music, and especially in music for the opera stage. European audiences of the 18th and 19th centuries were intrigued by the cultural practices of distant lands, and they had a limitless appetite for their representation in the arts. The East held particular fascination, such that the term **orientalism** has been coined to describe the stereotyped representation of Eastern cultures. Such representations, however, are seldom accurate or flattering. Instead, exoticism dehumanizes its subject so as to provide an escapist experience to the consumer. Europeans often perceived exoticized subjects as sexually licentious, primitive, and driven by their emotions— or, to put it another way, free from the strictures of society. In this way, exoticized subjects became an object of both adoration and loathing. They could give in to temptations that were denied to European viewers, but only because they were less than human.

Image 4.36: These dancers, who appeared in a 2012 concert performance of the Chinese dance, are wearing typical costumes and making a hand gesture that is often incorporated into *Nutcracker* choreography. At what point do these common presentational tactics become offensive, or downright racist?

Source: Marine Corps
Attribution: Isis M. Ramirez
License: Public Domain

All of this might seem a bit tangential to *The Nutcracker*, which, after all, tells a charming story set in an imagined candy land, but it is not. The ballet's representations of exoticized others—whether Romani people of Spain, or Arabs, or Chinese—contributes to a centuries-long practice that can still dehumanize these people today. This is best exemplified by a current controversy surrounding the performance of Tchaikovsky's Chinese dance, which usually relies on stereotyped costumes, makeup, and choreography that many people find offensive.

In 2017, yellowface.org was founded specifically to advocate for changes in how the Chinese dance is presented in productions of *The Nutcracker*. The organization encourages arts leaders to sign the "Final Bow for Yellowface" pledge, which is a commitment to end racist representations of the Chinese characters. It also provides resources for creating new costumes, makeup, and choreography for use in *Nutcracker* productions that reflect genuine Chinese cultural practices instead of racist stereotypes. The movement has gained support, but most productions—including that associated with this text—continue to present a stereotyped visual representation of Chinese culture alongside Tchaikovky's musical one.

Act II: Trepak

The final selection from the "Grand Divertissement" that we will examine here is the Russian dance, or Trepak. This time, Tchaikovsky took a model closer to home, for this dance is based on local Russian and Ukrainian folk practices.[13] Unsurprisingly, the Russian dance is Tchaikovsky's best imitation of the "real thing." Both his Russian dance and the authentic trepak are fast-paced and in duple meter, with a driving rhythm suited to high-energy dancing. We again hear the tambourine—now a symbol not of the Middle East but of native folk culture.

13.  In this video, you can see the kind of folk dance that inspired Tchaikovsky's Trepak.

JAVANESE TRADITIONAL, *THE LOVE DANCE OF KLANA SEWANDANA*

Like sung drama, danced drama can be found around the world. Some of the richest traditions hail from Southeast Asia, where one can find dozens of distinct varieties of danced storytelling. Our example belongs to the ***wayang wong***

Image 4.37: The *wayang wong* dance tradition developed in the courts of Yogyakarta and Surakarta, now the major cities of central Java.
Source: Wikimedia Commons
Attribution: User "Gobbler"
License: CC BY-SA 2.0

tradition, which developed in the courts of central Java, an island that is now part of Indonesia. Although *wayang wong* is unique to this small region, many of its musical and dramatic elements can be found across Java and throughout Indonesia. The most important of these is **gamelan** music, which is played on pitched gongs and keyed metallophones (marimba and xylophone are Western examples of such instruments).

Indonesia as Kingdom and Colony

Indonesia's performing arts traditions reflect its diverse cultural heritage. Civilization on the islands dates back thousands of years. Indonesia was at first ruled over by a series of Hindu and Buddhist kingdoms, but the arrival of Islam in the 15th century resulted in the gradual conversion of the population. Today, Indonesia is the largest Muslim nation in the world, although many inhabitants practice a form of the religion that contains traces of the region's Hindu and Buddhist heritage.

Javanese music is well known in the West due to the island's colonial history. Dutch traders began to visit the Indonesian islands in the 16th century. The profitability of trade led to an influx of Dutch settlers, who established a local government under the auspices of the United East India Company. When the company failed in 1800, the Dutch government formally annexed the Dutch East Indies—which included most of Java—as a colony. Under Dutch rule, indigenous courts were allowed to remain intact, but they were granted only ceremonial powers. While this denied Indonesians their political autonomy, it contributed to the flourishing of Indonesian art, which the Dutch encouraged. It also facilitated the spread of Javanese music and art to Europe.

During World War II, Indonesia was occupied by the Japanese, who drove out the Dutch in an attempt to claim the islands for themselves. At the conclusion of the war, the Indonesians proclaimed independence. The Netherlands attempted to reassert its claim to the territory by force, and a military conflict ensued. In 1949, however, facing intense pressure from other powers, the Dutch acknowledged Indonesia as an independent nation. The impact of Dutch colonialism on the spread of Javanese cultural products resonates into the present day, and *gamelan* music in particular can be heard throughout the world. Indeed, there are over one hundred *gamelan* ensembles in the United States alone.

Wayang Wong

The dance form we will explore here, *wayang wong*, developed during the colonial era and resulted from the conflict between indigenous and colonial powers. *Wayang wong* was created at the court of Hamengkubuwono I, the first Sultan of Yogyakarta. Hamengkubuwono was to inherit the throne of the Mataram Sultanate from his brother, Pakubuwono II, but instead led his followers in a civil war after Pakubuwono agreed to cooperate with the United East India Company. The war ended in 1755 with a treaty establishing courts at Yogyakarta and Surakarta. Although this was nominally a victory for Hamengkubuwono, the Dutch ultimately benefited by pitting the courts against one another over the next two centuries. All the same, Yogyakarta remained a stronghold of Javanese resistance, and today serves as the capital of an independent region of the same name.

Image 4.38: These *wayang wong* dancers are portraying a scene from the Mahabharata.

Wayang wong was initially conceived of as a decadent three-day spectacle celebrating and affirming the power of the newly-established Yogyakarta court. Although the first performance required dozens of dancers and lasted from dawn to dusk on each of the days, it has persisted in scaled-down forms. The term *wayang wong* literally means "human *wayang.*" This is in deference to the principal form of Indonesian theater, *wayang kulit*, which uses shadow puppets to act out traditional epics to the accompaniment of music.

All forms of *wayang* tell stories that have a long history in Indonesian culture. The principal sources are

Image 4.39: This view from behind the screen shows a *dhalang* manipulating the shadow puppets in a *wayang kulit* performance. The *dhalang*, who must be highly trained, not only moves the puppets but narrates, provides dialogue, and sings. His performances usually exceed eight hours in length, lasting from sunset to sunrise.

two Indian epics, the *Mahabharata* and the *Ramayana*. *Wayang* performances also draw from the Panji stories, which concern the life of a legendary Javanese prince. Each of these epics is much too long and complex to be related in a single performance. Instead, *wayang* performers select individual stories, which they often elaborate in ways that add novelty without disrupting the traditional narrative. Indonesian audiences are already familiar with the stories, and they appreciate seeing the characters and events presented with originality.

Gamelan

Our example presents an excerpt from the Panji stories, which we will consider in greater detail below. Before that, however, we owe some attention to the music that accompanies *wayang wong* dance. The instruments used in *gamelan* music date back to at least the 8th century, although they did not acquire their present form until the 15th or 16th century, when gamelan music became an important component of court life. Gamelan music is ubiquitous in traditional Indonesian culture. It can be performed on its own, but it is also used to accompany dance and theater. It is played for court celebrations and religious ceremonies, pursued by amateurs for their own enjoyment, and consumed by fans as entertainment.

A gamelan is a collection of bronze percussion instruments that are struck using a variety of mallets. The components of a gamelan include vertically-hung gongs of various sizes, smaller gongs suspended horizontally in wooden frames, and melodic instruments consisting of metal bars suspended over resonating chambers. The instruments of a gamelan are built together and they remain together. It is not possible for players to bring their own instruments, or for an instrument to be substituted. This is because there is no fixed pitch system in Indonesian music, so gamelan instruments

Image 4.40: Although it bears a superficial resemblance, the *saron* differs from the *gendèr* in many ways. The bronze keys rest directly on the instrument, and the resonating chamber is a space within the wooden body of the instrument. The keys are also struck differently.
Source: Wikimedia Commons
Attribution: Tropenmuseum, part of the National Museum of World Cultures
License: CC BY-SA 3.0

Image 4.41: The word "gong," several examples of which we see here, comes from Indonesia.
Source: Wikimedia Commons
Attribution: Tropenmuseum, part of the National Museum of World Cultures
License: CC BY-SA 3.0

Image 4.42: The *gendèr* is one of several gamelan instruments with bronze keys strung over bamboo resonators.
Source: Wikimedia Commons
Attribution: Tropenmuseum, part of the National Museum of World Cultures
License: CC BY-SA 3.0

Image 4.43: The *kenong* and *kethuk* are horizontally-suspended gongs used to mark the underlying rhythmic cycle in gamelan music.
Source: Wikimedia Commons
Attribution: Tropenmuseum, part of the National Museum of World Cultures
License: CC BY-SA 3.0

Image 4.44: The gongs of the bonang resemble those of the *kenong* and *kethuk*, but are strung together and tuned to allow the rendition of melodies.
Source: Wikimedia Commons
Attribution: Tropenmuseum, part of the National Museum of World Cultures
License: CC BY-SA 3.0

are tuned to one another by the original builder. Every gamelan therefore plays a distinct set of pitches.

In addition to being communally stored and maintained, gamelans are bestowed with names. This not only recognizes the gamelan's status as a complete ensemble but also signifies the traditional belief that a gamelan possesses a spirit. This spirit resides primarily in the largest suspended gong, the *gong ageng*, which might be provided offerings of food, flowers, and incense. The blacksmith who forges the bronze components of the gamelan instruments is traditionally understood to hold special powers, and he is expected to prepare for his task through fasting and self-purification. His carefully-tuned gongs and bars are then set in ornately-carved wooden frames.

Each instrument in a gamelan occupies a specific place in the musical texture. The vertically- and horizontally-suspended gongs are all used to mark the pulses of the rhythmic cycles that underlie gamelan music. These cycles, each of which is named, consist of patterns of timbres provided by the various gongs. The *gong ageng* always marks the end of the cycle, which repeats throughout a performance and provides the structure.

The other bronze instruments—which include two sizes of *bonang*, *gendèr*, *slenthem* (an instrument that resembles the *gendèr* but is pitched lower and has fewer keys), and two sizes of *saron*— play the same melody in heterophonic texture. However, each of these instruments interprets the melody in a markedly different way. Some play ornate versions, some play spare versions, and some play syncopated versions. The result is a complex texture woven out of the brilliant and resonant timbres of the many instruments.

Gamelan music also uses a few additional instruments, although these are not part of the main gamelan ensemble. Such instruments usually provide improvised melodies that follow the contour of the main melody but are otherwise independent. The instruments that might fill this role include the *rebab* (a bowed fiddle related to the Chinese *jinghu*), the *gambang* (a wood-keyed xylophone), and the *suling* (a type of flute). Finally, a male choir or female soloist might sing, drawing their texts from a body of poems and riddles that belong to the gamelan tradition. These texts, however, are not associated with any particular musical composition. Instead, they might be heard in a variety of contexts.

A gamelan performance is led by the drummer, who plays three different sizes of a drum known as *kendhang*. The drummer starts and stops performances, but his most important task is to control the pace and to signal the dramatic shifts in tempo that are characteristic of gamelan music. During performance, the ensemble will periodically slow to half of its former tempo or accelerate to twice the tempo. This is accompanied by changes in how the melody is interpreted by each of the instruments, which will add notes at slow tempos in order to maintain a consistent texture.

Image 4.45: A *kendhang* player.
Source: Wikimedia Commons
Attribution: Raimond Spekking
License: CC BY-SA 4.0

The Love Dance of Klana Sewandana

Time	Form	What to listen for
The Love Dance of Klana Sewandana Performance: The court dancers and musicians of Yogyakarta		
32'14"	Sekartaji alone in the forest	A few of the metallophones play a slow, simple melody; the rebab and solo female singer improvise high melodies; a percussionist taps rhythms on a wooden box
35'12"	Klana Sewandana enters and attempts to seduce Sekartaji	The music at first becomes faster and more rhythmically intense; this is followed by fluctuations in tempo and dynamic
36'08		A male solo singer enters and the rhythm becomes more regular

Page | 126

37'52	Prince Panji arrives and fights Klana Sewandana	The brighter/louder metallophones reenter the texture
38'21"		The male choir enters and most of the instruments drop out
39'06"		The rebab enters
39'35"		The solo female singer joins the male choir
[...]		Instruments and singers continue to leave and reenter the texture as the music fluctuates in intensity
45'30	Prince Panji and Sekartaji are reunited	The music slows in tempo, then accelerates
48'19		The music slows in anticipation of the final note

We are now prepared to turn to our example: A *wayang wong* performance that presents an episode from the Panji legends. *Wayang wong* is practiced both in masked and unmasked versions. This is obviously an example of the former. The use of masks in Indonesian dance dates back thousands of years. The masks are symbolically significant, and their shape, color, and details carry information about the character.

Many episodes of the Panji legend concern his romantic relationship with Sekartaji, who often finds herself separated from the Prince due to the intervention of malevolent forces. To survive, she frequently disguises herself as a man, at one point becoming the King of Bali and meeting Prince Panji on the battlefield. (There is also a long history of cross dressing in *wayang* dance itself.) The scene we will examine opens on Sekartaji alone in the forest. She has fled from the unwanted affections of King Klana Sewandana, whose obsession with her has driven him insane. Klana Sewandana attempts to seduce Sekartaji, but she rebuffs his advances. Luckily, Prince Panji has been drawn to the scene by his great love for Sekartaji. He fights and defeats Klana Sewandana, and the lovers are reunited.

The three dancers in the scene move differently, for they represent the three character types of *wayang wong*. As a female type, Sekartaji keeps her feet close to the ground while executing refined movements with her hands, neck, and head. Klana Sewandana is a strong male, as betrayed by his wide stance, large steps, and aggressive movements. Prince Panji, on the other hand, is a refined male. As such, he keeps his feet close to the ground and moves fluidly.

Throughout the episode, the gamelan provides a constant musical backdrop while accentuating the dramatic contour. Klana Sewandana's arrival in the forest, for example, is marked by an intensification of the music, which grows in volume and increases in tempo. Musical outbursts punctuate the fight scene, while a musical calm descends on the final scene between Panji and Sekartaji. From time to time we hear the *rebab*, the *suling*, and various singers, who can be seen seated behind the dancers. The words they are singing have nothing in particular to do with the drama unfolding onstage, but voices contribute an important aesthetic element to any performance.

RESOURCES FOR FURTHER LEARNING

Print

Brenner, Benjamin. *Music in Central Java: Experiencing Music, Expressing Culture*. Oxford University Press, 2007.

Church, Michael, ed. *The Other Classical Musics: Fifteen Great Traditions*. Boydell Press, 2015.

Lau, Frederick. *Music in China: Experiencing Music, Expressing Culture*. Oxford University Press, 2007.

Riley, Roland John. *Tchaikovsky's Ballets: Swan Lake, Sleeping Beauty, Nutcracker*. Clarendon Press, 1985.

Romano, Renee and Claire Bond Potter, ed. *Historians on Hamilton: How a Blockbuster Musical is Reshaping America's Past*. Rutgers University Press, 2018.

Whenham, John. *Claudio Monteverdi: Orfeo*. Cambridge University Press, 1986.

Song

Esther M. Morgan-Ellis and Arielle P. Crumley

INTRODUCTION

Song is perhaps the most familiar and universal form of musical storytelling. Unlike opera, it does not require a large space, costumes, or staging. It can be collaborative, but is often performed by a single person. It is also compelling, for we generally get a great deal of pleasure out of using our imaginations to visualize the characters and events of a story. In many times and places, in fact, song and storytelling have been considered inseparable: The storyteller could not imagine communicating through any means other than music.

The purpose of song, of course, is not always to tell stories. Many songs present philosophical ideas, or describe scenes, or support worship, or encourage dancing. In this chapter, however, we will focus on songs—and collections of songs—that outline clear narratives, and we will examine ways in which the music helps to communicate the story. As we will see, it can do this in many ways.

SONG CYCLES

We will begin by looking at collections of songs that work together to tell a story that is emotionally complex, if not heavy in plot detail. Such a collection can be called a **song cycle**. A song cycle usually consists of about eight to twenty songs that use carefully crafted texts and music to present a cohesive narrative. Each song is distinct from the others and the order cannot be changed. While the term song cycle is most often applied to works from the art music world, it is valid across many genres. When a popular artist releases an album of songs that accomplish the purpose of a song cycle, however, the product is referred to as a **concept album**.

The most important difference between a song cycle and concept album is that the former is most commonly conceived of with live performance in mind, whereas the latter is often developed in the studio and consumed as a recording. For this reason, a song cycle is more likely to have limited instrumentation, while producers of concept albums often have a wider variety of sound tools at their disposal. We will begin by considering a concept album that includes not only sounds but images and spoken poetry.

BEYONCÉ, *LEMONADE*

On April 23, 2016, popular music star Beyoncé released her sixth album, *Lemonade*. The release was accompanied by a 65-minute film of the same name that premiered on the popular television network HBO. This album, which was influenced by a range of genres spanning from hip-hop to country, became critically acclaimed for its musical variety, while the accompanying film was admired for its astounding visual cinematography. The work as a whole has also been lauded for its unapologetic celebration of womanhood and black culture.

At its center, *Lemonade* is a concept album revolving around infidelity, seemingly sparked by the infamous accounts of Beyoncé and husband Jay-Z's marital struggles. The songs, which mirror Beyoncé's personal experiences with infidelity, touch on themes such as heartbreak, revenge, and forgiveness. The

Image 5.1: Here we see Beyoncé performing onstage in 2013.
Source: Wikimedia Commons
Attribution: User "Nat Ch Villa"
License: CC BY 2.0

accompanying film follows the singer's journey from betrayal to healing by dividing the twelve songs into separate chapters: "Intuition," "Denial," "Anger," "Apathy," "Emptiness," "Accountability," "Reformation," "Forgiveness," "Resurrection," "Hope," and "Redemption." Though the album's focus is on Beyoncé's personal healing, there is also an underlying political theme, for the album recognizes the struggles of black Americans by addressing issues such as black womanhood and police brutality. Here, we will discuss several songs and consider their visual counterparts, exploring different stages of the story's development.

"Hold Up"

One of the most noteworthy aspects of *Lemonade* is the poetry that Beyoncé recites between each song. These poems help to tie the story together and clarify dramatic details. Beyoncé's recitations include excerpts from the poems of Warsan Shire, a Somali-British poet known for writing about not only personal experiences but also the struggles of women, refugees, immigrants, and other marginalized groups of people. Throughout the recitation, listeners are confronted both with abstract images and with descriptions of the emotions that prevail in each chapter. Consider, for example, the poetry that precedes the song "Hold Up,"[1] which Beyoncé recites in eerie, whispering tones.

<table>
<tr><td>1.</td><td></td><td>"Hold Up" from *Lemonade*
Performance: Beyoncé (2016)</td></tr>
</table>

Immediately following this passage, the song "Hold Up" begins. This upbeat single reflects the "Denial" chapter of Beyoncé's journey. The song at first seems optimistic: its playful, Reggae-inspired beat and major key make the song sound like a laid-back summertime hit. The lyrics of the chorus seem to convey a positive attitude, repeating the phrase, "Hold up, they don't love you like I love you/Slow down, they don't love you like I love you." However, the verses express more negative emotions. By considering the lyrics in their entirety and noticing the duality between the verses and the chorus, the listener gets the impression that Beyoncé is fighting with her emotions, bouncing back and forth between denial and anger.

The visual aspect of the song also reveals a dichotomous nature. Beyoncé herself seems to be a visual representation of lightheartedness, dressed in a long, flowing gown of bright yellow. However, her look is meant to be a representation of Oshun, a West-African goddess of fresh waters, love, and fertility (this characterization is further emphasized in the beginning of the scene where Beyoncé emerges from a building surrounded by cascading water). Although Oshun is viewed as a benevolent deity, folktales often discuss Oshun's harsh temper when she has been wronged. Beyoncé embodies this character throughout the song, smiling playfully as she bashes windows, fire hydrants, and cars with a baseball bat.

"Don't Hurt Yourself"

In the following song, "Don't Hurt Yourself,"[2] which is performed during the chapter titled "Anger," Beyoncé leaves behind her playful nature for full-on vengeance. The song, which features rock musician Jack White (known mostly for his association with The White Stripes), has definite rock-and-roll characteristics, including heavy rhythms and distorted vocals. Beyoncé expresses her anger in the song's opening lyric: "Who the f*ck do you think I is? You ain't married to no average b*tch, boy." The mood throughout the song remains the same: angry and vengeful. Beyoncé concludes with a final warning: "If you try this sh*t again/ You gon' lose your wife."

<table>
<tr><td>2.</td><td></td><td>"Don't Hurt Yourself" from *Lemonade*
Performance: Beyoncé (2016)</td></tr>
</table>

With these lyrics, it becomes apparent that Beyonce's anger is directed toward her cheating husband. However, this song also includes one of the first instances in which Beyoncé addresses the album's other theme: the struggles of being a black American, particularly a black American woman. In the middle of the first verse, Beyoncé interpolates an excerpt from Malcolm X's famous speech "Who Taught You to Hate Yourself:"

> The most disrespected person in America is the black woman. The most unprotected woman in America is the black woman. The most neglected person in America is the black woman.

Beyoncé's anger seems to be not only directed at her husband but also at the mistreatment of black women in America. This continues to be an underlying theme throughout the remainder of the album. For instance, in the following song, "Sorry" (one of the most popular singles from the album), the last lyric reads "you better call Becky with the good hair." The term "Becky" is a popular colloquialism for a white woman, and this lyric seems to imply that the other woman was white. This reflects the negative stereotype that black women are less desirable than other women, and it implies that Beyoncé was cheated on because of her blackness.

"Sandcastles"

The next few songs on the album, which belong to the chapters "Apathy" and "Emptiness," exhibit various emotions, but it is with the song "Sandcastles"[3] that Beyoncé arrives at the most difficult and important point in her journey: "Forgiveness." The music itself presents raw emotions, with its simple, bare piano accompaniment and expressive vocals. Beyoncé's singing style is very different in this song, her voice at times sounding shaky or raspy, reflecting the hurt that is inevitable when confronting a cheating partner. She sings of her damaged marriage, of the fights and broken hearts, yet she reveals her reluctance to walk away from it all by singing, "Oh, and I know I promised that I couldn't stay, baby/ Every promise don't work out that way." Like the music itself, the visual portion of this song is very personal, including loving scenes of Beyoncé and husband Jay-Z laughing together and embracing.

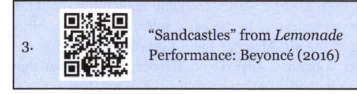

3. "Sandcastles" from *Lemonade*
Performance: Beyoncé (2016)

The following short song, "Forward," features English singer James Blake, who sings a heartbreaking melody. With the infidelity narrative reaching its conclusion in the previous song, this interlude pulls away from the story of Beyonce's struggles

Image 5.2: Beyoncé performing in 2007.
Source: Wikipedia
Attribution: Cornel Pex
License: CC BY 2.0

and introduces a new focus on the previously-mentioned underlying theme: the struggles of black Americans. The visual counterpart of the song features several important figures in the fight for equality and justice, including the mothers of Trayvon Martin, Eric Garner, and Michael Brown (Sybrina Fulton, Gwen Carr, and Lezley McSpadden respectively). Each woman is shown holding a photograph of her son who was killed by unnecessary violence and brutality.

The final chapters of Beyoncé's journey, "Hope" and "Redemption," feature upbeat and inspirational songs such as "Freedom" and the hit single "Formation." The powerful lyrics and gospel style of "Freedom" convey an inspirational message about continuing on in the midst of adversity. This message is not only a reflection of Beyoncé's power to move beyond her personal struggles while dealing with her husband's infidelity, it is also an anthem intended to uplift black Americans in their struggles against inequality. At the song's conclusion, there is an excerpt from a speech given by Hattie White, Jay-Z's grandmother, that elucidates the meaning of the album's title:

> I had my ups and downs, but I always find the inner strength to pull myself up. I was served lemons, but I made lemonade.

FRANZ SCHUBERT, *THE LOVELY MAID OF THE MILL*

Franz Schubert (1797-1828) lived a quiet life in Vienna, where he wrote over 600 songs for performance at intimate domestic gatherings. Although he died young, and without achieving significant fame outside of Vienna, his work became widely-known in the mid-19th century and today he is considered to be one of the finest composers of the era.

Song and National Character

Before we can look at Schubert's songs, we need to know something about the cultural context in which he was working. In the early 19th century, new ideas about national identity were in the air. Many of these ideas were rooted in the work of German philosopher Johann Gottfried von Herder, who argued that spoken language influenced an individual's character. He suggested, for example, that Germans all thought in roughly the same way because they spoke the same language, which in turn guided and structured their intellectual activity. From here, the notion that people who spoke the same language should participate in bounded, self-governing communities—nations, in fact—was not far removed.

During Schubert's time, neither Germany nor Austria existed in anything resembling their present forms, but the idea that communities of people who spoke a common language should constitute autonomous nations was quickly taking hold.

Herder also believed that the most authentic form of national character was to be found among those least corrupted by cosmopolitan influences—the peasants who worked the land. Before the late 18th century, impoverished rural folk were treated with contempt. It was not believed that they had anything to offer the ruling classes other than labor. Following Herder, however, they became the one true source of authentic "folk" culture, and therefore key to a nation's ability to understand itself.

Collectors began to scour the countryside for folk stories, folk poetry, folk dances, and folk songs. These were compiled and published for popular consumption. Perhaps the most famous of such collectors were the Brothers Grimm (Jacob Ludwig Karl and Wilhelm Carl), who were responsible for first recording many of the fairy tales—including Cinderella, Hansel and Gretel, Snow White, Rapunzel, and Sleeping Beauty—that have been ceaselessly told and retold around the world ever since.

All of this is important to our discussion of Schubert for two reasons. First, the elevation of the German language meant that German songs had the potential to become art. Before Schubert's time, songs were regarded as trivial popular entertainment. Schubert's songs, however, were taken seriously as cultural expression of the highest order.

Second, general fascination with folk culture and art influenced Schubert's approach to writing songs. He often chose texts that

Image 5.3: This posthumous portrait of Schubert was painted by Wilhelm August Rieder in 1875.
Source: Wikimedia Commons
Attribution: Wilhelm August Rieder
License: Public Domain

Image 5.4: The ideas of Johann Gottfried von Herder influenced the development of a German art song tradition.
Source: Wikimedia Commons
Attribution: Anton Graff
License: Public Domain

imitated folk poetry, or at least dwelt on rural subject matter, and he frequently set these to music in a folk-like style. Although some of his music seems very simple,

Schubert did not resort to the folk idiom because he lacked ability or imagination. Instead, he imitated genuine folk song to augment his storytelling.

We will see all of this influence at work in Schubert's 1824 song cycle *The Lovely Maid of the Mill*. Before turning to the story and music, however, we need to consider the setting in which the music was meant to be experienced.

Salon Culture

In the Vienna of Schubert's time, music lovers supported an economy of small, in-home concerts known as salons. A salon might be hosted by a wealthy family for the purpose of advertising their cultural and social capital. The performance would take place in the family's living room, where visitors could admire their furnishings and art. Hosting a salon was also considerably cheaper than maintaining a private orchestra, so it became the preferred means of cultural expression as Vienna's wealth slowly shifted from a small group of aristocrats to a larger middle class.

Naturally, certain types of music were preferable for salon entertainment. Only a few performers could fit in the venue at a time, and loud instruments were not welcome. A great demand arose, therefore, for solo piano music, chamber music (two to five individuals each playing their own part), and song, all of which Schubert produced in enormous quantities.

Image 5.5: This 1897 painting by Julius Schmid shows Vienna's upper classes garbed in their finest and crowded around the piano, at which Schubert himself is seated. All attention is clearly focused on the music, which is performed at intimate proximity. (Of course, Schmid was born much too late to attend a *Schubertiade*, and he was imagining the scene in question.)
Source: Wikimedia Commons
Attribution: Julius Schmid
License: Public Domain

All of Schubert's songs and chamber music were conceived of with this sort of environment in mind. In fact, he became so prominent in the salon scene that a special term, *Schubertiade*, was developed to describe a salon performance that featured only his music. Salons were comparatively informal, and listeners would gather around the performers in close proximity. Paintings of salon performances show listeners in rapt attention.

This type of engagement with music was typical more generally of Schubert's era, when the public held art in high regard and believed that artists were in a position to communicate profound truths. Schubert's listeners sought not only entertainment but also enlightenment, transformation, and catharsis. *The Lovely Maid of the Mill* offered all.

The Lovely Maid of the Mill

The poetry for this song cycle was written by Wilhelm Müller, a prolific author of song texts. Müller was one of many German poets who looked to folk models for inspiration, and the folk-like characteristics of his verse influenced Schubert's music. Müller's collection of twenty-five poems was first published in 1820, and Schubert began setting it to music just a few years later while he was recovering from a severe bout of illness. Schubert's spirits were low at the time he embarked on this project, for he feared that he would never fully regain his health. Indeed, he never did: Schubert succumbed to his illness five years later, just as he was on the brink of achieving success outside of Vienna.

In the poems, Müller tells the story of a young journeyman miller who has completed his initial apprenticeship and set out to find employment. He walks through the woods until he finds a stream, and then follows the stream to a mill, where he does indeed find a job waiting. He also finds the miller's daughter, and falls in love with her immediately. At first, she seems to reciprocate, and he is overjoyed to have won her affection. Slowly, however, the miller begins to suspect that the girl in fact loves the hunter, who has been hanging about the mill. As his suspicion turns to certainty, the miller experiences anger, grief, and finally resignation. Having lost his true love forever, he drowns himself in the brook.

It is worth noting that Schubert and Beyonce's songs cycles have a great deal in common. Both address the suffering that can come with love, and both express the intense emotions of the wronged party. It seems that we have never told enough stories about the difficulty of navigating a romantic relationship. The nuances of each musical story, however, are unique to the time and place in which each was crafted. Beyonce tells a tale of empowerment and reconciliation, while Schubert's protagonist seems to give up in the face of a romantic stymy.

The story told in *The Lovely Maid of the Mill*, however, exhibits a variety of 19th-century values. The period extending roughly from 1815 to 1900 is referred to in the arts as the Romantic era. In the realms of both literature and music, consumers expected insight into the inner emotional lives of individuals, whether they were fictional protagonists or the creators themselves. Two of the topics addressed in *The*

Lovely Maid of the Mill—love and suicide—were especially prevalent in the Romantic era, while the tale's rural setting exemplifies the Romantic interest in nature. While the story is not particularly interesting in its own terms, the music allows us to experience every nuance the protagonist's widely varying emotional states.

We will examine four songs: the first, the last, and two from intermediate points in the miller's emotional journey. In each case, we will look at how Schubert's musical decisions amplify and communicate the emotional and dramatic contents of the poetry.

"Wandering"

The first song is entitled "Wandering."[4] The poem reads as follows:

Wandering is the miller's joy,
Wandering!
A man isn't much of a miller,
If he doesn't think of wandering,
Wandering!

We learned it from the stream,
The stream!
It doesn't rest by day or night,
And only thinks of wandering,
The stream!

We also see it in the mill wheels,
The mill wheels!
They'd rather not stand still at all
and don't tire of turning all day,
the mill wheels!

Even the millstones, as heavy as they are,
The millstones!
They take part in the merry dance
And would go faster if they could,
The millstones!

Oh wandering, wandering, my passion,
Oh wandering!
Master and Mistress Miller,
Give me your leave to go in peace,
And wander!

translated by Celia Sgroi

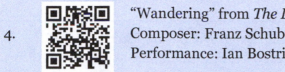

4. "Wandering" from *The Lovely Maid of the Mill*
Composer: Franz Schubert
Performance: Ian Bostridge and Mitsuko Uchida (2005)

The textual contents, frequent word repetition, and generous use of exclamation points all paint a picture of an enthusiastic (if naive) young man. His outlook is positive and he sees nothing but joy in his future. He also indicates a clear preference for individual liberty. He is not, in other words, the type of young man who is eager to take on the responsibilities of marriage.

Schubert translates all of this enthusiasm and simplistic good nature into his music. He seems to imagine the miller's words as constituting a folk-type song, which the young man literally sings as he walks through the woods. To do so, Schubert keeps his setting (the music crafted to suit a set of words) very simple. To begin with, he creates a **strophic** song, in which each stanza of the text is set to the same music. As a result, we hear the same melody and accompaniment five times in a row. This is a standard form for European and American folk music, which is traditionally learned by ear and memorized. One can easily master the melody, which can then be used to sing a limitless amount of text. This form is also common in the Christian hymn tradition. In all of these cases, the focus is meant to be on the meaning of the words.

Schubert's strophic melody is simple and catchy. The opening melodic phrase is heard twice, as is the last, while the middle section presents an additional melody in **sequence** (that is to say, it is repeated at a different pitch level—lower, in this case). In total, therefore, this song contains three short melodic ideas, all of which are repeated either verbatim or with a minor alteration.

Schubert's melody, however, does not *quite* imitate a folk song. It is in fact fairly challenging to sing, as it contains a number of difficult leaps in the first and third sections. His piano accompaniment also walks the line between simple and sophisticated. It utilizes a straightforward pattern of arpeggiated harmonies (a technique by which the notes in a triad are played from lowest to highest and/or vice versa), none of which challenge the ear, but it is denser and more varied than one would expect in the folk tradition.

Over the course of the song cycle, however, the listener comes to realize that the piano does more than just support the singer. Schubert encourages us to hear the piano as a second storyteller. Perhaps its arpeggiated accompaniments, which are present in almost every song, represents the gurgling of the brook. When the arpeggiations are absent, it is always for a significant reason. The brook itself turns out to be a very important character. In addition to being present in many of the texts, it actually becomes the narrator for the final poem. We don't know any of this when we first hear the opening song, but in retrospect we must think twice about what the piano has to contribute.

"Mine!"

		"Mine" from *The Lovely Maid of the Mill* Composer: Franz Schubert Performance: Ian Bostridge and Mitsuko Uchida (2005)
Time	**Form**	**What to listen for**
0'00"	Piano introduction	The arpeggios in the left hand of the accompaniment suggest the steady murmuring of the brook
0'10"	A "Brook, stop your murmuring!" . . .	A melodic motif is repeated at progressively higher pitch levels
0'28"	"Through the grove" . . .	Repetition of another motif culminates in the singer's repetition of the word "mine" on a loud, high note
0'49"	Transition	The music shifts to a new key (B flat major)
0'53"	B "Spring, are these all your flowers?"	This section, which rests briefly on a minor-mode harmony, seems more disturbed than the A section
1'19"	Transition	The music returns to the original key (D major)
1'24"	A	The A text and music return
2'01"	Coda	The singer repeats the word "mine;" the pianist provides a concluding passage

The eleventh song in the cycle is entitled "Mine!" This song marks the moment when the miller wins the heart of the girl (or so he thinks). The poem expresses his exuberance:

> Brook, stop your murmuring!
> Wheels, stop your thundering!
> All you merry woodland birds,

Large and small,
Stop your singing!
Through the grove,
In and out,
Only one phrase resounds:
The beloved miller's daughter is mine!
Mine!
Spring, are these all your flowers?
Sun, can't you shine any brighter?
Alas, then I must stand all alone,
With the blissful word mine,
Misunderstood in this vast universe.

translated by Celia Sgroi

Schubert brings this text to life with equally joyful music. He sets a brisk tempo, and the singer rushes through the words with a sense of youthful excitement. This is most certainly not a folk song. To begin with, it is not strophic, but **through-composed**—a term used to indicate a song that pairs a unique melody with each line of poetic text instead of repeating the same melody.

This song is also too complex to be perceived as a folk product. Schubert uses a ternary form (A B A), in which the first ten lines of poetry and their accompanying music constitute the A section and are therefore heard at the beginning and end of the song. The A section begins with another sequence. This time, a melodic fragment is heard at higher and higher pitch levels—an indication of the speaker's excitement. The A section ends with a rapid passage of notes that rocket to the highest pitch on the word "Mine!" The B section, apart from having a unique character, is in a different key than the A section (B-flat major instead of D major). This gives the song an added sense of wonder and delight. The piano accompaniment provides gurgling arpeggiated harmonies throughout.

"Withered Flowers"

		"Withered Flowers" from *The Lovely Maid of the Mill* Composer: Franz Schubert Performance: Ian Bostridge and Mitsuko Uchida (2005)
Time	**Form**	**What to listen for**
0'00"	A "All the flowers" . . .	The piano accompaniment is sparse and restrained

1'08"	A' "Ah, but tears don't bring" . . .	The music in this passage is identical to that of the first A section
2'09"	B "And when she strolls"	The mode changes from minor to major and the piano accompaniment becomes more active
2'44"	B	The text and music of the B section are repeated
3'18"	B "Then all your flowers"	The closing passage of the B section is repeated yet again
3'34"	Coda	The piano accompaniment transitions back to minor as it moves into the lowest range of the instrument

Next we will visit the eighteenth song, entitled "Withered Flowers." At this point, the miller has passed through various stages of suspicion and anger, and he has nearly resigned himself to his tragic fate:

> All you flowers
> That she gave to me,
> They should put you
> With me in my grave.
>
> Why do you all look at me
> So sorrowfully,
> As if you knew,
> What was happening to me?
>
> All you flowers,
> Why so limp, why so pale?
> All you flowers,
> What has drenched you so?
>
> Ah, but tears don't bring
> The green of May,
> Don't cause dead love
> To bloom again.

And spring will come,
And winter will go,
And flowers will
Grow in the grass again.

And flowers are lying
In my grave,
All the flowers
That she gave to me.

And when she strolls
Past my burial place
And thinks to herself:
He was true to me!

Then all you flowers
Come out, come out!
May has come,
And winter is gone.

translated by Celia Sgroi

The poem begins in a mournful, self-pitying vein, but the final stanzas introduce a glimmer of hope. The miller imagines a future time when his beloved, passing by his grave, will regret her cruelty. He will be dead, of course, but he will also be vindicated.

The form of this poem—a series of eight stanzas—suggests a strophic setting, but Schubert provides something quite different. He sets the first three stanzas to a slow, minor-mode melody that expresses their tragic sentiment. Then he repeats that melody for the next three stanzas. For the final two stanzas, however, he shifts to the relative major (that is to say, he moves from E minor to E major) and introduces a new melody, all of which is repeated for emphasis. At the climactic phrase "May has come," the singer soars to the highest notes in his range, and the vocal music concludes on a definitively triumphant note.

Once again, however, we would be remiss to ignore the piano accompaniment, which is particularly striking in this example. After seventeen songs in which the piano has sparkled and bubbled, now it has suddenly gone dead. We hear only dry, sparse chords for most of the song. This accompaniment reinforces the sorrowful mood of the miller, who has given up hope. The piano comes back to life with the final two stanzas, and builds in strength as the miller gains confidence. However, the piano also foreshadows the conclusion to this story, which will not be a happy one. Although the singer ends on a triumphant, major-mode cadence, the closing passage into the piano returns to E minor as it fades away and moves into the lower ranges of the instrument. The careful listener knows that the miller's hope is false.

"The Brook's Lullaby"

The final song in the cycle is entitled "The Brook's Lullaby."[5] The narrator is no longer the miller, who has drowned himself, but rather the brook, which promises to protect the disappointed lover and see that no more harm comes to him:

Rest well, rest well!
Close your eyes.
Wanderer, you weary one, you are at home.
Fidelity is here,
You'll lie with me
Until the sea drains the brook dry.

I'll make you a cool bed
On a soft cushion
In your blue crystalline chamber.
Come closer, come here,
Whatever can soothe,
Lull and rock my boy to sleep.

If a hunting horn sounds
From the green forest,
I'll rumble and thunder all around you.
Don't look in here
You blue flowers!
You trouble my sleeper's dreams.

Go away, depart
From the mill bridge,
Wicked girl, so your shadow won't wake him!
Throw in to me
Your fine scarf,
So I can cover his eyes.

Good night, good night,
Until everything wakes.
Sleep away your joy, sleep away your pain.
The full moon rises,
The mist departs,
And the sky above, how vast it is!

translated by Celia Sgroi

5. "The Brook's Lullaby" from *The Lovely Maid of the Mill*
Composer: Franz Schubert
Performance: Ian Bostridge and Mitsuko Uchida (2005)

For this final song, Schubert again provides a strophic setting, full of repeating melodic fragments. This time, however, he is imitating not a folk song but a lullaby. The melody is gentle and calming. It consists mostly of stepwise motion, and it is free of dramatic leaps and exciting runs. It *almost* sounds like a real lullaby, but not quite. Once again, Schubert makes things a bit too complicated by moving from E major to A major for the middle section, and by introducing a flatted pitch near the end that suggest E minor. The result is a particularly passionate lullaby with a hint of sadness.

BALLADS

The term **ballad** has been around for a long time, but it has meant different things in different times and places. The term comes from the French word meaning "to dance," for medieval French ballads were in fact dance songs. Today, we think of a ballad as being a slow, romantic song. That meaning of the term, however, dates only from the late 19th century. For most of history, a ballad has been some variety of lengthy song that tells a story. Ballad traditions of this sort are found across Europe and in North Africa, the United States, and Australia.

Here, we will examine three disparate musical examples that all, nonetheless, qualify as ballads in this sense. Our first example will be the most traditional, insofar as it has been passed down by means of oral tradition for many generations and exists in various versions on either side of the Atlantic. Our second example will be an adaptation of the folk ballad tradition by a 19th century European composer, and our third will be a recent ballad composed by an American singer. All three of these ballads tell stories, but each uses music in a different way.

"PRETTY POLLY"

We will begin with a ballad from the tradition of the British Isles. Discussing ballads such as "Pretty Polly," however, presents unique challenges. While each song from Beyonce's *Lemonade* or Schubert's *The Lovely Maid of the Mill* is a specific musical object that can be identified and described, such is not the case with traditional ballads.

Image 5.6: This 18th-century painting by William Hogarth depicts a woman singing ballads in a crowded street.
Source: Wikimedia Commons
Attribution: William Hogarth
License: CC0

This is because they belong to an **oral tradition** in which songs are passed down from generation to generation by word of mouth without reliance on written sources.

Oral tradition often works like an enormous game of telephone. Each time a new person learns the song, they make small changes to the text and/or music. These changes might be intentional or accidental. Some singers consciously decide to "improve" a melody or alter a few words of text, while others simply forget what they had originally been taught. At first, a song will still be recognizable, but over centuries and great distances it can acquire a text and melody that bear little relation to the original. In some cases, only a line of poetry or the name of a character betrays the link between two ballads that otherwise seem to have no connection.

This is the case with "Pretty Polly." We will be examining two versions of the ballad as it was recorded by American folk artists in the 20th century. Even these contemporary versions are significantly different, although a listener can easily recognize that each is a recording of the same song. These variations, however, only scratch the surface.

British Antecedents

"Pretty Polly" is a modern descendent of a much older British ballad entitled "The Gosport Tragedy." Like many ballads, "The Gosport Tragedy" narrated real-life happenings (although with a supernatural twist). Names and details

Image 5.7: This English broadside version of "The Gosport Tragedy" was printed in the early 19th century. A broadside is a single-sided sheet of paper that could contain the text of a ballad.
Source: Wikimedia Commons
Attribution: J.Turner
License: Public Domain

Image 5.8: This 18th-century engraving depicts a ballad singer making use of a visual aid as he seeks to captivate the crowd.
Source: PxHere
Attribution: Unknown
License: CC0

included in some versions of the ballad tie it to documented events that took place in 1726. Ballads were often used to commemorate tragedies, celebrate victories, eviscerate politicians, or spread the news of notorious crimes."The Gosport Tragedy" falls into this last category, for it tells the story of a ship's carpenter who murdered his pregnant girlfriend before himself perishing at sea. In the final stanzas of early versions, the spectre of the betrayed girl appears on board the ship to exact her revenge.

As such, "The Gosport Tragedy"—as well as its New World derivative, "Pretty Polly"—can be specifically categorized as a **murder ballad**. Just as television viewers today like watching shows about crime, so also regular folks of previous centuries enjoyed hearing about the salacious misdeeds of condemned criminals. As a result, the activities of notorious murderers provided fodder for countless ballads. Most murder ballads specifically tell of young women who lost their lives to deceitful lovers.

The purpose of these ballads was not only to thrill and horrify. They also served to instruct and warn. Mothers often sang ballads to their daughters, who received the message that they must withhold sexual favors from suitors until after marriage. The girls in the songs, after all, put their own lives at risk when they agreed to leave their homes for a young man who had not made a formal commitment. In this way, ballads provided entertainment while also enforcing social norms.

"The Gosport Tragedy" first appeared in print around 1760, but this should not be considered the "original" or "correct" version. One of the challenges facing those who wish to study the histories of traditional ballads is that there is never a preserved, authoritative work. While a particular ballad might have begun life as the creation of a specific individual, we almost never know the identity of that person. And, as described above, ballads begin to change immediately upon entering the oral tradition. Most scholars are more interested in examining the many versions of a ballad that proliferate throughout the repertoire than they are in identifying the most authentic version.

The story first told as "The Gosport Tragedy" has appeared under a variety of titles, including "The Cruel Ship's Carpenter," "Love and Murder," "Polly's Love," "Molly the Betray'd" and "The Fog-bound Vessel." Some versions have been published in print, while others have been collected by "ballad hunters," who visit rural areas to record and preserve products of the oral tradition.

The version known as "Pretty Polly" emerged in the Appalachian region of the United States. Many immigrants from the British Isles—especially the impoverished Scotch-Irish, who came from a region on the border between England and Scotland—paid for their voyage to the New World by serving as indentured laborers in Pennsylvania. After repaying their debt, they headed into the mountainous regions where land could be obtained for little or no cost. These immigrants had few physical possessions, but they brought in their memories a rich tradition of song.

We will examine two versions of "Pretty Polly" as sung by the traditional Appalachian musicians Dock Boggs (1898-1971) and Jean Ritchie (1922-2015). Both grew up in the region, and both learned the song as children from older musicians in their families or communities. Although the two versions were recorded in the same year and share many elements in common, they also contain significant differences. These differences reveal the influence of oral tradition and provide insight into the values and practices of folk music culture.

Dock Boggs

Dock Boggs was born in the small town of Norton, Virginia, the youngest of ten children. Boggs grew up in a musical household: His father sang and several of his older siblings played the banjo. However, none of the children received a formal music education. Instead, they taught each other or sought guidance from other musicians in the community. Boggs began playing on his oldest brother's banjo, and he learned "Pretty Polly"[6] from his family. He developed a unique playing style based on his observation of African American banjo players at dances, and he sought out the guidance of other black musicians who worked in the area. As a child, however, he never imagined that he might pursue a career in music.

Image 5.9: Dock Boggs often played a banjo very much like this one.
Source: Wikimedia Commons
Attribution: User "Arent"
License: CC BY-SA 3.0

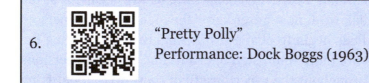

6.   "Pretty Polly"
      Performance: Dock Boggs (1963)

This changed in the 1920s, when parallel technological developments—radio and **field recording**—fed a booming market for rural Southern music. Radio revealed the enormous demand for rural music, especially among those who had moved to northern cities in pursuit of industrial jobs. Many stations began broadcasting regular "barn dance" programs, which eventually provided work to musicians. At the same time, record companies began sending field representatives into rural Southern communities in pursuit of marketable sounds. Before the 1920s, commercial recordings could only be made in studios, most of which were located in New York City. Beginning in 1923, however, Southern musicians were recorded on site using portable equipment.

Boggs had gone to work in the coal mines at the age of twelve, although he continued to play for dances—a source of conflict with his wife, who saw music as a sinful pursuit. During the 1920s, however, he began to see the possibility of a different life. Instead of waiting for a local opportunity, he travelled north to make his first recordings. In 1927 he recorded eight songs for Brunswick in New York City, and in 1929 he recorded a further four songs for Lonesome Ace in Chicago. Just as Boggs glimpsed a professional music career on the horizon, however, the stock market crash of 1929 inaugurated the Great Depression. Doors closed and he returned to the mines.

Although Boggs did not abandon music altogether, hard times lead him to pawn his banjo in the late 1930s, and he did not perform at all for the next quarter century. He had left the coal mines in 1954, ending a 44 year career during which he had miraculously escaped serious injury. Boggs settled down to a quiet retirement. In 1963, however, his fortunes shifted yet again. Beginning in the previous decade, an enthusiasm for Appalachian folk music had swept northern college campuses as part of what is known as the **folk revival**. One of the leading figures in the revival, Mike Seeger, had heard and appreciated Boggs's early recordings, and he set out to find him. Within weeks of their first meeting, Seeger had booked appearances for Boggs at all of the major folk festivals and begun to record his repertoire of songs. By the time he passed away, Boggs was firmly ensconced as a major figure in American folk music history.

"Pretty Polly" was among the songs that Boggs recorded in 1927, but for the purpose of sound quality we will examine his 1963 recording for Folkways records. Even these two performances by the same musician are quite different. Boggs does not sing the same set of verses in 1963 that he had sung in his youth, and his timing and inflection have also changed. This is probably not intentional. Folk musicians do not seek to replicate a single ideal performance, and they are prone to forget, discard, alter, and create verses.

Jean Ritchie[7]

Although she was a generation younger, Jean Ritchie's childhood was very similar to that of Boggs. She was the youngest of fourteen children born to a farming couple in Perry County, Kentucky. Her family carried on a rich tradition of ballad singing, and two of her older sisters were in fact recorded by the most famous Appalachian ballad hunter, Cecil Sharp, in 1917. Ritchie's family believed strongly in education, and she graduated from the University of Kentucky with a degree in social work in 1946. She took a job in her field, but also pursued music seriously, making her first of many recordings in 1952. Ritchie benefited from the folk revival, which provided a large and interested audience for her music.

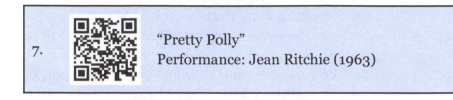

7.   "Pretty Polly"
Performance: Jean Ritchie (1963)

Ritchie was an accomplished ballad singer, but she is best remembered for her role in popularizing the instrument heard on this recording, the Appalachian dulcimer. The Appalachian dulcimer is a type of fretted **zither**, examples of which can be found in many traditions around the world. It is descended from a German instrument and was first built by immigrant craftspeople in Pennsylvania. The Appalachian dulcimer became popular in parts of the region because it is easy to build and play. The body is a simple box. Although the melody is only played on the highest string (or pair of strings), all of the strings are strummed at the same time. The dulcimer can be used to play simple tunes on its own or to accompany singing, although Ritchie in fact preferred to sing her ballads unaccompanied, as she had learned them.

Image 5.10: Jean Ritchie was the principal proponent of the Appalachian dulcimer in the second half of the 20th century.
Source: Wikimedia Commons
Attribution: Matthew Vanitas
License: CC BY-SA 3.0

Ritchie's father played the Appalachian dulcimer, but because he valued the instrument so highly he forbade his children to touch it. Ritchie, however, could not resist, and she taught herself to play in secret. After she had demonstrated a gift for the instrument, her father conceded to teach her. This story is typical of instrumentalists in the Appalachian folk tradition. Children were almost never encouraged to begin playing an instrument or provided with formal instruction. Instead, those who were interested would figure out how to play independently by listening, watching, and experimenting.

Comparing Two Renditions of "Pretty Polly"

The first difference between the Boggs and Ritchie recordings is the instrumental accompaniment: banjo for Boggs, dulcimer for Ritchie. Both singers, however, provide their own accompaniment, which is typical of ballad performances (when they are accompanied at all). Boggs uses the banjo to provide rhythms while at the same time picking out the melody as he sings it. The dulcimer also provides rhythm, but Ritchie does not play the melody while she sings. Instead, she plays various **countermelodies** on the dulcimer that are distinct from but compliment the sung melody. Both performers provide instrumental interludes between some of the verses.

The melodies sung by Boggs and Ritchie, however, are not quite the same. Each follows the same general shape, starting low, moving to a higher range, and returning to the low range, and the beginnings are almost identical. There are differences, however, in pitch, rhythm, and general timing. The two singers start at the same tempo, but Boggs gets considerably faster as he goes.

We might also compare Boggs and Ritchie as singers. Both sing in a plain, straightforward style, almost as if they are speaking. Neither uses **vibrato**. They also don't seem to put any particular effort into expressing the meaning of the text or creating an emotional effect. Instead, each simply sings the words, expecting the story to have an impact because of its dramatic contents, not because of the way in which those contents are communicated. All of this is typical of traditional Appalachian ballad singers.

The most obvious distinction between the recordings, perhaps, lies in the text. Boggs and Ritchie each start the song in quite a different way. Boggs begins with a first person recollection of courting Pretty Polly. This is reasonable, since he is a male singer, but also strange, since he reverts to the third person in the fourth verse. This is perhaps evidence that he learned several versions of the ballad over the years and combined verses from different sources. The first three verses in Ritchie's version are also in the first person, but this is because she is giving voice to the characters in turn. Her last four verses describe the conclusion of the scene in third person and offer a moralizing final thought. (Other singers, such as David Lindley, have been known to change the end of the story, allowing Polly to turn the knife on her assailant and walk away alive.)

Although the two recordings are obviously of the same song, they have only four verses in common—and even those are not identical. Boggs sings four verses that Ritchie does not, while Ritchie's final three verses were not sung by Boggs. This observation only applies to these specific recordings, of course. Both singers performed different sets of verses on different occasions, depending on either the setting or their ability to remember the words.

"Pretty Polly" as sung by Dock Boggs (1963)	"Pretty Polly" as sung by Jean Ritchie (1963)
Oh I used to be a rambler, I stayed around in town, I courted Pretty Polly, such beauty never been found.	
Pretty Polly, Pretty Polly, oh yonder she stands, With rings on her fingers and lily-white hands	
Pretty Polly, Pretty Polly come take a walk with me When we get married some pleasure to see	Polly, Pretty Polly, come go along with me, Before we get married some pleasure to see.
He led her over hills and valleys so deep At last Pretty Polly, she began to weep	
Oh Willie, oh Willie, I'm afraid of your way All minding to ramble and lead me astray	Oh Willie, Oh Willie, I'm 'fraid of your ways. I'm afraid you will lead my poor body astray.
Pretty Polly, Pretty Polly, you guessin' 'bout right, I dug on your grave two-thirds of last night	Now Polly, Pretty Polly, you're guessin' about right. I dug on your grave the best part of last night.

She went on a piece farther and what did she spy? A new-dug grave and a spade lying by She threw her arms around him and began for to weep At last Pretty Polly, sure fell asleep	Oh she stepped a few steps farther, and what did she spy, But a new dug-in grave, and the spade lyin' nigh. Oh he stabbed her through the heart and her heart's blood did flow, And into the grave Pretty Polly she did go. Now he threw a little dirt over her and started for home, Leaving no-one behind but the wild birds to mourn. It's a debt to the devil for Willie must pay For killing Pretty Polly and running away.

FRANZ SCHUBERT, "ELF KING"

For our next example, we will return to the Viennese composer Franz Schubert. We have already examined his approach to musical storytelling using the song cycle as a vehicle. Now we will see how he tells a complex story within a single song. Our example will be perhaps his most famous song, "Elf King" (1815; German: "Erlkönig"). This ballad was inspired by centuries of folk tradition, but also exhibits Schubert's thorough rejection of folk style.

Seeing as Schubert's career was addressed in the previous section, we will start right in with the ballad itself. Before we can discuss the music, however, we must examine the text. And before we can examine the text, we must know something about the famous and influential poet who wrote it, Johann Wolfgang von Goethe (1749-1832).

Image 5.11: This lithograph by Josef Kriehuber was completed in 1846—nearly two decades after Schubert's death.
Source: Wikipedia
Attribution: Josef Kriehuber
License: Public Domain

Johann Wolfgang von Goethe

For not being a musician himself, Goethe had an enormous influence on German song composers of the era. To begin with, he wrote hundreds of poetic texts that were intended to be set to music—and indeed, countless composers set his texts thousands of times. However, Goethe also had very strong opinions about *how* his texts should be set to music. These were informed by his fascination with folk culture, which—following the ideas of Herder—he esteemed highly.

Image 5.12: This portrait of Goethe was completed by Johann Heinrich Wilhelm Tischbein in 1786.
Source: Wikimedia Commons
Attribution: Johann Heinrich Wilhelm Tischbein
License: Public Domain

Goethe desired that composers setting his texts do their best to imitate folk style, which we have seen well represented in the ballad "Pretty Polly." Specifically, he thought that all such songs should be strophic, that they should be simple and accessible, and that the composer should make no effort to interpret the text through music. The purpose of the musical setting, in Goethe's mind, was simply to allow the text to be sung. The listener's focus should be entirely on the words, which the singer would interpret through subtle variations from verse to verse.

Goethe studied folk poetry closely and imitated a number of folk forms in his own song texts. One of these was the ballad. Goethe was particularly influenced by the ballad forms of northern Europe, which had a unique set of characteristics. The stories told in such ballads were preoccupied with supernatural forces and often included dialogue between human and non-human characters. They also ended in disaster. (All of this is true of "The Gosport Tragedy," which concludes with a ghost taking her revenge, although the supernatural element is absent in "Pretty Polly.")

"Elf King"

Goethe and other German poets who took their inspiration from European folk traditions often began by translating folk ballads into their own language. Such was the origin of "Elf King," which began life as a Danish folk ballad and was first translated by Herder. (The German title of the ballad, "Erlkönig," in fact represents a mistranslation from the Dutch original; "Erlkönig" means "King of the Alder Trees," while the original title, "Ellerkonge," means "King of the Elves.") Goethe's version of the ballad tells the same story as the Dutch original, but the specific words are entirely his own.

Here is the text to Goethe's poem. This literal translation does not capture the meter or rhyme scheme of the original, but it tells the story as Goethe intended:

Who rides so late through night and wind?
It is the father with his child.
He has the little one well in the arm
He holds him secure, he holds him warm.

"My son, why hide your face in fear?"
"See you not, Father, the Elf King?
The Elf King with crown and flowing cloak?"
"My son, it is a wisp of fog."

"You sweet child, come along with me!
Such wonderful games I'll play with you;
Many lovely flowers are at the shore,
My mother has many golden garments."

"My father, my father, and do you not hear,
What the Elf King quietly promises to me?"
"Be calm, stay calm, my child;
The wind is rustling the dry leaves."

"Won't you come along with me, my fine boy?
My daughters shall attend to you so nicely;
My daughters do their nightly dance,
And they will rock you and dance you and sing you to sleep."

"My father, my father, do you not see there,
Elf King's daughters in that dark place?"
"My son, my son, I see it definitely
It is the willow trees looking so grey."

"I love you; I'm charmed by your beautiful shape;
And if you are not willing, then I will use force."
"My father, my father, now he has taken hold of me!
Elf King has hurt me!"

The father shudders, he rides swiftly,
He holds in arm the groaning child,
He reaches the farmhouse with effort and urgency;
In his arms, the child was dead.

translation from CPDL

Image 5.13: Moritz von Schwind painted this scene, entitled *Der Erlkönig (The Elf King)*, in 1830.
Source: Wikimedia Commons
Attribution: Moritz von Schwind
License: Public Domain

In writing his version of the ballad, Goethe used simple language that reflected the speech of ordinary Germans. The structure of his poem, however, is fairly sophisticated. The first and last stanzas are spoken in the voice of an unidentified narrator. The first sets the scene, while the last delivers the tragic conclusion. The internal stanzas consist entirely of speech from the three characters: father, son, and Elf King. The father and son converse in stanzas two, four, and six, the son expressing his fear and the father offering assurances that there is no real danger. The Elf King seeks to tempt the child away in stanzas three and five. In stanza seven, the Elf King changes strategies and takes the child by force, provoking a frenzied response. The poem can be read literally or as a metaphor for childhood illness and death.

Goethe first created his ballad for use in a play entitled *The Fisherwoman* (1782). In the first scene of the play, the title character is seen washing dishes and singing a simple folk song ("Elf King"), as befits her lowly social status. The music was composed by the actress herself, Corona Schröter. In setting the poem, Schröter adhered closely to Goethe's preferences. She created a strophic setting in which every verse of the ballad is sung to the same melody. That melody, in turn, is charming in its simplicity. Schröter makes no effort to capture the drama or terror of the text in her music. In short, it is easy to hear her version[8] as being a "real" folk song.

8.  This first setting of Goethe's poem is quite unlike Schubert's "Elf King."

		"Elf King" Composer: Franz Schubert Performance: Dietrich Fischer-Dieskau, accompanied by Gerald Moore (1988 remaster).
Time	**Form**	**What to listen for**
0'00"	Introduction	The piano accompaniment seems to echo the beating of the horse's hooves and the blowing of the wind; use of the minor mode sets a serious tone
0'23"	Stanza 1	This stanza is delivered entirely in the narrator's voice, which is in the middle of the singer's range
0'56"	Stanza 2	This stanza is split between the father's voice (low range) and son's voice (high range)
1'29"	Stanza 3	This stanza is delivered in the Elf King's voice (high range); the music changes to the major mode and the volume decreases
1'52"	Stanza 4	This stanza begins in the son's voice and concludes in the father's voice; the music returns to the minor mode and the volume increases
2'14"	Stanza 5	This stanza is delivered in the Elf King's voice (high range); the music again changes to the major mode and the volume decreases
2'32"	Stanza 6	This stanza begins in the son's voice and concludes in the father's voice; the music returns to the minor mode and the volume increases
3'00"	Stanza 7	This stanza begins in the Elf King's voice and concludes in the son's voice; the music begins in the major mode but quickly returns to minor
3'24"	Stanza 8	This stanza is delivered in the narrator's voice

3'39"	The hoofbeats heard in the piano slow to a halt as the father arrives at his destination
3'47"	The final line is delivered without accompaniment; the piano provides a concluding cadence

By the time Schubert took on Goethe's ballad, the text was well known and had been set to music by many composers. Schubert was unknown at the time, but his innovative and compelling version of "Elf King" would attract a great deal of attention and establish him as an important composer of songs.

Schubert completely ignored Goethe's instructions. Instead of taking a folk-like approach, he went to great lengths to capture the characters and events depicted in the text. His setting begins with a turbulent piano introduction, in which we hear both the pounding hooves and raging storm. At the end of the song, we hear in the piano the gradual slowing of the horse as it comes to a clattering stop in front of the farmhouse. All of these are examples of **text painting**, a technique by which composers translate dramatic elements into sound. Text painting, of course, went against the folk tradition, as did using the piano to set a mood. In addition, Schubert's piano part is much too difficult to be genuine folk music. Only a highly accomplished player could ever hope to execute it well.

Schubert's disobedience does not stop there. His setting of the ballad is not strophic but through-composed, with each passage of music carefully designed to express the associated text. Schubert creates a sort of miniature, one-man opera with his setting. Although "Elf King" is performed by a solo singer, that singer assumes all four characters (narrator, father, son, and Elf King) and portrays each in their respective dramatic roles. This is done using a variety of means. To begin with, the voice of each character is heard in a unique range. The narrator sings in a neutral, middle range, while the father sings in the low range, with a deep, booming voice. The son sings in a high, childlike range, while the Elf King sings quietly in an even higher range.

Schubert also uses other techniques to distinguish his characters and bring the scene to life. While the father and son repeat the same melodies and rhythms, the Elf King constantly introduces new musical material as he tries various approaches to tempting the child away. The Elf King is also the only character who sings in the major mode—a musical embodiment of his charming speech. He does not shift to the minor mode until his final threatening words: "then I will use force."

The greatest musical disruption takes place with the final line of text. In order to maximize the impact of the story's tragic conclusion, Schubert silences the piano and has the singer deliver the news out of time and without accompaniment. Following the final two words, "was dead," the piano executes an abrupt cadence and the song is over.

BOBBIE GENTRY, "ODE TO BILLIE JOE"

By rejecting the norms of folk song and making an effort to develop nuanced musical characteristics, Schubert created a compelling ballad that has remained a popular favorite in the intervening centuries. That is not to say, however, that his approach to setting a ballad text is in any way superior to that of the folk tradition, nor that it was destined to replace the folk-inspired approach. Many later song composers used simple, strophic settings to amplify the emotional power of ballad texts and communicate effectively with listeners.

Image 5.14: Although singer-songwriter Bobbie Gentry maintained a successful career into the 1980s, she never surpassed her early hit "Ode to Billie Joe."
Source: Flickr
Attribution: User "oneredsf1"
License: CC BY-NC-SA 2.0

Although there are many excellent examples of 20th-century ballads composed in a folk style, we will examine only one: Bobbie Gentry's 1967 hit "Ode to Billie Joe."[9] Gentry was born in rural Mississippi, and many of her songs describe the difficulties of life in the impoverished regions of the South. She taught herself to play a variety of instruments as a child and wrote her first song at the age of seven. Although she later performed at nightclubs, her ambition was always to be a songwriter, not a singer. When she first recorded "Ode to Billie Joe" as a demo for Capitol records, she only sang the song herself to avoid the cost of hiring a performer.

9. "Ode to Billie Joe"
Performance: Bobbie Gentry (1967)

The producers at Capitol records commissioned arranger Jimmie Haskell to add strings to Gentry's recording, for which she had accompanied herself on acoustic guitar. Haskell wrote parts for four violins and two cellos, which were then recorded and **dubbed** on to the existing demo. Gentry's song also needed to be shortened in length, for the original recording was eight minutes long, containing eleven verses of Billie Joe's story. The final product, at four minutes and fifteen seconds, was still long for a pop single, but the song struck a popular nerve: It spent four weeks at the top of the charts and finished the year in third place.

The song's power lies in its storytelling. The first four verses describe a farming family coming together over the dinner table. In between passing the dishes, they comment on the news that a local boy, Billie Joe MacAllister, had jumped to his death from the Tallahatchie Bridge earlier in the day. Over the course of various dispassionate reminiscences, we learn that the song's female narrator was friends with Billie Joe, and in the fourth verse we are presented with the information that she was seen with Billie Joe just the day before, throwing something off of the same bridge from which he was soon to jump. The final verse takes us one year into the future, at which point the narrator's brother has moved away and her father has died. She reports that she spends most of her time dropping flowers off of the bridge.

The ballad's narrative is bleak throughout, and its portrayal of the characters' stagnation and hopelessness is compelling. The song's greatest power, however, has always lain in its mystery. What did the narrator and Billie Joe throw off of the bridge? Despite being asked throughout her career, Gentry always refused to say. She has also never explained why Billie Joe committed suicide—indeed, she has claimed not to know herself. While the listener is allowed to glimpse the daily life of the song's characters, we are not offered any insight into their thoughts or motivations.

Like "Pretty Polly," "Ode to Billie Joe" uses a simple, repetitive melody as a vehicle for a long, complex, and ultimately tragic story. In fact, the melodies are strikingly similar: Each begins with an ascending melodic gesture, and each repeats its opening melodic phrase at a higher pitch level before returning to the original, lower range. Gentry's melody is just a bit more complex, insofar as it moves to the high range twice and ends with a unique melodic phrase. In both cases, however, the melody serves the same purpose. On the practical side, it provides a vehicle with which the singer can tell the story. On the affective side, it sets an appropriate mood that adds to the story's impact.

While the minor mode of "Pretty Polly" is generally appropriate to a tragic narrative, Gentry takes a different approach. Although her melody contains **blues**-inspired inflections (the third scale degree is sometimes lowered and the seventh scale degree is always lowered), it is accompanied by major-mode harmonies. That, in combination with a lively tempo, produces a sound world that is not necessarily depressing. At the same time, however, the cheerfulness of the tune throws the darkness of the lyrics into sharp relief. According to Gentry, "Ode to Billie Joe" was a study in "unconscious cruelty" that explored the inability of the characters to communicate and empathize with one another. Each is isolated by their own grief. The inexpressive music, therefore, seems to emphasize the repressed emotions hidden by the narrator and her mother.

The various sounds of "Ode to Billie Joe" also give depth to the story and contribute to the song's impact on the listener. We might start with Gentry's voice, which is natural and unaffected. A touch of roughness adds an expressive character to her singing, while also helping the listener to identify her as a regular person. The fact that she is not overly trained as a performer makes her story and emotions seem more authentic. Her guitar accompaniment is sparse and rhythmic, propelling the music along with the minimum of effort. The strings were added to make the album commercially viable, but they also have a dramatic effect. The sliding harmonies emphasize the laziness of the scene, while the final spiraling descent illustrates the flowers falling from the bridge into the muddy water below.

EPIC RECITATION

Civilizations around the world have long used song as a vehicle for telling lengthy stories, or **epics**, many of which concern the founding of an empire. Here, we will consider two examples: an epic of ancient Greece, *The Iliad*, and an epic of the Mali Empire, *The Sunjata Story*. These two epics have a great deal in common, for each details the episodic struggles and triumphs of a great hero. The traditions themselves also seem to have elements in common. However, we cannot directly compare the recitation practices associated with these two texts for a simple reason: While the practice of sung epic recitation is alive and well in West Africa, it has not been practiced in Greece for two millenia, and we therefore can only guess at the details.

ANCIENT GREECE: *THE ILIAD*

In Chapter 4, we explored the origins of European opera and the influence of ancient Greek music on the genre. One of the aspects of ancient Greek music that directly inspired the creation of opera was the notion that ancient Greek poetry and drama were sung in their entirety, not spoken (like what is witnessed when attending a Shakespearean play). Although the lack of surviving musical notation from the period leaves us with little evidence as to how ancient Greek drama actually sounded, the few surviving musical fragments and our theoretical knowledge of both music and poetic recitation in ancient Greece provide us with a good idea as to how Greek poetry and drama might have been sung.

Greek drama grew out of a tradition of community gathering and singing, particularly during festivals and sacrifices in praise of gods such as Dionysus or Apollo. To accompany these celebrations, there would be songs of praise setting dramatic poetry pertaining to the celebrated figures or other mythical beings. Although the tradition began with the community singing these songs in a chorus setting, eventually solo singers would emerge from the chorus to act out the part of the god or hero, while the chorus acted as a narrator or took part in sung dialogue with the soloist. Thus, the beginnings of Greek theatre emerged, and the solo actor and chorus dynamic became a staple in the Greek theatre tradition.

Poetic Meter and Sung Recitation

Many Greek dramas have been preserved through their texts, and many have become well-known classics in today's world. However, through further study of some of the fragments of poetry from ancient Greece, it is now believed that the poetry and dramas were meant to be performed in musical settings. In later Greek dramas, melodic notation has preserved the ancient sung melodies, but there has yet to be found any surviving form of rhythmic notation from this time. It is understood, however, that the rhythm of the sung words was based off the **prosody** or meter of the poetry. Poetic meter, similar to musical meter, structures the rhythm of spoken (or in this case, sung) prose. A common example of a poetic meter used in Greek drama is **dactylic hexameter**. In this type of meter, a poetic phrase is divided into six **feet** (similar to measures in musical notation). Each foot is divided by what is called a dactyl, a long syllable followed by two short syllables (in this type of meter, a dactyl can also be substituted by a spondee, or two long syllables). When recited, the spoken or sung phrase would follow this pattern of long and short syllables, producing a steady rhythm:

> (long-short-short) (long-short-short) (long-short-short) (long-short-short)
> (long-short-short) (long-short-short)

One famous example of a Greek epic in dactylic hexameter is Homer's *Iliad*. The *Iliad* was written to be accompanied by a four-stringed lyre, and although there are no surviving fragments of actual melodic notation attached to the poetry, it is believed that this epic was meant to be sung in its entirety. In our example, an interpretation of a passage from the *Iliad*[10] by classicist Stefan Hagel, the consistent "long-short-short" rhythm of the dactylic hexameter is apparent. The sung melody is an improvisation based on the inflection of the text; for instance, if the approximate pitch goes up at the end of the word in natural speech, it likewise ascends to a higher note when sung. As in this example, the melodies of poetic recitations were probably folk-like in nature: that is to say, simple and repetitive. The tempo is set by the content of the text. In scenes of heightened tension the music may be fast, while the music used in describing a more solemn scene may be slow.

10.    *The Iliad*
Performance: Stefan Hagel (2017)

Although most of the musical elements of Homer's dramas are uncertain and therefore must be left up to the performer's interpretation, which is based on the nature of the text, there are several surviving fragments of poetry and drama written in stone or on papyrus that are accompanied by written musical notation. The ancient Greeks had a system of musical notation in which a pitch would be associated with a particular symbol, usually a symbol from the Greek alphabet. This pitch's symbol would be written above the syllable of the sung word. One of the few surviving fragments of music, written on papyrus, comes from Euripides's

Image 5.15: This stone tablet found in Delphi contains musical notation for a hymn to Apollo. The consistent line of text represents the poetry. The symbols above the text represent musical notes.
Source: Wikimedia Commons
Attribution: User "Ziggur"
License: Public Domain

Image 5.16: This fragment of papyrus contains a chorus from Euripides's drama *Orestes*.
Source: Wikimedia Commons
Attribution: User "Ziggur"
License: Public Domain

Orestes. The play tells the story of Orestes, the son of Clytemnestra and Agamemnon, who kills his mother to seek revenge for his father's death. The fragment is of a song sung by the chorus in unison. They sing of Orestes being chased by his mother's furies, or spirits of revenge.

Unlike the simple, repetitive melody that Homer's words would have most likely been performed to, the melody of the *Orestes* chorus,[11] believed to be composed by Euripides himself, is through-composed. The melody also differs from the Homeric poetry in that it doesn't follow the natural inflection of the spoken Greek text, though there are instances in which important words are sounded at a higher pitch for emphasis. The rhythm follows the dochmiac poetic meter, a meter typically used to convey agitation, anxiety, or distress. This sense of distress can certainly be heard in our example. There, we also see the choir accompanied by an aulos, a double pipe instrument. This instrument was often used to accompany choruses in dramatic productions.

Image 5.17: This piece of pottery, which dates to about 480 BCE, depicts a woman playing the aulos.
Source: Wikimedia Commons
Attribution: Marie-Lan Nguyen
License: CC BY 2.5

11.  Ancient Greek epic recitation can be contrasted with this surviving vocal composition, which does not follow the natural inflections of Greek text.

As is evident through this performance, with musical translation and a bit of reconstruction this ancient music is now able to be performed with near-perfect historical accuracy. The revival of the music alongside the poetry sheds a new light on the emotional impact of this drama on ancient audiences and allows modern audiences a glimpse of this once-forgotten art that inspired future forms of sung drama.

WEST AFRICA: *THE SUNJATA STORY*

Perhaps the richest extant tradition of epic recitation is to be found among the Mandinka people of West Africa, and their most valued epic is certainly the story of Sunjata, the founder of the ancient Mali Empire. A complete recitation of the Sunjata story can take between six and eight hours. The telling of the story is therefore a remarkable feat in and of itself—all the more so because its words are maintained entirely in the memories of the storytellers. The epic is the property of the *jali* caste, members of which are responsible for passing it from generation to generation.

Founded in 1240, the Mali Empire occupied all or part of half a dozen modern West African countries. It flourished until 1645, when conflict over accession to the throne resulted in the collapse of the empire. Although the Mali Empire was large and powerful, its history has largely been told from outside perspectives. This is because its inhabitants did not cultivate

Image 5.18: Here, a jali in Burkina Faso plays a typical instrument, the *balafon*.
Source: Wikimedia Commons
Attribution: User "PGskot"
License: CC BY-SA 4.0

written language, instead maintaining knowledge by means of oral transmission—a process that carries into the present day. The Mandinka, who currently number about 32 million, are the descendents of the Mali Empire, and they continue to celebrate their common heritage through story and song.

Mandinkan Social Structure and the Jali

Before we can examine Mandinkan storytelling practices, we need to know something about the people who tell those stories. Traditionally, Mandinkan

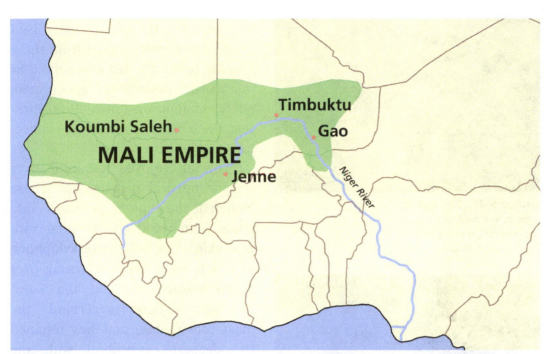

Image 5.19: This map indicates the territory governed by the Mali Empire between 1240 and 1645.
Source: Wikimedia Commons
Attribution: User "Roke~commonswiki"
License: CC BY-SA 3.0

society was organized according to a **caste system**, meaning that social roles were determined by birth and were strictly defined. Members of the jali caste were musicians and storytellers, and their role was to serve the aristocratic caste. (You might be familiar with the French term "griot," which is more widely used in the West, but members of the community generally prefer the term "jali.") Although the caste system is officially defunct today, it still exerts an influence on modern society, and jali continue to pass their knowledge and skills down through family lines.

The jali caste was not high ranking, but its members were considered to have special powers and to occupy a unique place in the community. They were considered ritually impure, and were prohibited from wearing the clothes of the aristocracy or sitting on their beds. When they died, they were buried separately from other members of the community. Jali also could not hold political office. At the same time, jali served as advisors to aristocrats and could therefore be very powerful. If a jali was captured in battle, they could not be killed or enslaved, but were expected to serve their captor as they had served their previous master.

The responsibilities of the jali were many. They were musicians, and as such they provided ceremonial music for naming ceremonies, marriages, and agricultural celebrations. They also entertained at dances and wrestling matches and sang the praises of the aristocrats they served. However, the primary role of the jali was to maintain and transmit the knowledge and traditions of the community, including histories, genealogies, proverbs, and laws. If the jali did not fulfill

Image 5.20: The *ngoni*.
Source: Wikimedia Commons
Attribution: User "Atamari"
License: CC BY-SA 4.0

Image 5.21: The *balafon*.
Source: Wikimedia Commons
Attribution: User "Redmedea"
License: CC BY-SA 3.0

Image 5.22: The *kora*.
Source: Wikimedia Commons
Attribution: Pongsapak Kiatpreecha
License: CC BY-SA 4.0

their function, therefore, society itself would disintegrate. Apart from these weighty tasks, the jali also served as moralists, counsellors, spokesmen, public announcers, mediators, messengers, buffoons, porters, tax collectors, and hairdressers.

The jali enjoyed dominion over specific musical instruments. These included the *ngoni* (a small lute made from wood and covered with goat skin), the *balafon* (a xylophone in which wood keys are strung over gourd resonators), and the *kora*. The last of these is certainly the most remarkable, and has retained the deepest connection with the jali tradition. The *kora* is a type of harp lute, the strings of which are suspended above a large resonator made out of a calabash gourd covered with cow skin. The strings are plucked with the thumb and index finger of each hand. All three of these instruments are used to play complex melodic patterns constructed out of complementary interlocking parts— parts that, at least on the balafon and kora, are each played with one of the two hands.

Traditionally, these instruments were only played by men. Boys would begin to learn from their fathers or uncles, and a jali's musical education would culminate in the building of his own instrument. A jali also needed to master the tuning systems, which are different for each instrument and quite unlike anything found in Europe. A result of this is that West African music can sound out of tune, although in fact each pitch is carefully positioned. Female jali were musicians too, but they were only trained to sing and play a percussion instrument called the *neo*. Today, of course, many women excel as performers on all of these instruments.

The Sunjata Story

The Sunjata story is well known, for it has been frequently published in both novel and verse form over the past century and is often included in world literature courses. It constitutes a mythologized retelling of how the historical figure Sunjanta unified the Mali Empire and became its first ruler. According to the epic, Sunjata—whose glorious conquests had been foretold by a soothsayer—was the son of the Mandinkan king's second wife. As a child, however, Sunjata could not walk, and when the king died it was his half brother who ascended to the throne. Sunjata and his mother were exiled and found a new home in the Mema kingdom, where Sunjata grew strong and gained such widespread support that he was designated heir to the throne. When the Mandinka kingdom was attacked by a malicious power, Sunjata came to the rescue while his half-brother fled in fear. Sunjata's coalition of small kingdoms defeated the aggressor and resulted in the founding of the Mali Empire.

There are not many recordings of the Sunjata story in existence, for it is carefully guarded. The epic is often related as part of religious ceremonies, and it is believed to bring blessings to all who hear it. Listeners, however, are prohibited from recording these performances. The recordings that are available have been made at formal concerts or recording sessions, and therefore lack many of the elements that would characterize a more authentic performance. These recordings tend to be brief, both because they often omit episodes from the story and because they lack the participatory embellishments that bring the story to life when it is shared in a communal context. Listeners, for example, might join together in singing hymns at appropriate points, or jali might shout out praise songs dedicated to historical figures as they enter the narrative. Participants will also interrupt the story to donate money in return for blessings.

In considering our recordings, therefore, we must be aware that they offer only a glimpse of Sunjata epic recitation as a living practice. Apart from being brief, they are in no way definitive. There are variations in the words that are used to tell the story and even in the events that are related (sometimes, for example, Sunjata and his mother are exiled from the Mali kingdom, while other times they choose to leave for their own safety). The epic is also not always sung to the same melody, nor is the accompaniment stable. The underlying instrumental music might be supplied by kora, balafon, ngoni, or even guitar, and the pattern played by these instruments—known as the **kumbengo**—can vary in large and small ways.

Comparing Two Renditions of *The Sunjata Story*

We will begin with a recording made of a 1987 performance in which jali Djelimady Sissoko recites the epic while Sidiki Diabaté accompanies him on the kora.[12] Like all performances, this begins with an instrumental improvisation. At first there is no pulse, but gradually the player settles in to the *kumbengo*. In this case, we hear the most typical *kumbengo* for a Sunjata epic recitation, that associated with the Sunjata praise song.[13] The praise song is entirely separate from the epic, but it might be sung during a ritual performance of the epic and the two are closely connected.

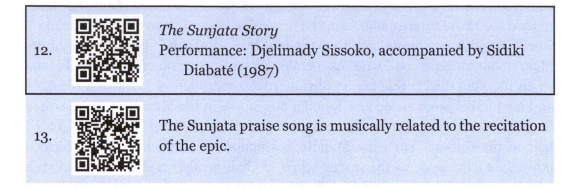

12.		*The Sunjata Story* Performance: Djelimady Sissoko, accompanied by Sidiki Diabaté (1987)
13.		The Sunjata praise song is musically related to the recitation of the epic.

The singer enters at the top of his range and then descends down the scale outlined in the accompaniment. This is the typical melodic shape for epic recitation, and it is influenced by the Mandinka language, which is tonal. This means that the inflection of vowel sounds changes the meaning of a word. Because most Mandinka words inflect in a downward direction, setting the words to music naturally produces a descending melody. The vocal ability of a singer is judged in terms of power and confidence. However, the most important quality for a singer to possess is truthfulness. A good singer, therefore, is one whose words are true, regardless of the sound of their voice. The truthfulness of Djelimady Sissoko's words is confirmed by Sidiki Diabaté, who fulfills the role of witness by chanting *naamu*, or "indeed," at the end of every sentence. (If the jali makes a mistake in telling the story, which frequently occurs, the witness must correct it.)

The "groove" is an important characteristic of this performance, as is the rhythmic interaction between the singer and kora player. However, these elements are not simple to perceive or explain. While the repetitiveness of the accompaniment makes it obvious that there is a regular pulse, that pulse is constantly shifting. Try tapping your foot along to the music, and you will soon find that you have lost the beat. This is the result of a concept of rhythm that is based on patterns, not European-style meter. West African musicians, for example, do not count beats in the way European musicians do, and they do not recognize a downbeat (the first and strongest pulse in a metrical grouping). Instead, they transform rhythmic patterns in the way that a kaleidoscope transforms images.

This concept of constant transformation is central to the practice of West African instrumentalists. In this recording, the kora player never repeats the *kumbengo* pattern unchanged for long. Instead, he makes constant alterations to the rhythmic and pitch content, adding syncopations and ornaments of unending variety. He also interjects virtuosic flourishes in between the phrases of the story. Periodically, the singer pauses to allow for an extended kora solo.[14] While the basic musical contents of the *kumbengo* are quite simple, therefore, the work of the kora player is complex and sophisticated.

We will briefly examine a second performance of episodes from the Sunjata story for the sake of comparison.[15] This rendition, recorded in 2014, is accompanied by the balafon. Although the balafon, which is a percussion instrument, is quite different from the kora in terms of construction, playing technique, and sound, it executes exactly the same function. Again, the performance opens with an extended solo by the balafon player, Fodé Lassana Diabaté, who eventually settles into a *kumbengo* that is very similar to that played on the kora. Again, the balafon player constantly alters his accompaniment, adding rhythmic and melodic variations. And again, he occasionally takes the opportunity to improvise extended instrumental solos in between sections of the recited text.

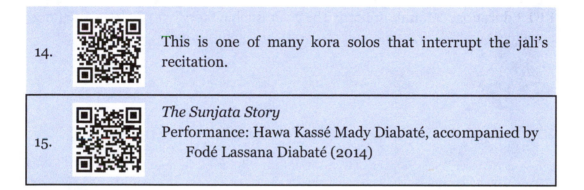

14. This is one of many kora solos that interrupt the jali's recitation.

15. *The Sunjata Story*
Performance: Hawa Kassé Mady Diabaté, accompanied by Fodé Lassana Diabaté (2014)

The work of the singer, Hawa Kassé Mady Diabaté, can also be compared to the previous recording. Most of her phrases begin high in her range and descend down the scale. She regularly enters during different parts of the *kumbengo* and does not align her phrases with the accompaniment. And her vocal production is powerful and commanding. She periodically plays a simple percussion instrument, known as a *shekere*, that consists of a gourd with a beaded cover.

Although this rendition is excellent, its context—amplified on a stage before a silent audience—is far removed from that in which the Sunjata story has thrived for eight hundred years. Jali storytelling is meant to be highly participatory, and this epic only lives when it is endorsed and enriched by the community.

RESOURCES FOR FURTHER LEARNING

Print

Church, Michael, ed. *The Other Classical Musics: Fifteen Great Traditions.* Boydell Press, 2015.

D'Angour, Armand and Tom Phillips. *Music, Text, and Culture in Ancient Greece.* Oxford University Press, 2018.

Fischer-Dieskau, Dietrich. *Schubert's Songs: A Biographical Study*. Limelight Editions, 1984.

Gaines, Zeffie. "A Black Girl's Song: Misogynoir, Love, and Beyoncé's Lemonade." *Taboo: The Journal of Culture and Education* 16, no. 2 (2017): 96-114.

Gustavson, Kent. *Blind But Now I See: The Biography of Music Legend Doc Watson*. Blooming Twig Books, 2012.

Stone, Ruth M. *Music in West Africa: Experiencing Music, Expressing Culture*. Oxford University Press, 2004.

Taruskin, Richard. *Music in the Nineteenth Century: The Oxford History of Western Music*. Oxford University Press, 2009.

Online

KET Education, "Mountain Born: The Jean Ritchie Story": https://www.ket.org/education/resources/mountain-born-jean-ritchie-story/

Stories without Words

Esther M. Morgan-Ellis

INTRODUCTION

Over the course of the past three chapters, we have examined a variety of musical forms and works that communicate narratives. These have included examples that rely on staged action, such as opera and ballet, and examples that incorporate a sung text. In this chapter, we will encounter music that tells a story without that aid of staged action or performed text. This music will use sound alone—perhaps supplemented by a written explanation—to communicate with the listener.

But how can sound tell a story? How can we know what music is about without seeing the story acted out or hearing the story told through words? In many ways, music is handicapped as a storytelling medium, for it cannot be specific. Sound cannot tell us the name of a character, or provide details about a dramatic setting, or convey dialogue, or even communicate a plot of any complexity. At the same time, sound can also be a particularly powerful storytelling medium. Because of its potential to provoke emotions in the listener, it can tell compelling stories on the emotional or psychological level. Music can also incorporate the sounds that would be heard in a specific setting or that might accompany a sequence of events, thereby recreating the aural experience of a story.

In general, music is able to communicate specific content using three techniques. While these have been primarily exploited in the European concert tradition, they are not unique to Western music. The three techniques are **mimesis**, **quotation**, and the use of **musical topics**. After an introduction to each in turn, we will see them at work in a variety of examples.

Mimesis is the simplest technique, and also the most common across traditions. In cases of mimesis, music imitates real-world sounds in order to call elements of the physical world to mind. These sounds might include birdsong, animal cries, trains, explosions, footsteps—anything that makes noise. Mimesis can be used to create a dramatic scene using sound alone.

In the case of **quotation**, one piece of music incorporates a passage from another. Quotation can be used in many different ways. Sometimes, the quoted music will have a text that the listener is expected to know. In this way, a composer can include specific dramatic content without employing text directly. Other times, the quoted music can be understood as part of a scene. For example, the American composer Charles Ives quoted the music of Wagner in his piano composition *Concord Sonata*. His intent was to recreate the living room of the Alcott family, with Louisa May playing her favorite tunes at the piano.

When a composer employs **musical topics**, they refer to recognizable musical styles or clichés in order to communicate with the listener. Some musical topics are associated with specific genres or traditions, such as military marches, waltzes, or Christian hymns. Upon hearing one of these styles referenced in a musical work, the listener might think of an army, or a ball, or a church service. In this way, the composer can transport an audience to a specific place.

Other musical topics rely on the use of standardized techniques to portray specific scenes, such as a storm, or a romantic tryst, or shepherds tending their flocks. This approach builds on the tradition of music for the theater. An operatic love scene, for example, is usually accompanied by slow, sweeping gestures in the strings, while shepherds appear to the accompaniment of droning bagpipes (usually imitated by orchestral instruments), flute, and double reeds (usually oboe or English horn). Musical topics often incorporate mimesis, although the technique is more complex. Hunting scenes, for example, were long set to music that used mimetic techniques to imitate the sounds of horses galloping and hunting horns blasting. The imitation of hoofbeats is an example of mimesis, but the hunting topic is associated not only with the sounds of hunting but also with the tradition of writing hunting music. The storm topic provides a similar example. While rapid chromatic scales, dynamic swells, and sudden accents can imitate wind blowing through the trees and lightning striking the ground, we recognize storm music primarily because we are familiar with the long tradition of this type of music being used to accompany storm scenes in opera, films, and cartoons.

In the European tradition, instrumental music that claims to tell a specific story or to otherwise communicate **extramusical** information is termed **program music**. This term was first employed in the 19th century, at which point in history a fierce debate took place between various European composers and critics concerning the purpose of music. Some argued in favor of program music, even going so far as to suggest that music could (and should) convey complex philosophical ideas. Wagner belonged to this school of thought. Others advocated on behalf of **absolute music**, or "music for music's sake"—that is, music that does not aspire to be more than sound, and that should be judged on the basis of its form and construction, not its power to communicate. Even in the 19th century, however, program music was not a new thing. As we shall see, earlier European composers had already established the various techniques with which music can communicate meaning. Similarly, composers and performers in other parts of the globe had long exploited sound as a storytelling vehicle.

We will begin, however, in 19th century Europe, with perhaps the most famous piece of program music to emerge from the concert tradition.

HECTOR BERLIOZ, *FANTASTICAL SYMPHONY*

When the French composer Hector Berlioz (1803-1869) premiered what was to be his most famous and influential work, he was only 27 years old. 1830, however, was a big year for the young composer. Not only was his *Fantastical Symphony* (French: *Symphonie Fantastique*) premiered in December at the Paris Conservatory, but he also won the Rome Prize (French: Prix de Rome), the top honor for French composers.

Image 6.1: This photograph of Berlioz was taken in 1863, many decades after his success with *Fantastical Symphony*.
Source: Wikimedia Commons
Attribution: Pierre Petit
License: Public Domain

However, Berlioz's training as a composer had been largely self-directed. His father had intended for him to become a physician, and it was to study medicine at the University of Paris that he had first moved to the city. Berlioz completed medical school, despite his disgust at the task of dissecting dead bodies, but he continued to pursue his musical interests throughout the course of his professional education. He gave up medicine upon graduating in 1824 and enrolled in the Paris Conservatory two years later.

During the **Romantic** era (roughly 1815 to 1900), audiences were fascinated by the personal lives of artists. They tended to understand artistic expression as autobiographical, and they perceived works through the lens of an artist's personal experience. In the case of *Fantastical Symphony* this was easy to do, for Berlioz was directly inspired by his own real-world experiences. Before discussing the symphony, therefore, we must dedicate some attention to Berlioz's love life.

The Origins of Berlioz's Symphony

In 1827, Berlioz attended a series of Shakespearean performances put on in Paris by a company of Irish actors. Over the course of several plays, he became obsessed with the actress Harriet Smithson, whom he saw in the roles of Ophelia (*Hamlet*) and Juliet (*Romeo and Juliet*). His subsequent behavior, which included moving into an apartment from which he could monitor her own dwelling and subjecting her to a deluge of correspondence, can only be described as stalking. She ignored his advances, however, and returned to London in 1829 without ever having met the composer.

Despite never so much as speaking to Harriet, Berlioz felt compelled to channel his passion into musical composition. He let it be widely known that *Fantastical Symphony*, which tells the story of a romantic obsession gone wrong (details later), was about Harriet Smithson.

Image 6.2: Given her fame as an actress, Harriet Smithson was painted many times. This portrait is by George Clint.
Source: Wikimedia Commons
Attribution: George Clint
License: Public Domain

Berlioz's romantic interests were intense but fleeting. He soon recovered from his infatuation with Smithson and in 1830 became engaged to Marie Moke. His status as the winner of the Rome Prize required that he spend several years studying composition in Italy, and while he was abroad he received word from Marie's mother that she was going to marry the wealthy piano manufacturer Camille Pleyel instead. Berlioz flew into a rage. He purchased guns, poison, and a costume, and boarded a train for Paris with the intention of sneaking into the Moke home dressed as a woman and murdering mother, daughter, and fiance before taking his own life. During the course of the trip, however, his passion cooled, and he abandoned the plan before arriving in Paris. He returned to Italy to complete the terms of his award.

Then, in 1832, Harriet Smithson found herself back in Paris. Berlioz saw that she was provided with a ticket to the premiere of his second symphony, entitled *The Return to Life* and conceived of as a sequel to *Fantastical Symphony*. She wrote him a letter complimenting the symphony and the two finally met. They began an affair and married in 1833, although it is widely suspected that Smithson only agreed to the union because of her dire financial situation. The two were not happy, and formally separated in 1843.

In the case of another composer, the above personal details might be gratuitous. In the case of Berlioz, however, they are essential. Not only did his audiences know about his love life, but they relished the opportunity to perceive his music as a window into his most intimate passions. Of course, *Fantastical Symphony* was not altogether autobiographical. In fact, most of the story, to which we will turn now, was lifted from books that Berlioz was reading at the time.

Berlioz went to great trouble to create, revise, and publicize the story told by his music. He published several versions, the last of which accompanied the 1855 version of the **score**. It was important to Berlioz that audiences were familiar with the story. For the 1830 premiere, he saw that his narrative was published in Parisian newspapers and distributed to audience members at the performance. (At this time, it was unusual for concert patrons to be provided with a printed program.) In the 1845 version of the score, Berlioz explained the importance of his narrative: "The following programme must therefore be considered as the spoken text of an opera, which serves to introduce musical movements and to motivate their character and expression." In short, he did not seem to believe that the music could speak entirely for itself.

The Structure and Story of *Fantastical Symphony*

Berlioz subtitled his *Fantastical Symphony* "An Episode in the Life of an Artist, in Five Parts." The artist in question was, of course, himself. The five parts were five distinct movements—an unusual design for a symphony. While most symphonies have four movements, Berlioz was self-consciously following in the footsteps of Ludwig van Beethoven, whose only program symphony—his Symphony No. 6 "Pastoral"—also had five movements. Beethoven's symphony told the story of a visit to the countryside, but it did so in very vague terms. The only texts were the five movement titles, which described the sensation of peace upon arriving in nature, a scene by a brook, a peasant festival, a thunderstorm, and feelings of relief after the storm had passed. To tell his story, Beethoven deployed musical topics associated with the countryside and incorporated mimetic gestures, including orchestral imitations of droning bagpipes and violent lightning strikes. Berlioz used the same techniques, but took the idea of writing a program symphony much further.

Berlioz's five movements are entitled "Reveries—Passions," "A Ball," "Scene in the Fields," "March to the Scaffold," and "Dream of a Witches' Sabbath." In the first movement, a young musician catches sight of his ideal woman and immediately falls in love with her. We learn from Berlioz's text that the musician always hears the same melody in his head when he sees or thinks of her—a melody "in which he recognizes a certain quality of passion, but endowed with the nobility and shyness which he credits to the object of his love." Berlioz termed this melody the "obsession" (French: *idée fixe*).

Image 6.3: This French lithograph imagines the scene at a ball captured in the second movement of Berlioz's symphony. The protagonist is clearly Berlioz himself.
Source: Wikimedia Commons
Attribution: Henri Fantin-Latour
License: CC0

The obsession melody returns in each of the five movements. In the second movement, we hear it when the protagonist glimpses the object of his affection at a ball. In the third movement, the protagonist sits alone in the countryside, listening to shepherds play their pipes. At first he feels hopeful about the future, but he is soon overwhelmed with suspicion and foreboding. The obsession melody reveals the subject of his disturbed brooding.

Because we will examine the fourth and fifth movement in detail, it is worth reading Berlioz's original description of each in full. His text to accompany the fourth movement reads as follows:

Convinced that his love is spurned, the artist poisons himself with opium. The dose of narcotic, while too weak to cause his death, plunges him into a heavy sleep accompanied by the strangest of visions. He dreams that he has killed his beloved, that he is condemned, led to the scaffold and is witnessing *his own execution.* The procession advances to the sound of a march that is sometimes sombre and wild, and sometimes brilliant and solemn, in which a dull sound of heavy footsteps follows without transition the loudest outbursts. At the end of the march, the first four bars of the *idée fixe* reappear like a final thought of love interrupted by the fatal blow.

It is here that we begin to depart notably from reality. Not only did Berlioz never personally have this experience, but it is known with reasonable certainty that he never took drugs of any variety. Instead, he got the idea for this movement from a book he was reading, Thomas De Quincey's *Confessions of an English Opium-Eater* (1821).

March to the Scaffold

	"March to the Scaffold" from *Fantastical Symphony* Composer: Hector Berlioz Performance: London Symphony Orchestra, conducted by Sir Eugene Goossens (2013)

Time	Form	What to listen for
0'00"	"The procession advances to the sound of a march. . ."	A rhythmic pattern played on the timpani sets the scene for a procession
0'28"	". . .that is sometimes sombre and wild, . . ." [March theme A]	This theme, on which we hear many variations, consists of a descending scale with a brief ascending motif at the end
1'40"	". . .and sometimes brilliant and solemn" [March theme B]	This theme, which is considerably louder and more triumphant, features the brass playing dotted rhythms

2'11"	March theme A	The A theme returns briefly, played by the strings and woodwinds in an interlocking texture
2'22"	March theme B	The B theme returns, this time with an active string accompaniment
2'52"	March theme A	The A theme returns as it did before
3'00"		The low brass play the descending scale of the A theme repeatedly at successively higher pitch levels, thereby building intensity
3'14"		The entire orchestra plays the A theme, first in its natural form and then upside down (an ascending scale)
3'40"	Coda	We hear a new theme at a faster tempo
4'17"	"...the first four bars of the idée fixe reappear like a final thought of love..."	We hear the obsession melody in the solo clarinet
4'26"	"...interrupted by the fatal blow."	The melody is cut off by a resounding chord, symbolizing the fall of the guillotine blade; triumphant chords from the brass represent the cheers of the crowd

"March to the Scaffold" exhibits all three of the communication techniques outlined above: mimesis, quotation, and the use of musical topics. For most of the movement, we hear two contrasting march themes, one (according to Berlioz's description) "sombre and wild" and the other "brilliant and solemn." These themes exemplify the use of musical topics. We are able to recognize them immediately as marches due to the tempo, the brisk character, and the instrumentation, which features percussion and brass. In the final passage of the movement, the tempo accelerates and the excitement builds. Then, out of nowhere, we hear the obsession melody played on a solo clarinet. This, of course, is an example of quotation. We are familiar with this melody and we know that it represents the protagonist's beloved. We can easily hear it, therefore, as his final thought of her. Before the melody can conclude, a great noise from the orchestra represents the guillotine blade crashing down. This is followed by two pizzicato "bounces" of the severed head and a series of raucous "cheers" from the crowd. All of this is mimesis, for Berlioz uses the orchestra to represent the sounds of the scene he is portraying.

"March to the Scaffold" was the most successful of the symphony's five movements, and it was frequently programmed as a standalone work during Berlioz's lifetime. However, the final movement, "Dream of a Witches' Sabbath," offers even better examples of our three communication strategies. It is also shows off Berlioz's extraordinary skill at using the orchestra. The music of Berlioz is still studied today by students of **orchestration**, and his 1843 *Treatise on Instrumentation* is still in print. He was also responsible for growing the orchestra in size. Although he wanted 220 musicians for the premiere of *Fantastical Symphony*, he had to settle for a mere 130. In addition to increasing the size of

Image 6.4: Berlioz's large orchestras were also loud. This became a frequent subject for humor throughout his lifetime, as in this 1846 cartoon that portrays the composer in the midst of brass, string basses, and a cannon.

Source: Wikimedia Commons
Attribution: User "Flopinot2012"
License: CC BY-SA 3.0

the string sections, Berlioz increased the number of required wind parts. *Fantastical Symphony* calls for four different types of clarinets, four bassoons, four harps, and an enormous percussion section, in addition to two instruments—the ophicleide (part of the tuba family) and the cornet à pistons (part of the trumpet family)— that were not typically included in the symphony orchestra. The final movement of *Fantastical Symphony* makes the most dramatic use of this extensive orchestral palette.

Dream of a Witches' Sabbath

"Dream of a Witches' Sabbath" from *Fantastical Symphony* Composer: Hector Berlioz Performance: London Symphony Orchestra, conducted by Sir Eugene Goossens (2013)		
Time	**Form**	**What to listen for**
0'00"	"Strange sounds, . . ."	Tremolo in the violins and violas

0'03"	"...groans, ..."	Upward sweeps in the cellos and basses
0'17"	"...outbursts of laughter;..."	Chromatic descent in the violins and violas
0'32"	"...distant shouts which seem to be answered by more shouts."	Call and response between woodwinds and a muted horn
0'53"		All of the preceding material is repeated, with some variations
1'37"	"The beloved melody appears once more, but has now lost its noble and shy character; it is now no more than a vulgar dance tune, trivial and grotesque"	We hear the opening of the obsession melody in the clarinet; it is played at a fast tempo with an uneven, dance-like rhythm
1'46"	"Roar of delight at her arrival"	The brass enter at top volume
1'58"	"She joins the diabolical orgy"	We hear the entire obsession melody in the high-pitched E-flat clarinet, accompanied primarily by double reeds
3'11	"The funeral knell tolls..."	The orchestra bells sound the tolling of the knell
3'39"	"...burlesque parody of the Dies irae..."	The opening phrase of the "Dies irae" melody is heard, first in the low brass, then in the trombones at twice the tempo, and finally in the woodwinds and pizzicato strings at twice the tempo again
4'18"		The second phrase of the "Dies irae" melody undergoes similar treatment

4'42"		The third phrase of the "Dies irae" melody undergoes similar treatment
5'20"	". . . the dance of the witches. . ."	A new theme emerges in the strings
5'38"		The new theme, which we recognize as "the dance of the witches," is presented first in the cellos, then the violins, then in the woodwinds
7'28"		A hint of the "Dies irae" melody return in the cellos and basses; the other strings play fragments of "the dance of the witches"
8'34"	"The dance of the witches combined with the Dies irae."	We hear complete statements of both melodies layered atop one another, "Dies irae" in the brass and "the dance of the witches" in the strings

Berlioz explained the action in "Dream of a Witches' Sabbath" as follows:

He sees himself at a witches' sabbath, in the midst of a hideous gathering of shades, sorcerers and monsters of every kind who have come together for his funeral. Strange sounds, groans, outbursts of laughter; distant shouts which seem to be answered by more shouts. The beloved melody appears once more, but has now lost its noble and shy character; it is now no more than a vulgar dance tune, trivial and grotesque: it is she who is coming to the sabbath... Roar of delight at her arrival... She joins the diabolical orgy... The funeral knell tolls, burlesque parody of the *Dies irae*, the *dance of the witches*. The dance of the witches combined with the Dies irae.

The movement opens exactly as Berlioz describes, with "strange sounds, groans, outbursts of laughter." Strange sounds are certainly heard in the violins. The players employ a technique known as **tremolo**, in which the bow is moved back and forth very quickly to produce a shaking effect. The cellos undeniably provide the groans, with their quick upward melodic sweeps. Both the violins and trombones can later be heard as laughing. Next we hear "distant shouts" in the high winds, echoed by "more shouts" from a muted horn. The opening passage, therefore, is constructed almost exclusively with the use of mimetic techniques.

When the obsession melody returns, it has indeed transformed in character. It is now a lively, impish dance tune played on the E-flat clarinet—an uncommon, high-pitched version of the instrument with a piercing sound quality. The tune is at first interrupted by a mimetic "roar of delight" from the orchestra, after which it is heard in full. In this case, quotation is combined with the use of a musical topic. We recognize the melody and understand what it represents, but the fact that it is presented as a dance tune adds meaning to its appearance.

After the dance dies away we hear the funeral bells. This barely even counts as mimesis, since Berlioz calls for actual bells to be struck. (He uses the tubular orchestra bells that are included in a standard large percussion section.) Next he employs a second quotation. This time he quotes a melody from outside the symphony—indeed, it is a melody that was composed more than 500 years before Berlioz was even born!

The "Dies irae" comes from the body of medieval Catholic church music known as **Gregorian chant**. This particular chant was composed in the 13th century and was associated with the funeral **Mass**, or **Requiem**. It was sung at the graveside and contains a particularly ominous text. The first three lines read as follows:

> A day of wrath; that day,
> it will dissolve the world into glowing ashes,
> as attested by David together with the Sibyl.
>
> What trembling will there be,
> when the Judge shall come
> to examine everything in strict justice.
>
> The trumpet's wondrous call sounding abroad
> in tombs throughout the world
> shall drive everybody forward to the throne.

The long text continues on to describe the coming of Judgment Day, when sinners are cast into Hell to endure eternal torment. Berlioz's audience in Catholic France would have recognized this melody immediately, and would likewise have known the associated text. For them, the "Dies irae" carried connotations of terror and hellishness. By using it in his symphony, therefore, Berlioz was able to take advantage of those connotations without incorporating text directly. The "Dies irae" provided the perfect backdrop for his triumphant witches.

Next Berlioz incorporates another dance topic, named in his synopsis as the "dance of the witches." We don't recognize the melody itself, but we have no trouble acknowledging that it is a dance, and Berlioz's description helps us to understand exactly what it going on. Finally, before the raucous conclusion, we hear the "Dies irae" and the "dance of the witches" juxtaposed, each sounding at the same time in a different part of the orchestra. The concluding passage also includes more unusual string techniques, including *col legno* (with wood), for which players turn their bows over and bounce the stick on their strings. This creates an eerie tapping effect.

Modest Mussorgsky, *Pictures at an Exhibition*

The Russian composer Modest Mussorgsky (1839-1881) was just a generation younger than Berlioz, and their careers overlapped for several decades. The two composers, however, lived in different worlds. Berlioz was French and worked in Paris, a major European cultural center. He received a formal music education and was well-connected with leading figures across the arts. Mussorgsky, on the other hand, was not even a professional composer, and was excluded from his country's growing musical establishment. His status as an outsider, however, only inspired Mussorgsky to find a unique artistic voice, and he emerged as one of the most important Russian composers of the 19th century.

Image 6.5: This portrait of Modest Mussorgsky was painted by Ilya Repin in 1881.
Source: Wikimedia Commons
Attribution: Ilya Repin
License: Public Domain

Mussorgsky and Russian Identity

Mussorgsky's career was split between military and civil service. He enrolled in Cadet School at the age of 13 and subsequently accepted a commission in the Russian Imperial Guard. He resigned his commission in 1858 so as to be able to focus more energy on music, but it was not feasible for him to compose for a living, so he instead took a series of administrative posts with the government.

Mussorgsky's main interest, however, was music. He studied composition with Miliy Alexeyevich Balakirev, who had emerged as the ideological leader of the nationalist movement in Russian music. Mussorgsky also developed close personal relationships with the other young composers in Balakirev's circle, all of whom saw themselves as anti-establishment figures in search of authentic Russian musical expression. Together, these composers were known as "the mighty handful"—an evocative nickname that has been identified with the progressive strain of late 19th-century Russian music ever since.

Despite their interest in developing a uniquely Russian school of composition, Mussorgsky and his colleagues were primarily influenced by European concert music. They studied the scores of Mozart, Beethoven, Schubert, Schumann, Chopin, Liszt, and Berlioz, the last of whom they particularly admired. Because they were largely self-trained and valued experimental approaches, however, these composers succeeded in adapting European forms and techniques to their own creative ends.

Capturing Visual Art in Music

Mussorgsky composed *Pictures at an Exhibition* after attending an art exhibit in commemoration of his friend Viktor Hartmann, who had died suddenly of an aneurism in 1873. Hartmann had belonged to the progressive school of Russian art, which sought to develop a uniquely Russian approach to the visual arts. It is natural enough, therefore, that Mussorgsky should have felt a kinship with Hartmann, for he and "the mighty handful" sought to accomplish the same thing in the realm of music. Mussorgsky had acquired a large number of Hartmann's paintings, which he allowed to be displayed as part of the exhibit in St. Petersburg.

After walking through the galleries, Mussorgsky was inspired to compose a piece of music that captured the experience in sound. He completed the work in only twenty days. *Pictures at an Exhibition* was initially conceived of as a ten-movement **suite** for piano. Each movement represents a Hartmann work, while a "Promenade" interlude between many of the movements symbolizes the act

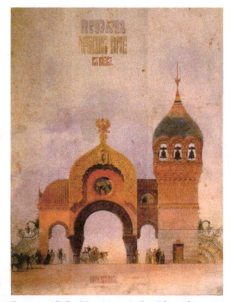

Image 6.6: A photograph of Russian architect and artist Viktor Hartmann.
Source: Wikimedia Commons
Attribution: Unknown
License: Public Domain

Image 6.7: Hartmann's painting of the Paris catacombs inspired the eighth movement of Mussorgsky's suite.
Source: Wikimedia Commons
Attribution: Viktor Hartmann
License: Public Domain

Image 6.8: Hartmann's *Plan for a City Gate* inspired the grandiose final movement of Mussorgsky's suite.
Source: Wikimedia Commons
Attribution: Viktor Hartmann
License: Public Domain

of walking from one painting to the next. Unfortunately, many of the paintings themselves have been lost, but Hartmann's work has lived on in this enormously popular musical composition.

Mussorgsky wrote for piano in part because he was not a skilled orchestrator. However, a large number of later composers took on that task, and as a result many different versions of *Picture at an Exhibition* have been performed over the past century. *Pictures* is heard most frequently as an orchestral work, and the most successful orchestration was created by the French composer Maurice Ravel in 1922. There are also versions for chamber orchestra, band, brass ensemble, and solo guitar. However, the popularity of *Pictures* has resulted in additional adaptations that live outside the concert hall. It has been performed by numerous rock bands—including Emerson, Lake, and Palmer, who recorded it live in 1971—and even formed the basis for early experiments in the world of electronic music.

For this reason, *Pictures at an Exhibition* presents a wonderful opportunity to consider the significance of **timbre**. We will examine two movements in depth, and for each we will compare four different versions: Mussorgsky's 1874 composition for piano, Ravel's 1922 orchestration, Japanese synthesizer artist Isao Tomita's 1975 interpretation, and German thrash metal band Mekong Delta's 1996 recording. All four versions contain exactly the same pitches and rhythms, but they sound quite different from one another due to the divergent sound qualities available from piano, orchestra, synthesizer, and rock band. It is impossible to argue that one version is the "best." Instead, each brings unique strengths to the task of sounding Mussorgsky's composition and each connects with different listeners.

Image 6.9: Here we see the album cover for Tomita's 1975 Pictures at an Exhibition.
Source: Flickr
Attribution: Jacob Whittaker
License: CC BY-NC-SA 2.0

The Gnome

		"The Gnome" from *Pictures at an Exhibition* Composer: Modest Mussorgsky Performance: Sergei Oskolkov (2003)

Time	Form	What to listen for
0'00"	A	This theme is loud, accented, and angular; it includes many descending and ascending leaps

0'18"	B	In this theme, the right hand repeats a descending figure that outlines an unusual scale
0'40"	A	
0'54"	C	This slow, ominous theme is played quietly in the low range of the piano; it is periodically interrupted by loud fragments of A
1'47"	D	The left hand descends chromatically while the right hand executes descending leaps; then the parts switch
2'11"	B	The B theme returns, but the left hand part is reminiscent of the C theme
2'37"	Coda	The movement concludes with a rapid passage in which the left hand descends and the right hand ascends

The first movement of *Pictures at an Exhibition* is entitled "The Gnome." Although the original Hartmann painting has been lost, it is known to have depicted a grotesque nutcracker with large teeth. It was undoubtedly disturbing. Mussorgsky captured the image in sound using a variety of techniques. "The Gnome" begins with a sequence of abrupt, angular melodic fragments. They are unpredictable and unpleasing, lurching about in a way that mimetically capture the motions of the creature they portray. A second, contrasting section contains an uneven descending melody with a dissonant, oscillating accompaniment. A third section vacillates ominously between low and high pitches, while a final section is loud and threatening. Fragments of the first section interrupt when least expected. Throughout, "The Gnome" is characterized by contrast and surprise, and it concludes with a frightening rush to the final cadence. The listener never knows what is going to happen next and is not given the opportunity to relax.

The piano version contains the unpredictable rhythms and rapid mood changes that are central to Mussorgsky's vision, but the instrument imposes several limitations. To begin with, striking the keys of a piano always produces essentially the same type of sound. While a piano can execute a large range of pitch and dynamic levels, its ability to do so does not compare to an orchestra, which can play higher, lower, louder, and softer. An orchestra, however, lacks the spontaneity and responsiveness of a solo pianist, who only has to coordinate with herself.

Ravel's orchestration[1] has emerged as the most common because, like Berlioz, he knew how to take full advantage of the ensemble's potential. He puts the opening melodic gesture in the low strings with an echo in the low brass, thereby creating a darker and more ominous sound quality than is available from the piano. Punctuations from the percussion section further heighten the tension. The next passage features the warm sounds of flute and celeste, with an accompaniment by the string section using **pizzicato** (a technique for which players pluck the strings instead of bowing them) and **glissando** (a technique for which players slide their fingers down the length of the string). Just as Berlioz used the low brass to make his "Dies irae" quotation sound threatening, Ravel uses them to increase the sense of danger and violence in his orchestration. Throughout, he never uses the same combination of instruments twice, thereby introducing an element of variety and surprise that was not available to Mussorgsky.

In his synthesizer version,[2] Tomita takes a similar approach, although of course he has a completely different set of sonic tools at his disposal. Like Ravel, Tomita explores a wide variety of sound qualities—some dark and muted, some percussive, some bright and zingy. He also applies modulatory techniques that transform those sounds, including **low-frequency oscillation**, glissandi, and **panning**. The end result is yet another gloomy sound world, full of contrast and surprise.

Mekong Delta[3] have a more limited sound palette with which to work, but it is well-suited to the task. They differentiate the sections of the piece primarily by changing the role of the drum set. In the first and second sections, the drummer mirrors the rhythms of the melody. In the third and fourth sections, however, the drummer sets up a steady rock beat, which lends the arrangement a sense of growing strength and determination. Other minor variations in instrumentation keep this version interesting throughout.

1.		"The Gnome" from *Pictures at an Exhibition* Composer: Modest Mussorgsky, orchestrated by Maurice Ravel Performance: Wiener Philharmoniker, conducted by Valery Gergiev (2002)
2.		"The Gnome" from *Pictures at an Exhibition* Composer: Modest Mussorgsky Performance: Isao Tomita (1975)
3.		"The Gnome" from *Pictures at an Exhibition* Composer: Modest Mussorgsky Performance: Mekong Delta (1996)

Ballet of the Unhatched Chicks

		"Ballet of the Unhatched Chicks" from *Pictures at an Exhibition* Composer: Modest Mussorgsky Performance: Byron Janis (1962)
Time	**Form**	**What to listen for**
0'00"	A	Discordant sounds are produced when the pianist plays two keys that are next to one another; this humorous effect calls to mind the chirping of chicks
0'15"	A	
0'30"	B	In this section, almost every note has a trill, meaning that the player oscillates quickly between two adjacent keys
0'41"	B'	Although the right hand plays a new melody, the left hand remains stable, indicating that this is a variation of B; this time, quick passages of notes resemble clucking
0'52"	A	
1'08"	Coda	The very brief coda provides a final cadence

The fifth movement of *Pictures at an Exhibition*, "Ballet of the Unhatched Chicks," is quite different. In this case, we still have the artwork that inspired the music. It is not a finished painting, but rather a sketch for a costume that Hartmann had designed for an 1871 production of the ballet *Trilby* at the Bolshoi Theater. The cast members were to portray unhatched baby chickens dancing in their shells.

Mussorgsky clearly saw the humor in this image, as well as in the dancing that one might imagine to have been performed in such a costume. His brief musical depiction, therefore, is highly comical. He employs a simple **ternary form** (A B A). Although the A and B sections of the form feature different melodies, we hear the chicks chirping and hopping throughout. While Mussorgsky used **dissonance** to

Image 6.10: Viktor Hartmann's costume design for the 1871 ballet *Trilby*.
Source: Wikimedia Commons
Attribution: Viktor Hartmann
License: Public Domain

signal fear and danger in "The Gnome," here he uses it to indicate the ridiculous nature of the scene. Occasionally, a lone, sustained note interrupts the dance—the voice of the mother hen, perhaps? An abrupt ending completes the comic effect.

For his orchestrated version,[4] Ravel chose to feature the high-pitched instruments whose voices most closely match those of the chicks being portrayed: violin, flute, clarinet, oboe, and bassoon. While he used percussion in "The Gnome" to accentuate the moments of greatest terror, here he uses percussion—cymbals in the A section, snare in the B section—to add comic touches.

Tomita[5] takes the idea of comedy the furthest. The same can be said concerning the idea of chickens, for—in an extreme case of mimesis—he uses a variety of simulated clucks and chirps to perform the melody. In the middle section of the form, he pans his chickens between audio channels and fades their voices in and out. Additional comic noises round out the scene.

The members of Mekong Delta[6] use rounded timbres in place of distorted ones to create a sound world for "Ballet of the Unhatched Chicks" that is surprisingly far removed from that of "The Gnome." The regular, energetic rhythmic underpinning from the drummer provides a sense of liveliness. Mekong Delta does not attempt to imitate the sounds of chickens in any way, but instead captures the lighthearted enthusiasm of the Mussorgsky composition.

4.		"Ballet of the Unhatched Chicks" from *Pictures at an Exhibition* Composer: Modest Mussorgsky, orchestrated by Maurice Ravel Performance: Wiener Philharmoniker, conducted by Gustavo Dudamel (2016)
5.		"Ballet of the Unhatched Chicks" from *Pictures at an Exhibition* Composer: Modest Mussorgsky Performance: Isao Tomita (1975)
6.		"Ballet of the Unhatched Chicks" from *Pictures at an Exhibition* Composer: Modest Mussorgsky Performance: Mekong Delta (1996)

ANTONIO VIVALDI, *THE FOUR SEASONS,* "SPRING"

Composers were writing program music long before Berlioz or Mussorgsky. In earlier periods, however, such compositions were generally perceived as entertaining novelties, not the future of concert art. The Italian violinist and composer Antonio Vivaldi (1678-1741) was particularly fond of program music, and he produced a great deal. His set of violin **concertos** known as *The Four*

Seasons (Italian: *Le quattro stagioni*, 1725) are the most famous. Indeed, they rank among the best known pieces of music from the European concert tradition.

Vivaldi's Career

Vivaldi spent his life in the city of Venice, which at the time was a wealthy and independent Republic. He initially trained as a Catholic priest, but ill health prevented him from performing many of his duties. However, he became highly skilled as a violinist and composer, and in 1703 he took the position of violin master at a local orphanage, the Devout Hospital of Mercy (Italian: Ospedale della Pietà; note that Hospital at this time does not indicate a center for medical care).

Venetian orphanages were not the squalid workhouses we know from Victorian literature. Indeed, quite the opposite. It was common—even acceptable—for Venetian aristocrats to keep mistresses, but the children of these relationships could not be brought up in the marital home. Instead, unwanted infants were deposited at orphanages via the *scaffetta*, which was an opening just large enough to fit a newborn. While not all of the surrendered infants were of high birth, the city's noblemen took an interest in the welfare of their illegitimate children, which meant that the orphanages were always well-funded. The children

Image 6.11: This portrait of Antonio Vivaldi was completed by Pier Leone Ghezzi in 1723. The text refers to Vivaldi as "The Red Priest," a nickname he was given due to his curly red hair.
Source: Wikimedia Commons
Attribution: Pier Leone Ghezzi
License: Public Domain

Image 6.12: This painting captures Venice in the time of Vivaldi. The coastal city is interwoven with canals and therefore largely navigable by boat.
Source: Wikimedia Commons
Attribution: Canaletto
License: Public Domain

Image 6.13: This 19th-century engraving depicts the orphanage at which Vivaldi was employed. The building no longer stands.
Source: Wikimedia Commons
Attribution: Unknown
License: Public Domain

were brought up with all of the advantages (except parents), and were prepared for comfortable lives.

The Devout Hospital of Mercy, at which Vivaldi took a position, was an orphanage for girls. His job was to teach them the musical skills that would allow them to secure desirable husbands. Vivaldi was exceptionally good at his job, and soon the girls at the orphanage became the best musicians in the city. He not only taught them how to play their instruments but wrote music for them to play. His primary vehicle was the concerto, which is a work for an instrumental soloist accompanied by an orchestra. Over the course of his career, Vivaldi wrote 500 concertos. About half were for violin, including 37 for his most successful protege, a virtuoso known as Anna Maria dal Violin. The other were mostly for bassoon, flute, oboe, and cello—all instruments played by girls at the Hospital.

Naturally enough, the citizens of Venice wanted to hear the girls perform. This, however, presented a serious problem. Women in Venetian society were generally prohibited from performing publicly. Some women took to the opera stage, but in doing so they were confirming their sexual availability and precluding the possibility of marriage. Most of the girls at the orphanage were destined for either husbands or a lifetime of service to the church, so they could not become soiled in this way. Those who did desire a career in music were likely to stay at the orphanage into adulthood, where they were provided with an opportunity to teach and perform. At least two girls who studied at the orphanage, Anna Bon and Vincenta Da Ponte, went on to become composers.

The orphanage developed a clever means by which to facilitate public performances without upsetting social convention. Each Sunday night, a public Vespers service was held for which the orchestra and choir provided music. Although this weekly church service was, for all intents and purposes, a public concert, the simple act of retitling protected the girls' honor. Members of high society came from across the region to hear the girls, who were physically isolated from the visitors to further ensure their chastity.

Vivaldi was promoted to music director in 1716, and he continued to teach at the orphanage even as he became quite famous outside of Venice. In addition to writing instrumental music, he wrote operas that were staged across Europe and provided choral music for Catholic church services. His long tenure at the orphanage was noteworthy, for male teachers at girls' orphanages usually got into trouble with one of their charges and eventually had to be dismissed. Vivaldi, on the other hand, developed a reputation for his ethical behavior.

For Vivaldi, the concerto was a relatively new genre. The first concertos had been written by Italian composers in the middle of the 17th century. At first, soloists were used primarily to add variation in volume to an orchestral performance—after all, a few players make less noise than many, and individual string instruments of the time did not have a large dynamic range. Vivaldi still valued the potential for concertos to include a great deal of variety, but he also used them as a vehicle for

Image 6.14: This 1720 depiction of a concert at the Devout Hospital of Mercy shows how the girls performed from high balconies, out of reach from visitors. Not well represented are the ornate grates that hid the girls from view.
Source: Wikimedia Commons
Attribution: Gabriele Bella, photographer Didier Descouens
License: CC BY-SA 4.0

virtuosic display. The solo parts, therefore, were often quite difficult, and allowed the player to show off her capabilities.

An early 18th-century concerto always followed the same basic form. It would contain three movements in the order fast-slow-fast. The outer movements would both be in **ritornello form**. "Ritornello" is an Italian term that roughly translates to "the little thing that returns," and it refers to a passage of music that is heard repeatedly. In a concerto, the ritornello is played by the orchestra. It is heard at the beginning and at the end of a movement, but also frequently throughout, although often not in its entirety. In between statements of the ritornello, the soloist plays. Although the ritornello always remains basically the same, the material played by the soloist can vary widely. The slow movement of a concerto would consist of an expressive melody in the solo instrument backed up by a repetitive accompaniment in the orchestra.

Spring

We will see an example of these forms in Vivaldi's "Spring" concerto. However, form is certainly not what makes this composition interesting. Vivaldi published his

Image 6.15: This 1723 portrait shows Vivaldi with his violin.
Source: Wikimedia Commons
Attribution: Unknown
License: Public Domain

Four Seasons concertos in a 1725 collection entitled *The Contest Between Harmony and Invention*. This evocative title was supposed to draw attention to novel aspects of Vivaldi's latest work. While eight of the twelve concertos contained in the collection were adventurous in purely musical terms, the first four were unusual for programmatic reasons.

Each of the *Four Seasons* concertos—one each for Spring, Summer, Autumn, and Winter—was accompanied by a sonnet. The poetry described the dramatic content of the music, and Vivaldi went to great trouble to indicate exactly how the music reflected the text. To do so, he inserted letter names beside each line of poetry and then placed the same letter at the appropriate place in the score. The correlation between musical and poetic passages, however, is easy to hear. This, in combination with the fact that no author is indicated, has led most scholars to believe that Vivaldi wrote the sonnets himself.

The sonnet for the "Spring" concerto reads as follows. The lines of poetry are broken up between the three movements, each of which is titled with an Italian tempo marking:

> I. *Allegro*
> Springtime is upon us.
> The birds celebrate her return with festive song,
> and murmuring streams are
> softly caressed by the breezes.
> Thunderstorms, those heralds of Spring, roar,
> casting their dark mantle over heaven,
> Then they die away to silence,
> and the birds take up their charming songs once more.
> II. *Largo*
> On the flower-strewn meadow, with leafy branches
> rustling overhead, the goat-herd sleeps,
> his faithful dog beside him.
> III. *Allegro*
> Led by the festive sound of rustic bagpipes,
> nymphs and shepherds lightly dance
> beneath the brilliant canopy of spring.

		"Spring," Movement I Composer: Antonio Vivaldi Performance: Anne-Sophie Mutter with the Wiener Philharmoniker, conducted by Herbert Von Karajan (2003)
Time	**Form**	**What to listen for**
0'00"	Ritornello - "Springtime is upon us."	The ritornello has an internal form of aabb; its simplicity and repetition suggest a folk dance
0'29"	A - "The birds celebrate her return with festive song, . . ."	The solo violinist and two violinists from the orchestra join together in imitation of birdsong
1'03"	Ritornello	The ritornello is slightly abbreviated in this and all future appearances
1'10"	B - ". . .and murmuring streams are softly caressed by the breezes."	The entire orchestra plays repetitive figures that rise and fall, imitating the murmur of the stream
1'33"	Ritornello	
1'40"	C - "Thunderstorms, those heralds of Spring, roar, casting their dark mantle over heaven, . . ."	The orchestra imitates thunder with low-range tremolo and lightning with quick ascending scales; the solo violinist shows off their virtuosity with rapid arpeggios
2'08"	Ritornello	This ritornello is in the minor mode
2'16"	D - "Then they die away to silence, and the birds take up their charming songs once more."	The solo violinist slowly ascends using repeated notes, suggesting calmness; the section ends with trills in the the violins, another imitation of birdsong

2'32"	Ritornello	This ritornello is the least stable, as it moves from one key to another
2'42"	E	This solo does not correspond with a passage of poetry; its sole function is to prepare the final ritornello
2'56"	Ritornello	The last thing we hear is the bb section of the ritornello

The opening ritornello in the first movement captures the spirit of the first line of poetry. It is joyful and exuberant. It is also simple and repetitive, giving the impression that it might really be folk music—the kind of tune one might hear at a country dance. The birds appear with the first solo episode, which requires two violinists from the orchestra to join with the soloist in imitating avian calls. After an orchestral ritornello, we hear some new music from the orchestra that captures the sounds of murmuring streams and caressing breezes. Another ritornello is followed by the thunderstorm. Rapid notes, sudden accents, and violent ascending scales in the orchestra are interrupted by energetic **arpeggios** in the solo violin, while shifts to the minor mode darken the mood of the passage. After another ritornello, the bird songs gradually reemerge, gaining strength as the storm clears for good. One more solo passage and a final ritornello close out the movement.

The second movement[7] is considerably simpler. The solo violin plays a beautiful, calm melody—suitable for the portrayal of a sleeping goat-herd. Underneath, the leafy branches rustle in the violins, who play undulating, uneven rhythms throughout, while the faithful dog barks in the violas. (This last touch is a little strange, for a barking dog would certainly wake the sleeper, but Vivaldi did not have any other tools with which to represent the animal.) The fact that no low strings or harpsichord are present in this movement gives it an ethereal feeling.

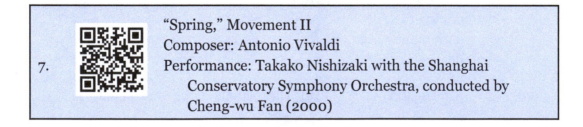

7. "Spring," Movement II
    Composer: Antonio Vivaldi
    Performance: Takako Nishizaki with the Shanghai
        Conservatory Symphony Orchestra, conducted by
        Cheng-wu Fan (2000)

The last movement[8] has the same form as the first, although the storytelling is considerably less intricate. In the opening ritornello, Vivaldi imitates a bagpipe by having the violas, cellos, and basses sustain long notes outlining the interval of a fifth. The sound is meant to remind the listener of a bagpipe's drone. The rhythms of the melody are appropriate for dancing, while the lively mood sets the scene for a celebration of spring. The soloist—other than momentarily imitating a bagpipe herself—does not contribute anything in particular to the storytelling. She seems content to interject lively, virtuosic passagework at the appropriate points.

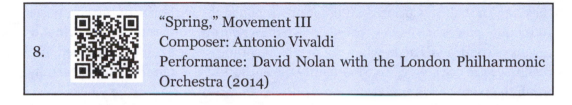

8.		"Spring," Movement III Composer: Antonio Vivaldi Performance: David Nolan with the London Philharmonic Orchestra (2014)

CHINESE SOLO REPERTOIRE, *ATTACK ON ALL SIDES* AND *SPRING RIVER IN THE FLOWER MOON NIGHT*

At the same time that European composers were producing vivid programmatic works, a parallel tradition of program music was flourishing in China. We will consider two examples from the literature for solo instruments, which is predominantly programmatic. One piece will portray a historical battle, while the other will reflect on the contents of a famous poem. Although Chinese music follows different rules than European music, is it not difficult for a Western listener to understand what this music is about. This is due both to the use of mimesis and to a cross-cultural agreement about the representation of calm and energetic moods in sound.

Image 6.16: Music has long been important in Chinese culture. Here, we see musicians in a 6th-century tomb painting.
Source: Wikimedia Commons
Attribution: Unknown
License: Public Domain

When we discuss this music, however, we will have to do so in slightly different terms than we have so far. Although Chinese musicians have developed a variety of notational systems that have allowed musical compositions to be preserved, they have not always prioritized notation or valued the authority of the composer. Individual pieces are usually passed down directly from performer to performer by means of **oral tradition**, while the names of composers are seldom recorded. As a result, we are not always able to identify the authors of this repertoire or determine when the pieces were written.

The history of music in China extends back for thousands of years, and some of the instruments date to antiquity. This is not to say, however, that the music has remained unchanged, or that all of the repertoire items are old. As we saw in Chapter 4, Beijing opera dates only to the late 18th century, and alternative opera traditions have continued to emerge and change. In the sphere of instrumental music, the use of individual instruments—as well as their physical structure—transformed with the passage of time. We will encounter two instruments, the pipa and the guqin. In doing so, we will consider their history, construction, and use in the performance of program music.

Pipa: *Attack on All Sides*

The pipa is a type of **lute** used in a variety of Chinese musical traditions. It dates back to at least the 3rd century, although it did not acquire its modern form until the 20th century. Like most of the instruments commonly used in Chinese music, the pipa was probably imported from Central Asia or India along the Silk Road trade route. At first, it was used only to accompany singing and dancing, but during the Tang dynasty (618-907) a repertoire of solo pipa music emerged. As such, the pipa repertoire is among the oldest in the Chinese tradition. The instrument was historically favored by both aristocrats and working musicians, and was long associated with women—specifically, courtesans.

The pipa has a distinctive, pear-shaped body and is played in an upright position. Modern instruments have twenty-four **frets** spaced according to the Western chromatic scale. The frets on the neck have a unique wedge shape, such that a player's finger does not in fact touch the neck when the string is depressed. The pipa's four strings can be tuned to a variety of pitches. Although they used to be silk, the fact that pipa strings have

Image 6.17: This 897 painting portrays the planet Venus, embodied as an elegant lady, playing the pipa.
Source: Wikimedia Commons
Attribution: Chang Huai-hsing
License: Public Domain

been manufactured out of steel since the 1950s gives the modern instrument a powerful sound. This is further accentuated by the fact that the player wears picks on the fingers of her right hand.

A great deal of the traditional pipa repertoire has survived into the present day due to the publication of four collections in the 19th century. The notation used in these collections, known as *gongche*, is completely unrelated to Western **staff notation**. Instead of mapping pitches and rhythms onto a graph, as staff notation does, it represents pitches with numbers and rhythms with dots and lines. In the context of a tradition that is primarily aural, however, such notation was used only to document music for preservation or reference. It was not used to learn unfamiliar music or in performance.

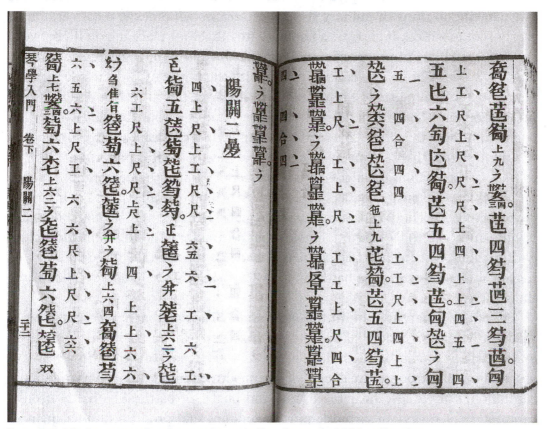

Image 6.18: An example of gongche notation from an 1864 collection.
Source: Wikimedia Commons
Attribution: Cheung Hok
License: Public Domain

Attack on All Sides[9] is the most popular piece in the pipa repertoire. It is also very difficult, however, and is usually only performed by the most accomplished players. The earliest notated version appears in an 1818 collection, but it is impossible to say when (or by whom) it was in fact composed. *Attack on All Sides* is an example of a "large" composition, containing many distinct sections. (The pipa repertoire also includes "small" compositions, which are shorter and have a single section.) While *Attack on All Sides* can always be recognized and identified, some published versions omit sections that are included elsewhere. Therefore, not every performance is identical. No single version can be identified as "correct." This can be contrasted with most music in the European concert tradition, for which there is generally understood to exist a single authoritative version.

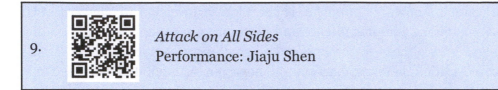

9. *Attack on All Sides*
Performance: Jiaju Shen

As with Beijing opera, pipa solos are divided into "civil" and "martial," the latter having to do with military themes. *Attack on All Sides* is most certainly a martial composition. It portrays a famous battle that took place in 202 BC between the armies of two Chinese provinces, Western Chu and Han, who were fighting for dominion over China. The conflict ended with the Battle of Gaixia, in which the Han troops kidnapped the Chu general's wife and used her to lure the enemy troops into a canyon. There, they fell victim to the "ambush from ten sides"—another common title for this piece. The battle itself hinged on musical warfare, for the Han sought to defeat their enemy by psychological means. To this end, they sang Chu folk songs throughout the night, with the effect of making the demoralized enemy homesick and inspiring soldiers to desert. The Chu general, Xiang Yu, is said to have composed a song of his own that same night. His lament, *The Song of Gaixia*, is still performed today. Tradition holds that he first sang the verses in alternation with his wife, who, feeling that she was at fault for the defeat, subsequently killed herself with his sword. The battle ended with Xiang Yu's suicide on the banks of the Wu river.

All of this is captured in *Attack on All Sides*. The fact that this composition is made up of many sections allows the performer to explore the various emotions and activities of the battle scene. In the first sections, we bear witness to the assembling Han troops. The energy of the music communicates their vitality and resolution, but we also hear the drums and bugles of battle. The battle itself is captured by a variety of virtuosic pipa techniques that produce rapid sequences of notes. After the battle, however, the music becomes mournful—a reflection of Xiang Yu's sorrow at his loss. The final word goes to the victor, however, and the piece concludes with a representation of the Han general's triumph.

Guzheng: Peng Xiuwen, *Spring River in the Flower Moon Night*

The oldest extant guzheng dates to about 500 BC. The guzheng is a type of **zither**, and its plucked strings run along the face of a resonant wood box. Each string passes over an individual wooden bridge, which can be moved to adjust the pitch. Players use picks on the fingers of the right hand to pluck the strings to

Image 6.19: A player uses finger picks to pluck the strings of the guzheng.
Source: Hanscom Air Force Base
Attribution: Mark Wyatt
License: Public Domain

one side of the bridges, while using the left hand either to pluck strings on the right-hand side or to press or pull the strings on the other side. This causes pitch fluxuations, which are carefully controlled and used to ornament the melody. As with the pipa, the strings of the guzheng, once silk, have been made of steel since the 1950s. They increased in number from thirteen to twenty-one around the same time. The strings are tuned to the pitches of the **pentatonic scale**, which is common in Chinese music. We might think of these as the first, second, third, fifth, and sixth notes of the major scale.

Because the modern guzheng is so different from the ancient instrument, performers tend to favor recently-composed pieces that make use of its full range. Such is the case with our example, *Spring River in the Flower Moon Night*, which is the work of Peng Xiuwen (1931-1996). Following the establishment of the People's Republic of China in 1949, Peng became a leading figure in the development of post-revolution Chinese music. In particular, he contributed to the development of the Chinese orchestra—an ensemble type that dates only to the 1930s. In most traditional forms of Chinese ensemble music, only one of each instrument is included, and the performers are granted the freedom to embellish their individual parts. In a Chinese orchestra, on the other hand, instruments of the same type are gathered into sections, and they use notated music to play in unison under the leadership of a **conductor**. This approach is obviously modelled on the European orchestra, and its popularity at first reflected Chinese admiration for Western technological achievements.

Peng became director of the China Broadcasting Chinese Orchestra, one of the most important ensembles of its type, in 1956, when he was only twenty-four years old. In addition to improving the tuning and balance of the orchestra, he arranged a large number of pieces from the European repertoire for Chinese orchestra and composed original pieces. One of these was *Spring River in the Flower Moon Night*,[10] which soon became even more popular with solo guzheng players. As we will see, its pentatonic pitch content and meditative mood suit the instrument well.

10.

Spring River in a Flower Moon Night
Composer: Peng Xiuwen
Performance: Bei Bei He (2016)

The title *Spring River in the Flower Moon Night* refers to a famous poem written by Zhang Ruoxu around the turn of the 8th century. The poem has inspired countless artistic interpretations over the centuries, including paintings and musical compositions. As the title might suggest, Zhang's poem describes the moonlit Yangtze river. After several evocative passages that conjure the beauty of the scene, however, he turns to themes of longing and loss, meditating on the ephemerality of life and the sorrows of travellers who leave their loved ones behind.

In his composition, Peng strives to evoke the full range of emotions contained in the poem. The guzheng version of *Spring River in the Flower Moon Night* requires a variety of techniques, including rapid tremolo picking on a single string, strums (both delicate and energetic), left-hand bends that add notes to the melody, and left-hand bends that are merely ornamental. Peng's ultimate goal is to leave the listener in the same state of sorrowful tranquility that they would experience upon reading the poem.

CATHERINE LIKHUTA, *LESIONS*

Although program music in the European tradition flourished most notably in the 19th century, many composers still conceive of their instrumental music in narrative terms. Composers continue to be inspired by stories and images from the physical world, and they continue to communicate those stories through sound. One such composer is Catherine Likhuta (b. 1981), who exclusively writes program music. We will examine a recent composition

Image 6.20: Catherine Likhuta was born in Ukraine. She currently lives in Australia.
Source: Catherine Likhuta
Attribution: Catherine Likhuta
License: © Catherine Likhuta. Used with permission.

of hers that tells a deeply personal story—that of her mother's struggle with the symptoms of Multiple Sclerosis.

Likhuta's Inspiration

Likhuta was born in Ukraine, where she studied music at the Kyiv Glière Music College and the Tchaikovsky National Music Academy of Ukraine. She then moved to Australia to pursue a doctoral degree at the University of Queensland. Likhuta is also an accomplished pianist, and she frequently premieres and records her own works, which are heard all over the world.

Like Berlioz, Likhuta chose to provide the listener with a description of her music. We will therefore allow her to explain its contents and purpose in her own words:

> *Lesions* was commissioned by Paul Dean for Ensemble Q and was written for Paul Dean, Trish O'Brien and Peter Luff.
>
> The term "lesions" refers to regions in organs and tissue which have suffered damage through injury or disease, such as a wound, ulcer, abscess or tumour. I first heard this term in 2004, when my mother (age 42 at that time) was diagnosed with an aggressive form of Multiple Sclerosis. While she had suffered from many disturbing, unexplainable and painful symptoms for sixteen years prior to that, the diagnosis of MS did not bring us any relief or closure.
>
> Virtually every family has a loved one who is suffering or suffered from an incurable illness. While this is a very heavy subject, I believe it is definitely worth talking about, for two simple reasons:
>
> 1. To show those who are affected that they are not alone and that there are millions of people in the world who are going through similar struggles;
> 2. To remind those lucky few who have not been affected that we have to keep looking for cures every day.
>
> Lesions is written in four parts that represent four most common stages of dealing with incurable illness: Sadness, Anxiety, Denial and finally Acceptance. The absence of a pause between the last two movements has an extra-musical meaning: though denial and acceptance are antithetical states of mind, many patients find themselves stuck between these two for a long time, sometimes for the rest of their lives. The new reality is too difficult to accept, yet the symptoms are just as difficult to deny.

As Likhuta explains, *Lesions* is more than just a piece of music. It also fulfills both therapeutic and advocacy roles. Writing this piece provided relief for Likhuta, as she was able to translate her difficult experience into expressive sound. At the same time, she hopes that it will bring comfort to others in a similar situation. *Lesions*, however, is not meant only to provide solace: Likhuta hopes that it will also inspire action on behalf of those who suffer from currently incurable illnesses.

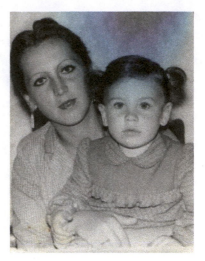

Image 6.21: This photograph of Likhuta and her mother was taken just before the latter was diagnosed with Multiple Sclerosis.
Source: Catherine Likhuta
Attribution: Catherine Likhuta
License: © Catherine Likhuta. Used with permission

It might seem odd that such a personal creation should result from a **commission**—the process by which a performer, producer, or organization hires a composer to create a new musical work. When a work is commissioned, the composer is often provided with specific guidelines concerning instrumentation, length, and level of difficulty. Sometimes these requirements impede creativity, but the best composers have always been able to suit their style and ambitions to the performers and situation at hand. In this case, the commissioning musicians were longtime collaborators of Likhuta's, and they were able to work together to bring her vision to life.

Likhuta has told us which emotions her music expresses, but she does not provide any details about how she captures feelings in sound. She presumes—correctly—that most listeners will easily perceive and understand the emotional states. Here, however, we will explicitly consider how these abstract emotions can be represented in musical terms.

Capturing the Stages of Grief in Music

		Lesions Composer: Catherine Likhuta Performance: Paul Dean, Peter Luff, and Trish O'Brien (2017)
Time	**Form**	**What to listen for**
0'00"	Sadness	This section at first seems calm and resigned, but grows in volume and intensity; the motif introduced at the beginning will return throughout the work

2'38"	Anxiety	The tempo immediately accelerates at the beginning of this section, which is generally unstable and unpredictable
5'17"	Anger	The energy of the work peaks in this section, which contains dissonant harmonies and aggressive rhythms
7'43"	Acceptance	This is the only section that is not preceded by a pause; the motif from "Sadness," now with a new character, transforms into a waltz before finally fading away

The first section, "Sadness," is characterized by a repeated **motif** in the clarinet and cello. Over the top of this, the horn enters with a mournful melody. At first, the music is calm and stately. The melody, however, becomes increasingly agitated as it is passed from the horn to the clarinet. The volume increases and the rhythm loses its stability, until eventually we hear cries of anguish from the clarinet. When the opening motif returns, it is with a sense of resignation.

The second section, "Anxiety," opens with a related motif, but the tempo is faster and the rhythm more agitated. This section is characterized by frequent change, as if the protagonist cannot get settled into place. Background motifs continually emerge, only to disintegrate and transform. There is no sense of key or tonal center. Instead, the pitches float uncomfortably in space.

"Denial," the third section, opens with a series of dissonant chords, after which an aggressive motif in the cello establishes a frenetic tempo. The energy continues to build, and the music is frequently interrupted by pauses and rhythmic shifts. When the motif from the opening of the piece returns, marking the beginning of the "Acceptance" section, it has been transformed: It is now loud, strong, and insistent. This statement is followed by a new, waltz-like melody in the clarinet that returns us to the opening motif, now restored to its original character. Following the emotional journey of the piece, however, the motif means something new. It communicates sadness, yes, but the self-conscious sadness of one who has come to terms with loss.

This is the first textbook ever to include the music of Likhuta—and it may be the last. She is still near the beginning of her career, and although she has been very successful, it is difficult to predict which composers or works will enter the permanent concert repertoire and which will not. There is no doubt that *Lesions* is an excellent piece of music that deserves to be heard for a long time. However, countless such pieces have flashed into existence over the centuries, only to disappear when they fail to attract the attention of an influential performer or publisher. Permanency is largely a matter of chance. This visit with Likhuta, therefore, is a valuable reminder that, for every "famous" composer or work of the past, there are thousands of wonderful compositions and creators awaiting (re)discovery.

ANOUSHKA SHANKAR, RAGA MADHUVANTI

We will conclude this chapter with a consideration of how cultural context can facilitate musical storytelling even in the absence of a specific text. Every example that we have considered thus far has been accompanied at some level by a description. In the case of Berlioz, we had a long prose explanation from the composer himself. In the case of Mussorgsky, references to the titles of paintings. In the case of Vivaldi, a poem. The titles of the two Chinese examples refer us to a historical event on the one hand and a poem on the other, while Likhuta explains how her composition connects with lived experience. This final example also has specific meaning, but it is only available to those initiated into the musical tradition from which it comes. While anyone can enjoy the sounds of "Raga Madhuvanti," its meaning is unveiled only when one positions it correctly within the web of North Indian musical and artistic practice.

Before we can approach our example, we need to know something about North Indian classical music. It is important to note that this text can provide only a shallow and perfunctory glimpse of a tradition that requires a lifetime of dedication to master. Like their Western counterparts, North Indian classical musicians immerse themselves in their tradition for decades before claiming any sort of authority. But as with European classical music, a listener does not need to master the theoretical nuances in order to enjoy a performance.

Raga Theory

The North Indian classical music of today combines relatively modern instruments and practices with a theoretical system that dates to the 9th century. Here, we will focus on the concept of **raga**, which is roughly analogous to the scale. Unlike the scale, however, which provides a composer or performer only with a set of pitches and some information about their hierarchy (the first note of the scale, for example, is the most important), a raga carries a great weight of information, both musical and extramusical (having to do with non-sounding elements). Ragas are sometimes used as the basis for fixed compositions, but more often they are explored in an **improvised** performance—a practice that we will explore below. It is impossible to determine the precise number of ragas in existence. About five hundred seem to be in use at any given time, while an individual musician might master a few dozen.

We will use Raga Madhuvanti[11] as an example. Raga Madhuvanti contains seven distinct pitches, just like the Western scale. However, the pitches found in Raga Madhuvanti are not found in any Western mode. If we were to imagine starting from a major scale, the third pitch would be flat but the fourth would be sharp, creating a large gap between them. In addition, the pitches contained in a raga vary depending on whether one is ascending or descending. The most important scale degree in Raga Madhuvanti is 1, while the second most important is 5.

| 11. | [QR code] | This video begins by demonstrating the ascending and descending forms of Raga Madhuvanti. It then demonstrates some of the typical melodic fragments before concluding with a sample song. |

This is already more information about performance practice than one can derive from a Western scale, but we have only begun. Each of the pitches indicated above must be precisely tuned, for North Indian music employs **microtones**, or pitches that fall between the keys on the piano. These must be learned by ear—and are unique to a given raga. Each pitch must also be approached and ornamented in the correct manner, for this is a rich vocabulary of slides, **vibratos**, and **trills**. Raga Madhuvanti also contains prescribed resting places for the melody as it develops. Any melody played in Raga Madhuvanti will be further shaped by a vocabulary of typical phrases that identify the raga. Finally, one cannot incorporate any additional pitches without destroying the raga.

But we have still only begun. It is now time to move on to the extramusical characteristics of Raga Madhuvanti. To begin with, Raga Madhuvanti is used to express gentle, loving, and romantic sentiments. In particular, it communicates the emotion that one feels for one's beloved. It is also considered sweet and playful. The root of the name, "madhu," translates to "honey." The character of the raga is captured in poetry and paintings known as **ragamalas**. The practice of personifying musical ragas through verse began in the 14th century, which in turn inspired the miniature paintings of the 16th and 17th centuries. There are no classical representations of Raga Madhuvanti, which was developed in the 1930s, but we can still link it to art. Ragas are organized into families, known as *thaat*, and Madhuvanti belongs to the Todi thaat. Ragas in a family share a variety of musical and extramusical characteristics. Raga Todi is

Image 6.22: A ragamala portraying Raga Todi, dating from 1591. In this image, she holds a rudra vina, which was the most important melody instrument from the 16th through the 19th centuries but which has now been replaced by the sitar. The presence of the instrument suggests the sound of the raga, even though it is unheard.
Source: Wikimedia Commons
Attribution: Anonymous
License: Public Domain

portrayed as a beautiful woman, the wife of Raga Hindol, who is separated from her lover. She is always surrounded by deer, and focuses her attention on the buck, who represents masculine virility.

At this point we've wandered a bit far from our topic—but all of this is relevant to the understanding of Raga Madhuvanti, which is traditionally considered to possess a spiritual existence independent of any performance or description. When we say that Raga Madhuvanti was "developed" in the 1930s, that is not quite correct. It might be better to say that it was "discovered," for most musicians would agree that ragas exist whether or not they are named and performed. When a musician begins to perform a raga, they embark upon the lifelong task of becoming acquainted with it, as if it were another human being. Every encounter reveals new facets of the raga, which cannot be fully captured in any single performance.

Finally, Raga Madhuvanti, like all ragas, is associated with a specific season and time of day. Raga Madhuvanti is an evening raga that should be performed during the fourth quarter of the day—or, roughly, between 4 and 8 pm. It is also considered appropriate for the summer season. At one time, these associations were taken very seriously. The North Indian classical tradition developed in the courts, where musicians played ragas that were suited to the moment. A morning raga for the monsoon season, for example, would be heard only on a monsoon morning. In the courts, musicians played constantly, and were therefore able to maintain correlations between ragas and time markers. With the rise of concert life in the 20th century, however, this became impossible, and North Indian classical musicians today generally perform ragas without concern for time or season. Nevertheless, these associations linger.

Tala Theory

This has been an overview of raga theory, which concerns the melodic and extramusical contents of a performance. Tala theory, which concerns rhythmic content, is equally complex, but we will largely pass over it here due to the fact that it is difficult for untrained listeners to perceive the rhythmic nuances of North Indian classical music. We will note only that a **tala** is a pattern of beats used in the performance of a raga. The number of beats in a tala can range from three to 128, although most contain between six and sixteen beats. Beats can be strong or weak, and each is characterized by a specific percussive sound. A tala, therefore, is best thought of as a cycle of timbres. This is simple enough, but a drummer will almost never play the cycle unadorned. Instead, they will improvise complex rhythms over the tala, which exists only in the imagination of the performers and listeners.

Ragas and talas are not paired up one-to-one, but only specific talas may be used with a given raga. We will be hearing a performance of Raga Madhuvanti paired with Rupak Tala, which contains seven beats divided into three groups containing three, two, and two beats respectively. North Indian classical musicians learn talas by reciting the syllables associated with each beat, which in turn represent that sound of the drum and indicate how it is to be struck to create that sound. The syllables for the seven beats of Rupak Tala[12] are Tin Tin Na Dhin Na Dhin Na. The most common percussion instrument in North Indian classical music is the tabla, which is a pair of small drums—one a bit larger than the other—that are played with the hands. "Tin" indicates a resonant stroke with the right hand, while "Na" is a damped stroke with the right hand and "Dhin" is a resonant stroke with both hands. An accomplished player will be careful to use the correct fingers with the appropriate force in exactly the right spot on the drum head.

12.   This video includes a demonstration of Rupak Tala. The tabla player only performs the basic 7-beat tala once. He then begins to introduce variations. However, you can track beats of the tala by tapping or clapping.

Instruments and Transmission

We are finally ready to consider a modern performance of Raga Madhuvanti. We will begin with the instruments, one of which—the tabla—has already been introduced. All North Indian classical music is performed over a drone, which usually consists of the two most important notes in the raga. In the case of Raga Madhuvanti, as noted above, those are the first and fifth scale degrees. The drone is most often performed on a tanpura. This long-necked lute is almost completely hollow and therefore extremely resonant. It has no frets and cannot be used to play melodies. Instead, the performer lightly plucks each of the four strings in turn to create a sustained drone. The tanpura is most often played by an apprentice of the soloist.

The sitar is capable of producing its own drone, but it is a much more complicated instrument and is used primarily to perform the raga. Today, the sitar is the most common North Indian melodic instrument. It was made famous in the second half of the 20th century by the virtuoso Ravi Shankar, who influenced The Beatles (see Chapter 8) and frequently performed at popular music festivals (including Woodstock, discussed in Chapter 7). The sitar, however, is not a particularly ancient instrument, dating only to the 18th century.

Like the tanpura, the sitar has a hollow neck and is highly resonant. Both instruments also produce a light, metallic buzzing sound that is essential to the timbre. Unlike the tanpura, the sitar has large, arched frets.

Image 6.23: The tanpura is held vertically by the player, who plucks the strings one at a time.
Source: Wikimedia Commons
Attribution: User "Martin spaink"
License: CC BY-SA 3.0

Melodies are played on the strings that run across them. These strings can either be pressed down, shortening the length of the string, or pulled to the side, increasing the tension on the string. Both actions change the note produced when the string is plucked, and they can be combined to produce the effect of sliding between pitches.

Sitars in fact have three different types of strings. The top three are used to play the melody. Below these are three or four strings that are used to produce the drone. Most interesting, however, are the twelve to fourteen **sympathetic strings** that run down the neck behind the frets. These strings are tuned to the pitches of the raga and resonate when the same pitches are played on the melody strings, thereby contributing to the vibrancy of the instrument's sound. They can also be strummed.

Mastering the sitar is comparable in difficulty to mastering the nuances of the raga and tala systems. Traditionally, aspiring musicians committed themselves

Image 6.24: Anoushka Shankar is one of the most famous living sitar players.
Source: Wikimedia Commons
Attribution: Harald Krichel
License: CC BY-SA 3.0

to a **guru**, or teacher, at a young age. The student would move in with the guru and become part of the family, completing household tasks in return for musical guidance. Although this system has largely been replaced by private lessons and music schools in the European model, both of the musicians we will discuss here learned their craft immersively in the traditional way. One is Ravi Shankar, who was apprenticed to sarod player Allauddin Khan, and the other is Anoushka Shankar, who learned from her father.

The Shankars

Ravi Shankar (1920-2012) is remembered as the performer who popularized North Indian music in the West. He began his regular tours of Europe and the United States in 1956. At concerts, he focused on educating audiences about his instrument—the sitar— and the North Indian classical tradition, winning fans in the process. In the 1960s he began to form relationships with popular musicians, including George Harrison of The Beatles. He was invited to participate in both of the major popular music festivals of the 1960s: the 1967 Monterey Pop Festival and the 1969 Aquarian Exposition, better known as Woodstock (see Chapter 7). His influence can be heard on a number of rock albums from the era, including The Beatles' *Sgt. Pepper's Lonely Hearts Club Band* (see Chapter 8).

Image 6.25: This photograph captures Ravi Shankar performing at the Woodstock festival in 1969.
Source: Wikipedia
Attribution: User "Markgoff2972"
License: CC BY-SA 4.0

Ravi's daughter Anoushka was born in London in 1981, when Ravi was sixty-one years old. She began training with him at the age of seven, and was soon appearing beside him onstage playing the tanpura. Anoushka gave her first solo performance at the age of thirteen, making her first studio recording shortly thereafter. Although she is certainly a master of the North Indian classical tradition, Anoushka has been primarily interested in cross-cultural collaborations, and has released a series of albums that explore the connections between different musical traditions. Like her father, she has also maintained connection with the world of popular music. Her most frequent collaborator is singer Norah Jones—who also happens to be her half-sister.

Raga Madhuvanti

We will focus on Anoushka's rendition of Raga Madhuvanti, made live at a Carnegie Hall concert in 2000. Ravi's recording will serve for comparison, for although both are performances of Raga Madhuvanti, they are quite different and cannot be considered to represent "the same piece." In the North Indian tradition, the roles of composer and performer are essentially indistinguishable. A player "composes" in the process of performing a raga, improvising melodic motifs and shapes. At the same time, the identity of the raga is paramount, and two performances of the same raga are therefore expected to communicate similar emotional and expressive content.

Both recordings are considerably shorter than a traditional performance, which might extend to an hour or more. This is typical of the modern era, for audiences desire variety and expect to hear several ragas on a concert. Both recordings, however, exhibit the traditional structure of a raga performance, which is in two large parts.

In the first part of a performance, termed the *alap*, Anoushka introduces the notes of Raga Madhuvanti.[13] This is done slowly and deliberately over the course of nearly ten minutes. She establishes the notes in order, ornamenting them with characteristics slides and melodic fragments. Because the notes of the raga must be presented from lowest to highest, her playing begins in the low range and gradually extends into the high. Once Anoushka has established all of the notes, she gradually introduces a regular pulse into the music. This pulse quickens, and she begins to play with increased rhythmic activity. As a result, the *alap*, which begins in a meditative mood, concludes with breathtaking excitement.

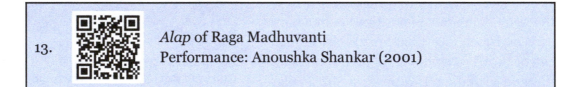

13.   *Alap* of Raga Madhuvanti
       Performance: Anoushka Shankar (2001)

Our recording of the *alap* closes with applause from the audience, but this is not the end of the performance. However, musicians in the North Indian classical tradition don't think of "performance" in the same way as Western classical musicians. There is seldom a clear beginning to the rendition of a raga, which instead emerges gradually from a process of strumming and tuning (activities that a Western player might describe as "warming up"). A performer will often continue to adjust their tuning throughout the *alap*. These habits reflect the continuity between "practice" and "performance" that is characteristic of the North Indian classical tradition. Every rendition of a raga—whether executed in privacy or before an audience—brings the performer and listener one step closer to really "knowing" it.

The second part of the performance is called the *jhala*.[14] Its beginning is marked by the entrance of the tabla, which establishes the tala (rhythmic cycle). In this case, we are hearing the seven-beat Rupak Tala, as described above. The role of the sitar also changes at this point. While Anoushka has been freely improvising thus far, now she plays a fixed melody called a *gat*. Such melodies are usually traditional, and they can be heard in many different performances of the same raga. For the remainder of the *jhala*, Anoushka improvises using fragments of the *gat* according to the rules associated with Raga Madhuvanti. One can recognize the *gat* from time to time as Anoushka works it into the fabric of her playing. As in the *alap*, she increases the rhythmic complexity and virtuosity of her improvisations as she builds to the exciting conclusion.

14.   *Jhala* of Raga Madhuvanti
Performance: Anoushka Shankar (2001)

Comparing Performances

A brief consideration of Ravi's performance of Raga Madhuvanti[15] reveals the flexibility that characterizes the North Indian classical tradition. His *alap* is very brief: less than two minutes, in comparison with Anoushka's ten. He establishes the pitches of the raga much more quickly, and his playing is lively from the start. At the beginning of the *jhala*, he plays a completely different *gat*, which then leads into an extremely long improvisation—twenty minutes—that, because it is founded on a different *gat*, sounds nothing like Anoushka's. In short, the two recordings of Raga Madhuvanti have very little in common. They are not, in a Western sense, recordings of the same piece of music.

15.   This performance of Raga Madhuvanti by Ravi Shankar offers an excellent opportunity to determine what constitutes the essential character of a raga. As the listener will easily observe, it is quite different from Anoushka's performance.

They are, however, recordings of the same raga, which brings us back to the question that opened this chapter: How can sound tell a story? An experienced listener will hear these two performances as both communicating aspects of the essential character of Raga Madhuvanti. Neither of these performances tells a specific story, containing a narrative, events, or characters (like we encountered in Berlioz's *Fantastical Symphony*). However, each is decidedly dramatic, insofar as it engages with and elucidates the extramusical character of the raga. A listener will know that Raga Madhuvanti is associated with the evening and that it expresses romantic love. They might also be familiar with the poetry or paintings that have captured and contributed to the raga's character. Each performance, therefore, adds to the grander narrative of Raga Madhuvanti—a narrative that stretches across generations and continents.

This example also presents an opportunity to discuss the non-universality of programmatic musical expression. Do you hear these performances as expressing the sentiment of romantic love? Do you hear them as playful? Do you connect them with the evening, or the summer? Do you even hear them as communicating the same emotional content as one another? The answer may very well be no. Most music communicates meaning within a cultural context. In this case, that meaning is determined by the listener's familiarity with North Indian classical music, with the raga system in general, and with Raga Madhuvanti in particular. A lifetime of exposure to this music will lead one to make the correct emotional connections. Those emotions, however, are not inherent in the music and not obvious to every listener. This is true of every musical tradition.

RESOURCES FOR FURTHER LEARNING

Print

Cone, Edward T., ed. *Fantastic Symphony: An Authoritative Score*. W. W. Norton & Company, 1971.

Church, Michael, ed. *The Other Classical Music: Fifteen Great Traditions*. Boydell Press, 2015.

Brown, David. *Mussorgsky: His Life and Works*. Oxford University Press, 2006.

Lau, Frederick. *Music in China: Experiencing Music, Expressing Culture*. Oxford University Press, 2007.

Robbins Landon, H. C. *Vivaldi: Voice of the Baroque*. University of Chicago Press, 1996.

Ruckert, George E. *Music in India: Experiencing Music, Expressing Culture*. Oxford University Press, 2003.

Taruskin, Richard. *Music in the Seventeenth and Eighteenth Centuries: The Oxford History of Western Music*. Oxford University Press, 2009.

Online

Catherine Likhuta's website: http://www.catherinelikhuta.com/

Unit 3

MUSIC FOR ENTERTAINMENT

Listening at Public Concerts

Esther M. Morgan-Ellis and Louis Hajosy

INTRODUCTION

Most of us know what a concert is, even if we've never been to one. They are common across categories of music and always follow the same basic formula: members of the public assemble at a given time and place to hear a soloist or ensemble present a prepared program of music. Concerts always tend to be **presentational** in nature (that is to say, there is a clear divide between performer and audience member), although behavioral norms vary across genres. Attendees at a Christian rock concert might get involved with worship, while hip-hop fans might dance, country fans might sing along, and audience members at an orchestral concert might sit in quiet contemplation or follow along with the printed score (a book of music that contains all of the orchestral parts). For the most part, concerts are intended to entertain ticket holders and to turn a profit for the artists and producers who present them.

In this chapter, we will examine four specific concerts that were staged in Europe and the United States between 1808 and 1969. We will consider the purpose for each concert, learn about the composers and producers involved in its presentation, and listen closely to a single musical work or performance. Each of these concerts was unique, and they span the gamut in terms of venue, audience, and repertoire. In order to set the stage for our encounter with concert culture, however, a brief overview of music as public entertainment is in order.

Despite the ubiquity of concerts today, musical performance as a major commercial venture has a relatively short history. In Europe, professional music first thrived in courts and churches. The wealthy staged elaborate musical presentations—such as the opera *Orpheus* (1607) at the court in Mantua, discussed in Chapter 4—for their own private consumption, but tickets were not put on sale. The Catholic church employed professional singers—such as Giovanni da Palestrina (1525-1594) at the Sistine chapel, discussed in Chapter 11—to provide music for worship services, but the music they produced was not intended to have entertainment value.

The first musical presentations for which members of the public could buy tickets were operas, which became available when the St. Cassiano Theater opened in Venice in 1637. Opera quickly became big business. Large crowds flocked to theaters to see the glamorous singers, fabulous costumes, and astonishing stage sets. However, there was one problem: In most places, the church authorities prohibited the performance of opera during the season of Lent. Lent, which constitutes the forty days preceding Easter, is the most solemn period in the church calendar. Members of most European Christian communities—most importantly, Catholics—were expected to abstain from frivolity and pass their time in spiritual contemplation. Opera was simply too exciting and fun.

Concerts, therefore, were first introduced as a solemn alternative to opera. The most successful early concert series was launched in Paris in 1725. It was titled the Concert Spirituel, and—as the name suggests—offered uplifting entertainment that would not offend the Catholic Church. These early concerts included a great deal of variety. In addition to choral works with a sacred message, the program was likely to include concertos, arias, and improvisations. Most of the music would have been recently composed and, despite the advertising, was not explicitly sacred. In order to replicate the thrills of opera as closely as possible, each concert began the same way as an operatic performance: The first thing on the program was always a *sinfonia* for orchestra in three parts, or movements, ordered fast-slow-fast. Over time, this became the **symphony**, perhaps the most important genre of composition for orchestra.

Image 7.1: This poster advertises a 1754 performance in the Concert Spirituel series. The program included a symphony, sacred Catholic music for choir, two violin concertos (one performed by an 11-year-old girl), and Italian songs. This type of variety was typical of early public concerts.

Source: Wikipedia

Attribution: Joseph-Nicolas-Pancrace Royer and Gabriel Capperan

License: Public Domain

During the 18th and 19th centuries, concerts became more and more important in European life. At the same time, orchestral music grew in prominence, and came to be understood as being more dignified and serious than opera. The idea of a concert as commercial entertainment, however, was never confined to the orchestra. In the 1830s, for example, the Hungarian pianist Franz Liszt began to give solo piano recitals across Europe (his career and music are discussed in Chapter 9). In the last 150 years, the concert model has been increasingly adopted by traditions outside of Europe. The first Chinese orchestra, the Shanghai Municipal Orchestra, was formed in 1879, while Indian classical musicians, who had formerly been employed by courts, began to stage public concerts near the turn of the century. These developments reflected a growing reliance on capitalistic economic models throughout the world, as musicians began to rely on ticket sales rather than aristocratic patronage.

The modern concert economy works in tandem with the recording industry, which has helped performing artists to gain international fame since the early 20th century. When you choose to buy tickets to a concert, it is usually because you already know and enjoy the music you are going to hear. This is a change from the earliest concerts, which were understood as an opportunity to introduce new music to the public. Such was the case with our first example.

1808: A CONCERT BY LUDWIG VAN BEETHOVEN

The Composer

In 1808, the German composer and pianist Ludwig van Beethoven (1770-1827) was at the height of his career. He was living and working in the city of Vienna, which at the time was emerging as the musical capital of Europe. He had moved there in 1792 at the age of 21 to study with the famous composer Franz Joseph Haydn (1732-1809). Unfortunately, Haydn had just departed to present a concert series in London, so the two composers ended up having very little contact. By the time Haydn returned, Beethoven was already well established as a virtuoso pianist and composer of piano music.

Image 7.2: The portrait of Beethoven was completed by Josef Willibrord Mähler when the composer was about 25 years old.
Source: Wikimedia Commons
Attribution: Joseph Willibrord Mähler
License: Public Domain

In 1798, however, an unforeseen health concern threatened to end Beethoven's career: He began to go deaf. While loss of hearing would be a hardship for anyone, for Beethoven it was catastrophic. As a pianist, he relied on his hearing to play with orchestras. And as a musician, hearing was the sense that he valued most. Growing deafness

Image 7.3: This Viennese vista was painted by Bernardo Bellotto shortly before Beethoven was born.
Source: Wikimedia Commons
Attribution: Bernardo Bellotto
License: Public Domain

took its toll not only on Beethoven's professional life but on his social life as well, and he began to avoid gatherings of people out of fear that his disability would be detected. In an 1802 letter to his brothers, Carl and Johann, Beethoven wrote about the shame he felt related to his hearing loss: "How could I possibly admit such an infirmity in the one sense which should have been more perfect in me than in others, a sense which I once possessed in highest perfection, a perfection such as few surely in my profession enjoy or have enjoyed - O I cannot do it."

This letter is known today as the Heiligenstadt Testament, due to the fact that it was written while Beethoven lived in the town of Heiligenstadt and was meant to serve as a last will and testament. It contains a great deal of insight into the composer's state of mind during these difficult years, including the fact that he considered ending his life out of despair at his deafness. However, as Beethoven wrote, "only art it was that withheld me," for "it seemed impossible to leave the world until I had produced all that I felt called upon me to produce."

Image 7.4: Although the Heiligenstadt Testament remained private during Beethoven's lifetime, its posthumous discovery revealed his tormented state of mind following his diagnosis.
Source: Wikimedia Commons
Attribution: Ludwig van Beethoven
License: Public Domain

It would seem that his intense need to compose music compelled him to carry on, in spite of his enormous loss.

The Heiligenstadt Testament remained unknown until it was found among Beethoven's papers following his death, for he never dispatched it to his brothers. However, it has since played an important role in cementing the public perception of Beethoven as an archetypical **Romantic** artist who became great through personal suffering. Before the 19th century, composers were seen as craftspeople. They created a product that was useful in everyday life, but they were not held in particularly high regard. Haydn, for example, although considered a great composer today, held the status of a servant for most of his lifetime (see Chapter 8).

In the early 19th century, however, things changed. The European public began to perceive prominent composers as "geniuses," and they treated them with heightened respect. Where Haydn had been a servant, Beethoven was invited to dine with wealthy aristocrats and treated as their equal, or even superior. This change was brought about by economic and social transformations. A growing middle class meant that more people had the leisure time and financial means to consume art music, while a new set of Romantic values prioritized individual emotional expression. The public became particularly interested in portrayals of heartbreak, illness, and personal struggle—the same experiences that were understood to inform great artistic expression.

Beethoven suited the new requirements to a tee. He not only suffered deafness, but also endured repeated rejection from women (he never married) and a tempestuous family life. One of his tragic love affairs was captured in another letter, written in 1812 and addressed to a lady identified only as the "Immortal Beloved." A few years later he lost his brother Karl to tuberculosis, despite his efforts to provide the best medical treatment. Following Karl's death, Beethoven embarked on a bitter court battle to win custody of his brother's son. After many years he prevailed, but the pressure he put on the child to follow in his own footsteps was so great that the boy attempted suicide. This is not the only example of Beethoven's bad behavior. He was generally rude and inconsiderate of others, and was frequently evicted from his various lodgings for noise violations. He also practiced poor hygiene and frequently appeared disheveled in public. All of this, however, was not only

Image 7.5: This 1820 portrait by Karl Joseph Stieler captures the Romantic view of Beethoven. The composer looks annoyed to have been interrupted at his solitary work. His hair is messy and his dress is informal. His surroundings reflect the high value placed on nature in this era.
Source: Wikimedia Commons
Attribution: Joseph Karl Stieler
License: Public Domain

forgiven but praised. Beethoven's antisocial behavior contributed to his reputation as a genius.

Scholars have long described Beethoven's career and output in terms of three periods: an early period, during which he primarily composed for the piano; a middle period, during which he focused on triumphant, large-scale works for public performance; and a late period, during which he became very experimental (indeed, some critics theorized that he had lost his mind). The 1808 concert that we about to explore marks the climax of Beethoven's middle period. At this time, his struggle with hearing loss was known to the public, and he had become famous across Europe for his dramatic and ambitious symphonic works.

The Concert

Beethoven's most famous concert took place on December 22, 1808, at the Theater an der Wien (Theater on the Banks of the Vienna River). For Beethoven, this concert was an invaluable opportunity to make some money and to premiere some of his recent compositions. However, circumstances in Vienna at the time made putting on a concert very difficult, and Beethoven faced a number of challenges in staging this event, which in the end was not particularly successful.

To begin with, competition from opera meant that a concert could only succeed if the opera houses were closed. That explains the date of this concert,

Image 7.6: This painting of the Theater an der Wien was completed in the early 20th century by Carl Wenzel Zajicek.
Source: Wikimedia Commons
Attribution: Carl Wenzel Zajicek
License: Public Domain

which Beethoven scheduled to take place during the Catholic season of **Advent** (the four weeks leading up to Christmas). Unfortunately, the timing also had two undesirable consequences. Because there was a rush to present concerts during Advent, Beethoven found himself in competition with a much more prominent event taking place on the same night, and as a result he was not able to hire the top Viennese musicians. (Others simply refused to work with him due to his corrosive personality.) Another challenge came with the weather, for the hall was freezing cold on the night of the performance.

Even during Advent, it was difficult to put together a public concert. To begin with, there were no permanent orchestras in Vienna, so the concert organizer would have to recruit each individual musician, organize the rehearsal schedule, and arrange for payment. Booking a hall was also difficult. Beethoven was only able to do so because he happened to have a personal relationship with the director of the Theater an der Wien, for whom he had done various favors over the course of the year. Finally, putting on a concert required special permits from the government, which exercised tight control over public gatherings.

Under these adverse circumstances, it comes as no surprise that the December 22 concert did not go off without a hitch. Beethoven had to settle for second-rate performers, including an inexperienced soprano who struggled to overcome her nerves. However, most of the difficulties were of his own doing. To begin with, the concert was four hours long, which even in 1808 was considered trying. Beethoven saw the concert as an opportunity to share as many of his new works with the public as possible, so he did not restrain himself in assembling the program. In fact, Beethoven completed the final piece on the program only a few days before the concert, which created a further problem: His orchestra did not have time to learn it properly, and the performance fell apart so badly that Beethoven (who also served as **conductor**) had to stop and restart the work.

In keeping with the common practice of the time, Beethoven brought together works from a variety of genres for his concert. He also met expectations by starting with a symphony and including sacred vocal music. The most unusual aspect of his concert was that it featured music by only a single composer.

The evening began with his Symphony No. 6, also known as the "Pastoral" Symphony. This programmatic five-movement work portrays a visit to the countryside and takes about 40 minutes to perform. Next was *Ah! Deceiver*, the concert aria with which the young soprano struggled. This was followed by the Gloria from his Mass in C major and his Piano Concerto No. 4, with Beethoven as soloist.

The second half of the concert began with Symphony No. 5. After the Sanctus from the same Mass, Beethoven performed an improvised fantasy at the piano. Due to his progressing deafness, this was to be his last public performance as a pianist. The concert concluded with his new *Choral Fantasy*, an ambitious work for orchestra, choir, and vocal soloists.

The concert did not elicit positive reviews. In general, patrons thought that it was too long, too loud, and a bit overwhelming. As one of Beethoven's supporters, the composer and critic J.F Reichardt, put it: "There we sat, in the most bitter cold, from half past six until half past ten, and confirmed for ourselves the maxim that one may easily have too much of a good thing, still more of a powerful one."

Symphony No. 5

Despite its many shortcomings, Beethoven's 1808 concert is remembered as one of the most remarkable of its era. December 22 marked both Beethoven's last performance as a pianist and the premiere of many influential works. Symphony No. 6 later inspired Berlioz when he wrote his own programmatic symphony, the *Fantastical Symphony* (discussed in Chapter 6). The *Choral Fantasy* foreshadowed Beethoven's Symphony No. 9, which transformed the genre with the addition of choir and vocal soloists.

Image 7.7: This engraving captures the premiere of Beethoven's Symphony No. 9 in 1824.
Source: Wikimedia Commons
Attribution: Bettmann
License: Public Domain

And Symphony No. 5, which we will examine in some detail, has become perhaps Beethoven's most famous composition.

Symphonies developed along with concert life. Due to their role as concert openers (and sometimes closers), 18th-century symphonies were usually lively and cheerful. They were almost always in the major mode. They were also fairly short, and composers tended to write a lot of them (Haydn composed 106). By the end of the 18th century, symphonies had four movements: a brisk opening movement, a slow second movement, a third movement inspired by dance, and an exciting finale.

While Symphony No. 5 is in many respects typical of the genre, it has a number of remarkable characteristics. Like other symphonies, it has four movements as outlined above. Unusually, however, these movements are linked by a single musical **motif** that is introduced at the beginning of the work: an ominous four-note pattern that was described by Beethoven's first biographer as fate knocking at the door. This "fate motif" returns throughout the first movement and then in the subsequent movements as well—an unusual characteristic, since the movements of a symphony were usually kept independent from one another.

The technique by which a composer develops a large-scale work out of a single musical motif is known as **organicism**. While Beethoven was not the first composer to work in this way, he took the technique further than any had before him. Organicism was highly regarded in the Romantic era, when listeners wanted art to mirror nature. Just as a tree might grow from a tiny seed, Beethoven's symphony grows from the opening "fate motif."

Symphony No. 5 is also notable for its drama and serious tone. Beethoven was responsible for elevating the symphonic genre, transforming symphonies from entertainment into the loftiest artistic expression. This is evidenced by his output: Beethoven wrote only nine symphonies, but each took years to complete and set new standards for length and complexity. Symphony No. 5 is in the key of C minor, which sets it apart from the cheerful curtain raisers of earlier composers, and the opening "fate motif" makes it clear that this is not just light entertainment. From the start, listeners felt as if the symphony was trying to communicate something. It seemed rife with conflict and action. To understand what it might communicate, however, we will have to look at the music.

Sonata Form

The first movement, like that of all symphonies (and most other instrumental works) of the time, is in what is known as **sonata form**. Sonata form developed gradually during the course of the 18th century. Nobody invented it: Instead, a variety of composers experimented with formal design until a consensus emerged. By the 19th century, the components of the form were firmly in place, and listeners knew what to expect from a first movement. This gave the composer a lot of power, for Beethoven was able to tell a story by satisfying or frustrating the expectations of the audience.

A movement in sonata form has at least three parts: an Exposition (heard twice), in which contrasting themes are introduced; a Development, in which those themes are explored and transformed; and a Recapitulation, in which the themes from the Exposition are heard for a second time. The form also includes two optional parts. Some sonata-form movements open with an introduction, which is usually slow and stately. And many sonata-form movements conclude with a Coda, in which anything can happen. (The term "**coda**" is derived from the Latin word for "tail.") Key areas are very important in sonata form. The Exposition starts with a Primary Theme in the home key, but moves to a different key for a Secondary Theme and Closing Theme. The Recapitulation, on the other hand, is entirely in the home key. The Development can move through a variety of key areas.

Minor-mode sonata form movements—such as the first movement of Beethoven's Symphony No. 5—are particularly interesting, because the composer has options for the key of the Secondary Theme. While the Primary Theme in the Exposition must be in minor, the Secondary Theme can be in minor or major. In other words, the Secondary Theme can have a sad/serious character or it can be cheerful/relaxing. If the Secondary Theme is presented in major in the Exposition, it can also be major in the Recapitulation—but the listener can't be sure until they hear it!

Movement I

	Symphony No. 5, Movement I
	Composer: Ludwig van Beethoven
	Performance: Dallas Symphony Orchestra,
	conducted by Jaap van Zweden (2012)

Time	Form	What to listen for
Exposition		
0'00"	Primary Theme	The first thing we hear is the four-note "fate" motif, which will return throughout the movements
0'43"	Secondary Theme	This major-mode theme starts with the same motif, but its character is at first calm and restful
1'05"	Closing Theme	This theme is jubilant—it seems to have recovered from the angst of the Primary Theme
1'23"	Repetition of Exposition	We hear all of the preceding music for a second time
Development		
2'45"		This section is dominated by the four-note "fate" motif, which we hear countless times
Recapitulation		
4'01"	Primary Theme	The Recapitulation opens with the "fate" motif, which comes crashing back in the full orchestra
4'17		The Primary Theme is mostly identical to that heard in the Exposition, with the exception of this dramatic oboe solo
4'49"	Secondary Theme	This theme is still in the major mode, suggesting that the movement might have a happy ending
5'15"	Closing Theme	This theme is also in the major mode, suggesting that the movement will conclude in major

Coda	
5'31"	The Coda turns almost immediately to minor; like the Development, it is dominated by the "fate" motif
6'01"	This entirely new theme suggests labor and struggle
6'33"	The movement ends almost exactly as it began

Beethoven used all of the sonata form tricks in the first movement of Symphony No. 5. The Primary Theme is stormy and anxious, not only because it is in C minor. The initial sounding of the fate motif by unison strings is obviously threatening, while the quick tempo and violent changes in dynamic that follow do nothing to calm the mood. The Secondary Theme, however, is in E-flat major, and it offers a moment of peace. Perhaps there is a chance to escape the storm.

In the Development, Beethoven was free to use any of the themes from the Exposition. However, he only explores the fate motif, which is heard dozens of times in all ranges and at all dynamic levels. Finally, he uses the fate motif to crash back into the Recapitulation. Following the Primary Theme, however, this is a plaintive, unmetered oboe solo that was not heard in the Exposition. This comes as a startling surprise, for the Recapitulation should not include any new musical material. What does it mean? Beethoven's audience must have wondered. The Secondary Theme, which could return in major or minor, is in C major, and the Recapitulation concludes in C major. This seems to suggest a "happy ending" for the movement.

However, Beethoven is not finished. A massive Coda—which listeners would not necessarily have expected—immediately returns us to C minor. A new, pounding theme is introduced. After about a minute, we hear the fate motif one last time, followed by the first measures of the Primary Theme and a final cadence. The happy ending has escaped us, and we find ourselves back in the terrifying sonic world of the opening measures.

The story told by the first movement of Symphony No. 5 is certainly not a happy one. Despite moments of respite (the Secondary Theme), the listener is haunted throughout by the fate motif, and the devastating conclusion to the Coda reveals that we have not escaped it. Indeed, we are left right where we started. However, the symphony as a whole tells a more uplifting story. The second movement—a theme and variations—is calm and beautiful. It offers repose after the stormy opening. The third movement uses the fate motif as the basis for an aggressive march. The movement concludes, however, with a mysterious passage that ultimately transitions triumphantly into the fourth movement, which is in a resounding C major.

Movement IV

		Symphony No. 5, Movement IV Composer: Ludwig van Beethoven Performance: Dallas Symphony Orchestra, conducted by Jaap van Zweden (2012)
Time	**Form**	**What to listen for**

Exposition

Time	Form	What to listen for
0'00"	Primary Theme	This theme opens with a triumphant statement in the brass that ascends through the pitches of a major triad before returning to the tonic; next, the violins repeatedly play an ascending major scale
0'30"	Transition Theme	Although transition themes are not always memorable, this one features a powerful motif in the low brass
0'53"	Secondary Theme	This theme is more relaxed than the Primary Theme; it has a dance-like lilt
1'17"	Closing Theme	The energy builds again with this theme

Development

Time	Form	What to listen for
3'27"		This section is dominated by the Secondary Theme
4'51"		This passage quotes Movement III; in it, we hear the short-short-short-long rhythmic motif that dominated Movement I

Recapitulation

Time	Form	What to listen for
5'20"	Primary Theme	This presentation is nearly identical to that in the Exposition
5'50"	Transition Theme	This presentation is similar to that in the Exposition, but it does not change key
6'16"	Secondary Theme	This presentation is nearly identical to that in the Exposition

6'40"	Closing Theme	This presentation is similar to that in the Exposition, but it is extended and builds into the Coda
Coda		
7'06"		The Coda begins with material from the Secondary Theme
7'33"		This passage contains new thematic material
8'12"		At this point, the tempo greatly accelerates
8'35"		We hear a fast-paced version of the motif that opened the movement; the Coda ends with a series of accented chords

To see how the story ends, we will take a close look at the fourth movement, which opens with a brilliant trumpet fanfare. The Exposition maintains a sense of joy and excitement throughout, but the Development introduces conflict as sections of the orchestra wrestle the themes through minor keys. The Development concludes with a repetition of the minor-mode march theme from the third movement. This was highly unusual for the time, and must have shocked Beethoven's audience. Once a movement was over, they didn't expect to hear its themes again. The march theme, which is presented in a quiet **pizzicato** by the strings, introduces a sense of uncertainty and discomfort, but it once again transitions into a triumphant Recapitulation. This time, the Coda—which accelerates to a breakneck tempo— provides the joyful ending that we were denied in the first movement.

Listeners in 1808 did not just hear Symphony No. 5 as a piece of music for orchestra. They heard it as an autobiographical account of Beethoven's personal struggle with hearing loss. The opening motif represented his own tragic fate, and the first movement expressed his suffering. The final movement, however, portrayed his victory over fate. He had struggled with his disability and had emerged triumphant. This narrative trajectory from darkness to light would later be imitated by other composers, including Pyotr Ilyich Tchaikovsky (Symphony No. 4) and Dmitri Shostakovich (Symphony No. 5, discussed in Chapter 10), each of whom also sought to tell a musical story about overcoming adversity.

1924: AN EXPERIMENT IN MODERN MUSIC

When bandleader Paul Whiteman put together his 1924 concert entitled *An Experiment in Modern Music*, he was trying to do much more than make money.

He was on a mission to legitimize his field of music: jazz. However, he wasn't concerned with promoting the interests of jazz's African American originators. Instead, he sought to convince white audiences that jazz—a suspect genre, due to its origins in the black community and associations with drinking and dancing—could be transformed into legitimate art by white composers and musicians such as himself. His concert, although profoundly racist in intent, is remembered for introducing one of the most beloved concert pieces of the 20th century: George Gershwin's *Rhapsody in Blue*.

Paul Whiteman and George Gershwin

Although few recognize his name today, Paul Whiteman was the most famous and successful bandleader of the 1920s. He specialized in what was known as "**sweet jazz**,"[1] a kind of lively dance music intended for white consumers. Most modern listeners would have a hard time identifying his music as jazz. Instead, we tend to reserve that term for the more rhythmically interesting performances put on by African American dance bands of the era—a type of music known at the time as "**hot jazz**."[2] To hear the contrast, one might compare Whiteman's biggest hit, "Whispering" (1920), with "East St. Louis Toodle-Oo" (1927) as recorded by Duke Ellington and his Washingtonians. Whiteman's recording is notable for its lively tempo, square rhythms, precise pitches, and instrumentation (his band included a violin section). "Whispering" is suitable dance music, to be sure, but it lacks the spontaneity and excitement of "East St. Louis Toodle-Oo."

Image 7.8: This 1934 photograph depicts Paul Whiteman with his characteristic mustache and extra-long baton.
Source: Wikimedia Commons
Attribution: Unknown
License: Public Domain

1. Whiteman's biggest hit, "Whispering" (1920), exemplifies his "sweet jazz" sound.

2. Duke Ellington's 1927 recording of "East St. Louis Toodle-Oo" provides a good example of "hot jazz."

Despite his massive success, Whiteman still faced considerable opposition as a jazz musician in the 1920s. Many white people were deeply worried about the dangerous effects that jazz might have on society. The rhythms of jazz prompted dancers to do things with their bodies that were not considered appropriate, while its association with nightclubs meant that it encouraged other immoral behaviors as well. However, the biggest concern—if often unspoken—was with the increasing influence of African American music on mainstream culture. To make jazz acceptable, therefore, Whiteman understood that he needed to make it white.

The purpose of Whiteman's concert was to illustrate the evolution of jazz from a rough and untutored product of African American culture into a sophisticated form of concert music. In order to tell this story, however, he needed a special piece with which to end his program—a piece that would combine elements of jazz with the European concert tradition, thereby synthesizing the two traditions and proving the potential for jazz to become art. He decided to approach one of the leading popular song composers of the day, George Gershwin, and requested that he write and perform a jazz-inspired piano **concerto**.

Image 7.9: This undated photograph depicts George Gershwin around the time that he composed Rhapsody in Blue.
Source: Wikimedia Commons
Attribution: Unknown
License: Public Domain

In 1924, George Gershwin (1898-1937) was still a young man, but he had already made a name for himself as a Broadway songwriter. Gershwin was born into a family of Russian Jewish immigrants who had settled in Brooklyn. He revealed a talent for music when his parents bought a piano for his older brother, Ira. While Ira had little interest in playing, George was fascinated with the instrument and demonstrated an uncanny ability to pick out familiar tunes on the keys. He subsequently took lessons in piano and composition.

In 1913, Gershwin left school to take a job as a **song plugger** with the music publisher Jerome H. Remick. At the time, the principle product of the popular music industry was sheet music, which allowed Americans to perform songs with piano accompaniment in their own homes. (Phonograph records were just beginning to sell in large numbers.) Music publishers, therefore, did whatever they could to build public interest in their products. Consumers were most likely to buy the sheet music for a song that they had heard and enjoyed at a theater or in a nightclub. The role of a song plugger, therefore, was to ensure that the songs published by a given company were heard as frequently as possible. Gershwin's job was to promote Remick songs to professional singers. Each day, performers would visit the publishing house to try out the latest products, and Gershwin would play new songs for them on the piano. If he was lucky, the performer would add a Remick song to their act, thereby providing valuable advertising for the sheet music.

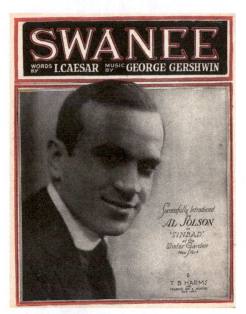

Image 7.10: The cover of the sheet music for Gershwin's 1919 hit "Swanee." A photograph of Al Jolson, the singer who made it famous, appears on the cover.
Source: Wikimedia Commons
Attribution: George Gershwin and Irving Caesar
License: Public Domain

Although Gershwin was good at his job, he was not content to play songs written by other people. He began composing his own songs, and had his first big hit in 1919 with "Swanee." As was always the case, "Swanee" began to sell when it was picked up by a star performer—in this case, the hottest singer of the decade, Al Jolson. The song was perfect for Jolson, for he specialized in blackface performances of numbers written from an imagined African American perspective. "Swanee" joined a long tradition of songs that expressed a nostalgic longing for the South. Indeed, Gershwin took the name "Swanee" from the famous Stephen Foster song "Old Folks at Home" (1851)—an early **"plantation song"** that used dialect to indicate the race of the narrator. Although the text to Gershwin's song is not in dialect, its stereotyped references to banjos, Dixie, and "Mammy" made it clear that the narrator was black. None of this proves that Gershwin harbored any racial animosity of his own. Instead, it exemplifies how common racist stereotypes were in mainstream entertainment of the era.

Following the success of "Swanee," Gershwin quickly made a name for himself as a leading composer of Broadway musicals. He worked primarily with his brother Ira, who wrote lyrics. Gershwin moved to Hollywood in 1936 to write music for film musicals, but died suddenly due to a brain tumor in July of 1937, when he was only 38 years old.

The Concert

Whiteman's *Experiment in Modern Music* took place on February 12 at Aeolian Hall in New York City. He intended for the concert to be a significant social and cultural event, so all of the prominent performers, conductors, and critics of classical music were invited. This was not Whiteman's regular audience of enthusiastic young dancers, but rather an audience of skeptical highbrows whom he hoped to win over. The afternoon began, therefore, with a lecture, in which Whiteman explained how his project would benefit the art music community and bring more listeners to the opera house and concert hall.

The program itself was divided into two parts. The first ostensibly illustrated the evolution of jazz, while the second presented various syntheses of jazz and classical music, culminating in the premiere of *Rhapsody in Blue*. The concert opened with a section entitled "The True Form of Jazz." Unsurprisingly, however, Whiteman's idea about what constituted "real jazz" was poorly informed.

The first number on the program was "Livery Stable Blues,"[3] a piece that has gone down in history as the first ever to be recorded and marketed as jazz. The record, made in 1917 by the Original Dixieland Jass Band (the spelling of "jazz" was inconsistent in early years), had been enormously successful, thereby launching the jazz craze in Northern cities. However, there was nothing particularly "original" about the band or the record. To begin with, all of the members of the band were white, while the style in which they played

Image 7.11: The exterior of Aeolian Hall in 1916.
Source: Wikimedia Commons
Attribution: Unknown
License: Public Domain

had most certainly originated in the black communities of New Orleans. (The band leader, Nick LaRocca, created controversy in the 1950s when he continued to aggressively push the ridiculous claim that he had personally invented jazz.) Although the members of the band came from New Orleans, they had settled in Chicago and made a living playing music for dances, and they made their first records in New York City—environments far removed from the birthplace of jazz. Finally, the song itself was a particularly hokey example of Dixieland jazz. In it, the instrumentalists imitate various barnyard animals, thereby perpetuating stereotypes of black music as primitive and ridiculous.

3.  "Livery Stable Blues" appeared on the B side of the Original Dixieland Jass Band's first record, recorded in New York City in 1917.

We will not examine the entire program in similar depth. Whiteman did not offer a particularly insightful survey of jazz history, and his concert was clearly designed to showcase the various capabilities of Whiteman's band above all else. It also served, as we have seen, to erase the black origins of the style that Whiteman was trying to legitimize.

The second part of the concert began with Victor Herbert's *A Suite of Serenades*—another piece that had been commissioned by Whiteman for the concert. Although

Image 7.12: The Original Dixieland Jass Band, right around the time they released their first record.
Source: Wikimedia Commons
Attribution: Unknown
License: Public Domain

not particularly jazzy, the suite allowed the band to show off their ability to play highbrow music. The suite's four movements—Spanish, Chinese, Cuban, and Oriental—reveal that the fascination with exoticism in music that we saw at work in Tchaikovsky's ballet *The Nutcracker* had not died away. This was followed by *Rhapsody in Blue*, while Edward Elgar's *Pomp and Circumstance March No. 1*—a piece that we all recognize from high school and college graduations—ended the program.

Rhapsody in Blue

Gershwin's *Rhapsody in Blue* almost never came to be. The composer's initial response to Whiteman's request that he write a jazz-inspired concerto had been quite sensible: He said no. After all, Gershwin was a popular song composer, and a busy and successful one at that. He knew that he didn't have the time to take on the project, and he wasn't sure that he would be able to do it well. However, just five weeks before the concert was to take place, Ira read an announcement in the *New York Tribune* that his brother was hard at work on a piece to be premiered as part of the program. After that, Whiteman was able to convince Gershwin to join his project, for he would have been publicly embarrassed if he did not produce the concerto that had already been advertised.

The Compositional Process

Luckily, Gershwin got some help from collaborators. Most importantly, while he composed a version of the concerto for two pianos (solo and accompaniment), he did not have to orchestrate it. That work was done by Ferde Grofé, a composer who was employed by Whiteman to produce arrangements for the band. Grofé was intimately familiar with the ensemble, so he was able to create parts that showed Whiteman's players to their best advantage. Because he had to use the musicians at hand, Grofé's initial **orchestration** was a little strange: He created parts for clarinet, various saxophones, trumpet, horn, trombone, tuba, string bass, percussion, piano, banjo, and eight violins. After the work proved successful, Grofé reorchestrated it, first for a small theater orchestra (1926) and then for full symphony orchestra (1942). When you hear *Rhapsody in Blue* today, you might be hearing any of these versions, although the last is the most common.

Grofé's contribution was the most important—especially since the young Gershwin did not yet have the skills necessary to write for a 23-part ensemble like Whiteman's. However, he was not the only collaborator to leave his mark on the concerto. The famous opening clarinet **glissando** was in fact the idea of the man who first played it, Ross Gorman. Although Gorman first added the glissando in rehearsal as a joke, Gershwin liked it and asked him to keep it for the performance. Finally, the concerto was given its name by Gershwin's brother Ira, who had recently seen an exhibition of paintings by James McNeill Whistler and was inspired by his color-centric titles (e.g. *Nocturne: Blue and Silver*).

The process by which *Rhapsody in Blue* came into being is interesting because

Image 7.13: Ferde Grofé had a long and successful career as a composer and arranger.
Source: Wikimedia Commons
Attribution: Bain News Service
License: Public Domain

Image 7.14: Clarinet player Ross Gorman is responsible for the glissando that opens Rhapsody in Blue.
Source: Wikimedia Commons
Attribution: Bain News Service
License: Public Domain

it sheds light on the collaborative nature of artistic production. We like to think of the composer as a puppet master, controlling all elements of the creation of a new work, but that is almost never the case. It is much more common for musical works to develop through a process of give and take between various creative personalities. This is particularly true in the world of musical theater and opera, where Gershwin himself felt most at home.

All the same, it was Gershwin who came up with the melodies and decided how to use them. In 1931, Gershwin described how the idea for the concerto came to him:

> It was on the train, with its steely rhythms, its rattle-ty bang, that is so often so stimulating to a composer – I frequently hear music in the very heart of the noise. [...] And there I suddenly heard, and even saw on paper – the complete construction of the rhapsody, from beginning to end. No new themes came to me, but I worked on the thematic material already in my mind and tried to conceive the composition as a whole. I heard it as a sort of musical kaleidoscope of America, of our vast melting pot, of our unduplicated national pep, of our metropolitan madness.

To create the concerto, it seems that Gershwin turned to his store of tune ideas left over from previous projects. This was a typical way for popular song writers to work. As Gershwin was developing songs for the musical theater stage, he would write dozens of melodies, although only some would end up in the final compositions. He never discarded a melody, however. Instead, he set it aside for future inspiration. This approach would have helped him to put together his concerto relatively quickly, since he wasn't starting from scratch: He already had the five themes that were to constitute the new work.

The Themes

For the sake of facilitating discussion of the music, analysts have named Gershwin's five themes, and they are known today as the "ritornello,"[4] "train,"[5] "stride,"[6] "shuffle,"[7] and "love"[8] themes. A **ritornello**, as you might recall from Chapter 4, is a theme that returns frequently throughout a work. The other themes are named after associations: the train theme has the propulsive rhythms of a train, the stride theme has the characteristics of stride-style piano playing (a descendent of ragtime piano playing), the shuffle theme would have been suitable for the contemporary dance of that name, and the love theme is slow and romantic.

4.  The "ritornello" theme.

5. The "train" theme.

6. The "stride" theme.

7. The "shuffle" theme.

8. The "love" theme.

Rhapsody in Blue
Composer: George Gershwin, orchestrated by
Ferde Grofé
Performance: Michael Tilson Thomas with the
Columbia Jazz Band (1976)

Time	Form	What to listen for
Part 1		
0'00"	Introduction	Clarinet solo featuring the famous ascending glissando
0'09"	Ritornello theme	Played by the clarinet
0'40"	Stride theme	Heard in the muted horns
0'54"	Ritornello theme	Played first by a muted trumpet, then the entire ensemble
1'10"	"The Man I Love" tag	This melodic fragment comes from Gerswin's hit song "The Man I Love"; it is heard throughout the concerto

1'24"	Piano solo	In these passages, the soloist demonstrates their virtuosity
1'46"	Ritornello theme	Heard in the solo piano
2'18"	Piano solo	
2'45"	Ritornello theme	This fast-paced version features various sections in turn
Part 2		
3'09"	Train theme	Heard first in the muted trumpets, then saxophone
3'29"	Stride theme	Heard first in the clarinet, then the full ensemble
4'12"	Shuffle theme	Heard first in the saxophones, then the trombones, then the full ensemble
4'55"	Piano solo	
5'10"	Stride theme	Heard in the solo piano
6'24"	Ritornello theme	Heard first in the piano, then in the ensemble with virtuosic piano accompaniment
7'14"	Shuffle theme	Heard in the solo piano
Part 3		
8'12"		At this point, the tempo greatly accelerates
8'27"	Love theme	Heard first in the strings, then in the full ensemble, then in the solo piano
Part 4		
11'02"	Piano solo	The virtuosic passage builds energy and transitions into the finale

11'54"	Love theme	The brass play a fast version of the theme, which is at first in the minor mode
12'50"	Stride theme	Following a dramatic build-up, the full ensemble plays this theme
13'16"	Ritornello theme	Heard in the full ensemble
12'28"	"The Man I Love" tag	Heard in the solo piano

All five themes are in major, but feature the added scale degrees—a flat third and seventh and a raised fourth—that are often heard in jazz. (This set of pitches is referred to as the **blues scale**.) The themes also contain **syncopated** rhythms, unexpected accents, and surprising shifts between duple and triple subdivisions. All of this, combined with the orchestration of the accompaniment, brings the sound of "jazz" to the concerto. What draws *Rhapsody* into the "classical" world is its length, internal variation, and formal complexity, for Gershwin used these themes to craft a 16-minute work that explores a variety of emotional states.

Although it is performed without any pauses, *Rhapsody in Blue* is in four distinct parts. The opening section features the ritornello theme. A second section brings in the train, stride, and shuffle themes. A third, slow section focuses on the love theme, and an exciting finale revisits the stride and love themes before concluding with the ritornello theme.

Reception

Following its premier, many critics accused *Rhapsody in Blue* of not having form. What they meant, however, was that it didn't meet their expectations for concert music. Writing in 1955, the composer and conductor Leonard Bernstein suggested that *Rhapsody* was not a real composition because it lacked the sense of inevitability that is communicated by Beethoven's music. While a work like Beethoven's Symphony No. 5 seems to move inexorably forward from beginning to end, Bernstein argued, the sections of *Rhapsody* could be reordered, rearranged, or even eliminated without damaging the overall work. Indeed, *Rhapsody* has been published, performed, and recorded in many different versions of various lengths, while Beethoven's Symphony No. 5 is a fixed work for a specific cast of players. Gershwin, however, was coming from a different musical world, and his values were not those of Beethoven (although he certainly knew much about the classical tradition).

Despite some pushback from critics, Whiteman's *Experiment in Modern Music* was a hit. After repeating the concert in various upscale New York venues,

Whiteman took it on a national tour. (*Pomp and Circumstance*, which reviewers found anticlimactic and gratuitous, was eliminated from the program.) The recording of *Rhapsody in Blue* sold millions of copies, and the work soon became a concert standard for piano soloists. In 1980, United Airlines negotiated for the use of *Rhapsody* in advertisements, and in 1999 the work was featured in the Disney film *Fantasia 2000*. Although Rhapsody's enormous popular success caused early critics to be suspicious of its status as art, it is recognized today as one of the masterpieces of the 20th century. However, we should not forget the disturbing racism of the concert project that brought this piece into existence.

1933: A CENTURY OF PROGRESS

Just a few years later, race became the focal point of another important concert. This time, however, the object was to celebrate the accomplishments of African American composers and performers in the overwhelmingly white world of European-inspired orchestral music. The concert in question took place as part of the 1933-34 Chicago World's Fair, titled "A Century of Progress," and it is remembered for the first performance of a symphony composed by an African American woman, Florence Beatrice Price.

Image 7.15: The poster for the 1933-34 Chicago World's Fair, "A Century of Progress."
Source: Wikipedia
Attribution: Weimer Pursell
License: Public Domain

The Composer

Florence Price (1887-1953) was born to upper-class parents in Little Rock, Arkansas. At the time, the population of Little Rock was one-third African American and the city had a thriving and self-sufficient black community. Her father was the city's only black dentist, while her mother was a successful real estate investor. Both of Price's parents had been born free, and both had enjoyed the advantages of a good education. As such, they considered themselves responsible for furthering the uplift of the black community in Little Rock by promoting education and the arts.

In 1903, Price left Little Rock to study music at the New England Conservatory, where she quickly rose to the top of her class. She was invited to study with the most exclusive composition teacher, and graduated in just three years with diplomas in piano teaching and organ performance. Upon completing her education, she returned home to carry on the uplift mission of her parents. She taught music at black colleges near Little Rock until 1910, when her father died. After a further two years teaching at Clark University in Atlanta, Price returned to Little Rock to marry the city's leading black lawyer. In keeping with social expectations, she gave up her college teaching career to raise children, but she also took the opportunity to return to composition.

The Prices settled in Little Rock, despite the fact that life was becoming increasingly difficult for the black community there. **Jim Crow** laws instituted in the 1890s had greatly reduced the opportunities for African Americans, and lynching became increasingly common. In 1927, the Prices determined that they could no longer tolerate the oppressive social climate and moved to Chicago, joining the wave of black Americans who left the South during the Jim Crow era.

In Chicago, Price quickly became involved with various organizations concerned with the advancement of African Americans and women in music. These included the Chicago Music Association (the local branch of the National Association of Negro Musicians) and the Chicago Club of Women Organists, of which she was the first black member. As her husband's career floundered, Price became the primary breadwinner. In addition to her serious concert music, Price composed popular songs, church music, and educational pieces for piano students, and during the Great Depression she took a job as a theater organist, accompanying silent films. Her husband did not adapt to his change in fortunes well, and soon became abusive. Price secured a divorce and custody of their two children in 1931.

Despite financial and personal struggles, the 1930s would see Price emerge as a composer of national significance. In addition to Symphony No. 1, Price composed other large-scale symphonic works, including her Piano Concerto in One Movement (1934) and her Symphony No. 3 (1938-40), both of which were premiered by major orchestras and praised by critics. In 1935 she returned in triumph to Little Rock, where she gave a concert of her piano music to benefit the underfunded black high school from which she had graduated. And in 1939, the renowned soprano Marian Anderson closed another famous concert, given from the steps of the Lincoln Memorial, with Price's arrangement of the African American spiritual "My Soul's been Anchored in de Lord." (Anderson sang at the Lincoln Memorial after the Daughters of the Revolution refused her permission to rent Constitution Hall on the basis of her race.) Anderson became a great admirer of Price and sang many of her songs, thereby further raising Price's visibility at the national level.

All the same, Price never broke into the very highest echelons of American concert life—those guarded by the elite institutions of New England. For a full decade, she wrote regular letters to the director of the Boston Symphony Orchestra, asking that he consider programming her music. In the most famous of these, written in 1943, she opened by directly addressing the two nearly insurmountable challenges that had impeded her career throughout her life: "To begin with I have two handicaps – those of sex and race. I am a woman; and I have some Negro blood in my veins." Price went on to clarify that she was not expecting special consideration, but asked only that her work be judged on its own merits. Despite her efforts, however, Price's orchestral music was not heard on the East Coast in her lifetime.

The Concert

In 1932, Frederick Stock, conductor of the Chicago Symphony Orchestra, was appointed music advisor for the upcoming Chicago World's Fair, "A Century of Progress." Stock had already made a name for himself as a champion of American music. Although the American concert establishment of the early 20th century was dominated by German-speaking emigres (Stock himself was born in Prussia), Stock broke new ground in 1917 by committing to include music by at least one American composer in each of his concerts. He was often ridiculed for doing so, as many critics still believed that European music was inherently superior. Stock doubled down with his vision for the World's Fair, however, promising to showcase "Chicago talent first and American talent second" while keeping European representation "drastically limited."

Stock became aware of Price that same year after her Symphony No. 1 took first prize in the orchestral division of the Rodman Wanamaker Competition, which since 1927 had offered recognition to the best African American composers. Price also earned an honorable mention in the same division and won prizes with two of her piano pieces, while the song prize was secured by her friend and student Margaret Bonds. In the end, these two Chicago women walked away with all of the top honors.

Stock immediately approached Price about premiering her Symphony No. 1 in connection with "A Century of Progress." He imagined it as part of a program celebrating the accomplishments of black composers and performers, with an emphasis on those with ties to Chicago. It seems that Stock was also interested in emphasizing the legacy of African American music, for he specifically programmed works that drew from black traditions such as jazz and spirituals.

Image 7.16: Frederick Stock, conductor of the Chicago Symphony Orchestra from 1905 to 1942.
Source: Wikimedia Commons
Attribution: Unknown
License: Public Domain

Image 7.17: Composer and pianist Margaret Bonds in 1956.
Source: Wikimedia Commons
Attribution: Carl Van Vechten
License: Public Domain

Image 7.18: Composer Samuel Coleridge-Taylor around 1905.
Source: Wikipedia
Attribution: Unknown
License: Public Domain

Image 7.19: Tenor Roland Hayes in 1954.
Source: Wikimedia Commons
Attribution: Carl Van Vechten
License: Public Domain

Before we examine Price's symphony, we must address the other components of the program. We will begin with the composers. Perhaps the best known in 1933 was Samuel Coleridge-Taylor (1875-1912), an English composer of mixed race. Coleridge-Taylor had visited the United States several times and was interested in the use of African American folk music in concert works. The program included an aria from his cantata *Hiawatha's Wedding Feast*—a decidedly American topic—and *Bamboula*, a piece inspired by African dance rhythms.

The other featured composer was John Alden Carpenter (1876-1951), whose jazz-influenced *Concertino for Piano and Orchestra* occupied the central position in the program. Carpenter was a white composer, but Stock clearly considered his work to display black musical influence. He was also a Chicago resident. Carpenter's *Concertino* was in the tradition of George Gershwin's *Rhapsody in Blue*, which had been performed the night before as part of an American program. In fact, Carpenter even brought Gershwin with him to the premiere!

The piano soloist was none other than Margaret Bonds, who had recently won composition prizes alongside Price. Performing Carpenter's *Concertino* was not Bonds's only contribution to the concert, however. She also spent many long nights helping Price to copy out the parts to her symphony. Price had a particularly busy year, and was not able to abandon her work as a pianist, lecturer, choir director, and radio arranger in order to focus on the premiere of Symphony No. 1. As a result, many members of the black musical community rallied to her aid.

At the top of the bill was Roland Hayes, a well-known tenor who would later become the first African American to record music from the European concert tradition. Hayes sung one such piece on the Chicago concert: an aria by the French composer Hector

Berlioz. By doing so, he demonstrated that he was the artistic equal to any white singer. His other selections, however, were all linked with black culture. Near the end of the program, Hayes sang two **spirituals**, "Swing Low, Sweet Chariot" and "Bye and Bye." The first had been arranged by the great African American singer and composer Henry T. Burleigh, while the second was Hayes's own arrangement. He also sang the Coleridge-Taylor aria.

There was one other piece on the program: John Powell's **concert overture** *In Old Virginia*. Powell (1882-1963) was another white composer, although he was known for incorporating Southern folk melodies—often of African American origin—into his music. Powell was also an outspoken white supremacist and advocate of eugenics. As an active contributor to Virginian political life, he helped to imagine and author the Racial Integrity Act of 1924, which set out to define and separate the "white" and "colored" races. According to the Act, even a single drop of non-white blood in an individual's ancestry qualified that person as "colored," meaning that they were subject to Jim Crow segregation and could not enter into marriage with a "white" person. This is but one item among many in Powell's anti-black legacy, and his inclusion on the "Century of Progress" emphasizes the great deal of progress that was still left to be made.

Price's symphony was well-received by both the public and the critics. Wearing an elegant, floor-length white gown, she was repeatedly called to the stage by a rapturous audience to take bows following the premiere. The black press generally praised her symphony as a great achievement on behalf of the African American community. Writing for the *Chicago Defender*, a black newspaper, Robert Abbott described what the premiere meant to his readers: "First there was a feeling of awe as the Chicago Symphony Orchestra, an aggregation of master musicians of the white race, and directed by Frederick Stock, internationally known conductor, swung in to the beautiful, harmonious strains of a composition by a Race woman." White critics tended to praise the music as a fine contribution to the European concert tradition. Eugene Stinson of the *Chicago Daily News*, for example, described Symphony No. 1 as a "faultless work" that "is worthy of a place in the repertory."

Symphony No. 1

Florence Price belonged to the cultural movement now known as the **Harlem Renaissance**, and much of her music exemplified its values. The Harlem Renaissance was driven by African American artists and intellectuals living and working in the Harlem neighborhood of Manhattan, although its influence spread across the nation. These cultural leaders took pride in their ancestry and encouraged the celebration of black heritage in literary and artistic works. By contributing to and elevating a rich tradition of African American culture, they hoped to improve life for the entire black community.

Symphony No. 1 provides a characteristic example of Price's engagement with her musical heritage. It was not her tendency to directly quote African American music in her compositions. However, she was deeply influenced by the tonal, rhythmic, and textural characteristics of such music, and she wove these elements into traditional European forms to create sophisticated concert works from a uniquely black perspective.

Because she was working in the European tradition, the overall form of Price's symphony is the same at Beethoven's. It begins with a long movement in sonata form. Next is a slow movement, followed by a dance movement, while the finale is fast-paced and exciting. We looked at the first and last movements of Beethoven's Symphony No. 5, so we will examine the two internal movements of Price's Symphony No. 1.

Movement II

		Symphony No. 1, Movement II Composer: Florence Price Performance: Fort Smith Symphony, conducted by John Jeter (2019)
Time	**Form**	**What to listen for**
0'00"	A	This hymn-like theme is played in the brass and accompanied by an African drum; clarinets and flutes echo each phrase in a call-and-response texture
1'57"	B	The strings play a mournful, descending theme that outlines a pentatonic scale and includes bluesy elements, including a slide and unusual harmonies
3'37"	A	
4'52"	Development	A phrase of the A theme leads into an extended development-like passage in which the A and B themes are explored and transformed
6'48"		The B theme returns, first in the oboe
9'31"	A'	This time, an active clarinet line accompanies the hymn-like theme, the phrases of which are interspersed with bells
11'22"	Coda	The entire orchestra plays the A theme; clarinet and cello solos lead into the final chord

The second movement begins with a theme that sounds like it might be a hymn. Several characteristics of the music combine to create this impression. To begin with, the melody is slow and stately. It is played on brass instruments, which have a long association with the church. Finally, the texture is that of a Christian hymn. The melody is clearly in the top voice, but all of the voices move in coordination, executing the same rhythmic patterns. This is called **homophonic texture**. Despite all of these clear indicators, however, what we are hearing is not a real hymn, but rather a hymn-like theme composed by Price.

Price had several good reasons to base her slow movement on such a theme. There was a long tradition of including hymn themes in symphonies, especially among composers who wished to demonstrate national pride. Ever since the early 19th century, music of the Christian church has been used to signify national identity by European composers. In addition, Price herself was deeply committed to her religious beliefs and would have been inclined to express herself in the musical language of the church. Finally, her orchestration in this movement reveals the influence of the church organ—an instrument that Price performed on and wrote for.

Price's hymn theme has several characteristics that betray African American influence. The first is the irregular length of its opening two phrases, each of which is five measures long. Similar phrasing can be found in African American spirituals, which seem to have provided Price with a model. Each of these phrases is followed by a short echo from the winds—an example of the **call-and-response** technique prevalent in black music. Finally, the hymn is accompanied by an African drum, one of several instruments that Price added to the standard orchestral percussion section. Another is the orchestral bells, which are heard later in the movement.

To complement the hymn theme, Price introduces a contrasting second theme in the violins, which play a descending melody that outlines a **pentatonic scale**. A pentatonic scale is a five-pitch subset of a major or minor scale; this one includes scale degrees 1 3 4 5 and 7 of a minor scale. Pentatonic scales are typical of indigenous music traditions found around the world, so the missing scale degrees give this theme a folk-like feel. At the same time, bluesy elements identify its character as uniquely African American. A descending slide is reminiscent of blues guitar playing. This is followed immediately by some blues-inspired harmonies, which include extended chords not often heard in European-style concert music and clashes between minor-mode melody and major-mode accompaniment.

The hymn theme returns, but this time it transitions into a lengthy development-like passage that explores the movement's two themes. First we hear the hymn motif move throughout the orchestra, acquiring various characters and expressions on its journey. Then the second theme returns in the oboe, although a re-harmonization means that it does not sound nearly as mournful. The movement concludes with a dignified return of the hymn theme, which resolves into a peaceful and satisfying final chord.

Movement III

		Symphony No. 1, Movement III "Juba Dance" Composer: Florence Price Performance: Fort Smith Symphony, conducted by John Jeter (2019)
Time	**Form**	**What to listen for**
0'00"	Rondo theme A	The violins play a syncopated pentatonic melody accompanied by minor-mode harmonies
0'18"	Rondo theme B	The trumpets play a contrasting major-mode melody
0'35"	C	The violins play a minor-mode melody accompanied by slide whistle
0'53"	Rondo theme A	The A theme returns in the winds, now with major-mode harmonies
1'01"	Rondo themes A & B	The trumpets enter with the B theme while the cellos continue to play the A theme
1'10"	Rondo theme B	The whole orchestra plays the B theme
1'27"	D	A new melody is heard in the horns
1'51"		The violins enter with a fragment of the B theme before picking up the D theme
2'08"	Rondo theme A	The whole orchestra plays the A theme, which is accompanied by major-mode harmonies
2'25"	Rondo theme B	The whole orchestra plays the B theme
2'40"	Coda	A surprising harmony begins the transition into a final triumphant statement of the B theme; the tempo decreases leading into the final cadence, which is underscored by rolls on the snare drum

The third movement is more explicitly African American in character. Price titled it "Juba Dance," in reference to a traditional dance performed by enslaved people that had roots in African culture. The specific steps of the Juba varied, but it usually contained elements of hand clapping, foot stomping, and body percussion (such as thigh slapping) that became known as "patting juba." Body percussion played an important role in 19th-century African American music, for it facilitated dancing even in the absence of other instruments. It also replaced traditional percussion instruments, which were outlawed in most of the South; slave holders feared that enslaved people might use drums to communicate between plantations for the purpose of coordinating revolts.

Although other composers had previously used Juba rhythms in their music, Price was the first composer to incorporate Juba influence into a symphony. She considered the rhythmic element in African American music to be of "preeminent importance." The third movement of Symphony No. 1 opens with a syncopated pentatonic melody in the violins, heard over a steady rhythmic pattern in the lower strings and percussion (we hear African drums again in this movement). The choice of violin for this melody calls to mind an enslaved fiddler, providing dance music on the plantation. The melody itself is intriguing, for it alternates between modes, first seeming to be in the minor mode but later resolving in the relative major. This characteristic is frequently encountered in folk music. Finally, "Juba Dance" requires yet another literal folk instrument: the wind whistle, which has roots in indigenous cultures.

"Juba Dance" is in **rondo form**, meaning that the opening pair of melodies return throughout. Each time, however, they undergo some sort of change. Different instruments perform the melodies, and they are accompanied by various countermelodies. In between, contrasting melodic material explores the diverse rhythmic possibilities of African American dance music.

1969: AN AQUARIAN EXPOSITION

Popular Music as Concert Art

All of the concerts we have examined so far have been relatively formal affairs. They have taken place in concert halls, and the audience members have been expected to sit quietly and give all of their attention to the music. This final aspect is the hallmark of concerts: They are primarily for listening—especially in the world of art music, wherein composers and performers generally expect to have the undivided attention of the audience.

There is a long history of concert presentation in popular music traditions as well. We will focus on those of the United States. In the mid-19th century, for example, the Hutchinson Family Singers became famous for their concerts of songs promoting abolition and women's rights. Their music was aimed at an educated, middle-class audience; those who wanted more lively entertainment would attend theatrical productions. Although most concerts featured singers, one could also hear brass band concerts in local parks—or, by the end of the 19th century, even attend one of the lavish concerts put on by the showman John Philip Sousa (see Chapter 12).

For the most part, however, American popular music has historically been found outside of the concert hall. In the early 20th century, one expected to hear the latest hit songs not in concert but as part of musical theater productions, variety shows, and motion picture programs. Likewise, the music played by ragtime pianists and jazz bands was mostly heard in drinking establishments and dance halls. This is one of the reasons that Paul Whiteman's *An Experiment in Modern Music* was such a noteworthy event: He expected his audience to sit and listen critically to music that had been consumed primarily in the context of social dancing. Whiteman also sought to blur the lines between popular and art music during a time when the two were considered to be fundamentally different.

Over the subsequent decades, however, this paradigm began to dissolve. Improvements in recording and broadcasting technology increased the flow of popular music into homes across the nation, and a powerful recording industry soon emerged. In the 1950s, a craze for rock 'n' roll swept the youth market. Television played an important role in building enthusiasm for the new musical style, but young people also wanted to see their favorite bands in person. At first, rock 'n' roll was primarily dance music. In the 1960s, however, the songs released by popular music labels became increasingly complex and sophisticated. (See, for example, the album *Sgt. Pepper's Lonely Hearts Club Band*, addressed in Chapter 7.) This music—termed rock—was, like classical music, meant primarily for listening.

Rock concerts grew in size and frequency during the 1960s for several reasons. One was technological. A symphony orchestra can be made louder by adding more instruments; that's how Hector Berlioz and Richard Wagner overwhelmed audiences in the 19th century. A rock band, however, gets louder by using amplification equipment that can produce sound at a higher wattage. The early 1960s saw significant developments in amplification technology that allowed bands to player louder than ever before. This in turn made it possible for rock bands to perform in larger venues, including stadiums and outdoor amphitheaters.

Americans also turned increasingly to popular music as they sought to understand and cope with the turbulent times in which they lived. The 1960s saw domestic upheaval on a level unprecedented since the Civil War of the 1860s. A series of high-profile political figures were assassinated, one after another: President John F. Kennedy in 1963, Malcolm X in 1965, and, in 1968, both Robert Kennedy and Martin Luther King, Jr. The Vietnam War provoked increasingly violent protests, which were to culminate in the Kent State massacre of 1970. The Stonewall riots of 1969 marked the start of the LGBTQ rights movement, while the decade also brought the women's liberation movement to the forefront of America's conscious. The civil rights movement saw victories, such as the Civil Rights Act of 1964, but black Americans continued to face discrimination and hate.

The "classical" music establishment of the 1960s was not well equipped to provide solace or emotional relief to listeners. After World War II, most serious composers abandoned audience-friendly styles in favor of experimental music. They did so for a variety of reasons: the fear that beautiful music could be turned to evil purposes (see, for example, Carl Orff's *Carmina Burana* in Chapter 10), the conviction that human beings were inherently corrupt and should not use music to express their emotions at all, an intense desire to break completely with the past after the horrors of the war, and sheer fascination with the mathematical and acoustic potentialities of sound. Some composers continued to write beautiful and expressive music that helped listeners to grapple with feelings of loss and disillusionment: Benjamin Britten's 1962 *War Requiem* is an excellent example. For the most part, however, listeners embraced popular performers whose music captured their hopes and frustrations.

As a result of all this, rock artists gained prestige and influence, and the rock concert became a mainstream cultural activity. Economically, 1960s rock concerts served the same purpose as Beethoven's 1808 concert: They made money for the band and its agents while winning new fans and developing interest in the music. People also attended for the same reasons (love of music and affirmation of social status), even if they behaved a bit differently. Near the end of the 1960s, concert promoters began to see the possibility of turning even bigger profits by organizing not just concerts but music festivals—multi-day celebrations that would bring together popular bands and attract tens of thousands of patrons.

The first major music festival was the 1967 Monterey International Pop Festival in Monterey, CA. This three-day event attracted 50,000 people and was immediately regarded as one of the great cultural landmarks of the decade. Its success inspired a slew of imitations. In 1968, the Newport Pop Festival and the Miami Pop Festival each attracted around 100,000 people, while the next year the Atlanta Pop Festival and the Atlantic City Pop Festival brought in closer to 110,000. However, all of these paled in comparison with the music festival that would go down in history as a watershed not only in the history of popular music but in the history of American culture: the 1969 Aquarian Exposition, better known as Woodstock.

The Festival

Woodstock began as a promotional idea for a new music recording business. Early in 1969, Michael Lang and Artie Kornfeld contacted New York City entrepreneurs Joel Rosenman and John P. Roberts for help financing a small recording studio in the town of Woodstock, NY. Rosenmann and Roberts were skeptical about the studio's potential for success, but their attention was captured by a passage in the business plan that sketched out a small-scale music festival intended to celebrate the studio opening. They encouraged Lang and Kornfeld to abandon their idea for a studio and instead focus on putting together a festival to take place in Woodstock. The four young men agreed that the idea was good, and they founded a company, Woodstock Ventures, to facilitate the project.

Lang already had some experience with the business end of music festivals, having co-organized the Miami Pop Festival in 1968. The Miami Pop Festival was small, attracting about 25,000, but it prepared Lang to anticipate the many logistical concerns that the team would face. And the festival at Woodstock wasn't supposed to be that much larger: The organizers hoped to attract 50,000 people at the most.

Things went wrong from the start. First, the organizers needed to find a location. It was important to them that the setting for the festival be attractive and bucolic, far away from the noise and pollution of the city. They wanted to sell the idea of an escape to nature, where participants could enjoy "3 days of peace & music." Lang and Kornfeld initially planned to hold the festival in Wallkill, NY, but local residents balked at the idea of a hippie invasion and were able to prevent them from securing the site. Next, they tried to book a venue in Saugerties, NY, but again the deal fell through,

Rosenman and Roberts, growing impatient with the other pair's failure to confirm a location, leased a 300-acre industrial park in Wallkill for the festival. The town's residents, however, launched a fierce attack against the project, and in July the Town Board passed a law requiring a permit for gatherings of more than 5,000. Later in the month, the Wallkill Zoning Board of Appeals banned the concert altogether on the grounds of sanitation concerns.

Finally, Rosenman and Roberts were introduced to dairy farmer Max Yasgur, who agreed to lease his 600-acre farm outside of Bethel, NY. Again, however, the organizers were met with local resistance, and they were unable to secure building permits from the Town Board until August 2—less than two weeks before the advertised start of the festival.

This left the organizers in a very difficult situation, for they simply did not have time to erect all of the infrastructure that is necessary for a large outdoor festival. However, people were coming: The conflict between the festival organizers and the authorities in Wallkill had been widely reported, with the result that far more people knew about the festival than might have otherwise. About 186,000 advance tickets had already been sold, and the organizers had reason to believe that a far greater number of people were planning to attend.

Image 7.20: This early advertisement lists the wrong location—Wallkill, NY—and omits many of the bands that eventually signed on to play.
Source: Wikimedia Commons
Attribution: Chic Chicas
License: CC BY-SA 4.0

The organizers decided to focus their resources on the most important piece of infrastructure, the stage—for what is a music festival, after all, without a stage for the performers. This meant that fencing (to keep out unticketed patrons) and ticket booths (to sell those tickets) were left unbuilt, and Woodstock became, practically speaking, a free festival. (Woodstock Ventures did eventually turn a profit, but most of this came from a documentary made at the festival and released in 1970.)

Although the organizers expected crowds, nobody could have imagined that people would flock to the festival in the numbers that they did. The morning of Friday, August 15, saw traffic jams that extended all the way back to New York City. Many people abandoned their cars and walked the final miles to the festival site, while the performers and sound crew had to be brought in by helicopter. Eventually, a state of emergency was declared in Sullivan County to deal with the unprecedented influx of people. The Governor of New York even threatened to call in the National Guard, but Roberts convinced him not to. All told, nearly 500,000 people attended the festival: ten times more than the organizers had anticipated.

It is on these half a million people that we will now focus. Why did they come? And why did so many of them come? It is certain that visitors to Woodstock made the pilgrimage for many different reasons. Some were attracted by the rural setting (previous festivals had mostly been in cities). Some were intrigued by rumors about the legal wranglings that had kept the festival out of Wallkill. Some were excited by the lineup of star performers. Whatever their individual reasons for attending, however, almost all of the visitors to Woodstock were seeking some kind of relief in the midst of growing social unrest. Many were disillusioned by President Richard Nixon's foreign policy, which had so far failed to bring the violence in Vietnam to an end. Others still grieved for Kennedy and King, whose murders came as a devastating blow to the civil rights movement. Woodstock, however, was not about politics—it was about music and community.

Naturally enough, the festival organizers and local government officials were worried about what might happen when nearly 500,000 people came together on a mere 600 acres. Similar gatherings had been marred by violence, and festivals were likely to attract troublemakers. Astonishingly, there were no violent outbreaks of any kind. This is even more remarkable when one considers the fact that the festival's troubles did not end with traffic. Because of the rush to construct the stage, other facilities were inadequate or non-existent. Camping was crowded, and few visitors were well-prepared. At first there was no food available on site at all; later, festivalgoers waited in line for hours to buy hot dogs.

In addition, it rained. Wind and rain on Sunday afternoon brought the festival to a halt for several hours. Stage hands rushed to cover expensive sound equipment, while audience members huddled under plastic sheets. The fields turned to mud. All of this could easily have led to discontent and rioting—but instead, the visitors peacefully waited out the storm until the musicians could return to the stage.

The Sunday storm also had a significant impact on Woodstock's musical legacy. The festival headliner, Jimi Hendrix, was supposed to close out the program on

Image 7.21: This photograph of the opening ceremony at Woodstock gives an idea of how enormous the crowds were.
Source: Wikimedia Commons
Attribution: Mark Goff
License: Public Domain

Sunday night. Because of storm delays, however, he did not take to the stage until 9 am on Monday morning. His set is remembered as the highlight of the festival. In particular, his rendition of "The Star-Spangled Banner" has become an iconic cultural artifact representing not only Woodstock but the entire 1960s. However, by Monday morning, only about 30,000 people remained in the audience—everyone else had gone home.

We will consider Hendrix and his performance in detail, but first it is necessary to survey the musical program in general. The first band to sign a contract was Creedence Clearwater Revival, whose fame quickly attracted other major artists to the festival. Other big names included Santana, Janice Joplin, The Grateful Dead, The Who, Jefferson Airplane, Sly and the Family Stone, and Crosby, Stills, Nash, and Young. Also on the program was the North Indian musician Ravi Shankar (discussed in Chapter 6), who had also played for enthusiastic crowds at the Monterey Pop Festival.

Just as interesting is the list of musicians who did *not* appear at Woodstock—especially those who are discussed in this book. Bob Dylan actually lived in Woodstock, but had planned a trip overseas to perform at the Isle of Wight Festival. Simon and Garfunkel were working on a new album. And The Beatles had already given up live performance for good.

Jimi Hendrix's Set: "The Star-Spangled Banner" and "Purple Haze"

Jimi Hendrix (1942-1970) was the most accomplished and influential guitar player of the 1960s. He entranced audiences with his virtuosic feats and inspired a new generation of performers to treat their instruments as tools not only for the production of melodies and harmonies but for the sculpting of sound. His influence was particularly strong on Jeff Beck, Eric Clapton, and Jimmy Page, all of whom responded to his unique ability to combine incredible musicianship with an innovative use of amplifier distortion and other effects to create sounds hitherto unheard. He experimented with a range of timbres that often crossed over into the world of pure noise, but which defined his playing and enlivened his studio albums—all five of which reached the Top 10 in the Billboard charts.

Image 7.22: This photograph of Jimi Hendrix was taken during a 1967 performance in Helsinki.
Source: Wikimedia Commons
Attribution: Hannu Lindroos
License: Public Domain

Henrix was born in Seattle, WA, where he began playing the guitar at the age of 15. He was particularly influenced by Elvis Presley and blues musicians such as Muddy Waters, and he spent his spare time learning their tunes by ear. Hendrix had a difficult childhood. His father was serving in the US Army at the time of his birth. Following his discharge at the conclusion of World War II, the family struggled financially and both parents took to abusing alcohol, resulting in Hendrix's mother's death at the age of 33. Hendrix himself joined the Army after getting into trouble with the law as a teenager. He trained as a paratrooper, but his unprofessional behavior (he played guitar constantly, slept at his post, and failed to report for inspections) led to an honorable discharge on June 29, 1962, just over a year after he had enlisted.

Freed from his military obligations, Hendrix took to music as a full-time pursuit. He first moved to Clarksville and then to Nashville, TN, where he had access to a variety of performance opportunities. Hendrix found work playing with bands that toured the Chitlin' Circuit, which was a collection of Southern and Midwestern music venues that were friendly to African American performers during the Jim Crow era.

All the same, Hendrix found his career opportunities limited by his race. In addition to the fact that he faced discrimination at performance venues, he also found that mainstream ideas about black musicians prevented him from playing the music he really loved. In Tennessee, Hendrix mostly played rhythm 'n' blues, the most prominent genre of popular music associated with the black community. However, he felt an affinity for rock music and considered himself to be a rock guitarist. It was therefore difficult for him to fit into the American music scene.

Image 7.23: Hendrix became known for his flamboyant stage antics, including playing the guitar with his teeth.
Source: Wikimedia Commons
Attribution: Marjut Valakivi
License: Public Domain

In 1966, Hendrix solved this problem by moving to London. There, he put together a rock trio with bassist Noel Redding and drummer Mitch Mitchell. They called themselves the Jimi Hendrix Experience and immediately made a splash on stage and in the recording studio. We have already seen how 1960s music was dominated by British bands in what has been termed the British Invasion. In a way, Hendrix himself became a British Invasion artist. His fame in the UK allowed Hendrix to remake his image and return to the United States under his own terms.

The Jimi Hendrix Experience made their US debut at the 1967 Monterey International Pop Festival, where Hendrix astonished music fans and performers alike with his ability as a guitarist (and his stage antics: he set his guitar on fire). He was therefore a natural choice for Woodstock, where he was paid the top fee of $18,000. Hendrix came to the festival with his new band, Gypsy Sun and Rainbows, although they were famously mis-introduced by the announcer as the Jimi Hendrix Experience. The band included several of Hendrix's associates from Tennessee, including bassist Billy Cox and second guitarist Larry Lee. Additional percussion was provided by Juma Sultan and Gerardo "Jerry" Velez.

However, Hendrix almost didn't go on stage. He was upset by media reports suggesting that the festival was in shambles, and discouraged by the number of attendees: Hendrix didn't like playing for large crowds. As of Saturday afternoon, he was still refusing to perform, but his manager finally talked him into fulfilling his contract. It took the band hours to make their way to the festival by car, where they found that no dressing rooms had been constructed. The newly-formed band was also under-rehearsed. According to Sultan, "We did not have a plan, we didn't know what he was gonna play." Although the set was recorded, two of Hendrix's numbers from Woodstock have never been released—his estate has declared that they do not meet the required performance standard and has persistently refused to allow publication.

Despite shortcomings, the two-hour performance has been described in transcendent terms by those who were there. Sultan provides the perspective of a band member: "It felt like three minutes, I walked out there, the sun was coming up and there was a sea of people, all this good energy, they were coming with the sun and light, it was overpowering. We could have played for hours more. . ." We will consider an eight-minute segment from near the end of Hendrix's set containing "The Star-Spangled Banner" and "Purple Haze."

"The Star-Spangled Banner"

Hendrix's performance of "The Star-Spangled Banner"[9] has been remembered as the culmination of Woodstock—a seemingly **improvised** expression conjured in the moment to express the hopes and fears of the crowds that had gathered there. In reality, Hendrix's "Star-Spangled Banner" was neither an improvisation—a rendition created in the act of performance—nor was it original to the festival. In fact, he had performed the national anthem more than thirty-five times in the month prior Woodstock, and would continue to include it in his concert appearances for the remainder of his career, making for a total of over sixty performances. What the audience heard was his carefully-considered **arrangement** of the national anthem for solo electric guitar.

| 9. | | "The Star-Spangled Banner"
Composer: John Stafford Smith/Francis Scott Key
Performance: Jimi Hendrix (1969) |

Before we can address his arrangement, however, we need to consider the equipment that Hendrix used to create his sounds. At Woodstock, Hendrix played a white 1968 Fender Stratocaster (serial no. 240981) that collectors call the "White One," owing to its Olympic White finish. Though he ate and wrote right-handed, Hendrix usually played guitar left-handed, strumming with his left hand. As seen in the documentary *Woodstock,* he played the "White One" (and most of his other guitars) upside down, restrung with light-gauge Fender "Rock 'n' Roll" strings for left-handed playing. Hendrix's Woodstock amplifier was a UK-built, 100-watt Marshall Super Lead, model 1959, known as the "Plexi" amp, which drove four 4-12 Marshall speaker cabinets that had been specially constructed for the festival.

Between his guitar and amplifier, Hendrix used a series of three effects devices. First came a Vox wah-wah pedal, his use of which is particularly audible in the "Voodoo Child (Slight Return)" introduction. The "small Fasel inductor coils in the Italian-made original were an important part of Jimi's distinctive tone," explains Paul Balmer. Next, there was a red Arbiter Fuzz Face,

> a primitive but effective mini amp, acting as a preamp stage [to overload the Marshall's front end,] generating a rich harmonic distortion. [Its] germanium transistors were either two NKT275s or [two] AC128s. This detail was important, as was the matching of these wayward early transistors: a good, well-matched pair sounded terrific, but if poorly matched, they sounded like a mistake. . . .
>
> The other [effect] on the Woodstock stage [was] a Uni-Vibe (an early four-stage phaser effect first developed in Japan by the Shin-Ei company): the second "volume pedal"-like device seen in the film footage at Woodstock is part of this Uni-Vibe rig.

Hendrix positioned "The Star-Spangled Banner" at the climax of his set. He began the anthem's four minute and thirty-eight second-long performance in a relatively subdued manner, with minimal **ornamentation** of the melody in the course of its first two phrases (that is, through the word "gleaming"). The first instance of what could be described as **text painting** occurs at the end of phrase 3, on the word "fight," at which point the undulating melodic motion in his descending run can be heard as a Vietnam-era representation of the conflict that Francis Scott Key had witnessed more than 150 years earlier. From this point, the performance intensifies, and Key's text provides ample opportunity for Hendrix to dazzle the crowd. At the beginning of phrase 5 (on the word "rockets"), he employs the wah-wah pedal for the first time, launching into a programmatic depiction of a fierce battle. Here, too, he first uses the Strat's whammy bar, to great effect. (This "**tremolo** arm" is attached to the guitar's bridge, allowing the player to produce **vibrato**. Because he typically played a right-handed guitar upside down, Hendrix, as clearly shown in *Woodstock,* developed a unique technique.) As the battle rages on, an even longer programmatic passage can be heard at the end of the fifth phrase, following the words "bombs bursting in air." By the end of the sixth phrase (with the words "flag was still there"), the battle has drawn to a close, and the time has come to bury the dead.

At this point, Hendrix interpolates the first half of "Taps."[10] "Taps" is a solo **bugle call** that, in its official version, is performed by members of the US military at military funerals and on a few other occasions. For older audience members, this quotation might also have been reminiscent of the first two lines in the **refrain** of the well-known patriotic song "Over There,"[11] by George M. Cohan (1878–1942). Cohen wrote "Over There" in 1917 to inspire military enlistment after the US entered the First World War. (The song enjoyed renewed popularity in the early 1940s, with the country's entrance into WWII.) Quoted below are Cohan's original lyrics for the refrain:

> Over there, over there,
> Send the word, send the word over there
> That the Yanks are coming, the Yanks are coming
> The drums rum-tumming ev'rywhere.
> So prepare, say a prayer,
> Send the word, send the word to beware
> We'll be over, we're coming over,
> And we won't come back till it's over over there.

10. This moving performance of "Taps" appears on the official YouTube channel of the U.S. Navy Band.

11. This early recording of "Over There" was made by soprano Nora Bayes on July 13, 1917.

Paired with their **arpeggio**-laden melody, the first two lines of this refrain comprise an obvious example of word painting: Cohan's melody resembles a military bugle or trumpet call.

Following Taps, Hendrix concluded his rendition of the national anthem with a rousing performance of its refrain. (Textually, as shown in Chapter 9, the final two lines of each of its four stanzas are very similar.) Here, in a vivid example of text painting on the word "wave," he uses the guitar's whammy bar to produce a steadily widening vibrato that clearly depicts a flag waving in the breeze.

Almost immediately, Hendrix's performance of "The Star-Spangled Banner" was widely criticized. Negative commentators focused on its non-traditional aspects, and some accused the guitarist of disrespecting our national anthem. In late August 1969, less than two weeks after Woodstock, Hendrix addressed the issue during a press conference promoting his upcoming benefit concert for the United Block Association (UBA) of Harlem (New York). Having been asked why he had chosen to perform "The Star-Spangled Banner" at the festival, Hendrix responded, comparing his interpretation to earlier, more traditional ones:

> Oh, because we're all Americans. We're all Americans, aren't we? It was written and played in a very beautiful, what they call a beautiful state. Nice, inspiring, your heart throbs, and you say, "Great. I'm American." But nowadays when we play it, we don't play it to take away all this greatness that America is supposed to have. We play it the way the air is in America today. The air is slightly static, isn't it?

This response is consistent with his others to similar questions about his decision, and taken together, they tend to reveal his iconic performance to be less about partisan politics and more about a longing for peace, a desire that all Americans can embrace. In his September 1969 appearance on *The Dick Cavett Show,*[12] Hendrix denied that the rendition was "unorthodox," adding, "I thought it was beautiful." Looking back twenty years later, Hendrix scholar Charles Shaar Murray praised the performance as "probably the most complex and powerful work of American art to deal with the Vietnam War and its corrupting, distorting effect on successive generations of the American psyche."

12.  Hendrix appeared on *The Dick Cavett Show* on September 9, 1969.

"Purple Haze"

After finishing his rendition of "The Star-Spangled Banner" at Woodstock, Hendrix transitioned directly into one of his biggest hits, "Purple Haze."[13] This song will serve as a good example of the **psychedelic rock** sound developed by Hendrix and his UK bandmates. It will also allow us glimpses of Hendrix the songwriter, the recording artist, and the live performer.

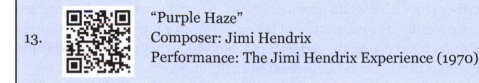

13. "Purple Haze"
     Composer: Jimi Hendrix
     Performance: The Jimi Hendrix Experience (1970)

Like many popular songs, "Purple Haze" emerged out of a collaborative experimental process. In late 1966, Hendrix was still seeking to develop his signature sound. The Jimi Hendrix Experience had landed their first hit on the UK charts in December, but Hendrix didn't think that the song, "Hey Joe," accurately reflected the band's character, and he promised fans that the next single would be something special. "Purple Haze" began as a guitar **riff**—a brief melodic fragment that eventually came to be repeated throughout the final song. Hendrix's producer, Chas Chandler, thought that the riff had potential and encouraged Hendrix to develop it into a song. According to Chandler, Hendrix finished writing "Purple Haze" in a backstage dressing room on December 26.

Image 7.24: The Jimi Hendrix Experience consisted of Hendrix, drummer Mitch Mitchell, and bassist Noel Redding.
Source: Wikimedia Commons
Attribution: VARA
License: CC BY-SA 3.0 Netherlands

On January 11, 1967, Hendrix taught the song to his bandmates and they made the initial recording in just three takes. The process, however, was far from finished. Chandler and Hendrix continued to discuss the track over the coming month, returning to the studio to record additional elements whenever they had an idea. Chandler then applied various effects to the recording. The final song, therefore, was the product of an extended period of studio experimentation, not a single recording session. This method of creating music had only recently become available with the advent of **multitrack recording**, which allows sounds recorded at different times to be combined.

Although the process by which "Purple Haze" came into the world is complicated, at least it can be explained. The same is not true of the song's lyrics. When asked what "Purple Haze" was about, Hendrix never gave the same answer twice. Once he said that the song was inspired by "a dream I had that I was walking under the sea." Another time he claimed that it captured a mythical scene, perhaps "the history of the wars on Neptune." Yet another time he said that it was a love song. Some have connected it with an episode from Hendrix's life, who claimed to have been the victim of a voodoo spell cast by a girl he met while living in New York City. Music scholar Harry Shapiro has argued that the song was inspired by a book Hendrix was reading at the time, Frank Waters' *Book of the Hopi* (1963), which describes Hopi rituals and legends. Finally, listeners have usually assumed that the song describes the experience of taking hallucinogenic drugs—something that Hendrix and other musicians certainly did, but which they could not explicitly reference in songs for fear of being banned from the airwaves.

To further complicate matters, Hendrix once claimed that "Purple Haze" originally had "a thousand" words, but that Chandler had forced him to reduce the length of the song by cutting verses. (Chandler did in fact help Hendrix to trim his lengthy tracks so that they would be suitable for radio play—a process that they both agreed made the songs better.) However, no additional verses to the song have ever surfaced.

The meaning of the lyrics probably doesn't matter all that much. Hendrix, after all, was a guitarist, and his songs were primarily vehicles for his virtuosic playing. It is certainly the guitar part that made this song a hit. The guitar introduction to "Purple Haze" features a sequence of dissonant harmonies (better heard on the studio recording than in our performance) followed by an angular melody that rises and falls. Next, Hendrix lays out the harmonic progression that will be heard under the verses—the first chord of which has in fact come to be known as the "Hendrix chord," due to its scarcity in the playing of others. The guitar is heavily distorted throughout, and Hendrix uses feedback as a musical device.

For reasons of video quality, we will consider Hendrix's performance of "Purple Haze" not at Woodstock but at the 1970 Atlanta Pop Festival. In some respects, a live performance of "Purple Haze" might be considered inferior to the studio recording: The overdubbed vocals are lost, as are the various post-production effects. What we gain, however, is Hendrix's extraordinary showmanship. To begin with, he doesn't play the guitar like other people. In addition to holding the instrument backwards, he employs a variety of unorthodox techniques, including playing passages without the use of his left hand. Even more striking is Hendrix's sexualized handling of the instrument, which he regularly positions between his legs.

The context of a stage performance also gives Hendrix the opportunity to improvise a long, unaccompanied guitar solo at the end of the song. The studio recording likewise ends with a guitar solo, but it is accompanied by drums and bass throughout and characterized by the use of an Octavia effects unit, which produces high, ringing overtones. In this performance, Hendrix appears to have relied on his guitar's inbuilt sound production capabilities. Although limited in his access to effects, Hendrix was no longer confined to the limited time frame of a pop single. He takes exactly the same amount of time—two minutes and ten seconds—in both the studio recording and stage performance to get through the scripted parts of the song: introductory riff, verse 1, guitar interlude, verse 2, guitar solo, verse 3. We can assume, however, that Hendrix conceived of the remainder of the song as a space for improvisatory exploration. In the Atlanta performance, he takes another minute and forty seconds to wow the audience with his bombastic playing.

His appearance at the Atlanta Pop Festival turned out to be one of Hendrix's final live performances. Just over two months later, he was found unresponsive in a London apartment. His death was attributed to asphyxiation following an overdose on barbiturates. The loss of Hendrix at the age of 27 is considered one of the greatest tragedies in the history of rock music. He was still at the beginning of what promised to be a dazzling career. In fact, he had just opened Electric Lady Studio in New York City and was looking forward to having greater creative autonomy as a recording artist. Hendrix, of course, was not the only victim of the drug-fueled popular music scene. His death reminds us that fame and success do not make life easy.

RESOURCES FOR FURTHER LEARNING

Print

Balmer, Paul. *The Fender Stratocaster Handbook: How To Buy, Maintain, Set Up, Troubleshoot, and Modify Your Strat*. Voyageur Press, 2012.

Brown, Rae Linda. "Lifting the Veil: The Symphonies of Florence B. Price." Forward to *Symphonies Nos. 1 and 3* by Florence Price. A-R Editions, 2008.

Clague, Mark. "'This Is America': Jimi Hendrix's Star-Spangled Banner Journey as Psychedelic Citizenship." *Journal of the Society for American Music* 8, no. 4 (2014), 435-478.

Lang, Michael. *The Road to Woodstock*. HarperCollins, 2009.

Murray, Charles Shaar. *Crosstown Traffic: Jimi Hendrix and the Post-War Rock 'n' Roll Revolution*. St. Martin's Press, 1989.

Roby, Steven, ed. *Hendrix on Hendrix: Interviews and Encounters with Jimi Hendrix*. Chicago Review Press, 2012.

Schiff, David. *Gershwin: Rhapsody in Blue*. Cambridge University Press, 1997.

Shapiro, Harry and Caesar Glebbeek. *Jimi Hendrix: Electric Gypsy*. St. Martin's Press, 1995.

Taruskin, Richard. *Music in the Early Twentieth Century: The Oxford History of Western Music*. Oxford University Press, 2009.

Taruskin, Richard. *Music in the Nineteenth Century: The Oxford History of Western Music*. Oxford University Press, 2009.

Online

Jas Obrecht, "Jimi Hendrix's Woodstock Setup: Guitar, Amps, Effects," Jas Obrecht Music Archive: http://jasobrecht.com/jimis-woodstock-setup/

Listening at Home and at Court

Esther M. Morgan-Ellis and Louis Hajosy

INTRODUCTION

Today, you can enjoy almost any kind of music in the privacy of your home. In fact, it seems likely that every kind of music is heard through headphones and stereo speakers more often than it is heard live. However, it is important to address the contexts for which music is created, and only certain types of music have traditionally been available for home consumption. In the previous chapter, we examined a series of public concerts and considered musical works that were created for the concert stage. In this chapter, we will focus on musical genres and works that were created explicitly for performance and enjoyment in domestic environments.

We've already encountered a few such pieces—Franz Schubert's "Elf King," for example (see Chapter 5), which was intended for performance at a living room concert before a small audience. The environment for which this song was created determined many of its characteristics. Because he knew the performance space would be small, Schubert wrote for just two performers. Much later, composers following in Schubert's footsteps would provide full orchestral accompaniment for their songs, but Schubert used only a piano. At the same time, Schubert's goals for this song could only be achieved by means of an intimate performance. He sought to communicate an intense drama to a rapt audience. This is not music for a noisy bar or a cavernous hall. Schubert wanted the singer and listener to be physically close and to share an emotional experience.

While we can enjoy public music in private or make private music public (baritone Dietrich Fischer-Diskau's most famous performance of "The Elf King" was broadcast on television), the experience is enriched by remembering how the music was meant to be consumed. Knowing about the original performance environment also helps us to understand why certain musical decisions were made. Such considerations will apply to all of the diverse examples in this chapter.

THE BEATLES, *SGT. PEPPER'S LONELY HEARTS CLUB BAND*

It might seem odd to start with an album by a famous rock 'n' roll band who once performed in front of 55,000 fans at Shea Stadium in Queens and appeared frequently on national television. No performers of the era were more public. However, this album represented a deliberate and explicit break with the concert model, and it was intended to be heard through headphones by attentive, isolated listeners.

Background

Frequently hailed as the greatest album ever recorded, *Sgt. Pepper's Lonely Hearts Club Band* (1967) epitomizes a musical work intended for domestic consumption. In fact, before even recording the album, The Beatles themselves knew that its contents would never be performed publicly. From the outset, according to producer George Martin, *Sgt. Pepper's* was intended to contain songs that "couldn't be performed live: they were designed to be studio productions." With their previous two albums, *Rubber Soul* (1965) and *Revolver* (1966), The Beatles had matured beyond the rock 'n' roll of their early period. (Chronologically and stylistically, *Revolver* marks the center of the band's career, and discussions of their discography tend to place it near the middle of a transitional period from *Rubber Soul* to *Sgt. Pepper's*.) The Beatles had become a rock band, and *Sgt. Pepper's* represents a continuation and acceleration of their progression away from Beatlemania and the British Invasion era.

By the time *Sgt. Pepper's* was released, The Beatles were well on their way to becoming the most influential band of all time. Along with *Rubber Soul* and *Revolver,* it is remembered as one of the first albums of the album era, a period from the mid-1960s to the mid-2000s during which the album, in various formats (LP, 8-track, cassette, CD), was the dominant medium for recorded music. Increasingly,

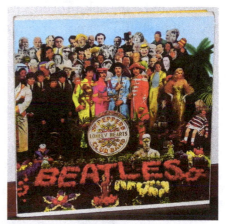

Image 8.1: The famous album cover for *Sgt. Pepper's Lonely Hearts Club Band* shows The Beatles dressed as the fictitious band members in flamboyant, military-style outfits. The crowd behind them includes influential political and cultural figures.
Source: Flickr
Attribution: Joe Haupt
License: CC BY-SA 2.0

Image 8.2: This press photo shows The Beatles in 1965.
Source: Wikimedia Commons
Attribution: EMI
License: Public Domain

albums came to be seen as more than just cost-effective vehicles for the distribution of hit-single compilations or collections of random songs. Artists had come to view their albums as extended works of art, in which each song was part of a unified whole, and The Beatles were at the forefront of this trend. With *Rubber Soul, Revolver,* and *Sgt. Pepper's,* the band, producer George Martin, and engineer Geoff Emerick succeeded in creating albums that were truly greater than the sum of their parts. (At Martin's request, Emerick was named The Beatles' engineer in April 1966, just before the *Revolver* sessions began.) Each album features songwriting that is more sophisticated and explores a wider variety of styles than its predecessor, and each reveals the band's ever-growing desire to experiment with the latest technological innovations. The impressive production and engineering skills of Martin and Emerick proved invaluable in this latter regard. By approaching the recording studio as another sort of musical instrument, they greatly facilitated The Beatles' attempts to realize their grand musical ideas. Although it took several hundred hours to record (an exorbitant amount of time by 1960s standards), *Sgt. Pepper's* was a huge hit in the Summer of Love, praised not only for bridging the cultural divide between popular music and high art but also for providing a musical representation of its generation and the contemporary counterculture.

The Beatles began recording *Sgt. Pepper's Lonely Hearts Club Band* on November 24, 1966, in Studio Two at EMI Recording Studios (now Abbey Road Studios), London. Still fresh in their minds were the previous summer's momentous

Image 8.3: This photo shows George Martin working with The Beatles in the recording studio sometime in the mid-1960s.
Source: Wikimedia Commons
Attribution: Capitol Records
License: Public Domain

events. On June 24, 1966, two days after completing their seventh album, *Revolver,* The Beatles had begun a tour of West Germany, Japan, the Philippines, and North America. The tour was relatively unsuccessful and plagued by weaker-than-expected ticket sales and run-ins with local authorities and protest groups. It ended with what became the group's final commercial concert, an eleven-song set at Candlestick Park in San Francisco on August 29. By then, each band member had agreed (probably in St. Louis, on August 21) that The Beatles would never again perform publicly. (They did, however, give one last public performance, from the rooftop of the London headquarters of Apple Corps, Ltd., their multimedia corporation, on January 30, 1969.) Many Beatles scholars consider the band's August 1966 decision to stop touring to be the most important one of their career. Within days of their August 31 return to London, they parted ways to begin a three-month break.

On November 19, 1966, five days before the *Sgt. Pepper's* recording sessions began, Paul McCartney conceived and began developing the idea of an Edwardian-era military band, namely, Sgt. Pepper's Lonely Hearts Club Band, whose members would be The Beatles' alter egos. The inspiration occurred "suddenly," during his return flight to London from a short safari vacation to Kenya with his then-girlfriend Jane Asher and Beatles assistant Mal Evans. In the following, McCartney recounts the episode:

> I got this idea. I thought, let's not be ourselves. Let's develop alter egos. [Let's] actually take on the personas of this different band. We could say, "How would somebody else sing this? He might approach it a bit more sarcastically, perhaps." . . . It would be a freeing element. I thought we [could] run this philosophy through the whole album: with this alter-ego band, it won't be us making all that sound, it won't be The Beatles, it'll be this other band, so we'll be able to lose our identities in this.
>
> [Mal and I] were having our [in-flight] meal, and they had those little packets marked "S" and "P." Mal said, "What's that mean? Oh, salt and pepper." We had a joke about that. So I said, "Sergeant Pepper," just to vary it, "Sergeant Pepper, salt and pepper," an aural pun, not mishearing him but just playing with the words.
>
> Then, "Lonely Hearts Club," that's a good one. [At the time, there were a] lot of those about, the equivalent of a dating agency now. I just strung those [words] together rather in the way that you might string together Dr. Hook and the Medicine Show. All that culture of the Sixties going back to those traveling medicine men, Gypsies. It echoed back to the previous century, really. I just fantasized, well, "Sergeant Pepper's Lonely Hearts Club Band." That'd be crazy enough, because why would a Lonely Hearts Club have a band? If it had been Sergeant Pepper's British Legion Band, that's more understandable. The idea was to be a little more funky. That's what everybody was doing. That was the fashion. The idea was just [to] take any words that would flow.

In late November 1966, when The Beatles began work on their eighth studio album, they had yet to choose its title. During the earliest sessions for what became *Sgt. Pepper's,* the band recorded "Strawberry Fields Forever" and "Penny Lane." When composing these songs, Lennon and McCartney drew inspiration from their memories of Liverpool, the band's hometown in Northwest England. For instance, Lennon, as a child, had played in the garden of Strawberry Field, a Salvation Army children's home (now closed) in Woolton, a Liverpool suburb. And Penny Lane is an actual street in south Liverpool: The song's lyrics vividly describe its associated characters. Also recorded during these early sessions was "When I'm Sixty-Four," a song from The Beatles' formative years and the only one of these three that appears on *Sgt. Pepper's.* Succumbing to management and record-company pressure, the band and producer George Martin agreed to release "Strawberry Fields Forever" and "Penny Lane" as a double A-side single on February 13, 1967. In his *Summer of Love: The Making of Sgt. Pepper,* Martin calls his agreement to leave these two songs off the album "the biggest mistake of my professional life."

Despite their exclusion from *Sgt. Pepper's,* "Strawberry Fields Forever" and "Penny Lane" were crucial in setting its overarching theme, one involving the band members' childhood experiences in Liverpool. ("Strawberry Fields Forever," as Martin recalls in *Summer of Love,* "set the agenda for the whole album.") In the first week of February 1967, The Beatles recorded what became the album's title track, "Sgt. Pepper's Lonely Hearts Club Band," yet another song evoking nostalgia for earlier times. More importantly, it was also the earliest realization of McCartney's alter-ego idea from the previous November 19, and he soon proposed that the entire album should represent a performance by the fictional band.

This qualifies *Sgt. Pepper's Lonely Hearts Club Band* as one of the first examples of a **concept album**—an approach to album design that would become increasingly important over the next few years and that persists into the present day. A concept album, like a song cycle (see Chapter 4), brings together a unified collection of songs to tell a story or capture an experience. Although *Sgt. Pepper's* does not present a specific narrative, it encourages the listener to imagine that they are present at a live concert—a concert, however, that they soon realize could never take place, due to the diversity of instruments and pervasiveness of studio editing.

"Sgt. Pepper's Lonely Hearts Club Band"

The scene is set by the opening track, "Sgt. Pepper's Lonely Hearts Club Band,"[1] which opens with ambient noises intended to create the illusion that a show is about to begin. Martin combined crowd noises he had recorded at a theatrical performance with the sounds of an orchestra warming up, which he captured in the studio while recording tracks for use in the album's final song. Of course, the ambient instrumentals aren't quite right: We seem to hear strings at the outset, but they are absent from the song itself, which features typical rock band instruments (electric guitars, electric bass, and drums). Our expectations are soon disrupted, however, when an ensemble of French horns joins the soundscape at the conclusion of the first verse. These are hardly at home in a rock lineup, and it is hard to imagine them being played onstage. The entrance of the horns is greeted by a cheer from the crowd, and crowd sounds punctuate the performance, reminding that listener that they are "present" at a live event.

| 1. | [QR code] | "Sgt. Pepper's Lonely Hearts Club Band" from *Sgt. Pepper's Lonely Hearts Club Band*
Composers: John Lennon and Paul McCartney
Performance: The Beatles (1967) |

Image 8.4: In imagining the Beatles's alter egos for the album, McCartney was inspired by traditional British brass bands. Here we see a horn player in the US Air Force Band.
Source: US Air Force
Attribution: Christina Brownlow
License: Public Domain

McCartney's lyrics—belted in a rock style—also reinforce the setting. He begins by providing a brief history of the band, after which he introduces it by name. Later, with lines like "we hope that you enjoy the show," "it's wonderful to be here," and "you're such a lovely audience," he clearly establishes the premise for the album. To further solidify the idea that we are hearing a live concert, McCartney concludes "Sgt. Pepper's Lonely Hearts Club Band" by transitioning directly into the second song. McCartney introduces a fictional singer, "the one and only Billy Shears" (voiced by Ringo Starr), who then launches into "With A Little Help From My Friends" to the sound of applause.

At this point, the concert conceit begins to evaporate. We no longer hear the sounds of the crowd, and we are gradually invited to forget the surroundings made real in the opening seconds of the album. While Starr's song is fairly conventional in terms of instrumentation and form, the third song begins the journey that will take the listener far away the concert stage.

"Lucy in the Sky with Diamonds"

		"Lucy in the Sky with Diamonds" from *Sgt. Pepper's Lonely Hearts Club Band* Composers: John Lennon and Paul McCartney Performance: The Beatles (1967)
Time	**Form**	**What to listen for**
0'00"	Introduction	Triple meter (through 0'47"); key of A major (through 0'31"); Paul's famous Lowrey organ part
0'06"	Verse 1	"Picture . . ."; George enters on tambura at about 0'17"
0'19"		"Somebody . . ."
0'32"	Bridge 1	"Cellophane . . ."; key of B-flat major (through 0'50")
0'43"		"Look . . ."
0'48"		"Gone"; quadruple meter (through 1'08")
0'51"	Chorus 1	"Lucy . . ." (3 times); key of G major (through 1'08")
1'07"		"Ahh"
1'09"	Verse 2	"Follow . . ."; triple meter (through 1'49"); key of A major (through 1'34")
1'22"		"Everyone . . ."
1'35"	Bridge 2	"Newspaper . . ."; key of B-flat major (through 1'52")

1'45"		"Climb . . ."
1'50"		"Gone"; quadruple meter (through 2'10")
1'53"	Chorus 2	"Lucy . . ." (3 times); key of G major (through 2'10")
2'09"		"Ahh"
2'11"	Verse 3	"Picture . . ."; triple meter (through 2'33"); key of A major (through 2'33")
2'24"		"Suddenly . . ."
2'34"		Quadruple meter (through fade-out); key of G major (through fade-out)
2'37"	Chorus 3	"Lucy . . ." (3 times)
2'52"		"Ahh"
2'57"	Chorus 3 (repeated)	"Lucy . . ." (3 times); fade-out begins at about 3'02"
3'12"		"Ahh"
3'17"	Chorus 3 (repeated; partial)	"Lucy . . ." (2 times); fades to silence

By the time they wrote and recorded *Sgt. Pepper's,* The Beatles had experimented with both cannabis and LSD, and the extent to which the band's use of these psychoactive drugs influenced its creation has long been debated. Of all the album's tracks, the third, "Lucy in the Sky with Diamonds," is the one most discussed in this regard. Many believe that the first letters of the nouns in the song's title, L, S, and D, are a reference to lysergic acid diethylamide, LSD. Lennon repeatedly denied this, maintaining that the title was derived from that of a pastel drawing by his three-year-old son, Julian, that depicted the boy's nursery-school classmate Lucy O'Donnell. During an episode of *The Dick Cavett Show* airing on September 21, 1971, Lennon recalled Julian's presentation of the drawing to him, which Starr witnessed:

This is the truth. My son came home with a drawing, and showed me this strange-looking woman flying around. I said, "What is it?" He said, "It's Lucy in the Sky with Diamonds," and I thought, "That's beautiful." I immediately wrote a song about it.

Whatever the case, the song itself is a masterpiece of **psychedelic rock**, due in no small part to its imaginative lyrics, with their "marmalade skies," "cellophane flowers," "rocking horse people," and "newspaper taxis." In writing them, Lennon was directly influenced by the literary style of Lewis Carroll's novels *Alice's Adventures in Wonderland* (1865) and its sequel, *Through the Looking-Glass and What Alice Found There* (1871), especially the latter's final chapter (chapter 12), "Which Dreamed It?"

Image 8.5: The Beatles embraced psychedelia not only in their music but in their image. Here we see a press photo from their Magical Mystery Tour.
Source: Wikimedia Commons
Attribution: Parlophone Music Sweden
License: CC BY-SA 3.0

Musically, "Lucy in the Sky with Diamonds" exemplifies The Beatles' artistic maturation over the period 1965–67. Its three main sections, the verse, the bridge, and the chorus, are in different keys: A major, B-flat major, and G major, respectively. Following a short introduction, this verse–bridge–chorus structure is heard for the first time, and is then repeated. A second repetition begins, but this time, the bridge is absent: verse 3 leads directly to chorus 3, which is then repeated through the fade-out. Moreover, the song employs **mixed meter**. The introduction, the verse, and the bridge (except its last measure) are in triple meter, while the bridge's last measure and the chorus are in quadruple meter, also known as common time. The technique of shifting from triple to quadruple meter one measure before the chorus is also used to connect verse 3 to chorus 3. Each meter-change is accompanied by a noticeable tempo shift.

"Lucy in the Sky with Diamonds" also reflects The Beatles' increasing tendency to utilize sounds and instruments infrequently heard in contemporary rock. The song's introduction, for instance, features a memorable keyboard part, brilliant in its simplicity, played by McCartney on a Lowrey DSO-1 Heritage Deluxe electronic organ. The ear-catching harpsichord- or celeste-like sound used for this part is (probably) a combination of the organ's harpsichord, vibraharp, guitar, and music-box stops. Then, about halfway through the first verse, Harrison enters on the tambura (tanpura), a long-necked, unfretted lute commonly associated with Indian music. Typically, as heard here, the player plucks the instrument's strings (usually four or five) in a continuously repeating pattern, producing a buzzing, overtone-rich drone. (In Western art music, the repetition of a musical pattern numerous times in succession is called **ostinato**.)

Image 8.6: Harrison became interested in North Indian music after encountering sitar master Ravi Shankar (discussed in Chapter 6). Here, they are pictured with President Gerald Ford during a 1974 White House visit.
Source: Wikimedia Commons
Attribution: David Hume Kennerly
License: Public Domain

Indian music's influence is again evident at the start of the first bridge. Here, as author Peter Lavezzoli explains, Harrison "mirrors Lennon's [lead] vocal with electric guitar, as if he were playing a sarangi behind a khyal singer." The Beatles' guitarist is known to have "liked 'Lucy in the Sky with Diamonds' a lot." In discussing his contributions to its arrangement, Harrison highlights the song's integration of non-Western elements:

> I particularly liked the sounds on it where I managed to superimpose some Indian instruments onto the Western music. . . . I like the way the drone of the tambura could be fitted in there.
>
> There was another thing: during vocals in Indian music, they have an instrument called a sarangi, which sounds like the human voice, and the vocalist and [the] sarangi player are more or less in unison in a performance. For "Lucy," I thought of trying that idea, but because I'm not a sarangi player, I played it on guitar. . . . I was trying to copy Indian classical music.

"She's Leaving Home"

We will pass over the next two songs, although of course they have many points of interest: "Getting Better" includes the Indian tambura and an unusual early electric keyboard instrument called the pianette, while "Fixing a Hole" opens with the sounds of a harpsichord. "She's Leaving Home,"[2] however, marks the first wholesale departure from the rock-band sound, for the accompaniment is provided exclusively by strings. The arrangement for four violins, two violas, two cellos, string bass and harp was created by Mike Leander, although George Martin was never happy with it. **Double tracking** on the chorus—a technique by which a melodic line is recorded twice—causes the voices of Lennon and McCartney to multiply, thereby providing a marked contrast with the more subdued singing in the verses.

<table>
<tr>
<td>2.</td>
<td></td>
<td>"She's Leaving Home" from Sgt. Pepper's Lonely Hearts Club Band
Composers: John Lennon and Paul McCartney
Performance: The Beatles (1967)</td>
</tr>
</table>

"Being for the Benefit of Mr. Kite"[3]

More extraordinary sounds await the listener in the next song, the lyrics of which describe the activities of circus performers. In seeking to evoke a carnival atmosphere, Martin naturally turned to the instrument most closely associated with fairgrounds: the calliope, or steam organ. To bring an actual calliope into the studio, however, would have been impossible, so he instead combined recordings of instruments made on-site with the reedy sounds of the studio organ. The timbral pallette is filled out by harmonium and four harmonicas.

Image 8.7: This British poster from 1874 depicts a horse-drawn calliope.
Source: Wikimedia Commons
Attribution: Gibson & Co
License: Public Domain

These instruments—and others—are heard at the beginning of the track and in two extended interludes, each of which transports the listener to the scene being described. The first interlude is in triple time—an unusual feature, since the rest of the song is in quadruple time. The change is explained by the line preceding the interlude: "And of course Henry the horse dances the waltz." We are hearing the music to which he is dancing (and perhaps seeing Henry in our minds). The second interlude has been described by Michael Hannan as having been designed "to conjure up the giddy experience of a hallucinogenic carousel ride." Any listener is likely to confirm this view, for Martin has overlaid a dense tapestry of recorded calliope sounds that fail to line up to the pulse in a meaningful way. The effect is dizzying.

| 3. | | "Being for the Benefit of Mr. Kite" from *Sgt. Pepper's Lonely Hearts Club Band*
Composers: John Lennon and Paul McCartney
Performance: The Beatles (1967) |

"Within You Without You"

We must consider, for a moment, the nature of the medium for which *Sgt. Pepper's Lonely Hearts Club* was intended. So far, all of the songs we have encountered appeared on the first side of the LP. "Being for the Benefit of Mr. Kite" closed out that side with its "hallucinogenic carousel ride." Next, the listener would have to take a brief break from listening in order to turn the record over. What they encountered next would represent the most distant point on their sonic journey.

The North Indian instruments heard in "Within You Without You"[4] are not new to the listener, but Harrison goes further in his efforts to absorb and reflect Indian musical influence, such that this song represents The Beatles' deepest foray into the world of Indian music. The Beatles' fascination (especially Harrison's and Lennon's) with Indian music and philosophy began in 1965. Like "Lucy in the Sky with Diamonds," the songs "Norwegian Wood (This Bird Has Flown)," from *Rubber Soul,* and "Tomorrow Never Knows," from *Revolver,* contain obvious examples of Indian musical influence. Written primarily by Lennon, all three are firmly rooted in the Western popular music tradition. Their "Indian" elements, though innovative, are essentially superficial, a sort of sonic flavoring, mainly involving the use of non-Western instruments (e.g., sitar, tambura).

| 4. | | "Within You Without You" from *Sgt. Pepper's Lonely Hearts Club Band*
Composer: George Harrison
Performance: The Beatles (1967) |

"Within You Without You" features a veritable orchestra of Indian and Western instruments, including three tamburas, two dilrubas (a bowed lute), a sitar, eight violins, three cellos, and tabla (a pair of hand drums). The unusual scales on which the melodies are based reflect Indian influence, as does the fact that the entire song is rooted in a persistent drone. Other Indian-derived elements include the slides we hear between pitches and the use of **call and response** between solo and grouped instruments. The lyrics convey Lennon's understanding of Eastern philosophy.

Image 8.8: The dilruba is a bowed lute.
Source: Wikimedia Commons
Attribution: J Singh
License: CC BY-SA 2.0

The inclusion, at Harrison's request, of the images of four Indian gurus on the album's iconic cover further attests to the culture's profound impact on the band at this time. The gurus appear there in a collage of several dozen celebrities and historical figures, before which The Beatles stand, posed as the fictional Lonely Hearts Club Band, in their brightly colored Edwardian-era military uniforms.

"A Day in the Life"

Near the end of the second side, "Sgt. Pepper's Lonely Hearts Club Band" returns as a reprise. It seems to the listener that this is the end of the concert—a message reinforced by the lines "we hope you have enjoyed the show" and "we're sorry, but it's time to go." The song sounds a little bit different than it did the first time: it's faster, shorter, and at a lower pitch level. The crowd sounds are back, however, and cheers at the end suggest that the concert has indeed concluded.

Instead, the music transitions directly into a final song—the longest and most complicated song on the entire album. "A Day in the Life"[5] begins with the spare texture of guitar and piano, but upon the words "I'd love to turn you on" the listener is gradually overwhelmed by a sound that grows in volume, pitch, and intensity with inevitable force. Although it is hard to identify, what we are actually hearing is forty orchestral musicians each recorded four times, for a total of 160 tracks. (It was during this recording session that Martin captured the ambient "warming up" noises heard at the beginning of the album.)

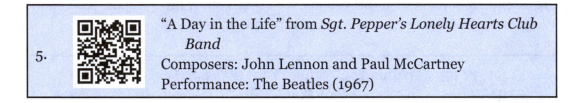

5. "A Day in the Life" from *Sgt. Pepper's Lonely Hearts Club Band*
    Composers: John Lennon and Paul McCartney
    Performance: The Beatles (1967)

Following the climax of the crescendo, we are returned to what seems to be a totally different song. It certainly bears little relation to what preceded the orchestral noise. This time, the words "I went into a dream" cue the return of orchestral instruments, which now underpin McCartney's floating vocals. The next section brings back the opening material, which again spills into a cacophonous orchestral crescendo. This time, however, it is followed up with a piano chord—in fact, a thrice overdubbed recording of three musicians playing three pianos—that slowly fades away over the course of forty-three seconds. The last thing we hear is some incidental studio chatter, which was originally cut into the outer groove so that it would loop indefinitely until the listener lifted the tonearm off of the disc.

Legacy

Few musical works in history have enjoyed the success of *Sgt. Pepper's Lonely Hearts Club Band*. After reaching number one on the UK's "Official Albums Chart" on June 10, 1967, it remained there for twenty-three consecutive weeks. In the U.S., *Sgt. Pepper's* began a fifteen-week run atop the "Billboard 200" album chart on July 1, 1967. Since that time, it has spent hundreds of weeks on both charts. Meanwhile, critical assessments of the album have remained almost universally positive for more than five decades. (To this day, its few negative critics are attacked as heretical pariahs, often publicly shamed by their colleagues.) As author Jonathan Gould explains, the critics' seemingly endless heaping of praise on *Sgt. Pepper's* began immediately after its release:

> The overwhelming consensus was that The Beatles had created a popular masterpiece: a rich, sustained, and overflowing work of collaborative genius whose bold ambition and startling originality dramatically enlarged the possibilities and raised the expectations of what the experience of listening to popular music on record could be. On the basis of this perception, *Sgt. Pepper['s]* became the catalyst for an explosion of mass enthusiasm for album-formatted Rock that would revolutionize both the aesthetics and the economics of the record business in ways that far outstripped the earlier Pop explosions triggered by the Elvis phenomenon of 1956 and the Beatlemania phenomenon of 1963.

Sgt. Pepper's has garnered a vast multitude of accolades. At the 10th Annual Grammy Awards ceremony (in February 1968, honoring 1967 releases), for example, it became the first rock album to be named Album of the Year (for The Beatles and producer George Martin). *Sgt. Pepper's* also received three other Grammys that night: Best Contemporary Album (again for The Beatles and producer George Martin), Best Engineered Recording—Non-Classical (for engineer Geoff Emerick), and Best Album Cover, Graphic Arts (for art directors Peter Blake and Jann Haworth). The Library of Congress added the album to the National Recording Registry in 2003, in recognition of its cultural, historic, and aesthetic significance, and in 2012, *Rolling Stone* ranked *Sgt. Pepper's* number one in its list of the "500 Greatest Albums of All Time." As of today, it has sold more than thirty-two million copies worldwide, making it one of the best-selling albums ever released.

COUNTESS OF DIA, "I MUST SING"

For most of history, of course, intimate music making has required live performers. As a result, various traditions of song accompanied by one or a few acoustic instruments have arisen in various times and places. We will examine several of these, beginning with the first secular song repertoire ever to be written down: that of the medieval troubadours, who wrote songs in what is now southern France.

Troubadours

In historical terms, troubadours were not professional musicians. They were noblemen and noblewomen who wrote and performed courtly songs for their own entertainment. The term "troubadour" comes from the Provençal language, which was spoken in the Duchy of Aquitaine. It literally means "one who finds," and was used to describe the work of poets, who were understood not to create their works but to discover them. Troubadours certainly dedicated most of their energy to crafting elaborate verses, but these were always set to music and sung, not recited.

Although troubadours wrote in dozens of distinct genres, they were primarily preoccupied with romantic concerns. The most significant genre of troubadour song was the **canso**, which expressed the courtly sentiment of *fin'amors* ("refined love"). Typically speaking, *fin'amors* was the passion that a knight felt for the lady he served. This passion was romantic and all-consuming, but it could never be satisfied, for the knight was pledged to serve his master and mistress—an obligation that precluded the possibility of intruding upon their marriage. Instead, the knight would suffer in song, lamenting the impossibility of winning the woman he desired but finding solace in dedicating his life to her service.

Image 8.9: The 12th-century troubadour Bernart of Ventadorn, as depicted in his vida.
Source: Wikimedia Commons
Attribution: Unknown
License: Public Domain

This ideal of unrequited passion was at the center of Aquitainian courtly life, as we see when we examine the biographies, or **vidas**, of the troubadours. These short narratives, which were only loosely grounded in historical truth, include few details about the troubadour's work or life. Instead, they focus entirely on the noble personages whom the troubadour loved and on behalf of whom the troubadour suffered. Take, for example, the vida of Bernart of Ventadorn, the most famous of all the troubadours. His rather long vida is dedicated entirely to his romantic life. It tells us how he first loved the wife of the Viscount of Ventadorn, about whom he wrote all of his songs. Upon the discovery of his passion, however, Bernart was dismissed and joined the court of the Duchess of Normandy—with whom he fell in love, of course, and about whom he wrote many more songs. Upon her departure for England, Bernart reportedly entered an order of monks and died of a broken heart.

Although troubadours are best remembered for their celebrations of idealized romantic suffering, they also sang about more earthly love affairs. The *alba* was a song about lovers interrupted by the dawn (and the return of the woman's husband), while the *serena* concerned a lover impatiently awaiting his partner's arrival in the evening. In a *pastorela*, a knight suggested to a peasant girl that they make love; sometimes she acceded, sometimes she did not. In sum, the repertoire makes it clear that troubadours didn't spend *all* of their time yearning for unobtainable aristocrats.

The troubadours were active throughout the 12th century, while the Duchy of Aquitaine flourished. During this period, their tradition was primarily **oral**. They wrote songs in their heads and performed them from memory, and those songs were then carried from place to place by **minstrels** who learned them by ear. In the early 13th century, however, an effort was made to preserve the songs of the troubadours. This is when the vidas were recorded. In addition, hundreds of poems and a smaller number of melodies were collected in richly-embellished manuscripts.

However, the need to preserve a fading tradition is not the only reason that the songs of the troubadours became the first secular music ever to be recorded. The troubadours and their supporters were also in the unique position of having access to the wealth and education necessary to write music down. In the medieval era, books were difficult and expensive to produce and were therefore enormously valuable. The pages were usually **velum** (dried sheep skin), and few people had the skills necessary to read or write. Music literacy in particular was largely restricted to clerics. While the troubadour repertoire is prized, we must remember that it offers only a glimpse into the rich traditions of song and dance music that flourished in medieval oral culture.

Although the songs of the troubadours were indeed preserved, we still have only shadowy ideas about what this music sounded like. This is because only the melodies were recorded, using a primitive form of notation that did not indicate

Image 8.10: Illuminations in medieval manuscripts shed light on performance practice. Here, we see musicians playing the rebec and cithar.
Source: Picryl
Attribution: Unknown
License: Public Domain

Image 8.11: The citole, portrayed here ca. 1310, was a type of lute, and therefore related to the modern guitar.
Source: Wikimedia Commons
Attribution: Robert De Lisle
License: Public Domain

Image 8.12: This illumination from ca. 1300 portrays a musician playing the vielle.
Source: Wikimedia Commons
Attribution: Unknown
License: Public Domain

rhythmic values. The extant manuscripts seem to suggest, therefore, that troubadours sang without accompaniment, but we know from illustrations that this was not the case. Manuscript illuminations depict troubadours and minstrels playing a variety of instruments, including the lute, citole, vielle, rebec, psaltery, harp, shawm, and bagpipes. It is clear that these instruments were used to accompany both dancing and singing. Today, therefore, performers use their imaginations when they approach the troubadour repertoire, creating appropriate accompaniments based on what we know about the instruments, styles, and practices of the time.

Mystery surrounds not only the songs but their creators. Most of the troubadours are known only by their brief vidas, which are highly unreliable. This is certainly the case of the Countess of Dia, who authored the canso that we will examine. Her vida reads as follows: "The Countess of Dia was the wife of Lord Guillem of Peitieu, a beautiful and good lady. And she fell in love with Lord Raimbaut of Orange and composed many good songs about him." This vida certainly tells us all that the author felt we needed to know: The Countess was beautiful and good (attributes commonly assigned to noblewomen), she loved a man who was not her husband, and she wrote songs about him. Unfortunately, scholars have been unable to identify the Countess, although competing theories thrive.

"I Must Sing"

The Countess of Dia's "I Must Sing" is the only song by a **trobairitz** (the female counterpart to a troubadour) to survive with music. However, it is clear that trobairitz thrived in the courts of Aquitaine, where men and women enjoyed relative equality. Although trobairitz were highly regarded for their poetic skill, they were discouraged from performing their songs in public—an activity considered unseemly for a woman. Instead, male performers would learn and share their music.

Image 8.13: The angels in this ca. 1320 illumination play nearly a full compliment of medieval instruments, including the guitar-shaped citole, violin-shaped vielle, psaltery, and trumpet .
Source: Wikimedia Commons
Attribution: the "Queen Mary Master"
License: Public Domain

Image 8.14: The musicians in this ca. 1310 illumination play harp, rebec, citole, psaltery, and perhaps a tambourine.
Source: Wikimedia Commons
Attribution: Unknown
License: Public Domain

Image 8.15: This is the vida of the Countess of Dia, accompanied by her image.
Source: Wikimedia Commons
Attribution: Unknown
License: Public Domain

Trobairitz also had to be a bit more circumspect regarding their declarations of courtly love. While troubadours could be fairly explicit, trobairitz sang in more general terms about the suffering that unrequited love caused them to endure.

"I Must Sing" follows the standard form for a canso. It is in five complete stanzas, the first of which clearly states the lover's complaint. A partial sixth stanza bids the listener farewell via an imagined messenger and offers a closing moral ("many people suffer for having too much pride"). In the intervening stanzas, the speaker reminds her errant lover of her many fine qualities and washes her hands of any blame for the separation:

> I must sing of what I do not want,
> I am so angry with the one whom I love,
> Because I love him more than anything:
> Mercy nor courtesy moves him,
> Neither does my beauty, nor my worthiness,
> nor my good sense,
> For I am deceived and betrayed
> As much as I should be, if I were ugly.
>
> I take comfort because I never did anything wrong,
> Friend, towards you in anything,
> Rather I love you more than Seguin did Valensa,
> And I am greatly pleased that I conquered you in love,
> My friend, because you are the most worthy;
> You are arrogant to me in words and appearance,
> And yet you are so friendly towards everyone else.
>
> I wonder at how you have become so proud,
> Friend, towards me, and I have reason to lament;
> It is not right that another love take you away from me
> No matter what is said or granted to you.
> And remember how it was at the beginning
> Of our love! May Lord God never wish
> That it was my fault for our separation.
>
> The great prowess that dwells in you
> And your noble worth retain me,
> For I do not know of any woman, far or near,
> Who, if she wants to love, would not incline to you;
> But you, friend, have such understanding
> That you can tell the best,
> And I remind you of our sharing.

My worth and my nobility should help me,
My beauty and my fine heart;
Therefore, I send this song down to you
So that it would be my messenger.
I want to know, my fair and noble friend,
Why you are so cruel and savage to me;
I don't know if it is arrogance or ill will.

But I especially want you, messenger, to tell him
That many people suffer for having too much pride.

Translated by Craig E. Bertolet. Used with permission.

As was always the case among troubadours, the Countess of Dia set her poem as a **strophic song**, meaning that each stanza is sung to the same melody. Although this means that there can be no direct correlation between text and music (since the music repeats), her melody is nonetheless expressive. She uses a standard troubadour form known as **bar form**, which follows an A A B pattern. The A section starts in the medium range and then descends—perhaps emblematic of the singer's sorrow. The B section ascends to the song's highest note by means of a series of leaps, creating a climactic moment before returning to the low range. The song is in the Dorian mode, which is very similar to the minor mode; only a single pitch in "I Must Sing" does not come from the minor scale.

In order to demonstrate the variety that characterizes modern performances of troubadour songs, we will consider two recordings of "I Must Sing." The first is very simple.[6] The female singer begins without accompaniment, but she is joined by a harp in the second A phrase of the first verse. The harp continues to play for the remainder of the performance. It provides simple harmonies, alternating between two chords derived from the pitches on which the phrases of the melody end. The singer chooses her rhythms based on the meaning of the text and sound of the words, while the harp follows her phrasing. This rendition could easily be performed by a single musician accompanying her own singing—just as we know these songs were often performed in the troubadour era.

6.	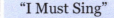	"I Must Sing" Composer: Countess of Dia Performance: New York's Ensemble for Early Music (2003)

The second recording is more complex.[7] First, we hear fragments of the melody played on a variety of stringed instruments, including lute, harp, and bass viol. When the singer enters, she interprets the melody with rhythmic freedom while the instruments add flourishes. In between verses, instrumental interludes feature a percussive pulse and the sounds of the *ney* flute and *kanun* zither, which perform a metered version of Dia's melody. Both the *ney* and the *kanun*—along with several other instruments heard on this recording—will be discussed in the next section, which addresses court music of the Ottoman Empire. The music director who created this recording, Jordi Savall, is renowned for his recreations of medieval European song using the instruments and performance techniques associated with Middle Eastern music of the same era. It is likely that the two musical traditions had many common elements in the 12th century. While troubadour practices were eradicated, however, those of Middle Eastern courts have persisted into the present.

7. "I Must Sing"
    Composer: Countess of Dia
    Performance: Montserrat Figueras with Hespèrion XXI,
    conducted by Jordi Savall (2010)

TANBURI CEMIL BEY, "SAMÂI SHAD ARABAN"

Where there are powerful rulers, there is music. We might select examples of court music from any of the great empires of history, for all have used music to advertise power, signify elite status, invest ceremonies with dignity, ornament daily life, and entertain guests. Many relevant instances are discussed elsewhere in this book: Claudio Monteverdi's *Orpheus* (Chapter 4), for example, was designed for the Gonzaga court at Mantua, while the *jali* of West Africa (Chapter 5) were principally occupied with serving the Mandinkan aristocracy.

Here, however, in keeping with the focus of this chapter on unstaged chamber music intended for small spaces and private audiences, we will consider a tradition that developed in the courts of the Ottoman Empire. This example will also help us to understand how troubadour songs (discussed in the previous section) are interpreted by performers today, for they often incorporate the instruments, textures, and ornamentation of Middle Eastern court music. Finally, this example will provide a point of reference for evaluating Pyotr Illyich Tchaikovsky's exoticized "Arabian" music in *The Nutcracker* (Chapter 4).

Music in the Ottoman Empire

The Ottoman Empire was founded in 1299 by the Turkish tribal leader Osman I. In 1453, the Ottomans captured the Christian city of Constantinople, which had until that point been the capital of the Byzantine Empire. Renamed Istanbul, that city became the capital of the Ottoman Empire: a centralized seat from which the sultan (Arabic for "supreme authority") could expand his reach. The Ottoman Empire achieved the height of its power in the late 16th century, at which point it extended from Central Europe across North Africa and well into the Middle East.

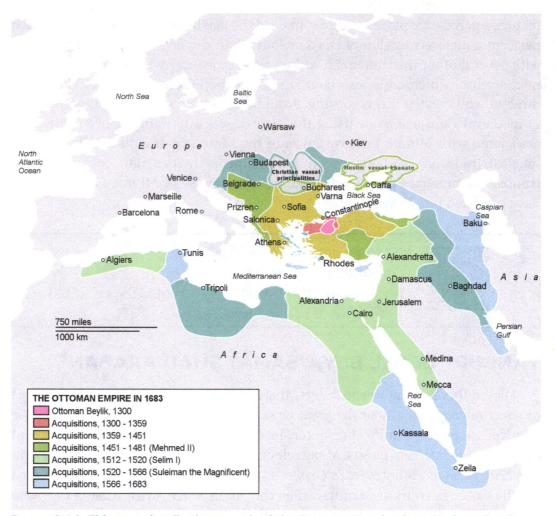

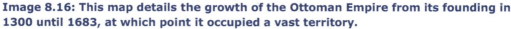

Image 8.16: This map details the growth of the Ottoman Empire from its founding in 1300 until 1683, at which point it occupied a vast territory.
Source: Wikimedia Commons
Attribution: Atilim Gunes Baydin
License: Public Domain

The 19th century, however, saw the Empire's gradual decline as it ceded power and territory to its neighbors. Following the Great War (later renamed World War I), the Empire was formally dissolved and ultimately replaced by the Republic of Turkey in 1923.

For several centuries, however, the Ottoman Empire mediated between European powers and the Far East. The Western border of the Empire came very near Vienna, which was a major European political and cultural center in the 18th and 19th centuries. As a result, Ottoman music had a significant impact in Europe. The Ottoman military band tradition, in particular, can be identified as the precursor to Western marching bands, while composers like Mozart and Beethoven frequently referenced Ottoman instruments and styles in their music.

The Ottoman Empire certainly cultivated rich musical traditions. Here, we will examine the most elite of those traditions: ***makam* music**, which was performed for (and sometimes even created by) the sultan and members of his court. As in

Page | 279

most great empires, the Ottoman rulers sought to manage cultural diversity, not eradicate it. As the Empire absorbed citizens from three continents, it simultaneously assimilated their cultural traditions. Ottoman musical practices, therefore, reflected Byzantine, Armenian, Arabic, Persian, and even European influence.

The term **makam** is itself derived from the Arabic *maqam*, which describes a system of musical **modes**. In European music, modes are scales, the most prominent of which in use today are major and minor. A *makam*, however, is more than just a scale. To begin with, there are many more *makams* than there are European modes—between 60 and 120. They are difficult to count because *makams* are always coming and going. An individual *makam* might fall out of use, or a new one might be developed.

The number of *makams* is so high because each contains a great deal of information about how music associated with it is expected to sound. A *makam* determines not only pitches but characteristic melodic motifs, ascending and descending melodic patterns, phrase endings, and the specific tuning of individual notes. This last element can be particularly striking, for the Turkish system divides each whole step into nine possible microtones (the European system divides it into only two). A note that is meant to be just slightly flat or slightly sharp, therefore, will sound out of tune to a Western ear, even though the performer has in fact placed it with perfect precision.

Makam music is performed using instruments that can be found across the

Image 8.17: This engraving captures Ottoman musicians of the mid-18th century.
Source: Wikimedia Commons
Attribution: Unknown
License: Public Domain

Mediterranean region. These include the *oud* (a type of lute), the *kanun* (a plucked zither), the *ney* (an end-blown reed flute), and the *rebab* and *kemençe* (both bowed fiddles), although these last instruments have been almost completely replaced by the violin. Percussion instruments are also important, for they mark the rhythmic cycle, known as the *usul*. These instruments include the pair of pot-shaped *kudüm* drums, the *bendir* (a circular frame drum), and the *def*, which is related to the tambourine. In the performance of *makam* music, only one of each instrument is typically present, and their unique timbres are easy to discern in the texture.

Ottoman musicians organized their court performances into suites of individual pieces. Such a suite is known as a ***fasıl***, and it might contain six or eight pieces, all in the same *makam*, totalling about thirty minutes of music. A traditional *fasıl* is full of variety: It contains different types of songs and several vocal and instrumental improvisations. Although most of the pieces feature a singer, the *fasıl* starts and ends with lengthy selections for the instrumental ensemble. The introductory *peşrev* is slow and stately, while the concluding ***saz semâisi*** contains passages in a lively dance tempo.

Samâi Shad Araban

We will consider a famous *saz semaisi* composed by Tanburi Cemil Bey (1843-1916). Cemil Bey was famous for his virtuosity as a performer. Although he began his training on the violin and kanun, he soon gained renown for his skill on the *tanbur*—a long-necked lute that developed in the Ottoman Empire—and *kemençe*. Cemil Bey lived late enough that he was able to leave behind recordings, made on 78 rpm discs. These attest to his ability and continue to influence performers today, who still employ techniques that he developed and popularized.

In addition to revolutionizing performance techniques, Cemil Bey left behind a large number

Image 8.18: The fretless *oud* is related to the European lute and guitar.
Source: Wikimedia Commons
Attribution: User "Tdrivas"
License: CC BY-SA 4.0

Image 8.19: The *kanun* is plucked using metal finger picks.
Source: Wikimedia Commons
Attribution: Benoît Prieur
License: CC BY-SA 4.0

Image 8.20: The Turkish *kemençe* is a small, pear-shaped fiddle. Like the *rebab*, it is held vertically.
Source: Wikimedia Commons
Attribution: Metin Sezgin
License: CC BY-SA 3.0

of compositions, many of which are among the most frequently performed in the Turkish classical tradition. Although Cemil Bey did not personally serve in the court of the sultan (the Ottoman Empire, after all, was well into its decline during his lifetime), he worked in the forms that had been developed for court entertainment. His "Samâi Shad Araban," therefore, has the typical characteristics of a *saz semâisi*, and by examining it we will be able to understand how this type of composition has functioned for hundreds of years. We will also have an opportunity to hear the typical Turkish instruments and consider how they are used in performance.

"Samâi Shad Araban" Performance: Omar Sarmini and Hames Bitar with the Ensemble Al-Ruzafa (2007)		
Time	**Form**	**What to listen for**
0'00"	A (Hane 1)	The violin, ney, oud, and kanun all play unique versions of the same melody
0'36"	Teslim	
1'12"	B (Hane 2)	
1'54"	Teslim	
2'30"	C (Hane 3)	Near the beginning of this passage we hear a "half-flat" pitch that some might perceive as out-of-tune
3'18"	Teslim	
3'54"	D (Hane 4)	In this passage, the meter changes to triple and short melodic passages are repeated
5'54"	Teslim	Played by the solo oud
6'31"	Teslim	Played by the entire ensemble

To begin with, we must consider the nature of composition in the Ottoman tradition. Like medieval Europeans (consider, for example, the Countess of Dia), Ottoman performers learned, composed, and taught music without the aid of notation. Although Ottoman music was notated as early as the 17th century, the purpose of notation has always been primarily to record compositions for future reference, and it is seldom used for teaching or performance. Even today, Turkish classical musicians rely on aural and oral processes—that is, listening, imitating, and correcting—to acquire techniques and repertoire.

A typical characteristic of music in oral traditions is variation. When a performer learns a tune by ear, they are likely to introduce minor alterations by accident. However, in the Ottoman tradition, variation is not only accepted but encouraged. The composer expects individual performers to interpret the melody in a way that reflects the characteristics of their instrument, their training, and their own personal preference. As a result, while a performance of "Samâi Shad Araban" is always recognizable, no two musicians will play exactly the same notes.

Another type of variation emerges due to the norms of Ottoman performance practice. A piece of music such as Clara Schumann's Piano Trio in G minor, discussed at the end of this chapter, is intended for a specific assortment of instruments: one piano, one violin, and one cello. Schumann also used notation to indicate exactly what each performer is supposed to do. Compositions in the Ottoman tradition, however, can be realized using any permutation of the classical ensemble. "Samâi Shad Araban," therefore, can be performed as a solo or by an ensemble. A typical performance will feature about six performers, with only one playing each of the instruments described above. However, a rendition by a smaller or larger ensemble is perfectly viable.

This flexibility is a characteristic of the **heterophonic** texture of Ottoman classical music, in which all pitched instruments play essentially the same melody. "Samâi Shad Araban," for example, can be **transcribed** (written down using staff notation) as a single melodic line. However, no two instruments play exactly the same pitches. Sometimes the variations have to do with the technical limitations of the instrument: a *rebab* player, for example, can slide between pitches, while a *kanun* player cannot. Other variations have to do with training or personal preference, as described above. The result is a complex musical texture in which the listener can easily perceive a core melody, even as the performers constantly alter that melody with diverse shadings and ornaments.

We will hear all of this in our recording of "Samâi Shad Araban." First, however, we must consider the typical characteristics of a *saz semâisi*. In terms of form, a *saz semâisi* always features a repeated melodic refrain (known as a *teslim*) that follows upon a series of disparate melodic passages (each of which is termed a *hane*, or "house"). The form of "Samâi Shad Araban" can be summarized as A T B T C T D T, in which T (for *teslim*) is the refrain.

While each of the *hane* are melodically distinct, the D *hane* is markedly different from the others. To begin with, it contains a great deal of internal repetition—each of the first three melodic phrases is repeated at least once. Most striking, however, is that it is in a different meter. While the predominant *usul* (meter) of a *saz semâisi* consists of a cycle of ten beats in a moderate tempo, the *usul* of the D *hane* has six beats and is performed at a significantly faster tempo. As a result, the penultimate passage of "Samâi Shad Araban" is more energetic and exciting than those that preceded it. This makes the *saz semâisi* a good piece of music with which to conclude a suite, for it always comes to a rollicking finish.

The melodic instruments in our recording are the violin, *ney*, *oud*, and *kanun*. Because the timbre of each is so different, it is fairly easy to pick the various instruments out of the texture. In addition, each adds unique, **improvised** ornaments. The *kanun* player periodically contributes melodic flourishes and rhythmic elements that are not played by the other instruments, while the violin player emphasizes their ability to slide between pitches. The *oud* is foregrounded near the end of the performance, when it renders a solo version of the *teslim* before we hear it one last time from the entire ensemble.

The percussion accompaniment to "Samâi Shad Araban"—and, indeed, to any *saz semâisi*—is not specified by the composer. Instead, the performers use their knowledge of the *usul* and the melody to improvise an accompaniment that demarcates the rhythmic cycle while also reflecting the character of the melodic phrases. In this recording, we can clearly hear the jingling sounds of the *def* above the regular beats of the various drums.

Finally, a word about mode. The *makam* of "Samâi Shad Araban" is indicated by its title, which tells us the type of piece that this is—a *saz semâisi*—and its mode, Shad Araban. (This is similar to the European convention of naming a piece of music something like Symphony in E Minor.) The pitches of Shad Araban[8] are not particularly similar to those of the major or minor scale. This *makam* features two intervals of an augmented second: a large interval that is not present in any European scale. It also contains a large number of half steps, the smallest European interval. As a result, melodies in Shad Araban move by intervals that seem alternately cramped and spacious.

8.   This video demonstrates the pitches of Shad Araban.

JOHN DOWLAND, "FLOW, MY TEARS"

John Dowland (1563-1626) was indisputably one of the finest lute players of his day. Although he was best known for his skill as a performer, he also wrote a great deal of music, both for his own instrument and for **viol consort** (an ensemble of string instruments that predated the modern violin family). He gained a reputation for writing exceptionally sad songs that celebrated melancholy.

Dowland's Career

Despite his widely-recognized skill, Dowland was repeatedly frustrated in his attempts to secure a position at the court of Queen Elizabeth I. This might have been due to the fact that he had converted to Catholicism, although Elizabeth, who was tolerant of religious diversity, employed other Catholic musicians. Whatever the case, he spent decades working on the European continent while continuing to publish his music in England. In 1594 he accepted a position at the court of the Duke of Brunswick-Lüneburg. Then, in 1598, he became lutenist at the court of Christian IV, King of Denmark, where he was held in high esteem and paid an astronomical sum.

Dowland returned to England in 1606, but it was not until 1612 that he was finally able to secure a position at the English court. By this time, he not only had an international reputation but had published a wealth of compositions. Writing music served Dowland's interests in several ways. By producing new music for his own instrument, the lute, Dowland increased his value as a court employee. By publishing music for the lute and other instruments, he created an additional source of income and strengthened his reputation. Finally, by dedicating his publications to wealthy aristocrats, he won their professional and financial support.

"Flow, My Tears"

The lute song "Flow, My Tears"[9] provides an excellent example of Dowland's professional savvy. The composition began life as a **pavan**[10] for solo lute entitled "Lachrimae" (a Latin term meaning "tears"). A pavan is a type of slow, stately court dance that was popular in Europe at the time. Although Dowland's music was not intended to accompany dancing, he was often influenced by the characters and styles of dance music. When "Lachrimae" became Dowland's most popular work, he took the opportunity to capitalize on his success by transforming it into a song.

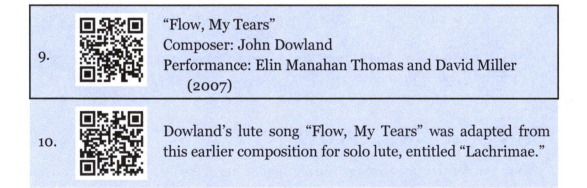

9. "Flow, My Tears"
Composer: John Dowland
Performance: Elin Manahan Thomas and David Miller (2007)

10. Dowland's lute song "Flow, My Tears" was adapted from this earlier composition for solo lute, entitled "Lachrimae."

"Flow, My Tears" was first published in Dowland's 1600 collection *The Second Booke of Songs or Ayres* (an **"ayre"** is a solo song with lute accompaniment). Dowland had previously developed a novel approach to typesetting his lute songs, many of which had more than one vocal part. Before Dowland, it was common practice to publish each vocal and instrumental part to a piece of music in a separate book, known as a "part book." Each performer therefore needed to possess the correct book, and could only see their own part. Dowland began printing all of the parts in a single book, which could be laid out on a table before the performers. In this way they could all read from the same page.

This tells us something important about how Dowland's music was used: He was writing for groups of friends or family members, who would perform his music gathered around a table in the home. Although today you are more likely to hear Dowland performed by professionals in a concert setting, that was never what he had in mind. He was producing music for the domestic entertainment market—music to fill the long evening hours when there was little else to do.

The layout of "Flow, My Tears" can help us to visualize a home performance, even if one cannot read the music. The lute and primary vocal part are paired together, since they might be performed by the same person. The lute part, as was typical of the era, is printed using **tablature** instead of staff notation. Lute tablature, much like guitar tab today, indicates where the fingers of the left hand go on each string of the instrument. It also includes rhythms. The extra vocal part is printed on the second page, and it faces in a different direction. This was for convenience: The additional singer would sit to the right of the lutenist, along the adjoining edge of the table.

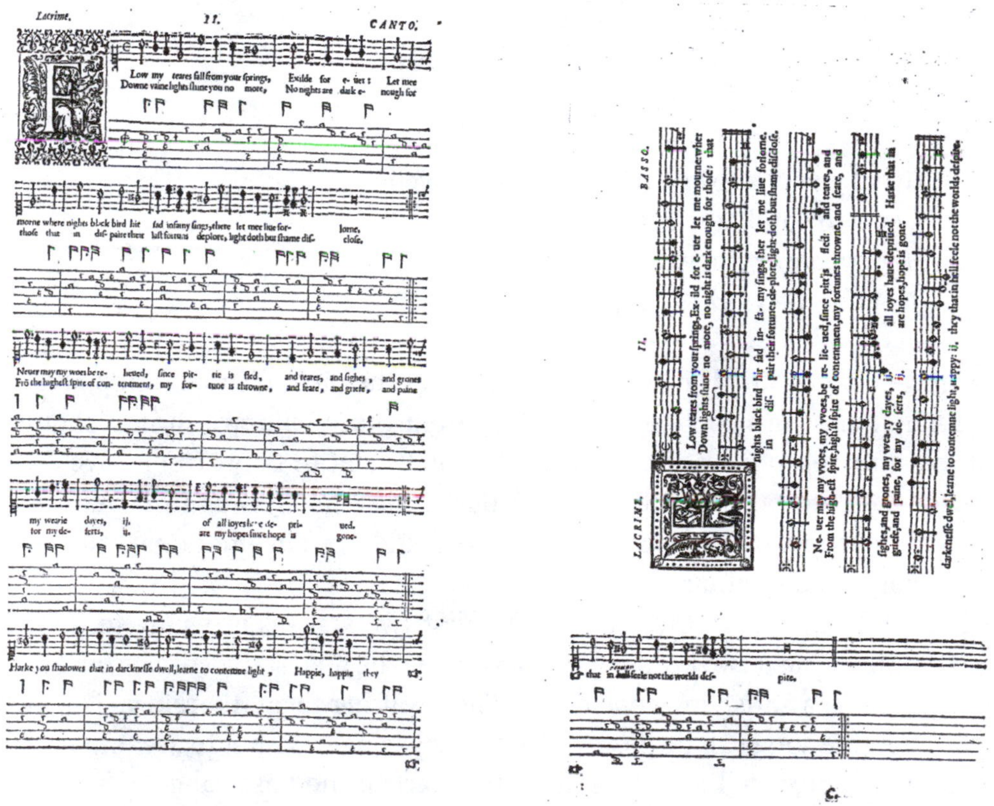

Image 8.21: As you can see, the additional vocal part in the original edition of Dowland's ayre faces a different direction than the lute and principal vocal parts. This facilitates an in-home performance for which the optional extra singer sits on the adjacent edge of a table.
Source: First Edition Scanned Image
Attribution: John Dowland
License: Public Domain

"Flow, My Tears" is a prime example of Dowland's work in terms of affect, form, and style. To begin with, the text is characteristically gloomy:

Flow, my tears, fall from your springs!
Exiled for ever, let me mourn;
Where night's black bird her sad infamy sings,
There let me live forlorn.

Down vain lights, shine you no more!
No nights are dark enough for those
That in despair their lost fortunes deplore.
Light doth but shame disclose.

Never may my woes be relieved,
Since pity is fled;
And tears and sighs and groans my weary days
Of all joys have deprived.

From the highest spire of contentment
My fortune is thrown;
And fear and grief and pain for my deserts
Are my hopes, since hope is gone.

Hark! you shadows that in darkness dwell,
Learn to condemn light
Happy, happy they that in hell
Feel not the world's despite.

Dowland—who wrote his own words—expresses the most profound hopelessness. The final stanza, in which he argues that even those who are in hell should be glad they are not in his position, takes this sentiment to the extreme. We do not, however, need to take this text too seriously. Melancholy was in fashion at the time. When people sang "Flow, My Tears," they indulged in emotional role-playing that probably had a cathartic effect.

Dowland's ayre is in three parts. The first two stanzas are sung to the same music, while the next two are sung to a new tune. The final stanza has its own music, which provides a satisfying conclusion. The resulting form, therefore, is A A B B C. Although the song can be performed by a solo singer with lute accompaniment, Dowland also provided an additional vocal part in the bass range, which would allow another performer to join in.[11] The vocal and instrumental parts are highly independent: Each is equally difficult and has its own rhythms and melodies.

11. In this rendition, we hear Dowland's song with both the primary soprano melody and the option bass melody.

The music, which is in the minor mode, is highly expressive. The opening melody descends, providing a musical portrayal of falling tears. In the B section, Dowland sets his list of sorrowful expressions (in the third stanza: "and tears, and sighs, and groans") to a melody that ascends by leap, accompanied by echoes from the lute. This technique communicates the passion and suffering behind these complaints. The highest pitch of the melody arrives in the C section with the word "happy"—but Dowland's descending melody indicates that he does not feel happiness himself.

In 1604, Dowland capitalized on the success of "Lachrimae" and "Flow, My Tears" yet again by publishing a further version of the work for viol consort. It appeared in a volume dedicated to Anne, the new Queen of England—an effort by Dowland to secure that elusive court position. This time, the composition became the first of a set of pavans entitled *Lachrimae, or Seven Tears*, all of which begin with the descending "tears" motif that we heard in the lute solo and song. The first pavan in the collection, "Lachrimae Antiquae" ("Ancient Tears"),[12] is essentially identical to "Lachrimae" and "Flow, My Tears." The additional six pavans explore different musical possibilities that are introduced by the "tears" motif. All are profoundly mournful in character. As if feeling the need to cement his reputation for melancholy, Dowland followed the set of *Lachrimae* pavans with a composition entitled *Semper Dowland semper Dolens*: Latin for "Always Dowland always mournful."

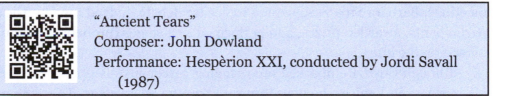

12. "Ancient Tears"
Composer: John Dowland
Performance: Hespèrion XXI, conducted by Jordi Savall (1987)

BARBARA STROZZI, *MY TEARS*

Barbara Strozzi (1619-1677), like Dowland, was a gifted performer who wrote music for her own use. Also like Dowland, she favored sorrowful laments that showcased her gifts, as a performer and composer, for extravagant emotional expression. Most of her vocal works concerned suffering caused by unrequited love. Strozzi's unique social position, however, meant that her artistic motivations were quite unlike Dowland's, while her geographic and temporal distance from him—Strozzi lived in Venice, and her career began shortly after Dowland's death—meant that her style was significantly different.

Strozzi's Career

Strozzi was the adopted daughter of the renowned poet and cultural luminary Giulio Strozzi. Her mother was a servant in Giulio's household. Although Strozzi's birth certificate indicates that her father was unknown, it was almost certainly Giulio himself. This sort of arrangement was not unusual in 17th-century Venice. Giulio himself was the illegitimate son of an illegitimate son, while Strozzi would in turn have four children out of wedlock. Whatever the case, Giulio took an active interest in his daughter's career as a singer and composer, writing texts for her to sing and facilitating her private performances before the city's artistic elite.

Image 8.22: This portrait by Bernardo Strozzi is entitled *Female Musician with Viola da Gamba*, but is believed to be of Barbara Strozzi.
Source: Wikimedia Commons
Attribution: Bernardo Strozzi
License: Public Domain

In 1637, Giulio established a formal **academy** dedicated to music over which his daughter presided. Academies were an important facet of intellectual life in Venice and other Italian-speaking cities of the era. They were not formal schools but, rather, gatherings of educated citizens who came together for discussion and debate. Giulio's named his association the *Accademia degli Unisoni*. This translates to "Academy of the Like-Minded," but also incorporates a music-themed pun on the word "unisoni," which can mean "unison" in the sense of multiple voices singing the same notes. At the academy meetings, Barbara Strozzi suggested topics for debate, judged the forensic skill of participants, awarded prizes, and performed as a singer (probably accompanying herself on the lute).

Although Strozzi embarked on a singing career just as opera was becoming big business in Venice, she never appeared on the opera stage. This is important. Although opera offered roles for women, taking to the stage meant social exclusion. A woman who performed in public was assumed to be a prostitute—and indeed, Strozzi herself faced such accusations as her fame grew. By confining her activities to the private sphere, she retained greater social capital. Her decision to perform only in domestic settings also influenced Strozzi's work as a composer, which focused on the chamber genres of **aria** (a strophic song) and **cantata** (an extended semi-dramatic work for soloist with accompaniment).

While it was typical for 17th-century Italian singers to write their own music, Strozzi pursued the task with unusual resolve. In fact, she published more solo vocal music than any other Venetian composer of her era. In total, she completed and published an astonishing eight single-author volumes of vocal music. Most of this was secular music with Italian texts (some of which she might have written

Image 8.23: This view of Venice's main plaza, named after the extravagant St. Mark's Basilica, was painted in the 1730s.
Source: Wikimedia Commons
Attribution: Canaletto
License: Public Domain

herself), although she also produced one collection of sacred works with Latin texts. Her volumes, which were published between 1644 and 1664, were highly regarded and widely consumed, and many of her most successful compositions were included in collections alongside the work of other great composers. While Strozzi performed before small groups of connoisseurs in a domestic setting, therefore, her music was also available for others to perform at home for their own entertainment, or for gatherings of family and friends.

My Tears

	My Tears Composer: Barbara Strozzi Performance: Emanuela Galli with Ensemble Galilei, conducted by Paul Beier (1998)	
Time	**Form**	**What to listen for**
0'00"	Refrain - "My tears. . ."	The melody starts high and descends via an unusual, tortured scale in a representation of falling tears; the singer embellishes the line with a variety of ornaments

0'39"	Recitative - "Why do you not let burst forth. . ."	The recitative passages are characterized by frequent changes in tempo and mood; there is no steady pulse; painful harmonies communicate the speaker's suffering
3'01"	Arioso - "And you, sorrowful eyes. . ."	The music settles into a triple meter
3'30"	Refrain	
4'03"	Aria - Verse 1: "Alas, I yearn for Lidia. . ."	The Aria is in quadruple meter
4'46"	Verse 2: "Because I wecome death. . ."	The Aria music repeats with new text
5'31"	Recitative - "But well I realize. . ."	
5'55"	Instrumental interlude	This interlude was not composed by Strozzi, but it is not inappropriate in a performance of her cantata, the accompaniment to which is largely improvised
6'45"	Arioso	Again, the music settles into a triple meter; the accompaniment centers on a four-note descending pattern
7'56"	Refrain	The singer repeats the entire opening passage of the cantata (Strozzi herself indicated only that the refrain should be repeated)

My Tears (Italian: Lagrime mie) appeared in Strozzi's seventh volume of music, which was published in 1659 and bore the title *The Pleasures of Euterpe* (in the mythology of ancient Greece, Euterpe was the Muse of Music). Pietro Dolfino's text is a lament for a beloved—Lidia—who has been imprisoned by her disapproving father:

Image 8.24: Here we see the title page of Strozzi's collection *The Pleasures of Euterpe*. The largest type sets the name of the dedicatee, from whom Strozzi might have expected payment in gratitude.
Source: Wikimedia Commons
Attribution: Barbara Strozzi
License: Public Domain

My tears, why do you hold back?
Why do you not let burst forth the fierce pain
that takes my breath and oppresses my heart?

Lidia, whom I so much adore,
Because she looked on me with a pitiable glance
is imprisoned by her strict father.
Between two walls
the beautiful innocent one is confined,
where the sun's ray can't reach her;
and what grieves me most,
and adds torment and pain to my agony,
is that my beloved
suffers on my account.

And you, sorrowful eyes, you don't cry?
My tears, why do you hold back?

Alas, I yearn for Lidia,
my idol whom I so much adore;

she's captured in hard marble,
she for whom I sigh and yet do not die.

Because I welcome death,
now that I'm deprived of hope;
Ah, take away my life,
I pray to you, my bitter pain.

But well I realize that to torment me
even more
Fate denies me even death.
Since it's true, oh God,
that vicious Destiny
thirsts only for my wailing,
My tears, why do you hold back?

Translation by Jennifer Gliere. Used with permission.

Like many secular cantata texts, this one features a **refrain**—"My tears, why do you hold back?"—that appears three times: once at the beginning, once in the middle, and once at the end. The melody to which the words "my tears" is sung descends from the top of the singer's range, dripping down in a vivid impression of falling tears. It is full of tortuous intervals and sigh-like ornaments that communicate the singer's distressed emotional state.

After the opening refrain, the singer carries on in the **recitative** style, allowing the rhythm and meaning of the text to determine her phrasing. Strozzi continues to employ text painting, such as with the drawn-out, descending chromatic line on the word "pain" (Italian: "dolore") and the gasping pause in the middle of the word "breath" (Italian: "respiro"). Strozzi finally settles in to a metered rhythm with the passage on the text, "And you, sorrowful eyes, you don't cry?" This type of music—more structured than recitative but less formal than an aria—is termed **arioso**. Again, Strozzi employs text painting in the form of repeated, descending sighs.

This is followed by the refrain, which leads into the aria. This is the most formal part of the cantata and the only passage of music in which two stanzas of text are sung to the same melody. The text concerned begins with "Alas, I yearn for Lidia" and concludes with "I pray to you, my bitter pain." The final passage of the text is set to music that continues to shift and bend in accordance to the singer's baleful emotions. The last thing we hear is the refrain—evidence that the singer's suffering has not lessened.

FRANZ JOSEPH HAYDN, STRING QUARTET, OP. 33, NO. 2 "THE JOKE"

Over the course of the 18th century, the demand for domestic music continued to grow. Instrumental music, in particular, saw a rise in popularity as entertainment for the concert hall, the court, and the home. New genres of instrumental **chamber music** came into existence, the most important of which was the string quartet. Chamber music differs from orchestral music in three important ways. First, it requires only a few players—usually between two and eight. Second, each of those players has their own part, while in an orchestra whole sections of string players are assigned the same part. Finally, chamber music does not require a conductor. Chamber music, therefore, is suitable for small spaces and emphasizes communication between the individual performers.

A **string quartet** is a type of chamber ensemble composed of two violins, a viola, and a cello. (The term "string quartet" can refer either to a group of players

Image 8.25: This 18th-century painting portrays Haydn himself (on the far right) playing viola in a string quartet. The players are intensely focused on the music making: Two of them look up while Haydn quickly turns a page. Others are listening, but their attitude is informal: Three women lean in from the right, while two additional admirers listen from beyond the door.

Source: Wikimedia Commons
Attribution: Anonymous
License: Public Domain

or to a composition.) Although today professional string quartets give concerts and make recordings, the genre was at first oriented primarily toward amateurs, who purchased sheet music and played at home for their own entertainment. Quartets also provided background music for dinners and social gatherings. The most important early composer of string quartets was Franz Joseph Haydn (1732-1809), whose creative contributions to the genre set the standard for generations to follow.

Haydn's Career

Image 8.26: This portrait of Haydn was painted by Thomas Hardy in 1791, when the composer was visiting London to put on a series of concerts.
Source: Wikimedia Commons
Attribution: Thomas Hardy
License: Public Domain

Haydn was born to working-class parents in a remote Austrian village. Neither his father (a wheelwright) nor his mother (a cook) had any musical training, but they recognized their son's talent and arranged for him to live with a relative who could provide educational opportunities. Then, in 1739, the music director at St. Stephen's Cathedral in Vienna—Georg von Reutter—heard Haydn sing and offered him a position in the Cathedral choir. For the next nine years, Haydn lived with Reutter, during which time he studied and performed music.

When Haydn's voice broke in 1749, however, he was suddenly out of a job, and he spent several difficult years trying to scrape together a living as a freelance musician. In mid-18th century Vienna, there were few opportunities for a musical career outside of church or court employment. In 1757, Haydn finally obtained the latter when he became music director for Count Morzin. His fine work with the Count's private orchestra won him a similar position four years later with the Esterházy family, whom he served for the remainder of his life.

The position of music director for the Esterházys was among the most desirable in the German-speaking world. (Although Haydn served informally as music director from 1761, he was not officially awarded the title until his predecessor passed away in 1766.) The Esterházy family was both wealthy and powerful, exercising great influence within the Habsburg Empire. In addition, Prince Nikolaus I, who headed the family from 1762 until 1790, was a great music lover and ardent support of Haydn. For this reason, Haydn was granted an unusual amount of creative freedom, and his work was met with appreciation. All the same, Haydn was a servant. As such, he was obliged to perform a variety of duties and occupied a low social rung.

Haydn did not just compose music. He was responsible for all musical entertainment, large and small, that took place in the Esterházy household. This included the weekly staging of an opera and two concerts, special performances in honor of guests, and the provision of chamber music for domestic entertainment. Prince Nikolaus was a musician himself: He played an unusual instrument called the baryton, which resembled a bass viol with extra strings that could be plucked. Although the baryton was never popular and soon disappeared altogether, the fact that it was favored by the Prince meant that Haydn had not only to compose music for the instrument but to accompany the Prince when he played. In total, he produced about 200 chamber works for baryton, most of which are trios for baryton, cello, and viola (Haydn's instrument). The baryton part is always prominent, but never too difficult—as suited the Prince's abilities and desires. These pieces are seldom performed today, and it is easy to look on them as a wasted effort. They remind us, however, that Haydn often composed on command, and that his own artistic inclinations were secondary to the requirements of his employer.

As a servant in the Esterházy household, Haydn followed the Prince as he moved between the various Esterházy estates. Principal among these were the ancestral palace in Eisenstadt (now in Eastern Hungary) and a new summer palace, Eszterháza, built by Prince Nikolaus in 1766. Although both palaces were well-equipped for musical performances, they were far from the urban center of Vienna, and Haydn's duties therefore meant that he was isolated from musical trends. As a result, he developed a unique approach to composition, innovating in terms of form and style. His fame slowly grew, and in 1779 he found himself in a position to renegotiate his contract with the Esterházys. Under the new terms, he was free to take outside commissions and to publish his music, which had previously been the property of his employers.

Image 8.27: This baryton is on display at the Esterházy palace. The extra strings are not visible because they run down the back side of the instrument, behind the panel that runs alongside the fretboard.
Source: Wikimedia Commons
Attribution: User "Rik86"
License: CC BY 2.5

Image 8.28: This view of the courtyard of Eszterháza Palace gives a sense of its enormous size.
Source: Wikimedia Commons
Attribution: User "Dguendel"
License: CC BY 3.0

String Quartet, Op. 33, No. 2 "The Joke"

Among the first of Haydn's publications were a set of string quartets, labelled as his Opus 33 ("**opus**" is the Latin word for "work," and it is often used to indicate the order in which published compositions appear). The label indicates that this was Haydn's thirty-third publication, but of course he had composed a great deal more music than that. Most of his works, however, were intended for the private use of his employer and were therefore never published. But when it came to the world of commerce, it made sense for Haydn to publish chamber works: There was a thriving market for sheet music intended for use in domestic entertainment.

Haydn's Opus 33 string quartets were dedicated to the Grand Duke Paul of Russia, and they were first performed in the Viennese home of his wife. In the dedication, Haydn explained that these quartets were composed in a "new and special manner." While this is exactly the sort of thing that a composer might say for the purpose of improving sales, it is true that Haydn's Opus 33 quartets are different from those that came before. Early quartets were essentially violin solos with accompaniment; in many cases, a professional was hired to take the first violin part, while amateurs filled in the others. The first violin is still prominent in Opus 33, but all of the parts are important and interesting, and they pass motifs from one to another. The resulting texture resembles a civilized conversation between intellectual equals—a musical representation of the rational discourse that was so valued during the Enlightenment era.

We will see all of this at work in the second quartet from Haydn's Opus 33 collection, which bears the subtitle "The Joke." This subtitle did not come from the composer himself, but rather from the Viennese publishing firm Artaria. Publishers often gave nicknames to instrumental works in this period, which otherwise were designated only by number. A nickname drew attention to a composition and gave the consumer an idea about its characteristics. Nicknames still help listeners today, for they tell us what a piece of otherwise abstract instrumental music is "about." We should always, however, take them with a grain of salt.

Haydn's Opus 33, No. 2 quartet was subtitled "The Joke" because of its fourth movement, which concludes with a bit of unmistakable musical comedy. The joke here is so obvious, in fact, that even listeners with no particular knowledge of music will get it. We should take a moment to marvel at the capacity of pure sound to be humorous. The quartet, of course, contains no words. It communicates purely through musical syntax, and the joke works by playing on our expectations regarding form, pulse, and phrasing.

Movement IV

The fourth movement is in **rondo form**, meaning that a refrain returns throughout.[13] In Haydn's time, this was a typical form for a final movement, and his listeners (and players) would have quickly recognized it. This would establish certain expectations—in particular, the expectation that the movement would end with a complete statement of the refrain.

13.      String Quartet, Op. 33, No. 2 "The Joke," Movement IV
Composer: Franz Joseph Haydn
Performance: Borodin Quartet (2010)

For the most part, the movement unfolds as anticipated. After a complete statement of the refrain (A), we hear a new passage (B), followed by the refrain (A), followed by another new passage (C), followed once more by the refrain (A). The refrain is lighthearted and dancelike, and the movement in general is fast-paced and jocular. At this point, however, something strange happens. There is a pause, followed by a halting passage in a slow tempo. Two loud entrances fade away into uneven rhythms. This strange interruption is followed once more by the refrain, but this time the two-bar sub-phrases are broken up by long pauses. The last thing we hear is a final statement of the opening two measures. At this point, however, the sequence of pauses has completely disrupted our ability to predict what is going to happen next, and a listener who is not looking at the music has no way of knowing that the piece is over. The comedy, then, comes from the weirdness of the final moments and the shock of realizing that the movement has in fact concluded.

In sum, our expectation regarding form is disappointed when we encounter the slow passage after the third A. Our expectation regarding pulse is disappointed by the frequent pauses near the end of the movement. And our expectation regarding phrasing is disappointed when the piece concludes one quarter of the way through the principal phrase of the refrain.

This last disappointment is particularly significant, for Enlightenment-era composers placed a high value on stable, symmetrical musical phrases. For composers such as Haydn, symmetry and balance—along with predictable harmonic progressions and clear textures—were signs of rational thinking. They also reflected the architecture of ancient Greece, which provided a model across the arts of the **Classical** era (1750-1815). We hear such phrases in the first movement of the quartet, which also contains humorous elements—although they are not quite so obvious to the average listener.

Movement I

		String Quartet Op. 33 No. 2 "The Joke," Movement I Composer: Franz Joseph Haydn Performance: The Coull Quartet (1995)
Time	**Form**	**What to listen for**
Exposition		
0'00"	Primary Theme	This theme, which is elegant and restrained, is in a balanced "a b a" form
0'28"	Transition	
0'46"	Secondary Theme	This theme is scattered and unfocused; it culminates in an explosive violin solo
1'05"	Closing Theme	The opening motif returns in this theme
1'15"	Repetition of the Exposition	
Development		
2'29"		Motifs in this passage are drawn from the a and b phrases of the Primary Theme
3'25"		The first violin again bursts into an inexplicable frenzy, which is curtailed by a rapid cadential progression

3'31"		The Primary Theme returns, but in a minor key
Recapitulation		
3'41"	Primary Theme	
3'58"	Transition	The transition unexpectedly interrupts the b phrase of the Primary Theme
4'16"	Secondary Theme	Again, this theme concludes with a wild violin solo
4'38"	Closing Theme	This time the Closing Theme is heard twice; the second time, the familiar motif is turned upside down
4'47"	Repetition of the Development and Recapitulation	It was common in this era to repeat the entire second half of a sonata-form movement

The first movement of the Opus 33, No.2 quartet is in **sonata form**, which was described and discussed in Chapter 7. The Primary Theme is in ternary (aba) form, and each of the phrases is four measures in length. The B phrase contains call and response between the parts: The first violin plays a **motif** that is echoed by the second violin and viola. The first sign of disruption—and humor—comes near the end of the Exposition, when the first violin launches into an uncharacteristically virtuosic and excited passage that momentarily spoils the mood of elegance and restraint.

More humor comes in the Development. After a particularly serious passage that explores the motifs of the Primary Theme, a return of the virtuosic and excited passage leads to an abrupt and unsatisfying cadence. This is followed by what seems to be the return of the Primary Theme and, therefore, the Recapitulation within the sonata form—but the theme is in minor, not major. As if realizing its mistake, the theme peters out and relaunches in the correct key, thereby inaugurating the Recapitulation.

These minor details would only be appreciated by those steeped in the musical traditions of the era. That, however, is exactly the kind of person for whom Haydn was writing. His consumers were the amateurs who played this music for their own amusement (and who therefore were intimately familiar with its conventions) and the aristocrats who enjoyed the chamber music that was performed in their homes on command. Today, aristocrats have been replaced by avid concertgoers, but amateurs still enjoy playing string quartets for no audience but themselves. The existence of organizations like the Associated Chamber Music Players, which serves to connect amateur chamber musicians and facilitate reading sessions and workshops, attests to the continued popularity of chamber music as domestic entertainment.

CLARA SCHUMANN, PIANO TRIO IN G MINOR

Clara Schumann (1819-1896) was the leading piano **virtuoso** of her day. Her legacy as a solo performer still impacts pianists, who learn selections from a repertoire that she established and give recitals according to her standards (Schumann was the first pianist to regularly perform from memory). Schumann also profoundly influenced the development of piano technique through her work as a teacher. As a composer, Schumann primarily created music for her own use, including a piano concerto, solo piano works, chamber music, and songs with imaginative piano accompaniments. Although her compositions were well received, Schumann always harbored misgivings about her abilities in that arena. Her self-doubt reflected a societal bias against female composers that was prevalent in the 19th century.

Image 8.29: This 1838 engraving by August Kneisel captures Schumann as a young woman.
Source: Wikimedia Commons
Attribution: August Kneisel
License: Public Domain

Schumann's Career

Schumann (born Clara Weick) was the daughter of renowned piano pedagogue Friederich Weick. From the moment of her birth, Weick planned to mold Schumann into a brilliant piano virtuoso. He provided her with daily instruction in all facets of music and required diligent practice. She was soon eliciting praise with her public performances, and was touring Europe to give concerts as a teenager.

At the age of nine, her performance in the home of one of Weick's friends inspired a listener—Robert Schumann—to abandon the study of law and enroll as a student of Weick. Robert, who was eighteen, moved into the Weick household and set about the task of becoming a piano virtuoso himself. He never succeeded, but he and Clara developed a close relationship, When she turned eighteen, Robert proposed and Clara accepted. Weick, however, was furious, and refused to permit the union. The couple took their case to court and were finally able to wed in 1840.

Schumann's marriage was happy, but also difficult. Over the course of the next fourteen years, she became pregnant ten times and bore eight children. She also supported the household financially by performing and teaching. Robert made a name for himself as a music critic and composer, but he suffered from an unidentified mental illness that produced bouts of depression, exaltation, and delusion. He attempted suicide in 1854 by leaping from a bridge into the Rhine river. He survived but insisted on being committed to an asylum, where he died two years later.

Throughout this period, Schumann continued to manage the household and support her husband. She composed little, although not because Robert discouraged her. Indeed, he thought she was a particularly gifted composer and lamented the fact that she was unable to commit more time and effort to the task. Schumann herself expressed doubts founded on her sex. In 1839, she famously wrote in her diary, "I once believed that I possessed creative talent, but I have given up this idea; a woman must not desire to compose—there has never yet been one able to do it. Should I expect to be the one?" Of course, there had been many successful female composers before Schumann, as we have seen in this chapter. She just didn't know about them, for they were ignored by the historians and audiences of the era.

After Robert's death, Schumann took responsibility for cementing his legacy as a composer, and it is due to her that Robert's music is still heard today. She toured extensively, often in partnership with the leading young performers of the day, and took a teaching position at the Hoch Conservatory. Schumann also mentored and supported the young composer Johannes Brahms, who would go on to become an influential figure himself. In addition to all of this, she raised two sets of grandchildren following the deaths of a daughter and son in the 1870s. Schumann continued to perform until 1891, despite increasing trouble with her arm, and taught up until her death at the age of 76.

Image 8.30: Here we see Schumann in 1857, after her husband's death.
Source: Wikimedia Commons
Attribution: Franz Hanfstaengl
License: Public Domain

Piano Trio in G minor

Schumann composed her piano trio during a particularly difficult period in her life. In 1846, the Schumanns were living in Dresden. They had left Leipzig due to concerns about Robert's physical and mental health, which was increasingly poor. Because Schumann was forced to accept fewer performance engagements while caring for Robert, she focused more of her creative energy on composition.

Image 8.31: Schumann frequently performed chamber music. This 1854 pastel by Adolph von Menzel portrays her in concert with one of her frequent collaborators, violinist Joseph Joachim.
Source: Wikimedia Commons
Attribution: Adolph von Menzel
License: Public Domain

Nevertheless, the task was not simple: Schumann gave birth to children in 1845 and 1846, suffered a further miscarriage, and lived in cramped quarters that contributed to conflict between her and her husband's creative endeavors. Despite challenges, Schumann's piano trio has been considered by many commentators to be her finest work, and it subsequently influenced Robert's first piano trio, which he composed in 1847.

Schumann performed both piano trios in public recitals throughout the remainder of her career, and her trio frequently appeared on programs given by other artists as well. However, it would have been heard most often in middle- and upper-class homes. The market for piano music, including both solo and chamber compositions, was largely driven by young women, who were expected to master the instrument as part of a respectable upbringing. A wife who could play the piano well was a considerable asset, for she could entertain family and friends within the domestic sphere. Chamber music also provided an opportunity for young couples to court. While unmarried couples were often kept under the watchful eye of a chaperone, playing music together allowed them to sit in close proximity.

In this context, we can witness Schumann's piano trio as a testament to her personal suffering, a reflection of her musical training and interests, and an example of domestic music. Her piano trio follows the standards of the day, and each of the four movements contains the expected characteristics. At the same time, she experiments with novel stylistic approaches and expresses herself with compelling sincerity.

Movement III

We will examine the third movement, which is the slowest in tempo.[14] This movement is in **ternary form** (A B A), allowing Schumann to explore contrasting emotions. The movement begins with a gracious, major-mode theme in the piano. A brief turn to minor suggests a hint of sorrow. After the theme has been introduced, it is repeated by the violin, with piano accompaniment. The cello enters with new material, further heightening the intensity of emotional expression with dynamic swells and an ascending **sequence** (a motif that is repeated at different pitch levels). The A section concludes with all three instruments cadencing together.

14. Piano Trio in G minor, Movement III
Composer: Clara Schumann
Performance: Storioni Trio, 2014

This cadence, however, is immediately destabilized by a new, faster tempo and turn to the minor mode. The B section exhibits anxiety and unrest. It features uneven, halting rhythms, accents, and frequent contrasts in dynamic level, texture, and mood.

When the A material returns, it is in the cello, with an accompaniment provided by the piano and **pizzicato** violin (a technique whereby the player plucks the strings instead of bowing them). After the violin and cello repeat their joint material from before, a **coda** containing new melodic material brings the movement to a peaceful conclusion.

RESOURCES FOR FURTHER LEARNING

Print

Bogin, Meg. *The Women Troubadours*. Paddington Press, 1976.

Church, Michael. *The Other Classical Musics: Fifteen Great Traditions*. Boydell Press, 2015.

Julien, Olivier, ed. *Sgt. Pepper and the Beatles: It Was Forty Years Ago Today*. Ashgate, 2008.

Landon, H.C. Robbins. *Haydn: His Life and Music*. Indiana University Press, 1988.

Poulton, Diana. *John Dowland*. University of California Press, 1982.

Reich, Nancy. *Clara Schumann: The Artist and the Woman*. Cornell University Press, 1985.

Taruskin, Richard. *Music in the Seventeenth and Eighteenth Centuries: The Oxford History of Western Music*. Oxford University Press, 2009.

Unit 4

MUSIC FOR POLITICAL EXPRESSION

National Identity

Esther M. Morgan-Ellis and Louis Hajosy

INTRODUCTION

In a sense, all music is political. No form of musical expression is detached from issues of class, race, nationality, and identity. If we argue that a Mozart string quartet is free from all political concerns, we ignore the fact that Mozart lived and worked in Vienna, the powerful, German-speaking seat of the Austro-Hungarian Empire. We ignore the fact that 18th-century string quartets embodied Enlightenment-era political values regarding equality and rational discourse. And we ignore the fact that Mozart's music is used today to represent elite cultural values.

In this chapter and the next, however, we will be exploring forms of musical expression that are explicitly political. We will examine a variety of musical works that were created to express or challenge political values. We will also encounter musical works that were not intended by their creators to contribute to political discourse, but that were coopted and repurposed by political actors.

In this chapter we will be considering the power of music to define and identify nations. The idea that music can express something important about a community has a long history. The ancient Greeks, for example, believed that the unique musical styles of each regional tribe represented the characteristics of that tribe. Moreover, they believed music to be so powerful that anyone who heard music from a particular tribe would in turn exhibit the characteristics of its members. Of course, for us to believe that music can express something about a group of people, we must first agree that all members of the group share something fundamental in common. This can be dangerous, for it invites the exclusion of any member who does not conform. Any claim

Image 9.1: This image shows ancient Greeks.
Source: Wikimedia Commons
Attribution: Albert Racinet
License: Public Domain

that a piece or style of music represents a nation should be met with the question, "What members of the nation does this music fail to represent?"

NATIONAL ANTHEMS

The most explicitly political genre of music is the national anthem. Almost every country has one today, but national anthems have actually not been in use for very long. The first official national anthem was "God Save the Queen," adopted by Great Britain in 1745. European countries began adopting anthems in the mid-19th century. This is the same period during which many modern European countries first came into existence, including Germany and Italy. This was also a period of growing **nationalism**. Artists, philosophers, and politicians generally agreed that people who shared an ethnic and linguistic heritage were somehow bound together and should belong to the same nation. Populations that shared such a heritage—the Hungarians, for example, who were governed by German speakers, or the Poles, who were governed by Russians—began to campaign for independence. Members of all ethnic groups generally agreed that art could express the characteristics of their people, whether or not they had secured autonomous rule. An official anthem became a means of documenting national values and expressing national pride.

National anthems can play an important role in shaping an individual's relationship with the nation. To begin with, anthems are often sung in unison by large groups of people. Recent research has revealed that singing in a community increases levels of oxytocin, a hormone that is closely associated with interpersonal bonding. Singing together, therefore, actively promotes feelings of closeness and community solidarity. Group singing also causes participants' breathing and heart rates to synchronize. Finally, studies have revealed that singing with other people promotes altruism, raises trust levels, and improves cooperation. It even raises pain thresholds. When groups of people sing the national anthem, therefore, they are not inspired only by the words or music. The experience of singing together itself reinforces national identity.

National anthems can also play a more abstract role in binding a nation together. The ritual of singing or hearing the anthem at sporting events and ceremonies helps us to feel connected with the nation and with one another. Whenever we sing or hear the anthem, we can imagine millions of our fellow citizens doing the same. We will never meet or even see the vast majority of these people, but the national anthem unites us, for it is the one song that everyone in the nation knows. That fact gives it great symbolic power.

Of course, the specific words and tunes of anthems are also of significance. It is difficult, however, to make generalizations about anthem texts and melodies, for there is a great deal of variety. To understand how the character and history of an anthem can reflect a nation's identity, we will look at some examples.

United States of America: "The Star-Spangled Banner"

As is the case with almost every national anthem, the words and the tune to "The Star-Spangled Banner"[1] were created by different people at different times. The tune is several decades older than the text, but our story will begin with the famous poem by Francis Scott Key (1779–1843). During the War of 1812, Key travelled with a delegation to the British flagship HMS *Tonnant* to negotiate a prisoner exchange. Although Key and his compatriots were successful in their mission, they were held captive after overhearing British officers plan an attack on the city of Baltimore. Key subsequently witnessed the nighttime battle from aboard a British ship. Famously, he knew that the American forces had emerged victorious when he saw their flag flying over Fort McHenry in the morning light on September 14, 1814. Key began his poem onboard the ship and finished it shortly after his release from captivity. The text of its earliest surviving draft appears below, transcribed from his handwritten manuscript.

1.  "The Star-Spangled Banner"
Composer: John Stafford Smith
Lyricist: Francis Scott Key
Performance: Whitney Houston with The Florida
Orchestra, conducted by Jahja Ling (1991)

O say can you see, by the dawn's early light,
What so proudly we hail'd at the twilight's last gleaming,
Whose broad stripes and bright stars through the perilous fight
O'er the ramparts we watch'd, were so gallantly streaming?
And the rocket's red glare, the bomb[s] bursting in air,
Gave proof through the night that our flag was still there,
O say does that star[-]spangled banner yet wave
O'er the land of the free and the home of the brave?

On the shore dimly seen through the mists of the deep,
Where the foe's haughty host in dread silence reposes,
What is that which the breeze, o'er the towering steep,
As it fitfully blows, half conceals, half discloses?
Now it catches the gleam of the morning's first beam,
In full glory reflected now shines in the stream,
'Tis the star-spangled banner—O long may it wave
O'er the land of the free and the home of the brave!

And where is that band who so vauntingly swore,
That the havoc of war and the battle's confusion
A home and a Country should leave us no more?

Their blood has wash'd out their foul footstep's pollution.
No refuge could save the hireling and slave
From the terror of flight or the gloom of the grave,
And the star-spangled banner in triumph doth wave
O'er the land of the free and the home of the brave.

O thus be it ever when freemen shall stand
Between their lov'd home and the war's desolation!
Blest with vict'ry and peace may the heav'n rescued land
Praise the power that hath made and preserv'd us a nation!
Then conquer we must, when our cause it is just,
And this be our motto—"In God is our trust,"
And the star-spangled banner in triumph shall wave
O'er the land of the free and the home of the brave.

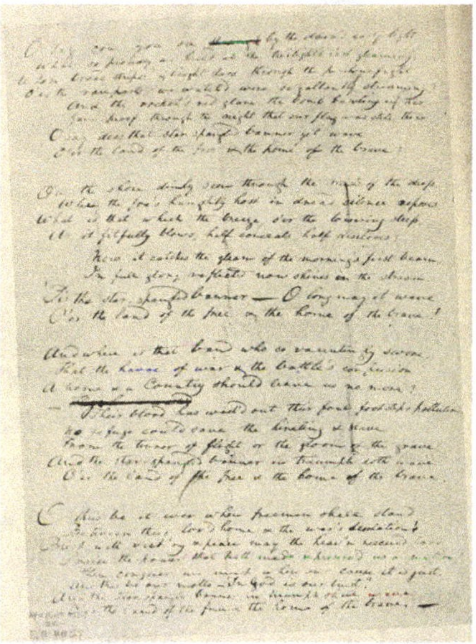

Image 9.2: The autograph manuscript of Key's poem can be viewed at the Maryland Historical Society.
Source: Wikipedia
Attribution: Francis Scott Key
License: Public Domain

Originally untitled, Key's poem was first printed in Baltimore a few days later, probably on September 17, in a **broadside** entitled "Defence of Fort M'Henry." Broadsides—single sheets of paper printed on one side only—were commonplace in larger cities during the 18th and 19th centuries. Their texts often dealt with topics of the day, and they frequently carried news of a recent scandal, accident, crime, or execution. Such texts could be written, typeset, printed, and distributed very quickly, so broadsides were an effective means of spreading information. More specifically, "Defence of Fort M'Henry" was printed as a **broadside ballad**, so in addition to providing a ballad text (Key's poem, in this instance), it named the popular tune to which the text was to be sung. Because buyers already knew the currently popular tunes, they could immediately sing the new lyrics. (This type of songwriting differs greatly from the approach common today, in which a single person typically creates both the lyrics and the melody—or at least works with a songwriting partner who provides the missing half. Reusing another composer's melody would not only seem to lack creativity but would probably result in a lawsuit.)

It is not clear that Key himself had any particular melody in mind when he wrote "Defence of Fort M'Henry," or that he ever intended for it to be sung. However, he had written song texts before. Indeed, various lines and images included in his September 1814 poem first appeared in his 1805 song "When the

Warrior Returns." Perhaps for this reason, the 1814 poem had the same pattern of syllables and rhymes as Key's previous effort, and therefore fit the same tune. In the "Defence of Fort M'Henry" broadside, between an introduction describing the fort's bombardment and the poem's text, there appears the indication "*Tune—Anacreon in Heaven.*" Pairing the text with this melody produces a **ballad**—a narrative, strophic song. A **strophic song** is one in which each stanza of text is sung to the same melody.

This tune, which we recognize today as the melody of "The Star-Spangled Banner," was composed by John Stafford Smith (1750–1836) around 1776 and first published, with lyrics by Ralph Tomlinson (1744–78), as "The Anacreontic Song" around 1779. The song was also widely known as "To Anacreon in Heaven," which are the opening words. Tomlinson's lyrics celebrate the ancient Greek poet Anacreon, who wrote about love, wine, and

Image 9.3: "The Anacreontic Song" is clearly identified as a drinking song by the text across the top of this sheet music, which reads "as sung at the Crown & Anchor Tavern in the Strand."
Source: Wikimedia Commons
Attribution: Poem by Ralph Tomlinson, music by John Stafford Smith
License: Public Domain

amusements. Smith and Tomlinson created their song for the Anacreontic Society, a London gentlemen's club founded around 1766. Its members were amateur musicians who desired to promote the arts and enjoy one another's company. Their meetings included a concert, dinner, and light entertainment, and they sang "To Anacreon in Heaven," the society's "constitutional song," after finishing their meal (the point at which the fun really began). Although the Anacreontic

Image 9.4: Meetings of the Anacreontic Society were famously raucous, as captured in this 1801 caricature by James Gillray.
Source: Wikimedia Commons
Attribution: James Gillray
License: Public Domain

Society occasionally aspired to higher things, it was essentially a drinking club—and a rather lively one by all reports. The Society was shut down in 1792 after a visit by the Duchess of Devonshire provoked controversy over some lewd after-dinner songs. Though the Society had lasted for only a few decades, "To Anacreon in Heaven" was a hit. It quickly became popular with the creators of broadside ballads and accumulated a large number of texts. When "Defence of Fort M'Henry" appeared, therefore, the tune's indication allowed any purchaser to immediately sing the ballad.

"The Star-Spangled Banner," as it came to be known, joined a pantheon of patriotic 19th-century songs. It quickly gained popularity, but was generally overshadowed by "Hail, Columbia" and "America" ("My Country, 'Tis of Thee"). "The Star-Spangled Banner" faced significant criticism as a national song. The leading objection was that it was simply too difficult to sing. Indeed, its **melodic range** (an octave and a fifth) is unusually wide for a national anthem, and all but professional singers struggle to reach the highest notes. The melody is also characterised by **disjunct motion**—that is to say, the notes of the melody do not simply move up and down the scale, but instead are separated by large intervals. Others complained that its text, too specifically tied to a unique historical event, failed to reflect national values more generally. Finally, it has been criticized for its militaristic subject matter. All the same, the song slowly gained traction, first becoming popular at Independence Day celebrations. In 1899, the the US Navy adopted "The Star-Spangled Banner" for official use, and in 1916 President Woodrow Wilson ordered that it be played at all military events.

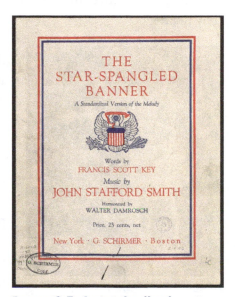

Image 9.5: A standardized version of "The Star-Spangled Banner," with a harmonization by Walter Damrosch, was published in 1918.
Source: Library of Congress
Attribution: Francis Scott Key, John Stafford Smith, Walter Damrosch
License: Public Domain

By the early 1900s, many variations of the song's tune had arisen, so in 1917, President Wilson commissioned five prominent musicians—Walter Damrosch, Will Earheart, Arnold J. Gantvoort, Oscar Sonneck, and John Philip Sousa—to agree on and publish a standardized version. Baseball fans began singing the song at games beginning in 1918. Finally, on March 3, 1931, President Herbert Hoover signed a bill designating "The Star-Spangled Banner" as the national anthem of the United States. The legislation had been championed by Rep. John Linthicum of Baltimore, who, understandably, had taken an interest in promoting a local song. He was successful only following extensive debate over the song's merits and deficiencies and the consideration of several alternatives, including "America the Beautiful."

Performing "The Star-Spangled Banner"

There have been countless performances of "The Star-Spangled Banner:" most indifferent, but some exceptionally good or bad. It seems that a video of another "national anthem fail" circulates about once a year. But what is it that makes a "bad" performance? Sometimes, as in the case of Christina Aguilera's performance at the 2011 Super Bowl, it's because the singer forgets the words. Sometimes, as in the case of Victoria Zarlenga's rendition at in international soccer match in 2012, it's because the singer can't stay on key. And sometimes, as in the case of

Fergie's performance at a 2018 NBA All-Star game, it's because the singer takes an interpretive approach that is considered inappropriate (Fergie's "sexy," jazz-inspired version of the anthem provoked laughter and backlash).

So what makes a "good" performance"? These vary as well, but they usually share certain characteristics. First, of course, all of the notes and words are correct. Second, the accompaniment—if present at all—is in appropriate style; many successful renditions use military band instruments, which are conducive to patriotic expression. Third, the singing style needs to come across as dignified. This can mean several things. Singers with various backgrounds, including R & B, pop, rock, and opera, have all given successful performances. But the singer can't sound like they're showing off, and they can't sound like they are trying to entertain. These unspoken rules can turn performing the national anthem into a nerve-wracking experience, for it is difficult to predict how audiences will interpret what they hear.

Image 9.6: Here, Whitney Houston performs for a London audience in 2010.
Source: Wikimedia Commons
Attribution: User "Egghead06"
License: CC BY 3.0

One of the most highly-praised renditions of the anthem was given by Whitney Houston at the 1991 Super Bowl. In examining her performance, we will consider how she blended her personal style with patriotic signifiers to satisfy the crowd.

Houston's performance starts off with the sounds of the snare drum—a clear reference to marching music that simultaneously signifies the US military and captures the mood of disciplined patriotism that would attend a military review. The sound might also spark a sense of pride in the listener, or perhaps responsibility. It might make them stand up a little bit straighter. A trumpet **fanfare** precedes Houston's entrance. When she does begin to sing, she is accompanied by a full brass ensemble, which underpins her lyrics with the power, volume, and brilliant timbre of a military band.

This orchestration remains consistent through the first A section of the musical form, but with the second A section ("Whose broad stripes. . .") there is a significant change in the sound of the performance. Suddenly, Houston is backed by not a military band but soaring strings, whose shimmering timbre and connected articulation contrast with what we have just heard. And that's not all: The strings also play harmonies that are significantly more adventurous and less predictable than those provided by the brass ensemble. The second A, therefore, is more meditative and introspective. It replaces an expression of military might with one of emotional complexity.

Houston emphasizes this contrast with her vocal production. She sings the first A section in a fairly straightforward manner, using the full power of her voice. In the second A section, however, she both reduces her volume and increases her use of **ornamentation**. Melodic ornaments, in this case, are any notes that are not included in the most basic version of "The Star-Spangled Banner"—the version you might sing at a sporting event or patriotic celebration. You can also hear how Houston changes her vocal production. Her sound becomes breathy and subdued— the result, in some cases, of using **head voice** instead of **chest voice**.

The mood changes again when we arrive at the B section ("And the rockets. . ."). The brass and percussion rejoin the strings, while Houston abandons her airy timbre and gives us the full power of her voice. The orchestra is primarily there to accompany the singer, but every once in a while a brass fanfare emerges from the texture. The climax of the anthem is accentuated by both the singer and the orchestra. On the word "free," Houston adds a melodic ornament that takes her to the highest note of the performance—an interval of a fourth above the top note in the official version. Then, when she arrives at "brave," the orchestra plays an unexpected harmony that prolongs the final cadence. In other words, we have to wait a few extra seconds before it feels like the song is really over.

Germany: "The Song of the Germans"

While "The Star-Spangled Banner" traced a long path to its status as national anthem, the process was fairly straightforward. The same cannot be said of many other countries. The current national anthem of Germany is titled "The Song of the Germans" (German: *Das Lied der Deutschen*). However, it was not the first national anthem, and it has not been in continuous use. Its history offers an excellent example of how transformations in the identity, contents, and use of an anthem can reflect the complex political journey of an individual nation.

Although it traces its history back for many centuries, the modern nation of Germany came into existence in 1871. By this time, it was typical for European nations to adopt national anthems, and the Germans were certainly not to be excluded from this practice. At first, they adopted the Prussian national anthem. They did so to symbolize the unification of previously-independent Prussian principalities under a single nation. The title of the anthem was "Hail to Thee in the Victor's Crown," and it featured the refrain "Hail to thee, emperor!" The melody, however, was that to which "God Save the Queen" is currently sung—a sign of the close ties between European monarchies.

Image 9.7: This map indicates the original borders of Germany, following the country's unification in 1871. Much of what was once Eastern Germany is now Poland.
Source: Wikipedia
Attribution: Users "Wiggy!" and "kgberger"
License: CC BY-SA 2.5

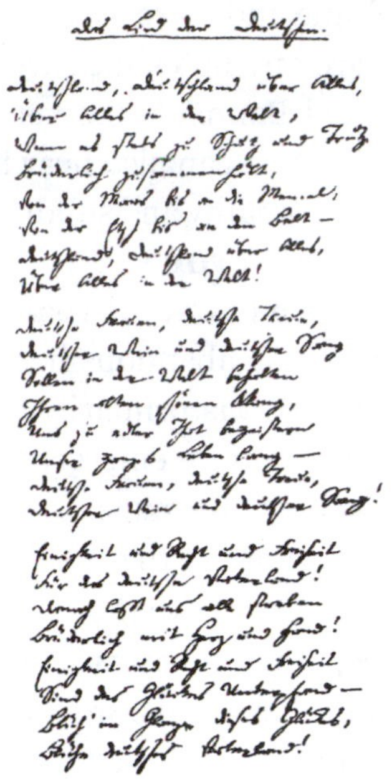

Image 9.8: Here we see Fallersleben's original manuscript for "The Song of the Germans."
Source: Wikimedia Commons
Attribution: Hoffmann von Fallersleben
License: Public Domain

World War I, in which Germany was defeated, prompted major political reorganization. The emperor abdicated in 1918 and was replaced by a constitutional government known as the Weimar Republic. The new government required a new anthem—but the song selected for the role was in fact very old. The words to "The Song of the Germans" were written in 1841 by August Heinrich Hoffmann von Fallersleben, a Prussian academic. The text was initially subversive. Fallersleben lived and worked in a monarchy, but his song called for the unification of the German-speaking lands under democratic rule. During his own time, this was a dangerous message, and Fallersleben was dismissed from his post for promoting it. Following the unification of Germany, however, the call became patriotic and Fallersleben's song was celebrated.

Like Key, Fallersleben wrote his text to fit a preexisting melody. Because he was making a political plea, he selected a political tune: the national anthem of the Austro-Hungarian Empire, which carried a text entitled "God Save Emperor Francis." By rewriting this important anthem, Fallersleben sought to rewrite political reality. The tune, incidentally, had been composed in 1797 by one of the most important of all Austrian composers, Franz Joseph Haydn. It would continue to serve as the national anthem of Austria, although with different texts to suit changes in government, until World War II.

World War II also brought changes to Germany, which was divided at the close of the war into East Germany and West Germany. The government of East Germany commissioned an entirely new anthem, entitled "Risen from the Ruins," while West Germany ceased to use an anthem altogether. Although unusual, it is not difficult to explain this development. Anthems tend to represent patriotic feeling and pride in one's country—sentiments that seemed inappropriate in a post-Holocaust Germany. Various songs—including Ludwig van Beethoven's

Image 9.9: Here we see the 1797 manuscript of Haydn's hymn, now in the Austrian National Library.
Source: Wikimedia Commons
Attribution: Joseph Haydn
License: Public Domain

"Ode to Joy,"[2] now the anthem of the European Union—were used to mark state occasions in West Germany, but "The Song of the Germans" was not officially readopted until 1952.

2. Beethoven's "Ode to Joy" is the official anthem of the European Union. Here it has been recorded with the original German text, but it is also sung in other languages and performed as a textless instrumental.

When it did enter back into use, it was accompanied by significant conflict over the text. The first stanza in particular had become controversial. It opens with the line, "Germany, Germany above all, above all in the world." To Fallersleben, this meant that the promise of a united German nation must be held above the petty interests of minor German monarchs. To the Nazis, however, it was a call for Germany to take over the world. The second verse, which celebrates German women, wine, and song, perhaps lacks the dignity required of an anthem. After the war, therefore, the third verse was favored:

> Unity and justice and freedom
> For the German fatherland!
> Towards these let us all strive
> Brotherly with heart and hand!
> Unity and justice and freedom
> Are the safeguards of fortune;
> Flourish in the radiance of this fortune,
> Flourish, German fatherland!

Controversy over the words, however, has come to stand in for larger political battles. In this way, "The Song of the Germans" simultaneously unites and divides the country, while embodying its difficult past.

Performing "The Song of the Germans"

To consider "The Song of the Germans"[3] in use, we will look at a performance that is, in most respects, very similar to Houston's rendition of "The Star-Spangled Banner." This performance also took place at a major sporting event—a match between two teams in the national German soccer league. The anthem was again sung by a popular performer. Namika, who was born Hanan Hamdi to Moroccan immigrant parents, is a well-known singer and rapper who has landed several hits since 2015. Like Houston, she performs the anthem in her own individual style. She introduces melodic ornaments but makes a conscious effort not to distract from the dignity of the text. And, finally, the orchestration of the accompaniment is remarkably similar, for Namika is also backed by the militaristic combination of brass and snare drums, and her rendition is likewise punctuated by trumpet fanfares.

| 3. | [QR code] | "The Song of the Germans"
Composer: Franz Joseph Haydn
Lyricist: August Heinrich Hoffmann von Fallersleben
Performance: Namika at Bundesliga match between FC Bayern Muenchen and Bayer 04 Leverkusen in Munich (2017) |

There is, however, one very significant difference: Namika is joined by the fans, whose voices can clearly be heard throughout the performance. While Houston was admired as a soloist, Namika is leading a sing-along. Why this difference? It is certainly not the case that Germans are more patriotic or more musical. The German anthem, however, is considerably more singable than "The Star-Spangled Banner." Given that it outlines a range of only an octave and that the melody is largely **conjunct**, containing few large melodic leaps, "The Song of the Germans" can be sung by an untrained musician. It is likely that these musical differences have contributed to contrasting cultural traditions: Germans join in, while American leave anthem singing up to the professionals.

South Africa: "National Anthem of South Africa"

The story of "National Anthem of South Africa"[4] is equally tortuous, although the narrative details—and the resulting anthem—reflect a different type of national strife. While Germany came into conflict with the world, the South African conflict was entirely internal, unfolding as a white ruling minority sought to disenfranchise the non-white majority. This conflict and its resolutions were captured in a trio of official and unofficial anthems.

| 4. | [QR code] | "National Anthem of South Africa"
Composers: Enoch Mankayi Sontaga & Marthinus Lourens de Villiers
Lyricists: Enoch Mankayi Sontaga & C.J. Langenhoven
Performance: Ndlovu Youth Choir (2019) |

The roots of modern South Africa are to be found in the 17th century, when Dutch colonists first settled on its shores. The descendants of these colonists, who both displaced and intermingled with the native Africans, speak a language known as Afrikaans that combines elements of Dutch and indigenous languages. In the early 19th century, British colonists displaced the Dutch, and South Africa became a part of the British Empire. In this way, English became an important language, and it has continued to be widely spoken even since South Africa gained independence in 1931.

In total, eleven official languages are spoken in South Africa: Afrikaans, English, and nine indigenous African languages. This, of course, creates problems for the selection of a national anthem. The language of the anthem will naturally reinforce the power and the prestige of the citizens who speak that language, while symbolically excluding those who speak other languages. Language, therefore, plays an important role in the history of South Africa's national anthems—and in that of other polyglot nations.

Image 9.10: The nation of South Africa is located at the southern tip of the African continent.
Source: Wikipedia
Attribution: User "Amada44"
License: Public Domain

The political parties that came to power upon South Africa's independence from Great Britain represented the interests of the Afrikaner and English-speaking minorities. A decade of increasing tension between ethnic groups culminated in the 1948 election of the National Party, an Afrikaner ethnic nationalist party that instituted the policy of **apartheid** (the Afrikaans word for "separateness"). Apartheid was a form of white supremacist segregation whereby every South African citizen was legally classified as "white,"

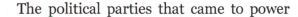

Image 9.11: "The Call of South Africa" was the official anthem under apartheid.
Source: Wikimedia Commons
Attribution: Various
License: Public Domain

"black," "colored," or "Indian." A citizen's racial classification then determined where they were allowed to live and what jobs they were allowed to hold. Public spaces were segregated, with preference given to "white" South Africans, and non-whites had limited power to vote. In addition, interracial marriages and sexual relationships were prohibited.

The National Party also adopted a new national anthem. South Africa had been using "God Save the King/Queen," a legacy of its colonial status, but a political desire to distance British influence resulted in the 1957 designation of "The Call of South Africa" (Afrikaans: "Die Stem van Suid-Afrika") as the national anthem. The text to "The Call of South Africa" was a 1918 Afrikaans poem by C.J. Langenhoven. The musical setting was created three years later by Marthinus Lourens de Villiers. The poem reflects an

Afrikaner perspective, and it celebrates ownership of the South African land—which was taken from the native inhabitants by colonizing forces. As a result, "The Call of South Africa" was and continues to be deeply offensive to many black South Africans.

At the same time that "The Call of South Africa" was gaining popularity among Afrikaners, black South Africans were coalescing around an alternative anthem. "Lord Bless Africa"[5] (Xhosa: "Nkosi Sikelel' iAfrika") began life as a Methodist hymn. The tune, first verse, and chorus were composed in 1897 by Enoch Mankayi Sontaga, a teacher at a mission school. Sontaga, who was of Xhosa descent, was influenced by the British hymn tradition, and he described "Lord Bless Africa" as a combination of European four-part harmony with a repetitive, African-style melody. It quickly gained popularity among church congregations, and in 1912 was adopted by the South African Native National Congress, a political party that advocated the rights of black South Africans. In 1927, "Lord Bless Africa" was published in an expanded version that included seven additional Xhosa-language verses by Samuel Mqhayi. During apartheid, the hymn—which was banned by the National Party—became a symbol for resistance to the racist policies of the government. Many considered it to be the true national anthem.

5.  This video captures a performance of "Lord Bless Africa" by Paul Simon and the group Ladysmith Black Mambazo to close Simon's 1987 African Concert.

Apartheid officially came to an end with a 1992 referendum, and the first open elections of the post-apartheid era, which took place in 1994, put the previously-banned African National Party into power. Nelson Mandela, who had played a leading role in negotiating the end of apartheid, became President. Mandela had been imprisoned by the National Party for his anti-government activities from 1964 until 1990. As President, however, he was committed to the principles of reconciliation and equality. For this reason, he declared that "The Call of South Africa" and "Lord Bless Africa" would both hold the status of national anthem, and for several years both songs were performed at state and sporting events.

Although symbolically significant, having dual anthems was logistically difficult. The combined performance took about five

Image 9.12: After being imprisoned by the National Party for more than a quarter of a century, Mandela became President of South Africa.
Source: Wikipedia
Attribution: South Africa The Good News
License: CC BY 2.0

minutes, and the question about performance order was politically charged. In addition, the two languages represented by the anthems fell significantly short of reflecting the linguistic diversity of the South African populace.

In 1997, therefore, Mandela commissioned a new anthem. He required that it combine the two existing anthems, contain verses in a variety of language, expunge controversial references to colonialism, and emphasize national unity. He also insisted that it be no longer than one minute and forty-eight seconds in length.

The resulting "National Anthem of South Africa" is in two parts, the first taken from "Lord Bless Africa" and the second from "The Call of South Africa." It includes two verses from "Lord Bless Africa." The first half of the first verse is in Xhosa, while the second half is in Zulu. The second verse is in Sethoso. At this point, the anthem **modulates** to a new key and we hear the first four lines of "The Call," sung in Afrikaans to the original melody. The final lines of the anthem, which are in English, contain a new text calling for the people of South Africa to come together in order to "live and strive for freedom."

Performing "National Anthem of South Africa"

Our rendition comes from the Ndlovu Youth Choir. This ensemble was founded in 2009 as an after-school program for impoverished children in the rural village of Moutse. The goal of the organizers was to provide these young people with the same quality of music education that was available to affluent youth and to thereby give them a means with which to express themselves and find a meaningful path in life. In 2019, the choir won international fame by advancing to the final round of *America's Got Talent*. Many performances of "National Anthem of South Africa" feature a vocal soloist singing in a popular style and an orchestral accompaniment including brass and percussion—that is to say, they are stylistically identical to the anthem performances we have already examined in this chapter. The Ndlovu Youth Choir, however, developed a unique arrangement of "National Anthem of South Africa" that exhibits various indigenous singing styles.

"National Anthem of South Africa" is certainly unusual. It contains two unrelated melodies in different keys and verses in five languages. All the same, it reflects the diversity of the nation and speaks to a troubled past. It provides a musical representation of a nation that has been fractured and reunited.

Israel: "The Hope"

One additional national anthem will provide an opportunity to consider the connection between music and nation. This time, our analysis will reveal little about the complex history of the nation, as was the case with "Song of the Germans" and "National Anthem of South Africa." Instead, it will shed further light on the difficulty of assigning national identity to a melody.

The national anthem of Israel, entitled "The Hope"[6] (Hebrew: "Hatikvah"), has a brief and uncomplicated history. It was immediately adopted on an unofficial basis when the nation of Israel was founded in 1948, and it became the official national anthem in 2004. The text was written in 1878 by the Polish poet Naphtali Herz Imber, and it expresses yearning for a return to the Jewish homeland. "The Hope" was used as an anthem by several Zionist groups, and beginning in 1897 it was sung at the Congresses of the World Zionist Organization, which advocated for the founding of an autonomous Jewish nation. As such, it came to represent Zionist sentiment throughout the Jewish diaspora.

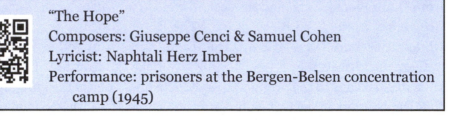

6.   "The Hope"
Composers: Giuseppe Cenci & Samuel Cohen
Lyricist: Naphtali Herz Imber
Performance: prisoners at the Bergen-Belsen concentration camp (1945)

The deep significance that "The Hope" had for Jewish people is evidenced by several stories from WWII-era concentration camps. In one recorded incident, a group of Czech Jews sang "The Hope" as they were escorted into the gas chamber at Auschwitz. The guards were enraged and beat them, but could not stop the singing. Reports from other camps indicate that the song was sung frequently by Jewish prisoners and that it brought them solace. When Bergen-Belsen was liberated, the inmates also sang "The Hope"—a recording of which was captured and broadcast to the world.

Image 9.13: This 1907 edition of "The Hope" paired it with another popular Zionist song.
Source: Library of Congress
Attribution: Jacob Kamenetzky and A. H. Fromenson
License: Public Domain

The melody to which Imber's text has always been sung was provided by Samuel Cohen in 1888. He did not compose it but rather adapted it from a melody he had heard sung in Romania. The tune, however, is not Romanian. In fact, it can be traced to a 16th-century Italian song entitled "La Mantovana," which has been attributed to the singer Giuseppe Cenci and was first published around 1600. The melody quickly became popular and soon had been paired with texts in Dutch, Polish, Ukranian, Romanian, and English.

Bedřich Smetana, "The Moldau"

"The Moldau" from *My Homeland*
Composer: Bedřich Smetana
Performance: The Budapest Philharmonic Orchestra
conducted by Ádám Medveczky (1987)

Time	Form	What to listen for
0'00"	A	This passage represents the emergence of the Moldau from two small springs that join together to form a powerful current; the principal melody is shared with Israel's national anthem, "The Hope"
4'06"	B	This passage represents the rural landscapes through which the Moldau passes; the folk-like melody is meant to evoke the celebration of a farmer's wedding
5'34"	C	This passage represents a scene described by the composer as "the round dance of the mermaids in the night's moonshine"
8'44"	A'	The principal melody returns
10'44"		The melody shifts into the major mode
11'12"		This passage quotes from Smetana's symphonic poem "Vyšehrad," which is the first in the cycle *My Homeland*; it serves both to connect the works thematically and to represent the literal presence of the Vyšehrad castle, which stands on the banks of the Moldau

Most famously, the melody was used by the Czech composer Bedřich Smetana (1824-1884) as the main theme for his nationalist **symphonic poem** "The Moldau" (1874), which belongs to a larger cycle of works entitled *My Homeland*. Here we begin to see the complexities surrounding "The Hope." Decades before this tune came to communicate Jewish identity, and more than half a century before it would represent the nation of Israel, it was used to signify Czech identity and national sentiment.

Smetana's "The Moldau" is an example of program music. It describes in sound the course of the famous Moldau river as it winds its way through the countryside and ultimately joins the Elbe river. "The Moldau" contains a succession of distinct sections. First, we hear the river emerge from a pair of warm and cold springs. It

Image 9.14: This photograph captures Smetana around the time that he wrote "The Moldau."
Source: Wikimedia Commons
Attribution: Unknown
License: Public Domain

slowly gains strength until a mighty, expressive melody—that used for "The Hope"—bursts forth to represent the river. Next we hear the sounds of dance music as it might be played at a country wedding, followed by a nocturnal passage representing mermaids in the moonlight. Finally, the river theme returns, first in its original minor mode and then in a triumphant major.

How can an Italian melody develop and sustain both Jewish and Czech nationalistic connotations—all while continuing to be periodically mistaken for a Flemish, Polish, Ukranian, Romanian, and Scottish folk song? The answer has to do both with musical style and with the power of association. "La Mantovana" is an exceptionally simple tune. It contains two parts, one lower and one higher (a typical characteristic in many folk traditions). Both parts have a limited range and move primarily using stepwise motion. All of these attributes allow "La Mantovana" to be adapted in conformance with the conventions of various national styles.

However, association is more powerful than style. Listeners who first encountered this melody as representing the Moldau river and Czech identity will have a hard time hearing it in a different way. It has a similarly powerful (although quite different) meaning for Jews who grew up singing the Zionist lyrics. The multiple identities of the tune have created consternation in the Jewish community, and many have objected to its pairing with Imber's text. All the same, efforts to find or create a new musical setting have always met with failure, and this melody continues to exercise enormous emotional power over a global population.

NATIONAL REPRESENTATION IN WESTERN ART MUSIC

As we have already seen, anthems are only the most obvious and explicit example of national representation in music. There are many ways in which music can come to stand for a nation. Sometimes, composers or performers set out to capture national character in sound. They seek to develop an individual work or a broader style that is uniquely tied to their national identity. Other times, those in power identify and promote music that is determined to represent the nation. In such cases the music is not created with the nationalistic intent, but rather repurposed. Finally, we might differentiate between musical representations created by the people who belong to nations or ethnic groups versus those created by outsiders.

We are not talking here about **exoticism**, wherein an artist represents an ethnic group for the purpose of voyeuristic entertainment, but rather contributions to national style made from a foreign perspective.

Contesting the Representation of Hungary

We will begin by looking at two compositions for piano, each created by a Hungarian composer who sought to express his national identity in music. Both composers turned to Hungarian folk music for inspiration, but they disagreed about which Hungarian folk tradition best represented Hungarian identity. This type of disagreement has larger implications about who "counts" as a citizen and whose culture can be understood to represent the nation.

It is important to note that the political nation of Hungary did not exist when either of these pieces were composed. Instead, Hungary was ruled by German-speaking monarchs, first as a territory of the Austrian Empire and then as a subservient partner in the Austro-Hungarian Empire. Modern Hungary first gained independence upon the dissolution of the Austro-Hungarian Empire following World War I. Throughout the 19th century, however, Hungarians sought greater autonomy by means of political protest and armed revolt. Efforts to represent Hungarian identity in the arts were part of a larger nationalist movement that had ties to the quest for independence.

Franz Liszt, *Hungarian Rhapsody No. 2*

		Hungarian Rhapsody No. 2 Composer: Franz Liszt Performance: Tiffany Poon (2014)
Time	**Form**	**What to listen for**
0'00"	A	This introductory passage is dramatic and mysterious
	Lassan	This part of the rhapsody is characterized by unexpected harmonies and flexible tempos
044"	B	The tempo stabilizes into a slow march
1'27"	C	This theme begins in the major mode
1'44"	D	This theme imitates the sound of a cimbalom; it accelerates in tempo

2'30"	A	
3'04"	B	This theme returns in the low register of the piano
3'41"	C	
4'36	A	This theme returns in the lowest register of the piano
	Friska	This part of the rhapsody is characterized by stable harmonies and fast tempos
5'12"	D	This theme returns in the high register of the piano; as is accelerates in tempo, the harmony stabilizes
6'00"	E	This passage includes a large number of closely related themes; all are accompanied by the same harmonic pattern, which oscilates between the I and V chords
8'45"		The tempo slows and the melody briefly turns to the minor mode
9'02"		The major mode returns, the tempo accelerates, and the volume builds, leading into an explosive final cadence

Franz Liszt (1811-1886) is an unusual candidate for "most famous Hungarian composer," although he certainly merits the title. To begin with, he did not speak Hungarian. Although the village of Doborján in which Liszt was born was located in the Kingdom of Hungary, the inhabitants spoke German. Furthermore, Liszt lived in Hungary for only the first decade of his life. He demonstrated great musical talent as a child, so his parents took him to Vienna at the age of 11 to cultivate his gifts. He returned only on concert tours. All the same, Liszt was proud of his Hungarian heritage and expressed it frequently in his compositions for piano.

Liszt's extraordinary career set new standards for piano playing and public

Image 9.15: This 1839 portrait by Henri Lehmann captures Liszt as a young man.
Source: Wikimedia Commons
Attribution: Henri Lehmann
License: Public Domain

performance. After a successful Viennese debut in 1822, he completed his education and embarked on what might have been a typical career of teaching, composing, and performing. In 1832, however, he happened to attend a recital in Paris by the Italian violin virtuoso Niccolò Paganini. Liszt was astonished by Paganini's extraordinary technique, and he committed to becoming Paganini's equal at the piano. To this end, Liszt gave up concertizing and went into seclusion to refine his technique.

When Liszt returned to the stage in 1838, he was indeed heralded as the greatest living pianist. He embarked on a decade-long tour of Europe, during which he established a reputation for flamboyant and thrilling performances. It was Liszt's practice to appear on stage with two pianos, for he played with such force that he would break strings and need to change instruments. Before Liszt, solo recitals were practically unheard of. Audiences preferred variety, and it was considered foolish to imagine that anyone would attend a concert with only one performer. Liszt, however, provided his own variety, combining piano **transcriptions** of symphonies with **improvisations**, classics by the great composers of the past, and showy new compositions by himself. Liszt also possessed a great deal of sex

Im Concertsaale!

Image 9.16: This 1842 engraving captures the spirit of a Liszt recital: The audience is made up almost entirely of women, who blow kisses, throw flowers, and faint in ecstasy.
Source: Wikimedia Commons
Attribution: Theodor Hosemann
License: Public Domain

Page | 326

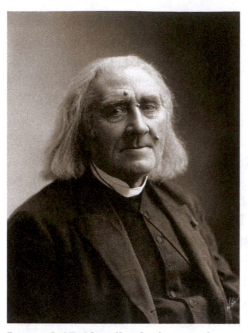

Image 9.17: Liszt lived a long and productive life—long enough to be photographed in 1886.
Source: Wikimedia Commons
Attribution: Nadar
License: Public Domain

Image 9.18: Although Liszt gave up his public touring career in 1848, he continued to play piano in more intimate settings. He is pictured here with the American violinist Arma Senkrah.
Source: Wikimedia Commons
Attribution: Louis Held
License: Public Domain

appeal. He was particularly popular with society ladies, who went into hysterics at his concerts and fought over his discarded items. Due to his enormous success, Liszt became the first performing artist to require a manager.

Liszt composed piano music in a variety of genres. His fantasies explored operatic themes written by other composers, while his etudes showcased specific piano techniques. He also produced nineteen *Hungarian Rhapsodies*, each of which was inspired by the Romani music that Liszt heard as a child. Liszt was not the first composer to write "Hungarian" music, which had been in fashion for decades. However, his Hungarian compositions were more personal than those of German composers, who used Hungarian musical elements to flavor their works. Liszt made it clear that his music was a personal statement that reflected his national identity.

We will examine Liszt's *Hungarian Rhapsody No. 2*, which is certainly his best-known effort in the genre. In it, Liszt uses the scales, rhythms, and forms of Hungarian music as a vehicle for dazzling piano technique. A good performance of *Hungarian Rhapsody No. 2* is entertaining and astonishing. Before looking at Liszt's composition, however, we need to know something about the folk tradition on which the piece is based.

Liszt was influenced by a style of dance music known as **verbunkos** that he associated with the itinerant Romani musicians of his childhood home. The Romani—known colloquially as Gypsies— live across Europe, although they are often excluded from mainstream society and actively persecuted. In the village where Liszt grew up, Romani musicians played verbunkos music in cafes as entertainment for the upper classes. Their traditional instruments included violin and cimbalon, a type of hammered dulcimer. Although verbunkos music is unique to Hungary, therefore, it is closely associated with the Romani people, who are not ethnic Hungarians.

Verbunkos music has a variety of distinctive characteristics. To begin with, it is divided into two sections: an opening *lassan* and a concluding *friska*. The lassan is slow and melancholic, featuring dramatic harmonic shifts. It lacks a pulse and has an improvisatory feel. The friska, on the other hand, builds in volume and tempo, becoming increasingly exciting as it approaches a conclusion. The harmonies are simple, alternating between the tonic and dominant chords.

Verbunkos music also employs different scales than European concert music. While 19th-century composers of art music used only the major and minor scales, Romani musicians used various scales—mostly related to minor—that featured raised or lowered pitches and, as a result, contained augmented intervals (that is to say, intervals greater than a whole step, which is the largest possible distance between two notes in a major or minor scale). Such scales sounded exotic to Liszt's audience, as they still do to many Westerners today.

Liszt's *Hungarian Rhapsody No. 2* exhibits the influence of verbunkos dance music in a variety of ways. To begin with, it takes the two-part form of a *lassan* and *friska*. The *lassan*, which is exceptionally dramatic, features a march-like theme

Image 9.19: This group of Romani musicians was photographed in 1865.
Source: Wikimedia Commons
Attribution: Unknown
License: Public Domain

that is occasionally interrupted by unmetered flights of fancy. The music sounds as if it might be improvised, but in fact Liszt wrote out every note. In addition to these rhythmic characteristics, Liszt occasionally introduces unusual scales that echo Romani practice. The *friska* begins with a passage that is meant to imitate the sound of a Hungarian cimbalom. From there, Liszt finds his way to the major mode and provides a virtuosic conclusion.

Béla Bartók, *Romanian Folk Dances from Hungary*[7]

By the time Béla Bartók (1881-1945) was growing up in southern Hungary, Liszt was a national hero. Hungarians were proud of his monumental success across Europe and his influence on the elite musical establishment. They had also come to accept his musical representations of Hungarian identity—such as we observed in *Hungarian Rhapsody No. 2*—as authentic and correct. As a music student, therefore, Bartók took Liszt as a model and sought to express his Hungarian identity using a similar musical language.

---

7.  *Romanian Folk Dances from Hungary*
Composer: Béla Bartók
Performance: Béla Bartók, Welte piano roll (1927)

In 1904, however, Bartók had an experience that changed his thinking about how Hungarian identity should be represented in art music. While visiting a summer resort, he happened to hear a nanny sing folk songs from the region of Transylvania. It was unlike any music he had ever heard before—and was certainly far removed from the verbunkos dance music of the urban cafes. He immediately set out to discover and document as much Eastern European folk music as he could find, becoming in the process one of the earliest **ethnomusicologists** (a scholar who specializes in indigenous music traditions).

Bartók found a like mind in fellow composer Zoltán Kodály, with whom he travelled the countryside recording the music of rural singers and instrumentalists. They sometimes used a primitive recording device that captured sound by carving grooves into a wax cylinder, but they also wrote down melodies using Western **staff notation** and they transcribed song texts. In 1906, they

Image 9.20: This photograph of Bartók was taken in 1922.
Source: Wikimedia Commons
Attribution: Unknown
License: Public Domain

Image 9.21: Here we see Bartók recordings the songs of Slovak peasants in 1908.
Source: Wikimedia Commons
Attribution: Unknown
License: Public Domain

Image 9.22: This 1905 photograph captures Bartók and Kodály shortly after their partnership was formed.
Source: Wikimedia Commons
Attribution: Aladár Székely
License: Public Domain

published *Hungarian Folk Songs*, a collection of peasant songs with simple piano accompaniments. Their intent was to spread awareness about the existence of the music, which they valued highly.

Following his studies, Bartók began to criticize Liszt's version of Hungarian musical identity. Verbunkos dance music, he argued, was not the real Hungarian folk music. His objection was less to the ethnic identity of the Romani musicians who performed it as to the commercial context in which verbunkos music had developed and thrived. It flourished in the cities and was sponsored by the aristocracy as official Hungarian culture. True Hungarian folk music, argued Bartók, was to be found among the disenfranchised rural peasantry.

Bartók was interested both in promoting the cause of Hungarian independence and in developing his own unique voice as a composer. While he took genuine pride in the folk culture of Eastern Europe, he also saw it as grist for his own creative mill. His omnivorous appetite for folk music attracted some criticism from Hungarian nationalists. They were pleased when he promoted Hungarian folk music, but less supportive when he strayed beyond the bounds of the ethnic Hungarian population.

Again, however, we must ask, "Who counts as Hungarian?" This is not a question of literal citizenship, but a question of belonging. Which ethnic groups are to have their cultural products privileged as representing the nation? The borders of the Austro-Hungarian empire extended far beyond those of modern Hungary, encompassing a variety of ethnic groups and spoken languages. Bartók was not interested in deciding who counted as Hungarian. His mission was to collect and popularise as broad a selection of folk music as possible and to integrate that music into his own compositions.

Image 9.23: This map depicts the distribution of ethnic groups within the Austro-Hungarian empire in 1910. It reveals the significant presence of non-Hungarian ethnic groups within the borders of modern-day Hungary.
Source: Wikimedia Commons
Attribution: User "Andrein"
License: Public Domain

To see one of Bartók's compositional techniques in action, we will take a look at his *Romanian Folk Dances from Hungary*. It features tunes that he collected from the region of Transylvania, which was a part of Hungary for the first two decades of the 20th century. (Bartók shortened the title to *Romanian Folk Dances* when Romania annexed the region following World War I.) Like Liszt's *Hungarian Rhapsody No. 2*, this is a piece for solo piano based on Hungarian folk music. The similarities end there, however, for the purpose behind Bartók's composition was completely different.

Romanian Folk Dances contains six independent movements. They are entitled "Joculcu bâtă" (Stick Dance), "Brâul" (Sash Dance), "Pe loc" (In One Spot), "Buciumeana" (Dance from Bucsum), "Poarga Românească" (Romanian Polka), and "Mărunțel" (Fast Dance). The melody of each movement is taken from a Transylvanian fiddle tune. Bartók did not alter the melodies, transcribing them as he had heard them. He then supplied an original accompaniment, which is usually heard in the left hand of the piano. Bartók described this approach as similar to crafting a piece of jewelry in order to show off a beautiful gem. His musical settings were supposed to exhibit the inherent beauty and interest of the folk tunes. All the same, his unusual harmonies are what make these pieces enjoyable and interesting for most listeners.

Because Bartók was unwilling to make changes to the borrowed folk tunes, each movement is short and simple in terms of form. Although only the second movement repeats literally in its entirety, all of the movements contain some melodic repetition. As in the Liszt example, we hear unusual scales and rhythms, which Bartók derived from the folk music he studied. Bartók, however, was not a virtuoso pianist, and he was not writing music for the purpose of popular entertainment. His emphasis was on fidelity to his source material, not show.

There are, of course, other reasons for which the music of Liszt and Bartók sounds quite different. Liszt was composing at the height of the **Romantic** era, when music was expected to be highly expressive while also adhering to certain rules about the use of harmony. Bartók, writing in the early 20th century, was a **modernist**. He sought to break new ground by replacing **common-practice tonality**—the typical chord progressions we are familiar with from most Western music—with a new harmonic language of his own invention. *Romanian Folk Dances* is an early example of his experimental work.

Contesting the Representation of the United States

Antonín Dvořák, Symphony No. 9 "From the New World"

Throughout the 19th century, Europeans considered the United States to be a cultural backwater. Americans, of course, were preoccupied not with artistic innovation but with expanding and stabilizing their nation. Those who did pursue the arts were expected to receive their training in Europe and to imitate European models. In the late 19th century, however, American composers became increasingly interested in developing a unique national voice.

None of this is to say that there was no distinctively American music in the 19th century. There certainly was—much of which is explored elsewhere in this volume. Hymn composers in New England and the South had already developed several new strains of church music, while diverse folk traditions flourished in rural areas. In addition, there were the rich musical traditions of Native Americans, who faced eradication on a national scale, and African Americans, whose influence was first felt in the sphere of popular and dance music. However, none of this mattered to members of the arts establishment. They valued European-style concert music and sought a way to express American identity in that context.

Surprisingly, the composer who is usually cited as launching the American school of composition was not an American at all, but a Czech. Although he did not actually break new ground, Antonín Dvořák (1841-1904) tends to get credit for the bizarre reason that he was European, and therefore commanded greater respect and attention from his contemporaries than did American composers. In fact, Dvořák was brought to the United States for the express purpose of guiding the development of American music.

Dvořák was a prime candidate for teaching Americans how to express national identity in music, for he had first made a name for himself by doing the same for the Czech musical establishment. His first successful composition was a series of orchestral pieces ostensibly based on Slavic dances. For Dvořák, however, his national identity was a source of frustration. He struggled to be accepted not as a Czech composer but as a *good* composer.

When Dvořák came to New York City in 1891, he was at the height of his career. He had been invited to serve as the first director of the National Conservatory of Music, which was to train American musicians in the European concert tradition. He was also expected to contribute to the development of American concert music. Dvořák produced two

Image 9.24: This photograph of Dvořák was taken in 1882.
Source: Wikimedia Commons
Attribution: Unknown
License: Public Domain

monumental "American" works during his stay in the United States, both of which were premiered in 1893. One was his String Quartet No. 12, known as the "American Quartet" (a work composed, ironically, during his visit to a Czech community in the midwest). The other was his Symphony No. 9 "From the New World." The symphony in particular exemplifies Dvořák's ideas about what was American in music.

Dvořák was regularly asked for his views on this subject, and in 1895 he published an article entitled "Music in America" that contained his advice to American composers wishing to develop a national style. He recommended, unsurprisingly, that they draw inspiration from folk music: specifically, that of African Americans and Native Americans. Dvořák, of course, knew very little about American folk traditions—he was completely ignorant of folk music in most parts of the country, while his ideas about Native American music were more fantasy than fact. His observation that Native American and African American musics were "practically identical" betrays his shallow thinking on the subject.

The one thing Dvořák really did know something about was African American **spirituals**. He encountered this repertoire through Harry Burleigh, who was a student at the National Conservatory of Music during the time that Dvořák served as director. Burleigh had learned to sing spirituals from his grandfather, who had been born a slave but had purchased his freedom in the 1830s, and he later gained international fame both for his concert arrangements of spirituals and for his original art songs. At Dvořák's request, Burleigh frequently sang for him in his home. He reported that "Swing Low, Sweet Chariot," apparently the composer's favorite item in his repertoire, was the basis for the theme in the first movement of Symphony No. 9. The second movement, which we will consider in detail, also features a spiritual-like theme. In fact, it was such a convincing fake that it was

HARRY T. BURLEIGH

Image 9.25: This photograph of Harry Burleigh was taken in 1936, many years after his youthful association with Dvořák.
Source: Wikimedia Commons
Attribution: Maud Cuney-Hare
License: Public Domain

frequently mistaken for a genuine spiritual after a student of Dvořák's wrote a text for it, titled "Goin' Home," in 1922.

Dvořák's Symphony No. 9 also has a Native American connection, although it is romanticized and inauthentic. Dvořák, like most Europeans, was familiar with Henry Wadsworth Longfellow's 1855 epic poem *The Song of Hiawatha*, in which the poet provides a largely fictionalized account of the life of an Ojibwe warrior. *Hiawatha* had been translated into Czech in 1870, and Dvořák was familiar with it before his visit to the United States. Although Symphony No. 9 is an example of absolute music and should not be understood to communicate a specific, coherent narrative, Dvořák told interviewers that the two internal movements were both influenced by *Hiawatha*, and that he intended the second movement as a sketch for a dramatic setting of the text (a project

Image 9.26: This illustration was included in an 1891 edition of *The Song of Hiawatha*.
Source: Wikimedia Commons
Attribution: Houghton Mifflin Company
License: CC0

that he never in fact pursued). Although Dvořák offered few specifics, it has been argued that the two themes of the second movement—one gentle and romantic, one distraught and funereal—portray the wooing and death of Hiawatha's bride, Minnehaha.

Symphony No. 9 "From the New World," Movement II
Composer: Antonín Dvořák
Performance: Berliner Philharmoniker, conducted by Ferenc Fricsay (1960)

Time	Form	What to listen for
0'00"	Intro	The brass play a sequence of sustained harmonies
0'53"	A	The spiritual-inspired theme is heard in the English horn; it has a form of aba'
2'44"	Intro	The woodwinds repeat the sequence of harmonies
3'12"	A	Muted strings play the b section of the A theme; the English horn concludes with the a' section
4'54"		The horns play the opening motif of the A theme
5'20"	B	This plaintive, minor-mode theme, played by the oboe, is accompanied by tremolo strings
5'56"	C	For this minor-mode theme, pizzicato strings provide the steady pulse of a funeral march
6'45"	B	The B theme returns in the muted violins
7'52"	D	This theme, also cast as a funeral march, is played by the muted violins
8'48"	B	The B theme briefly returns in the muted strings
9'11"	E	Various instruments and sections, beginning with the oboe and flute, imitate birdsong
9'27"		The cyclical theme, which returns in each movement, is heard in the low brass, while the A theme is heard in the trumpets

| 10'08" | A | This theme returns in the English horn; the b section is played by muted strings; the a' section begins in solo strings |
| 12'43" | Intro | The opening passage is repeated in the brass; it resolves via an ascending string passage into a quiet, low-range final chord |

Dvořák's Symphony No. 9 follows the standard four-movement pattern for a European symphony, two examples of which were examined in Chapter 7. We will take a look at the slow movement, which Dvořák placed second. This movement is in **ternary form**, with a brief introductory passage that also serves as the conclusion. The introduction consists of a series of seven chords, played slowly by the brass section. The harmonies, which are unexpected and dramatic, seem to lift the curtain on a magical scene.

The first section features Dvořák's spiritual-inspired theme. It is first played by the English horn—a double reed instrument that can be thought of as a low-pitched oboe. The theme itself is also in ternary form (a b a'). The a' section concludes with an ascent in the melody that brings it to a satisfying close. The first statement of the theme is followed by a repetition of the introductory chords in the winds, the b section of the theme in the strings, and the conclusion of the theme in the English horn. The tempo throughout is extremely slow (marked Largo by Dvořák), and the mood is peaceful.

The middle section of the movement offers a marked change in mood, as Dvořák increases the tempo and switches from the major to the minor mode. This section is primarily in **rondo form**, meaning that a principle theme alternates with secondary themes. The principle theme is agitated and mournful, featuring a repeated descending figure, while the secondary themes are accompanied by a steady bass line that could belong to a funeral march. After the final abbreviated statement of the principle theme, Dvořák inserts a major-mode passage in which the winds and strings imitate birds. Dvořák frequently included birdsong in his compositions, and his "American Quartet" also features such imitations. In this case, the birdsong can be directly related to *Hiawatha*, which includes the telling of a myth in which people are turned into birds.

Next, Dvořák includes a reference to the first-movement theme based on "Swing Low, Sweet Chariot," overlaid with the spiritual-like theme from this movement. By stating the two themes simultaneously, Dvořák draws our attention to their similarity. Both, after all, reflect the same African American influence. Dvořák is also continuing the practice of connecting the movements of a symphony, known as **cyclical technique**, that we first saw at work in Berlioz's *Fantastical Symphony*.

The closing section contains the last statement of the spiritual theme, although this time the b passage is laced with pauses. These convey the impression that the "singer" of this wordless song is overcome with emotion, needing perhaps to sob or catch their breath. Finally, the opening chords are heard once more, the last of which is repeated and sustained.

This movement—and Symphony No. 9 as a whole—can be taken as Dvořák putting his own advice to American composers into action. Those composers, however, did not necessarily appreciate his guidance. Their negative reactions were largely understandable. To begin with, the American arts establishment had already been grappling with the task of developing a unique national voice. That a foreigner would step in and tell them what to do was, to many, unpalatable. Composers also objected to Dvořák's specific advice. The music of Native Americans and African Americans, they argued, was not the music of all Americans. It represented only a small portion of the populace and could not stand in for the country as a whole. While certain individuals objected for racist reasons, most simply did not accept Dvořák's argument that a national style could be derived from these narrow sources.

Amy Beach, *Gaelic Symphony*[8]

One of many composers who rejected Dvořák's approach was Amy Beach (1867-1944). As we will see, Beach preferred to found an American style on the folk music of her ancestors, who hailed from the British Isles. Before examining her response to Dvořák's Symphony No. 9, however, we need to learn something about this extraordinary woman.

Beach counts among the many composers who began their careers as child prodigies. Born into a well-to-do New Hampshire family, she demonstrated a thorough grasp of pitch before she could talk and was harmonizing melodies at the age of two. She composed her first piano music—a set of waltzes—at the age of four, and was soon giving public piano recitals that attracted the attention of the press. When her family moved to a Boston suburb in 1875, Beach was able to receive professional training in music, although she was to remain almost

Image 9.27: This undated portrait of Amy Beach is held at the Library of Congress.
Source: Wikimedia Commons
Attribution: George Grantham Bain Collection
License: Public Domain

entirely self-taught as a composer. She would learn by analyzing newly-published music from Europe and studying Berlioz's textbook on orchestration.

8.  *Gaelic Symphony*, Movement II
Composer: Amy Beach
Performance: Royal Philharmonic Orchestra, conducted by Karl Krueger (2011)

Image 9.28: This photograph of Beach was taken a few years after she married and gave up her performing career.
Source: Wikimedia Commons
Attribution: Unknown
License: Public Domain

Beach gave her debut performance with the Boston Symphony Orchestra at the age of sixteen, and might have gone on to become the great piano **virtuoso** of her era. Instead, at the age of 18, she married. Her husband, Dr. Henry Harris Aubrey Beach, was twenty-four years her senior and, in Beach's own words, "old-fashioned." He believed that it was a man's honorable obligation to support his wife, and he was not willing to allow Beach to pursue a career performing or teaching piano. He supported her work as a composer, however, and did a great deal to promote her success. For the twenty-five years of their marriage, therefore, Beach committed herself to composition. She won accolades from both the press and her peers, and was warmly accepted into what has been termed the Second New England School of composers.

Beach first gained attention in 1892 with her Mass in E-flat major, which was the first work by a woman ever to be performed by Boston's prestigious Handel and Haydn Society. Then in 1896 the Boston Symphony Orchestra premiered her *Gaelic Symphony*, the first to be composed by an American woman. Although it is only fair to acknowledge Beach's role as a trailblazer, many now consider the *Gaelic Symphony* to be the first great American symphony, regardless of the composer's identity. Beach preferred not to write or speak about her experiences as a female composer in an era when women were discouraged from entering the field, and later stated only that she had met with no particular difficulty. In 1900, Beach appeared as soloist with the Boston Symphony Orchestra in her Piano Concerto in C-sharp minor—a rare public performance during her married years. The extreme difficulty of the work attests to Beach's virtuosic abilities.

Upon her husband's death in 1910, Beach resumed her performance career. She toured Europe in the 1910s, where she was praised as a rare American composer whose work equalled that of Europeans in quality. Both her *Gaelic Symphony* and her Piano Concerto—again with the composer at the keyboard—were well received. Back in the United States, Beach continued to compose and perform while also developing music programs for children and mentoring younger composers.

Beach—like all American composers active in the 1890s—was well aware of Dvořák's advice and intimately familiar with his Symphony No. 9. In 1893, she was one of a number of prominent composers interviewed by the *Boston Herald* on the topic of Dvořák's recent call for music based on the melodies of African Americans (he would only later praise Native American influence). Each was asked what they thought about Dvořák's advice and what they saw as the future of American concert music. Beach acknowledged that spirituals were beautiful and expressive, but she rejected them as the basis for an American style. Instead, as she put it, "We of the North should be far more likely to be influenced by the old English, Scotch, or Irish songs inherited with our literature from our ancestors." She agreed, it seems, with Dvořák's call to incorporate folk influences, but disagreed about which folk music embodied American identity—or, at least, her identity. Beach's response indicates that, while Southern composers might be differently influenced by their musical environment, the music of the plantations meant nothing to her.

Beach put her theory into practice with the *Gaelic Symphony*. She began by studying Irish folks tunes, which were to form the basis of her work. She eventually incorporated four melodies that had been published in an 1841 Dublin magazine. However, it was her intent not only to quote genuine Irish folk melodies but also to absorb their musical language and use it in her original themes. Beach began by writing the second movement, which we will examine. Her symphony, like Dvořák's, is traditional in its overall structure. It opens and closes with lengthy movements in sonata form, while the third movement is slow and expressive.

The second movement begins with a complete presentation of an Irish folk tune titled "The Little Field of Barley." After a brief introduction by the horn and strings, the tune is played by the oboe—a choice of instrument perhaps inspired by the English horn in the second movement of Dvořák's symphony. Accompanying drones in the clarinets and bassoon can be heard as imitating a bagpipe. At the conclusion of the melody, the tempo changes, suddenly becoming much faster. We then hear a series of variations on the tune. The first is provided by the violins, who play rapid series of high, sparkling notes. Next we hear from the winds, who pass the theme back and forth with the violins. The horn and English horn then take the theme to the minor mode. Upon the recovery of the major mode, the tempo slows and we hear the original tune once more from the English horn. At this point the music swells dramatically, although a concluding fast passage featuring flutes and violins means that the movement ends with a smile.

NATIONAL REPRESENTATION IN STYLE AND INSTRUMENTATION

In the previous section, we looked at four individual works that can each be understood to express something about national identity. All four of these works, however, belong generally to the tradition of Western art music. When Liszt and Bartók wrote for solo piano, they contributed to the repertoire for pianists trained in the classical style. When Dvořák and Beach composed symphonies, they adhered to norms developed by two centuries of European composers. In other cases, however, entirely new musical traditions come to represent a nation's identity. Such traditions have unique characteristics and practices, and sometimes unique instruments as well. They become inextricably linked with national identity on an international level and can serve to further the political interests of a nation. Such is the case with the tradition of steelband music, which developed in and came to represent the nation of Trinidad and Tobago.

Steelband Music of Trinidad and Tobago

Like South Africa, the nation of Trinidad and Tobago is largely defined by its colonial past. The modern nation consists of two islands (Trinidad is the larger, Tobago the smaller). These islands were first claimed as a Spanish colony in 1498. The invaders rewrote the demographics of the region, essentially eradicating the indigenous population while bringing vast numbers of enslaved Africans overseas to work in the agricultural sector. For this reason, citizens of African descent now make up about 40% of the population.

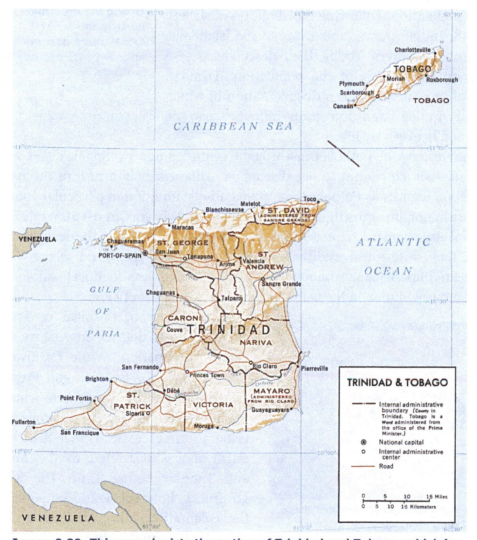

Image 9.29: This map depicts the nation of Trinidad and Tobago, which is located off the coast of Argentina.
Source: Wikimedia Commons
Attribution: CIA
License: Public Domain

By the end of the 18th century, Spain struggled to supply enough settlers to oversee its island's industries. To this end, in 1783 the Spanish King invited French settlers to take over agricultural lands on the islands, resulting in French cultural influence. In 1797, however, the British took military control of Trinidad and Tobago, and the islands remained part of the British empire until independence in 1962.

As a result of British colonialism, English is the official language of Trinidad and Tobago, although most residents speak a creolized form that reflects the influence of several African languages. However, citizens of British descent make up only a small portion of the population. Following the abolition of slavery in 1838, Indian immigrants came to the islands as indentured laborers. Today, their descendants also make up about 40% of the population. Trinidad and Tobago, therefore, is a diverse nation in which African, Indian, and European influence can be discerned in everyday life.

Image 9.30: Carnival participants wear extravagant costumes adorned with sequins and feathers.
Source: Wikimedia Commons
Attribution: User "Idobi"
License: CC BY-SA 4.0

The vestiges of Catholicism—brought centuries ago by Spanish and French colonists—will be central to our discussion. Although only a fifth of the nation's population identify as Catholic today, one Catholic tradition in particular continues to have a major impact on the music of Trinidad and Tobago: **Carnival**. We discussed Carnival elsewhere in Chapter 4, for it played a significant role in the development of opera. Diverse Carnival traditions have arisen around the world in the wake of European imperialism. Although no two traditions are identical, all facilitate exuberant celebration in the period leading up to the start of Lent.

Image 9.31: Groups of revelers dress in matching costumes, which are painstakingly crafted in the months leading up to Carnival.
Source: Wikimedia Commons
Attribution: User "Jean-Marc /Jo BeLo/Jhon-John"
License: CC BY 2.0

The history of Carnival in Trinidad and Tobago is tied to the history of the islands' occupation. While Carnival was celebrated by the Spanish and French, it was suppressed by the British, who were not Catholic and did not approve of the celebration's excesses. Under British rule, Carnival was restricted to the Monday and Tuesday before Lent. The islands' governors, however, could not put down the celebrations altogether, and during the 19th century they became increasingly exuberant—sometimes even violent. The early 20th century saw Carnival transformed into a more respectable event.

This was accomplished through the institution of competitions for Carnival participants, with perhaps the most coveted title—Calypso Monarch—going to the performer of the best new calypso song.

Music was always very important to Carnival. The **calypso** tradition developed among enslaved Africans, and has roots in the sung storytelling of West Africa. Here, however, we will focus on the dance music associated with Carnival—in particular, that performed on the nation's indigenous instrument, the steelpan.

Steelpans developed out of an older tradition of dance music known as *tamboo bamboo*. Both traditions had something important in common: The instruments could be constructed at no cost out of readily available materials. *Tamboo bamboo* was performed using hollow

Image 9.32: Today, most of the music in Carnival parades is blasted from sound trucks.
Source: Wikimedia Commons
Attribution: User "Jean-Marc /Jo BeLo/ Jhon-John"
License: CC BY 2.0

bamboo sticks, which were stamped on the ground to create complex rhythmic patterns. The various dimensions of the sticks meant that they produced different tones. *Tamboo bamboo* developed after drums were banned by the British in 1834, but the practice was itself banned a century later as part of the ongoing attempt to quell the Carnival festivities.

Although the origins of steelpans—like those of most musical traditions developed by disenfranchised populations—are shrouded in mystery, it is certain that impoverished Afro-Trinidadian youth began building drums out of discarded biscuit tins in the late 1930s. The first experimenters entered into intense competition with one another, and each sought to create a drum that could play more individual pitches than that created by his rival. Notes could be produced by hammering raised bumps into the bottom of the tin, the size of which determined the pitch. Oil barrels, which were readily available due to the presence of a US naval base on the island, soon replaced biscuit tins as the material of choice. Before long, these musicians had developed drums that could play complete melodies—and were extremely noisy.

At first, the British government reacted to steelpans with the same disdain they had cast upon tamboo bamboo and drums in the past. There was general concern that the new instrument would fuel street violence and lead to civil unrest. In 1946, however, a steelpan musician named Winston "Spree" Simon played the British national anthem, "God Save the King," for the governor. By performing a European melody on the instrument (and a patriotic one at that), Simon proved that steel pans could be respectable. The British immediately saw the instrument's potential for the promotion of national pride and set about establishing the steelpan as a national instrument.

Image 9.33: In this photograph taken by David Stanley, we see members of the group NGC Steel Xplosion playing in the 2014 Panorama competition.
Source: Flickr
Attribution: David Stanley
License: CC BY 2.0

The process began in 1949, when a Government Steelband Committee was formed to promote steelpan music. The Committee in turn formed the Trinidad and Tobago Steelband Association and founded the Trinidad All Steel Percussion Orchestra. In 1952, a steelband category was added to the national Trinidad Music Festival, which had been established in 1948 to celebrate and encourage the European concert tradition. When steelbands participated in the Music Festival, they played European classics arranged for steelpans. Finally, in 1963, the Panorama competition was founded to celebrate the independence of Trinidad and Tobago. Panorama is a highlight of the annual Carnival celebrations, and it continues to honor the band who gives the best performance of a recent dance hit.

Over the first few decades of its existence, the steelpan became an extraordinarily flexible instrument. It had to be, seeing as it was used to play both nuanced symphonic classics and energetic dance music. An individual instrument has a full set of **chromatic** pitches (analogous to the keys on a keyboard) spanning at least one octave. Pans come in a variety of sizes, from the small tenor or lead pan to the bass pan, which requires multiple physical drums with just a few pitches each. A steelband will contain dozens of pans in a variety of sizes. The pans are played using rubber-tipped mallets, which are often "rolled" (repeatedly struck in a rapid pattern) on the instrument to create a sustained pitch.

Image 9.34: In some of the higher-range instruments, the pitches are spread across two pans.
Source: Wikimedia Commons
Attribution: User "Roland zh"
License: CC BY-SA 3.0

Image 9.35: In this photograph, we see musicians in Saint-Martin playing multiple sizes of instruments, with the large bass pan in the foreground.
Source: Wikimedia Commons
Attribution: Grégory Rohard
License: CC BY-SA 4.0

Steelpan musicians have always valued their ability to play classical music. From the beginning, the performance of concert music demonstrated the sophistication of the instrument and the musicians—who at first were all members of the black community—in front of an international audience that was skeptical of their worth. In fact, the desire to play classical music well steered the development of the instrument, and many of its contemporary features, such as the suspension of the pans from metal frames, exist to facilitate concert performance. However, steelbands (or steel orchestras, as they are often called) don't take on classical repertoire primarily to prove themselves. The musicians play concert music because they love it and because it is deeply meaningful to them.

Invaders: Ludwig van Beethoven, Symphony No. 5, Fourth Movement[9]

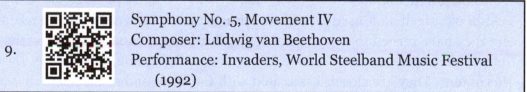

9.

Symphony No. 5, Movement IV
Composer: Ludwig van Beethoven
Performance: Invaders, World Steelband Music Festival
(1992)

We will examine a performance from the 1992 World Steelband Music Festival, which developed out of the Trinidad Music Festival in 1964 (one year after Trinidad and Tobago gained independence). This festival celebrates the diverse capabilities of the instrument, for each competing band must perform both an arrangement of a calypso and a selection from the European concert repertoire. However, this structure has not been without conflict. In the years following independence, some representatives of the Afro-Trinidadian community insisted that steelbands should only play indigenous music, not that of the colonizers. Other factions were unwilling to sacrifice music they loved in order to make a political statement, and believed that European influence could make Afro-Trinidadian music better. These kinds of political concerns still preoccupy performers in the European tradition in all parts of the world.

In 1992, the Invaders chose the fourth movement of Bethoven's Symphony No. 5 for their Festival performance. The Invaders are one of the oldest steelbands in Trinidad, tracing their lineage back to the earliest days of steelpan development. They have been equally successful performing concert repertoire and dance music, taking prizes at both the World Steelband Music Festival and Panorama.

For this performance, the Invaders add percussion instruments taken from the symphony orchestra, including a set of timpani. They dress in a manner that reflects concert hall practice (tuxedos for men, elegant matching jackets for women) and are led by a **conductor**. None of these elements would be present if the Invaders were competing at Panorama, but they are all considered appropriate for a performance of Beethoven. They do not read from sheet music, as orchestral musicians would, but have instead memorized their parts. The Invaders play all the notes just as Beethoven wrote them. The sound of the ensemble, however, is quite unlike anything Beethoven could have imagined.

Trinidad All Stars: Ultimate Rejects, "Full Extreme"

Our second performance, from the 2017 Panorama competition, it quite different. At Panorama, it is typical for a steelband to perform an arrangement of a hit song from the previous year. These arrangements are more than just transcriptions for steelband: That is to say, the members of the ensemble do not simply play the notes of the song on their instruments. Instead, steelband arrangers use the song as a starting point from which to craft elaborate variations. The resulting composition is usually about ten minutes long (in contrast to the three-minute popular song on which it is based) and demonstrate the full range of the ensemble's capabilities.

Although steelbands used to perform arrangements of calypso songs, in recent years they have turned to a new genre of Carnival music: **soca**. Soca is a variety of electronic dance music. Unlike calypso, soca songs value danceability over lyric content. They are closely associated with Carnival, and often celebrate the spirit of freedom and joy that imbues the festivities. During Carnival, the new songs for that year are blasted from speakers carried through the streets on truck beds. Although recorded soca has largely displaced live steelband performances in Carnival parades, the musical practices continue not only to coexist but to influence one another.

In 2017, the Trinidad All Stars took first place in the Panorama competition with their arrangement of the soca song "Full Extreme,"[10] which was released that same year by the band Ultimate Rejects. The song is characterized by its lively beat and repetitive melodic and textural refrains. The lyrics, which reflect a local English, dialect, celebrate the party spirit that cannot be quenched even by recession and disaster. The music video reinforces this message, as costumed carnivalgoers dance despite the oppressive presence of uniformed police. The refrain "We jammin still" captures the power of Carnival to overcome centuries of attempted repression.

10. This is the music video for the 2017 Ultimate Rejects song "Full Extreme."

The extended performance of "Full Extreme"[11] by the Trinidad All Stars fully captures the soca song's energy, even though it includes no text. Central to the performance, of course, is the arrangement itself. Steelpan arrangers are highly regarded in the pan community, and the best are competitively recruited by the bands who hope to win Panorama. This 2017 arrangement of "Full Extreme" was created by Leon "Smooth" Edwards. Edwards was born in the capital of Trinidad and Tobago, Port of Spain, where he became involved with steelpan music at a young age. He played with the Trinidad All Stars from 1968 until 2002, continuing to participate in Carnival even after immigrating to the United States in 1988. Edwards began arranging in 1975, and won his first Panorama as an arranger in 1980. "Full Extreme" was his ninth win.

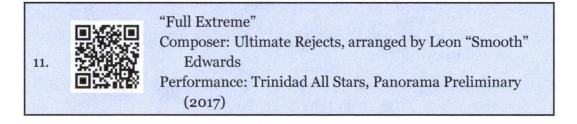

11. "Full Extreme"
Composer: Ultimate Rejects, arranged by Leon "Smooth" Edwards
Performance: Trinidad All Stars, Panorama Preliminary (2017)

In Edwards' arrangement, you can hear the basic melodic elements of the Ultimate Rejects' song. However, his arrangement is considered "good" because of the many ways in which it departs from the original, which is too repetitive to be very interesting in a purely instrumental version. In particular, Edwards makes use of the chromatic capabilities of the steelpan, writing passages that require players to strike almost every note on the instrument. He also contributes **variations** on the melody of the song. Finally, he occasionally interrupts the rhythmic groove, with has the effect of heightening the rhythmic excitement of his arrangement. The Trinidad All Stars' performance is strong not only because they play all the correct notes at the correct times but because they exude energy throughout. The best steelpan players—like the best performers in many traditions—become physically involved in the music.

There are a number of additional noteworthy differences between the All Stars' performance of "Full Extreme" and the Invaders' performance of Beethoven. The players wear a coordinated uniform, but it is t-shirts, not tuxedos. They do not require a conductor, but are instead lead by the rhythm section—which contains a drum set and various timekeeping instruments, not timpani. Before the performance begins, we can hear the succession of metallic strikes that set the music in motion. (Appropriately, the rhythm section in this type of steelband is referred to as the "engine room.") The level of dedication and professionalism, however, is the same, as steelbands practice intensely—and in secret—in the months leading up to Carnival.

RESOURCES FOR FURTHER LEARNING

Print

Beckerman, Michael B. *New Worlds of Dvořák: Searching in America for the Composer's Inner Life*. W.W. Norton & Company, 2003.

Block, Adrienne Fried. *Amy Beach, Passionate Victorian: The Life and Work of an American Composer, 1867-1944*. Oxford University Press, 1998.

Dudley, Shannon. *Carnival Music in Trinidad: Experiencing Music, Expressing Culture*. Oxford University Press, 2003.

Ferris, Marc. *Star-Spangled Banner: The Unlikely Story of America's National Anthem*. Johns Hopkins University Press, 2014.

Hang, Xing. *Encyclopedia of National Anthems*. Scarecrow Press, 2003.

Riley, Matthew, and Anthony D. Smith. *Nation and Classical Music: From Handel to Copland*. Boydell Press, 2016.

Shadle, Douglas W. *Orchestrating the Nation: The Nineteenth-Century American Symphonic Enterprise*. Oxford University Press, 2015.

Taruskin, Richard. *Music in the Nineteenth Century: The Oxford History of Western Music*. Oxford University Press, 2009.

Online

Patriotic Melodies Collection, Library of Congress: https://www.loc.gov/collections/patriotic-melodies/

Jewish Music Research Centre: https://www.jewish-music.huji.ac.il/

Support and Protest

Esther M. Morgan-Ellis

INTRODUCTION

In the previous chapter, we examined various ways in which nations can be represented by musical means. Our examples included national anthems, pieces of art music that draw from folk sources, and a complete musical tradition with national significance. In this chapter, we will turn our attention to the role of music in political action, and we will see how music can not only represent a nation but also directly influence its character and future.

As we already discussed in the context of national anthems, music can bring people together and inspire them to feel sympathetic toward one another. Music—especially participatory music—can create community. Music can also inspire an emotional response in the listener. These capacities are combined to great effect when music is used to urge a group of people to think or act along specific political lines.

Sometimes, music is employed in support of a political candidate or ideology. The most prominent examples of this include campaign songs, music played at political rallies, and the soundtracks to political advertisements. In all of these cases, music is used to inspire sympathy with a cause or candidate and win the support of the listener. However, the creators of the music in question do not always have a say in its political use. More often than not, music is coopted for political purposes and used in ways that the original artist had never imagined (and may not approve of). In such cases, we see the capacity of music to express meaning beyond its creator's intent.

Other times, music is used to combat a dominant political force. The most prominent example of this is the **protest song**, which is used to inspire resistance to an ongoing political action. When music is used to protest ruling powers, however, there is always an element of danger. Those who position themselves in opposition to governments or bosses risk serious reprisal. For this reason, protest music is not always easy to decipher. Sometimes it is **overt** in its meaning, clearly indicating the objectionable situation and the desired action. Sometimes, however, it is **covert**, instead disguising its meaning so that only certain listeners will receive the message. In such cases, it can be difficult to determine exactly what a piece of music "means" or even to prove that it is subversive at all. We will examine both overt and covert examples in this chapter.

MUSIC AS POLITICAL ADVOCACY

Campaign Songs

The use of music to rally support for a political cause has a long history. Music has been used around the world to display the power of monarchies, to urge soldiers into battle, and to inspire patriotic support for all manner of governments. Here, we will focus on the role of music in American politics, with special attention given to specific songs that have been used by candidates seeking election to the presidency.

Although we are focusing on campaign songs, those are not the only musical tools that have been employed by American political candidates. Before the rise of mass media, campaigning was conducted in person at events such as rallies, parades, and whistle stops, often to the accompaniment of a local brass band playing popular and patriotic tunes. Today, we are more likely to hear campaign music via television, whether we are watching a televised campaign event or a paid political advertisement. At events, candidates are likely to use popular songs that convey a relevant message, set the right mood, or speak to a desired voting base. In advertisements, we are more likely to hear **underscoring** similar to that used in television shows and movies. Such music attracts less attention than a popular song, but it plays an equally important role in communicating the candidate's message.

To see underscoring at work, we might examine two recent television advertisements from a 2016 Republican candidate for governor of Georgia, Casey Cagle. In a spot from early in the campaign, titled "Difference,"[1] Casey touts his humble beginnings, strong personal ethic, and political accomplishments. The music behind his voiceover is bouncy and cheerful. The major mode tells us that this is a message of optimism, while the mid-tempo drumbeat and repetitive, **staccato** melody notes are reassuring and uplifting. Later in the campaign, however, Cagle—in response to a strong showing by his rival—attempted to construct a new public persona for himself, one that emphasized strength and determination. These qualities are reflected in the television advertisement "About,"[2] which features music that would be equally at home in an action film. The minor mode and suspenseful harmonies keep the listener on edge, while periodic percussive strikes suggest danger and unrest. As musicologist Naomi Graber has observed, the music builds to a climax in parallel with Cagle's rousing speech, suggesting that Cagle himself is the superhero in this narrative.

1. In this 2016 campaign ad for Georgia gubernatorial candidate Casey Cagle, the music is bouncy and cheerful.

2.  In this ad from later in Cagle's campaign, the music is suspenseful.

Candidates are sometimes musicians themselves and are therefore able to exploit their own musical skills to win the sympathy and support of the public. In 1886, for example, two brothers—Alf and Bob Taylor—ran against one another in a bid to become governor of Tennessee. Both men were excellent fiddlers, and they not only performed frequently throughout the campaign but also used their love of folk music to establish a down-home identity and connect with rural voters. More than a century later, President Bill Clinton advertised himself as fun-loving and cool by playing saxophone on *The Arsenio Hall Show*, while Democratic presidential candidate Martin O'Malley garnered attention by playing guitar and singing Taylor Swift's "Bad Blood" on *The View*. Although the genres (and skill levels) of these candidate-performers varied widely, all used music to paint themselves as good-humored and relatable.

When it comes to conveying a specific political message through music, song is clearly

Image 10.1: Alf and Bob Taylor fiddling at one of their campaign events in 1886. Bob won the election, but Alf was elected governor of Tennessee in 1920.

Source: Wikimedia Commons
Attribution: George Simons
License: Public Domain

Image 10.2: Bill Clinton famously played saxophone on The Arsenio Hall Show in 1992. The sunglasses further underscore Clinton's message to voters.

Source: Flickr
Attribution: Rogelio A. Galaviz C.
License: CC BY-NC 2.0

Image 10.3: Martin O'Malley singing on the campaign trail in 2014.

Source: Flickr
Attribution: Karen Murphy
License: CC BY-ND 2.0

the best choice, and it has been in use since the beginning of American electoral politics. In the earliest years, election songs were usually **parodies**. As early as George Washington's reelection campaign in 1792, supporters advocated their candidates' causes by writing new words to recent popular songs. This technique could be very effective. Because the melody was already familiar, parody lyrics were quickly learned, sung, and spread. The success of a popular song could even contribute to the success of the campaign that chose to parody that song. In 1840, William Harrison's campaign song "Tippecanoe and Tyler Too," which parodied the familiar "Three Little Pigs," became so popular that it was widely credited with winning him the presidency.

There is also a long history of presidential candidates relying on endorsements by celebrity musicians to boost their popularity. The earliest example of this came in 1860, when the famous abolitionist singer Jesse Hutchinson wrote a parody song in support of Abraham Lincoln. The song—"Lincoln and Liberty, Too," set to the tune of "Rosin the Beau"—was a hit, but Hutchinson's popularity probably contributed just as much to Lincoln's victory.

New songs have also been written in support of presidential candidates. While this practice dates to the early 20th century, it is particularly widespread today, when anyone can write a song, record a performance, and upload their contribution to social media. Technology has always influenced the role of music in presidential elections. Beginning in the 1930s, the prevalence of radio (and later television) led campaigns to employ songs that were already popular—an approach that proved more effective than the creation of a new song that might or might not prove a hit.

In this chapter, we will consider three such songs. These songs are all quite different in style and message, but they share one important thing in common: None of them were written with any political end in mind. In each case, the presidential campaign coopted the song because it supported the campaign's political message.

Milton Ager and Jack Yellen, "Happy Days Are Here Again"

The first presidential candidate to coopt a popular song for his campaign was Franklin Delano Roosevelt, who in 1932 adopted the recent hit song "Happy Days Are Here Again"[3] to represent his political agenda. Although the song was not created for his campaign and did not communicate an explicitly political message, Roosevelt found that it perfectly captured the spirit of his presidential bid.

3. "Happy Days Are Here Again"
    Composers: Milton Ager and Jack Yellen
    Performance: Annette Hanshaw (1930)

It is no surprise that Roosevelt should have been the first presidential candidate to use a popular song in his campaign. The 1920s and 1930s were a time of

Image 10.4: This 1932 photograph shows Roosevelt giving a campaign speech in Topeka, KS.
Source: Flickr
Attribution: FDR Presidential Library & Museum
License: CC BY 2.0

extraordinary growth in the music recording and broadcast industries, with the result that popular songs were more influential than ever before. The first commercial license was issued to a radio station in 1921, while 1925 saw the invention of the electrical microphone and an accompanying improvement in the quality of recorded and broadcast sound. Due in part to the economic downturn of 1929, radio soon eclipsed the phonograph in popularity. The most successful programming in that era consisted of live musical performances. Roosevelt was the first presidential candidate (and later president) to take full advantage of the radio as a platform for connecting with Americans and spreading his message.

The decision to play "Happy Days Are Here Again" at the 1932 Democratic National Convention was made spontaneously after the man who introduced Roosevelt gave a lifeless and dour speech. Roosevelt's campaign managers had originally intended to brand him with "Anchors Aweigh" (a nod to his Navy service), but they felt that the occasion called for something more lively and selected "Happy Days Are Here Again" at the last moment. The song proved effective and was used for the remainder of the campaign. In fact, it was such a success that "Happy Days Are Here Again" was associated with the Democratic Party for many years to come.

Image 10.5: Here we see Roosevelt making a radio broadcast from his home in 1943.
Source: Wikimedia Commons
Attribution: Unknown
License: Public Domain

In 1932, a song like "Happy Days Are Here Again" would have had particular resonance with Americans, who were experiencing the worst effects of the Great Depression. The 1930s saw a public clamor for escapist films, theater, and songs. Almost no popular songs from this era reference the difficulties that plagued Americans following the stock market crash of October 1929. Instead, they celebrate good times, affluence, and carefree living.

The authors of "Happy Days Are Here Again"—composer Milton Ager and lyricist Jack Yellen—were themselves the beneficiaries of fortunate timing, for they wrote their song just before the onset of the Great Depression. "Happy Days" was commissioned by MGM for inclusion in an early sound film, *Chasing Rainbows* (1930). While waiting for the film to be released, however, Ager and Yellen provided their new song to bandleader

Image 10.6: Band leader George Olsen premiered "Happy Days are Here Again" on the day of the 1929 stock market crash.
Source: Wikimedia Commons
Attribution: Unknown
License: Public Domain

George Olsen, who performed regularly at Hotel Pennsylvania in New York City. Olsen's band premiered "Happy Days" on October 24, 1929—the day of the crash. Olsen supposedly called on his soloists to "sing it for the corpses," a reference to the morose diners who had just lost their life savings. As Yellen recalled, "After a couple of choruses, the corpses joined in, sardonically, hysterically. Before the night

Image 10.7: This undated photograph depicts a building in Tin Pan Alley that housed many of the era's leading music publishers.
Source: Wikimedia Commons
Attribution: Unknown
License: Public Domain

was over, the hotel lobby resounded with what had become the theme song of ruined stock speculators as they leaped from hotel windows."

"Happy Days Are Here Again" went on to become a major hit. It appealed to listeners who reveled in the irony of the lyrics ("happy days" were certainly *not* anywhere to be seen), but it also embodied the American spirit of optimism and perseverance in the face of extreme difficulty. The lyrics—like those of most successful songs—are not about any particular event or situation. Instead, they speak in broad terms, bidding farewell to "sad times" and "bad times" before celebrating the fact that "the skies above are clear again" and calling on all to "tell the world" that "happy days are here again."

"Happy Days Are Here Again" was a project of a songwriting industry known as **Tin Pan Alley**. The main product of Tin Pan Alley song

Image 10.8: The sheet music cover for "Happy Days Are Here Again" (1929).
Source: Flickr
Attribution: Stewart Harris
License: CC BY-NC-SA 2.0

publishers was sheet music, which consumers would purchase so as to be able to perform hit songs in their own homes. By 1929, sheet music sales had already been eclipsed by phonograph sales, and radio was further eating into the popular music market share. Still, songwriting teams, usually in the employment of Tin Pan Alley publishers, continued to crank out potential hits into the 1940s. (The name "Tin Pan Alley" refers to the discordant sounds of cheap pianos being played in the many publishing houses located on a single block in Manhattan.)

During the Tin Pan Alley era, songs were not often associated with individual performers. Instead, hit songs were recorded by all of the prominent singers, each of whom was expected to perform a common repertoire. "Happy Days Are Here Again" was first recorded in November 1929 by Leo Reisman and His Orchestra, but this was only the first in a parade of renditions by a variety of popular singers. We will consider the 1930 recording by Ben Selvin and His Orchestra, with Annette Hanshaw on vocals.

Ben Selvin (1898-1980) holds the honor as the most productive recording artist in American history, having recorded as many as 20,000 individual tunes. It is difficult to make an exact count because Selvin recorded under dozens of different names for all of the major record labels of his era. This was a typical practice, since performing artists were required to sign exclusive contracts with recording companies. The use of pseudonyms allowed an artist to triple or quadruple their income by recording with a variety of labels. As a producer at Columbia Records, Selvin also oversaw the creation of recordings by other artists. His catalog includes some of the finest records made in the early 1930s.

Annette Hanshaw (1901-1985) was among the countless singers who performed and recorded with Selvin's band. She was also very famous in her own right, being voted the best female popular singer in a 1934 *Radio Stars* magazine poll. Hanshaw, however, later confessed that she detested performing and could not stand her own records. She loved music but became very nervous in front of

Image 10.9: At the time this photo was taken in 1934, Annette Hanshaw was one of the most popular singers on the radio.
Source: Wikimedia Commons
Attribution: Unknown
License: Public Domain

a microphone and was dissatisfied with her abilities as a singer.

Selvin and Hanshaw's recording of "Happy Days Are Here Again" is typical of 1920s-era **sweet jazz**. This type of music was intended primarily for dancing, and it could be heard in upscale urban hotels, ballrooms, and on the radio. Selvin's band contains instruments that we associate with jazz today, such as saxophones, trumpets, trombones, and piano, but—in keeping with the standard of the era—it also contains a violin section, and the bass line is played on the tuba instead of the string bass. The tempo is lively and the beat is clearly articulated by the rhythm section (piano and tuba).

Ager and Yellen's jazz-influenced tune is highly **syncopated**, meaning that melody notes often fall between beats. We can hear this in the chorus: The word "happy" falls on the beat, but the words "days" and "are" come after the beat.

Image 10.10: Ben Selvin, pictured here in 1945, might have recorded as many as 20,000 tunes over the course of his career.
Source: Wikimedia Commons
Attribution: Unknown
License: Public Domain

(Try clapping the pulse while reciting the lyrics in rhythm to see how this works.) This pattern is repeated with the next phrase, in which "here" falls on the beat but the second syllable of "again" come off the beat. Selvin's band makes this pattern sound even more exciting by shortening the melody notes that fall on the beat.

The form of this recording is also typical of the era. Although the song "Happy Days Are Here Again" technically begins with a **verse**, Selvin chooses to open his rendition with the much catchier **chorus**. After singing through the chorus once, Hanshaw sings the verse, which is much shorter than the chorus and also in the minor mode. This provides welcome contrast, but the change in mood doesn't last long. Next, we hear a rendition of the chorus by an anonymous trio of male singers. Finally, we get an instrumental version, with the male singers joining in for the closing phrase. In short, most of the recording is taken up by three complete turns through the chorus—which, by the end of the three minutes, is firmly lodged in the listener's head.

This approach to the production of popular music—extreme repetition, softened by a brief excursion into contrasting material—is still with us today. Although the forms, sounds, and lyrics have all changed, record producers continue to foreground the most memorable musical material while finding opportunities to introduce contrast. This delicate balance between too much repetition (which would make a song annoying) and too little (which would prevent it from being memorable) characterizes the eternal formula for successful popular music.

Paul Simon, "Bridge Over Troubled Water"

Successful campaign songs always combine a relevant text with music that sets an appropriate emotional tone. It is easy to see how a song like "Happy Days Are Here Again" could serve this purpose well: It is bright and cheerful, and exhibits unchecked optimism about the future. The 1970 Simon & Garfunkel hit "Bridge Over Troubled Water"[4] is a less obvious choice for a political campaign. While the song's lyrics touch on themes that a candidate might want to emphasize, the music lacks the energy of a typical campaign song. We will begin, therefore, by examining the song itself. Then we will consider why George McGovern, the Democratic challenger to President Richard Nixon, might have selected it for his 1972 campaign.

4.   "Bridge Over Troubled Water"
      Composer: Paul Simon
      Performance: Simon and Garfunkel (1970)

In 1969, Paul Simon and Art Garfunkel were two of the biggest stars in American popular music. Their recent albums *Sounds of Silence* (1966) and *Parsley, Sage, Rosemary and Thyme* (1966) had both proved major hits, and they were at the forefront of the **folk rock** genre. Although both men sang and made contributions to the duo's **arrangements**, Simon was the lead songwriter—a fact that caused some friction, as Simon increasingly felt that Garfunkel was not making an equal contribution to the partnership. The duo broke up in 1970 just as their fourth album, *Bridge over Troubled Water*, was rapidly climbing the charts.

Image 10.11: Paul Simon and Art Garfunkel in 1968.
Source: Wikimedia Commons
Attribution: GAC-General Artists Corporation and Columbia Records
License: Public Domain

Simon wrote "Bridge over Troubled Water" very quickly in 1969. He later recounted that the basic idea took him about twenty minutes to work out, while the whole song was finished in under two hours. The title lyric was inspired by a line from the 1958 Swan Silvertones song "Mary Don't You Weep," in which Claude Jeter sings, "I'll be your bridge over deep water if you trust in me." Simon's source ended up shaping not only the lyrics but the sound of his new song. The Swan Silvertones were an African American gospel group, and their music drew from the rich tradition of black church music. Although Simon and Garfunkel did not attempt a wholesale imitation of this style, they wanted their recording to reflect the influence of gospel (a style discussed in Chapter 11).

"Bridge over Troubled Water" contains three verses, the last of which was added at the request of Garfunkel to support the song's dramatic musical climax. Simon wrote the verse, but never cared for it—his message was communicated in its entirety in the first two verses. These vow to the listener that, although they may be "weary, feeling small," "down and out," or "on the street," the singer will always "take your part" and "lay me down / Like a bridge over troubled water." In short, the song promises solace and support for anyone who is experiencing difficulties in life.

Although Simon wrote the song using his favored instrument, the guitar, he chose to make the recording with a piano played in the gospel style. The instrumental introduction, with its grandiose chords and syncopated rhythms, could indeed preface the entrance of a gospel singer. Instead, we hear the voice of Garfunkel, which Simon thought was better suited to the tune than his own. The first verse is accompanied only by piano. The second verse is additionally supported by vibraphone, which adds warmth and resonance without changing the character of the song.

At the conclusion of the second verse, however, the music takes a new direction. First, a drum set crashes onto the soundscape. Strings enter next, followed by an electric bass. The full instrumental forces grow in energy throughout the third and final verse, which also features Simon singing a harmony part. In the final seconds of the song, the tempo slows as the strings ascend to their highest note, producing a triumphant conclusion.

Despite the drama that Simon and Garfunkel were able to produce in their studio recording of "Bridge over Troubled Water," the song itself is not particularly energetic. It features a slow tempo, a sustained vocal line, and lyrics that encourage the listener to feel calm and resolute. It's not a song one would play to rile up a crowd or to encourage enthusiastic support for a cause.

Image 10.12: In 1972, George McGovern ran an unsuccessful presidential campaign to unseat Richard Nixon.
Source: Wikimedia Commons
Attribution: Warren K. Leffler
License: Public Domain

All the same, George McGovern chose "Bridge over Troubled Water" as the theme song for his 1972 presidential bid, and he played it at his rallies throughout the campaign. The song certainly embodied many of McGovern's values. He ran on a platform of national unification and healing, advertising his ability to reach across the aisle and bring opposing factions together. The preceding years had indeed been characterized by devastating internal conflict, including the 1968 assassination of

Martin Luther King, Jr., the 1969 Stonewall riots, and growing unrest concerning the war in Vietnam—unrest that culminated in the 1970 Kent State massacre in which National Guardsmen killed four student protesters. McGovern positioned himself as a staunchly anti-war candidate who would bring peace to the nation. For this reason, "Bridge over Troubled Water" was uniquely suited to his campaign. At one point, McGovern even quoted the song directly, stating, "I want, indeed, to become a bridge over troubled waters."

McGovern was able to use "Bridge over Troubled Water" in another way as well. He invited Simon and Garfunkel to participate in a benefit concert that took place in Madison Square Garden on June 14, 1972. (Simon actively supported McGovern's candidacy; Garfunkel was less enthusiastic but eager to perform before a large crowd.) McGovern naturally benefitted from having star performers take the stage, just as he profited from associating himself with a song that was heard constantly on the radio. However, McGovern was also able to polish his image by bringing the sundered duo back together for the first time since their partnership had ended. He, after all, was the candidate of reconciliation and peace making. McGovern's ability to restore the Simon and Garfunkel partnership therefore attested to his potential skills as a national leader.

"Bridge over Troubled Water," therefore, was perhaps not as bizarre a choice for a campaign song as one might think. Unfortunately for McGovern, the song does not seem to have done him any good: He was soundly defeated in the 1972 election by incumbent Richard Nixon, who won over 60% of the vote and took every state except Massachusetts and the District of Columbia.

Tom Petty and Jeff Lynne, "I Won't Back Down"

In contrast with Simon and Garfunkel's soulful ballad, Tom Petty's 1989 hit "I Won't Back Down"[5] is an obvious choice for a political candidate. In fact, it is so well-suited to the campaign trail that half a dozen candidates have employed it in just the first two decades of the 21st century. It was also used to voice a non-partisan political message following the September 11 terrorist attacks. At the same time, at least one candidate's attempt to coopt the message and popularity of "I Won't Back Down" backfired. We will try to understand why this song has been so useful in the context of political discourse and consider the risks of coopting the creative work of a celebrity for partisan purposes—especially when that celebrity is politically active.

5.  "I Won't Back Down"
Composer: Tom Petty and Jeff Lynne
Performance: Tom Petty and the Heartbreakers (1989)

By the time he released "I Won't Back Down," Tom Petty (1950-2017) was already a rock music superstar. Petty was born and raised in Gainesville, FL, where he dropped out of high school to join a band. He was inspired by Elvis Presley and The Beatles, whose success proved to him that it was possible for a regular, working-class kid to make it in music. Although Petty only achieved local celebrity in his first decade as a rock musician, the late 1970s saw the meteoric rise of his band Tom Petty and the Heartbreakers, which recorded a string of successful albums between 1976 and 1987. Although the Heartbreakers would reconvene in the early 1990s and continue to release albums until just a few years before Petty's 2017 death, Petty took a hiatus in 1988 to join George Harrison's group the Traveling Wilburys.

Image 10.13: Petty continued to perform up until his death. He is pictured here on stage in 2012.
Source: Wikimedia Commons
Attribution: Ирина Лепнёва
License: CC BY-SA 3.0

During this same period, Petty also released his first solo album, *Full Moon Fever*. The lead single from this album was "I Won't Back Down."

Half of the songs on *Full Moon Fever* were cowritten by Tom Petty and Jeff Lynne, an English musician and founding member of the Traveling Wilburys. It is common for popular songwriters to work in pairs. This strategy has proved successful since the early 20th century, when Tin Pan Alley songwriters teamed up to produce hits. Many songwriters find that this approach aids productivity, since the contributors can help one another out of creative difficulties and suggest improvements to the music or lyrics. Lynne also produced the album and is, therefore, in part responsible for the sound of "I Won't Back Down."

The success of "I Won't Back Down"—both as a popular song and as a political soundtrack—can be traced to its straightforward message. Like "Happy Days Are Here Again," "I Won't Back Down" does not refer to any particular event or circumstances. We don't know what the singer is standing up for, or against whom he is resisting, or why he is in a position that requires he stand his ground. All we know is that, despite "a world that keeps on pushin' me around" and "draggin' me down," the singer "won't back down."

The music admirably communicates this message of steadfast endurance. "I Won't Back Down" is set to a medium rock tempo—not so fast as to feel frantic but not so slow as to feel lethargic. The music sounds as if it—like the singer—could carry on this way forever. The sung melody has a protracted melodic rhythm, meaning that the individual note values are long and unhurried. Petty's unaffected drawl further convinces us that he is not to be moved, while the relaxed guitar solo underscores the point. "I Won't Back Down" is, naturally enough, in the major mode, but the accompaniment prominently features a minor chord, heard under the word "won't" in the title line. This tinges the lyric with seriousness of purpose. Although the singer is not overly concerned, he is not taking the threat lightly.

"I Won't Back Down" first made political headlines in 2000, when George W. Bush used it at events during his presidential campaign. The song seemed an excellent choice, but it became a liability when Petty protested, sending the campaign a cease-and-desist letter and demanding that they quit using his music. Bush's campaign staff might have known better: Petty had already indicated a penchant for political speech as a musician and had aligned himself with various activist causes. In 1979, Tom Petty and the Heartbreakers performed in a Madison Square Garden concert intended to raise support for the dismantling of nuclear power plants, while in 1985 they took to the stage for the famous Live Aid concert in Philadelphia, which raised funds to combat famine in Ethiopia. And in 1992, Petty had written the song "Peace in L.A." in response to the Rodney King riots, donating all proceeds to charity. Although none of these were explicitly left-wing causes, Petty was certainly aware of his power as a political agent, and he knew that music could make a difference in a political struggle. After the 2000 election, Petty performed "I Won't Back Down" at Al Gore's concession speech, thereby clearly sending the message that he intended to retain control over how his music was used.

Image 10.14: The 1985 Live Aid concert raised funds to combat famine in Ethiopia.
Source: Wikimedia Commons
Attribution: User "Squelle"
License: CC BY-SA 3.0

Petty, however, did not always interfere when politicians coopted his music. During the 2008 presidential campaign, for example, "I Won't Back Down" was used by Democratic candidates Hillary Clinton and John Edwards, but also by Republican candidate Ron Paul. In 2012, he again made no comment when "I Won't Back Down" was played at the Democratic National Convention. That same year, however, he issued another cease-and-desist letter to Representative Michele Bachmann, who used his song "American Girl" to launch her presidential campaign. Petty, of course, was not the first rock star to object to the coopting of his hits—and also not the last. All modern presidential campaigns are accompanied by a chorus of popular recording artists asking that candidates stop using their music. It's not clear why Petty accepted some uses of his songs and rejected others, but it is entirely clear that he understood the power of his music and celebrity.

CARL ORFF, *CARMINA BURANA*

Although popular song has been the preferred political vehicle of the past century, art music is also ripe for exploitation. Indeed, much of the music that we enjoy in concert halls and opera houses today was created on behalf of political regimes for the purpose of cementing their power. Monteverdi's opera *Orpheus*, for example, was intended to display the wealth of the Gonzaga court and solidify its position in the eyes of visitors. Although the plot of *Orpheus* is not explicitly political, many of the Italian operas of the following two centuries portrayed monarchs as benevolent and wise father figures ordained by God for the safekeeping of their people—an image that did much to mediate potential unrest. The modern symphony orchestra, in its own turn, might be traced to a court in Mannheim, where an orchestra was used to advertise the splendor of Charles III Philip, who ruled a large region in what is now Germany.

Image 10.15: This photograph of Carl Orff was taken in 1940, the same year that *Carmina Burana* began to be used at Nazi rallies.
Source: Wikimedia Commons
Attribution: Hanns Holdt
License: Public Domain

Orff and the Nazi Party

Here, however, we will examine a 20th century instance of concert music turned to political use. While Carl Orff (1895-1982) did not set out to write a political piece of music, his **scenic cantata** *Carmina Burana* was embraced by the Nazi Party, the leaders of which believed that it conveyed many of their values and could be put to use for the purpose of riling up crowds and building communal sentiment. Beginning in 1940, *Carmina Burana* was frequently performed at Party rallies and government functions, in which context it both exemplified "good" Nazi music and was used to boost enthusiasm for the government and its activities.

Carl Orff was not himself a member of the Nazi Party. After the war, he was investigated by the American denazification authorities, who cleared him of collaboration charges and authorized him to continue his professional work. All the same, Orff thrived under the Nazi regime, and he certainly didn't use his position of relative influence to resist the regime's activities. He never denied the Nazis permission to use his work, and on several occasions actually wrote music on their behalf. Any attempt at subversion, of course, would probably have culminated in Orff's execution. In short, he behaved as many Germans of the era did, neither supporting nor condemning the Nazis.

Orff wrote a large number of theatrical works, many of which expressed his theory of "elemental music." In attempting to recapture the power of ancient Greek drama, Orff advocated for a unified stage art that combined music, dance, poetry, image, design, and theatrical gesture. If this sounds familiar, we have already seen other creative figures attempt to revive the arts of ancient Greece (the Florentine Camerata, discussed in Chapter 4) and develop an all-encompassing approach to musical theater (Richard Wagner, discussed in Chapter 3). Indeed, Orff himself was responsible for the 1925 revival of the most famous opera produced under the Camerata's influence, Claudio Monteverdi's *Orpheus*. His greatest impact, however, was in the field of music education. He co-founded the Günther School in Munich in 1924 and taught music there until the end of his life. The techniques he developed for working with young children are still in use today.

Carmina Burana

Carmina Burana—certainly Orff's most successful composition—is what he termed a "scenic cantata." A **cantata** is a multi-part work for voice(s) and accompaniment. We examine two cantatas elsewhere in this volume: Barbara Strozzi's *Lagrime mie* for solo soprano and basso continuo (Chapter 8) and Johann Sebastian Bach's *Sleepers, Wake* for soloists, choir, and orchestra (Chapter 11). Cantata, however, is a flexible designation. Just as Strozzi and Bach's cantatas have little in common, Orff's cantata will in turn bear only a limited resemblance to other cantatas you might have encountered. His addition of the term "scenic" indicates that his cantatas are meant to be staged. Orff envisioned dramatic performances complete with sets, costumes, pantomime, and dancing. *Carmina Burana* was indeed presented as a dramatic spectacle in its early days, although now you are more likely to encounter it as an unstaged concert work.

Today, *Carmina Burana* seems to have completely shed its wartime significance. Few people know that it was ever used as Nazi propaganda, and it is widely enjoyed by audiences and performers. This is in part possible because the text has nothing whatsoever to do with politics, war, or Nazi values. Indeed, the text is nearly a thousand years old: Orff extracted it from a medieval manuscript of

Image 10.16: This scenic sketch was created for a 1959 production of Carmina Burana in Munich.
Source: Wikimedia Commons
Attribution: User "UweJuergens"
License: CC BY-SA 3.0

the same name. "Carmina Burana" is Latin for "Songs from Benediktbeuern," and refers to a volume of poems written primarily in the 11th and 12th centuries. The manuscript containing the poems was discovered at a Benedictine monastery in Benediktbeuern (now a municipality in Bavaria) and is prized as one of the most significant collections of what are known as **goliard** songs.

Goliards were, in modern terms, carousing college dropouts. Many were younger sons from wealthy families. Because only the eldest son could inherit, younger sons were sent to monasteries or Catholic universities, where they were educated in theology and prepared to enter the clergy. Many of these young men, however, had no affinity for the religious life and instead preferred to pursue more earthly pleasures. Because they had been well educated, goliards were able to leave a record of their satirical poems and racy songs. Most of these were written in Latin, the language of the Catholic church, although some are in the vernacular languages spoken by the goliards.

The songs in the *Carmina Burana* manuscript address all of the topics that might be of interest to young men who enjoy having a good time: the fickleness of fortune and wealth, the ephemeral nature of life, the joy of the return of Spring, drinking, gluttony, gambling, and lust. Few of the texts can be associated with specific melodies, meaning that a composer who wanted to borrow them would

Image 10.17: Fortune, as portrayed in the Carmina Burana manuscript. Her wheel raises kings to the heights while crushing peasants below. However, because the wheel is constantly turning, those on the bottom can hope for an improvement in their fortunes, while those on the top must remember that they will not remain there.
Source: Wikimedia Commons
Attribution: Unknown
License: Public Domain

be obliged to create new musical settings. Orff did so, although he often sought to imitate the melodic shapes and modes of Gregorian chant (see Chapter 11 for an example).

Taken as a whole, however, Orff's music is far removed from that of the medieval Catholic church. He wrote for an enormous ensemble consisting of three vocal soloists, three choirs (two mixed and one boys'), and a large orchestra complete with an eighteen-piece percussion section and two pianos. His music was inspired by Igor Stravinsky's primitivist ballets (see Chapter 3), which used repetitive melodic figures (**ostinatos**) and jarring rhythms to evoke a pre-modern social order.

To create his scenic cantata, Orff first chose twenty-three poems from the manuscript and organized them into scenes, which address the topics of fate, springtime, drinking, and love. The first and last scenes are identical, for they portray "Fortune, Empress of the World." The vision of fortune as a great wheel that turns incessantly can be found throughout the *Carmina Burana* manuscript, where it is represented both in verse and image. It therefore seemed natural to Orff that his cantata should end as it had begun, with a mighty chorus announcing the power of fate to shape our lives. We will examine four musical selections, one representing each of the four themes explored in *Carmina Burana*.

"O Fortune"

The opening chorus, "O Fortune,"[6] is certainly the most famous part of *Carmina Burana*. It has featured in dozens of films, television shows, commercials, and video games, and has even been employed by professional sports teams. Its text consists of three stanzas:

6.  *"O Fortune" from Carmina Burana*
Composer: Carl Orff
Performance: Orchestra and choir of the Deutsche Oper Berlin, conducted by Eugen Jochum (1968)

O Fortune, like the moon of ever changing state, you are always waxing or waning; hateful life now is brutal, now pampers our feelings with its game; poverty, power, it melts them like ice.

Fate, savage and empty, you are a turning wheel, your position is uncertain, your favour is idle and always likely to disappear; covered in shadows and veiled you bear upon me too; now my back is naked through the sport of your wickedness.

The chance of prosperity and of virtue is not now mine; whether willing or not, a man is always liable for Fortune's service. At this hour without delay touch the strings! Because through luck she lays low the brave, all join with me in lamentation!

Translation by Gavin Betts. Used with permission.

The music is simple in the extreme. After a shockingly loud introduction, in which the full chorus and orchestra sound a series of accented chords, the instruments of the orchestra set an ostinato into motion. The ostinato contains only four pitches, each of which is sharply accented. Over the top of this ostinato, the chorus sings a melody constructed out of repeated melodic and rhythmic fragments. Almost all of the melodic motion is **conjunct** and the entire melody occupies the tiny range of a fifth. Some commentators have compared this melody to Gregorian chant, while others have remarked upon its folk-like qualities.

The first two verses are musically identical, but the third is marked by an explosion in volume. The sopranos repeat their melody, but they do so an octave higher than before. Likewise, high-register instruments join the ostinato. In the final moments of the movement, the pattern finally breaks as a new six-note ostinato takes us to the final thrilling chord. Orff's music certainly conveys the power and inescapability of fate!

"Dance"

The next selection we will consider has quite a different mood. It is an instrumental movement from the springtime scene entitled simply "Dance."[7] All the same, "Dance" shares a great deal in common with "O Fortune." Orff opens the movement with a series of dramatic chords, after which he uses ostinatos to underpin a melody that is itself full of melodic repetition. And once again, that melody

Image 10.18: This pastoral illustration appears in the Carmina Burana manuscript.
Source: Wikimedia Commons
Attribution: The Yorck Project
License: Public Domain

moves primarily by step and occupies only a small range. "Dance" feels a bit more rhythmically unpredictable than "O Fortuna." This is due to the fact that the meter changes frequently, which prevents a steady pulse from being established (try tapping your toe along to the music—it should be very difficult). A further sense of liveliness is produced by metric disagreements between the ostinato and the melody: Often, the strong pulses in each layer do not line up.

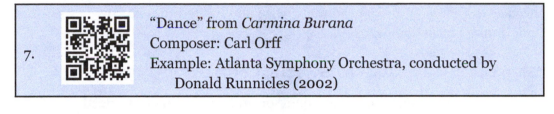

7. "Dance" from *Carmina Burana*
Composer: Carl Orff
Example: Atlanta Symphony Orchestra, conducted by
Donald Runnicles (2002)

"Dance" is in a ternary (A B A) form. The first A section features strings, which composers often employ to bring pastoral scenes to life. The flute, which carries the melody in the B section, is even better suited to shepherd life. This middle passage is unusual, for we hear only the flute and timpani—a rare paring to be sure. Finally, the A melody returns in the horns and trumpets. As in "O Fortune," the music builds to an exciting and noisy final chord.

"Once I had Dwelt on Lakes"

Our third example will provide still further contrast, for it features one of the humorous texts that Orff chose to include in his cantata. "Once I had Dwelt on Lakes"[8] is narrated from the perspective of a roast swan as he awaits his fate on a banquet table:

8. "Once I had Dwelt on Lakes" from *Carmina Burana*
Composer: Carl Orff
Performance: Gerhard Stolze, Orchestra and choir of the
Deutsche Oper Berlin, conducted by Eugen Jochum (1968)

Once I had dwelt on lakes, once I had been beautiful, when I was a swan. Poor wretch! Now black and well roasted!

The cook turns me back and forth; I am roasted to a turn on my pyre; now the waiter serves me. Poor wretch! Now black and well roasted!

Now I lie on the dish, and I cannot fly; I see the gnashing teeth. Poor wretch! Now black and well roasted!

Translation by Gavin Betts. Used with permission.

Each of the three stanzas concludes with a refrain, which is sung by the men of the choir. The part of the swan is played by the tenor soloist, who sings at the top of his range. The resulting sound, which is often tense and pinched, can be heard as an imitation of the swan's own voice. We also hear the swan in the opening bassoon solo—played at the top of *that* instrument's range. Finally, the fluttering sound in the strings and flute might capture the swan's trepidation as he contemplates his impending fate. Once again, repetitive melodies—melodies that are also, in the case of that sung by the choir, stepwise and limited to a narrow **range**—are underpinned by ostinatos.

"It is the Time of Joy" & "Sweetest of Men"

Finally, we will examine a selection—or, to be fair, a pair of selections—from the scene dealing with love. We are not talking about romantic love, however, but carnal lust. The texts to "It is the Time of Joy"[9] and the short response number "Sweetest of Men"[10] outline the courtship of a woman by a young man who is consumed with desire. She ultimately accedes:

9.		"It is the Time of Joy" from *Carmina Burana* Composer: Carl Orff Performance: Gundula Janowitz, Dietrich Fischer-Dieskau, Orchestra and choir of the Deutsche Oper Berlin, conducted by Eugen Jochum (1968)
10.		"Sweetest of Men" from *Carmina Burana* Composer: Carl Orff Performance: Gundula Janowitz, Orchestra of the Deutsche Oper Berlin, conducted by Eugen Jochum (1968)

It is the time of joy, O maidens, now enjoy yourselves together, O young men.
Refrain: Oh, oh, I am all aflower, now with my first love I am all afire, a new love it is of which I am dying.
I am elated when I say yes; I am depressed when I say no. **Refrain**
In the time of winter a man is sluggish, when spring is in his heart he is wanton. **Refrain**
My innocence plays with me, my shyness pushes me back. **Refrain**
Come, my mistress, with your joy; come, come, fair girl, already I die. **Refrain**

Sweetest of men,
I give myself to you wholly!

Translation by Gavin Betts. Used with Permission.

This musical example is dominated by percussion and piano, which keep up a lively rhythmic accompaniment. The verses are sung alternately by the women and the men of the choir, while the **refrain** is sung alternately by the baritone soloist and the boys' choir. The complete vocal forces come together for the final verse/refrain pair. Every pair is sung to the same melody, but the timbral variations introduced by the changes in singers keeps the music from getting stale.

"Sweetest of Men" could hardly be more different from "It is the Time of Joy." In place of the percussive ostinatos, the orchestra sustains a single harmony. The solo soprano soars to the top of her range, carrying the fifth vowel of her text through a long passage of notes. This is known as a **melismatic** passage, and it contrasts sharply with the **syllabic** character of the previous number, in which every syllable was paired with a single note. The selection can be heard in fairly graphic terms as the satisfying fulfillment of a sexual encounter, which was communicated by all the bumps and bangs of the previous number.

This particular moment almost got Orff into trouble with the authorities, for the Nazi regime did not take kindly to the glamorization of improper social behaviors. (The Soviet regime was equally prudish, as exemplified by its response to Dmitri Shostakovich's opera *Lady Macbeth of the Mtsenk District*, which is detailed in the final section of this chapter.) In fact, Herbert Gerigk, a leading ideological voice in the Nazi Party, registered several objections to *Carmina Burana* when he reviewed the premiere: He found fault in the language of the text, which was incomprehensible to German listeners; the primitive character of the music, which he considered to reflect the influence of jazz (a musical style that was widely denigrated and strictly forbidden); and the "loose morals" on exhibit in the cantata.

Nonetheless, it was another interpretation of *Carmina Burana* that won official acceptance. The Nazi official Horst Büttner regarded the work as exemplifying "the radiant, strength-filled life-joy of the folk." He also pointed out that the poems were artifacts of German folk heritage, and therefore to be treasured as national literature. Finally, Büttner connected the rhythms and melodies with German folk music, thereby identifying *Carmina Burana* as an authentic expression of German identity.

When used in the context of political gatherings, *Carmina Burana* had the added value of encouraging powerful and unambiguous collective emotional reactions. It seemed to echo Hitler's call for Germans to "think with your blood." This was the kind of music that could inspire support for the regime on a purely physical level.

MUSIC AS POLITICAL PROTEST

Just as music can be used to express confidence in a candidate or government or to win support for a political cause, it can also be used to protest the actions of those in power. Because these two objectives are similar, campaign songs and protest songs generally have certain characteristics in common. The elements that usually make for a good campaign song—non-specific lyrical content, catchy melody, energetic rhythms, hopeful mood—also tend to make for an effective protest song. In both cases, after all, the song is supposed to inspire those who hear it to rally in support of a political action.

However, there are some important differences in the ways that campaign songs and protest songs are used. Campaign songs are usually broadcast over loudspeakers at live events or perhaps performed by a band. They might also be included in television advertisements. In all of these contexts, campaign songs are passively consumed by the audience. They play an important role in setting a mood and establishing a campaign's brand, but their potential effectiveness is limited to their sound and lyrics.

Protest songs, on the other hand, are most often performed by the protesters themselves. They are not passively consumed but collectively voiced in a **participatory** context. Therefore, the sound of the song as a commercial product is not of paramount importance. What *does* matter is that the song be fairly simple in terms of text and melody so that participants can quickly learn it, and so that even the least accomplished singer will be able to join in.

Protest songs differ from campaign songs in another important way as well, for they are likely to be expressly written for political use. At the same time, protest songs are often coopted by movements that are far removed from their original context and may or may not have the explicit support of the song's creator. And, just as a non-political song can be adopted by a campaign, a non-political song can be deployed in support of a protest movement. Once again, therefore, we will see how creative artists cannot be guaranteed to retain control over the meaning or use of their own works.

Protest Songs

Florence Reece, "Which Side Are You On?"

Our first example was certainly intended as a protest—and a pointed, personal protest at that. The creator of this song was not a popular performing artist but an impoverished union organizer in rural Kentucky, unknown outside of her own community until long after the song was written. She did not have commercial success on her mind but, rather, the immediate survival of her family, which had been targeted for destruction by a powerful oppressive force.

Florence Reece (1900-1986) was the daughter and wife of coal miners. Born in Tennessee, she married Sam Reece at the age of sixteen and moved with him to Harlan County, Kentucky. It was here that a bloody conflict between mine workers and owners, now known as the Harlan County War, would play out between 1931 and 1939. In addition to fighting to protect her family, Florence documented the period in poems and songs that both reflected her desperate situation and called on fellow members of the mining community to maintain the struggle.

During World War I, the coal mining industry enjoyed a boom in production. Coal, after all, was needed for the production of steel, of which the war effort required an endless supply. Although coal companies saw the greatest profits, individual coal miners also lived comfortably during this period: Because there was enormous demand for their labor, the United Mine Workers (UMW)—the union that represented coal miners—was able to secure high wages on their behalf.

Following Armistice, however, coal companies failed to scale back their production, with the result that the market was overwhelmed and prices dropped precipitously. Many coal miners were fired, while those who remained on the job saw their wages cut again and again. Then, in 1929, the Great Depression hit, and conditions for mine workers became even worse. The UMW found that it had lost its bargaining power and withdrew, leaving workers without advocacy.

Miners who lost their jobs or found the conditions intolerable could not simply leave. To begin with, work was scarce in the early 1930s. It was the structure of the mining industry, however, that posed the greatest challenges. Miners lived in company towns that were owned and operated by the mining conglomerates. They could not buy their own homes and were reliant on the company store for household goods and groceries—stores that often inflated prices and encouraged mine employees to go into debt. Miners who wanted to leave often were not able to do so, since they owed money to their employer, while those who lost their jobs simultaneously became homeless.

Another union stepped in to fight on behalf of the desperate miners, whose labor was still necessary to keep the industry going. That union, the National Miners Union, was backed by the American Communist Party, and it was

Image 10.19: These Harlan County miners were photographed in 1946.
Source: Wikimedia Commons
Attribution: Russell Lee
License: Public Domain

Image 10.20: Miners endured difficult living conditions with no prospects for future wealth.
Source: Wikimedia Commons
Attribution: Russell Lee
License: Public Domain

Image 10.21: Coal mining was difficult and dangerous work.
Source: Wikimedia Commons
Attribution: Russell Lee
License: Public Domain

willing to undertake extreme actions. The mine owners, on the other hand, were able to buy the support of local sheriffs, the state militia, and the court system. They even hired Chicago gangsters to take out union leaders. The ensuing conflict resulted in countless deaths on both sides, including hundreds of children and infants who starved to death or were denied medical services by the company doctors.

One particular skirmish prompted Florence Reese to create "Which Side Are You On?"[11] Sam Reece was a union leader and, therefore, a target for the company-backed law enforcement. One day, Sheriff J.H. Blair arrived at the Reece home with his men. They ransacked the house in front of Florence and her seven terrified children and then settled in to wait for Sam, with the intention of shooting him dead when he arrived. Sam, however, had been warned about the raid and did not return home that day. After the men left at nightfall, Florence tore a calendar off the wall and wrote the text to her song on the back.

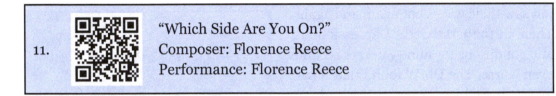

11. "Which Side Are You On?"
     Composer: Florence Reece
     Performance: Florence Reece

Florence Reece was a lyricist, not a composer, and when she wrote songs, she sang the words to familiar pre-existing melodies. For "Which Side Are You On?" she chose the melody of an old Baptist hymn, which she knew as "Lay the Lily Low." The same melody is also used for the traditional ballad known variously as "Jack Munro," "Jack Went A-Sailing,"[12] and "The Maid of Chatham." The ballad is probably of British origin and, therefore, can be considered a likely source for the hymn melody known to Reece.

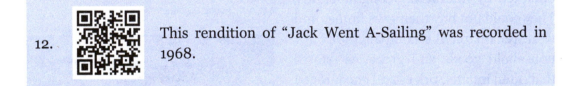

12. This rendition of "Jack Went A-Sailing" was recorded in 1968.

The hymn melody was a natural and effective choice. As a committed Christian, Reece would have been likely to select tunes that she had learned in the context of worship. This particular tune is simple and easy to sing. It is also a bit ominous, given its minor mode and descending melody—the last note of each phrase is the lowest. As a result, the tune cannily captures the spirit of Reece's message

Reece's message is straightforward and unadorned. She does not rely on poetic imagery or metaphor—and she doesn't need to. In the first stanza, she praises the union. In the second, she announces that victory is assured. In the third, she makes it clear that everyone involved in the conflict must choose a side, calling out the sheriff who threatened her family by name. In the fourth, she brings in her concern about the children of miners. In the fifth, she exhorts miners to be honest and brave. In the sixth, she proclaims her mining heritage—and incorporates her only flight of poetic fancy, referring movingly to her deceased father as "in the air and sun." And in the seventh (not heard in our recording), she returns to the theme of collective strength through unionization. The chorus—a simple question, repeated four times—drives home the message without any ambiguity.

Reece did not record her song until much later in life. When she did so, she sang in the simple, unadorned style of many Appalachian ballad singers. She sings without accompaniment, just as she would have in 1931. Her words have a force that comes not only from her personal experiences but from her knowledge that they continue to be relevant. Although the Harlan County miners emerged victorious in 1939, another conflict would take place in 1973, when 180 miners employed by the Eastover Coal Company's Brookside Mine and Prep Plant went on strike for improved working conditions and decent wages. Reece joined the strikers in solidarity, and her rendition of "Which Side Are You On?" before a crowd of miners and their families was recorded in the documentary *Harlan County, USA*.

Image 10.22: Pete Seeger, who led the Almanac Singers, went on to have a remarkable career as a singer, songwriter, and activist.
Source: Wikimedia Commons
Attribution: Fred Palumbo
License: Public Domain

Reece's song first gained mainstream popularity when it was recorded in 1941 by the Almanac Singers,[13] a **folk revival** group based in New York City and led by a young Pete Seeger. The Almanac Singers were actively engaged with left-wing politics, and they were interested in supporting the labor movement. Their version employs guitar and banjo accompaniment and features a large group of singers on the chorus—a sonic representation of the collective workers represented by the union. The song was later recorded by dozens of other artists, and it has been used in protests around the world.

13.   "Which Side Are You On?"
       Composer: Florence Reece
       Performance: The Almanac Singers (1955)

Bob Dylan, "Blowin' in the Wind"

It is not surprising that a folk revival group like the Almanac Singers would record Reece's protest song. Participants in the folk revival movement were almost universally preoccupied with social justice issues, and its singers would both record and create countless protest anthems. In fact, it is difficult to select a representative example. Bob Dylan's classic "Blowin' in the Wind,"[14] however, will serve our purpose well. It will allow us to consider the connection between style and message, to examine the typical characteristics of a successful protest song, and to consider the ways in which a protest song can mean something to listeners (and singers) that was never intended by its creator.

14.   "Blowin' in the Wind"
        Composer: Bob Dylan
        Performance: Bob Dylan (1963)

The folk revival movement began in the 1930s, when young people in northern cities began to take an interest in the songs and tunes of rural Southern musicians. The movement was largely driven by field collectors, the most prominent of whom were the father-son team of John and Alan Lomax. Collectors would travel through rural communities recording folk artists. In fact, it was Alan Lomax who collected "Which Side Are You On?" from Florence Reece in 1937. Sometimes, collectors would actually bring rural performers up north to perform on college campuses and at folk festivals. For the most part, however, the folk revival was driven by northern musicians performing the songs they learned from field recordings, using the same acoustic instruments—especially guitar—that were common in the south.

Image 10.23: This photograph of Bob Dylan was taken at the 1963 March on Washington.
Source: Wikimedia Commons
Attribution: Rowland Scherman
License: Public Domain

Although the folk revival was sparked during the Great Depression, it did not exert mainstream influence until the 1960s, when the counterculture movement adopted folk music as a favored means of expression. The 1960s saw extraordinary social upheaval, as young people rebelled against the conservative social values of the post-WWII era, marginalized groups fought for civil rights, and anti-war activists protested US involvement in Vietnam. Folk music quickly became an important vehicle for political speech.

Most of the central figures in the folk revival did not become famous performing authentic folk music. Instead, they wrote and recorded original songs in a folk style. Perhaps the most influential and respected of these artists was Bob Dylan, who produced an extraordinary catalog of songs featuring his own evocative poetry.

Image 10.24: "Blowin' in the Wind" appeared on Dylan's second album, *The Freewheelin' Bob Dylan*.
Source: Flickr
Attribution: Martin Beek
License: CC BY-NC-ND 2.0

Dylan was regarded as a folk singer because he accompanied himself on acoustic guitar and harmonica, but he was more interested in expressing himself creatively than in preserving music of the past.

Bob Dylan was born Robert Allen Zimmerman to Midwestern Jewish parents in 1941. He moved to New York City in 1961, where he legally changed his name while still using a variety of pseudonyms to record and publish his creative work. Dylan's eponymous first album, released in 1962 by Columbia Records, consisted mostly of familiar folk and gospel songs. It was hardly a success, barely breaking even in financial terms, and skeptics within Columbia recommended that his contract be terminated. Dylan's producer stood by him, however, and his second album, *The Freewheelin' Bob Dylan* (1963), was considerably more successful. The album's songs were decidedly topical, addressing political concerns ranging from integration to the Cuban missile crisis. The first song on the album was "Blowin' in the Wind."

"Blowin' in the Wind" is in three stanzas, each of which concludes with a refrain. Each of the stanzas consists of a series of three questions, the answer to which is promised by the refrain, even though it is never in fact provided. Within each stanza, the questions become increasingly pointed and specific. The first in each set tends to be vague: It does not connect with a social issue and cannot be ascribed specific meaning. The later questions, however, begin to make explicit reference to ongoing political crises. Mentions of "cannon balls" and "deaths" clearly conjure the image of war, while the lament that some people are still not "allowed to be free" elicits scenes of oppression at home and abroad.

However, despite the growing specificity and attendant urgency of the questions, Dylan never makes the subject of his song exactly clear. He is concerned about war, but which war? He laments oppression, but whose? We can easily guess what was on his mind in 1962, when he wrote this song. The Vietnam War, which had been ongoing since 1955, was beginning to attract significant opposition in the United States, while the civil rights movement was quickly gaining momentum. Dylan became particularly involved in the struggle for racial equality. He performed at the 1963 March on Washington, and his third album, *The Times They Are a-Changin'* (1963), contained a number of songs that addressed the struggles and victories of equal rights campaigners.

We might, therefore, imagine that we know what this song meant to Dylan, but that does not mean that the significance of "Blowin' in the Wind" is limited to the Vietnam War and the civil rights movement. Dylan himself ensured that his song could speak to political issues beyond his own time and place. He did so by refraining from mentioning the social causes of his day and instead speaking in broad, almost universal terms. His concerns about war and freedom apply just as well to ancient struggles as they do to those that have yet to take place. We might draw a contrast here with Reece's song, which explicitly mentions mining and even names one of her adversaries.

Dylan's music suits his message: Each of the questions begins with the same melodic phrase and ends on an inconclusive pitch, indicating that there is more to be said, while his refrain, which promises an answer, ends on the home pitch (the tonic scale degree). The melody is highly repetitive, making it easy to learn. It also encompasses only a small vocal range and moves almost entirely by step (conjunct motion), making it easy to sing. Finally, the simple guitar accompaniment can be replicated by a moderately competent player. In short, this song, which requires neither special equipment nor advanced musical training, can be performed by almost anyone.

However, Dylan's melody also carries meaning on a deeper level. Like Reece, he did not write his melody from scratch, but rather adapted it from another song. His source, the African American **spiritual** "No More Auction Block,"[15] provides us with additional insight into what the song might mean, for "No More Auction Block" describes the relief of a formerly-enslaved person who has escaped from slavery and is no longer to be subjected to humiliations and abuses. According to Alan Lomax, the song originated in Canada, where it was sung by former slaves after the practice was abolished there. It later spread to the United States. Dylan's melody is not identical, but one can easily hear that he borrowed the opening melodic phrase. When we listen through the lens of the spiritual, we can feel even more confident about the relationship between "Blowin' in the Wind" and the civil rights movement.

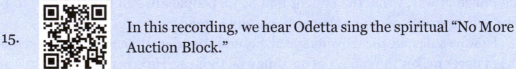

15.   In this recording, we hear Odetta sing the spiritual "No More Auction Block."

But we can't go too far in ascribing specific meaning to "Blowin' in the Wind." Dylan himself refused to explain what the song meant, or even to admit that it meant anything in particular. When the song was published in *Sing Out!* magazine in 1962, it was accompanied by the following note from Dylan:

> There ain't too much I can say about this song except that the answer is blowing in the wind. It ain't in no book or movie or TV show or discussion group. Man, it's in the wind — and it's blowing in the wind. Too many of these hip people are telling me where the answer is but oh I won't believe that. I still say it's in the wind and just like a restless piece of paper it's

got to come down some ... But the only trouble is that no one picks up the answer when it comes down so not too many people get to see and know ... and then it flies away. I still say that some of the biggest criminals are those that turn their heads away when they see wrong and know it's wrong.

In other words, "Blowin' in the Wind" is about searching for answers, not providing them.

Dylan went even further in distancing his song from the political turmoil of the early 1960s, stating clearly before its first ever performance, "This here ain't no protest song or anything like that, 'cause I don't write no protest songs." It's easy to understand why Dylan, an artist with a wide-ranging creative vision, would not want to be pigeonholed as a writer of protest songs. All the same, his claim rings hollow, especially in light of the many activists who were inspired by his song and the social movements that have adopted it.

We will examine two recordings of "Blowin' in the Wind," both made in 1963. First, we will listen to Bob Dylan's own version, which was released as a single and included as the lead track on his second album. This version was moderately successful: *The Freewheelin' Bob Dylan* peaked at 22 on the Billboard album charts. However, Dylan's songs have almost always done better when sung by other performers. We will also listen to the version by the folk trio Peter, Paul & Mary, who can be considered responsible for making "Blowin' in the Wind" a hit. Their recording reached number 2 on the Billboard singles charts.

Dylan's version is remarkably simple and unpolished. He plays a regular rhythm on the guitar, choosing the most obvious chords (he uses only three). At the end of each verse, he pauses to blow a few notes on the harmonica. His timing as a singer was always idiosyncratic, and sometimes the words don't fall on the beat, as you would expect. His voice is rough, and he doesn't seem to put any effort into expressing the meaning of the text.

The version recorded by Peter, Paul & Mary is considerably more sophisticated.[16] Although the group also accompanies their singing with guitars, they use two instruments, not one, and the guitars are played using a refined finger-picking style that is far removed from Dylan's simple strumming. We hear the guitars right at the beginning, when they provide an extended introduction to the song. Peter, Paul & Mary also chose more nuanced and compelling harmonies than Dylan had. As a result, their version is significantly more difficult for an amateur to replicate.

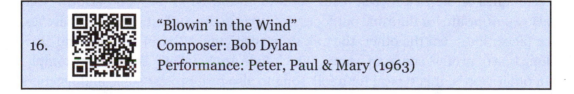

16. "Blowin' in the Wind"
Composer: Bob Dylan
Performance: Peter, Paul & Mary (1963)

All three members of the group were singers, and they used this to their advantage by varying the vocal texture phrase by phrase. The first verse begins

Image 10.25: This photograph of the folk trio Peter, Paul & Mary was taken in 1970.
Source: Wikimedia Commons
Attribution: ITA-International Talent Associates
License: Public Domain

Image 10.26: Peter, Paul & Mary had great success with their version of Dylan's "Blowin' in the Wind."
Source: Flickr
Attribution: Joe Haupt
License: CC BY-SA 2.0

in two-part harmony with Mary Travers on the melody, but grows in volume and energy when a third voice enters to underscore the final question. Then the men sing the first refrain without Mary, who subsequently sings the first question in the second verse alone. All three take the second question in unison and the third in harmony before Mary sings the second refrain as a solo. The third verse builds to a climax as Mary moves from the melody to a high harmony, after which she sings the final refrain alone. All three provide a final unison refrain to close out the recording. The changes in texture draw the listener's attention to some of the more important questions (the one about freedom is especially forceful), while also making the song more interesting.

Finally, Peter, Paul & Mary's version has a polish that is lacking in Dylan's. The rhythms are regular and predictable, while the voices of the singers are carefully controlled and perfectly in tune. This is not to say that Peter, Paul & Mary's version is better, and many people prefer Dylan's recording for its simplicity and honesty. However, this comparison gives us some insight into what makes a hit: It is not only the song that matters, but the arrangement and performance.

Bob Marley and Peter Tosh, "Get Up, Stand Up"

In our previous example, style played an important role in the construction of a successful protest song. On the one hand, the acoustic instruments and simplified techniques of the folk revival made "Blowin' in the Wind" easy to perform—and also appropriate for informal outdoor renditions in the context of rallies, marches, or picket lines. On the other, the folk style positioned "Blowin' in the Wind" in a long line of protest songs, of which "Which Side Are You On?" is an early example. In other words, it is typical for a folk song to also be a protest song, and listeners therefore have an easy time accepting "Blowin' in the Wind" in this role.

Style will also be important to our next example. Some characteristics of the **reggae** style, which relies on a range of amplified electric instruments, make "Get

Up, Stand Up" (1973)[17] somewhat more difficult to use in the context of an on-the-ground protest. At the same time, reggae itself is deeply connected with social rebellion and resistance to oppressive ruling powers—so much so that the genre itself might be considered a protest. In the case of this song, therefore, a knowledge of the reggae style and its historical context is vital to understanding the message of the music.

17.      "Get Up, Stand Up"
Composer: Bob Marley and Peter Tosh
Performance: Bob Marley and the Wailers (1973)

Reggae has been around since 1968, when it emerged as the most widely-performed and influential style of popular music in Jamaica. Reggae represented a synthesis of various music traditions of Central and North America. Jamaican listeners had easy access to American popular music, which was imported on recorded discs and broadcast on the radio, and they were particularly enthusiastic about rhythm 'n' blues and jazz. Following Jamaican independence in 1962, however, Jamaicans were increasingly interested in developing unique popular music styles that represented their national identity. The first of these were ska (an uptempo style featuring jazz instrumentation and off-beat accents) and rocksteady (a slower version of ska), both of which influenced reggae. Ska and rocksteady also drew from the Caribbean traditions of mento and calypso—as did reggae in its own turn.

The meaning of the Jamaican English term "reggae" has been much debated. It can be used to refer to a person who is poorly dressed, or to a quarrel. It has also been connected with the term "streggae," which can describe a loose woman. The term was first used in a musical context in the Maytals's 1968 song "Do the Reggay," which also established the stylistic conventions of what would become a major new genre. The lead singer of the group, Frederick "Toots" Hibbert, provided his own definition of the term: "Reggae just mean comin' from the people, an everyday thing, like from the ghetto. When you say reggae you mean regular, majority. And when you say reggae it means poverty, suffering, Rastafari, everything in the ghetto. It's music from the rebels, people who don't have what they want." Reggae music, therefore, would speak to regular Jamaicans, and it would address their rebellious desire to overthrow the forces that kept them in poverty.

Hibbert also mentions **Rastafarianism**, which is another vital ingredient to reggae. We can understand neither the reggae worldview nor the specific lyrics of reggae songs without addressing this movement. Rastafarianism can trace its roots to the "Back to Africa" movement of the 1920s. The leader of the movement was Marcus Garvey, a fiery political orator of Jamaican origin who advocated for pan-African unity. In his view, those of African descent in all parts of the world should take pride in their heritage and throw off the yoke of white colonial oppression. He sought independence for black majority colonial states but also encouraged members of the African **diaspora** to return to Africa, where he imagined the founding of a single unified African state with himself at the head. While organizing in the United States, Garvey went so far as to establish a shipping company, the Black Star Line, for the express purpose of returning African Americans to the African continent. This project, however, led to Garvey's 1923 conviction for mail fraud, after which he was deported.

Back in Jamaica, Garvey prophesied that the liberation of the entire African diaspora would be sparked by the crowning of a black king in Africa. He founded his claim in an interpretation of the Book of Revelation, which foretells the rise of the Lion of Judah. When the Ethiopian regent Ras Tafari Makonnen became Emperor Haile Selassie I in 1930, therefore, Garvey and others believed that the prophecy had been fulfilled. Selassie, whose full title includes the designation "Lion of the Tribe of Judah," traced his own lineage back to King Solomon and the Queen of Sheba.

Selassie himself was an Ethiopian Orthodox Christian, and he disdained the prophecies that were emanating from the New World. In Jamaica, however, Selassie's coronation sparked a wave of renewed black pride and confidence that the end of colonial oppression must be at hand. Selassie's former title and name

Image 10.27: This photograph of Ras Tafari Makonnen was taken a few years before he became Emperor Haile Selassie I.
Source: Wikimedia Commons
Attribution: American Colony (Jerusalem)
License: Public Domain

soon lent itself to the new movement, which was part political ideology and part religion.

Rastafarians adhere to the teachings of the Bible, which they believe to have originally been written in an Ethiopian language. They reject colonial domination and seek to recover a shared black identity. However, there is no centralized authority within the Rastafarian community, and there are no administrative hierarchies or orthodox beliefs. Rastafarians are not even agreed about the identity of Emperor Haile Selassie: Some believe that he is Christ reincarnate, while others regard him as a prophet. (The fact that Selassie was assassinated in 1974 led some to lose their faith, but devout followers maintained either that his death had been faked or that he survived in a spiritual form.)

Despite the negligible status of Rastafarianism as a religion (there are at most one million practitioners around the world), it has attracted significant attention due to the popular success of reggae music. Many Jamaican musicians of the 1960s found themselves drawn to the ideology, and reggae music soon came to embody Rastafarian identity and beliefs. Rastafarians were also quick to establish a wide variety of symbols—the green, yellow, and red colors of the Ethiopian flag, dreadlocks, and cannabis use—that helped identify practitioners to the larger community. All of these symbols came to be associated with reggae as well. When reggae gained popularity abroad following the success of the 1973 film *The Harder They Come,* a wide variety of cultural symbols were therefore available for use in identifying and promoting the new musical style.

For most people, it is the sound of reggae music that initially attracts them to the genre. All reggae songs have a moderate, laid-back tempo. They are in quadruple meter, but the emphasis is on the off-beat, which is usually marked by two sharply articulated strums on the electric guitar. The bass also plays an important role, accentuating strong beats and contributing countermelodies, while the drums hold the groove in place. Other typical instruments include the electric organ, which often fulfills a similar role to that of the guitar, and jazz-derived horns including the saxophone and trumpet.

The rhythms in reggae emerge from the interactions of these various instruments, each of which contributes one element to a complex groove. No single instrument is responsible for the rhythmic character of a song, but each has a unique role in sustaining the beat. At the same time, individual players are free to vary their rhythms, the result of which is a flexible groove that shifts in form while maintaining its essential identity. In reggae, various rhythmic patterns—termed "riddims"—have specific names and coded meanings, known only to those initiated into the tradition. The essential structure of the rhythmic texture, however, is derived from African practices and can be found in various musical traditions of the African diaspora.

We will hear this type of groove in our recording of "Get Up, Stand Up." Before considering the sound the the song, however, we must address the lyrics. The message of "Get Up, Stand Up" is embodied in its short chorus, which calls on the listener to "stand up for your rights," with the added encouragement, "don't give up the fight!" All three verses also conclude with the "stand up for your rights" refrain, which echoes both the text and music of the chorus.

While the chorus and concluding refrains are unambiguous, the three verses contain references to the Rastafarian belief system that might be lost on the uninitiated. The first verse opens with a derisive reference to a "preacher man," who symbolizes the institutionalized (and white) Christian church, which Rastafarians regard as an oppressive force. It continues on to warn that "not all that glitters is gold," a reflection of the Rastafarian disdain for worldly possessions. The second verse mocks those who await the second coming of Christ, while the third makes the observation that "almighty Jah is a living man"—both expressions that rest on the common Rastafarian belief that Emperor Haile Selassie is (or was) God incarnate.

In sum, therefore, "Get Up, Stand Up" is a song steeped in the Rastafarian tradition that calls for the listener to pursue both spiritual and political freedom.

Image 10.28: This photograph of Bob Marley was taken in 1980, at which point he was an international celebrity.
Source: Wikimedia Commons
Attribution: Ueli Frey
License: CC BY-SA 3.0

Image 10.29: Peter Tosh is pictured here in 1979.
Source: Flickr
Attribution: Rogelio A. Galaviz C.
License: CC BY-NC 2.0

The call to protest embodied in its chorus is broad and might be applied to any number of specific situations. The verses, however, outline a uniquely Rastafarian worldview that few listeners are likely to accept. In this way, "Get Up, Stand Up" might be considered a deeply flawed protest song, for it seems to be intimately tied to the time and place of its origin. While "Blowin' in the Wind" could be about any war or any oppressive situation, "Get Up, Stand Up" is explicitly about the Jamaican experience.

The creators of "Get Up, Stand Up," however, would not have seen this specificity as a flaw. They were committed to giving voice to the oppressed among the African diaspora, and they couldn't care less about whether their song could be conveniently exploited by others. "Get Up, Stand Up" was the creation of two of reggae's chief architects, Bob Marley (1945-1981) and Peter Tosh (1944-1987). The song was initially inspired by the suffering of impoverished Haitians, whose condition Marley witnessed when touring the island in the early 1970s. Marley recorded several versions of the song with his group, The Wailers, while Tosh released his own solo version. We will

Image 10.30: Bob Marley's group The Wailers, seen here performing at London's Crystal Palace in 1980, contained several guitars, electric bass, electric organ, a variety of percussion instruments, and three female backup singers.
Source: Wikimedia Commons
Attribution: User "Tankfield"
License: CC BY-SA 3.0

consider the first recording of "Get Up, Stand Up," which appeared on The Wailers' 1973 album *Burnin'*.

The track begins with a few drum hits, after which the basic pulse is established by various electric guitars. The groove—with all of its parts in place—enters along with Marley's voice. Although most of the instruments in the band are occupied with the groove, a guitar—the sound of which is processed by a "wah-wah" pedal—occasionally interjects melodic riffs, while an electric bass periodically fills in between sung phrases. Marley's voice is recorded on several tracks, which allows him to converse with himself in a **call-and-response** style: While one Marley sings the chorus, another provides encouragement. His informal yet impassioned vocal delivery is meant to connect emotionally with the listener and spur them into action. The idea of collectivity is reinforced by **double-tracking** on the chorus. Because we actually hear more than one voice singing the call to protest, we easily imagine a crowd—and just as easily join in ourselves. The chorus, after all, is very easy to sing. It contains only four pitches, and the melody outlines the stepwise ascent of a scale.

The harmonies, likewise, are easy to play. The entire song essentially rests on a single minor **triad**—a harmony that reinforces the seriousness of the song's message, and that literally anyone could provide using a guitar or piano. Here, however, we run into some difficulty, for while it is easy to replicate the harmony and melody of the chorus to "Get Up, Stand Up," it is very difficult to replicate the style. To do so requires a broad array of electric instruments, each played by an expert with perfect timing and a deep knowledge of their role in the groove. This can only be accomplished in a staged setting. While Peter Yarrow was able to strum his guitar and lead a sing-along of "Blowin' in the Wind" at a 2011 Occupy Wall Street protest,[18] for example, "Get Up, Stand Up" is more likely to be blasted over loudspeakers, as it was during the 2011 teachers' strike in Madison, WI.[19]

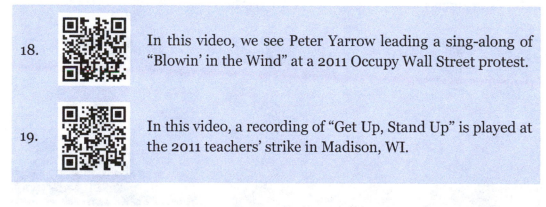

18. In this video, we see Peter Yarrow leading a sing-along of "Blowin' in the Wind" at a 2011 Occupy Wall Street protest.

19. In this video, a recording of "Get Up, Stand Up" is played at the 2011 teachers' strike in Madison, WI.

DMITRI SHOSTAKOVICH, SYMPHONY NO. 5

One of the most famous pieces of protest music in the European concert tradition might not have been a protest at all. Experts still debate the meaning of Shostakovich's Symphony No. 5. Some believe that it was a harsh rejection of the totalitarian regime under which he lived and worked, while others are skeptical of this interpretation. Because Symphony No. 5 is a piece of **absolute music** (instrumental music that does not narrate an explicit story), it can be interpreted in many different ways. While this leaves the message in question, it has also permitted the work to have a powerful impact on generations of listeners.

Music in the Soviet Union

Dmitri Shostakovich (1906-1975) was born shortly before the 1917 Bolshevik Revolution, in which the longstanding Czarist regime was overthrown and the Soviet Union was born. The revolution brought hope to many Russians. Life under the Czars had been difficult for all but the aristocracy, with no chance for upward mobility and little freedom. The new government promised to improve the lot of Russia's working class, bringing opportunities for education and economic success.

Soon, however, the Soviet Union ran into trouble. After the first decade, economic hardships led to dissatisfaction. At the same time, Joseph Stalin, who had become head of the government followed the death of Vladimir Ilyich Lenin in 1924, set out to consolidate his power. While the Soviet Union was meant to be governed by a committee, Stalin soon had absolute control. Part of his strategy was to deflect blame for the nation's struggles onto others. In the 1930s, he

Image 10.31: This photograph of Dmitri Shostakovich was taken in 1950.
Source: Wikimedia Commons
Attribution: Roger & Renate Rössing, credit Deutsche Fotothek
License: CC BY-SA 3.0 Germany

Image 10.32: In this photograph we see Lenin hearing the demands of the masses.
Source: Wikimedia Commons
Attribution: Internet Archive Book Images
License: Public Domain

Image 10.33: Stalin, pictured here in 1941, quickly consolidated his power and became a dictator.
Source: Wikimedia Commons
Attribution: Unknown
License: Public Domain

held a series of public "show trials" in which prominent members of the government were convicted of crimes against the Soviet people. In this way he purged the government of all those who did not support him while positioning himself as an advocate of the people.

This is the environment in which Shostakovich finished his education and began his career. Shostakovich gained international fame at the age of 19, when his Symphony No. 1 was well received not only in the Soviet Union but in Europe as well. At first, unsurprisingly, the young composer produced music in support of the government. Many of his early works explicitly praised Soviet leaders and celebrated the revolution. It seems that he personally felt optimistic about his nation's future.

The arts, however, faced difficult times under Stalin. Stalin believed in the power of artists to influence public opinion and encourage dissent. For this reason, he went to great lengths to keep creative workers under control. He did so through a combination of censorship, intimidation, and outright murder.

Stalin's strategy for taking control of the music establishment was very clever indeed. He began in 1929 by reforming the nation's music conservatories (prestigious schools that trained performers, conductors, scholars, and composers). His first move was to fire the faculty and replace them with partisans. Next he changed the admission standards, such that only students from working-class backgrounds were permitted to attend. These reforms were to be short lived, but he had made his point. When the professors were allowed to return to their posts, they understood that Stalin had total power over their careers (and lives) and were ready to fall into line.

In 1932, Stalin formed the Union of Soviet Composers (USC), a national organization in which all composers were required to participate. The purpose of the USC was to ensure that members only created music that upheld the values of the government and portrayed it in a positive light. Members were required to hold each other accountable and report any deviant behavior to the authorities. With all of the composers living in fear and spying on one another, Stalin was in a position to dictate the messages that were being broadcast in concert halls and opera houses.

All composers were required to uphold the doctrine of **Socialist Realism**. Exactly what constituted Socialist Realism was never made entirely clear, which is what gave the doctrine its power. Stalin always had the final say concerning any individual work, and his judgment alone could determine whether the composer had met the required standard or not. All artistic works, however, were expected to portray the communist revolution in a positive light. They were to be optimistic and uplifting. And they were certainly not permitted to criticize the Soviet Union or depress the consumer. Stalin also required that concert music be accessible to all citizens, and he preferred that it be based on popular or folk styles. If a musical work was condemned as **formalist**, then it had failed to achieve these goals, and the composer would face serious repercussions.

Shostakovich's Condemnation

Following the success of his Symphony No. 1, Shostakovich continued to climb the ranks of Soviet composers. By the 1930s, he was certainly the best known and most influential. When he finally ran afoul of the government, therefore, it was a major event.

In 1934, Shostakovich premiered an opera (his second) entitled *Lady Macbeth of the Mtsenk District*. The opera was based on an 1865 novella by Nicolai Leskov that centered on Katerina, the neglected wife of a well-to-do merchant. In the novella, Katerina has an affair that ultimately leads to her and her lover committing a series of murders to protect their secret. After they are captured, convicted, and sent to a prison work camp, the man leaves Katerina for another female prisoner. Overcome with fury and grief, Katerina seizes him and leaps into an icy river, where they both perish.

In short, *Lady Macbeth of the Mtsenk District* featured a typical operatic narrative, full of romance and violence and ending in tragedy. The opera was a huge success in Leningrad and Moscow, performing to enthusiastic audiences for two years. Then, in 1936, Stalin himself attended a performance in Moscow. He had recently attended a performance of Ivan Dzerzhinsky's opera *Quiet Flows the Don*—an overtly pro-government work with little artistic merit. (Ironically, much of the opera had been orchestrated by Shostakovich, who stepped in to help his

Image 10.34: This photograph was taken at the Stockholm premiere of *Lady Macbeth of the Mtsenk District* in 1935.
Source: Wikimedia Commons
Attribution: Unknown
License: Public Domain

less-adept colleague.) Stalin publicly demonstrated his support, giving the piece a standing ovation and insisting upon meeting the composer. Nine days later, he saw *Lady Macbeth*. This time, Stalin did not even stay to the end.

The next day, an article entitled "Muddle Instead of Music" appeared in *Pravda*, the official government newspaper. The article was unsigned, but readers understood that it spoke for Stalin himself. The article began by condemning Lady Macbeth in terms of subject matter and musical expression. The opera celebrated corruption, reveled in degradation, and lacked musical clarity. Next the author began to attack past works of Shostakovich, arguing that he had been working against the doctrine of Socialist Realism for many years. Finally, the article included a clear warning for the composer: If Shostakovich did not mend the error in his ways, he might find himself in serious trouble.

This anonymous article raises some questions. Why did *Lady Macbeth* come under condemnation two years after it had premiered and after it had been well received? How was it that many of Shostakovich's pieces that had previously been accepted as "good" were suddenly denounced as "bad"? What was the purpose of this article? Although we can never know for sure, it seems likely that Shostakovich had simply become too successful—and therefore too powerful. With a single anonymous article, Stalin was able to put him in his place.

The article meant an immediate halt to all aspects of Shostakovich's career. Performances of his work were cancelled and commissions were withdrawn. The composer himself called off the premiere of his Symphony No. 4, which had been

СУМБУР ВМЕСТО МУЗЫКИ

Об опере «Леди Макбет Мценского уезда»

Image 10.35: This is the *Pravda* article, "Muddle Instead of Music," that stalled Shostakovich's career and threatened his life.
Source: Wikimedia Commons
Attribution: User "Huydang2910"
License: CC BY-SA 4.0

about to take place. He lost all standing in the Union of Soviet Composers and was essentially blacklisted.

Shostakovich also feared for his life. In fact, for a month following the publication of the article he spent nights on his porch so that the police would not wake up his children when they came to arrest him. His fears were justified, for many other composers had already disappeared, having been taken away to prisons or work camps. However, the police did not come, and after a time Shostakovich's thoughts turned to the revitalization of his career. In order to be readmitted to the music establishment, he needed to be formally rehabilitated. This process required a public apology and the creation of a new work that would demonstrate his contrition. With rehabilitation in mind, he began work on his Symphony No. 5.

Symphony No. 5

When Symphony No. 5 premiered in Leningrad in 1937, it was accompanied by another article, this time signed by the composer. The article was entitled "An artist's creative response to just criticism." In it, Shostakovich (or, more likely, a government agent writing on his behalf) admitted that he had strayed from the path illuminated by Socialist Realism but proclaimed that he had seen the error in his ways and desired to reform. He described Symphony No. 5 as an autobiographical account of his personal suffering and rebirth, culminating in a return to optimism.

The **symphony** does indeed follow a general trajectory from darkness to light—the same trajectory as Beethoven's Symphony No. 5, which clearly served as a model (see Chapter 7). The first movement is angsty and tormented. Its jagged melodies and sparse instrumentation seem to portray devastation and hopelessness. The brief second movement is a bizarre waltz. The third and fourth movements, however, bring the listener through catharsis to a possible triumph, and it is these that we will examine closely.

Movement III

According to reports, the audience wept throughout the third movement of Symphony No. 5.[20] The music is certainly sorrowful. A dirge-like tempo combines with winding melodies in the minor mode to express an unmistakable despair. Sometimes the instruments imitate speech, as if they are attempting to put into words an emotion that cannot be spoken. Shostakovich's orchestration is sparse: He includes only strings, harp, and a few solo winds, each of which take their turn with the melody.

20.  Symphony No. 5, Movement III
Composer: Dmitri Shostakovich
Performance: San Francisco Symphony, conducted by
Michael Tilson Thomas (2009)

However, there is another explanation for the listeners' reaction. In this movement, Shostakovich captures the sound of Russian Orthodox funeral music.[21] This would have resonated with his audience on several levels. To begin with, times were very difficult in the late 1930s, as the Soviet population was devastated by famine and disease. Everyone in the hall knew someone who had died, and everyone was mourning. At the same time, the government had abolished the Russian Orthodox religion and closed the churches. Nobody had heard this music for decades. As such, it also represented the past and all that had been lost. Despite its portrayals of agony, however, the third movement concludes on a note of hope. The final minutes are calm, and the closing chords are in the major mode.

21.   This funeral chant by Pavel Chesnokov is typical of Russian Orthodox music.

Movement IV

Symphony No. 5, Movement IV
Composer: Dmitri Shostakovich
Performance: The New York Philharmonic, conducted
    by Leonard Bernstein (1959)

Symphony No. 5, Movement IV
Composer: Dmitri Shostakovich
Performance: Royal Liverpool Philharmonic
    Orchestra conducted by Vasily Petrenko (2000)

Bernstein	Petrenko	What to listen for
0'00	0'00"	The finale starts with a trill in the winds that leads to pounding timpani and an aggressive brass theme; the energy continues to grow as the tempo increases
3'03"	3'23"	The tempo slows and the energy dissipates
4'46"	5'24"	The violins quote from Shostakovich's song "Rebirth"
6'40"	7'42"	The build to the Coda begins; Bernstein takes a quick tempo from the start, while Petrenko takes a relaxed tempo
8'10"	10'54"	The Coda begins; Bernstein's tempo is more than twice that of Petrenko

The fourth movement begins with a terrifying crash, as pounding drums introduce a militaristic minor-mode theme in the brass. The music grows in excitement for several minutes before giving way to a period of calm. In this middle section, Shostakovich introduces a **quote** from a song he had composed years before using a text by the poet Alexander Pushkin. The title of the song is, in fact, "Rebirth," and it describes the process of peeling away an outer layer accumulated over time to reveal the true substance beneath. After this interlude, the music regains momentum, building to a dramatic major-mode conclusion. It is here, however, that we must pause to debate what this music really means.

The closing passage of Symphony No. 5 features the ringing, high notes of trumpets, backed up by the entire orchestra. Played at a fast tempo, as it often is, the music is thrilling and triumphant. However, this approach to performing the **coda** seems to have derived from a misprint in the first published version of the symphony, which indicated a lively tempo of 188 quarter notes per minute. In reality, Shostakovich wanted this passage to be performed at a tempo of 184 eighth notes per minute, which, at less than half of the misprinted tempo, is quite slow. At this speed, the music sounds not triumphant but painful. The trumpet players agonize as they blast out their high notes, while the string players saw back and forth for minutes on end. One can literally hear the suffering of the musicians. When the symphony finally ends, it is with a sensation of exhaustion, not overcoming, as if the orchestra has been beaten into submission. Some commentators have described the passage as a false smile, put on because the authorities have required as much—but not a true representation of joy.

What does it mean?

The controversy over the tempo is only part of the story. For many decades, fans of Shostakovich have wanted to hear Symphony No. 5 as protest music and to believe that the composer was defying the government. They received confirmation in 1979, when Soviet musicologist Solomon Volkov published a book entitled *Testimony*. Volkov claimed that he had sat with Shostakovich during his final weeks and written down the composer's reminiscences. In *Testimony*, Volkov confirmed that Shostakovich had always stood in opposition to the Soviet regime and that Symphony No. 5 was indeed meant to protest its oppressive rule. However, Volkov was almost immediately discredited by Shostakovich's wife, who said that he and her husband were hardly even acquainted. Few continue to take his account seriously.

The response following the concert was also mixed. Some critics did not feel that Shostakovich had successfully communicated the personal metamorphosis outlined in his article. The third movement, they felt, was simply too sad, while the fourth movement failed to offer the transformative rebirth that was promised. However, the audience was thrilled, and gave the symphony a thirty-minute standing ovation. Perhaps for this reason, the government officially accepted Shostakovich's apology and declared him rehabilitated. He was able to return to his work—although with the knowledge that Stalin could end his career (and his life) if he failed to keep in line.

The controversy surrounding Symphony No. 5 is possible because of its status as absolute music. On the one hand, it is just a symphony—just music, just sound. It is titled with a number, and the movements are marked only with their tempos. It is therefore impossible to prove that the music is about one thing or another. The symphony's various contexts, however, which include its role as Shostakovich's rehabilitation piece, the accompanying article, the musical references, and its expressive language, give us a great deal of material to use in debate. The symphony must be about something. To this day, however, noone has conclusively proven what Shostakovich meant to communicate with his Symphony No. 5.

RESOURCES FOR FURTHER LEARNING

Print

Hevener, John W. *Which Side Are You On?: The Harlan County Coal Miners, 1931-1939*. University of Illinois Press, 2002.

Hilburn, Robert. *Paul Simon: The Life*. Simon & Schuster, 2018.

Kasper, Eric T., and Benjamin Schoening, eds. *You Shook Me All Campaign Long: Music in the 2016 Presidential Election and Beyond*. University of North Texas, 2018.

McDougal, Dennis. *Dylan: The Biography*. Wiley, 2014.

Schoening, Benjamin, and Eric T. Kasper. *Don't Stop Thinking About the Music: The Politics of Songs and Musicians in Presidential Campaigns*. Lexington Books, 2011.

Taruskin, Richard. *Music in the Early Twentieth Century: The Oxford History of Western Music*. Oxford University Press, 2009.

Turino, Thomas. Music as Social Life: The Politics of Participation. University of Chicago Press, 2008.

White, Timothy. *Catch a Fire: The Life of Bob Marley*. Holt Paperbacks, 2006.

Wilson, Elizabeth. *Shostakovich: A Life Remembered*. Second edition. Princeton University Press, 2006.

Yurchenco, Henrietta. "Trouble in the Mines: A History in Song and Story by Women of Appalachia." *American Music*, Vol. 9, No. 2 (1991): 209-224.

Zanes, Warren. *Petty: The Biography*. Griffin, 2016.

Online

Trax on the Trail: http://www.traxonthetrail.com/

Dana Gorzelany-Mostak et al., "Making Trax in 2016 and Beyond," *Bulletin* of the Society for American Music, Volume XLIV, No. 3 (Fall 2018): https://www.american-music.org/general/custom.asp?page=Bulletin443Fall2018

NPR, "'A Song For Any Struggle': Tom Petty's 'I Won't Back Down' Is An Anthem Of Resolve": https://www.npr.org/transcripts/721228788?storyId=721228788?storyId=721228788

Unit 5

FUNCTIONAL MUSIC

Music for Spiritual Expression

Esther M. Morgan-Ellis

INTRODUCTION

Religious practitioners around the world have long used music to express their spiritual convictions. Music plays a particularly significant role in the context of worship. This is hardly surprising: Music has the power to encourage a wide variety of emotional states, ranging from meditative calm to frenzied excitement. It can help participants in worship to feel close to each other and to their deity. It also aids in the memorization and communal recitation of texts, which often define religious practice. Individual creative artists also draw inspiration from their religious convictions, even if the music they produce is not intended for the purpose of facilitating worship.

In this chapter, we will explore a variety of examples related to Christian worship and beliefs. The focus on Christianity is the result of the Western and classical bias of this text. Christianity has been the dominant religion of Europe since the 4th century, when it was legalized by the Roman emperor Constantine the Great. Most of the influential composers in the classical tradition belonged to Christian denominations, and many wrote beautiful music for use in church services. As a result, church music through the ages has both reflected and shaped broader musical practices. The stylistic variety of this music is nearly infinite. This variety results from the combined forces of general musical taste, the requirements of religious authorities, and the needs and histories of congregations.

This chapter will be dedicated to the examination of worship music from different eras. Although today we are more likely to hear most of this music in concert halls or on recordings, much of it was first intended for practical use in church services. To understand how this music came to be and what it meant in its time and place, we will consider each example in its religious context.

HILDEGARD OF BINGEN, "O STRENGTH OF WISDOM"

Histories of European music almost always begin with the chants that were used in medieval Catholic churches. This is for the simple reason that **Gregorian chant**, as it is most commonly known, was the first music to be written down using the early form of staff notation from which modern musical notation is descended.

As such, it is the earliest European music to have been preserved, and therefore the earliest music that is available for close examination.

Gregorian Chant

Gregorian chant constitutes an enormous body of music for use in Catholic worship services. In musical terms, it is fairly simple to characterize. The rhythms of Gregorian chant are determined by the natural stresses of the text, and it therefore does not have a regular pulse or meter. The melodies tend to have a small range and feature conjunct motion, making them accessible to untrained singers. Gregorian chants are often in modes other than major and minor, which can make them sound unusual to modern ears. Finally, Gregorian chants are **monophonic**, meaning that each was written down as a single, unaccompanied vocal line to be sung by a group in unison or by a soloist. (Although we known that countermelodies and accompaniments were often improvised, these were not recorded using notation.)

The name "Gregorian chant" derives from a popular legend concerning the origins of this body of music. According to tradition, the Holy Spirit regularly visited Pope Gregory I in the form of a dove so as to impart divine wisdom. Following the unification of state and church powers as the Holy Roman Empire in 800, the entire body of chant began to be attributed to Gregory, and was thereafter named for him. This attribution—which was taken as fact by most believers—served an important purpose, for it suggested that the style of chant preferred in Rome came straight from God. However, there are some problems with this story. The practices of Gregorian chant predated Gregory I, who served as Pope from 590 to 604, by centuries, and it continued to grow and develop long after his reign. In fact, it is today considered unlikely that Gregory I contributed anything to the repertoire that bears his name.

Image 11.1: This 12th-century manuscript illumination shows the Holy Spirit, in the form of the dove, whispering into the ear of Pope Gregory I.
Source: Wikimedia Commons
Attribution: Unknown
License: Public Domain

The use of chant is common across many religious traditions. Within Christianity, there are a variety of chant styles, including Russian Orthodox chant, the Byzantine chant of Greece, Ethiopian Orthodox chant, and Anglican chant. In Judaism, congregants chant from the Torah. In Islam, the call to prayer is chanted five times a day from the minaret of the mosque. In Buddhism, monks chant together to facilitate their meditative practice. In Hinduism, practitioners chant when they perform religious rituals in the home. All of these forms of chant have elements in common, due to the fact that each uses the human voice to sound a sacred text on an occasion of great solemnity.

Image 11.2: These Buddhist monks are chanting as part of a religious ceremony.
Source: Flickr
Attribution: Joy Holland
License: CC BY 2.0

Gregorian chant began to develop in the Benedictine monasteries of Italy, the first of which was founded by St. Benedict of Nursia in 529. All monks and nuns withdraw from the world to dedicate their lives to God by means of regular prayer and humble living. Those belonging to Benedictine orders live according to the Rule of St. Benedict, a book that describes the organization of monasteries and monastic life. In particular, the Rule of St. Benedict punctuates each day with eight worship services known as the **Canonical Hours**. Each of the Hours has a different purpose and contents, but all include the chanting of Psalms—all 150 of which are chanted each week. The Hours also include other types of chant, the texts of which are in Latin and are primarily derived from the Bible.

But why chant? All of these texts could just as easily be recited. What does the act of singing contribute to the worship experience? There are a number of

Image 11.3: Monasteries, like this 9th-century example in Armenia, were often built in remote locations so that monks and nuns could fully remove themselves from society.
Source: Wikipedia
Attribution: User "Stevage"
License: CC BY-SA 3.0

good reasons for which monks began to chant. To begin with, the act of communal singing creates a shared physical experience. Participants breathe together and their heart rates begin to coordinate. Singing also has a calming effect. In addition, singing helps with the memorization of text. Although monastics were often literate and had access to books, they did not usually read words (or music) in the context of worship. Books were valuable and rare, and were reserved for close study, not daily use. Singing also helps words to carry through a large space—such as the cavernous interior of a medieval church. Finally, singing helped the monks to stay awake. Monastic life allowed for very little sleep, and several of the Canonical Hours took place when most would rather be in bed.

Benedictines and other Catholics had been chanting for centuries before any of this music was written down. The Catholic church first became concerned with recording its repertoire of chant after the founding of the Holy Roman Empire in 800. As the church spread across Europe, the authorities in Rome began to worry about losing control over distant congregations. In order to maintain centralized authority and prevent churches from breaking away, it was necessary for the **liturgy**—all of the words, music, and actions that constitute church services—to be standardized. Texts could be written down and actions described, but music remained ephemeral.

Before the development of music notation, chants were passed on and preserved by means of **oral tradition**. Practitioners would learn and memorize the music through repeated hearings. A monk or priest could then bring the chant to a distant community and teach it to the Christians there. This was risky, however, for music in the oral tradition usually changes over time and distance as individual musicians forget how it goes, commit errors, or make intentional alterations. Catholic authorities worried that the emergence of unique musical traditions would lead churches to desire independence in other ways as well.

A solution to this problem was finally recorded around 1026 by the Italian monk Guido of Arezzo. Guido sought to create a system by which monks and choristers could more easily learn Gregorian chants. To facilitate learning, he assigned syllables to the first six pitches of what today we call the scale. These syllables—ut, re, mi, fa, sol, and la—were drawn from the Latin text to a hymn, and they are still in use today ("ut" was replaced by the more singable "do" in the 17th century). He then began positioning the pitches on a lined staff that indicated their relative distance from one another. Guido's system of notation was not quite like that in use today: His staff had only four lines, his noteheads looked quite different, and he had no way of indicating rhythms. Modern notation, however, is directly descended from this medieval invention.

Image 11.4: Although this example dates from about 200 years after Guido of Arezzo, it illustrates the principles of his music notation system.
Source: Wikimedia Commons
Attribution: User "Juandelaencina"
License: Public Domain

Beginning in the 11th century, therefore, the melodies of Gregorian chant could be preserved on paper. Although we take musical notation for granted today, it transformed the development of music in the Western world. For the Catholic church, it offered a guarantee that Gregorian chants would be

Image 11.5: This famous image from *Scivias* portrays Hildegard receiving a vision from god.
Source: Wikimedia Commons
Attribution: Unknown
License: Public Domain

sung in the same way across Europe. Over time, however, notation would develop to allow for the construction and preservation of increasingly complex musical structures containing many simultaneous melodies, such as we will encounter with the next example. It also allowed for composers to emerge as significant and powerful figures.

All of this took time, however, and it was typical in the medieval era for chant composers to remain uncredited and anonymous. This was in part due to the myth that assigned authorship of all chant to Pope Gregory I, and in part due to the fact that individual creativity was not highly esteemed. But there is one major exception to this rule: the abbess Hildegard of Bingen (1098-1179), who not only composed dozens of extraordinary chants but also exerted far-reaching influence within the Catholic church.

Hildegard's Extraordinary Life

Hildegard was born into a minor noble family in what is today southern Germany. As a child she was pledged to the Benedictine monastery at Disibodenberg—perhaps as a tithe (tradition holds that she was the tenth child), perhaps as a ploy by her parents to gain favor, or perhaps because she had experienced spiritual visions from the age of three. Hildegard was trained by Jutta, an older woman who served as abbess at the monastery and who was also an **anchor**. As such, she was permanently enclosed in a small hut adjoining the monastery. An opening allowed food to be passed in and waste to be passed out, but Jutta herself remained in place until her death in 1136.

Hildegard was elected to replace Jutta as abbess. Disibodenberg, however, was home to monks as well, and the entire community was under the authority of the abbot. Hildegard wanted greater independence for herself and her nuns, and asked that they be allowed to move to Rupertsberg. When the abbot refused her request, Hildegard went to the archbishop instead. Although the archbishop granted his permission, the abbot still refused to allow the women to depart. Hildegard then became very ill to the point of total bodily paralysis. The abbot took this to be a sign from God, and finally permitted the nuns to leave Disibodenberg. Hildegard officially founded her monastery at Rupertsberg in 1150, followed by a second at Eibingen in 1165.

At Rupertsberg, the nuns had need for only a single male monastic, who visited in order to give communion and hear confession. This monk, Volmar, also served

Image 11.6: This illumination captures Hildegard's vision of the angelic hierarchy.
Source: Wikimedia Commons
Attribution: Unknown
License: Public Domain

Image 11.7: This illustration of the earth and heavens appeared in Hildegard's third and final theological compendium, *Book of Divine Works*.
Source: Wikimedia Commons
Attribution: Hildegard von Bingen
License: Public Domain

as Hildegard's scribe and encouraged her to record her visions. She finally did so in the 1151 compendium *Scivias* (Latin for "Know the Ways"), which included rich illustrations and a number of musical compositions. This was followed by two additional volumes of theological writing. Pope Eugene III accepted Hildegard's recorded visions as church doctrine, thereby according her unusual status in the church for a woman. Hildegard also wrote on the topics of botany and medicine, created recipes, recorded church history, and invented her own secret alphabet. She was finally recognized as a Saint and Doctor of the Church in 2012, following a centuries-long canonization process.

Hildegard's music is remarkable for its creativity and expressivity. Her best-known work is a musical drama called *Ordo Virtutum* (Order of the Virtues), which portrays the struggles of a human soul to resist mortal temptation. The play's single male role—the devil, who speaks instead of singing to indicate his nature—was probably played by Volmar. Hildegard also composed a wide variety of chants for use in church services. These are notable for their melodic complexity, extensive vocal ranges, frequent variations, and **text painting** (the practice—unusual for the time—of expressing the meaning of the text in music). In short, Hildegard broke all of the rules for chant composition, and as a result created unusually compelling works.

"O Strength of Wisdom"

We will examine her **antiphon** "O Strength of Wisdom" (Latin: "O Virtus Sapientiae").[1] An antiphon is a short chant that can be used in various ways throughout the course of the Canonical Hours. Antiphon texts were usually drawn from the Psalms, but Hildegard always wrote her own chant texts. The imagery is inspired by her visions and makes reference to her theological writings:

> O strength of Wisdom
> who, circling, circled,
> enclosing all
> in one lifegiving path,
> three wings you have:
> one soars to the heights,
> one distils its essence upon the earth,
> and the third is everywhere.
> Praise to you, as is fitting,
> O Wisdom.

> *Translation by Kate Quartano Brown.*

1.		"O Strength of Wisdom" Composer: Hildegard of Bingen Performance: Rebecca Ramsey, Armonico Consort, Choir of Gonville & Caius College, Cambridge (2019)

Divine Wisdom (Latin: Sapientia), embodied by a woman, was a prominent allegorical character in Hildegard's writings. For her, Sapientia was the life-giving force that animated the cosmos. The three-winged figure might refer to an illustration that appeared in *Scivias*, which in turn represented the "Jealousy of God" as he battled the devil. The number three is always associated with the Holy Trinity of God the Father (who "soars to the heights"), God the Son (who is found "upon the earth"), and God the Holy Spirit (who "is everywhere")—the three natures of the single creator.

Image 11.8: This illumination appeared in *Scivias*, Hildegard's first theological work.
Source: WikiArt
Attribution: Hildegard von Bingen
License: Public Domain

This chant is in the Phrygian mode, which is similar to minor but also contains a lowered second scale degree. This can give music in the Phrygian mode a dark and ominous character, but Hildegard's chant is essentially joyful in terms of text and music. It begins with a long **melisma** on the invocation "O." (A melisma is a sequence of notes sung on a single syllable.) This sets a reverential mood. She uses melismas throughout to emphasize important words—the first mention of "Sapientiae," for example, contains sixteen pitches. Melismas also draw out the text so that the listener has an opportunity to meditate on its meaning: Without them, the poem would be sung too quickly. Hildegard employs text painting when she elevates her melody to its highest note with the words "to the heights," and then down nearly to its lowest to illustrate the passage "upon the earth."

GIOVANNI DA PALESTRINA, *POPE MARCELLUS MASS*

Next we will consider a famous piece of choral music composed in the late 16th century for use in the Sistine Chapel, which is located within the Vatican in Rome and used by the Pope himself. This piece of music is not only beautiful but historically significant. To understand how it came to be composed and why it has the characteristics that it does, we must take a look at the religious politics of the era.

The Reformation

Beginning in 800, with the foundation of what would later be known as the Holy Roman Empire, the Catholic Church was the dominant religious force in Europe. During the 16th century, however, the Catholic Church began to run into trouble. One by one, factions began to break off, forming new denominations and rejecting the authority of the Pope.

Image 11.9: This portrait of Martin Luther was painted by Lucas Cranach the Elder in 1529.
Source: Wikimedia Commons
Attribution: Lucas Cranach the Elder
License: Public Domain

The first sign of defection came in 1517, when Martin Luther, a Catholic priest, posted his 95 theses to the door of a church in Wittenburg, Germany (or so the story goes—it is likely that his writings were in fact disseminated in a less flamboyant manner). Luther's 95 theses were a list of complaints about the Catholic Church. Some of his objections were to practices that amounted to outright corruption. The most famous of these was the sale of indulgences, whereby priests would forgive the sins of their parishioners in return for money. Luther also objected to the complexity of the Catholic hierarchy, which he saw a preventing Christians from experiencing a direct relationship with God. Finally, he had concerns about the services, which were in Latin (a language that was not understood by most members of the public), and the music, which he worried was overly complex and exclusive.

Luther had no intention of founding a new church. His only desire was to convince the Catholic Church to reform itself. However, he unwittingly began a chain of events that led to the creation of the Lutheran Church—the music of which we will explore in the next section. The English soon followed the Germans in abandoning Catholicism. The Anglican Church was founded in 1534 by King Henry VIII when the Pope refused to annul his marriage to Catherine of Aragon. And in Switzerland, the Calvinists were defecting from the Catholic Church during this same period.

All of this constituted a crisis for the Catholic Church, which saw the first major challenge to its authority in Europe. To address the crisis, the Pope convened an ecumenical council of high-ranking church officials to reform Catholic doctrine. The Council of Trent was held between 1545 and 1563. It debated a number of issues, and in fact adopted some of the reforms first suggested by Luther.

In 1562, the Council turned its attention to music. It determined that music for worship had come to inappropriately resemble that intended for entertainment. To correct this, the Council banned the use of musical instruments, which were associated with dancing and secular song and were therefore considered inappropriate for worship. Instruments, however, were not the only concern. Church composers had developed the habit of including popular tunes in their music, usually to demonstrate how clever they were at reworking preexisting musical material into something new. Their compositions were also becoming virtuosic and extravagant, and the Council was concerned that the focus of church music was on fancy singing, not the meaning of the text.

The Council was particularly critical of **polyphonic** music, in which each vocal part has an independent melody. In such compositions, the sopranos, altos, tenors, and basses each sing the words of the text at different times, which can make those words almost impossible to understand. Such music is beautiful, but it was perceived to be undermining the goals of the church service.

The Council of Trent briefly considered banning polyphonic music altogether, but ultimately did not, instead issuing strict rules about how such music must be composed. They required that music for the church be sober and restrained, avoiding the showy excesses that were characteristic of music for entertainment, and that the text always be comprehensible. They encouraged styles that were **syllabic**, meaning that each pitch corresponds to a single syllable of text, and **homorhythmic**, meaning that all of the voices move in rhythm together, each singing the same text at the same time.

Image 11.10: This 1588 painting by Pasquale Cati depicts the Council of Trent.
Source: Wikimedia Commons
Attribution: Pasquale Cati
License: Public Domain

Luckily for the Catholic Church, a composer was ready to take on the challenge of creating compelling music that met their requirements. Giovanni da Palestrina (1525-1594) spent his entire life in the employment of the Catholic Church. He served as organist, singer, and choir director at a variety of churches in Rome, including St. Peter's basilica, the largest church in the world. It is worth noting that women were prohibited from singing in the choir at St. Peter's. Instead, the high vocal parts were performed by boys, by men who sang in a high **falsetto** range, or by men known as **castrati** due to the fact that they had been castrated before puberty with the result that they retained voices in the soprano range. In total, Palestrina served ten Popes—a testament to the longevity and impact of his career.

Image 11.11: In this engraving we see Giovanni da Palestrina presenting his work to Pope Julius III.
Source: Wikimedia Commons
Attribution: Unknown
License: Public Domain

Palestrina and his Music

Palestrina was an advocate of a musical style known as the ***ars perfecta***, or "perfect art." Members of this school of composition believed, first and foremost, that music—like human beings—could be perfected. They sought to develop and formalize a style that was rational and aesthetically pleasing. Palestrina, after all, lived and worked at the height of the Italian **Renaissance**, a period during which the sciences and arts both flourished as intellectuals revived the values of ancient Greek and Roman civilizations. Adherents to the *ars perfecta* developed a set of rules for composers to follow. The resulting music was calm, free of dissonance, and fairly predictable. It radiated a sense of self-control and rationality. It also all sounded pretty much the same. Perfection, after all, cannot be improved upon.

Palestrina's enormous body of music is considered to exemplify the peak of achievement in the *ars perfecta* style. His compositions were particularly influential due to the invention in 1501 of a technique for printing music. Rome was home to one of the first music publication firms, meaning that Palestrina's compositions could easily be published and distributed across Europe. Palestrina was enormously productive. He wrote over four hundred motets—stand-alone choral pieces with Latin texts that are

Image 11.12: This lithograph of Palestrina was produced by Henri-Joseph Hesse in 1828.
Source: Wikimedia Commons
Attribution: Unknown
License: Public Domain

intended for use during church services. He also created at least 104 settings of the Mass Ordinary, the most famous of which we will examine here.

The **Mass Ordinary** contains all of the words that are spoken or sung at every Catholic Mass, which today we can think of as the typical Sunday morning service. The entire text of the service, including the parts that change from day to day, is termed the **liturgy**. The Mass Ordinary, like the rest of the service, is principally in Latin, and it contains five parts: Kyrie, Gloria, Credo, Sanctus, and Agnus Dei. Each part contains a text that is considered central to the Catholic faith, and which parishioners must speak, sing, or at least hear every time they attend a service.

Pope Marcellus Mass

We will examine the Kyrie and Credo from Palestrina's *Pope Marcellus Mass*. Out of Palestrina's many Masses, this one is the most closely associated with the Council of Trent and its musical reforms. Indeed, it is fabled that the Council decided not to ban polyphony after hearing this Mass, although most historians doubt the truth of this story. However, this Mass was certainly composed with the musical values of the Reformation in mind, and it satisfied the Council's requirements.

It is not certain when Palestrina composed this Mass, but it is named for Pope Marcellus II, who reigned for only twenty-two days in 1555. Marcellus's brief papacy happened to span Holy Week, the most sacred period in the Catholic calendar. Holy Week encompasses the seven days leading up to Easter. The most austere of these is Good Friday, on which day the faithful remember Jesus's crucifixion. Following the 1555 Good Friday service in the Sistine Chapel, Pope Marcellus berated the

Image 11.13: This 1555 engraving captured Pope Marcellus II during his brief reign.
Source: Wikimedia Commons
Attribution: Giulio Bonasone
License: CC0

choir for singing music that he found inappropriate given the seriousness of the occasion. Apparently they had chosen music that was complex and virtuosic, while the Pope would have preferred something simple and modest.

This Mass, therefore, was a direct response to the Pope's complaint, but also a more general response to concerns that were later expressed by the Council of Trent. By the time it was published in 1567, it was a model for Catholic composers everywhere. With the *Pope Marcellus Mass*, Palestrina satisfied the new requirements of the Catholic Church without abandoning his musical values. His

MUSIC FOR SPIRITUAL EXPRESSION

Mass was beautiful and expressive, but also modest and clear. He has succeeded in producing art that served the requirements of worship.

To see how this music worked, we will consider the Kyrie and the Credo. These are the most disparate movements of the Mass. The Kyrie has the shortest text: It translates in its entirety to "Christ have mercy, Lord have mercy, Christ have mercy." The text is also unusual because it is in Greek, not Latin. The Credo has the longest text, for it details all of the core Catholic beliefs. This text is also known as the Nicene Creed, for it was adopted by the First Council of Nicea in 325. In the context of a musical setting, however, this movement is always termed the Credo. The Latin verb "credo," which opens the text, means "I believe." The Credo goes on to summarize the story of Christ and state the essential tenets of the faith. The current English version of the Nicene Creed as used by the Catholic Church reads as follows:

> I believe in one God,
> the Father almighty,
> maker of heaven and earth,
> of all things visible and invisible.
>
> I believe in one Lord Jesus Christ,
> the Only Begotten Son of God,
> born of the Father before all ages.
> God from God, Light from Light,
> true God from true God,
> begotten, not made, consubstantial with the Father;
> through him all things were made.
> For us men and for our salvation
> he came down from heaven,
> and by the Holy Spirit was incarnate of the Virgin Mary,
> and became man.
> For our sake he was crucified under Pontius Pilate,
> he suffered death and was buried,
> and rose again on the third day
> in accordance with the Scriptures.
> He ascended into heaven
> and is seated at the right hand of the Father.
> He will come again in glory
> to judge the living and the dead
> and his kingdom will have no end.
>
> I believe in the Holy Spirit, the Lord, the giver of life,
> who proceeds from the Father and the Son,
> who with the Father and the Son is adored and glorified,
> who has spoken through the prophets.

I believe in one, holy, catholic and apostolic Church.
I confess one Baptism for the forgiveness of sins
and I look forward to the resurrection of the dead
and the life of the world to come. Amen.

Kyrie

		Pope Marcellus Mass, Kyrie Composer: Giovanni da Palestrina Performance: The Sixteen, conducted by Harry Christophers (2003)
Time	**Form**	**What to listen for**
0'00"	"Lord have mercy"	Each of the six parts enters independently; it is impossible to say which has the melody
1'17"	"Christ have mercy"	This section begins with the soprano and bass in homorhythm, but soon becomes polyphonic
2'37"	"Lord have mercy"	This section has the same texture as the first "Lord have mercy," but the musical contents are different

For his setting of the Kyrie, Palestrina did not take particular concern with the clarity of the text. The reason is evident enough: The text is very brief, and it is instantly recognizable by its first word, which appears nowhere else in the liturgy. In keeping with the three-part structure of the text, Palestrina uses a ternary musical structure. He repeats the short text many times within each section, such that the listener hears the Greek words dozens of times.

The nature of the text allows Palestrina to do two things with his music that were otherwise frowned upon by church authorities. First, his Kyrie is highly **imitative**, each vocal part entering independently. There are six vocal parts, meaning that the texture quickly becomes dense. First, we hear the altos. Next, the highest sopranos, followed by the lowest basses. Within half a minute, everyone is singing. No single part has the melody. Instead, as is typical of polyphonic music, every part is equally important, and melodic fragments are passed around. This also means that the text does not line up between vocal parts. Second, his vocal lines are melismatic, meaning that many notes are sung on a single syllable of text.

All the same, Palestrina is careful not to show off. The music is noble and stately. The melodies are modest and restrained, while the harmonies move slowly and deliberately. The movement has a single, introspective mood. Palestrina aims to create an atmosphere in which churchgoers can ponder the meaning of the words and prepare for worship.

Credo

Time	Text	What to listen for
\[*Pope Marcellus Mass*, Credo Composer: Giovanni da Palestrina Performance: The Sixteen, conducted by Harry Christophers (2003)\]		
0'00"	"I believe in one God. . ."	The opening line is chanted by a solo male voice
0'07"	". . .the Father almighty. . ."	We seldom hear all six voice parts at the same time; instead, groups of three to five voice parts take turns singing phrases in homorhythm
2'31"	". . .and by the Holy Spirit. . ."	The note values lengthen and the rhythmic complexity lessens
3'27"	"For our sake he was crucified. . ."	The texture is reduced to four voices; at first, we hear only the low parts
5'11"	"I believe in the Holy Spirit. . ."	The texture expands to six voices; this passage is sprinkled with melismas
7'53"	"Amen"	The texture becomes increasingly polyphonic

The Credo is quite different. To begin with, although the Credo text is about thirty times as long as the Kyrie text, the Credo movement is only about twice as long as the Kyrie. This is because Palestrina does not repeat text and does not draw out words using melismas. Instead, he focuses on moving through the text from beginning to end with the maximum of clarity.

Palestrina achieves this clarity in several ways. First, he seldom uses the entire choir, instead limiting the texture to three or four vocal parts. Second, he uses a homophonic texture in which all of the parts sing the same words at the same time. Finally, he avoids melismas, using them only at the ends of phrases once the meaning has already been communicated.

The Credo contains more musical diversity than the Kyrie. Palestrina divides it into four sections. The first includes the opening text, the second begins with Christ's incarnation, and the third describes his crucifixion, resurrection, and ascension. The final section lists the core Catholic beliefs. Because the third section contains the text most essential to Christianity, it receives the most serious treatment. Palestrina reduces his choir to four parts and uses long note values for the passage about Christ's burial, followed by more rapid rhythms to symbolize his return to life.

Palestrina's *Pope Marcellus Mass* provides an excellent example of how the values of the Christian church influenced the development of music. Palestrina's Latin-texted compositions are frequently performed by choirs today, and they are widely admired for their elegance and beauty. However, Palestrina might never have produced music in quite this style were it not for pressure from his employers.

JOHANN SEBASTIAN BACH, FUGUE IN G MINOR AND *SLEEPERS, WAKE*

About 150 years later, another composer of church music was also guided by the needs and preferences of his faith community. The church music of Johann Sebastian Bach (1685-1750) is quite different from that of Palestrina, however, both because musical tastes had changed in the intervening years and because Bach worked not for the Catholic but for the Lutheran Church. We will take a look at two of his most famous creations: a piece of music for the organ and a composition for choir and orchestra.

Image 11.14: This portrait of Johann Sebastian Bach was painted in 1746 by Elias Gottlob Haussmann.
Source: Wikimedia Commons
Attribution: Elias Gottlob Haussmann
License: Public Domain

Bach's Legacy

Today, the music of J.S. Bach is performed more frequently than that of almost any other composer from the European tradition. Ensembles all over the world are dedicated to his music, while countless books have detailed his life and works. He is esteemed by many as the greatest composer of all time (although, as will be discussed in the final chapter of this book, it is nearly impossible to define "greatness" in music).

All of this would have very much surprised the composer himself. During his lifetime, Bach was not particularly famous or respected, and he struggled constantly with difficult working conditions and low pay. He was better known as an organist than as a composer: While Bach was respected as a virtuoso

Image 11.15: During his lifetime, Bach was best known as an organist. He is depicted at the console in this 1725 engraving.
Source: Wikimedia Commons
Attribution: Unknown
License: Public Domain

performer, his compositions were considered old-fashioned and stuffy. Only a handful of his works—mostly for keyboard—were published before his death, and he had no reason to expect future generations to take any interest in his music.

Bach's fortunes shifted in the early 19th century, when German musicians began to revive and popularize his music. The most significant such event took place in 1829 when the composer Felix Mendelssohn staged a performance of Bach's *St. Matthew Passion* in Berlin. Like *Sleepers, Wake* (German: *Wachet auf*), which we will examine, the *St. Matthew Passion* was a work for choir and orchestra intended for use in a Lutheran church service. Bach never imagined that any of his church music would be performed in concert halls or consumed as either art or entertainment. He sought only to support the work of the church. Since the time of Mendelssohn, however, Bach's choral compositions have been a staple of the concert repertoire, and today's listener can access thousands of recordings.

A brief examination of Bach's life and career will serve to contextualize his work as a composer. Bach was born into a large family of German musicians that extended back for many generations. His father, grandfather, great-grandfather, uncles, and other male ancestors were all performers and in most cases composers, while his sons were all to become composers as well. From the time of his birth, therefore, there was no doubt about Bach's future career. Musicians of his time and place generally found employment with either a court or a city, in which capacity they would produce new compositions, oversee performances, and participate in those performances as instrumentalists or singers.

Bach's Career

Bach never lived outside the region of Thuringia, which today is located in central Germany, and he never travelled beyond the borders of the modern German nation. Following an education in Eisenach, he took a series of five professional posts. First he served as a church organist in the cities of Arnstadt (1703-1707) and Mühlhausen (1707-1708). His next position was at the ducal court in Weimar (1708-1717), where he played the organ and served as music director. After this he became music director at the court of Prince Leopold in Köthen (1717-1723). Finally, Bach took the position of music director at the St. Thomas Church in the city of Leipzig, where he remained until his death.

Famously, Bach was not the city council's first choice for the job. They initially offered the post to a composer—Georg Philipp Telemann—whose music is only seldom performed today, but who at the time was considered to be more fashionable. Bach was in turn loathe to accept the job, which was less prestigious than the post he held in Köthen. He made the move to Leipzig, however, out of concern for his family. Bach, who was married twice, had a total of twenty children, ten of whom survived into adulthood. Leipzig had excellent schools, and he knew that his sons would have better prospects in that city. Bach's second wife, Anna Magdalena, was herself a highly-skilled musician. She provided her husband with invaluable assistance, copying out parts by hand each week so that the church musicians could perform his music during the Sunday service.

Image 11.16: Today, this statue of Bach stands outside of the St. Thomas Church in Leipzig.
Source: Wikimedia Commons
Attribution: User "Appaloosa"
License: CC BY-SA 3.0

In Leipzig, Bach was required to perform a variety of tasks on behalf of the municipal government. He was principally responsible for music at the St. Thomas Church, but also oversaw music at the city's other three churches. As music director, Bach produced instrumental and vocal compositions for use in the church, hired musicians, ran rehearsals, and played the organ. He also taught music and Latin at the St. Thomas School, which was attached to the church. Finally, he was obliged to produce music for civic occasions, including commemorations of important events and celebrations of esteemed visitors.

Bach frequently complained about his immense workload and limited resources. He felt that the city did not provide adequate funds with which to hire

Image 11.17: The interior of the St. Thomas Church looks much the same today as it did in Bach's time.
Source: Wikimedia Commons
Attribution: User "S-kay"
License: Public Domain

Image 11.18: This 1723 engraving depicts the St. Thomas Church and adjoining School, where Bach taught music and Latin.
Source: Wikimedia Commons
Attribution: Johann Gottfrieg Krügner
License: Public Domain

the musicians that he needed, and he often had to limit his instrumentation due to budgetary concerns. Although today one can hear Bach's music rendered by the best choirs and orchestras in the world, Bach himself was seldom able to arrange for high-quality performances of his music. He relied primarily on students from the St. Thomas School and from the nearby Leipzig University.

We will examine two pieces of church music from two different parts of his career. Bach's Fugue in G minor dates from his early years as a church organist in Arnstadt. Like most of Bach's music, it has survived only as a handwritten manuscript. The same it true of *Sleepers, Wake*, which was created in 1731 for use at the St. Thomas Church in Leipzig.

Fugue in G minor

		Fugue in G minor Composer: Johann Sebastian Bach Performance: Wolfgang Rübsam (1977)
Time	**Form**	**What to listen for**
0'00"	Exposition	The subject is heard first in the soprano voice, then alto, then tenor, then bass
0'51"	Episode	All of the episodes consist largely of sequences
0'58"	Subject	After a false entrance in the tenor, the subject is heard in the soprano
1'11"	Episode	
1'17"	Subject	Heard in the alto
1'28"	Episode	
1'36"	Subject	Heard in the bass
1'47"	Episode	
1'59"	Subject	Heard in the soprano
2'10"	Episode	This is the most diverse and lengthy episode
2'31"	Subject	Heard in the bass; the tempo slows before the final cadence

Bach wrote hundreds of fugues, most of which had nothing to do with his work as a church musician. The term **fugue** refers to a compositional technique that can be applied across genres. Bach wrote most of his fugues for keyboard instruments such as the harpsichord, which resembles a small piano in appearance but creates sound using quite a different process: When the player depresses a key, it causes a string to be plucked with a quill or piece of hard leather. Most famously, Bach twice wrote keyboard fugues in every major and minor key. His two collections, known as *The Well-Tempered Clavier* Book I (1722) and Book II (1742), were intended to demonstrate a new method for tuning the harpsichord. Bach also wrote fugues for solo string instruments, orchestra, and choir. One of Bach's final works, entitled *The Art of Fugue*, was left incomplete at his death but nonetheless demonstrated his ultimate mastery of the technique.

Fugal technique was widely employed in the 18th century. It is simple in principle, but very challenging to execute. Whether a fugue is written for instrumentalists or singers, we always speak of its "voices" and use the typical choral designations: soprano, alto, tenor, and bass. Most fugues have four voices, although Bach wrote for as few as two and as many as six.

Every fugue begins with a solo melody in one of the voices. This melody is called the **subject**. The composer will introduce the subject in each of the voices in turn until all have entered the texture. This section of the fugue is called the **exposition**. For the remainder of the fugue, sections that do not contain the subject, which are known as **episodes**, will alternate with statements of the subject, which constitute the **development**. The subject will appear in many different keys and sometimes in different forms (for example, the melody might be turned upside down) until finally it is heard one last time in the original key and the fugue concludes. A fugue might have many episodes or none at all, and there is no predetermined length or precise form.

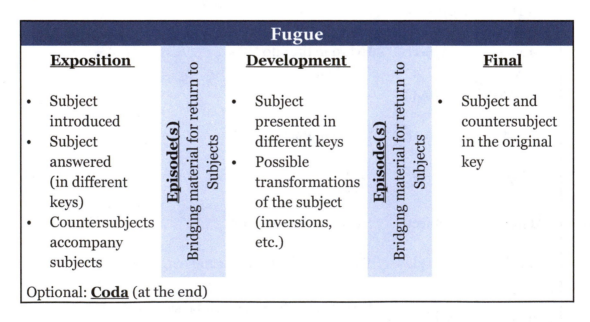

Fugue				
Exposition	Episode(s) — Bridging material for return to Subjects	**Development**	Episode(s) — Bridging material for return to Subjects	**Final**
• Subject introduced • Subject answered (in different keys) • Countersubjects accompany subjects		• Subject presented in different keys • Possible transformations of the subject (inversions, etc.)		• Subject and countersubject in the original key
Optional: **Coda** (at the end)				

Fugues are difficult to write because the composer must follow complex rules concerning the relationships between the voices. These rules concern the distances between simultaneous pitches, the directions in which voices move, the special treatment of notes that do not belong to chords, and the keys in which the subject must appear. Because the subject itself can never be altered, the composer must employ all of their skill to avoid breaking rules. (These rules are not arbitrary, but rather emerged over decades of practice and guide the composer in creating a fugue that sounds good.) Bach seems to have enjoyed the challenge of fugue writing, and he often created subjects that were especially difficult to work with.

Although a fugue is not necessarily an example of church music, Bach composed

Image 11.19: Although the church in Arnstadt was known as the New Church during the time that Bach worked there, in 1935 it was renamed the Bach Church in honor of the composer.
Source: Wikimedia Commons
Attribution: Michael Sander
License: CC BY-SA 3.0

organ fugues for use in Lutheran church services. We will examine a fairly simple fugue that he composed in his capacity as church organist for the city of Arnstadt. He would have played his Fugue in G minor at the beginning or end of services, but also on organ recitals that were intended not for worship but for the enjoyment of the audience. While this piece of music sets a mood that is appropriately serious for worship, its complexities also reward careful listening.

In Arnstadt, Bach played on an organ that had just been installed by the builder Johann Friederich Wender. All organs work by blowing air through pipes, which might be made out of wood or metal, be of various shapes, or contain reeds. These

Image 11.20: The organ in the New Church at Arnstadt.
Source: Wikimedia Commons
Attribution: User "Mtag"
License: CC0

variations allow organs to produce many different sounds. Most organs have multiple keyboards, each of which can be linked to one or more sets of pipes. In this way, the performer can quickly change from one sound quality to another by moving between keyboards. Sets of pipes are activated or deactivated by adjusting wooden rods known as stops. Organs also have an additional keyboard, termed the pedalboard, that is operated using the feet. The pedalboard is typically linked to pipes that sound in the lowest register.

Despite its complexity, the organ is actually one of the oldest instruments found in Europe. Organs were first developed in ancient Greece over two thousand years ago. Although early organs were small and portable instruments, they began to grow in the 14th century when the first permanent organ was installed in a church. By the 19th century organs had become enormous instruments capable of producing a great range of volumes and timbres.

Bach's organ in Arnstadt is still played today. Like other Baroque organs, it is fairly small, although still capable of producing a wide variety of sounds. It has two keyboards and a pedalboard, which together give the player access to twenty-one sets of pipes. Baroque organs are not capable of gradual changes in dynamic. The performer can suddenly alternate between loud and soft by changing keyboards, but all notes played using a given set of pipes are the same volume. Fugues, therefore, are most often performed without any dynamic changes.

Bach's Fugue in G minor (often called the "Little" Fugue in G minor, to distinguish it from others in the same key) has a five-measure subject. The subject begins with long note values, but gradually incorporates shorter and shorter note values as it proceeds. This creates an impression of increased activity, even though the tempo does not accelerate. The fugue has four voices, which enter from highest to lowest in the order soprano-alto-tenor-bass. The texture quickly becomes dense, and—after the opening measures—at least one voice is moving rapidly at all times. Although the fugue is short, therefore, one needs to listen to it several time to hear everything that is going on. It can be challenging to pick out the subject, even once it has become familiar.

Bach was noted for the density and complexity of his music. Indeed, that was the characteristic that earned him scorn in his own time—just as it earned him respect a century after his death. He also preferred to establish and then maintain a single mood with each piece of music. As such, there is little expressive variation within the Fugue in G minor. Once the engine starts, it runs steadily and unerringly until the final cadence.

Sleepers, Wake

During the early years of his employment in Leipzig, J.S. Bach dedicated most of his energy to the creation of **Lutheran church cantatas**. This was a big job because the churches there required a new cantata every week. The Lutheran liturgical calendar is organized into a year-long cycle of Biblical readings, and the cantata corresponded with the topic of the readings and the sermon. For this reason, Bach needed to produce an appropriate cantata for every Sunday morning Mass and for special services, making for a total of sixty cantatas a year.

After his first year on the job, Bach could have begun to reuse old cantatas—but instead he completed a whole second cycle and most of three additional cycles. Bach had also written church cantatas at several of his previous jobs. However, none of his church cantatas were ever published. As a result, about two hundred are extant today, while hundreds more might have been lost.

A **cantata** is a multi-part work for voice(s) and instrumental accompaniment. Bach's Lutheran church cantatas are multi-movement works for choir, soloists, and orchestra. Bach always used texts in German, the language of his congregation. He did not write the texts himself, however, but rather selected them from among the works of various theological poets. Each cantata is thirty to forty minutes long and usually contains four to seven movements. Some of the movements use the entire choir, while others feature solo singers, often paired with solo instruments.

Bach's cantatas constituted the musical focus for worship at St. Thomas and other churches in Leipzig. Although forty minutes of choral music might seem excessive, the services themselves lasted four hours. The centerpiece was a one-hour sermon, which was preceded by opening prayers, hymns, readings, and the performance of the cantata. Communion followed the sermon.

The cantata had a very specific purpose: It reflected on the Biblical readings for the day, interpreted their meaning for the congregation, and prepared listeners to understand and appreciate the sermon. As stated above, Bach in no way regarded his cantatas as entertainment—or even, strictly speaking, art. He was deeply committed to his Lutheran faith and he understood his role in the service to be essentially spiritual. His cantatas shaped churchgoers' understanding of their relationship with God.

We will see Bach's approach to cantata composition in *Sleepers, Wake*. Although many of Bach's cantatas are difficult to date, we know that this one was first performed on November 25, 1731. The occasion was the 27th Sunday after Trinity—a day that occurs only in years during which Easter falls very early, for in regular years the liturgical season of Advent will have already commenced. This explains why Bach had to write this cantata several years after having completed his annual cycles, for the 27th Sunday after Trinity had not occurred since 1704. *Sleepers, Wake* was performed only once in Bach's lifetime, at Leipzig's St. Nicholas Church.

The Epistle reading for the 27th Sunday after Trinity is 1 Thessalonians 5: 1-11, while the Gospel reading is Matthew 25: 1-13. Both exhort Christians to be prepared for the return of Christ. In Paul's letter to the Thessalonians, he warns that the Lord will come "like a thief in the night," without any warning. Matthew records the parable of the wise and foolish virgins. All had gathered together to await the coming of the bridegroom (an allegory for Christ), but the foolish virgins had failed to bring extra oil for their lamps. While they were away buying oil, the bridegroom arrived and the wedding feast commenced. The wise virgins, who were prepared for the arrival, were welcomed into the hall, but the foolish virgins were shut

Image 11.21: Bach was also responsible for music at the large St. Nicholas Church in Leipzig.
Source: Wikimedia Commons
Attribution: Dr. Bernd Gross
License: CC BY-SA 3.0

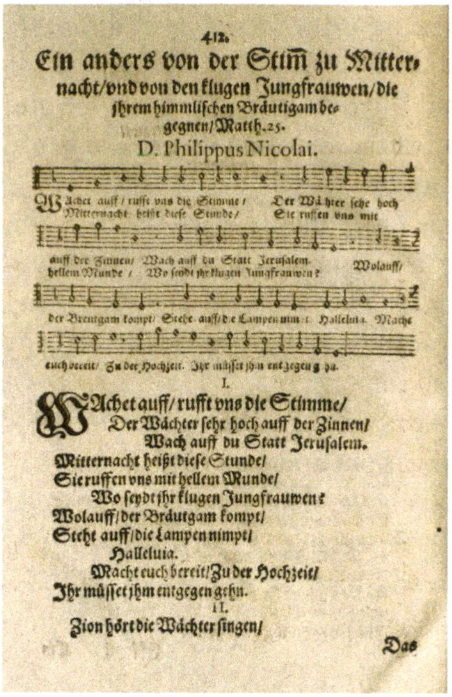
412.

Ein anders von der Stim zu Mitternacht/vnd von den klugen Jungfrauwen/die jhrem himmlischen Bräutigam begegnen/Matth.25.

D. Philippus Nicolai.

I.

Wachet auff/rufft vns die Stimme/
Der Wächter sehr hoch auff der Zinnen/
Wach auff du Statt Jerusalem.
Mitternacht heißt diese Stunde/
Sie ruffen vns mit hellem Munde/
Wo seydt jhr klugen Jungfrauwen?
Wolauff/der Bräutgam kompt/
Steht auff/die Lampen nimpt/
Halleluia.
Macht euch bereit/Zu der Hochzeit/
Jhr müsset jhm entgegen gehn.

II.

Zion hört die Wächter singen/

Das

Image 11.22: Here we see the original 1599 publication of the chorale "Sleepers, Wake."
Source: Wikimedia Commons
Attribution: Philip Nicolai
License: Public Domain

out in the darkness. The message is clear: Christians must be prepared for Christ's coming. If they are not, they will be excluded from heaven and denied eternal life.

Bach's cantata reflects on this parable using a variety of musical and dramatic techniques. He began by selecting an appropriate **Lutheran chorale** on which to base his cantata. Chorales are unison hymns sung by the congregation, and they were first developed by Martin Luther himself in the early years of the church. One of Luther's objections to Catholic worship was that the music was performed in Latin by professional choirs. He preferred participatory music in the language of the congregants. To develop a repertoire of chorales, he wrote new tunes, adapted Gregorian chants, and even borrowed popular melodies. Luther saw no problem with using secular music for worship. As he supposedly put it, "Why should the devil have all the good tunes?"

Because *Sleepers, Wake* is based on a Lutheran chorale, it is a special type of cantata known as a **chorale cantata**. Bach primarily wrote chorale cantatas while in Leipzig, and he developed a unique approach to their construction, of which *Sleepers, Wake* is a fine example. The cantata contains seven movements, three of which—the first, fourth, and seventh—include text and music from a 1599 chorale of the same name. Bach selected this chorale because it, too, comments on the parable of the wise and foolish virgins, thereby offering another layer of interpretation. Everyone in the congregation at St. Thomas would have known the chorale well and would have instantly recognized the words and music. Because the chorale is in A A B form, each of the movements based on it is in that same form.

I. Wake up, the voice calls us

Bach spreads his references to the chorale throughout the cantata, and he integrates it with his own music differently on each occasion. In the first movement, we hear the choir sing the first verse of the chorale text:

> Wake up, the voice calls us
> of the watchmen high up on the battlements,
> wake up, you city of Jerusalem!
> This hour is called midnight;

they call us with a clear voice:
where are you, wise virgins?
Get up, the bridegroom comes;
Stand up, take your lamps! Hallelujah!
Alleluia!
Make yourselves ready
for the wedding,
you must go to meet him!

Translation by Francis Browne

We also hear the chorale melody, but it is buried in a dense texture of newly-composed music. While Bach's congregation would have recognized the chorale, many modern listeners have a hard time even picking the melody out.

	I. "Wake up, the voice calls us" from Sleepers, Wake Composer: Johann Sebastian Bach Performance: American Bach Soloists (2007)	
Time	**Form**	**What to listen for**
0'00"	Ritornello	The violins and oboes exchange melodic material in a call-and-response texture
0'28"	A "Wake up, the voice calls us. . ."	The sopranos sing the chorale melody while the altos, tenors, and basses sing newly-composed material
1'32"	Ritornello	This ritornello is identical to that which opened the movement
2'00"	A "This hour is called midnight. . ."	The A music repeats with a new texts
3'04"	Ritornello	This ritornello sounds different because it moves through several key areas

	B	
3'24"	"Get up, the bridegroom comes. . ."	We hear exclamations of "get up" and "stand up" from the choir
3'57"	"Alleluia!"	This passage is especially ornate; the chorale melody does not enter until near the end
4'42"	"Make yourselves ready. . ."	The texture returns to normal
5'32"	Ritornello	We hear the complete ritornello one last time
2'10"	Episode	This is the most diverse and lengthy episode
2'31"	Subject	Heard in the bass; the tempo slows before the final cadence

The first movement starts with orchestral music, the uneven dotted rhythms of which suggest a wedding march. Dotted rhythms were also associated with royalty in this era—another appropriate connotation for music about Christ's coming. This opening passage is in fact a **ritornello**. In this movement Bach combines ritornello form, in which an orchestral melody returns throughout a piece of music, with the A A B form of the chorale. The resulting form is: rit A rit A rit B rit. The orchestra also provides short interjections between the verses within each section. Although a congregation might sing the first verse of the chorale in less than two minutes, the first movement of the cantata takes nearly four times as long to perform. This is due to the slowed-down chorale melody and frequent orchestral interruptions. As a result, however, the congregation has an opportunity to meditate on the text, the meaning of which is reinforced by Bach's musical setting.

Image 11.23: This bassoon part in Bach's own hand is one of only a few extant original manuscripts for *Sleepers, Wake*.
Source: Wikimedia Commons
Attribution: Johann Sebastian Bach
License: Public Domain

The first movement is texturally very dense. There are active parts for strings, winds, and voices, and it is seldom possible to identify a single, dominant melody. The opening ritornello contains three distinct layers. Underpinning everything is the **basso continuo**, a feature of almost all music composed in the Baroque era (1600-1750). Basso continuo is always performed by some combination of low-pitched instruments and instruments that can play chords. In this case, we hear cello, bassoon, organ, and harpsichord. While Baroque bass lines can be simple, Bach's seldom are. This one contains a variety of interesting rhythmic and melodic elements, thereby attracting an unusual amount of the listener's attention. Above that, the violins and oboe trade melodic motifs back and forth in a six-part texture.

When the singers enter, the orchestra begins by repeating the musical material from the ritornello. The already-dense texture suddenly becomes much more complex. First we hear the sopranos with the familiar chorale melody. While the sopranos sing in slow, even note values, the altos, tenors, and basses sing quickly. These other voices occasionally integrate text painting as well, such as with their ascending cries on the text "wake up". Also notable is the passage on the text "Alleluia," which features excitable melismas in the altos, tenors, and basses.

Ritornello Form: Movements I & IV of Bach's *Sleepers, Wake*						
ritornello orchestra	**A** *from chorale* lines 1-3 of text with accompaniment	**ritornello** orchestra	**A** *from chorale* lines 4-6 of text with accompaniment	**ritornello** orchestra	**B** *from chorale* lines 7-12 of text with accompaniment	**ritornello** orchestra

IV. Zion hears the watchmen sing

The chorale disappears until the fourth movement,[2] when we hear the second verse sung by the tenor section:

> Zion hears the watchmen sing,
> her heart leaps for joy,
> she awakes and gets up in haste.
> Her friend comes from heaven in his splendour,
> strong in mercy, mighty in truth.
> Her light becomes bright, her star rises.

Page | 418

Now come, you worthy crown,
Lord Jesus, God's son!
Hosanna!
We all follow
to the hall of joy
and share in the Lord's supper.

Translation by Francis Browne.

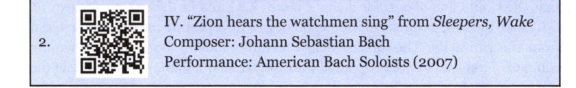

2.

IV. "Zion hears the watchmen sing" from *Sleepers, Wake*
Composer: Johann Sebastian Bach
Performance: American Bach Soloists (2007)

This movement is much simpler than the first movement. In place of the orchestral ritornello, with its call-and-response texture, we have a unison ritornello melody from the violins and violas. The chorale melody, instead of being buried in a complex texture, is clearly presented without competition from other vocal parts. All the same, this movement is by no means simple. The two melodies—one in the strings, one in the tenors—weave around one another in unpredictable and extraordinary ways. While their phrases never start or end together, the parts always complement one another.

VII. May gloria be sung to you

We finally hear a straightforward presentation of the chorale in the seventh movement,[3] in which the entire choir—and perhaps the congregation as well—sing the third verse in four-part harmony:

May gloria be sung to you
with the tongues of men and angels,
with harps and with cymbals.
The gates are made of twelve pearls,
in your city we are companions
of the angels on high around your throne.
No eye has ever perceived,
no ear has ever heard
such joy.
Therefore we are joyful,
hurray, hurray!
for ever in sweet rejoicing.

Translation by Francis Browne

3.   VII. "May gloria be sung to you" from *Sleepers, Wake*
      Composer: Johann Sebastian Bach
      Performance: American Bach Soloists (2007)

Although Bach borrowed chorale melodies from the Lutheran tradition, he always created his own harmonizations. In practice, this means that the soprano part is borrowed, but the alto, tenor, and bass parts are original. Bach has the orchestral musicians double the vocal parts, playing the same melodies that are being sung. This makes the ensemble sound exceptionally full and rich without distracting from the chorale melody: a fitting culmination to the cantata.

II. He comes

Although there are four movements that do not contain the chorale melody or text, we will look at only two of them. The text was supplied by an unknown poet. It includes many references to the Song of Solomon—a passage of Biblical love poetry that was understood by Bach and his contemporaries to be a metaphor for the love between Jesus and the faithful soul. To set this expressive new text, Bach used musical forms from the opera stage: **recitative** and **aria**. Bach never wrote an opera and did not think highly of the form, but he often adapted operatic conventions for his own purposes.

The second movement[4] of *Sleepers, Wake* is a recitative for solo tenor:

> He comes, he comes,
> the bridegroom comes!
> You daughters of Zion, come out,
> he hastens his departure from on high
> to your mother's house.
> The bridegroom comes, who like a roedeer
> and a young stag
> leaps on the hills
> and brings to you the wedding feast.
> Wake up, rouse yourselves
> to welcome the bridegroom!
> There, see, he comes this way.

Translation by Francis Browne.

4.   II. "He comes" from *Sleepers, Wake*
      Composer: Johann Sebastian Bach
      Performance: American Bach Soloists (2007)

He announces the coming of the bridegroom with a series of exuberant melodic leaps, accompanied only by basso continuo. This movement contains no repetition and has no particular form. In fact, the singing—as is always the case with recitative—is not particularly melodic at all. Instead, its purpose is to declaim the text with the utmost expressive force.

III. When are you coming, my salvation?

		III. "When are you coming, my salvation?" from *Sleepers, Wake* Composer: Johann Sebastian Bach Performance: American Bach Soloists (2007)
Time	**Form**	**What to listen for**
0'00"	Ritornello	This ritornello features a virtuosic violin obbligato
0'26"	A "When are you coming. . ."	The soprano and bass exchange lines while the solo violin line weaves about them
1'46"	Ritornello	This ritornello is similar to that which opened the movement, but it is in a different key
1'59"	B "Open the hall. . ."	This passage has the same texture as A, but the music and text are different
2'32"	Ritornello	This passage is not closely related to the opening ritornello
2'46"	B'	This passage is similar to B, but it is in a different key
3'18"	Ritornello	This ritornello is very brief, for it is interrupted by the return of the A text
3'25"	A' "When are you coming. . ."	This passage echoes A, but is not musically identical
4'25"	Ritornello	The closing ritornello is identical to that which opened the movement

The recitative serves to introduce the third movement, which is a duet for soprano and bass. Just as recitative developed within the operatic tradition, this is clearly an operatic duet—specifically, the type of duet sung by two characters who are in love. The soprano and bass call back and forth to one another, expressing their mutual desire. Bach's lovers, however, are a Soul (soprano) and Jesus (bass), and they offer a dramatic enactment of the desire that all Christians are meant to feel for their savior.

Because the third movement is based in operatic conventions, it has the **da capo form** of an opera aria. "Da capo" literally means "from the head," and it serves as an instruction to the performers to repeat the first of two parts, resulting in an A B A form. (The second A is not written out.) Bach accompanies his aria with basso continuo and an **obbligato** (or "obligatory") instrumental solo. He intended the obbligato part in the fourth movement to be performed on the violino piccolo, a type of small violin that is tuned higher than a modern instrument. However, it can also be performed on a standard violin. The instrumental soloist provides ritornellos before, between, and after each of the sung sections, but also supplies a virtuosic accompaniment to the vocal soloists. The resulting music is beautiful and expressive—even if the text is a bit corny:

> Soul: When are you coming, my salvation?
> Jesus: I come, your portion.
> Soul: I wait with burning oil.
> Jesus: Open the hall
> Soul: I open the hall
> Both: to the heavenly feast.
> Soul: Come, Jesus!
> Jesus: Come, lovely soul!

> *Translation by Francis Browne.*

JOHN NEWTON, "AMAZING GRACE"

So far, we have examined compositions for use in Christian worship that are fixed in terms of their musical details. Two recordings of *Sleepers, Wake*, for example, might differ slightly in terms of tempo or timbre, but they will sound essentially the same. They will certainly contain all of the same pitches and rhythms, and will be similar in length. These are all characteristics of the classical tradition, in which the composer exercises a great deal of control over the musical work.

Next, however, we will examine an example of Christian worship music that has changed dramatically as it has been adopted and adapted by different religious communities. In fact, the only element of "Amazing Grace" to remain consistent throughout its lifetime has been the words, although all of the versions under consideration here also use the same melody—that which will be familiar to those who know the hymn. This stylistic flexibility is typical of music in the **vernacular** tradition, which permits the reinterpretation and transformation of musical compositions by individual performers.

No-one has ever performed *Sleepers, Wake* without being aware that it was composed by J.S. Bach, but people sing "Amazing Grace" every day without knowing who penned the words or music. Indeed, those are not easy questions to answer—the text, although initially written by John Newton (1725-1807), was later expanded by an anonymous author, while people still debate the identity of the tune's composer. People who know this hymn are more likely to identify it with one of its great interpreters, such as Aretha Franklin, whose version we will encounter below.

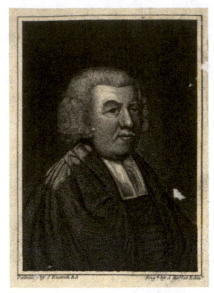

Image 11.24: This engraving of John Newton by John Moffat was published around 1788.
Source: Wikimedia Commons
Attribution: John Moffat
License: Public Domain

Newton's Life

The story of "Amazing Grace" begins with John Newton, who wrote six verses—some familiar from modern usage, some not—in 1772. Newton was a clergyman in the Church of England. He served as curate in the village of Olney, where his parishioners were largely impoverished and uneducated. Newton gained a reputation for impassioned preaching that spoke to the personal moral struggles of his congregants. Unlike other preachers, Newton willingly shared sins from his own past—and those were certainly in no short supply.

Newton took to the sea as a ship's apprentice at the age of eleven, but was pressed into service with the Royal Navy after refusing to obey his captain's orders. After deserting the Navy to visit a young lady, Polly Catlett, he was traded to a slave ship, where he developed a reputation for writing obscene songs and using language that shocked even sailors. Newton had renounced his Christian faith early in his seagoing career, but in 1748 a near-death experience aboard the ship *Greyhound* inspired him to reconsider his beliefs. He was further encouraged by his love for Polly, whom he married in 1750. All the same, it was many years (and another brush with death) before Newton reformed in any meaningful way, and he continued to work in the slave trade well into the 1750s. Newton began studying theology in 1756 and was finally successful in securing ordination and his position at Olney in 1764.

At Olney, Newton began writing hymns for his congregation to sing together at weekly prayer meetings. Newton's hymns used simple language that was easily intelligible to his parishioners, and many of his texts were written in the first person. They focused on the confession of sins and the joys of salvation. Although

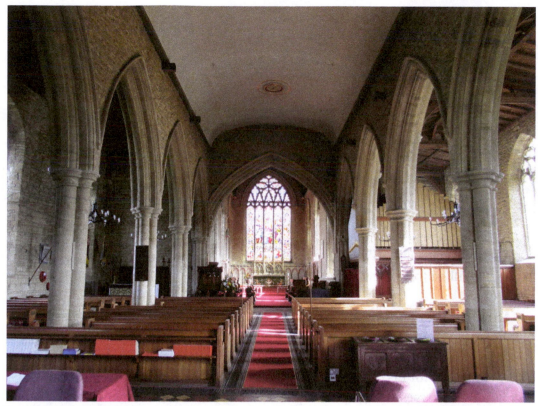

Image 11.25: Here we see the interior of St. Peter and St. Paul's Church in Olney, where Newton served as curate.
Source: Wikimedia Commons
Attribution: User "Poliphilo"
License: CC0

the quality of his verse was criticized by some, Newton's hymns became quite popular. They first appeared in print as part of the 1779 collection *Olney Hymns*, which included "Amazing Grace":

> Amazing grace! (how sweet the sound)
>   That sav'd a wretch like me!
> I once was lost, but now am found,
>   Was blind, but now I see.
>
> 'Twas grace that taught my heart to fear,
>   And grace my fears reliev'd;
> How precious did that grace appear
>   The hour I first believ'd!
>
> Thro' many dangers, toils, and snares,
>   I have already come;
> 'Tis grace hath brought me safe thus far,
>   And grace will lead me home.

The Lord has promis'd good to me,
   His word my hope secures;
He will my shield and portion be
   As long as life endures.

Yes, when this flesh and heart shall fail,
   And mortal life shall cease;
I shall possess, within the veil,
   A life of joy and peace.

The earth shall soon dissolve like snow,
   The sun forbear to shine;
But God, who call'd me here below,
   Will be forever mine.

Although it is known that Newton's congregation used his "Amazing Grace" text beginning in 1773, we have no idea what tune or tunes the text was sung to. It certainly was not the tune we know today. Newton was not a composer, but he always intended for his devotional poems to be sung. Like other hymn text authors, he crafted his verses using specific patterns of syllables and rhymes so that they could be sung to preexisting melodies. This system of interchangeable texts and tunes meant that any hymn text could be sung to a variety of tunes and any tune could be supplied with a variety of texts. Only over time have specific texts and tunes in the hymn tradition come to be paired off, such that churchgoers expect a text—"Amazing Grace," for example—always to be sung to the same melody.

"Amazing Grace"[5] in the Sacred Harp Tradition

5.   "Amazing Grace"
Performance: Texas Sacred Harp Singers, Southwest
Sacred Harp Singing Convention (2011)

The pairing of "Amazing Grace" with its tune took place in 1835, when William Walker published a version in his hymnal *Southern Harmony*. The name of the tune was "New Britain" and it had already been in circulation for some time, although in the company of different texts. The authorship of "New Britain" is still contested. It was based in turn on two older melodies that first appeared in the 1829 hymnal *Columbian Harmony*. These tunes are unattributed, which indicates that they might be the work of hymnal compilers Charles H. Spilman and Benjamin Shaw. It is equally likely, however, that the tunes derive from folk tradition and might trace their origin to the British Isles. The "New Britain" tune also appears in an 1828 manuscript compiled by hymn composer Lucius Chapin, who has been proposed as yet another potential author. It is unlikely that a composer will ever be identified—if, indeed, "New Britain" was even the product of a single composer, which we have reason to doubt.

By the time William Walker published his version in 1835, the "Amazing Grace" text had already become very popular in the United States. It was widely used during the Second Great Awakening, which saw the staging of revivals across the country. These revivals featured charismatic preachers, who swayed crowds using emotionally charged speech punctuated with song. The verses of "Amazing Grace"—which embodied the personal, confessional approach to conversion favored by these preachers—were paired with simple refrains and sung to familiar tunes without the aid of hymnals.

Walker was not personally associated with the Second Great Awakening, but he made his living as a hymn publisher and singing teacher, and was therefore aware of trends in the world of Protestant worship music. Walker belonged to the American hymn tradition known as **shape-note singing**, which encompasses a unique form of notation, an approach to music education, and a compositional style.

The notation used in the shape-note tradition was first developed in late-18th century England for the purpose of simplifying the task of reading music. As its name suggests, shaped notation employs various shapes—each paired with a syllable—to represent the different pitches. In its original form, the system used only four shapes, even though a scale contains seven distinct pitches. The shapes were repeated in a way that maintained consistent patterns of intervals between shapes. If a singer could learn the intervallic distance between two shapes, they could easily sing music at sight. The syllables provide an additional tool for singers and also make it easy to teach the system. (The use of syllables to learn melodies actually dates back to ca. 1026, when the Italian monk Guido of Arezzo proposed a system that used six syllables—including the four later adapted by shape-note enthusiasts.)

Image 11.26: These are the four distinct shapes used in Sacred Harp-style notation.
Source: Wikimedia Commons
Attribution: User "Opus33"
License: Public Domain

Shaped notation was adopted in the United States as part of a movement to improve church music. During the second half of the 18th century, music lovers in New England began to lament the sorry state of American congregational singing. Churchgoers were largely illiterate, and they did not have access to hymnals or instruments. The most common method of hymn singing, known as **lining out**, required a songleader to call out a musical phrase, which the congregants would then repeat in unison. Activists wanted to restore four-part harmony to the worship service, but this would require music literacy and access to printed notation.

To fulfill both of these needs, entrepreneurs began to publish hymn books and offer singing schools. A singing master would travel around a region, spending two weeks at a time teaching anyone who was interested how to read using the shape-note system. Singing schools were usually hosted by a church, and classes would meet daily. These schools not only paved the way to better church music, but also provided much-needed entertainment to farming communities during the winter months and facilitated interactions between young men and women, who had few opportunities to encounter one another unchaperoned. The students would not only pay tuition to the singing master but would purchase hymn books—another important source of income.

The hymns composed in the American shape-note tradition were unique. Most of the composers—William Billings (1746-1800) and Daniel Read (1757-1836) were the most famous to emerge from the First New England School—were self-taught, and they gleefully rejected the conventions of European harmony and part writing. Their hymns contain unusual and harsh sounds (the result of breaking voice-leading rules), uneven phrases, and incomplete chordal harmonies (open fifths in place of triads). The shape-note composers also adhered to the ancient practice of putting the melody in the tenor part instead of the soprano—an approach, dating back to medieval church polyphony, that had already disappeared from European choral music.

The singing school movement was launched in New England, but by the early 19th century had come to be regarded as outdated. The North, after all, aspired to a cosmopolitan identity and was embarrassed by the primitive efforts of its shape-note composers. The movement, however, found a new home in the South, where rural singing masters flourished up until the Civil War. It was there that the most influential hymn books were published. William Walker's *Southern Harmony* was among these, but without question the most important shape-note hymnal was *The Sacred Harp* (1844), published in Georgia by Benjamin Franklin White and Elisha J. King. Unlike other such hymnals, *The Sacred Harp* has remained popular into the present day, and enthusiasts around the world regularly gather to sing from its pages. As such, the tradition of shape-note singing is today most commonly referred to as **Sacred Harp singing**.

Image 11.27: Pictured here are participants in a 19th-century singing school that took place in Keene, New Hampshire.
Source: Wikimedia Commons
Attribution: Keene Public Library and the Historical Society of Cheshire County
License: Public Domain

Participants in modern Sacred Harp sings adhere to a number of practices that originated in the singing school movement. To begin with, their purpose is not worship but music marking. Many Sacred Harp enthusiasts also profess Christian beliefs,

Image 11.28: In this photograph by Brent Moore, we see a song leader standing in the center of the hollow square. He is beating time with his arm.
Source: Flickr
Attribution: Brent Moore
License: CC BY-NC 2.0

and sings often begin and end with prayer, but Sacred Harp thrives because participants are committed to the music.

At a typical sing, participants sit in a formation known as a "hollow square," with singers—seated according to vocal part—facing a central open space. Although the vocal parts are gendered in typical choirs, this is not the case in Sacred Harp: Women will frequently sing the tenor part up an octave, while men will sing the soprano part down an octave. There is no conductor. Instead, participants will take turns selecting hymns, which each will direct from the central position. The person who chooses the hymn will specify which verses are to be sung, and someone will provide the starting pitches for each part. Then the group will sing through the hymn once on the syllables before turning to the text.

The vocal style associated with Sacred Harp singing is also unusual. Participants do not tend to approach their task with nuance. Instead, each sings as loudly and exuberantly as they can, often accenting the rhythms with physical movement (something that is expressly prohibited in choral singing). The tempos are steady. Finally, there is never instrumental accompaniment.

"Amazing Grace," paired with the tune "New Britain," appears in both *Southern Harmony* and *The Sacred Harp*. The *Southern Harmony* version contains only three voice parts (soprano, tenor, and bass), but editions of *The Sacred Harp* eventually added an alto part. (Experienced singers might notice that the soprano part is very high. This notation, however, is not meant to be taken literally, and

Image 11.29: The *Southern Harmony* version of "Amazing Grace," published in 1835, contains only three voice parts.
Source: Wikimedia Commons
Attribution: William Walker
License: Public Domain

Image 11.30: The *Sacred Harp* version of "Amazing Grace," published in 1844, contains four voice parts.
Source: Wikimedia Commons
Attribution: User "Opus33"
License: Public Domain

most groups will sing the hymn in a lower key.) The familiar melody is in the tenor in both versions, while the other parts provide harmony above and below. As a result, a performance of this version of the hymn strikes most listeners as familiar, but somehow strange.

Our rendition of "Amazing Grace" was recorded at the Southwest Sacred Harp Singing Convention in McMahan, TX, in 2011. After an initial pass using the syllables, the participants sing the first four verses of Newton's text.

"Amazing Grace" in the Southern Gospel Tradition[6]

Soon after the 1844 publication of *The Sacred Harp*, a rift emerged in the Southern hymn publishing community. In 1846, Jesse Aiken published *The Christian Minstrel*, which introduced a new shape-note system using seven shapes. This development seemed natural enough. As one advocate for the new system put it, "Would any parent having seven children, ever think of calling them by four names?" Aiken's hymnal provoked a virulent debate. While some publishers refused to adopt the new system, others were won over. William Walker himself switched to seven-shape notation with his 1866 hymnal *Christian Harmony*. Eventually, the seven-shape system emerged victorious.

6.		"Amazing Grace" Performance: The Inspirations (1976)

Other changes came upon the hymn publishing industry as well. By the late 19th century, the stark harmonies of *The Sacred Harp* had largely been eschewed in favor of more pleasing harmonies derived from popular music. Hymn composers moved away from the minor mode—which dominates the pages of *The Sacred Harp*—and began to write in a more cheerful vein. Composers also abandoned the archaic practice of placing the melody in the tenor voice, instead putting it in the soprano and supporting it with accompaniment in the lower parts. Finally, piano accompaniment was introduced in the early 20th century as churches gained access to instruments.

All of these characteristics describe the **Southern gospel** tradition, which continues to flourish. Southern gospel music is driven by hymn composers and publishers, who supply a steady diet of new hymns. These are sung at conventions, which attract vast numbers of singers eager to test their reading ability on unfamiliar music. At the same time, Southern gospel devotees enjoy singing old favorites, such as "Amazing Grace." Although Southern gospel music does not belong to a single Christian denomination, it is closely associated with evangelical branches such as the Southern Baptist Convention.

In the early 20th century, Southern gospel publishers began sponsoring professional quartets to sing their music. These quartets—which were at first all-male—toured the singing conventions, where they would perform the latest hymns from a particular publisher. They also participated in revivals, gave concerts, sang on the radio, and released commercial recordings. It might be argued that Southern gospel transformed from a **participatory** musical tradition to a **performative** one, for today many people think of Southern gospel primarily as a commercial music genre. At the same time, collective singing of Southern gospel music continues to take place in churches and at singing conventions.

Image 11.31: Although Southern gospel quartets were traditionally all male, modern singing groups typically include women.
Source: Picryl
Attribution: Library of Congress
License: Public Domain

Our example was recorded by the Inspirations in 1976. The Inspirations follow solidly in the model established in the early 20th century by publishers' quartets. The group was formed in 1964 when Martin Cook, a high school chemistry teacher in Bryson City, NC, began singing gospel music with four of his students. A couple years later they founded a gospel music festival, Singing in the Smokies, and by 1969 the Inspirations were a full-time professional group. A string of number-one gospel hits in the early 1970s cemented their reputation.

The Inspirations' recording of "Amazing Grace" was created during a live performance in Warner Robbins, GA. This is important, both because the sounds of the audience contribute to the effectiveness of the recording and because the release of live albums is a meaningful practice in the gospel tradition. After all, this music is intended to have a profound and personal impact on the listener. The Inspirations describe themselves as "an enthusiastic, sincere, clean-cut group of fundamental conservative Christian gentlemen with a desire and an objective to witness to a needful and sinful world through the medium of Gospel Music." They make music not to entertain an audience but to save it.

The first verse is sung by lead tenor Archie Watkins. As is typical of the genre, he sings the melody in the highest part of his range. This means that the top notes sound almost like cries. We can hear that he is straining to reach them—an effort that is emotionally compelling and communicates the sincerity of the message. This type of singing has roots in the tradition of secular Appalachian music-making, and can be heard in banjo songs and bluegrass. Watkins does not sing with a steady pulse, as we heard in the Sacred Harp rendition, but takes his time to express each individual word.

For the second verse, the ensemble enters to supply a wordless harmony, switching to text only for the final two words. The third verse is sung on text by the entire ensemble, although Watkins high melody still stands out from the texture. We also hear the low bass singing of Mike Holcomb—another characteristic feature of the Southern gospel music.

The third verse sung by the Inspirations, however, is not the third verse of Newton's text:

> When we've been there ten thousand years,
> Bright shining as the sun,
> We've no less days to sing God's praise,
> Than when we first begun.

In fact, this verse wasn't written by Newton at all. It was first published in the 1790 Virginian hymnal *A Collection of Sacred Ballads*, in which it was incorporated into the much older hymn "Jerusalem, My Happy Home." (In *The Sacred Harp*, the verse appears as part of "Jerusalem, My Happy Home" and "Ninety-Fifth Psalm," but is not included in "Amazing Grace.") The first person to associate this verse with "Amazing Grace" was Harriet Beecher Stowe, author of the 1852 anti-slavery novel *Uncle Tom's Cabin*. In Stowe's narrative, Uncle Tom sings three verses of "Amazing Grace"—two of Newton's verses and the new one—to mark his moment of greatest spiritual need.

It is typical for favorite verses to appear in more than one hymn. This is the result of oral tradition. A certain verse—memorable for its imagery or message—sticks in a singer's head. They then add the verse to another hymn, one that has a tune with the same pattern of strong and weak beats. It is believed that Stowe was drawing from African American oral tradition in particular when she included this verse in "Amazing Grace." However, it was not included in a hymnal until the 1910 *Coronation Hymns*.

"Amazing Grace" in the Black Gospel Tradition[7]

Black gospel is not unrelated to Southern gospel. The two traditions share a great deal in common and have always influenced one another. In the period during which these traditions developed, however, American society was highly segregated—by Jim Crow laws in the South and by less visible means in the North. It is unsurprising, therefore, that a unique tradition of music, based in part on African American musical tradition, should have arisen among black worshippers.

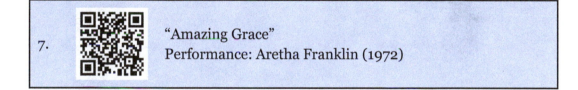

7.   "Amazing Grace"
      Performance: Aretha Franklin (1972)

The style of music making that would come to be known as black gospel emerged first in the Holiness churches of the early 20th century. These congregations traced their roots to the revival meetings of the Second Great Awakening, in which many African Americans had participated. They favored a highly expressive and emotional form of worship, in which individual congregants might be moved to speak or sing.

During the 1920s, musicians in Holiness churches began to incorporate popular influences into worship. These included styles of piano playing derived from ragtime, percussion and brass instruments associated with jazz, and blues-inspired vocals. Although some churchgoers were skeptical about the inclusion of secular sounds in worship, the music gained popularity with the success of early recordings by artists like Arizona Dranes, a blind pianist and singer who belonged to the Church of God in Christ.

In the 1930s, male quartets—much like those in the Southern gospel tradition—and choirs came to the fore as black gospel gained followers. Although the style borrowed from popular music, it maintained strict separation from the commercial

Image 11.32: The Golden Gate Quartet, seen here performing in 1964, was founded in 1934 and remains active today, although with new members.
Source: Wikimedia Commons
Attribution: F.N. Broers / Anefo
License: CC0

world, and gospel singers who made secular recordings were often shunned by the church community. At the same time, black gospel exercised enormous influence on the development of popular music. This influence is especially evident in the singing styles that emerged in rhythm 'n' blues and, later, soul. It is no wonder that many successful gospel artists were attracted by the possibility of mainstream popular success.

Aretha Franklin (1942-2018) was among the most prominent of these crossover singers, although anxieties about secular music had largely subsided by the time her career took off. Franklin was the daughter of a Baptist minister, C.L. Franklin, and she first sang in the church. Her father was something of a celebrity, and Franklin got to know many of the great gospel singers while she was still a child. At the age of 12, she began accompanying her father on preaching tours, for which she would provide stirring music. At 18, however, she decided to leave gospel behind for a career in popular music. With her father's support, she moved to New York City and signed with Columbia Records.

Franklin did not flourish at Columbia, and it was not until she moved to Atlantic Records in 1967 that her career took off. Her version of "Respect," which topped the R&B and pop charts that year, was just the first in a chain of hit singles and albums. At the height of her success, however, Franklin returned to her roots and recorded a gospel album, the 1972 *Amazing Grace*. It was to be the top-selling album of her entire career.

Image 11.33: This 1967 photograph shows Aretha Franklin five years before she recorded "Amazing Grace."
Source: Wikimedia Commons
Attribution: Atlantic Records
License: Public Domain

Amazing Grace was recorded live over the course of two evening concerts at the New Temple Missionary Baptist Church in Los Angeles. Franklin was backed up by the Southern California Community Choir and the prominent gospel singer Reverend James Cleveland. The title track, "Amazing Grace," is the longest on the double album, clocking in at nearly eleven minutes. (Our version, taken from the master recording, is over sixteen minutes long.) The selection was featured near the end of the first evening's concert, and was without doubt the high point of the show.

As with the Inspirations' recording discussed above, the fact that Franklin's "Amazing Grace" was recorded live is important. The sounds of the audience help us to visualize the church setting and remind us that this is worship music. We don't just hear the song—we also hear people being moved and transformed by the song. The shouts and applause of the listeners are integral to the performance. The audience noise also helps us to understand the motivations of the singer. Aretha is not just performing a song: She is expressing her deeply held beliefs in an intensely personal way. Finally, we can hear how the audience shapes the performance. As they respond to Franklin's singing, they also inspire her to new heights of expression.

Franklin's singing style is emblematic of the black gospel tradition. She in fact only sings two verses of the hymn: the first and third. However, she weaves them into an epic drama, full of twists and turns. Every vowel of the text is drawn out in a long **melisma** containing many notes, and there is never a sense of pulse. Although the first verse is elongated and intense, we soon find out that Franklin was only getting started. The emotional energy builds with the third verse, in which Franklin brightens her timbre as she moves to the top of her range. She also adds a great deal of new text, which gives the impression of having been improvised on the spot. With these added words, she personalizes the message and seems to confess her own sins. She speaks directly to the people in the room through music.

In the final line of the verse, however, Franklin abandons the texts and insteads hums an additional iteration of the melody. By doing so, she draws down the emotional energy for the purpose of producing an even more dramatic final conclusion. Upon returning to the text of verse three, Franklin inaugurates a series of call and response passages between herself and the choir/audience. Again, the verse fails to conclude, and the choir enters with the third-line text. It seems almost as if they are trying to provide Franklin with the strength to finish the hymn. When Franklin returns with the first line of the verse, she builds her singing into shouts and cries before finally arriving "home."

These three renditions of "Amazing Grace" are remarkably different. Variations in performing forces—choir vs male quartet vs solo female vocalist with piano accompaniment—do not even begin to explain the variations in aesthetic and emotional impact. Instead, we have to examine the vocal styles that are characteristic of each performing tradition—styles that in turn make sense only in the context of worship practices that are each unique to a time and place. In the end, we see how a hymn written centuries ago by a reformed slave trader can embody and express the spiritual values of diverse individuals and sects.

JOHN COLTRANE, *A LOVE SUPREME*

All of the compositions we have examined in this chapter were originally intended for practical use in a worship service. In our exploration of "Amazing Grace," however, we encountered instances of performances—Aretha Franklin's, for example—that brought the hymn into less formal realms. Franklin's concerts probably provided a worship experience to some of those present, and her performance was an expression of deeply held belief. The essential purpose of the concerts, however, was to create a commercial recording, which is in turn available for consumption as entertainment.

Image 11.34: Coltrane is pictured here in 1963.
Source: Wikimedia Commons
Attribution: Hugo van Gelderen (Anefo)
License: CC0

With our final example, we will encounter a similar instance of personal belief influencing the commercial output of a performing artist. John Coltrane's album *A Love Supreme* (recorded in 1964, released in 1965) was certainly never intended for use in a place of worship. All the same, it was clearly intended by the performer as an *act* of worship, although the specifics of Coltrane's belief system—outlined below—continue to elude researchers.

John Coltrane (1926-1967) was one of the great jazz innovators of the 20th century. He began playing saxophone as a teenager in Philadelphia. Coltrane joined the Navy during World War II, where his talent was recognized and he received the rare honor of being permitted to play with the base swing band even though he had not enlisted as a musician. Upon leaving the military, he toured with various bands and began to meet and play with the jazz luminaries of the era.

Coltrane began his post-war career playing bebop, a high-intensity form of jazz in which virtuosic soloists exhibit their skills. Bebop is performed by **jazz combos**—small ensembles with a single performer per instrument. A combo will almost always include piano, bass, and drums, with the addition of one more players on a melody instrument (saxophone, trumpet, and trombone are the most common). In bebop, the combo will begin by playing a set melody, usually underlaid with complex harmonies. This composition is termed a **head** and is notated on a **lead sheet**. Then the members of the ensemble will take turns improvising solos over the chord progression. Coltrane composed and recorded perhaps the most difficult of all bebop heads, "Giant Steps,"[8] in 1959 (released on the album *Giant Steps* in 1960).

8.  "Giant Steps" (1959) is perhaps Coltrane's most famous composition—and performance.

Like many jazz musicians of the era, Coltrane struggled with drug and alcohol abuse, and he became a heroin addict. In 1957, however, Coltrane quit heroin cold turkey, locking himself in his Philadelphia home to battle withdrawal. He later described "a spiritual awakening which was to lead me to a richer, fuller, more productive life." He indeed went on to produce his greatest work, and religious themes would increasingly dominate his music for the rest of his career. Coltrane's most compelling spiritual statement, by all accounts, was his 1965 album *A Love Supreme*.

In the liner notes to *A Love Supreme*, Coltrane described his 1957 experience: "At that time, in gratitude, I humbly asked to be given the means and privilege to make others happy through music. [. . .] This album is a humble offering to Him. An attempt to say "THANK YOU GOD" through our work, even as we do in our hearts and with our tongues." There is no doubt that Coltrane intended his album as an expression of his profound spiritual thanksgiving to god—but it is not clear exactly who or what "god" was to Coltrane.

Both Coltrane's maternal and paternal grandfathers were pastors in the African Methodist Episcopal church, and there is no doubt that his childhood experiences with Christian worship influenced both his beliefs and musical expression. However, Coltrane became increasingly interested in non-Christian spiritual beliefs in his adult years. His first wife, with whom he maintained a close friendship even after they divorced, was a Muslim convert. Later he took to studying Eastern religions, and he was known to pore over the religious texts of Christianity, Islam, Judaism, Hinduism, and Buddhism with equal fervor. In the liner notes to his 1965 album *Meditations*, Coltrane stated bluntly, "I believe in all religions."

Image 11.35: The album cover for *A Love Supreme* is stark and serious.
Source: Flickr
Attribution: Gilles Péris y Saborit
License: CC BY-NC 2.0

A Love Supreme is in four parts: "Acknowledgement," "Resolution," "Pursuance," and "Psalm." For this reason, the complete work is often described as a suite. The parts range from seven to eleven minutes in length, and were recorded in a single session on December 9, 1964. The performers, in addition to Coltrane, were McCoy Tyner on piano, Jimmy Garrison on bass, and Elvin Jones on drums. This ensemble, known today as the "classic quartet," recorded many of Coltrane's greatest albums.

Although *A Love Supreme* is generally regarded as a unique artistic work that cannot easily be categorized, it can also be understood as an example of **modal jazz**. In modal jazz, the traditional chords of bebop are replaced by harmonies built on modal scales—those other than major and minor. With the emphasis shifted away from harmony, performers focus more on melodic development, rhythmic intricacy, timbral variation, and emotional expression. Examples of modal jazz tend to be slower and more exploratory than bebop recordings. Throughout, *A Love Supreme* avoids explicit melodic statements or clear rhythmic frameworks. There is no "tune," and the listener cannot easily find a downbeat or identify the meter. Instead, the recording gives the impression of transcending the confines of "jazz" and offering a window directly into the players' souls.

"Acknowledgement"[9] opens with the reverberation of a gong and cymbal rolls. Out of this wash of sound emerge Tyner's piano chords and Coltrane's improvisation on a four-note figure. Next we hear the primary theme of the album: a four-note, repeated motif played by Garrison on the bass. When Coltrane enters again, it is with the same four notes we heard him play at the opening of the track. He slowly adds notes and builds in energy, eventually using the technique of **overblowing** to create squawking notes in the high range of the instrument. We hear the same rhythmic patterns again and again throughout his solo. Finally, Coltrane plays the four-note motif from the bass again and again, in dozens of different keys. The track concludes with members of the combo singing the motif on the text "a love supreme" before Garrison plays a closing bass solo. By singing, the performers reveal what had hitherto been a secret meaning behind the motif that dominates the composition.

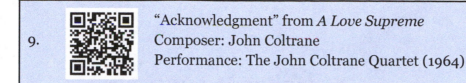

9.		"Acknowledgment" from *A Love Supreme* Composer: John Coltrane Performance: The John Coltrane Quartet (1964)

The final part, "Psalm,"[10] also has a secret text. This time, the text is a poem of praise authored by Coltrane and included in the album's liner notes. It uses phraseology and language that is familiar from Christian worship, but at no point does it explicitly indicate that Coltrane is worshipping the Christian god. Similarly, the title "Psalm"—a reference to the Psalms of Christian and Jewish tradition—clearly refers to something other than a literal Biblical Psalm. Although there is no sung text in the recording, the listener can easily follow the words as Coltrane plays, since his phrasing closely matches that of the poem.

10.		"Psalm" from *A Love Supreme* Composer: John Coltrane Performance: The John Coltrane Quartet (1964)

RESOURCES FOR FURTHER LEARNING

Print

Cobb Jr., Buell E. *The Sacred Harp: A Tradition and Its Music.* University of Georgia Press, 2004.

Goff, James R. *Close Harmony: A History of Southern Gospel.* University of North Carolina Press, 2002.

Kahn, Ashley. *A Love Supreme: The Story of John Coltrane's Signature Album.* Penguin Books, 2003.

Reed-Jones, Carol. *Hildegard of Bingen: Woman of Vision.* Paper Crane Press, 2004.

Ritz, David. *Respect: The Life of Aretha Franklin.* Back Bay Books, 2015.

Taruskin, Richard. *Music from the Earliest Notations to the Sixteenth Century.* Oxford University Press, 2009.

Taruskin, Richard. *Music in the Seventeenth and Eighteenth Centuries: The Oxford History of Western Music.* Oxford University Press, 2009.

Wolff, Christoph. *Johann Sebastian Bach: The Learned Musician.* W.W. Norton & Company, 2001.

12

Music for Moving

Esther M. Morgan-Ellis

INTRODUCTION

Any music that has a regular pulse can cause listeners to tap their feet or clap in unison. Sometimes, however, such coordination of physical activity is the primary purpose of music. This is the case when soldiers sing together while they march, or when a DJ blasts music onto a crowded dance floor. Work songs can coordinate practical labor, such as chopping wood or sowing seeds, while dance music brings people together in an enjoyable social activity. All music related to movement, however, has certain elements in common, for it must relate to the mechanical functions of the human body.

Image 12.1: Prisoners at the Parchman Penal Farm in Mississippi, such as these photographed in 1911, often sang call-and-response songs to coordinate their physical labor and keep up their endurance.
Source: Wikimedia Commons
Attribution: Unknown
License: Public Domain

MUSIC FOR MARCHING

Music can have a powerful impact on the energy and coordination of marching groups. It not only keeps participants stepping in time but can provide them with motivation as they become tired. For this reason, militaries around the world have accompanied marching with music for untold centuries. No matter when or where such music is created, it is always essentially similar. Music for marching, after all, must be in **duple meter** (for humans have two legs) and must feature a pulse at a walking pace—brisk for a drill, perhaps, or stately for a ceremony. The pulse must always be clear, strong, and regular, so that marchers can hear and respond to it. Music for marching cannot contain tempo variations, or it would no longer be of use. Music for marching also needs to be loud. Because of its military connections, marching music tends to be firmly associated with a specific nation, for which it can provide patriotic expression. This is true of both examples that we will explore.

Image 12.2: Marching bands are a typical feature of parades, such as this 2007 parade that took place at the Texas State Fair.
Source: Wikimedia Commons
Attribution: Terry Shuck
License: CC BY 2.0

JOHN PHILIP SOUSA, "THE STARS AND STRIPES FOREVER"

	"The Stars and Stripes Forever" Composer: John Philip Sousa Performance: United States Navy Band (2013)

Time	Form	What to listen for
0'00"	Intro	The march starts with a unison melody played by the ensemble

0'04"	A	A variety of instruments play the melody
0'19"	A	The A strain is repeated
0'34"	B	The volume drops as the clarinets and euphoniums take the melody
0'50"	B	The second pass through the B strain, featuring the trumpets, is considerably louder
1'05"	C	The volume diminishes again as single-reed instruments take the melody
1'37"	D	Unison trombones lead off this passage
2'01"	C'	A piccolo countermelody is added to the C strain
2'31"	D	The D strain is repeated
2'55"	C"	A trombone countermelody is added to the C strain; in addition, the trumpets take over the melody, thereby increasing the volume

The most prolific and influential composer of **marches** in the United States was John Philip Sousa (1854-1932). Although he began his career as a military musician, most of Sousa's marches were intended for concert performance by his band, which toured the world for decades around the turn of the 20th century. For this reason, his marches are particularly interesting to listen to, but they still meet the requirements for functional marching music.

Sousa was born in Washington, D.C., where his father served as a trombone player in the Marine Band. Following some initial private music instruction, Sousa enlisted as a musical apprentice in the United States Marine Corps at the age of 13. He left the military in 1875 to pursue a career in theater music, and over the next five years

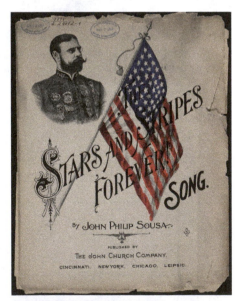

Image 12.3: Sousa's "The Stars and Stripes Forever" was premiered in 1897.
Source: Wikimedia Commons
Attribution: John Philip Sousa
License: Public Domain

he performed on the violin and began to develop his ability as a conductor. During this period, Sousa also became an expert **arranger**—a skill that would serve him well for the remainder of his career. At first he produced **orchestrations** of popular operas, but later he would make a name for himself as a composer. In 1880, Sousa was asked to produce a series of arrangements of operatic selections for the Marine Band. On the strength of his excellent work, he was invited to rejoin the Corps, this time as director of the Marine Band.

The United States Marine Band

The United States Marine Band has a remarkable history of its own. Established in 1798, it is the oldest of the formal United States military bands, which today number well over one hundred and are attached to all five branches of the military. Of course, the United States military employed musicians long before the Marine Band was formed—and indeed, long before the United States itself came into existence. As early as 1633, the Virginia militia relied on drummers to coordinate drills and maneuvers, and beginning in 1687 the Virginia colonists provided public funds for the purchase of military instruments. The first record of a complete military band dates from 1747, when the Pennsylvania colonists formed regiments.

Both drummers and bands supported American troops throughout the Revolution. In fact, musicians have been credited with some of the major victories. At the 1777 Battle of Bennington, for example, the drummers and fifers accompanied troops directly into battle, inspiring the soldiers to soundly defeat the British in what has since been recognized as a turning point in the war. That same year, buglers were added to cavalry units and tasked with coordinating maneuvers by means of **bugle calls**. At the conclusion of the war, General Washington proclaimed that all military musicians were to be allowed to keep their instruments in recognition of the great hardship they had endured.

Image 12.4: This photograph of Sousa was taken in 1900.
Source: Wikimedia Commons
Attribution: Elmer Chickering
License: Public Domain

Image 12.5: This photograph of the Marine Band was taken in 2019.
Source: The United States Marine Corps
Attribution: Travis Miller
License: Public Domain

Image 12.6: This painting, created by Archibald Willard in 1857, depicts drummers and fifers in the Revolutionary War.
Source: Wikimedia Commons
Attribution: Archibald Willard
License: Public Domain

The 19th century saw significant improvements both in military music programs and in the construction of the instruments used by military bands. As of 1815, when music was introduced to the West Point curriculum, a military band was likely to include flutes, oboes, bassoons, clarinets, French horns, serpents, bass drums, and tambourines. Soon, however, improved brass instruments—most notably the trumpet, which could now play complex melodies—led to their inclusion in the standard band line-up. These technical developments were the result of new production techniques associated with the Industrial Revolution, and they benefited wind musicians in all settings by greatly expanding the capabilities and ranges of their instruments.

By the time Sousa began his career, therefore, the military band was a large and sophisticated ensemble capable of great flexibility and nuance. Sousa himself aided in the creation of the sousaphone, which is essentially a tuba that has been modified to increase its capacity such that it can be heard over a band. The status of military musicians was also on the rise. General Phillip Sheridan had credited musicians with Union victories in the Civil War, stating that "music has done its share, and more than its share, in winning this war." The Civil War was certainly fought to diverse musical accompaniment: 28,000 musicians serving in 618 bands accompanied troops into battle, played for ceremonies, and provided entertainment at military encampments.

Sousa's Career

As director of the Marine Band, Sousa was primarily responsible for providing ceremonial music. Since 1801, the Marine Band has boasted a unique attachment to the White House, earning the nickname "The President's Own." The Marine Band plays for all Presidential inaugurations, state funerals, and military funerals at Arlington National Cemetery. It also marks the arrival of visiting heads of state and participates in state dinners and formal receptions. As the premier national music ensemble, it serves as a symbol of military and political might.

Sousa, however, also expanded the public-facing role of the Marine Band. In 1891 he took the band on a concert tour, inaugurating an annual tradition that has carried into the present day. Under Sousa, the Marine Band also released commercial recordings under the auspices of the Columbia Phonograph Company. This was a point of significant contention for Sousa himself. On the one hand, his Columbia recordings made him famous: It was as a direct result of his success as a recording artist that Sousa was able to launch a lucrative private career upon leaving the military in 1892. At the same time, Sousa believed that recording technology marked the inevitable decline of live music as both a professional and amateur pursuit.

For decades to come, Sousa would publicly resist the steady growth of the recording industry while simultaneously profiting from it. 1906 saw the publication of Sousa's most famous attack on the industry, an article entitled "The Menace of Mechanical Music." That same year he made the following remarks at a congressional hearing:

Image 12.7: Here we see Sousa's band in 1893.
Source: Wikimedia Commons
Attribution: Unknown
License: Public Domain

These talking machines are going to ruin the artistic development of music in this country. When I was a boy—I was born in this town—in front of every house in the summer evenings you would find young people together singing the songs of the day or the old songs. To-day you hear these infernal machines going night and day. We will not have a vocal cord left. The vocal cord will be eliminated by a process of evolution, as was the tail of man when he came from the ape.

Sousa conjured up an apocalyptic image of parlor pianos fallen silent and children divested of the ability to sing their childish songs. He warns of a future where all music will come from the "talking machine." At the same time, however, Sousa's own band was releasing recordings—although Sousa himself almost never conducted the ensemble at recording sessions and was able to proudly state that he was in no way personally associated with the gramophone companies.

Although this might seem hypocritical, the subject of the congressional hearing mentioned above—a new copyright law, intended to protect the rights of composers in the realm of recorded music—casts the controversy in a different light. While Sousa may indeed have genuinely feared the effects of "canned music" on amateur participatory music making, he was primarily concerned with the rights of composers, who were losing income due to that fact that they could not claim

royalties on recordings of their works. Until 1909, anyone could make and sell unlimited recordings of a published musical composition or literary work upon purchasing a single copy of the printed product. Composers, lyricists, song writers, and authors were not entitled to royalties, and instead had to watch those in the recording industry get rich from their creative work. In making the above argument, Sousa was trying to appeal to the public and win support for the passage of updated legislation. He was eventually successful: The Copyright Act of 1909 guaranteed compensation to composers and authors whose work was reproduced in a recorded medium.

Sousa also worried that "canned music" would prevent people from attending live performances by the Sousa Band, for such concerts were the main source of income for Sousa and his musicians. The Sousa Band toured constantly, making visits not only to all parts of the United States but to countries around the world. In total, the band gave well over 15,000 concerts between 1892 and 1931. A typical concert would include transcriptions of popular orchestral works, operatic excerpts (complete with vocal soloists), virtuosic instrumental solos, and—most thrilling of all—newly-composed marches by Sousa himself.

Image 12.8: This program outlines a typical concert by the Sousa Band. The audience, however, would have heard more than just the single march listed here: Sousa interpolated marches in between most of the more serious numbers.
Source: Ann Arbor District Library
Attribution: University Musical Society
License: CC BY-NC-SA 2.0

The Stars and Stripes Forever

We will consider Sousa's most famous march, "The Stars and Stripes Forever." According to Sousa, he composed this march in his head in late 1896, shortly after hearing about the death of his manager and friend David Blakely. It was premiered in early 1897 and met with immediate success. Ninety years later, in 1987, "The Stars and Stripes Forever" was designated as the National March of the United States of America by an act of Congress.

In addition to performing "The Stars and Stripes Forever" at concerts, the Sousa Band made several recordings of the march. Even more profitable, however, were Sousa's various arrangements for performance by amateur musicians. These included versions for piano (two, four, or six hands), zither (solo or duet), one or two mandolins (solo or with piano accompaniment), guitar (solo or duet), banjo (solo or duet), and banjo with piano. In addition, Sousa published full band arrangements for all of his marches—although he was careful to include many part duplications between the instruments, so that even a small town band with only a few members would be able to give a successful performance.

"The Stars and Stripes Forever" provides a typical example of a Sousa march. Its form might be summarized as: intro A A B B C D C' D C". It begins with a brief but loud introduction by the whole band. This is followed by three distinctive melodic passages, or "**strains**," the first two of which (A and B) are repeated. Each of the strains is in the major mode, and each—naturally—features the regular pulse of percussion and low brass. Next, an interlude (D) interrupts the pleasant mood of the strains: Blasting brass belt out chromatic scales and dissonant chords, exploring minor-mode territory while climbing to successively higher pitch levels. It is a relief, therefore, when the third strain returns (C'), now with a piccolo countermelody floating over the topic. Another interlude (D) sets up a final rendition of the C strain. Now elaborated upon even further, C" features both the piccolo countermelody and an additional countermelody in the trombones. The resulting cacophony is undeniably exciting.

SCOTTISH TRADITIONAL, "SCOTLAND THE BRAVE"

Our previous example, "The Stars and Stripes Forever," might just as well have been discussed in Chapter 9 as an example of music embodying national identity. Not only is it the official National March of the United States, but it has come to be associated with patriotic events, especially Independence Day. Our next example would be even more at home in Chapter 9: Both the tune—"Scotland the Brave"[1]—and the musical tradition—Scottish Highland bagpiping—are intimately connected with Scottish history and identity. This is, of course, hardly surprising. When we talk about marches, we are often talking about military tradition, and it is nearly impossible to disentangle military history and practice from national identity and pride.

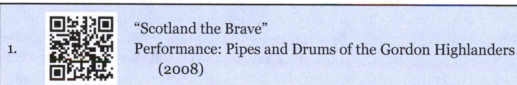

1. "Scotland the Brave"
   Performance: Pipes and Drums of the Gordon Highlanders (2008)

Scottish Highland Bagpipes

Scottish Highland bagpipes are certainly a military instrument. The first written account of bagpipes being carried into battle dates from 1549, when the piercing sound of bagpipes was found to carry across the battlefield even better than that of a trumpet. Pipers were regularly attached to combat regiments, and they could be heard on both sides of the famous Jacobite rising of 1745, when Charles Edward Stuart sought to regain the British throne. In this conflict, bagpipes served not only to urge troops into battle but to mark the identity of the combatants: the Jacobites

Image 12.9: The Scottish Highland bagpipes are particularly loud and powerful.
Source: Flickr
Attribution: User "jpellgen"
License: CC BY-NC-ND 2.0

carried Scottish Highland bagpipes, while the British troops carried Lowland bagpipes (a related instrument that has fallen out of use).

Pipers continue to serve in the British military into the present day, although their role is now only ceremonial and they are no longer deployed in combat. The last appearance of pipers on the front line took place during a 1967 uprising in the British protectorate of South Arabia (now part of Yemen). Pipers also led assaults during both of the World Wars, but the practice was largely abolished due to the high casualty rate.

There is no question that the Scottish Highland bagpipes are an outdoor instrument. They are extremely loud. Scottish bagpipes seem to have come into use during the 1200s, although it is unknown whether they were adapted from a Roman instrument or developed independently. The basic principle of any bagpipe is the same: An air reservoir (usually a bag) is squeezed so as to force air through a series of pipes, thereby producing sound. Most of the pipes are tuned to a fixed pitch, but one is equipped with holes that allow the piper to sound specific notes. While bagpipes can be found around the world, the Scottish instrument and associated tradition has certainly gained the greatest prominence. Today, pipe bands can be found in almost all former British colonies and throughout the United States.

In Scottish Highland bagpipes, the air reservoir is filled when the piper blows into a long **air pipe**. Although the piper must regularly refill the reservoir, this action has no impact on the sound of the instrument, which is continuous and always at the same volume. This is because the sound is produced by air from the bag—which is kept under a constant pressure—flowing out through the pipes. The fixed-pitched pipes are three in number, and they all play the same note, although in two different octaves. The other pipe—termed the **chanter**—allows the piper to play nine distinct pitches spanning just over an octave.

The fact that the melodic capabilities of the Highland pipes is so limited means that performers must either play repertoire suited to their instrument or adapt other melodies by changing some of the notes. For example, pipers frequently play the melody from Dvořák's Symphony No. 9 "From the New World" (Chapter 9), which is usually retitled "Goin' Home."[2] However, the Highland pipes do not have a pitch that is required to correctly perform the middle section of the melody. Instead, pipers simply play the closest pitch that is available on the instrument, which happens to be one half step lower than the pitch Dvořák had intended.

2.  "Goin' Home" is a popular selection for Highland pipers.

It is typical for pipers to borrow tunes from other repertoires. In fact, the two tunes most frequently played on Scottish Highland bagpipes—"Amazing Grace" and "Scotland the Brave"—began life and became popular independent of the piping tradition. "Amazing Grace," discussed in Chapter 11, is a Christian hymn. Although the lyrics were written by an English preacher, they were paired with their melody in the United States, which is also where the hymn became popular. In a sense, therefore, "Amazing Grace"—like "Goin' Home"—is a musical import.

Scotland the Brave

"Scotland the Brave," on the other hand, seems to have been written in Scotland in the 1890s, although it was initially played on other instruments. The tune first appeared in the 1895 *Gesto Collection of Highland Music*, in which it was titled "Scotland Forever" and labelled as a "trumpet march." Around 1911, it was included in a collection of pipe music published by the Boys' Brigade Bands of Glasgow—an indication that Scottish pipers were playing it. The tune, however, did not become famous until 1951, when Cliff Hanley added a patriotic text so that it could be sung in a theatrical production. "Scotland the Brave" quickly became a hit, and in 2006 placed second in a public poll to select an unofficial national anthem for Scotland.

"Scotland the Brave" bears all of the typical characteristics of a march. It is in duple time, to facilitate the tramping of feet. It is in a bright major mode (although the tuning of pipes is not always equivalent to that of a piano). The melody is rhythmically straightforward: There is a note on every strong beat, meaning that the melody will coordinate with the steps of marchers, and the notes that fall between the beats are placed sparsely and predictably. After all, a complex melody would be lost in the noise of an outdoor march, and would confuse the regular rhythm of the movement. It might even prove catastrophic to coordination. The melody also features uneven, or **dotted**, rhythms, which have long been associated with royalty and pomp.

"Scotland the Brave" is also packed with repetition. It is in a **rounded binary form**, meaning that its two parts both end with the same melodic phrase. That phrase also constitutes the first half of the first part, such that the tune can be diagrammed as [A A'] [B A']. In a single turn through the tune, therefore, we hear the A phrase three times—and the B phrase is closely related, bearing the same rhythmic characteristics. Although this form is common in folk music of the British Isles, the melody of "Scotland the Brave" is particularly effective. Both the A and B phrases include the lowest and highest notes of the tune, although they reverse the melodic contour. The A phrase ascends immediately from the low octave to the high and then back down, while the B phrase begins in the high octave and plummets to the low—twice. The result is dizzyingly triumphant.

When we hear pipers play "Scotland the Brave," we hear more than just the notes of the melody as it might be sung or played on the trumpet. That is because pipers deploy a variety of **idiomatic** melodic ornaments that are uniquely available on their instruments. These sometimes sound like glitches or hiccups, but they are in fact specific sequences of between one and four pitches that are quickly and precisely added to the melody using the finger holes on the chanter. Each ornament has a name and is considered appropriate for a specific type of music, and pipers in large bands perform ornaments in perfect unison. In "Scotland the Brave," ornaments help to emphasize the march rhythm. After all, the Scottish Highland bagpipes can only produce sound in a constant, uninterrupted stream. Ornaments break up the sound and introduce rhythmic excitement.

We hear several other instruments on our recording. The pipers are aided by a line of drummers, who keep the pulse steady while also emphasizing the rhythmic contour of the melody. The second time through the melody the pipers are joined by the instruments of a marching band, including brass and flutes. These instruments play a simpler, unornamented version of the tune. We can detect subtle clashes when the pitch produced by the bagpipes, which are tuned according to a unique system, disagrees with that produced by the other instruments.

MUSIC FOR DANCING

Dance music has many of the same demands as march music. It needs to be loud, so that the dancers can hear it over the sounds of their movements. It needs to have a steady tempo, so as to propel the dance forward. It shouldn't be too melodically complex, since the dancers won't be playing close attention. And it often needs to be repetitive, so that dancing can carry on at length.

Unsurprisingly, bagpipes are just as well suited to dancing as they are to marching. In Scotland they are used to accompany the various folk dances, each of which is characterized by a specific meter and rhythm. Reels,[3] for example, are in a fast **quadruple meter** with an emphasis on beats one and three and a melody that moves in steady rhythm at twice the pace of the underlying pulse. Jigs,[4] on the other hand, are in compound duple meter, meaning that each pulse is subdivided into three sub-pulses. These characteristics, of course, are not randomly assigned: They reflect the steps of the dance.

3.  In this example, an Irish pipe band plays a pair of reels.

4.    Here, a Scottish-style pipe band plays a jig.

Because dancing often takes place indoors, Scottish Highland bagpipes are not always the most desireable instrument. One is more likely to hear an instrument that has been used to accompany dancing throughout Europe for many centuries: the violin. The violin is terrifically convenient as a dance instrument. It is small, and therefore highly portable. It can play a fast melody, but is also capable of providing harmonies. It is fairly easy to hear, given its high range and bright timbre. And it can be played standing up—perhaps even by the same person who is calling out the dance instructions. For all of these reasons, violin has emerged as the most popular instrument to accompany dancing from Hungary to Texas.

We will begin our tour of dance music in the United States, therefore, with one of the oldest traditions: The fiddle-driven dance music of the **Southern Appalachians**.

DANCE MUSIC IN THE UNITED STATES

Appalachian Square Dancing: Tommy Jarrell, Fred Cockerham, and Kyle Creed, "Arkansas Traveler"

To see the violin at work as a dance instrument, we will first visit an influential fiddler who lived in North Carolina, Tommy Jarrell (1901-1985). Jarrell developed a unique fiddling style that was both loud and rhythmically exciting, and which was therefore well suited to Appalachian square dancing. We will also consider a recording made by two other musicians from the same region, Fred Cockerham (1905-1980) and Kyle Creed (1912-1982). Although their style was at first limited to Surry County, NC, it has since been adopted by fiddlers and banjo players around the country.

Before we can consider either Appalachian dancing or the music that accompanied it, we need to understand how the instruments used in this tradition found their way into the Southern Appalachian mountains. In addition to the fiddle, mountaineers soon took up the open-backed banjo—an instrument, unlike the violin, that is indigenous to the American South. The combination of fiddle and banjo proved ideal for dancing: Both instruments can play melody while also maintaining rhythmic drive.

The Fiddle

The fiddle was brought to the New World by immigrants from the British Isles and mainland Europe (particularly Germany). Some were lucky enough to bring physical instruments, but many instead brought the recollection of how a violin looked and sounded. These individuals then built their own instruments using available materials. Such homemade fiddles had their shortcomings, but they attest to the importance of music in the lives of impoverished mountaineers who had few material possessions.

The fiddle was played with equal enthusiasm by black and white Americans. As early as the 1690s, enslaved people were tasked with mastering the instrument so that they could provide music for dances. These performers were expected to supply the latest European dance tunes, but they would introduce rhythmic characteristics that have their roots in West African music. They also played their fiddles for entertainment within the enslaved community—often under the fascinated gaze of white onlookers, who sought to imitate their playing. In this way, a uniquely American style of dance music emerged on Southern plantations. When African Americans left the plantations and moved into the mountains, whether enslaved or free, they brought their music with them.

The Southern Appalachians were populated primarily by poor immigrants from the Ulster province of Ireland. These individuals, known in the United States as the Scotch-Irish, crossed the Atlantic as indentured servants, after which they repaid the cost of their passage by working on plantations in Pennsylvania. Upon fulfilling their labor contracts, Scotch-Irish immigrants travelled into the mountains in search of available land. There, as they labored side-by-side with free and enslaved blacks, music often became an important point of exchange. Tunes and playing styles alike were shared across racial lines, with the result that the Scotch-Irish repertoire was soon transformed, reinterpreted, and expanded.

Image 12.10: African Americans began to play the fiddle in the early years of American slavery, when they were expected to provide dance music for their masters. In this image we see a young man playing a homemade instrument for his own amusement.
Source: Flickr
Attribution: User "Okinawa Soba (Rob)"
License: CC BY-NC-SA 2.0

Image 12.11: William Sydney Mount, who traveled through the South in the mid-19th century to sketch scenes for his paintings, has left us with extensive documentation of the interracial musical exchange that was taking place. In this scene, an African American listens surreptitiously to a white fiddler. We can imagine that he is a fiddler himself, and is perhaps listening in order to learn the tune.
Source: Wikimedia Commons
Attribution: William Sidney Mount
License: Public Domain

The Banjo

While the fiddle is a European instrument that underwent change in the hands of Southern African Americans, the banjo is an African American instrument that was transformed by professional white performers in the North. The earliest banjos were built by enslaved people and played for their own amusement. The first recorded mention of a banjo dates from 1781, when Thomas Jefferson noted that the instrument had been "brought hither from Africa." The banjo is indeed derived from West African lutes, including the *akonting* and the *ngoni*. These instruments share important features with the early banjo, including a round neck and strings of unequal length (one is shorter than the others and used to provide a regular drone).

The 19th century saw the transformation and popularization of the banjo in the hands of white musicians. The process began in the 1830s, when the banjo was adopted by **minstrel show** performers as the representative instrument of plantation life. Over the next few decades, **blackface minstrelsy** swept the nation, becoming the most popular form of theatrical entertainment in the United States. Minstrel shows were premised on the imitation of African American music, dance, and speech. Although minstrels advertised their authenticity, most knew little of life in the South and instead borrowed their materials from the Ango-American comedic and musical traditions. In order to portray various stock characters, performers would blacken their faces with burnt cork and dress in the rags of the slave or the finery of the free Northern dandy. They would also accompany their singing and dancing with the instruments of slavery—most notably the banjo.

As a minstrel instrument, the banjo underwent several important changes. It borrowed the flat neck and **frets** of the guitar, which facilitated the performance of melodies. A fifth string was added, thereby expanding the instrument's range. And the body of the banjo developed its characteristic round shape: The instruments built by enslaved people were often constructed out of gourds, but 19th-century

Image 12.12: This modern *akonting* is descended from the same West African instrument as the banjo.
Source: Wikimedia Commons
Attribution: Olivier Epron
License: CC BY 3.0

Image 12.13: The *ngoni* has a canoe-shaped body and short neck, but is also closely related to the banjo.
Source: Wikimedia Commons
Attribution: User "Atamari"
License: CC BY-SA 4.0

Image 12.14: A costumed performer in blackface poses with his banjo.
Source: Wikimedia Commons
Attribution: Unknown
License: Public Domain

minstrels began to stretch skin heads across discarded cheese hoops. The instrument was played in a style known as **clawhammer** or *frailing* in which the performer uses the nail of their index finger to strike melody strings on strong beats while sounding the short fifth (or drone) string with their thumb in between melody notes.

The popularity of blackface minstrelsy is complicated to explain. The practice certainly traded on racist stereotypes and derogatory humor, but it also reflected a genuine interest in black culture and creativity. Consumers of minstrelsy believed that they were getting an authentic glimpse of plantation life—and they often found the characters sympathetic and appealing. The most vicious characterizations arose after the Civil War, when Northerners began to fear an influx of newly-liberated African Americans. At the same time, black performers sought to gain acceptance (and make a living) by putting on minstrel shows of their own. Incredibly, they had to wear dark makeup and imitate the antics of white minstrels in order to be considered authentic.

The impacts of minstrelsy were felt throughout the American popular music landscape. Indeed, they continue to resonate into the present day. Here, however, we will focus on the popularization of the banjo, which soon became a mainstream instrument. In fact, by the late 19th century, it had become an acceptable alternative to the piano for young ladies, while both male and female banjo orchestras proliferated into the 1920s. The banjo became a staple in early jazz, and could be heard in every dance band. The banjo also spread throughout the rural South, where white players were influenced both by traveling minstrels and by the African American musicians in their midsts.

Dancing and Mountain Life

This brings us back to the Southern Appalachians, where rural mountain dwellers played the fiddle and banjo both for entertainment and for profit. The image of the carefree hillbilly strumming a banjo on his porch is, of course, profoundly misleading: Mountaineers worked hard and lived precariously, and they often did not have the leisure to indulge in music. All the same, if they wanted to be entertained, they had to entertain themselves, and music helped to pass the time at home.

Musicians could also earn money by playing at dances. **Square dancing—** although frowned upon by certain churchgoers—was a popular form of entertainment. A dance would usually take place inside of a home on a Saturday night, and people would walk great distances to attend. All of the furniture would be moved outside, and the floor might be sprinkled with cornmeal. The musicians—or perhaps just a single fiddler—would stand in a central doorway and play as loudly as possible. To play for a dance, a fiddler only needed to know one tune, which could be repeated all night if necessary. Dances could become quite rowdy, and young women were often prohibited from attending. Those who did show up would pay a little money, some of which would be handed over to the musicians—unless they were simply compensated with dinner.

Appalachian square dancing[5] is descended from social dances of Europe and the British Isles, although it has taken on unique forms. The dancers are organized either into squares of four couples or large circles containing any number of couples. They engage in a variety of familiar and repetitive interactions, usually following the instructions of a **dance caller**. Dancers might grasp hands to turn around one another, exchange places, dance in couples, gallop up and down lines, or weave amongst one another. The dances can go on indefinitely, although the caller usually brings them to an end after ten or fifteen minutes.

5.  In this video, a caller leads participants through the figures of a square dance to the accompaniment of "Arkansas Traveler."

Such dances require music with a steady pulse, a fast pace, and an emphasis on the off-beat: Dancers move with a continuous down-and-up motion, and they frequently add individualized footwork between the basic steps. While it does not matter which specific tune is played for a dance, the style of the performance is therefore very important.

The Musicians of Surry County, NC

This brings us, finally, to Tommy Jarrell, Fred Cockerham, and Kyle Creed, all of whom contributed to the development of a unique and highly danceable style in Surry County, NC, in the early 20th century. Of the three, only Cockerham was a professional musician. Indeed, it was very uncommon for mountaineers to pursue music as an occupation. There was more money to be made in manual labor, with the result that only those with physical handicaps (most often blindness) were likely to resort to music as a primary source of income. Like many rural musicians of the era, Cockerham found work with a traveling medicine show, advertising a rhubarb salve made by the South Atlantic Chemical Company. It was grueling work that required constant travel and frequent live radio performances in distant cities.

Creed was an expert carpenter and stone mason, and he made a living in construction. In the 1960s, however, Creed built a banjo for his friend Fred

Cockerham. It was a success, and over the next two decades Creed applied his carpentry skills to the production of about two hundred banjos. His work as a **luthier**, or instrument builder, was enormously influential. Creed's banjos, which are highly prized, had several unique features, including a shorter neck than had previously been typical. Today, most open-backed banjos are built following his design. Creed was also an expert fiddler and banjo player. Like many Appalachian musicians, he learned to play from older male relatives, including his father, uncle, and grandfather.

Jarrell charted the most typical course through life. As a boy, he learned to play banjo and fiddle from his father, who made a living as a farmer. Jarrell would often provide dance music with his father and his uncle: The three men would stand in different rooms, each playing the fiddle at top volume. Upon his marriage in 1923, however, Jarrell took a job in road construction, operating a motor grader for the North Carolina Highway Department, and played fiddle and banjo only for his own entertainment. Work like his, however, hardly left the laborer with excessive time and energy for leisure pursuits, and Jarrell largely gave up music for much of his adult life. He returned to his instruments only in the 1960s, following the death of his wife. His exuberant style attracted many admirers, and aspiring musicians began to visit him at home, where Jarrell's legendary hospitality won him many friends.

Arkansas Traveler

"Arkansas Traveler"
Performance: Tommy Jarrell

Time	Form	What to listen for
0'01"	A	Jarrell establishes a lively dance rhythm with his bow; this remains consistent throughout the performance
0'10"	A	Jarrell repeats the A strain
0'18"	B	The B strain is in a higher range, as is typical
0'27"	B	Jarrell repeats the B strain
[...]	AABB etc.	Jarrell continues to play in this pattern for the remainder of the video

We are going to consider two performances of the tune "Arkansas Traveler." This is one of the best-known Appalachian fiddle tunes, and it is characteristic of the repertoire. Like almost all fiddle tunes, "Arkansas Traveler" is in **binary form**. Each of the two sections in repeated, resulting in an A A B B pattern. Both the A and B sections end with the same concluding gesture, however, which becomes one of the characteristic elements of this tune. It is also typical for the two sections of a fiddle tune to be played in different ranges. In "Arkansas Traveler," the A section is in the low range, while the B section is high. (Fiddlers traditionally referred to these as the "course" and "fine" sections, in reference to the relative thickness of the low and high strings.) The whole tune can be repeated as many times as desired.

"Arkansas Traveler" is additionally interesting because of its connection to a popular minstrel show sketch. The origins of the tune itself—first published in Cincinnati, OH, in 1847—are unclear. It gained popularity, however, as part of a humorous skit in which a city gentleman stops to ask a mountaineer for directions. The mountaineer routinely misunderstands the traveler and delivers a series of humorous punchlines at his expense. The skit entered circulation as early as the 1820s, and initially portrayed an interracial encounter. Later, when the "Arkansas Traveler" tune and accompanying fiddle-driven story were added (the mountaineer cannot remember how to finish the tune, and is grateful when the

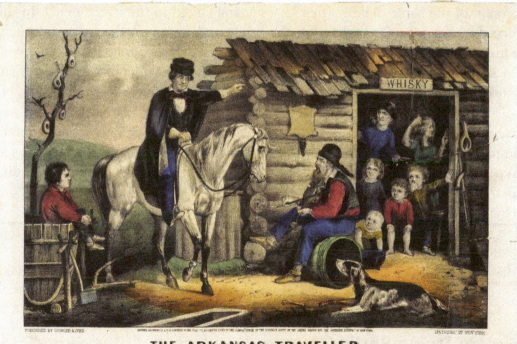

Image 12.15: In this famous 1870 portrayal of the "Arkansas Traveler" sketch, a well-dressed city gentleman encounters a fiddling "hillbilly." The image is crowded with hillbilly stereotypes. These include the mountaineer's beard, fiddle, dog, tumble-down shack, large family, and threatening wife. A sign reading "whiskey" suggests that he is a moonshiner.
Source: Wikimedia Commons
Attribution: Edward Washburn
License: Public Domain

traveler takes up the fiddle and plays the final phrase), it was reworked to address anxieties surrounding class relations. Some versions portrayed the mountaineer sympathetically—others, less so.

We will begin with Jarrell's fiddle version of "Arkansas Traveler." Jarrell's influence on the old-time fiddling tradition cannot be overstated, and his style has a number of distinct features. First, he almost never plays on just one string. Instead, he adds harmonies by bowing on two (or even three) strings at the same time, or by dipping his bow to sound the lower strings while he plays a melody in the high range. Second, he prioritizes rhythm over melody. Although you can hear the notes of the tune, Jarrell never sacrifices rhythmic drive. He also emphasizes the off-beats, changing the direction of his bow in between the rhythmic pulses of the tune and thereby introducing **syncopation**. You can imagine how he could play for a dance all by himself. There is no need for additional instruments to supply harmony or rhythm: Jarrell does it all.

The second most common dance configuration would be fiddle and banjo. The practice of combining fiddle and banjo was first documented among enslaved people in 1774, and it developed first in the African American community. The fiddle and banjo produce a **heterophonic texture**, since each plays an idiomatic version of the same melody (that is, a version suited to the instrument). In this recording we hear Cockerham on the fiddle and Creed on the banjo (although both men played both instruments, and they often switched roles).[6] Unlike Jarrell, Cockerham plays only the melody notes, although his bowing patterns also create syncopated rhythmic patterns. Creed closely follows the melody on the banjo, but because his instrument works so differently he does not play exactly the same notes. In between beats, he periodically hits the short fifth string with his thumb, thereby emphasizing the syncopated character of the music. Occasionally, he produces an **arpeggio** by slowly strumming across the strings from lowest to highest, ending on the melody note.

6.  "Arkansas Traveler"
    Performance: Fred Cockerham and Kyle Creed

Swing: Irving Berlin/Fletcher Henderson, "Blue Skies"[7]

In the previous section, we talked about the social dance practices of rural America, where workers gathered in private homes and danced to the sounds of fiddle and banjo. The same desire to engage in social dancing as a form of leisure was also prevalent in cities. Whether one worked on a farm or in an office, dancing offered an opportunity to have fun, drink alcohol, and socialize with the opposite sex. In cities, however, dance practices developed along quite different lines. After all, there was a great deal more money to made, and dance musicians were in constant competition to provide dancers with the most novel and exciting music. This, in combination with technological developments on the one hand and a large, youthful consumer base on the other, led to rapid developments in the urban dance music of the early 20th century.

7.		"Blue Skies" Composer: Irving Berlin (arr. Fletcher Henderson) Performance: Benny Goodman and His Orchestra (Remastered 1991)

1920s Social Dancing

We have already visited with a 1920s dance band: That led by Paul Whiteman (Chapter 7), whose "sweet jazz" records swept the market. By the 1930s, however, Whiteman's style was already out of date. To begin with, new inventions were changing the instrumentation of dance bands. The electronic microphone allowed the plucked string bass to replace the tuba. The string bass had a more percussive articulation and could play at faster tempos, with the result of intensifying dance music. The banjo, which had featured a built-in resonator that allowed it to project, was replaced by the developing electric guitar. Strings and woodwinds, such as the clarinet and oboe, disappeared in favor of saxophones and brass, which came to be organized into large sections. The size of bands increased to about seventeen players, while the drummer took on an more active role in maintaining rhythmic energy.

All of these changes took place in response to the dancers, who were developing increasingly energetic and athletic steps. The most influential new dance of the era was the **Lindy Hop**,[8] which was introduced by a pair of African American dancers in 1928. Early dancers—mostly young African Americans in Harlem—sought to outdo one another in an attempt to impress white "slummers," who got a thrill from visiting clubs and ballrooms in black neighborhoods. The Lindy Hop went mainstream in the 1930s and young people across the country imitated wild new steps that they saw in ballrooms, on stage, or in films.

8.		The Lindy Hop has been a competitive dance since its inception. Today, dancers from around the world face off in formal competitions.

The new musical style that developed to accompany the Lindy Hop and other related dances was soon known as **swing**, a term that now refers both to the dances themselves and to the characteristic uneven, or "swung," rhythms of the music. These rhythms reflected the relaxed and informal movements of the dancers, who rejected the upright posture and precise steps of older styles. The term, however, was first used by African Americans to describe well-played music and the euphoric emotions it produced. The widespread adoption of the term—along with expressions such as "cool," "hip," and "in the groove"—paralleled the growing interest in black culture and music among white musicians and audiences.

Goodman, Henderson, and the Rise of Swing

Despite enthusiasm among urban young people, it took a while for swing music to catch on. In 1935, however, clarinetist and bandleader Benny Goodman (1909-1986) was able to connect with a demographic of young white listeners who propelled swing music into the forefront of the American conscious. The key to Goodman's success was the radio. In 1934, he secured a spot on the national radio program *Let's Dance*. The show featured three bands, each of which played a different style of popular dance music: Latin, sweet, and hot. Goodman's band represented the "hot" style, but listener response indicated that the other styles were generally preferred. A disastrous national tour in the summer of 1935 confirmed the band's poor reception. Upon arriving in Hollywood, however, Goodman was greeted by cheering fans. These

Image 12.16: Benny Goodman around the year 1970.
Source: Wikimedia Commons
Attribution: Unknown
License: Public Domain

young West Coast listeners had been listening religiously to Goodman's band, which always played after midnight on the East Coast and therefore had received little exposure in all but the westernmost time zone.

Goodman's style was derived from the work of African American arranger Fletcher Henderson (1897-1952). During his years working as a pianist and bandleader in New York City, Henderson produced creative and danceable arrangements of hit popular tunes. Although these arrangements were first intended for his own band to perform and record, Goodman purchased Henderson's catalog outright in the mid-1930s and introduced the arranger's hard-driving, rhythmic style to a mainstream audience. Henderson also produced new arrangements to suit Goodman's needs. In 1939, Henderson joined Goodman's band, which was one of few integrated bands active in the Swing Era.

Image 12.17: Goodman performing with his ensemble in 1946.
Source: Library of Congress
Attribution: William P. Gottlieb
License: Public Domain

Image 12.18: Goodman's band, members of which are pictured rehearsing in 1952, was one of few integrated swing bands.
Source: Wikimedia Commons
Attribution: Fred Palumbo
License: Public Domain

Henderson was one of the key architects of the swing style. He abandoned the free-wheeling improvisation of Dixieland jazz in favor of carefully-scripted parts for instruments organized into sections. Although he also produced original compositions, Henderson based most of his arrangements on the melodies of popular songs. We will be considering his treatment of Irving Berlin's 1926 "Blue Skies."

Blue Skies

Irving Berlin (1888-1989)—a Russian immigrant to New York City—was one of the leading song writers of the early 20th century. Although "Blue Skies" first gained traction on the musical theater stage, the song really took off with Al Jolson's 1927 performance in *The Jazz Singer*—the first commercially successful "talking picture." Today, "Blue Skies" is regarded as a jazz standard. Its popularity among jazz musicians, however, is due expressly to the success of Henderson's brilliant arrangement, which he created for Goodman in 1935.

Henderson's "Blue Skies" opens with an introduction in which the trumpets and clarinets call back and forth to one another over a pounding rhythmic pulse. The **chorus** of "Blue Skies" is then presented by the band. The melody is in A A

Image 12.19: Here we see a young Irving Berlin seated at the piano in 1906.
Source: Wikimedia Commons
Attribution: Life magazine
License: Public Domain

B A form, which Henderson reflects in his instrumentation. The first two A sections are played by the trumpets, while the two phrases of the B section are played by the saxophones and trombones respectively. Finally, the saxophones round out the melody with the final A section. Henderson, however, does not merely reproduce Berlin's tune. He adds melodic flourishes, unusual harmonies, and—most importantly—unpredictable syncopations. By doing so, Henderson reimagines what was already an outdated song for a new generation of dancers.

The remainder of the arrangement consists of repeated passes through Berlin's tune, each more creative than the last. The melody itself slowly recedes from the foreground, although snippets are always audible. For the second pass, the trumpets (now muted) take the A section again, but this time with constant interruption from the saxophones, resulting in a **call and response** texture. A solo saxophone player provides the remainder of the melody, but during the final A section he substitutes an improvised alternative melody. What should have been a third turn through the "Blue Skies" tune begins with an improvised trumpet solo, backed up by saxophone interjections. The melody returns with the B section, which is introduced by the trumpets and finished by the saxophones. The concluding A phrase is likewise split between those instruments. A final turn through the melody begins with a clarinet solo by Goodman himself, but ends with the entire band playing the concluding A phrase. The effect is exciting: We hear the full force of Goodman's horns, backed up by the driving power of the rhythm section.

Disco: Chic, "Good Times"

African American musicians and dancers have had an outsized impact on American popular music since the turn of the 20th century. We have already considered ragtime, Dixieland jazz, and swing—all dance-rooted styles that attracted large audiences and influenced the course of musical development. The trend continued: In the 1950s, black rhythm 'n' blues artists laid the groundwork for rock 'n' roll. Soul emerged as gospel singers brought the sounds of the black church into the mainstream, while funk developed from the combination of soul-infused vocals with jazz harmonies and the interlocking rhythmic layers common in African-derived traditions. Also in the 1960s, producer Berry Gordy created his signature sound at Motown Records in Detroit and built a roster of black performers who were able to withstand the British Invasion.

Disco Dancing

We will pick up the story in the 1970s, when black artists contributed significantly to another dance tradition: **disco**. Disco, however, is decidedly multiethnic. It bears traces of funk, but also the rhythms of Latin America, and it was first associated with a community that was bound together not by race but by sexual orientation. Eventually, it would come to be embraced as the musical style of the 1970s counterculture, and discos would become meetings places for people from all walks of life.

The birth of disco dancing and music can be traced to 1970, when New York City DJ David Mancuso began throwing private parties in an underground venue. His clientele consisted primarily of members of the gay community, most of whom were black, and all of whom were regularly harassed by the police when they visited commercial gay bars and clubs. Disco soon captured the interest of other groups, including Latina/o/x and Italian Americans, and venues proliferated in cities like Philadelphia and San Francisco. By 1975, disco has become a national craze, appealing to everyone who sought an escape from the political and economic pressures of the decade.

Disco music is primarily characterised by its fast tempo, "four-on-the-floor" beat (meaning that every pulse in a quadruple meter framework is emphasized), and dense textures. Disco tracks are usually founded on a rhythmic groove consisting of chicken-scratch guitar (a playing technique used to produce a rhythmic, pitchless sound), a variety of percussion instruments, and electric guitar **riffs**. This is underpinned by a syncopated electric bass line. In addition, however, one might hear piano, electric guitar, electric piano, synthesizers, and orchestral instruments. The resulting music is irresistibly groovy, but also full of variation, since the instruments enter and leave the texture throughout a given track. In short, it is exactly the kind of music that makes people want to dance.

Because disco music was intended for dance clubs, not radio play, it was released in a different format than rock music. Rock singles were usually about three minutes long, and were released on 45 rpm 7-inch discs. Rock albums—which were oriented toward listeners, not dancers—featured a curated selection of songs on a 33 ⅓ rpm 12-inch disc. Dancers, however, required long stretches of music, and the 7-inch single was not convenient for use in clubs. Disco producers, therefore, because designing their songs for 12-inch discs. Instead of offering variety, however, they would stretch out a single track until it took up an entire side—about twenty-two minutes. DJs would then facilitate smooth transitions between discs to keep a crowd dancing through the night.

Chic was one of the most successful disco bands. The group was formed by guitarist Nile Rodgers and bassist Bernard Edwards in 1970, although it was not until 1976 that they took the name Chic. In 1977 they were joined by drummer Tony Thompson, and soon thereafter by singers Luci Martin and Alfa Anderson. The band had a string of hits in 1978 and 1979, but disbanded following the rapid decline in disco's popularity.

Image 12.20: Chic is still active. Here, we see the band performing in 2012.
Source: Wikimedia Commons
Attribution: Alex Marshall
License: CC BY-SA 3.0

Good Times

We will examine their 1979 song "Good Times."[9] It is a fine representative of the disco style in its own terms, but it also proved seminal in the development of hip-hop, which we will consider next. The members of Chic publicly stated that every one of their songs contained a "deep hidden meaning," which could be discerned through careful examination of the lyrics. The lyrics to "Good Times" are, on the surface, a series of straightforward calls to party and enjoy oneself. However, they contain several quotes from Depression-era songs, including the title line of "Happy Days Are Here Again," which we examined in Chapter 10. According to Rodgers, these references were a commentary on the dismal economic situation of the late 1970s, which paralleled that of the 1930s. In this light, "Good Times" takes on something of a grim character: It invites the listener to engage in escapist party behavior, but also offers a reminder that the challenges of life will still be waiting.

Image 12.21: Nile Rodgers (left) performing with Chic in 2014.
Source: Wikimedia Commons
Attribution: Drew de F Fawkes
License: CC BY 2.0

9.  "Good Times"
Composers: Nile Rogers and Bernard Edwards
Performance: Chic (1979)

Of course, there is no reason to assume that the average consumer would give any attention to the words. "Good Times" was a hit because of its danceable beat. After an opening synth swoosh, the track launches into a groove consisting of handclaps, drumset, a repetitive guitar riff, and a funky bass line. A piano occasionally enters the mix, while the sound of strings wafts above. The vocals are delivered in a detached, **staccato** manner that further contributes to the song's rhythmic energy. Near the middle of the track, the texture is reduced to handclaps, drums, and bass. One by one, the other layers—Fender Rhodes electric keyboard, piano, guitar, and strings—are reintroduced, with the effect of rebuilding the energy level in this 12-inch dance club version of the single. "Good Times" was one of the last disco songs to top the Billboard Hot 100 singles chart.

Hip-Hop: The Sugarhill Gang, "Rapper's Delight"

Hip-hop was also born in New York City, although it grew out of the needs and creative impulses of another disenfranchised community: black youth in the Bronx. During the 1970s, poor neighborhoods in New York City were devastated by cuts to municipal and federal funding. The city itself faced dire budget shortfalls, with the result that one fifth of all public workers were laid off in 1975 alone. This meant that police and fire forces shrank, classrooms became more crowded, and basic utilities fell into disrepair. Landlords—no longer able to maintain decaying tenements—turned to arson, while rates of homelessness, prostitution, and crime all skyrocketed. By 1979, the New York subway—home to 250 felonies every week—was the most dangerous public transportation system in the world. In what has been termed "white flight," those with the means to flee the city left for more hospitable communities. This depletion of the tax base plunged the city even further into debt—a debt now shouldered only by the residents without the money or connections needed to begin a new life elsewhere.

The Birth of Hip-Hop

The hardest-hit neighborhood was the Bronx, which by 1977 had become, in the words of the *New York Times*, "a symbol of America's woes." The demographics of the Bronx were radically transformed during this decade. Overall, the population plummeted by 20%. This was largely due to "white flight": While white residents numbered over a million in 1970, making up 73% of the borough's population, over half left the Bronx, reducing the white population to only 47% by 1980. At the same time, the black and hispanic populations grew, constituting 32 and 34% of the population respectively by 1980. Many of the new residents immigrated from Caribbean nations and from Puerto Rico, bringing with them the popular music styles of Latin America.

Hip-hop emerged when impoverished youth living in the Bronx sought ways to express and entertain themselves. The music and dance that we will consider here were part of a complex of practices that also included visual art (graffiti) and characteristic modes of dress and speech. All of these served to identity the practitioners, build and enforce community bonds, and provide a creative outlet.

Image 12.22: This photograph captures President Jimmy Carter on his 1977 tour of the Bronx, which was intended to draw attention to the neighborhood's economic woes.
Source: Wikimedia Commons   .
Attribution: Unknown
License: Public Domain

Hip-hop culture was also extremely competitive, and those active as musicians and dancers worked constantly to develop new techniques, sounds, and moves that would distinguish a practitioner from the crowd.

The first pioneers of hip-hop music were DJs, who borrowed their tools and techniques directly from the disco. DJs would provide music for block parties and community dances by playing the disco, salsa, and funk records that the dancers loved. In playing records, however, these DJs played careful attention to crowd reactions and developed unique approaches that stimulated dancers to greater activity. DJ Kool Herc (Clive Campbell, b. 1955 in Jamaica), for example, noticed that dancers' energy increased during the **breaks**—passages in dance music in which the melody recedes and we hear only the rhythm section. To take advantage of this, he began to play two identical records at the same time, **backspinning** one to repeat breaks while the other continued to sound over the loudspeakers. Later, Theodore Livingston (b. 1963) noticed that backspinning created a scratching sound that could be used to add rhythmic excitement to the track. In this way, DJs transformed recorded music and laid the groundwork for a completely new style.

At first, DJs confined themselves to operating the turntables. DJ Kool Herc and a few others, however, began reciting rhymes over the breaks, thereby becoming the first rappers. Soon, DJs began recruiting dedicated rappers known as **MCs** (an abbreviation of "master of ceremonies"). Many of their rhymes were connected with the African-derived tradition of the "toast," in which a skilled orator tells a story celebrating a protagonist's cunning and resource. Although the toasting tradition had largely died out in black culture, it survived in prisons and was captured on the hit 1973 album *Hustler's Convention*,[10] which had an enormous influence on early MCs.

Image 12.23: DJ Kool Herc, pictured here in 2009, was one of the pioneers of hip-hop.
Source: Wikimedia Commons
Attribution: User "Bigtimepeace"
License: Public Domain

The dance style that developed alongside hip-hop was highly individual and expressive. **"Breaking"** derived its name from the rhythmic breaks isolated by DJs, whose music came to be known as "breakbeat." Dancers, known as "b-boys" and "b-girls," performed increasingly acrobatic moves in response to the DJ's looped breaks, which in turn inspired the DJ to generate more intense rhythms. Individuals and crews often entered into direct competition with one another, engaging in dance battles that took place within a circle of onlookers.

10. The 1973 album Hustler's Convention captures the toasting tradition and had an enormous influence on early hip-hop.

Image 12.24: Breaking remains central to hip-hop culture.
Source: Wikimedia Commons
Attribution: E. Başak
License: CC BY-SA 2.0

For most of the 1970s, hip-hop was regarded as a **performance practice**, not a genre of music. It was an approach to the presentation of dance music that involved looping breaks, scratching records, and reciting rhymes. The early DJs and MCs, however, never considered the possibility of recording their music or seeking commercial success outside of the Bronx. In fact, most refused invitations to enter the recording studio. For this reason, the first hip-hop records were made not by the pioneers of the style but rather by relatively unknown performers working with studio musicians.

Rapper's Delight

This was the case with the first hip-hop hit, "Rapper's Delight."[11] In 1979, New Jersey-based producer Sylvia Robinson recruited three local MCs—Michael "Wonder Mike" Wright, Henry "Big Bank Hank" Jackson, and Guy "Master Gee" O'Brien—to create a hip-hop record for Sugarhill Records. The group called themselves the Sugarhill Gang, and they recorded "Rapper's Delight" in a single take with a live band hired for the occasion. In keeping with the disco model, the fifteen-minute single was released on a 12-inch disc. It sold over two million copies in the United States, peaking at 36 on the Billboard Hot 100 charts and proving that there was a large commercial market for hip-hop.

Image 12.25: The MCs who called themselves the Sugar Hill Gang.
Source: Flickr
Attribution: Russell Mondy
License: CC BY-NC 2.0

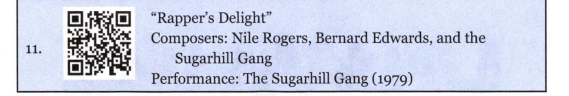

11.   "Rapper's Delight"
      Composers: Nile Rogers, Bernard Edwards, and the
            Sugarhill Gang
      Performance: The Sugarhill Gang (1979)

MCs usually rapped over breaks from pre-existing songs. It is therefore not surprising that "Rapper's Delight" should borrow from a recent hit: Chic's "Good Times." In this case, the original record was not used directly. Instead, the studio players performed the handclaps, drumset pattern, bass line, piano riffs, and synth hits from "Good Times" live while the MCs took turns rapping. All the same, the borrowed music is immediately recognizable. Nile Rodgers certainly recognized it when he heard a DJ playing "Rapper's Delight" in a New York club. At first he was extremely angry and threatened to sue, but the matter was quickly settled and Rogers and Bernard Edwards were credited as co-authors. Later, Rogers came to admire "Rapper's Delight," citing its originality and cultural significance.

The lyrics to "Rapper's Delight" are typical of early hip-hop. The MCs boast about their skills and accomplishments, encourage the listeners to dance, celebrate the party lifestyle, and play with patterns of rhythmic syllables. At one point, the rapping gives way to a break, which could have been looped in live performance to facilitate dancing. Most characteristic of this record, however, is the fact that it is founded on pre-existing music. Hip-hop artists would continue to borrow and reimagine musical material for the purpose of paying homage, providing commentary, and exhibiting their own creativity. The resulting tradition is rich with **intertextual** references.

DANCE MUSIC IN CONCERT SETTINGS

In the last section, we considered four musical examples that were all created expressly to facilitate dancing. That doesn't mean that this music can't be enjoyed by a listener—indeed, it often is. However, these have been examples of practical dance music.

In the next section, we will consider dance rhythms and forms adapted to purely musical ends. This essentially takes us back to where the chapter started, with John Philip Sousa's concert marches. Here, however, we take a look at two dramatically different composers who each used the popular dance styles of their time and place to inform music that was meant primarily for listening.

Johann Sebastian Bach, Cello Suites

We have already considered the career of J.S. Bach, one of the most respected and influential composers in the European tradition. In Chapter 11, we examined two pieces of music that he created for use in the Lutheran church. Bach held a series of positions as organist or music director with various courts and municipalities, and in each of these positions he was required to compose music of various types in order to satisfy the needs of his employer.

Image 12.26: This engraving by August Weger was produced after the composer's music became popular with 19th-century audiences.
Source: Wikimedia Commons
Attribution: Joseph Weger
License: Public Domain

Bach and the Baroque Dance Suite

Although most of his jobs required the production of church music, one did not: his position as music director at the court of Leopold, Prince of Anhalt-Köthen,

Image 12.27: This grandiose portrait depicts Bach's employer, Prince Leopold.
Source: Wikimedia Commons
Attribution: Unknown
License: Public Domain

which he held from 1717 to 1723. Because the Prince was a Calvinist, he had little need for church music; Calvanist churches of the time rejected musical instruments and restricted singing to the modest chanting of Psalms. A piece of music like "Sleepers, Wake" (Chapter 11), therefore, would not have been welcome. The Prince, however, maintained a lavish court, and he was particularly fond of music. He sang and played the violin, viola da gamba, and harpsichord. Although his parents had declined to spend money on music, Prince Leopold assembled a large court orchestra of eighteen musicians and recruited the finest composer in the region: Bach. During Bach's employment, Prince Leopold called upon him to produce instrumental music and cantatas for the purpose of entertaining guests, celebrating anniversaries, and generally ornamenting life in the palace.

While at the Prince's court, Bach adopted the practice of composing **dance suites**. The popularity of dance suites stemmed from the desire of minor German monarchs to emulate the court of the French king, which was renowned for its sophistication and luxury. The dance suite was pioneered by the German composer Johann Jacob Froberger (1616-1667), who traveled throughout Europe absorbing and adapting the musical styles that he heard at courts in France, Italy, England, and Belgium. Froberger was able to bring this music to German courts in the form of dance suites, which were associated with cosmopolitan sophistication. Unlike Froberger, Bach never left left Germany. All the same, he became a master of musical forms and styles from throughout the continent.

The dance suite consists of movements inspired by court dances from various European countries. At the core of the dance suite are the Allemande, Courante, Sarabande, and Gigue. To these may be added any number of other dances, including the Menuet, Bourée, Gavotte, and Loure. In addition, some dance suites begin with a Prelude, which establishes the key area for the suite and sets the mood.

The sources of the four required movements reveal the international character of the dance suite. The Allemande traces its origins to Germany, although by the time it was integrated into the dance suite it had been adopted and transformed by French courts (the French name for Germany is *Allemagne*). Although the Allemande was initially a fast-paced dance in quadruple meter, the French slowed it to a stately tempo. The Courante can be of two types, French or Italian. While both are in **triple meter**, the French is slow and dignified, while the Italian is

Image 12.28: In this 1772 engraving by James Caldwell, aristocrats dance the Allemande.
Source: New York Public Library
Attribution: James Caldwall and Michel Vincent Brandoin
License: Public Domain

quick and lively. The Sarabande originated in Mexico, where it was a quick and salacious dance accompanied by castanets. After being banned from the Spanish courts for alleged obscenity, however, it was reinvented as a slow and dignified triple-meter dance with rhythmic emphasis placed on the second beat. And finally, the Gigue traces its roots to the English and Irish jig, a fast dance in **compound duple meter** (meaning that each pulse is divided into three sub-pulses).

In the context of a dance suite, all four of these movements are always cast in binary form. Each part is repeated, with the resulting form of A A B B. This should strike the reader as familiar, for it is also the form of the Appalachian dance tune "Arkansas Traveler." Likewise, it can be found in the folk dances of the British Isles and Europe. Bach refined the form in his own dance suites, starting both the A and B sections with similar melodic material in different keys. Bach's B sections usually start in the **dominant** key, which is based on the fifth scale degree of the original key. For example, if the suite is in the key of C major, each A section will start in the key of C, while each B section will start in the key of G.

Bach wrote a large number of dance suites for many different configurations of instruments. These include four suites for orchestra, twenty-eight for keyboard, three for lute, six for violin, six for cello, and one for flute. A word of caution, however, for it is in fact very difficult to count Bach's suites. He gave such works a variety of titles, including Suite, Partita, and Overture, and only a handful—six keyboard partitas—were published in his lifetime. The others have survived only in manuscript form, since they were intended for private court performance, not widespread distribution.

In the court of Prince Leopold, dance suites were performed solely as musical entertainment. The dances themselves had largely fallen out of fashion, but their rhythms and gestures lived on in the suites. We will consider two movements from two of Bach's suites for solo cello: the Courante from Suite No. 2 in D minor and the Sarabande from Suite No. 4 in E-flat major.

Bach's Cello Suites

The six suites for solo cello are among Bach's most influential compositions. All cellists play at least some of the suites, although the last two present major challenges: Suite No. 5 in C minor requires that the cellist change the pitch of their highest string, while Suite No. 6 in D major seems to have been written for a related but higher-pitched string instrument, with the result that it is exceedingly difficult to perform on a modern cello. Today, it is common to hear these pieces in performance, and they have been recorded countless times.

Despite their ubiquity, however, a great deal of mystery surrounds the origin of the cello suites. To begin with, in the time of Bach it was very uncommon to write music featuring the cello, and essentially unheard of to write for solo cello. The cello was part of the **basso continuo** section, and was therefore relegated to strictly accompanimental roles. Bach would have written these suites for a specific performer (or performers) at the court of Prince Leopold, so we can assume that he had a close relationship with one or more accomplished players who would have been able to bring the music to life.

The legacy of these suites is further complicated by the fact that the original manuscripts have not survived. Instead, we have been left with copies made by Bach's second wife, Anna Magdalena. It is worth considering her role in his life with some care. When Bach joined Prince Leopold's court, he brought with him his first wife, Barbara. In 1720, however, Barbara died while Bach was traveling with the Prince. Anna Magdalena was the daughter of a court trumpeter and a court singer herself. She married Bach in 1721, at the age of 20. In addition to raising their many children, Anna Magdalena provided Bach with invaluable services as a **copyist** and perhaps

Image 12.29: The only surviving manuscripts containing the cello suites are in the hand of Bach's second wife, Anna Magdalena.
Source: Wikimedia Commons
Attribution: Anna Magdalena Bach
License: Public Domain

even collaborator. She would copy out individual parts from his orchestral scores and also make clean copies of his roughly worked-out draft manuscripts. Because the only surviving manuscripts for the six cello suites are in her hand, there has been some controversy concerning the accuracy of the bowings and articulations, which have a significant effect on the performance of the music. Anna Magdalena's copy is also free of dynamic markings and other phrasing instructions, with the result that modern performers have to make many important decisions about how to interpret these pieces.

It is hard to determine exactly how the Courante was danced. On the one hand, dance notation is notoriously vague. On the other, there were many variations of the Courante, and it is known to have transformed over time. However, we can make generalizations. The word *courante* (or the Italian *corrente*) means "running," and the dance has been described as containing quick back-and-forth steps, little leaps, and stately glides. It was performed by couples. Bach's Courante from Suite No. 2 certainly reflects the activity of such a dance: The melody moves at a quick but regular pace, offering few chances for repose.

Courante from Cello Suite No. 2 in D minor Composer: Johann Sebastian Bach Performance: Phil Snyder (2019)		
Time	**Form**	**What to listen for**
0'00"	A	The tempo is steady throughout, and there is not much rhythmic variety
0'31"	A	The A section is repeated
0'59"	B	The B section starts with the same melodic motif as the A section, but it is in a higher range
1'28"	B	The B section is repeated

Although the Sarabande was initially, in the words of one priest, "a dance and song so loose in its words and so ugly in its motions that it is enough to excite bad emotions in even very decent people," by Bach's time it had been thoroughly reformed. The Sarabande[12] from Suite No. 4 reflects the slow, stately dance that had been popular in French courts of the previous century. It contains uneven dotted rhythms throughout—rhythms that were intimately associated with French royalty and pomp. This contributes to the movement's serious and dignified tone.

12.		Sarabande from Cello Suite No. 4 in E-flat major Composer: Johann Sebastian Bach Performance: Phil Snyder (2019)

Johann Strauss II, *Tritsch-Tratsch-Polka* and *The Blue Danube*

In 19th-century Vienna, Johann Strauss II (1825-1899) was known as "The Waltz King." His dance-inspired compositions were enormously popular, and by the time of his death he had accumulated countless honors and plaudits. Strauss's music is also uniquely tied to Viennese identity: It is played by the Vienna Philharmonic every New Year's Eve and presented on nightly concerts for the benefit of tourists to the city. In total, Strass composed over 400 **waltzes**, **polkas**, and quadrilles. Although his orchestra did sometimes play for balls, Strauss's fame and influence resulted from concert performances, and many of his compositions are not suited to dancing.

Image 12.30: The photograph of Johann Strauss II was taken in 1899 by Franz Luckhardt.
Source: Wikimedia Commons
Attribution: Fritz Luckhardt
License: Public Domain

Strauss's Career

Strauss carried on the legacy of his father, Johann Strauss I (1804-1849), who was largely responsible for transforming the waltz from a rustic country dance into a dance for the sophisticated urban ballroom. Johann I, however, forbade his sons from pursuing careers in music. He knew from experience that a musician's life was strenuous, and he wanted stable, middle-class business careers for his own children. When he caught Johann II practicing the violin one day, therefore, he beat him severely. Johann II, however, was not to be deterred. Throughout his youth he secretly studied violin and composition with members of his father's orchestra, and in 1844 he assembled his own orchestra and put on a concert at Dommayer's Casino (a venue in which his father had frequently appeared, but that he subsequently boycotted).

The concert, which included popular selections of the day in addition to four of Strauss's own com-

Image 12.31: This 1894 caricature by Theo Zasche captures Strauss II as "The Waltz King."
Source: Wikimedia Commons
Attribution: Theo Zasche
License: Public Domain

positions, was a great success, but the young orchestra leader still found it difficult to compete with his father. He spent much of the first few years of his career touring outside of Vienna, and was only able to build his local reputation following his father's death. Soon, however, Strauss had established himself as a musical trend-setter in the city, and in 1863 he was finally appointed Music Director of the Royal Court Balls—a position that had in fact been created for his father, but which Strauss was long denied due to his support for the rebels during the 1848 Vienna Revolution.

We will consider two of Strauss's most famous compositions: *Tritsch-Tratsch-Polka* (1858) and *The Blue Danube* (a waltz composed in 1866). Both of these works were created for concert performance. While it would be possible to dance to them, at least in part, each contains elements that are intended to appeal to the listener and that might even foil any attempt to dance.

Tritsch-Tratsch-Polka

Invention of the polka is traditionally attributed to a housemaid working in Czech-speaking Bohemia. According to legend, she attracted attention with a lively dance set to a regional folk song. Admirers asked her to teach it to them, and the dance quickly spread throughout the countryside. Whatever its origins, the polka was certainly a fixture in Prague ballrooms by 1837, and it was being danced in Vienna by 1839. Next to the waltz, the polka was certainly the most successful European ballroom dance of the 19th century. Within a few decades, it was being danced throughout central and western Europe, up north in the Netherlands and Russia, to the east in India, and in the New World, where it was popular from Mexico to the midwestern United States.

Image 12.32: The polka, represented here in a print from the 1840s, was originally a rural folk dance.
Source: Wikimedia Commons
Attribution: J. Rigo et Cie
License: Public Domain

The term "polka" is believed to be derived from the Czech word for "half," and therefore probably refers to the duple meter of polka music. The dance is performed by couples, who embrace while performing a distinctive step (evocative of tripping or galloping) as they whirl around the room. Dancers tend to bob up and down in time to the beat. The polka is always performed at a fast tempo, and it is one of the more energetic 19th-century ballroom dances.

Strauss composed his *Tritsch-Tratsch-Polka*[13] for performance in Pavlovsk, Russia, where he had the honor of conducting the summer concert season at the Vauxhall Pavilion every year between 1856 and 1865. These performances often stimulated his creativity, and Strauss created some of his most memorable works for these concerts. In 1858, he was inspired to write a polka that captured the excitement and thrill of gossip—for which "Tritsch-Tratsch" (an equivalent to "chit chat") was current Viennese slang.

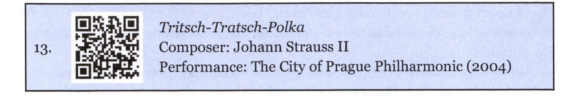

13.		*Tritsch-Tratsch-Polka* Composer: Johann Strauss II Performance: The City of Prague Philharmonic (2004)

Tritsch-Tratsch-Polka is certainly full of energy. Its characteristic **motif**—heard right at the beginning—is a rapidly ascending octave. The melody is played primarily by high-pitched instruments, such as the violin and flute, while the tinkling triangle emphasizes the **offbeats**. The polka is in a ternary form (A B A), each section of which contains its own repeating melodies. The A section has an internal form of a b c a, while the B section has the form d d e d e d. In short, Strauss deploys an excellent balance of contrast and repetition. The polka starts with an exuberant trill and ends with a hilarious sequence of outbursts from the flutes, oboes, and brass. The regular duple pulse in a fast tempo is maintained throughout, with occasional emphasis from the snare drum or cymbals.

The many musical details of *Tritsch-Tratsch-Polka* make it worth listening to. If one is dancing, it is more difficult to appreciate Strauss's clever and delightful orchestration. At the same time, this music is perfectly suitable for dancing—although in such a case the orchestra might choose to repeat the B and A sections one or two times more before playing Strauss's remarkable ending. In this case, therefore, we have music that was created for the concert stage but that could also live in the ballroom with minimal adjustment.

The Blue Danube

		The Blue Danube Composer: Johann Strauss II Performance: Wiener Philharmoniker, conducted by Karl Böhm (1973)	
Time	**Form**	**What to listen for**	
0'00"	Intro	Flutes and horns hint at the first waltz theme; tremolo strings shimmer in the background	
1'27"	Waltz 1	Internal form: abb	
2'34"	Waltz 2	Internal form: aaba	

3'34"	Waltz 3	Internal form: aabb
4'33"	Waltz 4	Internal form: intro aabb
5'43"	Waltz 5	Internal form: intro aab
6'56"	Coda	Unlike the preceding waltzes, the coda—which revisits many of their themes—contains no direct repetition and includes many transitional passages
8'16"		The theme from Waltz 1 returns; after a passage of calm, it builds to an exuberant climax

The Blue Danube has additional features that tie it to concert performance. Before considering those, however, we need to consider the waltz as a ballroom dance. Like the polka, the waltz seems to have originated in the Bavarian countryside, although it is somewhat older, perhaps dating to the mid-18th century. When the waltz first entered urban ballrooms, it proved something of a shock: Never before had pairs of dancers held each other in such a close embrace. In older ballroom dances, such as the minuet, the dancers kept a respectful distance from

Image 12.33: This illustration appeared in Thomas Wilson's 1816 manual *Correct Method of German and French Waltzing*.
Source: Wikimedia Commons
Attribution: Unknown
License: Public Domain

one another, but when waltzing a man actually put his hand around his partner's waist. Soon, however, dancers had become accustomed to this new style, and by the 1780s the waltz was common in Vienna and beginning to spread around Europe. It was Strauss himself, however, who—building on the legacy of his father—ensured the dance's popularity throughout the 19th century.

The waltz calls for smooth, gliding motions, and is therefore quite unlike the polka. A mid-19th century waltz was energetic but stately—the tempos, therefore, were moderate. The waltz is in a characteristic triple meter, with dancers moving down and forward on the first beat, but rising up on the second and third. This is reflected in the music, for the first beat (or **downbeat**) is usually stronger and sounded in a lower range than the others (often intoned as "boom-chuck-chuck"). In Vienna, it became typical for the orchestras play the second beat just a little early, thereby producing a sense of weightlessness in the last part of the pattern.

The Blue Danube actually began life as a choral piece. It was commissioned by the Vienna Men's Choral Association, with whom Strauss had already enjoyed a two-decades-long association. While Strauss was supposed to be at work on his choral waltz, Austria suffered a bitter defeat in the Seven Weeks' War with Prussia. The conflict sapped morale in Vienna, with the result that the choirmaster encouraged Strauss to write an exceptionally joyful and lighthearted piece in order to lift the audience members' moods. A satirical text was added by the Choral Association poet, although it was apparently disliked by both the singers and the audience. As a result, the reception accorded *The Blue Danube* at its premiere on February 15, 1867, was surprisingly tepid for a waltz that would become Strauss's most popular composition. A more serious text—that sometimes sung today—was appended in 1889. However, *The Blue Danube* is most often heard in its purely orchestral form, and it was as an instrumental piece that it became famous following a performance at the World Exhibition in Paris later in 1867.

Image 12.34: This 1910 edition of *The Blue Danube* includes the vocal parts.
Source: Wikimedia Commons
Attribution: Johann Strauss and Franz von Gernerth
License: Public Domain

Unlike *Tritsch-Tratsch-Polka*, *The Blue Danube* is a fairly lengthy piece with a complex form. Like Strauss's other waltz-inspired concert pieces, it consists of a string of independent, self-contained waltzes—five, to be precise—preceded by an introduction and followed by a lengthy **coda**. The introduction hints at the theme of the first waltz, while the coda revisits themes from the first four waltzes, concluding with a grandiose statement of the same theme with which the piece timidly opened.

One could not dance to this version of *The Blue Danube*: The introduction starts too slowly and is too tentative, while the coda would confuse dancers with its unorthodox form and frequent transitions. The individual waltzes, however, could easily be extracted for ballroom use. Each is in binary form, the A and B sections of which each contain the correct sixteen measures and expected repeats. Although each of the waltzes contains two distinct themes, the standard waltz rhythm ("boom-chuck-chuck") is never absent.

RESOURCES FOR FURTHER LEARNING

Print

Bierley, Paul E. *The Incredible Band of John Philip Sousa*. University of Illinois Press, 2010.

Dils, Ann and Ansley Cooper Albright. *Moving History/Dancing Cultures: A Dance History Reader*. Wesleyan University Press, 2001.

Jamison, Phil. *Hoedowns, Reels, and Frolics: Roots and Branches of Southern Appalachian Dance*. University of Illinois Press, 2015.

Lott, Eric. *Love & Theft: Blackface Minstrelsy and the American Working Class*. 20th anniversary edition. Oxford University Press, 2013.

Malone, Jacqui. *Steppin' on the Blues: The Visible Rhythms of African American Dance*. University of Illinois Press, 1996.

Siblin, Eric. *The Cello Suites: J. S. Bach, Pablo Casals, and the Search for a Baroque Masterpiece*. Grove Press, 2011.

Taruskin, Richard. *Music in the Seventeenth and Eighteenth Centuries: The Oxford History of Western Music*. Oxford University Press, 2009.

Turino, Thomas. *Music as Social Life: The Politics of Participation*. University of Chicago Press, 2008.

Unit 6

EVALUATING MUSIC

What is Good Music?

Esther M. Morgan-Ellis and David R. Peoples

WHAT IS GOOD MUSIC?

It seems as if one of the objectives of this book should be to reveal what the difference is between "good" music and "bad" music. However, if you have read this entire book and still have no idea, don't worry—the authors don't know either. Or, at least, we are not able to make any generalizations about what is good and what is not, even if we are adept at identifying quality in specific instances. This is because music is so diverse in its forms and objectives that there cannot be a single standard of quality. When we ask, "Is this music good?," what are we asking? Although this particular question is vague and unhelpful, asking questions can help us to judge the quality of a specific composition or performance.

First, we should think about the purpose behind a given composition. Is it supposed to make people dance? Is it supposed to provoke an emotional reaction? Is it supposed to make listeners feel patriotic? Is it supposed to incite rebellion? Is it supposed to be intellectually engaging? Then we should ask the question, "Is this piece of music successful at achieving its objective?" This way we can avoid pointless comparisons between pieces of music that serve completely different functions. There is no value in saying that a symphony by Beethoven is "better" than an Appalachian fiddle tune.

Second, we can measure a composition against others of its type. While it is misguided to compare a Bach cantata to a hip-hop track, we can argue that Bach wrote better cantatas than other 18th-century German church composers, or that Ice-T is a better rapper than Vanilla Ice. To do so, we need to agree on some specific criteria used to determine quality. This is very difficult. Most classical musicians agree that Bach is the greatest composer of his era, if not of all time. They will argue that his music is better than that of his contemporaries because it is more complex, or more expressive. But who decided that complexity and expressivity were desirable qualities? Bach was not highly regarded in his own time, when listeners preferred a more restrained approach to composition. Should that matter to us today? There's a further problem. Although Bach's music was not widely studied or performed until eighty years after his death, it now forms the bedrock of the classical music industry and educational system. Can those of us who grew up playing and listening to Bach's music judge its quality, when that same music has been used to define and teach "goodness" in classical music? Or are we only able to judge less familiar composers in comparison to Bach?

Third, we might compare a piece of music to others of its kind by considering originality. When we find a pop song or a string quartet or a gamelan composition that we really love, we are probably attracted to it because, while representative of its type, it is somehow different in an appealing way. All songs played on Top 40 radio have a great deal in common, but a "good" song is likely to have something special that sets it apart from the others. All string quartets composed in the 18th century will share formal and stylistic features, but a "good" one will stand out as unique. What it means to be original and how innovations might be received will depend on the type of music.

Fourth, we can consider the skill of the composer or performer. Certain types of music—four-voice fugues, for example—are objectively difficult to craft, and we can empirically judge their quality. However, this is often not the case, as this type of evaluation requires strict criteria. We can also judge the skill with which music is performed. In the classical tradition, we tend to separate the quality of a performance from the quality of the music being performed. In other traditions, however, such is often not the case. The music of John Coltrane is "good" not because he wrote exceptional tunes but because his recordings are extraordinary. If he had spent his career publishing printed music, no-one would have noticed. Because he worked with a team of highly-skilled musicians to record and release groundbreaking performances, however, we hold his music in high esteem. And how do we know that his recordings are "good"? This again requires some level of agreement between members of the jazz community concerning the goals of their music.

Finally, we can take into account the impact that music has on listeners and society. We can argue that "good" music is important to someone, or plays a role in the development of art or culture. It has certainly been argued that the music of Wagner is "good" because it heavily influenced the next generation of composers. It has also been argued that Wagner is a "good" composer because many people love his operas. However, influence and popularity are often determined by factors that are independent of the music itself. Wagner happened to be a German male (which allowed him to be taken seriously) with a royal patron (which allowed him to focus on his work and to stage lavish productions of his most ambitious operas). These circumstances contributed significantly to his legacy. If Wagner had written all of the same operas, but they had never been staged and were forgotten today, would those operas still be "good"? Were there other composers writing at the same time who, due to less fortunate circumstances, have been forgotten, but who's music was just as "good" or "better"? Is it even possible to know? To turn to another example, young people are often criticized for listening to "bad" (that is, popular and ephemeral) music. This has been going on for many generations, but no amount of criticism can stop anyone from listening to music that they love and that has meaning for them. Does the fact that a piece of music is important to someone make it "good"?

As these questions reveal, it is no easy task to determine whether a piece of music is "good" or not. It is tempting to paraphrase the words of Supreme Court Justice Potter Stewart, who famously declined to define pornography in a 1964 decision but instead stated "I know it when I see it." Many of us would like to say of good music, "I know it when I hear it"—and sometimes we do. However, we should never forget the limitations of our individual perspectives, and we should keep our ears open to all of the good music that is waiting to be discovered.

THE PULITZER PRIZE

Despite the problems inherent in trying to identify the "best" music, we have long insisted on doing so. This is evidenced by countless competitions and awards across all genres of music. Perhaps the most prominent award given to a composer of art music is the Pulitzer Prize for Music, which has been awarded annually since 1943. The current criteria indicate that this award is "For a distinguished musical composition by an American that has had its first performance or recording in the United States during the year." The history of Pulitzer Prize winners, therefore, should be a history of the best music composed in the last 75 years. In truth, of course, many of the composers and works to receive the Pulitzer have been forgotten, while many great musicians were never considered because their music was not considered to be art.

1945: AARON COPLAND, *APPALACHIAN SPRING*

Of all the compositions ever to win the Pulitzer Prize, none may have been so warmly embraced by the listening public as Aaron Copland's *Appalachian Spring*. This orchestral work—first conceived of as a **ballet**, but more frequently performed on the concert stage—has never left the repertoire, and it is regularly performed in versions for both **chamber orchestra** and full orchestra. *Appalachian Spring* also helped to solidify Copland's reputation as a composer of explicitly "American" music. Indeed, Copland-esque soundtracks have been used to accompany on-screen cowboys and ranchers ever since the 1940s, and we have long accepted that the sound of Copland is the sound of rural America.

Image 13.1: This photograph of Copland was take in 1946, one year after he won the Pulitzer Prize.
Source: Picryl
Attribution: Victor Kraft
License: Public Domain

Copland's Career

Aaron Copland (1900-1990) did not start off his career writing folksy-sounding concert pieces. His earliest interest lay in synthesizing jazz and classical idioms, as we saw George Gershwin do with his 1924 *Rhapsody in Blue*. Copland, however, did not meet with Gershwin's success. Gershwin was an uneducated popular song composer who rose to the challenge of writing a sophisticated concert work and was therefore lauded for his accomplishments. Copland, on the other hand, had the benefit of a rigorous education, and in 1924 was concluding three years of study in Paris with the most renowned composition teacher of the 20th century, Nadia Boulanger. When he incorporated jazz into his early works, therefore, he was scorned by highbrow critics who thought that by doing so Copland was degrading his art. Copland gave up the project and instead wrote sophisticated concert music in a modern style for the rest of the 1920s.

The Great Depression convinced many composers of art music to adopt a more commercial style. They did so both out of necessity and for ideological reasons. It was not practical to write elite music for small audiences during a period of such hardship, but it also seemed unethical. What was the purpose of art if not to comfort people in their time of suffering? Copland was also interested in using music to further left-wing political causes in which he had taken an interest. He was particularly influenced by the rising interest among young progressives in American folk music, which was understood to represent the common people and their struggles.

Folk tunes had a major impact on Copland as he began to develop his unique musical language. All three of the ballets that cemented his reputation as a composer used folk melodies to portray rural America. *Billy the Kid* (1938) combines a variety of cowboy songs with Mexican folk music to tell the story of the famous outlaw. *Rodeo* (1942), also set on the Western frontier, features an Appalachian fiddle tune called "Bonaparte's Retreat" in its final scene. And *Appalachian Spring* (1944) contains a set of variations on the Shaker hymn tune "Simple Gifts."

Image 13.2: Like many composers, Copland was also active as a conductor. He is pictured here working with bass-baritone William Warfield in 1963.
Source: Picryl
Attribution: Library of Congress
License: Public Domain

Appalachian Spring

Before looking inside *Appalachian Spring*, however, we need to know a little more about how this ballet came to be. In 1942, Copland was commissioned to write a ballet "on an American theme" by dancer Martha Graham and music

Image 13.3: Martha Graham was among the most famous American dancers of the 20th century.
Source: Picryl
Attribution: Barbara Morgan
License: Public Domain

Image 13.4: This portrait of Elizabeth Sprague Coolidge was completed by John Singer Sargent in 1923.
Source: Wikimedia Commons
Attribution: John Singer Sargent
License: Public Domain

patron Elizabeth Sprague Coolidge. Copland completed the 25-minute score without a narrative in mind—his aim was simply to write music that sounded "American" and contained dramatic contrasts. In fact, he had no idea what the ballet was to be about until he saw it just a few days before the October 1944 premiere at the Library of Congress in Washington, D.C. He later loved to talk about the compliments he received from listeners who felt that he had perfectly captured the Appalachian mountains in music, when in fact no such idea had been in his mind while composing.

The dramatic narrative, which was developed by Graham after she heard the music, concerns the marriage of a young farming couple. The eight brief scenes portray the community coming together to celebrate the wedding, the various emotions felt by the bride and groom, and the adventure of embarking upon married life. The title, which replaced Copland's working title, *Ballet for Martha*, was drawn from a line of Hart Crane's 1930 poem "The Dance."

Scene One

We will take a look at the first, second, and seventh scenes to get an idea about how Copland created "American"-sounding music. After seeing the ballet performed, he wrote his own summaries of the music and action incorporated into each scene. To describe scene one, he wrote "Very slowly. Introduction of the characters, one by one, in a suffused light."[1] In this excerpt, we can hear several of the techniques that characterize Copland's music. He creates the impression of a wide open space by juxtaposing high and low sounds. He captures a sense of stillness by writing music that moves slowly and seldom changes harmony. Finally, his melodies outline triads in different key areas. This means that scene one is not in any particular key, and is therefore **polytonal**. But the music is not jarring or uncomfortable, like that which we heard in *The Rite of Spring*. Instead, Copland creates a floating effect: we often don't know where we are or where we are going, but the experience is pleasant.

1.		Scene One from *Appalachian Spring* Composer: Aaron Copland Performance: Harmonie Ensemble/New York, conducted by Steven Richman (2004)

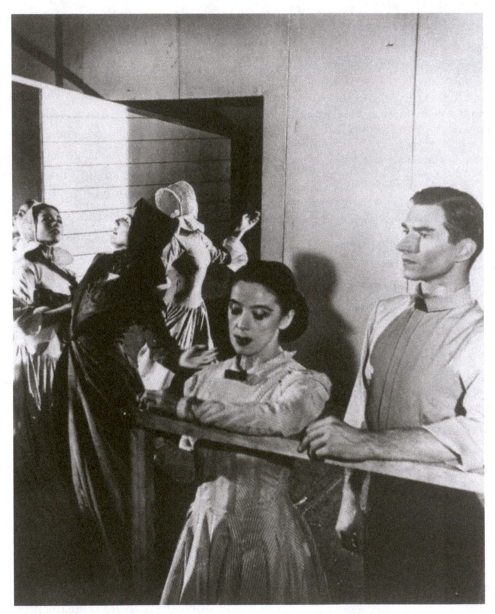

Image 13.5: This snapshot captures a scene from the premiere of Appalachian Spring.
Source: Picryl
Attribution: Library of Congress
License: Public Domain

Scene Two

The mood suddenly changes with scene two, which Copland described as follows: "Fast/Allegro. Sudden burst of unison strings in A major arpeggios starts the action. A sentiment both elated and religious gives the keynote to this scene."[2] Copland continues to employ polytonality, but we are now dancing instead of floating. He introduces a variety of exciting rhythmic elements, including **mixed meter**, that make it difficult (or even impossible) to tap your foot along to the music. The elated sentiment that Copland describes is communicated by means of fast tempos and **disjunct** melodies that include large leaps. The religious sentiment is communicated through a sequence of powerful, emotive harmonies.

2. Scene Two from *Appalachian Spring*
    Composer: Aaron Copland
    Performance: Harmonie Ensemble/New York, conducted by Steven Richman (2004)

Scene Seven

Copland's use of a traditional tune comes in scene seven:[3]

Calm and flowing/Doppio Movimento. Scenes of daily activity for the Bride and her Farmer husband. There are five variations on a Shaker theme. The theme, sung by a solo clarinet, was taken from a collection of Shaker melodies compiled by Edward D. Andrews, and published under the title "The Gift to Be Simple." The melody borrowed and used almost literally is called "Simple Gifts."

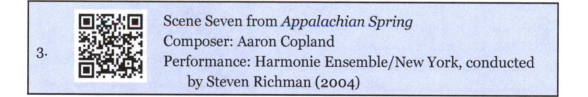

3. Scene Seven from *Appalachian Spring*
    Composer: Aaron Copland
    Performance: Harmonie Ensemble/New York, conducted by Steven Richman (2004)

Copland regularly relied on the work of scholars and song collectors. In this case, he turned to Dr. Andrews's 1940 volume *The Gift to Be Simple: Songs, Dances and Rituals of the American Shakers* for source material. Copland first presents the hymn tune in the solo clarinet. Like Bartók (see Chapter 9), he does not alter the melody at all, but he does provide an original and very modern harmonization. Copland then leads the listener through a series of **variations**, each of which is more rhythmically exciting and virtuosic than the last.

It is interesting to note that Copland was in fact one of the early champions of music appreciation as a subject of study. He sought to reveal the secrets of the concert hall to as many new listeners as possible, and he dedicated much of his

Image 13.6: This group of New York Shakers was photographed around 1880.
Source: Wikimedia Commons
Attribution: James E. Irving
License: Public Domain

time to talking and writing about music for the public. His 1937 volume *What To Listen For In Music* is an early classic of the music appreciation literature and is still in print.

1965: THE DUKE ELLINGTON CONTROVERSY

After Copland, the Pulitzer Prize was awarded to a long list of highly-educated white male composers writing in the European concert tradition. Clearly, jury members considered the production of "good music" to be linked to genre, race, and class. The winning works included symphonies, concertos, cantatas, and operas. However, the 1960s saw growing unease among listeners, performers, and scholars with this narrow definition of what could be "good" in music. Jazz, in particular, had developed into a sophisticated concert genre, and a number of composers were producing music that was, by many measures, just as "good" as that coming out of the classical sphere. The primary differences lay in instrumentation (jazz band instead of orchestra), **harmonic** language (jazz composers used different scales and chords), and the incorporation of **improvisation**.

Image 13.7: Duke Ellington playing the piano and smiling at the Hurricane Club in New York, N.Y., in May 1943.
Source: Wikimedia Commons
Attribution: Farm Security Administration/ Office of War Information Collection
License: Public Domain

This tension came to the forefront in 1965. Upon considering the various nominated works, the Pulitzer jury concluded that none of them was worthy of the prize. Instead, they recommended that a special citation be granted to Duke Ellington (1899-1974) in recognition of his lifetime of accomplishment in the field of music. Ellington had initially been nominated by Viola Lomoe, the wife of a newspaper editor and a dedicated fan of jazz. She had suggested that the jury consider Ellington's recent *The Far East Suite*, which she described as "being one of the larger forms of orchestral music" and therefore eligible for recognition. However, she also suggested that Ellington's entire career was prize worthy. "If the whole body of Ellington work can be considered," she wrote, "that can be heard anywhere, any time. In fact, it's inescapable, though often it's played or sung without a credit line."

Ellington's Career

Image 13.8: The Cotton Club, pictured here in 1930, opened in 1920 as a Harlem night spot for white "slummers."
Source: Wikimedia Commons
Attribution: The New Movie Magazine
License: Public Domain

Lomoe made a valid point about the ubiquity of Ellington's music, which has become ingrained in American culture. He composed over 3,000 popular songs in his lifetime, the best-known of which is perhaps "It Don't Mean a Thing (If It Ain't Got That Swing)" (1931). Ellington first rose to national prominence as a pianist and band leader in 1927, when his group became the house band at the Cotton Club in Harlem. The Cotton Club was one of several 1920s-era establishments that catered to white New Yorkers who were attracted by the perceived danger and excitement of dabbling in African American culture. While the club only admitted white patrons, the musicians, dancers, and servers were all black. Patrons and employees were not permitted to mix, however, and the advertising and decorations established the Cotton Club as a place where white New Yorkers could safely encounter the exotic black other. Although Ellington and his musicians were sometimes required to play up to stereotypes, they were still able to create masterpieces in the jazz idiom, and their music was heard across the country via regular radio broadcasts.

For several decades after leaving the Cotton Club in 1931, Ellington and his band toured internationally and made popular recordings. Ellington always thought of his music as art, and he resisted the jazz label, instead describing his own creations as "beyond category." While his songs gained the greatest popularity, many of his compositions relied on the extended forms of classical music.

The Far East Suite

Image 13.9: Duke Ellington is pictured here with his ensemble in 1963.
Source: Wikimedia Commons
Attribution: Hans Bernhard
License: CC BY-SA 3.0

The Far East Suite, recorded in 1966, is one such work. It contains nine movements, ranging from two-and-a-half to eleven-and-a-half minutes in length, and was inspired by world tours undertaken by Ellington's group in 1963 and 1964. The suite was a collaboration between Ellington and Billy Strayhorn, his longtime creative partner. While cowriting is common in jazz, the fact that *The Far East Suite* had two composers sets it apart from the classical tradition, in which instrumental compositions are always the work of an individual.

Each selection on the album represents Ellington's impressions upon visiting a foreign country. Commenting on the trip, Ellington stated, "The cats in the band go crazy about everything they see." In essence, each piece took a geographic area as an artistic starting point, resulting in continuous contrast and the ongoing transformation of accompanimental ideas. *The Far East Suite* includes an array of constantly evolving interactions between soloists (whether improvising or not) and unique combinations from within the ensemble.

Image 13.10: This photograph of Ellington were captured during a 1963 tour stop in India.
Source: Flickr
Attribution: U.S. Embassy New Delhi
License: CC BY-ND 2.0

A feature of Ellington's compositions is the thoughtful use of each instrument's unique voice. In the suite, each of the instrumental voices conjures up an element of the travel experience. The first movement of the suite, entitled "Tourist Point of View,"[4] sets the mood by contrasting comforting and disorienting sounds. In the introduction, we hear **dissonant** chords played by the brass. Upon the entrance of the saxophone soloist, these are replaced by bright, high harmonies in the winds, which in turn give way to a call-and-response texture that pits the two sections against one another. The constant changes in texture and timbre suggest an onslaught of new and unfamiliar experiences. In the foreground, we hear smooth solos that use intervals similar to those in Eastern melodies, although the airy sound of the tenor saxophone serves as a touchstone of familiarity. The energy reaches a peak with Cat Anderson's high trumpet playing, but the track concludes with a general decrescendo until finally the bass and drums fade out.

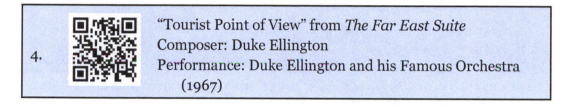

4. "Tourist Point of View" from *The Far East Suite*
    Composer: Duke Ellington
    Performance: Duke Ellington and his Famous Orchestra
        (1967)

As the suite progresses, each movement takes on a new story, which is illustrated using a combination of unique musical elements. These range from the use of a clarinet in "Bluebird of Delhi" to portray the song of a bird, pitted against a swinging ensemble (typical of Ellington/Strayhorn's sound), to the muted brass improvisations in "Amad," which suggest the Muslim call to prayer against a persistent piano **ostinato**.

"Isfahan"[5] (a city in Iran) is captured with a slow jazz ballad that showcases the sound of Johnny Hodges on alto saxophone against a relaxed and relatively soft ensemble. This movement has an easygoing atmosphere. Dramatic harmonies, produced by winds and muted brass, are paired with heavy rhythmic punctuations and ostinatos. Gravity is provided by occasional full ensemble interjections, some of which are echoed by unaccompanied melodies in the saxophone. ("Isfahan" is still popular among jazz artists today and is regularly performed by ensembles of varying size).

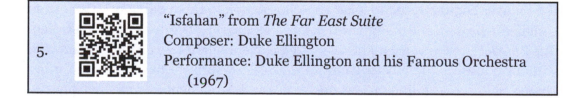

5. "Isfahan" from *The Far East Suite*
    Composer: Duke Ellington
    Performance: Duke Ellington and his Famous Orchestra
        (1967)

Image 13.11: Isfahan is home to some of the great architectural marvels of the Middle East, such as the Shah Mosque, pictured here.
Source: Flickr
Attribution: User "Amirpashaei"
License: CC BY-SA 4.0

We hear the influence of music from the 1960s in the rock inflections (especially in the drums) and non-swung beat divisions of "Blue Pepper." But the suite quickly mellows in "Agra," and concludes with what might be described as a sequence of cadenzas in the final movement, "Ad Lib on Nippon." *The Far East Suite* took elements that had developed over the course of a decades-long collaboration between the artists Strayhorn and Ellington—in particular, the use of slowly-shifting ensemble colors that interacted with and influenced solo improvisations—to a new level, illustrating a story shaped by personal experience.

Disappointment

However, 1965 is not remembered as the first year in which a jazz composer was recognized with a Pulitzer Prize. This is because, despite the jury's recommendation, the Pulitzer board refused to issue a special citation to Duke Ellington. Two jurors resigned in protest, and many more felt that a serious injustice had been perpetrated. The Pulitzer Prize was meant to recognize excellence in American music. Jazz was, without question, the most significant musical art form to have emerged in the United States, and Ellington was one of its most prominent and creative figures. If the purpose of the Pulitzer Prize was to celebrate excellence in American music, on what grounds was Ellington to be denied recognition? The man himself joked, "Fate is being kind to me. Fate doesn't want me to be famous too young." (He was 66 years old.) However, Ellington was offended—not because the board had rejected him, but because they had rejected a form of music that he valued highly. "Most Americans still take it for granted that European music—classical music, if you will—is the only really respectable kind," he later said in an interview. "By and large, then as now, jazz was like the kind of man you wouldn't want your daughter to associate with." Ellington firmly believed that jazz could constitute "good music" and that criteria could be established by which the determine quality in jazz.

1997: WYNTON MARSALIS, *BLOOD ON THE FIELDS*

Despite the uproar, it was still to be several decades before a jazz composer would win the Pulitzer Prize for Music. By the 1990s, it was well established that the Pulitzer in music usually went to compositions for symphony orchestra. Occasionally, small chamber ensembles, choirs, and even solo piano were selected. Only once had the award gone to an electronic composition: Mario Davidovsky's *Synchronisms No. 6 for Piano and Electronic Sound* (1970). It comes as no surprise that many musicians detected a sense of exclusiveness and prejudice on behalf of the Pulitzer committee.

In 1994, notable composer and performer Gunther Schuller (who had performed with jazz musicians Dizzy Gillespie and John Lewis) was awarded the Pulitzer for his *Of Reminiscences and Reflections*, a composition for large orchestra. Although Schuller was a member of the jazz community, his winning composition contained few jazz elements. In particular, it lacked a jazz sound and performance style. As a result of his win, however, Schuller was invited to adjudicate for the 1997 Pulitzer in Music. The other jury members included a jazz critic, a jazz performer, and two traditional composers. With a majority of jury members having extensive experience in jazz, the panel finally chose to award the Pulitzer to a jazz musician.

Developing *Blood on the Fields*

Several years earlier, the Lincoln Center had **commissioned** jazz artist Wynton Marsalis (b. 1961) to present a new composition. The 32-year-old Marsalis was already well known as a jazz trumpeter and composer; indeed, he had established the Lincoln Center's own summer jazz series in 1987, and had made great progress in his mission to institutionalize jazz as a respected American art form. Although Marsalis grew up in New Orleans and interacted with important jazz musicians from a young age, most of his early training was in classical music, and it was with the intent of pursuing an orchestral

Image 13.12: The Jazz at the Lincoln Center Orchestra, captured here in a photograph by Adam Bowie, was founded and is still led by Wynton Marsalis.
Source: Flickr
Attribution: Adam Bowie
License: CC BY-NC-SA 2.0

Image 13.13: Wynton Marsalis is a virtuoso trumpeter who performs in a variety of styles, including jazz and classical.
Source: Flickr
Attribution: Evert-Jan Hielema
License: CC BY-NC-ND 2.0

career that he enrolled in the Juilliard School in 1979. Although he soon decided that his future lay in jazz, Marsalis's background prepared him to create music that drew from a diversity of traditions, styles, and forms. In response to the Lincoln Center commission, therefore, he decided to create a work in the European **oratorio** tradition. Oratorios employ an orchestra and vocal soloists to tell a story, although their presentation does not incorporate costumes, sets, or acting. Instead, the story is communicated entirely through sound.

For his oratorio, which was premiered in 1994, Marsalis crafted a narrative that related the experiences of an enslaved couple. His story begins on a slave ship and ends with the protagonists striking out for the north and freedom. The two main characters are Leona and Jesse, the latter of whom was a prince before his enslavement. Over the course of *Blood on the Fields*, the two aid each other in adjusting to their new lives, finding hope for the future, and eventually escaping from bondage. Originally, Marsalis had intended *Blood on the Fields* to be "tragic the whole way through, with no redemption." Following extensive study and reflection, however, he concluded that optimism was "a very important part of the jazz expression." Marsalis's attitude—as well as his music—was deeply influenced by Duke Ellington, whose work he perceived as being essentially optimistic.

In creating the music for *Blood on the Fields*, Marsalis drew from a variety of African American traditions, including New Orleans jazz, blues, funk, chants, **field hollers**, work songs, and **spirituals**. He wrote for a jazz orchestra of forty musicians, with an important role for himself on the trumpet. In addition to playing their instruments, the orchestra members also recite text in unison to prepare each scene. Marsalis patterned this approach on the tradition of ancient Greek theater, which employed a chorus to narrate and reflect upon events.

Work Song (Blood on the Fields)

We will consider "Work Song (Blood on the Fields),"[6] which is the sixth scene of the oratorio's twenty-one. In this scene, Leona and Jesse are working in the fields, and they describe their monotonous labor and lament their unbearable situation. Although the scene follows quickly upon that in which they are purchased at auction, we are informed that in fact fourteen years have passed.

6.	[QR code]	"Work Song (Blood on the Fields)" from *Blood on the Fields* Composer: Wynton Marsalis Performance: The Lincoln Center Jazz Orchestra (1997)

The first thing we hear is Marsalis's trumpet. The growling sound he produces using a plunger mute is modelled on the playing of James "Bubber" Miley, who pioneered this style as a member of Ellington's band in the 1920s. Marsalis's improvisatory melody imitates the shapes and sounds of blues singing, although of course his playing communicates emotion without the benefit of words. In between his phrases, the members of the orchestra recite in unison.

Soon, the members of the orchestra establish a groove, which remains fairly consistent for the remainder of the scene. Throughout *Blood on the Fields*, Marsalis makes an effort to represent the motions and elements of each scene in music. In this case, we hear the regular rhythms of field labor. Punctuated brass exclamations and forceful drum hits emphasize the heaviness and effort of the work, while the unevenness of the rhythmic pattern suggests strain and sudden movements. The groove itself is rooted in the practices of various African and African-derived musical traditions. The process by which many distinct instruments each contribute a fragment to a complex musical whole is known as **hocket**, and is characteristic of black musical styles ranging from jali recitation to funk.

The regular interjections of other instruments suggest the sound and texture of New Orleans jazz, in which no single instrument carries the melody. Instead, each member of the ensemble contributes a distinct line to the texture, all of which combine to produce a rhythmic cacophony. In the case of "Work Song," we might also hear the instruments as the voices of other enslaved workers, joining the two vocalists in protest.

2013: CAROLINE SHAW, *PARTITA FOR 8 VOICES*

The 2013 Pulitzer Prize attracted an unusual amount of attention. To begin with, at 30 years old, Caroline Shaw (b. 1982) was the youngest composer ever to win a Pulitzer. In addition to that, she was only the fifth woman to win in the seventy years of the competition. (Ellen Taaffe Zwilich was the first, in 1983.) Finally, the work itself was out of the ordinary. *Partita* requires amplified singers to employ unusual and non-Western vocal techniques, and at the time of the award only one vocal ensemble—Roomful of Teeth, of which Shaw herself is a founding member—had ever performed it. In fact, Roomful of Teeth had not even premiered the complete work, but had programmed individual movements as they were completed. *Partita* had also not been published and could only be heard on Roomful of Teeth's eponymous 2012 album, which itself won a Grammy for Best Chamber Music/Small Ensemble Performance in 2013. In this way, *Partita* was more like a pop song than a classical composition. As a result, it inspired discussion not only about whether or not it was "good" but about whether it even had the necessary characteristics to satisfy the criteria used to evaluate compositional quality.

Roomful of Teeth

We can't understand *Partita* without understanding the history and mission of Roomful of Teeth. The group was founded in 2009 by Brad Wells, who had a vision for an eight-part vocal ensemble that would break new ground in the world of art music. Most choirs adopt a uniform vocal production technique derived from the European tradition. However, the human voice is capable of producing an extraordinary range of sounds, and there is boundless variety in the techniques used by non-Western and popular singers. The members of Roomful of Teeth learn these techniques from world-renowned experts. In the past decade, the group has studied Tuvan **throat singing**, yodeling, Broadway **belting**, Inuit throat singing, Korean P'ansori, Georgian singing, Sardinian cantu a tenore, Hindustani music, Persian classical singing, and Death Metal singing. All of these techniques have been incorporated into their performances. To accomplish this, Wells commissions composers to write music expressly for the group. Much of this work takes place during an annual gathering at the Massachusetts Museum of Contemporary Art (MASS MoCA) in North Adams, Massachusetts, where teachers, singers, and composers come together to create new music.

As you can imagine, not just any choir can sing the repertoire that is created for Roomful of Teeth. Although the music is notated, the techniques required to perform it are highly specialized, and any vocal ensemble that wants to take on the challenge will require training. For this reason, few other choirs have ever performed *Partita*. Roomful of Teeth, on the other hand, continues to perform the work regularly. Some of their concerts are traditional in format, but they also engage with experimental performance techniques. In January of 2019, for example, they performed *Partita* outdoors in Times Square to the accompaniment of the LEIMAY Ensemble, a contemporary dance troupe.

Image 13.14: Roomful of Teeth is an experimental vocal ensemble founded in 2009.
Source: Roomful of Teeth
Attribution: BONICA AYALA
License: © Rooomful of Teeth. Used with permission.

Shaw and her Inspirations

Caroline Shaw (b. 1982) was among the first composers to write for Roomful of Teeth. Her training at the time she began work on *Partita*, however, was oriented towards violin performance, not composition (or even vocal performance). She only entered a PhD program in composition in 2010. This also makes her unusual. Most previous Pulitzer winners were established figures with degrees, university positions, and long lists of major works. Shaw was essentially unknown.

Image 13.15: Caroline Shaw is still at the beginning of her career.
Source: Original Work
Attribution: Caroline Shaw
License: © Caroline Shaw. Used with permission.

The inspiration for *Partita* came from several sources. The first was Sol LeWitt's *Wall Drawing 305*, which can be viewed at the MASS MoCA, where Roomful of Teeth completes an annual residency. *Wall Drawing 305* is not a work of visual art in the traditional sense (just as Shaw's *Partita* is not a traditional choir piece), and might be categorized as **conceptual art**. The "work" is, in fact, a set of instructions intended to guide draftsmen in placing one hundred points on a wall. These instructions can be followed by anyone in any space to create the drawing. LeWitt was interested in randomness, and he sought to prevent the emergence of patterns in the visual product. No two realizations of any work in his *Wall Drawing* series will be the same.

Shaw was attracted to LeWitt's artistic vision, and she used several of his instructive texts in *Partita*. Her description of the work also ties it to *Wall Drawing 305*: "Partita is a simple piece. Born of a love of surface and structure, of the human voice, of dancing and tired ligaments, of music, and of our basic desire to draw a line from one point to another." However, she also cites Times Square as a source for the work:

> Since my very first years living in New York City, I have spent a lot of time in Times Square. I used to walk through the area right after I moved there just to take in its unique combination of chaos and magic. It is truly unlike any place in the world. I love to see how many people come to the city and visit Times Square, who are always looking up in awe and confusion and wonder. It is that mix of confusion and wonder that is also deeply in Partita. . . I also like to think about the traffic patterns that move through Times Square, intersecting, crossing, and pausing in different ways, just like the text in the first movement. . .

Finally, Shaw took the title and form of *Partita* from the tradition of Baroque **dance suites**. Bach used the terms partita and suite almost interchangeably, although his partitas are somewhat looser in form. Shaw would have encountered the term partita as a violinist, since that is how Bach labelled his suites for solo violin. Three of Shaw's movements share the names of typical Baroque dances: "Allemande," "Sarabande," and "Courante." The final movement, titled "Passacaglia," links *Partita* with a different Baroque form, for a passacaglia is a set of variations over a repeating bass line. We do not find passacaglias in genuine Baroque dance suites.

Passacaglia

To get a sense of how *Partita* sounds, we will consider the last of the four movements, "Passacaglia."[7] The movement opens with the ensemble presenting a cycle of harmonies. They sing the same **chord progression** three times, but each time using a different vocal timbre. The first time through, they produce warm, rounded sounds. The second time, they shift timbres mid-pitch, switching from bright to subtle. The third time, they sing in a chest style derived from Bulgarian choral practice, producing a piercing and aggressive sound followed by a gasping sigh.

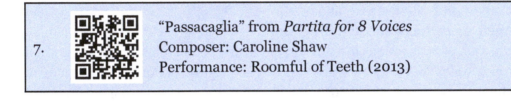

7. "Passacaglia" from *Partita for 8 Voices*
Composer: Caroline Shaw
Performance: Roomful of Teeth (2013)

Next we hear the chord progression again, but this time it is overlaid with oscillating figures in half of the voices. These carry into the subsequent section, providing the backdrop for a high melody sung in octaves and then for spoken text extracted from LeWitt's *Wall Drawing 305*. During this passage we also hear harmonic **overtone singing** from the men, who manipulate low pedal tones to produce a rainbow of high-pitched sounds. One by one, the singers switch to reciting LeWitt's text, until we are left with a cacophony of speaking voices. Isolated pitches extracted from the opening chord progression occasionally pierce the texture.

The cacophony is only resolved by the production of a grating sound derived from Korean *pansori* singing. This builds in strength before transforming into the opening chord, which inaugurates one final pass through the harmonic progression in chest voice. A second pass begins, but is derailed by the introduction of new chords. More overtone singing ornaments the final harmony of the piece.

2018: KENDRICK LAMAR, *DAMN.*

The 1997 decision to grant the Pulitzer Prize to a jazz composer certainly broke new ground, but the 2018 decision represented an even bolder divorce with tradition. There were, as always, three finalists. The most conventional work under consideration was Michael Gilbertson's *Quartet*, a work for **string quartet** in the concert tradition. The next contender was Ted Hearne's *Sound from the Bench*. This **cantata** for chamber choir, two electric guitars, and drums is a bit

less conventional. In it, Hearne combines text from landmark Supreme Court decisions with excerpts from ventriloquism textbooks to comment on the evolving legal notion of corporate personhood. Despite any eccentricities, Gilbertson and Hearne are both conservatory-educated composers who write concert works for traditional ensembles, and are therefore typical Pulitzer Prize contenders.

Image 13.16: Kendrick Lamar's album *DAMN.* won the Pulitzer Prize in 2018.
Source: Wikimedia Commons
Attribution: User "Rena3xdxd"
License: CC BY-SA 4.0

More Controversy

Neither Gilbertson nor Hearne won the competition, however. Instead, the jury awarded the Pulitzer Prize to Kendrick Lamar for his hip-hop album *DAMN*. In doing so, they rejected 75 years of received wisdom about what kind of music is prize-worthy, instead making the bold assertion that hip-hop has the potential to be "good" music and that there are criteria for judging the relative quality of hip-hop artists and tracks. How else could they identify Lamar as being the "best"? However, this effort to bring hip-hop into the world of the Pulitzers presented challenges. To begin with, *DAMN.* is not a literate musical work. That is to say, it did not begin life as notes on a page, and musical notation does not play a role in its preservation. This, of course, is true of most popular genres, and that leads us to the next point.

Up until 2018, only works in art music genres had been considered for the prize. Jazz, of course, was not always considered to be "art music," but by the 1960s there was at least a strong argument being made that it ought to be, and it was possible to obtain a college degree in jazz studies. Furthermore, the specific Ellington work cited in 1965 was

Image 13.17: This photograph of Lamar was taken at the 2018 Pulitzer ceremony.
Source: Wikimedia Commons
Attribution: User "Fuzheado"
License: CC BY-SA 4.0

not a popular song, but rather an adventurous instrumental composition, while Marsalis's 1997 composition was even more self-evidently a work of "art." Jazz in general was not exactly popular by the time is was recognized with a Pulitzer, and the works in question were particularly cerebral. Hip-hop, on the other hand, is decidedly a popular genre.

Furthermore, Kendrick Lamar is decidedly a popular hip-hop artist. He is not a fringe figure, producing artsy, experimental tracks in the hip-hop vein for a small group of admirers. With scores of Grammy nominations, over a dozen Grammy wins, multiple million-selling albums, and a string of singles at the top of the Billboard Hot Rap charts, Lamar's music is mainstream. In this respect, he was a new type of Pulitzer Prize winner. Before, the jury had often recognized artists who were well-known in the world of concert music, but it had never selected a winner who was genuinely *popular*. This raised questions not only about how "good" music can be identified but also about the purpose of the Pulitzer. In the past, it had served to boost the careers of little-known composers, or at least provided support to those creating music in a field that offered few opportunities for financial gain. Lamar needs neither fame nor money. What purpose could be served in providing him with more of both?

The answer, of course, is that the art music establishment—represented by the Pulitzer Prize jury—was seeking to make a statement about its own values. By extending the honor to Lamar, they both acknowledged the profound impact that hip-hop has had on art music composers and suggested that the categories of "art" and "popular" might not even make sense anymore. Good music is good music—so why should anyone get hung up on genre? The gap between the worlds of art and popular music still exists, of course. Nowhere is this more evident than in the awkward phrasing of the Prize jury's citation, which describes *DAMN.* as "a virtuosic song collection unified by its vernacular authenticity and rhythmic dynamism that offers affecting vignettes capturing the complexity of modern African-American life." This is not language that would speak to the average hip-hop fan. However, it does speak to classical music aficionados, and it positions *DAMN.* within the lineage of Pulitzer Prize-winning works.

DNA

The jury selected "DNA"[8] as the emblematic track from the album, so we will consider that example. Most hip-hop is highly collaborative: **Producers**, rappers, and studio musicians work together to create individual tracks, each shaping the final product in different ways. There is seldom a single artist who decides exactly how it will sound. In the case of "DNA," Lamar worked with Michael Len Williams II (b. 1989), a producer and rapper who has also collaborated with Gucci Mane, Miley Cyrus, Rihanna, and Beyoncé (he contributed to "Formation," mentioned in Chapter 5). "DNA" grew out of a beat that Williams had originally prepared for Gucci Mane, but that he offered to Lamar while they were working on tracks that would eventually become part of *DAMN.* Lamar was inspired by Williams's work and created the first part of "DNA." In the recording studio, however, Lamar began rapping *a capella*, subsequently asking Williams to build a beat around his words.

---

8.   "DNA"
    Composers: Kendrick Lamar & Michael Len Williams II
    Performance: Kendrick Lamar (2017)

The result is a single track in two distinct parts. At the midway point, the pulse breaks down. We hear an excerpt from a televised attack against Lamar, made by Geraldo Rivera on Fox News: "This is why I say that hip-hop has done more damage to young African Americans than racism in recent years." Seemingly in response, Lamar's rapping accelerates and the rhythms become staggeringly complex. Williams later stated that he "wanted it to sound like he's battling the beat," which it certainly does. The pulse recedes into the background during this section, encouraging the listener to focus entirely on the intense rhythmic exchanges between Lamar and his environment. The lyrics in "DNA" are wide-ranging, but they return repeatedly to issues of disenfranchisement and generational trauma in the black community. Lamar uses hip-hop to shine a light on these problems— mocking Rivera's reactionary dismissal in the process.

GREATNESS AND GENRE

The preceding discussion about the Pulitzer Prize for Music has essentially been a discussion about "greatness" and genre. For most of the twentieth century, the Pulitzer committee restricted their concept of "greatness" to classical music. In the late twentieth century they expanded it to include jazz, and in the twenty-first century that have expanded still further to include hip-hop. What will come next? We can only wait and see. However, it is clear that the committee has historically perceived some genres as superior to others, and continues to see "greatness" only in specific realms.

Some of the best performing artists, however, clearly do not place these same limitations on music. In this section, we will explore the work of individual artists and performing ensembles that have excelled in the realm of classical music, but have put as much (or more) energy into other genres. All of these artists would disagree that any one musical genre is superior to another. Instead, they hear good music everywhere and are inspired by a variety of styles and approaches.

ALARM WILL SOUND

Alarm Will Sound is an instrumental ensemble based in New York City. The group was initially formed by students at the Eastman School of Music in Rochester, NY. While pursuing degrees in music, founders Gavin Chuck and Alan Pierson

Image 13.18: This photograph of Alarm Will Sound was taken in 2011 by Michael Clayville.
Source: Wikimedia Commons
Attribution: User "Mclayville"
License: CC BY-SA 3.0

got into conversation about the limited opportunities for the performance of **New Music** (a standard term for recent, often experimental, art music compositions, many of which might be classified as **avant-garde**)—and especially **minimalist**

music. They recruited a group of interested performers and started a concert series. Upon graduating from Eastman, the members of the ensemble decided that they wanted to keep working together, and in 2001 Alarm Will Sound was founded.

The group's first concert under their new name took place on May 24, 2001, in New York City's Miller Theater. Unsurprisingly, given their collective interests, the program explored the music of minimalist composer Steve Reich (b. 1936). Reich was at the forefront of the development of minimalism in the 1960s. Although minimalist composers take a variety of approaches to their work, they share an interest in developing extended compositions from limited musical material. Reich himself has always detested the term

Image 13.19: Steve Reich in 1976.
Source: Wikimedia Commons
Attribution: Hans Peters / Anefo
License: CC0

"minimalism," preferring the more descriptive "pattern and process music." This is fitting: Most minimalist composers employ fixed transformative processes in their work.

Reich's Compositional Processes

Reich's earliest experiments were completed using **tape loops**. He discovered that if he played two identical loops of audio tape at slightly different speeds, he could produce a dazzling and constantly shifting array of effects, opening up a world of sound that could never be detected in the untransformed material. Reich's first completed tape piece did not even use musical sounds. Instead, he built *Come Out*[9] (1966) using a clip from an interview with Daniel Hamm, one of the Harlem Six—a group of black men (mostly teenagers) who were coerced into confessing to a 1964 murder and denied adequate representation by the courts. Although the men were convicted by an all-white jury in 1965, all but one of the charges were eventually overturned. In *Come Out*, we hear Hamm explaining the means to which he had to resort in order to convince police that he and his co-defendants had been beaten in jail and required medical attention.

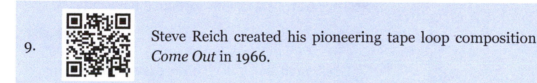

9.   Steve Reich created his pioneering tape loop composition *Come Out* in 1966.

Come Out was initially a byproduct of a sound collage that Reich built at the request of civil rights activist Truman Nelson, but it ended up being a broadly influential minimalist experiment. Over the course of the 13-minute work, Hamm's voice slowly dissolves into a cacophony of rhythms and timbres. The words soon become unintelligible as the listener's interest shifts to the element of pure sound. Although it is almost impossible to detect the gradual changes that are taking place, no two seconds of the recording are the same. Sustained attention is rewarded with an inimitable sonic experience.

Reich soon applied similar techniques to musical material, at the same time developing new approaches to facilitating gradual change over extended periods of time. Reich was a highly trained musician, having studied at the Juilliard School in New York City and Mills College in Oakland, CA. He also had omnivorous tastes: He was equally enthralled with jazz, the music of Bach and Vivaldi, rock, and Stravinsky's *The Rite of Spring*. Later, he took opportunities to study non-Western traditions, including Balinese gamelan and West African drumming. All of these influenced his mature style.

Tehillim

		I. Psalm 19:2-5, "The heavens declare the glory of God" from *Tehillim* Composer: Steve Reich Performance: Alarm Will Sound (2011)
Time	**Form**	**What to listen for**
0'00"	Melody	The Psalm text is presented by a solo singer and accompanied by tambourine and clapping
0'36"	Melody (repetition)	Another singer repeats the melody, which is now doubled by clarinet
1'12"	Canon in 2 voices	The two singers perform the melody in canon
1'47"	Canon in 2 voices (two repetitions)	The strings enter with sustained harmonies
2'59"	Canon in 4 voices	The tempo slows; each phrase is repeated many times; the voices are doubled by reed organ and accompanied by maracas; the string harmonies continue
8'49"	Melody	The solo singer is doubled by clarinet and accompanied by tambourine, clapping, and maracas
9'24"	Melody (repetition)	The string harmonies return
9'58"	Melody (repetition)	A second singer harmonizes below the melody
10'32"	Melody (final statement)	The texture thins as elements disappear one by one

On their inaugural concert, Alarm Will Sound performed two large-scale Reich works for orchestral ensemble and singers: *Tehillim* (1981) and *The Desert Music* (1983). We will consider *Tehillim*, which, by Reich's own account, represented his first attempt to engage musically with his Jewish heritage. The texts, sung in Hebrew by four female voices, are taken from the Book of Psalms (the original Hebrew word for which is "Tehillim," which literally means "praises"). In the first movement, we hear four lines from Psalm 19:

> The heavens declare the glory of God;
>   the skies proclaim the work of his hands.
> Day after day they pour forth speech;
>   night after night they reveal knowledge.
> They have no speech, they use no words;
>   no sound is heard from them.
> Yet their voice goes out into all the earth,
>   their words to the ends of the world.
> In the heavens God has pitched a tent for the sun.

At first, a solo voice is accompanied only by a tambourine without jingles (intended by Reich to evoke the small drum mentioned in Psalm 150) and clapping—another mode of rhythmic accompaniment that was in use during Biblical times. We hear the entire Psalm text sung to a continuous melody, which is shaped by the rhythms of the Hebrew words. This is an atypical way for Reich to open a piece of music, but he soon begins applying transformations.

The second time through the melody, the singer is doubled by a clarinet, while a second percussive accompaniment of tambourine and clapping enters in **canon** with the first. Next, we hear the melody in a two-voice canon, one singer echoing the other. Soon after the canon begins, the strings enter with sustained harmonies. At the conclusion of this turn through the complete melody, the tempo slows and the texture fractures into a four-voice canon. The four singers repeat each individual line of the Psalm many times. They are doubled by electric organ, which contributes a reedy timbre, and accompanied by maracas. The sustained string harmonies gradually shift, seemingly out of time with the voices. Finally, the original soloist—again doubled by clarinet—assumes the melody once more, to the accompaniment of drums and maracas. She is briefly harmonized by one of the other singers, but the movement ends much as it began.

While *Tehillim* is quite different from *Come Out* in all surface respects, we can see how Reich's basic compositional process is consistent. The textures in *Tehillim*—as in *Come Out*—are created from the increasingly complex layering of limited sound material. In the case of *Tehillim*, Reich relies on rhythmic and melodic canons, augmented by slow-moving, kaleidoscopic harmonies.

Orchestrating Aphex Twin

The members of Alarm Will Sound were brought together by their love for music like *Tehillim*, and in their early years they found a great deal of success staging concerts that highlighted the work of individual living composers. However,

Image 13.20: Aphex Twin performs at Coachella in 2008.
Source: Wikimedia Commons
Attribution: Octavio Ruiz Cervera
License: CC BY-SA 2.0

they also shared a passion for popular music—in particular, the innovative electronic dance music of Aphex Twin. Members of the ensemble began discussing the possibility (and purpose) of recreating Aphex Twin's music using acoustic instruments.

According to founder Gavin Chuck, the idea was controversial: "There were heated debates about the nature of digital vs. acoustic sound, and of machine precision vs. human expressiveness. There were disagreements about whether we should be as faithful as possible to the originals, or interpret them more openly." Despite the varied opinions about the merit of such a project, Alarm Will Sound eventually took it on. Their work culminated in the 2005 album *Acoustica*, which primarily featured arrangements taken from Aphex Twin's 2001 album *Drukqs*.

Whether or not all of the work required to make and record these arrangements was worthwhile is debatable. We will consider the opening track from *Acoustica*, "Cock/Ver10."[10] One might argue that Alarm Will Sound's limited sound palette and acoustic means of production are inferior to the programmed beats, digitally-refined timbres, and studio effects of Aphex Twin's original[11]—or one might prefer the sounds of orchestral instruments. It is hard not to be impressed by the skill of the arranger, Stefan Freund, who translated Aphex Twin's track into an orchestral score, and by the individual performers, who place complex rhythms and melodic gestures in exactly the right place.

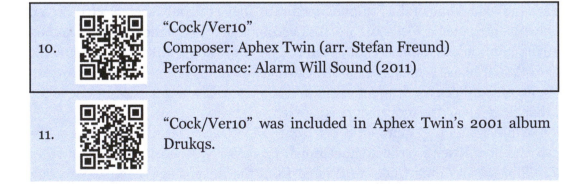

10.   "Cock/Ver10"
      Composer: Aphex Twin (arr. Stefan Freund)
      Performance: Alarm Will Sound (2011)

11.   "Cock/Ver10" was included in Aphex Twin's 2001 album *Drukqs*.

From Chuck's perspective, the strength of the project lay in its capacity to connect the ensemble with new audiences and put their artistic values on display. It became, in his words, "an important platform from which to pursue a wide-ranging artistic vision that doesn't worry too much about genre—electronic vs. acoustic, high-modernist vs. pop-influenced, conventional classical concert vs. multimedia experience." In short, by recording the works of Aphex Twin, Alarm Will Sound proved that they were eager to embrace good music from unexpected quarters.

YO-YO MA

Perhaps the most visible and influential individual to make a career as a classical crossover artist has been cellist Yo-Yo Ma. His work has embraced a range of folk and non-Western musical styles, with the result that he has successful bestowed his own cultural prestige on a large number of performers and traditions that might otherwise not have come into contact with the classical establishment. His projects have resulted in the creation of a lot of excellent music and the introduction of new sounds to classical audiences.

Image 13.21: Cellist Yo-Yo Ma was born in Paris in 1955.
Source: Flickr
Attribution: World Economic Forum
License: CC BY-NC-SA 2.0

Image 13.22: Yo-Yo Ma performing in 2008.
Source: Wikimedia Commons
Attribution: World Economic Forum
License: CC BY-SA 2.0

Classical Mastery

Yo-Yo Ma was born in Paris to Chinese parents, but his family immigrated to the United States when he was seven. He first gained prominence as a child prodigy. Almost immediately after his arrival in the States, Ma played for Presidents John F. Kennedy and Dwight D. Eisenhower at a Kennedy Center benefit concert that was broadcast on national television.[12] This was the first in a series of prominent performances and television appearances that introduced Ma to the American public.

12.  A young Yo-Yo Ma played cello on live television in 1962.

After earning his bachelor's degree at Harvard University in 1976, Ma embarked on what could have been a typical concert career. He appeared as a soloist with orchestras around the world, collaborated with chamber musicians, and released recordings, eleven on which won Grammys between 1985 and 1998. The first of these award-winning recordings offered Ma's interpretation of the complete Bach cello suites (see Chapter 12)—a rite of passage for any cellist who wants to be counted among the greats.

Ma still performs these pieces regularly. He has presented the complete suites to crowds numbering in the tens of thousands at the Hollywood Bowl in Los Angeles and the Jay Pritzker Pavilion in Chicago, but he also played movements from the suites at the one-year national September 11 memorial service, the funeral for Senator Edward M. Kennedy, and the service held to honor victims of the 2013 Boston Marathon bombing. In 2019, he featured the Prelude to Suite No. 1 in G major[13]—certainly the best-known movement from the suites—in a video meant to express the many ways in which the arts bring communities together. He issued an invitation for people around the world to submit videos on the theme of self-expression and community building. Many of these were then integrated in the final video.

13.  Yo-Yo Ma has proven his mastery of the classical cello literature. Here he plays the Prelude to Bach's Suite No. 1.

Despite his success on the concert stage, however, Ma soon embarked on a series of collaborations that brought him into contact with non-classical performers and genres. By doing so, he clearly indicated his belief that examples of "good music" can be found in all traditions, and that quality is determined by the level of execution and creativity that characterize a performance. Early in his journey, Ma collaborated with a team of world-class tango musicians to record *The Soul of the Tango* (1997). This Grammy-winning album contributed to the elevation of tango from its undeniably humble roots.

Tango

Tango originated in the slums of Buenos Aires, Argentina, in the late 19th century. A popular dance style, the tango was inherently international: It was driven by an instrument brought to South America by German immigrants, the *bandoneon* (a type of push-button accordion) and capitalized on the **syncopated** rhythms of rural *gauchos* (cowboys) and African slaves. The lyrics to early tango songs described the hardships of life in the slums, while the accompanying dance reflected the violence of knife duels, the characteristic posture of the good-for-nothing young man, and the ritualistic domination of the female dancer by her male partner. The tango rhythm is built on a **quadruple-meter** framework with an emphasis on the second half of the second beat.

The tango was at first treated with contempt in its native Argentina. The dance and its accompanying music, after all, were associated with poverty, seedy establishments, and questionable morals. In 1907, however, the tango made a hit in Paris, where it acquired cultural cachet. By the 1920s, it had been embraced around the world, but in the 1930s its popularity began to fade (in part because the Great Depression excited an appetite for more cheerful music). Later in the century, however, Astor Piazzolla (1921-1992) would reinvent the tango for the concert hall, composing nuanced and dramatic pieces that were intended for listening, not dancing.

We will consider Yo-Yo Ma's recording of Piazzolla's famous "Libertango," which he recorded with Leonardo Marconi on piano, Antonio Agri on violin, Hector Console on bass, Horacio Malvicino on guitar, and Néstor Marconi on bandoneon. The title incorporates the Spanish word for "liberty"—a reference to Piazolla's new style, which he launched with the 1974 publication and recording of this composition. Any performance of "Libertango" is immediately recognizable, due to the catchy ostinato played by the bandoneon. The compositions itself is fairly simple: After an introduction, which establishes the ostinato and harmonic progression, we hear the A section twice. This is followed by the B section, which begins with contrasting material but concludes with a variation on the first half of the A melody. Then the ostinato returns, serving as a basis for improvisation.

	"Libertango" Composer: Astor Piazzola Performance: Yo-Yo Ma, Leonardo Marconi, Antonio Agri, Hector Console, Horacio Malvicino, Néstor Marconi (1997)

Time	Form	What to listen for
0'00	Ostinato	The bandoneon establishes the ostinato while the piano plays a syncopated rhythm known as the tresillo
0'26"	A	The A melody is played in the cello
0'54"	A	The A melody is played by the cello and violin in octaves
1'22"	B	The B melody is played by the bandoneon

1'37"	A'	The bandoneon plays a variation on the first half of the A melody, which is now combined with the ostinato; the cello and violin play a countermelody
1'50"	Ostinato	This time, the cello and violin double the bandoneon on the ostinato
2'18"	Ostinato with improvisation	The guitar player improvises a solo over the ostinato

Throughout the recording, we can clearly hear the **tresillo** rhythm that is characteristic of much Latin American music. This rhythm has its roots in West African music, and it entered the Latin American mainstream when the traditions of enslaved Africans combined with the folk and popular practices of both indegenous peoples and colonial powers. The same rhythm can also be heard in African-derived musics of the United States, such as ragtime. The tresillo rhythm can be counted as 3+3+2. Each count is a half-beat, such that one measure in quadruple meter contains eight counts. In our recording of "Libertango," the tresillo rhythm is heard primarily in the piano.

Appalachian Music

At about the same time, Ma also turned his attention to the folk music of the United States. He teamed up with celebrity fiddler Mark O'Connor and renowned bass player Edgar Meyer to record two albums, *Appalachia Waltz* (1996) and *Appalachian Journey* (2000), each of which contains fiddle tunes, songs, and new compositions inspired by the American folk sound. The trio did not attempt to reproduce authentic performing styles. Instead, they brought their own skills and backgrounds to the creation of unusual arrangements that balanced traditional material with novel interpretation.

We will consider their rendition of "Fisher's Hornpipe" from *Appalachian Journey*. This tune has been convincingly attributed to James A. Fishar, who served as music director at Covent Garden opera house in London in the 1770s. It appeared as "Hornpipe #1" in his 1778 collection of dance tunes. Whether or not Fishar composed the tune, it quickly gained popularity. Today it can be heard all over the British isles, in Canada, and in the United States, where it first appeared in print in 1796. There are countless versions—a symptom of the **oral tradition**, in which tunes are learned not from notation but by ear. Appalachian fiddlers would most likely have learned "Fisher's Hornpipe" from travelling dance musicians and adapted it to their own tastes.

For comparison, we might consider Tommy Jarrell's version of "Fisher's Hornpipe,"[14] which he learned from his father. This is an example of the traditional fiddling style known today as Round Peak, named after a prominent geological feature near Mt. Airy, NC. Jarrell provides harmony by playing multiple strings at the same time and rhythm by employing syncopated bowing patterns. As such, he doesn't particularly require accompaniment.

14.  This recording of "Fisher's Hornpipe" by Tommy Jarrell provides a good example of a traditional Appalachian rendition.

Ma and company's rendition is quite different. O'Connor is joined on the fiddle by bluegrass legend Allison Kraus. Although they play the same instrument as Jarrell, their technique could not contrast with his more greatly than it does. Each plays only a single melodic line, and does so with great precision and clarity. The slower tempo allows each note to sparkle. Occasionally we can hear vibrato—a technique that Jarrell would never employ. When accompanying other instruments, O'Connor and Kraus evoke some of the same rhythms as Jarrell, but their rendition of the melody is less syncopated.

Perhaps most importantly, the version of "Fisher's Hornpipe" on *Appalachian Journey* takes the original tune far outside of its folk framework. When Jarrell plays "Fisher's Hornpipe," he simply repeats the A and B strains until he decides that it is time to stop. His version is in the key of D, and it most certainly stays there. O'Connor and Kraus (soon joined by Meyer and Ma) begin with a fairly straightforward rendition of the tune, but after a few times through they switch to a groovy rhythmic pattern. Then, as Ma takes the melody, they **modulate** (change keys)—twice. Next, each player takes a turn with the A or B section, adding ornaments as if trying to outdo the person who played before. After this, they break into a **polyphonic**, four-part version of the tune that includes several countermelodies. The recording ends with even more key changes and virtuosic, high-range playing from Ma.

		"Fisher's Hornpipe" Composer: James A. Fishar (arr. Mark O'Connor) Performance: Yo-Yo Ma, Edgar Meyer, Mark O'Connor, Alison Krauss (2000)
Time	**Form**	**What to listen for**
0'00"	A	The two violins play the A strain in harmony (note: Jarrell begins with the other strain, making this his B strain)
0'10"	A	Addition of bass pizzicato

0'21"	B B	Addition of cello harmony
0'42"	B' B'	The two violinists play a variation on the B strain
1'04"	A' A'	The two violinists play a variation on the A strain
1'25"	A	The key modulates up one step and the cello plays the A strain, which is extended by a brief concluding passage
1'39"	A	The key changes again as a solo violin plays the A strain
1'49"	A	The other violin plays the A strain with additional ornamentation
1'59"	B	The cello plays the B strain
2'09"	B	The bass plays the B strain
2'21"	B B	One violin plays the B strain while the other instruments provide new countermelodies in a polyphonic texture; the key changes for the second statement of the B strain, the last phrase of which is repeated
2'46"	A' A	The A' variation returns for one statement before the cello plays the A strain
3'08"	A' A	The key modulates up by one step for another A' statement; it modulates up by yet another step for a cello statement of the A strain
3'30"	Coda	A concluding passage echoes the opening motif of the A strain

Silk Road Project

Ma's most significant and lasting foray outside of the European concert tradition, however, began in 1998 and has carried into the present day. He founded the Silk Road Project with the aim of bringing together musicians and cultures from across the regions formerly traversed by the **Silk Road**—the trade route, spanning from Italy to Japan, that shaped Europe, the Middle East, North Africa, and Asia beginning in the second century BCE. For Ma, the Silk Road was a symbol of intercultural exchange. For two millennia, the Silk Road moved

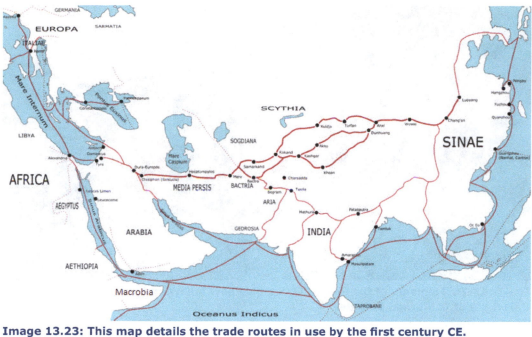

Image 13.23: This map details the trade routes in use by the first century CE.
Source: Wikimedia Commons
Attribution: User "Shizhao"
License: CC BY-SA 3.0

clothing, artifacts, musical instruments, songs, stories, and religious beliefs from one end of the known world to the other. Ma has described the historical Silk Road as "a model for productive cultural collaboration, for the exchange of ideas and traditions alongside commerce and innovation"—values that he wants to promote in the modern world.

Although the Silk Road Project has grown into a multifaceted arts organization—Silkroad—that pursues a variety of initiatives, we will consider only the activities of the Silkroad Ensemble, a collective of international **virtuosi** who blend the instruments, styles, and techniques of various musical traditions. The ensemble contains nearly sixty members (although only a dozen or so perform together on any given occasion) and has been active across the globe. Its members record albums (seven in the first two decades), give concerts, host festivals, and conduct clinics for students of all ages.

The music played by the Silkroad Ensemble comes from a variety of sources. Sometimes, individual members share traditional pieces from their own cultural backgrounds. The various performers then find a way to interpret that music in a way that makes sense to each of them, and the ensemble works together to develop creative arrangements. Sometimes, the Silkroad Ensemble—like Roomful of Teeth, discussed above—commissions composers to write works for their unique performing forces and abilities. And sometimes, the ensemble adapts pieces of music that have been written for other performers. In all cases, their repertoire blends cultural influences. However, it is very important to Yo-Yo Ma that the Silkroad Ensemble treat its sources with respect and avoid exoticizing

Image 13.24: Members of the Silkroad Ensemble bow following a 2011 concert at the University of California, Berkeley.
Source: Flickr
Attribution: User "rocor"
License: CC BY-NC 2.0

non-Western musical traditions—like we saw happen in Tchaikovsky's *The Nutcracker* (Chapter 4).

We will consider one of the Silk Road Ensemble's most popular numbers, "Arabian Waltz." This piece was written and recorded by the Lebanese composer and oud player Rabih Abou-Khalil in 1996. Although well-versed in traditional Arab music, Abou-Khalil is equally knowledgeable of Western traditions, having studied flute at the Academy of Music in Munich, Germany. His compositions blend Arab scales, textures, and rhythms with influences from jazz, rock, and European concert music. "Arabian Waltz" was written for oud, string quartet (a European ensemble), and traditional Arab frame drums.

Image 13.25: Rabih Abou-Khalil is a well-known oud player and composer.
Source: Wikimedia Commons
Attribution: Lior Golgher
License: CC BY-SA 2.5

The original recording[15] featured Abou-Khalil in collaboration with the Balanescu Quartet—an ensemble led by Romanian violinist Alexander Bălănescu that specializes in experimental music.

15.		"Arabian Waltz" Composer: Rabih Abou-Khalil Performance: Rabih Abou-Khalil, The Balanescu Quartet (1996)

Image 13.26: The shakuhachi is related to the Persian ney, discussed in Chapter 8.
Source: Wikimedia Commons
Attribution: User "Yuzu696"
License: CC BY-SA 4.0

Image 13.27: The janggu is played here by a performer in traditional garb.
Source: Wikimedia Commons
Attribution: User "m-louis"
License: CC BY-SA 2.0

Clearly, "Arabian Waltz" was a cross-cultural work from its inception. In the hands of the Silkroad Ensemble, however, it has absorbed an even greater depth of international influence. We will consider a live performance that the ensemble gave in 2009 at the Park Avenue Armory in New York City. The ensemble, on this occasion, consisted of two violins, viola, cello, string bass, pipa (a Chinese lute—see Chapter 6), sheng (the Chinese mouth organ—see Chapter 4), shakuhachi (a Japanese flute), tabla (North Indian drums—see Chapter 6), various Middle Eastern frame drums (see Chapter 8), and janggu (a Korean drum). This is unquestionably an extraordinary assortment of instruments, each played by a master of the respective tradition.

The Silkroad Ensemble's performance of "Arabian Waltz"[16] begins just as Abou-Khalil's had, with the sound of Arab frame drums. From the start, however, the ensemble members leave their unique stylistic fingerprints on this rendition. The principal melody is first heard in the shakuhachi, played by Kojiro Umezaki. Umezaki plays the melody—itself unmistakably Middle Eastern—in a Japanese style, introducing the typical embellishments that are **idiomatic** to the shakuhachi. Another remarkable contribution comes from the tabla player, Sandeep Das, who likewise plays his instrument just as he would in a North Indian context. In the second half of the performance, Das is featured in a solo that combines the sound of the tabla with the other drums, producing an unprecedented aggregation of percussive timbres.

16.		"Arabian Waltz" Composer: Rabih Abou-Khalil Performance: Yo-Yo Ma, The Silkroad Ensemble (2009)

CONCLUSION

These case studies have explored the expansive definitions of "good music" offered by recent Pulitzer committees, a leading art music ensemble, and one of the most famous living classical musicians. All have agreed that quality can be found in many genres and traditions. We might sum up their values according to the five criteria presented in the introduction.

Was every example in this chapter successful at fulfilling its stated purpose? We've looked at a lot of dance music—did it inspire you to dance? Did Shaw's *Partita* change the way you think about the possible uses for the human voice? Did Marsalis's "Work Song" cause you to feel the suffering of his oratorio's protagonists?

Was each of these examples exceptional when compared to others of its type? Is Lamar the best hip-hop artist, and was *DAMN.* the best hip-hop album of 2017? Is *Tehillim* a particularly compelling example of minimalist composition? Are the works of Aphex Twin superior to those of other electronic music artists?

Were this examples particularly original? Do they stand out from the field? Is there something about the musical details of *Libertango* that make it stick in your head? Does the originality of the vision behind Ellington's *Far East Suite* qualify it as "better" than other jazz compositions of the era?

The skill of the performer—whether we are talking about Lamar's accomplished rapping, Roomful of Teeth's polished singing, Alarm Will Sound's clever orchestrating, or Ma's exquisite cello playing—certainly contributes to the quality of each of these examples. Ma in particular has exhibited singular dedication to identify and collaborating with the most accomplished performers from each global tradition. Flawless execution is central to his cross-cultural vision. But what about the skill of the composers? How can we judge that?

Finally, what impact has this music had on society? As an enormously popular performer, Lamar has certainly had an impact—will his legacy shape the future of hip-hop? Copland certainly defined the sound of "Americanness" for generations of composers. That makes him important, but does it make him good? Shaw is still at the beginning of her career—will her future influence determine the quality of *Partita* in some way?

This book ends as it began: with a long list of questions. None of these questions can be definitively answered, but they are all worth asking. They are worth asking because we listen to music every day, meaning that every day we have the opportunity to engage with an art form that human beings have used to communicate, entertain, and even shape the course of history for tens of thousands of years. We can either listen passively or we can ask questions of what we hear. These questions lead us to listen with greater care, extract more from the music in our lives, and discover new things about the world around us.

RESOURCES FOR FURTHER LEARNING

Print

Hasse, John Edward. *Beyond Category: The Life and Genius of Duke Ellington.* Da Capo Press, 1995.

Online

Andrew Granade and David Thurmaier, *Hearing the Pulitzers* podcast: http://hearingthepulitzers.podbean.com/

Caroline Shaw: https://carolineshaw.com/

Jazz at Lincoln Center: https://www.jazz.org/

Pulitzer Prizes for Music: https://www.pulitzer.org/prize-winners-by-category/225

Roomful of Teeth: https://www.roomfulofteeth.org/

Silkroad Ensemble: https://www.silkroad.org/

Wynton Marsalis: https://wyntonmarsalis.org/

 **Instruments of the Orchestra**

INTRODUCTION

The symphony orchestra has been a fixture of Western concert music since the early 18th century. It grew in size over the course of the 19th century as composers added new instruments and increased the number of players. Today, a professional orchestra is likely to contain about a hundred musicians. These are divided into sections of various sizes based on the instruments they play.

Orchestras include four different types, or families, of instruments. These are known as the **strings**, **woodwinds**, **brass**, and **percussion**. The instruments contained in each family share a means of sound production, but they come in different sizes and might be made of different materials. As a result, they play in different ranges and with different timbres. Each instrument of the orchestra also has different strengths and weaknesses. Some can play with great agility, while others are better suited to sustained pitches. Some are loud and piercing, suited to prominent solo lines, while others are more subtle. Composers who write for the orchestra must carefully consider the characteristics of each instrument. When the symphony orchestra is used well, however, it is capable of producing an extraordinary variety of sounds.

To hear each of the instruments in the orchestra and see a demonstration of its capabilities, please visit this webpage maintained by the London-based Philharmonia Orchestra: https://www.philharmonia.co.uk/explore/instruments.

THE STRING FAMILY

All orchestral string instruments produce sound when a vibrating string causes a hollow wooden body to reverberate. On all instruments except the harp, the strings are usually set into motion with a bow, although they can also be plucked. Modern bows are strung with horsehair, while the strings themselves are made out of various metals. Because string instruments are not very loud, there are usually a lot of them in an orchestra.

Violin

The violin is the smallest modern string instrument. It has four strings and plays in a high range. In an orchestra, there are two sections of violin players: the first violins and the second violins. The first violins often have the melody, while the second violins are more likely to play harmony in a lower ranger.

Viola

The viola looks nearly identical to the violin, but it is somewhat larger. Although it also has four strings, they sound at a lower pitch. As a result, the viola plays in a lower range and produces a richer timbre.

Cello

The cello sounds one octave lower than the viola. It is also much bigger, and is held vertically between the knees instead of on the shoulder. It is supported by a metal rod called an endpin.

Bass

The bass is the largest member of the string family, and it sounds in the lowest range. Although it looks somewhat like a large cello, the shape is different: notice how the upper part of the body slopes into the neck. The bass is also tuned differently. It is the least agile of the string instruments and seldom gets time in the spotlight, although a virtuoso performer can do amazing things with it.

Harp

The harp is only distantly related to the other string instruments. Each of its 40+ strings is tuned to a different pitch, and they are plucked to produce sound. The harp is inaudible when the rest of the orchestra is playing, but it is often assigned important solo passages.

THE WOODWIND FAMILY

All woodwind instruments produce sound when the player blows into the instrument, thereby causing the column of air to vibrate. All woodwinds were at one point in history made of wood, except for the saxophone, which has always been made of metal. However, this is not why they are classified together as a group. The reason for this is their similar construction, which constitutes a tube with holes. The more holes that are covered by fingers or keys, the lower the pitch, while the fewer holes that are covered, the higher the pitch. Additionally, the shape of the tube will influence the timbre: cylindrical instruments produce clear and brilliant timbres, while conical instruments produce round, vocal-like timbres. The inner dimensions of the flute and clarinet exhibit cylindrical bores (the tubing is of a consistent diameter) and the oboe, bassoon, and saxophone exhibit conical bores (the tubing gradually expands in diameter throughout the length of the instrument).

In many woodwinds, the use of a single or double reed further modifies the timbre. Over time, orchestral composers came to prefer a system of paired woodwinds—2 flutes, 2 clarinets, 2 oboes, 2 bassoons—as the standard woodwind section, adding other instruments as they desired for color.

Flute

Flutes can be made of various metals, although most professionals prefer solid silver. The player produces sound by blowing across an open hole near the closed end of the tube, and controls pitches both by depressing keys and increasing or decreasing wind pressure.

Flutes come in many sizes. It is typical for orchestral music to contain parts for the standard flute and a small, high-pitched flute called a piccolo. However, there are also larger flutes, including the alto, bass, and rare contra-bass flutes.

Clarinet

Clarinets are typically made of wood with metal keys. The player creates sound by blowing air into a mouthpiece with a piece of cane (a **single reed**) attached, which causes the reed to vibrate.

Like flutes, clarinets come in various sizes. Orchestras typically include a soprano clarinet (also called a B-flat clarinet) and a bass clarinet, which is twice as large (pitched one octave lower). Composers also write for other sizes, including the alto clarinet (which falls between the standard and bass clarinets) and the high-pitched E-flat sopranino clarinet.

Saxophone

The saxophone uses a single-reed mouthpiece similar to that of the clarinet, and the body of the instrument is made out of brass. Most sizes feature an upturned bell. The instrument's unusual name comes from its inventor, Adolphe Sax, who in the 1840s was seeking to create an instrument to blend the agility of the woodwind family with the large dynamic range of the brass family.

The saxophone is seldom found as a permanent member of the woodwind section in the orchestra, often appearing only as a soloist. However, it has become increasingly prominent in art music of the 20th and 21st centuries. It is best known for its use in jazz and popular music.

Oboe

The oboe is similar to the clarinet in construction and appearance, but in place of a mouthpiece containing a single reed it utilizes a pair of reeds protruding from one end. The player blows through these reeds, causing them to vibrate and produce the distinctive nasal timbre of the oboe. All instruments that utilize this method of sound production are referred to as **double reeds**.

The English horn is a related double-reed instrument. It is somewhat larger than the oboe and produces a lower, richer sound.

Bassoon

The bassoon is the largest double-reed instrument. It gets its own entry here because, unlike the English horn, it is one of the core instruments of the orchestra and is used in almost every piece of music. The bassoon has a distinctive appearance: Its long resonating column rises considerably above the head of the player. Although the bassoon produces pitches in a very low range, composers sometimes employ an even lower-pitched version, the contra-bassoon.

THE BRASS FAMILY

All instruments in the brass family feature a cup-shaped metal mouthpiece into which the player blows air in a way that causes their lips to vibrate. As the family name suggests, the instruments are typically made of brass, and, although they come in many shapes and sizes, each essentially constitutes a long tube with a bell at the end. Brass instruments vary in terms of range (which is determined in part by the length of the tube) and the method by which the player controls the pitch. They also vary in the brightness of their timbre, which depends on whether the instrument is cylindrical bore (the tubing is of a consistent diameter until it opens into the bell) or conical bore (the tubing gradually expands in diameter throughout the length of the instrument).

Trumpet

The trumpet is the smallest—and therefore highest-pitched—member of the brass family. As a cylindrical-bore instrument, it has a brilliant, piercing sound. The performer controls pitch by depressing valves that open and close, which changes the length of the tubing, and by buzzing their lips faster or slower.

French Horn

The French horn plays in a range that is similar to that of the trumpet, but it sounds quite different. This is due in part to the fact that it is conical bore and in part to the fact that the length of tubing is much greater. A horn player holds the instrument with one hand in the bell, which allows them to additionally control pitch and timbre.

Trombone

Like the trumpet, the trombone is a cylindrical-bore instrument with a bright sound. Its greater size and length mean that it produces lower pitches. The most striking difference between the two instruments, however, has to do with the method by which the player controls the pitch. While all other brass instruments have valves that allow or prevent air from passing through lengths of tubing, a trombone player manually extends or shortens the length of their instruments by moving a large slide.

Euphonium

The euphonium is a conical bore brass instrument that fills the middle-low register of the brass section. It is similar in construction to a tuba, sounding one octave higher. It is not a standard member of the orchestral brass section, but it plays an important role in American and British wind bands.

Tuba

The tuba is the largest instrument in the brass family and plays the lowest notes. The tuba was introduced into the modern orchestra in the mid-19h century and is therefore one of the newest members of the brass family. Although it is operated much like a trumpet, the fact that it is conical bore and features an upward facing bell contributes to its more muted timbre.

THE PERCUSSION FAMILY

All percussion instruments create sound when a resonating body is set into motion following an impact. If this description seems vague, it is because percussion instruments employ an extraordinary variety of methods to produce sound. The simplest percussion instrument is a pair of clapping hands, while the most complex require extensive mechanical workings.

In general, percussion instruments can be grouped into pitched and unpitched classes. Pitched percussion instruments sounds specific pitches and are therefore able to play melodies and harmonies, while unpitched are used only to sound rhythms.

PITCHED

Piano

The piano is the most common percussion instrument. Indeed, it is usually classed by itself, for—unlike other percussion instruments—it is played by specialists who perform an enormous repertoire of solo music that has been created for the piano over the past three hundred years. What identifies the piano as a percussion instrument is its method of producing sound. When a player depresses a key on the piano, it causes a hammer to strike a metal string, the vibrations of which produce sound within the wooden body of the instrument. The keyboard is laid out in a way that gives the player access to every pitch of the chromatic scale, while the mechanical action allows performers to control the dynamic level and sustain of each note.

The piano is closely related to other keyboard instruments that are discussed in this book, including the harpsichord and organ. These are described in the context of specific examples.

Mallet Percussion

Most of the pitched percussion instruments are laid out like a piano keyboard, but produce sound when the player strikes a key with a mallet. This in turn causes a metal tube positioned below the key to vibrate and produce sound. The marimba has wooden keys and a large range. Its timbre is mellow and resonant. The xylophone looks similar to the marimba, but it has a smaller range and produces a more articulated and piercing sound. The glockenspiel is smaller still and has metal keys that produce a bell-like sound.

Timpani

The timpani have a long history in the orchestra, and they are arguably the most important instrument in the percussion section. The timpani constitute a set of three to five drums with large copper bowls and taut resonating heads. Each drum is tuned to sound a specific pitch. Although the timpanist seldom plays melodies, the drums are often used to reinforce the harmonic structure of the music.

Unpitched

The list of unpitched percussion instruments is nearly endless. One of the most common is the snare drum, which has two taut resonating heads, the lower of which is strung with metal beads that produce a rattling sound. The player uses two sticks to perform rhythms on the upper head. Also common is the bass drum, which likewise has two heads and is played with a large, soft mallet. Various gongs and cymbals are made out of metal and either struck with a mallet or crashed together.

Western Art Music

This appendix is designed to assist instructors who seek to craft alternative pathways through this textbook. In particular, it will facilitate the design of a chronologically-ordered music appreciation course focused on Western art music. Under the heading "Western Art Music," such works are first grouped according to their respective style periods (see also the accompanying figure, "A Timeline of Western Art Music") and then listed alphabetically (by the last name of their composer(s) in most cases, by some other designator in the others). Additionally, listed under "Other Musical Works," instructors designing the type of course mentioned above will find relevant works of Western folk music and popular music, non-Western music, and cross-cultural music. List entries beginning with an asterisk (*) are works mentioned but not discussed at length; all other works listed are covered in great depth and are represented by an official listening example. Each entry includes the work's date(s) of composition, premiere, or publication and the chapter(s) in which the work is mentioned.

The style-period dates given in this guide are widely accepted and correspond to those used in "A Timeline of Western Art Music." On this timeline, each style period is represented by a semi-oval proportional in size to its period's duration. Because the evolution of musical style takes place over time, each period fades gradually into the next. This process produces smaller, transitional periods of varying lengths (the overlapping areas of the semi-ovals), within which the dates of the large style periods are positioned (though not necessarily centered). During these transitional periods, older composers writing in a fully developed style are working concurrently with the avant-garde, a younger generation of composers innovating toward the emerging style. At the apex of each semi-oval there appears a date marking a significant milestone in the period.

A Timeline of Western Art Music

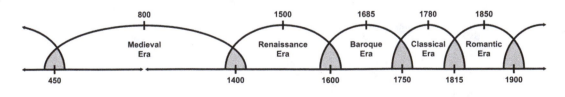

WESTERN ART MUSIC

The Medieval Era (450–1400)

Countess of Dia, "A chantar m'er" [I must sing] (ca. 1200) (chapter 8)

* Dies irae [Day of wrath], the sequence of the Requiem Mass (chapter 6)

Hildegard of Bingen, "O virtus Sapientiae" [O strength of Wisdom] (ca. 1150) (chapter 11)

* Hildegard of Bingen, *Ordo virtutum* [Order of the virtues] (ca. 1150) (chapter 11)

The Renaissance Era (1400–1600)

John Dowland, "Flow, My Tears" (1600) (chapter 8)

John Dowland, *Lachrimae, or Seven Tears* (1604) (chapter 8)

* John Dowland, *Lachrimae* (1596) (chapter 8)

Giovanni da Palestrina, *Missa Papae Marcelli* [Pope Marcellus Mass] (published 1567) (chapter 11)

The Baroque Era (1600–1750)

* Johann Sebastian Bach, *Die Kunst der Fuge* [The art of fugue] (completed 1749; published 1751) (chapter 11)

Johann Sebastian Bach, Fugue in G minor ("Little"), BWV 578 (composed by 1707) (chapter 11)

Johann Sebastian Bach, Six Suites for Solo Cello, BWV 1007–12 (ca. 1720) (chapter 12)

* Johann Sebastian Bach, *St. Matthew Passion* (performed 1727) (chapter 11)

Johann Sebastian Bach, *Wachet auf* [Sleepers, wake], BWV 140 (1731) (chapter 11; see also chapter 10)

* Johann Sebastian Bach, *Das wohltemperierte Klavier* [The well-tempered clavier], Book 1 (1722) and Book 2 (1742) (chapter 11)

* Giulio Caccini, *Euridice* (1602) (chapter 4)

* George Frideric Handel, *L'Allegro, il Penseroso ed il Moderato* [The cheerful person, the thoughtful person, and the moderate person] (1740) (chapter 2)

* George Frideric Handel, *Water Music* (premiered 1717) (chapter 4)

* George Frideric Handel, *Music for the Royal Fireworks* (performed 1749) (chapter 4)

Claudio Monteverdi, *L'Orfeo* [Orpheus] (1607) (chapter 4; see also chapter 10)

* Jacopo Peri, *Dafne* (1597) (chapter 4)

* Jacopo Peri, *Euridice* (1600) (chapter 4)

Barbara Strozzi, *Lagrime mie* [My tears] (1659) (chapter 8)

Antonio Vivaldi, *Le quattro stagioni* [The four seasons], nos. 1–4 (of 12) from *Il cimento dell'armonia e dell'inventione* [The contest between harmony and invention] (1725) (chapter 6)

The Classical Era (1750–1815)

* Ludwig van Beethoven, *Ah! perfido* [Ah! Deceiver] (1796) (chapter 7)

* Ludwig van Beethoven, *Choral Fantasy* (1808; revised 1809) (chapter 7)

* Ludwig van Beethoven, Mass in C Major (1807) (chapter 7)

* Ludwig van Beethoven, Piano Concerto No. 4 (1804–6/7) (chapter 7)

Ludwig van Beethoven, Symphony No. 5 (1807–8) (chapter 7; see also chapter 9)

* Ludwig van Beethoven, Symphony No. 6 ("Pastoral") (1802–8) (chapters 6 and 7)

Franz Joseph Haydn, String Quartet, Op. 33, No. 2 ("The Joke") (1781) (chapter 8)

* Wolfgang Amadeus Mozart, *La clemenza di Tito* [The clemency of Titus] (1791) (chapter 4)

* Wolfgang Amadeus Mozart, *Così fan tutte* [All women do it] (1790) (chapter 4)

* Wolfgang Amadeus Mozart, *Don Giovanni* (1787) (chapter 4)

* Wolfgang Amadeus Mozart, *Le nozze di Figaro* [The marriage of Figaro] (1786) (chapter 4)

Wolfgang Amadeus Mozart, *Die Zauberflöte* [The magic flute] (1791) (chapter 4)

The Romantic Era (1815–1900)

* Ludwig van Beethoven, Symphony No. 9 (1822–24) (chapter 7)

* Hector Berlioz, *Le retour à la vie* [The return to life] (1831–32) (chapter 6)

Hector Berlioz, *Symphonie fantastique* [Fantastical symphony] (1830) (chapter 6; see also chapters 7 and 9)

* Antonín Dvořák, String Quartet No. 12 ("The American") (1893) (chapter 9)

Antonín Dvořák, Symphony No. 9 ("From the New World") (1893) (chapter 9)

Franz Liszt, *Hungarian Rhapsody No. 2* (1847) (chapter 9)

Modest Mussorgsky, *Pictures at an Exhibition* (1874) (chapter 6)

Franz Schubert, "Erlkönig" [Elf king] (1815) (chapter 5)

Franz Schubert, *Die schöne Müllerin* [The lovely maid of the mill] (1824) (chapter 5)

Clara Schumann, Piano Trio in G Minor (1846) (chapter 8)

Bedřich Smetana, *Vltava* [The Moldau] (1874), from *Má vlast* [My homeland] (1874–79) (chapter 9)

Johann Strauss II, *An der schönen, blauen Donau* [The blue Danube] (composed 1866; premiered 1867) (chapter 12)

Johann Strauss II, *Tritsch-Tratsch-Polka* (1858) (chapter 12)

* Pyotr Ilyich Tchaikovsky, *Iolanta* (1891) (chapter 4)

Pyotr Ilyich Tchaikovsky, *The Nutcracker* (1892) (chapters 4 and 7)

* Pyotr Ilyich Tchaikovsky, *The Nutcracker [Suite]* (1892) (chapter 4)

* Pyotr Ilyich Tchaikovsky, *Sleeping Beauty* (1890) (chapter 4)

* Pyotr Ilyich Tchaikovsky, *Swan Lake* (1877) (chapter 4)

* Pyotr Ilyich Tchaikovsky, Symphony No. 4 (1877–78) (chapter 7)

Richard Wagner, *Der Ring des Nibelungen* [The ring of the Nibelungs] (1848–74), the Ring Cycle, including *Das Rheingold* [The Rhinegold], *Die Walküre* [The Valkyrie], *Siegfried*, and *Götterdämmerung* [Twilight of the gods] (chapter 3)

The Twentieth Century and Beyond (1900–Present)

Alarm Will Sound, *Acoustica: Alarm Will Sound Performs Aphex Twin* (2005) (chapter 13)

* Alarm Will Sound, *Steve Reich, Tehillim/The Desert Music* (2002) (chapter 13)

Béla Bartók, *Romanian Folk Dances from Hungary* (1915) (chapter 9)

Amy Beach, *Gaelic Symphony* (1894–96) (chapter 9)

* Amy Beach, Mass in E-flat Major (1890) (chapter 9)

* Amy Beach, Piano Concerto in C-sharp Minor (1899)

* Benjamin Britten, *War Requiem* (1962) (chapter 7)

* John Cage, *4'33"* (1952) (chapter 1)

* John Cage, *Williams Mix* (1952) (chapter 1)

* John Alden Carpenter, *Concertino for Piano and Orchestra* (1915; revised 1948) (chapter 7)

* Samuel Coleridge-Taylor, *Bamboula* (1911) (chapter 7)

* Samuel Coleridge-Taylor, *Hiawatha's Wedding Feast* (1891) (chapter 7)

* John Coltrane, *Giant Steps* (album, released 1960) (chapter 11)

John Coltrane, *A Love Supreme* (album, released 1965) (chapter 11)

Aaron Copland, *Appalachian Spring* (ballet, 1943–44) (chapter 13)

* Aaron Copland, *Billy the Kid* (ballet, 1938) (chapter 13

* Aaron Copland, *Rodeo* (ballet, 1942) (chapter 13)

* Henry Cowell, *Dynamic Motion* (1916) (chapter 1)

* Mario Davidovsky, *Synchronisms No. 6 for Piano and Electronic Sound* (1970) (chapter 13)

* Ivan Dzerzhinsky, *Quiet Flows the Don* (1934) (chapter 10)

* Edward Elgar, *Pomp and Circumstance March No. 1* (1901) (chapter 7)

Duke Ellington (and Billy Strayhorn), *The Far East Suite* (recorded 1966); released as Duke Ellington and His Orchestra, *Duke Ellington's "Far East Suite"* (1967) (chapter 13)

* Duke Ellington and His Famous Orchestra, "It Don't Mean a Thing (If It Ain't Got That Swing)" (released 1932) (chapter 13)

* Duke Ellington and His Washingtonians, "East St. Louis Toodle-Oo" (1927) (chapter 7)

* George Gershwin, *An American in Paris* (1928) (chapter 1)

George Gershwin, *Rhapsody in Blue* (premiered 1924) (chapter 7)

* Gustav Holst, *The Hymn of Jesus* (composed 1917; premiered 1920) (chapter 3)

Gustav Holst, *The Planets* (1914–16) (chapter 3)

Catherine Likhuta, *Lesions* (2017) (chapter 6)

Wynton Marsalis, *Blood on the Fields* (premiered 1994) (chapter 13)

Carl Orff, *Carmina Burana* (1936) (chapter 10; see also chapter 7)

* John Powell, *In Old Virginia* (1921) (chapter 7)

Florence Price, Symphony No. 1 (1931–32) (chapter 7)

* Florence Price, Symphony No. 3 (1938–40) (chapter 7)

* Florence Price, *Piano Concerto in One Movement* (1934) (chapter 7)

Maurice Ravel, orchestration (1922) of Modest Mussorgsky's *Pictures at an Exhibition* (1874) (chapter 6)

Steve Reich, *Come Out* (1966) (chapter 13)

Steve Reich, *Tehillim* (1981) (chapter 13)

* Steve Reich, *The Desert Music* (1983) (chapter 13)

Caroline Shaw, *Partita for 8 Voices* (in four movements, each premiered individually between 2009 and 2011); released as Roomful of Teeth, *Roomful of Teeth* (2012) (chapter 13)

* Dmitri Shostakovich, *Lady Macbeth of the Mtsensk District* (1930–32) (chapter 10)

* Dmitri Shostakovich, Symphony No. 1 (1924–25) (chapter 10)

* Dmitri Shostakovich, Symphony No. 4 (1935–36) (chapter 10)

Dmitri Shostakovich, Symphony No. 5 (1937) (chapter 10; see also chapter 7)

* Igor Stravinsky, *L'oiseau de feu* [The firebird] (1910) (chapter 3)

* Igor Stravinsky, *Petrushka* (1911) (chapter 3)

Igor Stravinsky, *Le sacre du printemps* [The rite of spring] (1913) (chapter 3)

* Ellen Taaffe Zwilich, *Symphony No. 1 (Three Movements for Orchestra)* (1982) (chapter 13)

OTHER MUSICAL WORKS

Western Music

"Amazing Grace" (three renditions) (chapter 11)

* Aphex Twin, *Drukqs* (2001) (chapter 13)

"Arkansas Traveler" (two renditions) (chapter 12)

The Beatles, *Sgt. Pepper's Lonely Hearts Club Band* (1967) (chapter 8)

Irving Berlin, "Blue Skies" (1927) as arranged by Fletcher Henderson (1935) (chapter 12)

Chic, "Good Times" (1979), from the album *Risqué* (1979) (chapter 12)

* George M. Cohan, "Over There" (1917) (chapter 7)

* Concert spirituals performed by Roland Hayes (chapter 7):

"Swing Low, Sweet Chariot," arranged by Henry T. Burleigh (see also chapter 9)

"Bye and Bye," arranged by Roland Hayes

* Emerson, Lake & Palmer, *Pictures at an Exhibition* (1971) (chapter 6)

"Fisher's Hornpipe" (two renditions) (chapter 13)

Jimi Hendrix, "Purple Haze" (live, 1970) (chapter 7)

Jimi Hendrix, "The Star-Spangled Banner" (live, 1969) (chapter 7)

* Victor Herbert, *A Suite of Serenades* (1924) (chapter 7)

Kendrick Lamar, *DAMN.* (2017) (chapter 13)

* Lightnin' Rod (pseudonym of Jalal Mansur Nuriddin), *Hustlers Convention* (album, 1973) (chapter 12)

Yo-Yo Ma, *Soul of the Tango: The Music of Astor Piazzolla* (1997) (chapter 13)

* Yo-Yo Ma, Edgar Meyer, and Mark O'Connor, *Appalachia Waltz* (1996) (chapter 13)

Yo-Yo Ma, Edgar Meyer, and Mark O'Connor, *Appalachian Journey* (2000) (chapter 13)

Mekong Delta, *Pictures at an Exhibition* (1996) (chapter 6)

National anthems (various) (chapter 9)

* The Original Dixieland Jass Band, "Livery Stable Blues" (1917) (chapter 7)

"Scotland the Brave" (ca. 1890s) (chapter 12)

John Philip Sousa, *The Stars and Stripes Forever* (1896) (chapter 12)

Steelband music of Trinidad and Tobago (chapter 9)

The Sugarhill Gang, "Rapper's Delight" (single, 1979) (chapter 12)

Isao Tomita, *Pictures at an Exhibition* (1975) (chapter 6)

John Williams, *Star Wars [A New Hope] (Original Motion Picture Soundtrack)* (1977) (chapter 3)

John Williams, *Star Wars: The Empire Strikes Back (Original Motion Picture Soundtrack)* (1980) (chapter 3)

John Williams, *Soundtrack to Star Wars: Return of the Jedi (Original Motion Picture Soundtrack)* (1983) (chapter 3)

* John Williams, music for numerous films directed by Steven Spielberg, beginning with *The Sugarland Express (Original Motion Picture Soundtrack)* (1974) (chapter 3)

Non-Western Music

Tanburi Cemil Bey, "Samâi Shad Araban" (ca. 1900) (chapter 8)

Chinese solo repertoire:

    "Attack on All Sides" (composed by 1818) (chapter 6)

    * "The Song of Gaixia" (composed ?) (chapter 6)

    Peng Xiuwen, "Spring River in the Flower Moon Night" (ca. 1957) (chapter 6)

Tian Han, *Baishe zhuan* [The story of the white snake] (1958) (chapter 4)

Javanese traditional (gamelan) music, *The Love Dance of Klana Sewandana* (chapter 4)

"Raga Madhuvanti" (two renditions) (chapter 6)

"The Sunjata Story" (two renditions) (chapter 5)

Cross-Cultural Music

Arabian Waltz (two renditions) (chapter 13):

    Rabih Abou-Khalil, featuring the Balanescu Quartet et al. (released 1996)

    Yo-Yo Ma and The Silk Road Ensemble (live, 2009)

Definition of Terms

Absolute music - Instrumental music that does not claim to be about anything other than its own form and sound; the opposite of program music.

Academy - In 16th- and 17th-century Italy, a society of like-minded intellectuals dedicated to pursuits including discussion, debate, and engagement with the arts.

Achievement - What a person does with their aptitude.

Advent - In the Catholic church calendar, the four weeks leading up to Christmas.

Air pipe - The pipe extruding from a set of bagpipes into which the player blows air.

Allegory (in music) - The use of musical sounds to signify hidden meaning.

Alto - A singer with a range somewhat lower than that of a soprano, usually female.

Anchor - A monastic who lives their entire life in a small room adjoining a monastery, thereby "anchoring" the community.

Antiphon - A short Gregorian chant that can be used in various ways throughout the Canonical Hours and in the Mass.

Apartheid - The system of legalized racial segregation that was in place in South Africa from 1948 into the early 1990s.

Aptitude - The ease and speed with which the brain processes certain kinds of information.

Aria - A work for solo vocalist that follows a set form. Arias are most common as components of operas and oratorios, but can also be composed as stand-alone works.

Arioso - A passage of vocal music that is more structured than recitative but less formal than aria; usually brief in comparison with an aria.

Arpeggio - A musical gesture that sounds the pitches of a chord one at a time, either ascending or descending.

Arranger - Someone who takes a melody or work created by another composer and makes limited alterations; arrangements are usually created for specific ensembles and include some new musical material, although the original material is still easily detected.

Arrangement - A version of a composition designed for performance by a specific set of instruments or voices. Arrangements can be made by the original composer, but are usually produced by a collaborator or successor.

Ars perfecta - A style of vocal composition that reached maturity in 15th-century Italy. Music in this style is polyphonic and follows a robust set of rules concerning the treatment of dissonance.

Articulation - The manner in which a pitch is begun, sustained, and released.

Auditory cortex - The area of the brain in which sound is first processed.

Avant-garde - From the French for "advance guard"; used to refer to works of art that break with norms and explore new creative territory.

Ayre - A solo song with lute accompaniment common in the Baroque English tradition.

Backspinning - The practice employed by DJs of spinning a record in reverse in order to repeat a passage.

Ballad - A song that tells a story.

Ballet - A style of presentational dance, the current form of which emerged in 18th-century France. Ballet is often used to tell stories by means of gesture and music, and is characterized by unique apparel, including tutus and pointe shoes.

Bar - A unit determined by meter that contains the basic grouping of pulses (e.g. a bar in triple time will contain three beats). Synonymous with "measure."

Bar form - A musical form, A A B, common in troubadour songs and Lutheran hymns.

Bar lines - In notated music, vertical lines that indicate the beginning and end of each bar.

Baroque - A period in Western music history that is typically bookmarked by the invention of opera (ca. 1600) and the death of J.S. Bach (1750).

Belting - A style of singing employed by women for which the performer uses their chest voice to produce pitches in a high range to powerful effect; common in Broadway productions beginning in the mid-20th century.

Basso continuo - A type of instrumental accompaniment developed in the Baroque era. Basso continuo is most often performed using two instruments:

one that can play harmonies (e.g. harpsichord) and one that can play a bass line (e.g. cello).

Beijing opera - A style of Chinese opera that was developed in the Beijing court in 1790; relies on stable character types and incorporates symbolic actions, costumes, and makeup.

Binary form - A two-part musical form, usually mapped as A B.

Blackface minstrelsy - The practice of portraying African American stereotypes with the aid of dark makeup. Although primarily associated with the 19th-century minstrel show, neither blackface nor minstrelsy have entirely disappeared from American society.

Blue note - A lowered note (usually the third, fifth, or seventh scale degree); typical of the blues style.

Blues - An African American musical style dating from the early 20th century. Distinctive characteristics of this style include lowered notes, slides, and a 12-bar structure.

Break - A passage in dance music in which the melody recedes and we hear only the rhythm section.

Breaking - The athletic style of dancing that developed alongside hip-hop music.

Broadside - A single-sheet publication format popular from the 16th to 19th centuries.

Broadside ballad - A broadside containing the text to a new song, usually meant to be sung to a familiar melody that is named but not notated.

Broca's area - The area of the brain that controls the physical production of speech. This area takes in sound, converts it to neuronal representations, then translates it to the physical motion involved in making speech sounds.

Bugle call - A brief melody played on the bugle or trumpet for the purpose of signalling a military maneuver or structuring military life. The best-known bugle call, "Taps," is played at US military funerals.

Cadence - A harmonic gesture that brings a phrase to an end.

Call and response - A texture in which two parts exchange melodic material.

Calypso - A song tradition associated with Trinidadian Carnival. Although the musical style of calypso songs has changed over the past two centuries, their lyrics are characterized by clever wordplay and sociopolitical topics.

Canon - A texture in which all parts carry the same melody, but enter at points separated by a set distance.

Canonical hours - A sequence of eight daily church services that structure life in a Benedictine monastery.

Canso - A type of troubadour song that addresses the hopeless love a knight feels for the noblewoman he serves. Such love, termed *fin'amor*, cannot be consummated, for the knight has sworn fielty to the woman's husband.

Cantata - A multi-part work for voice(s) and accompaniment. 17th-century cantatas were often for solo voice and basso continuo, while later cantatas were more often for soloists, choir, and orchestra. Cantatas can be secular (a chamber cantata) or sacred (a church cantata).

Carnival - The public celebration that immediately precedes the period of Lent in many Catholic-majority countries.

Castanets - Small wooden clappers that are held in each hand and used to tap rhythms in the flamenco tradition.

Caste system - A system of social organization in which roles are hereditary and immutable. Caste membership generally determines an individual's social class, marriage prospects, and trade.

Castrati - Male singers who were castrated before puberty to prevent their voices from changing. Castrati were first used in Catholic church choirs, but later took the leading male roles in Italian opera. The practice was made illegal in Italy in 1861.

Cerebral cortex - The outermost layer of the brain. It is this area that controls complex thought.

Cerebrum - The outermost layer of the brain that gives it a wrinkled appearance. Both Broca's and Werneike's Areas are situated in the Cerebrum.

Chamber music - Music intended for one-on-a-part performance in a small space; usually refers to compositions that require between two and eight performers.

Chamber orchestra - A small orchestra, containing around twenty performers.

Chanter - The pipe on a set of bagpipes that contains holes, allowing the player to sound nine distinct pitches.

Conceptual art - A work of art to which the underlying idea is more important than its visual characteristics.

Chest voice - A mode of vocal production used to access notes in the medium and low ranges; so named because the singer feels the vibrations in their chest. When chest voice is carried into the high range, it sounds quite different from head voice.

Chord - A collection of pitches, usually three or four, that belong to the same mode, are separated by intervals of a third, and are often sounded simultaneously to support a harmony.

Chord progression - A sequence of chords; certain chord progressions are common, while others are unusual and might sound displeasing.

Choreographer - The person who determines the physical movements (choreography) of a dance.

Chorus - In most popular songs, the part of the melody that is frequently repeated, and always with the same text; usually the most memorable part of a song.

Chromatic - Using notes beyond those included in the major or minor scale.

Classical - A period in Western music history that is typically considered to extend from 1750 to 1815. This period is characterized by restrained harmonies, balanced phrases, and transparent textures.

Clawhammer - A style of banjo playing for which the performer sounds melody notes by striking the four melody strings with the fingernail of their index or middle finger and sounds drone notes by plucking the short fifth string with their thumb.

Coda - A concluding passage added to the end of a composition that otherwise adheres to a set musical form or process.

Col legno - A technique for playing a string instrument that involves turning the bow upside down and bouncing the wooden stick on the strings.

Commission - The process by which a performer, producer, or organization hires a composer to create a new musical work.

Common-practice tonality - The system that governed the use of harmonies in Western music between the 17th and early 20th centuries; still relevant to most music produced today.

Compound duple meter - A type of duple meter in which each of the two pulses is subdivided into three subpulses; can be counted ONE-two-three-FOUR-five-six.

Concept album - An album (collection of songs) that is unified by a coherent narrative or mode of presentation.

Concert overture - A descriptive single-movement orchestral work.

Concerto - A work for instrumental soloist(s) with orchestral accompaniment.

Conductor - An ensemble leader who does not play an instrument but instead keeps time, often using a baton, and guides the performance using gestures.

Conjunct motion - Melodic motion in which the pitches move up and down the scale; the opposite of conjunct motion.

Contrast - The relationship between two musical passages that do not share recognizable melodic, harmonic, or rhythmic features.

Copyist - The person who copies out a written work; before printing technology became cheap and accessible, this role was crucial to the proliferation and performance of musical works.

Corpus callosum - A bundle of fibers that divide the two halves of the brain and transmit messages from one side of the brain to the other.

Countermelody - A secondary melody that complements the principal melody.

Covert - A term applied to a work of art that has a hidden meaning.

Crescendo - The process of gradually getting louder.

Cyclical technique - An approach to composition in which the various parts of a large-scale work are unified by recurring melodic material.

Da capo form - A form used principally in 17th- and 18th-century arias containing two contrasting sections and an instruction to the singer to repeat the first section upon reaching the end of the notated music. The form can therefore be diagrammed A B A.

Dactylic hexameter - A poetic meter in which a phrase is divided into six feet, each of which contains a long and two short syllables.

Dance caller - The person who calls out instructions to dancers while they perform a social dance with established moves, most of which require the interaction of partners; common in square dancing and contra dancing.

Dance suite - A genre of music in which each movement is inspired by a courtly European dance. Every dance suite contains an Allemande, Courante, Sarabande, and Gigue, in addition to other dances. This genre emerged in 17th-century Germany.

Decrescendo - The process of gradually getting softer (interchangeable with "diminuendo").

Development - In sonata form, the middle passage between the Exposition and the Recapitulation, in which themes from the Exposition are explored and transformed. In a fugue, the bulk of the composition, between the exposition and the final subject entrance, during which the subject is heard in a variety of keys and possibly undergoes specific transformations.

Diaspora - All members of a population that has been spread across various nations or regions (e.g. the African diaspora contains all people of African ancestry found throughout the world).

Diegetic music - Music that is part of a dramatic scene and is therefore audible to the characters in that scene.

Diminuendo - The process of gradually getting softer (interchangeable with "decrescendo").

Disco - A style of dance music that emerged in New York City in the 1970s; characterized by a fast tempo, quadruple meter, syncopated bass lines, and dense textures.

Disjunct motion - Melodic motion in which the pitches do not simply move up and down the scale but are instead separated by large intervals; the opposite of conjunct motion.

Dissonance - The effect produced by simultaneously-sounded pitches that are separated either by a very small interval (e.g. a minor or major second) or an interval not present in triad-based harmonies (e.g. an augments fourth or major seventh). Although the perception of dissonance is rooted in musical context and personal taste, it strikes most listeners as uncomfortable.

Dominant - The fifth degree (note) in a major or minor scale, or the harmony based on that note.

Dotted rhythm - A rhythmic pattern in which pairs of notes are of unequal length, the first being three times as long as the second.

Double reed - A type of instrument that utilizes a pair of reeds protruding from one end to produce sound. The player blows through these reeds, causing them to vibrate. This family includes the oboe, English horn, and bassoon.

Double tracking - An audio recording technique in which a performer sings or plays along with their own prerecorded performance, usually to produce a stronger sound than can be obtained with a single voice or instrument.

Downbeat - The first beat in a measure or bar.

Dubbing - The process by which additional audio tracks are added to a studio recording.

Duple meter - A meter in which pulses (beats) are grouped by twos, usually in a strong-weak pattern.

Dynamic level - The loudness or softness of a musical passage.

Epic - A lengthy story concerning a quest or heroic adventure. Epics are often ancient, having been orally transmitted for many generations, and are frequently associated with a nation or ethnic group.

Episode - In a fugue, a passage in which the subject is not heard.

Ethnomusicologist - A scholar who specializes in indigenous music traditions.

Exoticism - The exploitation of a culture for the purpose portraying it as foreign, unusual, exciting, or titillating; relies on stereotypes instead of authentic representation.

Exposition - In sonata form, the section in which the Primary and Secondary Themes are introduced in their respective keys. In a fugue, the opening passage in which the subject is heard once in every voice.

Extramusical - Anything related to a musical work that is not explicitly conveyed in a performance.

Fanfare - A short, martial melody, usually played on trumpets or other brass instruments, that most often emphasizes the first, third, and fifth scale degrees; can introduce a performance or be integrated into a larger work as a dramatic signifier.

Fasıl - A suite of six to eight movements in the Ottoman tradition.

Falsetto - The head voice range in male singers; this technique allows men to sing in what is typically a female range.

Field holler - A style of unaccompanied singing, often improvised, used by enslaved African Americans to accompany work, communicate, or express emotions.

Field recording - The act of making recordings on location, usually of non-professional musicians in the rural communities where they live and work; also the recorded object itself.

Fixed composition - A musical work the contents of which are firmly established ahead of performance by a composer. Every performance of a fixed composition will be recognizable as a performance of the same work.

Flamenco - A style of music and dance native to Spain that features guitar accompanied by complex rhythms both clapped and played on the castanets.

Florentine Camerata - A group of intellectuals who gathered in Florence in the late 16th century and are responsible for developing European opera.

Folk revivals - In the United States, a period of widespread interest in folk music beginning in the 1930s and peaking in the 1960s.

Folk rock - A genre that emerged in the United States in the 1960s that blends elements of folk and rock music, usually by adding electric guitars and drums to songs that would otherwise qualify as folk.

Foot - In poetry, the basic metric unit; analogous to a measure or bar in music.

Forbrain - The anterior (forward-most) region of the brain.

Form - The organization of a musical work in time; can be mapped using terms or letter names.

Formalist - A term used in the Soviet Union to condemn art that did not meet the expectations set forth by the doctrine of Socialist Realism. Formalist art was usually described as being preoccupied with its own qualities instead of advancing the goals of the revolution.

Forte - A loud dynamic.

Fortissimo - A very loud dynamic, louder than forte.

Freemasonry - A system of secret fraternal organizations that traces its roots to the stonemasons' craft guilds established in the fourteenth century. Freemasonry is rich with lore and symbolism, and initiates progress through degrees as they become privy to its secrets.

Fret - A raised piece of wood or metal on a fingerboard that allows the player to easily stop the string at a specific point in order to sound a pitch. Frets are common on instruments in the lute class (e.g. the guitar).

Frontal lobe - The anterior (forward-most) lobe of the brain.

Fugue - A type of composition in which a melodic subject is introduced in each of the voices (usually numbering three or four) at the outset. Statements of the subject then alternate with episodes in which the subject is not present.

Gamelan - An instrumental ensemble native to Indonesia, consisting primarily of bronze gongs and metallophones.

Genre - A way of categorizing musical works based on perceived characteristics, use, or market.

Gesamtkunstwerk (German; English: "total artwork") - Composer Richard Wagner's term for an all-encompassing work that brings together varied art forms--music, dance, gesture, poetry, image--into a single, ideal medium of artistic expression. He used this term to describe his late operas.

Glissando - When an instrumentalist slides from one pitch to another.

Goliard - A medieval cleric who had studied at a European university but then grew disaffected with religious life. Goliards are remembered for their satirical poems and songs.

Gregorian chant - A body of monophonic vocal music developed in the medieval Catholic church.

Guru - In the North Indian tradition, a master who passes on musical knowledge to an apprentice.

Harlem Renaissance - A 1920s intellectual, social, and artistic movement centered in the Harlem neighborhood of Manhattan, New York City.

Harmonics (string technique) - A technique whereby the player touches the string lightly at a specific place while bowing, thereby producing an airy, high pitch.

Harmony - The pitches that support the melody; can refer generally to non-melodic voices or specifically to chords.

Head voice - A mode of vocal production used to access notes in the high range; so named because the singer feels the vibrations in their head.

Head - In jazz, a composition that is used as the basis for improvisation.

Heterophonic texture - A musical texture in which all melodic instruments/voices perform essentially the same melody at the same time, but with individual variations determined by the capabilities of the instrument.

Hindbrain - The posterior (back) region of the brain.

Hocket - A technique by which two or more voices contribute different notes to a single continuous melody.

Homophonic texture - A musical texture in which a single prominent melody is supported by accompaniment.

Homorhythmic - A musical texture in which all of the voices move in the same rhythm.

Hot jazz - In the 1920s, social dance music played primarily by African American bands; defined in contrast to sweet jazz, which was played primarily by white bands and was more rhythmically and timbrally restrained.

Idiomatic - Tailored to the capabilities and limitations of a specific instrument.

Imitation - A compositional technique whereby the voices in a polyphonic texture enter one at a time with similar melodic material.

Impresario - An impresario takes on the presentation of art as a financial venture, overseeing all elements of a production.

Improvisation - Composition during the act of performance. Improvisation is usually guided by norms and practices that belong to a given tradition.

Intertextual - Concerning connections or exchanges between distinct creative works.

Interval - The distance between two pitches.

Jali - In West Africa, a member of a hereditary caste of musicians responsible for transmitting stories and songs.

Jazz combo - A small jazz ensemble with one player per instrument.

Jim Crow - Legalized racial segregation in the United States. Jim Crow laws were in place between 1877 and the mid-1960s and were most common in the South.

Kumbengo - The repetitive melodic pattern--usually played on a kora, balafon, or ngoni--that underpins various types of singing in the West African jali tradition.

Lead sheet - A notated composition in the jazz tradition. A chart indicates the melody and harmonies of a composition, but it does not indicate instrumentation. In addition, performers will alter the melody and improvise solos over the harmonies, meaning that various performances of the same chart will sound quite different.

Legato - A smooth, connected form of articulation.

Lent - In the Catholic church calendar, the forty days of fasting and penitence that lead up to Easter.

Libretto - The words that are sung in a musical drama, such as an opera or oratorio.

Lining out - A hymn-singing practice in which a leader calls out fragments of text before the congregation slowly sings the passage. This approach to hymn singing was common before hymnals were readily available and churchgoers had the ability to read music.

Liturgy - All of the required words, music, and actions that constitute a church service.

Lindy Hop - An influential dance of the Swing era, introduced in 1928 by a pair of African American dancers.

Low-frequency oscillation - In synthesized music, the use of low frequencies to produce a pulsing or vibrating effect

Lute - A class of plucked string instruments in which the strings extend along a neck and pass over a closed resonating chamber; the guitar is a member of the lute class.

Lutheran chorale - A hymn for use in the Lutheran church; all chorales were originally monophonic.

Lutheran chorale cantata - A special type of Luthern church cantata that incorporates chorale texts and melodies.

Lutheran church cantata - A multi-movement work for soloists, choir, and orchestra intended for use in a Lutheran worship service; typical in 17th- and 18th-century Germany.

Luthier - A craftsperson who builds and repairs wooden musical instruments.

Major mode - A collection of pitches that can be used to craft melodies and harmonies. The major mode is characterized by a specific sequence of intervals between scale degrees and is often heard as happy, cheerful, or confident.

Makam - The system of modes in Turkish music, developed in the Ottoman Empire.

Makam music - The classical music of the Turkish tradition.

March - A musical composition in duple meter performed at a steady, moderate tempo to which one could march, whether the composition is intended for practical use or concert performance.

Mass - Originally, the Catholic church service that includes Communion; other denominations have also adopted this term, and today Mass typically takes place on Sunday morning.

Mass Ordinary - The texts that are recited or sung during every Catholic Mass.

MC - Short for "master of ceremonies"; in hip-hop, the original designation for the performer, now known as a rapper, who improvises spoken lyrics over the beat.

Measure - A unit determined by meter that contains the basic grouping of pulses (e.g. a measure in triple time will contain three beats). Synonymous with "bar."

Melisma - A sequence of notes all sung on a single vowel.

Melismatic - Vocal music in which there are many pitches per syllable.

Melodic motion - Described in terms of the intervallic relationship between adjacent pitches, which can produce either conjunct or disjunct motion.

Melodic range - The span between the low and high notes of a melody; can be small, medium, or large in size.

Melodic shape - The shape of a melody, which is determined by the trajectory of the pitches in terms of highness and lowness.

Melody - A coherent sequence of notes that, if embedded in a complex texture, is clearly of primary importance.

Meter - The grouping of pulses into stable units usually containing two, three, or four pulses.

Mezzo forte - A medium-loud dynamic.

Mezzo piano - A medium-quiet dynamic.

Microtones - Intervals smaller than a half step.

Midbrain - The middle region of the brain.

Mimesis - The imitation of real-world sounds with instruments or voices.

Minimalism - An approach to composition in which a process of gradual transformation is applied to limited musical material.

Minor mode - A collection of pitches that can be used to craft melodies and harmonies. The major mode is characterized by a specific sequence of intervals between scale degrees and is often heard as tragic, ominous, or serious.

Minstrel - In 12th-century Aquitaine, a travelling musician who spreads the songs of the troubadours.

Minstrel show - In the 19th-century United States, a form of entertainment in which performers (usually white) enacted African American stereotypes by darkening their faces with burnt cork or greasepaint, speaking in pseudo-dialect, and portraying established character types through song, dance, and comical sketches.

Mixed meter - The alternation between various meters, such that meter is not felt consistently throughout a musical composition.

Modal jazz - A jazz genre in which the traditional chords of bebop are replaced by harmonies built on modal scales. Performers focus on melodic development, rhythmic intricacy, timbral variation, and emotional expression.

Mode - In music, a system for organizing pitches. The most common modes in Western music are major and minor. Non-Western modal systems include makam and raga.

Modernism - An artistic movement of the early 20th century that glorified progress and presented an optimistic view about the future.

Modulation - The act of changing from one key (a set of pitches determined by a scale) to another.

Monophonic - Having a single melodic line with no accompaniment or countermelodies.

Multitrack recording - A technique by which each instrumental or vocal part is recorded on a different track, often not simultaneously, allowing for the creation of a studio recording that cannot be replicated in live performance.

Murder ballad - A ballad that tells the tale of a murder, most often concerning a young woman who has been murdered by her lover.

Music therapy - The clinical and evidence-based use of music interventions to accomplish individualized goals within a therapeutic relationship by a licensed music therapist.

Musical topic - A compositional style or technique that has come to be associated with a specific subject matter (e.g. chromatic scales to represent wind, or horn calls to connote hunting). Topics were first theorized by musicologist Leonard Ratner.

Nationalism - Identification with one's own nation and support for its interests, especially to the exclusion or detriment of the interests of other nations.

New Music - Experimental art music produced recently by living composers.

Non-diegetic music - Music that is heard in tandem with a dramatic scene but that is not a part of the scene and therefore not audible to the characters in that scene.

Obbligato (Italian; English: "obligatory") - A term used in the 17th and 18th centuries to refer to a solo instrumental countermelody incorporated into an aria. The term references the fact that such accompaniments cannot be omitted without seriously detracting from the work.

Octave equivalence - The idea that pitches whose frequencies are related by powers of two (e.g. 220, 440, 880) are the same note and, to a degree, interchangeable; pitches separated by an octave are therefore assigned the same letter name.

Offbeat - A weak pulse (two or four) in quadruple meter, or the weak pulse (two) in duple meter.

Opera - A form of staged music drama in which all or part of the text is sung.

Opus - Latin for "work;" used to number compositions, usually in the order of creation (e.g. Beethoven's Symphony No. 5 is his opus 67).

Oral tradition - The means by which stories, customs, and music are passed from generation to generation by word of mouth.

Oratorio - An unstaged dramatic work for solo vocalists, choir, and accompanying ensemble that tells a story using sung text and music.

Orchestration - The act of adapting a composition for orchestra, which involves assigning elements of the melody and harmony to different instruments; also the resulting product.

Organicism - A compositional technique by which all parts of a musical work are interconnected; in typical cases, the work seems to grow out of a single motif.

Orientalism - The stereotyped representation of Eastern cultures in Western works of art.

Ornamentation - The addition of trills, runs, or other embellishments to a melody. Ornamentation is sometimes indicated in the notated score but often not.

Ostinato - A repeating melodic or rhythmic figure.

Overt - A term applied to a work of art the meaning of which is entirely apparent.

Overtone - A higher-pitched frequency that is activated when a pitch is produced.

Overtone series - A sequence of higher-pitched frequencies that are activated every time a pitch is produced.

Overtone singing - A style of singing employed primarily by men for which the performer produces a single low pitch but changes the shape of their mouth to accentuate various overtones.

Overture - An instrumental work that opens a musical drama. Overtures precede operas, oratorios, ballets, musicals, and other forms. Overtures can also be composed as stand-alone works.

Panning - A technique used in two-channel recording by which a sound gradually transitions from one channel to the other; this effect is most evident when one listens using headphones, in which case the sound will move from one ear to the other.

Parody - A musical parody is produced when someone supplies new lyrics to a familiar melody.

Participatory - A music event in which the boundary between the roles of performers and audience members is indeterminate or nonexistent; with "presentational," one of two ends of a spectrum of music event types.

Pavan - A type of slow, stately court dance popular in 16th-century Europe.

Pentatonic - A melody that uses only five pitches.

Performance practice - Non-notated practices that are essential to the accurate presentation of a musical work.

Period instruments - Instruments that were used in a specific historical period. This term is most often applied to performances of works from before 1900 on instruments built to meet historic specifications.

Piano - A quiet dynamic.

Pianissimo - A very quiet dynamic, quieter than piano.

Pitch - The "highness" or "lowness" of a sound; can be represented as a frequency or a note name.

Pizzicato - A technique for playing a string instrument by which the performer plucks the strings with their finger.

Plantation song - A popular song written ostensibly from an African American perspective that expresses a nostalgic yearning for plantation life in the South.

Such songs, often written using dialect and performed in blackface, were popular between the mid-19th century and the early 20th century.

Polka - A fast dance in duple meter, performed by couples, that was first popularized in the 1830s.

Polyphonic texture - A musical texture in which no single voice has the melody and all are equally important.

Polytonality - When harmonies in multiple keys are sounded at the same time.

Presentational - A music event in which there is a clear boundary between the roles of performers and audience members; with "participatory," one of two ends of a spectrum of music event types.

Producer - In contemporary popular music, the person who designs the overall sound of a track. A producer might program beats, adjust audio levels, or contribute in a variety of other ways before, during, and after the recording process.

Program music - An instrumental composition that tells a story or paints a picture. Program music never includes a sung or spoken text, but it is always associated with a printed text. This might range from a descriptive title to a lengthy essay.

Prosody - The pattern of accented and unaccented syllables in poetry.

Protest song - A song intended to protest a corporate or political action or regime. Such songs can carry overt (apparent) or covert (hidden) meaning.

Psychedelic rock - Rock music inspired by or representative of psychedelic culture, which centers on the use of mind-altering substances; a category associated primarily with the late 1960s US.

Pulse - A regularly-spaced rhythmic emphasis; synonymous with "beat."

Quadruple meter - A meter in which pulses (beats) are grouped by fours, usually in a strong-weak-medium-weak pattern.

Quadratonic - A melody that uses only four pitches.

Quotation - The technique of incorporating a familiar melody into a composition for the purpose of conveying information to the listener.

Raga - A musical mode in the North Indian system. Ragas are organized into families, and each has a unique name. Unlike the Western scale, a raga contains more than just a set of hierarchically-organized pitches. It also contains information about pitch order, how to approach and ornament pitches, characteristic melodic motifs, and affective associations.

Ragamala - A miniature painting that captures the character of a raga.

Rastafarianism - A belief system that emerged in Jamaica when regent Ras Tafari Makonnen was crowned Emperor Haile Selassie I of Ethiopia in 1930; combines biblical faith with the belief that Selassie is (or was) Christ.

Recapitulation - In sonata form, the section in which all of the themes from the Exposition are heard for a second time, but in the home key.

Recitative - A style of singing that is modelled on dramatic speech. In recitative, there is minimal repetition and seldom a recognizable melody. The rhythm is determined by text stresses. Recitative is usually sparsely accompanied, using only a few instruments. It is used in opera and oratorio to propel the plot forward.

Refrain - A passage of music that returns throughout a vocal work.

Reggae - A genre of music that developed in Jamaica beginning around 1968; characterized by a medium tempo, quadruple meter, off-beat accents, electric instruments (organ, guitars, bass) that play interlocking rhythmic patterns, and lyrics concerning social justice and Rastafarian beliefs.

Register - A part of an instrument or vocalist's range; can by high, middle, or low.

Renaissance - A period in Western music history that is typically bookmarked by the rise of humanist thought (ca. 1400) and the invention of opera (ca. 1600).

Repetition - The relationship between two identical musical passages.

Reprise - The return of a musical number in the context of a theatrical performance.

Requiem - The Catholic funeral Mass.

Rhythm - The temporal aspect of sound; can be described as the pattern of "on" and "off" states exhibited by any sound as time passes.

Riff - A brief, repeated melodic fragment in popular music.

Ritornello - A passage of instrumental music that returns throughout a composition. This term is usually applied to music of the Baroque era.

Romantic - A period in Western music history that is typically considered to extend from 1815 to 1900. This period is characterized by expressive harmonies, experimental forms, and the rise of program music.

Rondo form - A musical form in which a refrain, introduced at the outset, alternates with contrasting material (e.g. A B A C A B A).

Rounded binary form - A type of two-part form in which both parts end with similar melodic material (e.g. [a a'] [b a"]).

Royalties - The profit share due to creative artists when their work is sold or reproduced in any form, including sheet music, recordings, and live performances.

Sacred Harp singing - A shape-note singing practice that relies on the Sacred Harp hymnal, first published in 1844.

Salon - A gathering in the home of a wealthy art lover for the purpose of engaging with elite culture in intimate surroundings.

Saz semâisi - The concluding movement in a *fasıl* suite of the Ottoman tradition. The form alternates between unique *hane* passages and a *teslim* refrain. The final *hane* is in a lively dance meter.

Scale - A sequence of pitches containing the principle notes that can be used to compose or improvise in a given key. A scale is characterized by the intervals between the notes, which are usually major or minor seconds but can also be thirds.

Scenario - The sequence of scenes in a ballet.

Scenarist - The person who develops the scenario for a ballet.

Scenic cantata - A staged dramatic work for vocal soloists, choir, and orchestra that includes costumes, pantomime, and dancing; developed by Carl Orff.

Score - A document in which all parts of a composition are notated. In most cases, only the conductor reads from the score, while instrumentalists read from individual parts that include only their own music and singers read from vocal scores that include only the voice parts.

Session musician - A professional musician who makes studio recordings for use in film, television, or the popular music industry.

Sequence - The repetition of melodic material at a different pitch level.

Shape-note singing - A tradition of hymn singing that relies on notation in which the scale degrees are indicated with differently-shaped noteheads; flourished in the 18th and 19th centuries, but still widely practiced today.

Silk Road - The trade route, spanning from Italy to Japan, that shaped Europe, the Middle East, North Africa, and Asia beginning in the second century BCE.

Single reed - A type of instrument that utilizes a single reed embedded in a mouthpiece to produce sound. The player blows across the reed, causing it to vibrate. This family includes the clarinets and saxophones.

Singspiel - A form of German comic opera in which sung arias are interspersed with spoken dialogue; can be translated as "song play."

Soca - A dance music genre associated with Trinidadian Carnival that dates to the 1970s.

Socialist Realism - The Soviet doctrine requiring that all art portray the communist revolution in a positive light. Art was also expected to be optimistic and accessible.

Sonata form - A typical form for the first movements of instrumental works in the European tradition of the 18th and 19th centuries. The form contains three principal sections (the Exposition, Development, and Recapitulation) and an optional fourth (the Coda). The thematic contents and key areas of the Exposition and Recapitulation are tightly controlled.

Song cycle - A set of songs that work together to tell a story or explore an emotional state.

Song plugger - In the first half of the 20th century, a music publishing company employee who was responsible for advertising songs either by performing them in public or convincing professional singers to adopt them.

Soprano - A singer with a high range, usually female.

Source music - Music in a film or television show that is generated from within the scene and is therefore audible to both the viewer and the characters.

Southern Appalachians - The mountainous region traversing the states of Alabama, Georgia, South Carolina, Tennessee, North Carolina, Kentucky, Virginia, and West Virginia.

Spiritual - A folk hymn from the African American tradition.

Square dancing - A form of social dancing in which four sets of couples face one another as the sides of a square and engage in a sequence of interactive movements.

Staccato - An articulation that is short and accented.

Staff notation - A system of notation that developed in Europe beginning in the 11th century and is in common use today. Noteheads are placed on a 5-line staff to indicate pitch and register. Rhythm is indicated by the appearance of the note.

Stop time - A style of accompaniment in jazz and blues that is characterized by chords sounded on the downbeat and followed by space that is occupied only by a soloist.

Strain - In certain forms, including those of marches and ragtime, the term used for a unique section (e.g. the B strain).

String quartet - Can refer either to a chamber ensemble made up of two violins, a viola, and a cello, or to a piece of music composed for such an ensemble.

Strophic song - A song in which all verses are sung to the same melody.

Subgenre - A means of dividing musical genres into increasingly specific subcategories.

Subject - In a fugue, the unaccompanied melody that is introduced at the outset and then heard in all voices over the course of the composition.

Suite - A multi-movement instrumental work that does not adhere to a standard formal structure (e.g. symphony).

Sweet jazz - In the 1920s, social dance music played primarily by white bands; defined in contrast to hot jazz, which was played primarily by African American bands and was more rhythmically and timbrally daring.

Swing - A style of dance music that emerged in the 1930s and is characterized by "swung" rhythms, which are produced when the first in a pair of notes is held for twice as long as the second, resulting in a long-short pattern; also refers to the accompanying style of dance.

Syllabic - Vocal music in which there is one pitch per syllable.

Sympathetic strings - Strings on an instrument that are intended to vibrate in sympathy with sounded pitches, thereby influencing the timbre and resonance of the instrument.

Symphonic poem - A descriptive single-movement orchestral work that portrays a scene, tells a story, or communicates a philosophical idea; popular in the late 19th century.

Symphony - A genre of orchestral music. A symphony usually contains four movements, the first of which is in sonata form. The interior movements are respectively slow and dance-inspired, although the order is not set. The final movement is fast.

Syncopation - A rhythmic pattern that deemphasizes strong beats and emphasizes off-beats (that is, the second halves of beats).

Syntax - The orderly arrangement of sounds in a system.

Tablature - A type of instrument-specific notation that provides the player with visual instructions regarding where to place their fingers on a fretboard or keyboard. Guitar tablature, or "tab," is common today.

Tango - A style of dance and music that emerged in the slums of Buenos Aires, Argentina, in the late 19th century.

Tape loops - Short audio recordings made on magnetic tape that can be endlessly looped. The use of tape loops was common amongst early minimalist composers.

Tempo - The rate at which the pulse is felt.

Ternary form - A three-part form that can be diagrammed as A B A.

Text painting - A technique by which the composer translates the meaning of a text into sound (e.g. sets the word "falling" to a descending melodic line).

Throat singing - Any of several variants of overtone singing, for which the performer produces a single low pitch but changes the shape of their mouth to accentuate various overtones.

Through-composed - A vocal composition in which each stanza of the poem is sung to unique music, in contrast to a strophic setting.

Timbre - The quality of a sound, determined by its overtones.

Tin Pan Alley - The music publishing industry that flourished in New York City between the 1890s and 1940s; so named because many of the publishers stationed their headquarters on the same block, and the sound of their many pianos was said to resemble the clanging of tin pans.

Tonic scale degree - The first and most important note of a scale; the "home" pitch to which melody and harmony tend to return.

Transcription - The act of notating music.

Tremolo - Rapid articulation on a single pitch or, sometimes, quick alternation between two pitches. On string instruments, tremolo involves moving the bow back and forth very quickly to produce a fluttering sound.

Tresillo - A syncopated rhythm common in Latin American music. This rhythm, which occurs in a duple- or quadruple-meter framework and can be counted as 3+3+2, has its roots in West Africa.

Trill - A rapid oscillation between two adjacent pitches.

Triple meter - A meter in which pulses (beats) are grouped by threes, usually in a strong-weak-weak pattern.

Trobairitz - A 12th-century Aquitainian noblewoman who wrote refined love songs; the female counterpart to a troubadour.

Underscoring - Music in a film or television show that is audible to the viewer but not to the on-screen characters.

Variation - The relationship between two musical passages that share recognizable melodic, harmonic, or rhythmic features, but that are not identical. Also, a compositional technique in which a foundational piece of music is altered in a ways that distinguishes it from the source while leaving the source recognizable.

Velum - A common material in the production of medieval manuscripts; most often made from dried sheep skin.

Verbunkos - A style of dance music performed by Romani musicians; can be roughly divided into two parts: the slow, expressive *lassan* and the lively *friska*, which features simple harmonies and increases in tempo.

Vernacular - The language spoken by the people in a given area; can also refer to folk or popular music traditions that are comprehensible to the average citizen.

Verse - In most popular songs, the part of the melody to which the same words are never sung twice; usually alternates with the chorus.

Vibrato - A wobble added to a pitch.

Vida - A medieval biography of a troubadour.

Viol consort - An ensemble of viols of various sizes, ranging from treble to bass. This was a common chamber ensemble in 16th-century Europe.

Volume - The loudness or quietness of sound; can be specified in terms of amplitude (specific) or dynamic marking (contextual).

Virtuoso - One who is highly skilled at playing an instrument.

Waltz - A moderately-paced dance in triple meter, performed by couples, that dates from the 18th century.

Wayang wong - A narrative dance tradition from Java, performed to the accompaniment of gamelan music.

Wernicke's Area - The specific area of the brain that processes understanding of language and construction of meaningful thoughts.

Zither - A class of plucked or hammered string instruments in which the strings extend across a closed resonating chamber; familiar examples include the autoharp and hammered dulcimer.

CPSIA information can be obtained
at www.ICGtesting.com
Printed in the USA
LVHW061731040822
725212LV00006B/40

9 781940 771311